Sociology

"Dear Professor Henslin . . ."

The following are excerpts from letters and emails to Jim Henslin from students who have used various versions and editions of *Sociology: A Down-to-Earth Approach*.

Dear Dr. Henslin,

I am a nursing student in Broward Community College. I had to take sociology in the summer before I could start my RN program in August. I had a wonderful time reading *Sociology: A Down-to-Earth Approach*. I never thought sociology would interest me much. I thank you for spectacularly presenting different religions, caste, cultures, and their norms very tactfully. I read all the chapters that were on my syllabus entirely. I learned a lot from this book and hope it will make the rest of my education journey easier.

Sincerely,

Abuasad Haque

Hi Mr. Henslin,

I hope this is still your email address. I am a student at Greenville Technical College in Greenville, South Carolina. I am currently taking Introduction to Sociology here at Tech and I must tell you, your book rocks!!!! It is the most fun I have ever had reading any textbook in my life!

Sincerely,

Kim B

Dear Professor Henslin,

I am a student at Stony Brook University in New York and I'm working toward a major in Sociology. I just completed an introductory summer course in Sociology that was taught with your textbook. I found your book to be incredibly interesting—so much that I am now reading the chapters we skipped over in class.

Thanks again,

Anna Maria Huertas Kormoski

Mr. Henslin,

I am a student at Texas Pan American University in Edinburg, Texas. I just want to take the time to write and say how much I have enjoyed your book. Not only is it very simple to understand, it is also very interesting. I was reluctant to take the class but through the text, I enjoy the class so much more.

Sincerely,

Julissa Rodriguez

Dear Mr. Henslin,

My name is Sydney Conley. I'm a student at Midlands Technical College in Columbia, South Carolina. I'm studying for a test that I have tomorrow in Sociology and I just thought you might like to know that I find your book *Essentials of Sociology* very interesting. Thanks to your book, I'm considering continuing my study of Sociology.

Thanks again

Sydney Conley

Hello Professor Henslin,

My name is Marta Holiday and I am a student at Marymount College in Tarrytown, NY. I am taking Introduction to Sociology at Nassau Community College to earn extra credits and your text was required reading for our class. I just wanted to tell you how much I enjoyed your book. I found the chapters fun and interesting—especially how you opened each with a sketch or a personal vignette.

It was a pleasure to read your work. I felt as though I became acquainted with you through your words.

Sincerely,

Marta A. Holliday

I am currently a freshman at Dordt College, a liberal arts college in Sioux City, Iowa. I really enjoy your book so far. It is very easy to read and understand. I especially appreciate the "down-to-earthiness" of this book. I have found that I can apply the things I have learned [from your text] to my Psychology 201 class also. Thanks for your dedication to making the field of sociology more exciting to learn about.

Joya Gerritsma

Sociology

third edition

A DOWN-TO-EARTH APPROACH
CORE CONCEPTS

James M. Henslin
Southern Illinois University, Edwardsville

PEARSON

Boston   New York   San Francisco
Mexico City   Montreal   Toronto   London   Madrid   Munich   Paris
Hong Kong   Singapore   Tokyo   Cape Town   Sydney

Executive Editor: Jeff Lasser
Series Editorial Assistant: Lauren Houlihan
Senior Marketing Manager: Kelly May
Development Editor: Jenn Albanese
Editorial Production Service: Nesbitt Graphics, Inc.,
 Dusty Friedman
Composition Buyer: Linda Cox
Manufacturing Buyer: Megan Cochran
Electronic Composition: Nesbitt Graphics, Inc.
Interior Design: Carol Somberg
Photo Researcher: Kate Cebik (interior),
 Laurie Frankenthaler (chapter openers)
Cover Administrator: Linda Knowles

For related titles and support materials, visit our online catalog at www.ablongman.com.

Between the time website information is gathered and then published, it is not unusual for some sites to have closed. Also, the transcription of URLs can result in typographical errors. The publisher would appreciate notification where these errors occur so that they may be corrected in subsequent editions.

ISBN-13: 978-0-205-57135-2   ISBN-10: 0-205-57135-2

Printed in the United States of America
10 9 8 7 6 5 4 3 2   RRD-OH   11 10 09 08

What's New?

Because sociology is about social life and we live in a changing global society, an introductory sociology text should reflect not only the most recent sociological research but also the national and global changes that engulf us, as well as new sociological research. This revision of *Sociology: A Down-to-Earth Approach, Core Concepts* has over 60 new suggested readings, 350 new references, 260 new instructional photos, and 115 updated illustrations. Here are some of the new topics, illustrations, tables, and boxed features.

CHAPTER 2
New Cultural Diversity box: Culture Shock: The Arrival of the Hmong

CHAPTER 3
New topic: *Anime* in the socialization of children

CHAPTER 4
New topics:
• Shooting deaths at an Amish school
• Cultural diversity in smiling
• Applied body language: training of airport personnel and interrogators
• Applied impression management: Helping women executives get promoted

CHAPTER 5
New topics:
• Torture warrants
• Groupthink applied to the acceptance of torture by U.S. officials
• No-Sneeze kittens mentioned as a new product

CHAPTER 6
New topic: Online shaming sites
New Cultural Diversity box: "What Kind of Prison Is This?"

CHAPTER 7
New illustration: Figure 7.8, illustrating births to single women by education

CHAPTER 8
New tables:
• Table 11.3 Age of Rape Victims
• Table 11.4 Relationship of Rapists to Victims

CHAPTER 9
New topics:
• First Latino to compete for the Democratic candidacy for President
• *Proposition 2* of the Michigan state constitution
New Down-to-Earth Sociology box: The Man in the Zoo
New Cultural Diversity box: The Illegal Travel Guide

CHAPTER 10
New topics:
• Finding brides for dead sons (China)
• Housework, child care, and paid labor data from Bianchi et al. research
New Down-to-Earth Sociology box: Caught Between Two Worlds: The Children of Divorce
New Technology box: Finding a Mate: Not the Same as It Used to Be

To my fellow sociologists, who do such creative research on social life and who communicate the sociological imagination to generations of students.

With my sincere admiration and appreciation,

Jim Henslin

Brief Contents

Contents

4   Social Structure and Social Interaction   96

THROUGH THE AUTHOR'S LENS

When a Tornado Strikes: Social Organization Following a Natural Disaster

When TV news announced that a tornado had ripped apart a town just hours from my own, not only destroying buildings but also taking lives, I wondered how the people were adjusting to their sudden loss. These photos, taken the next day, show a community in the process of re-building. (Page 122)

5 Societies to Social Networks 126

6 Deviance and Social Control 152

7 Social Stratification 184

THROUGH THE AUTHOR'S LENS

The Dump People: Working and Living and Playing in the City Dump of Phnom Penh, Cambodia

I learned that people were living in the city dump of Phnom Penh, the capital of Cambodia. This photo essay reveals their life far better than words ever could. These men, women, and children are not only scavenging trash, but also they are participating in a community. (Page 196)

THROUGH THE AUTHOR'S LENS

Work and Gender: Women at Work in India

Like women in the West, women in India are not limited to the home. Their work roles, however, stand in sharp contrast with those of women in the West. This photo essay illustrates some of the amazing differences I saw. (Page 238)

Boxed Features

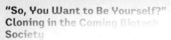
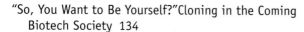

Guide *to* Social Maps

Social Maps illustrate the old Chinese saying, "A picture is worth ten thousand words." They allow you to see at a glance how social characteristics are distributed among the fifty states or among the nations of the world. The U.S. Social Maps are a concise way of illustrating how our states compare on significant factors.

These Social Maps are unique to this text. I have produced these Social Maps for you from original data. At a glance, you can see how your state compares with your region and the other states—or you can see how the United States compares with other countries. I hope that you will find these Social Maps informative. If you have any suggestions for other Social Maps that you would like to see in the next edition, please share them with me.

To the **Student** *from the* **Author**

WELCOME TO SOCIOLOGY! I've loved sociology since I was in my teens, and I hope you enjoy it, too. Sociology is fascinating because it holds the key to so much understanding of social life.

If you like to watch people and try to figure out why they do what they do, you will like sociology. Sociology pries open the doors of society so that you can see what goes on behind them. *Sociology: A Down-to-Earth Approach, Core Concepts* stresses how profoundly our society and the groups to which we belong influence us. Social class, for example, sets us on a path in life. For some, the path leads to better health, more education, and higher income, but for others, it leads to poverty, dropping out of school, and even a higher risk of illness and disease. These paths are so significant that they affect our chances of making it to our first birthday, as well as of getting in trouble with the police. They even influence how our marriage will work out, the number of children we will have—and whether or not we will read this book in the first place.

When I took my first course in sociology, I was hooked. Seeing how marvelously my life had been affected by these larger social influences opened my eyes to a new world, one that has been fascinating to explore. I hope that this will be your experience, also.

From how people become homeless to how they become presidents, from why people commit suicide to why women are discriminated against in every society around the world—all are part of sociology. This breadth, in fact, is what makes sociology so intriguing. We can place the sociological lens on broad features of society, such as social class, gender, and race-ethnicity, and then immediately turn our focus on the small-scale level. If we look at two people interacting—whether quarreling or kissing—we see how these broad features of society are being played out in their lives.

We aren't born with instincts. Nor do we come into this world with preconceived notions of what life should be like. At birth, we have no ideas of race-ethnicity, gender, age, or social class. We have no idea, for example, that people "ought" to act in certain ways because they are male or female. Yet we all learn such things as we grow up in our society. Uncovering the "hows" and the "whys" of this process is also part of what makes sociology so fascinating.

One of sociology's many pleasures is that as we study life in groups (which can be taken as a definition of sociology), whether those groups be in some far-off part of the world or in some nearby corner of our own society, we constantly gain insights into our own selves. As we see how *their* customs affect *them,* the effects of our own society on us become more visible.

This book, then, can be part of an intellectual adventure, for it can lead you to a new way of looking at your social world—and in the process, help you to better understand both society and yourself.

I wish you the very best in college—and in your career afterward. It is my sincere hope that *Sociology: A Down-to-Earth Approach, Core Concepts* will contribute to that success.

James M. Henslin
Department of Sociology
Southern Illinois University, Edwardsville

P.S. I enjoy communicating with students, so feel free to comment on your experiences with this text. Because I travel a lot, it is best to reach me by e-mail: henslin@aol.com

To the Instructor from the Author

REMEMBER WHEN YOU FIRST GOT HOOKED on sociology, how the windows of perception opened as you began to see life-in-society through the sociological perspective? For most of us, this was an eye-opening experience. This text is designed to open those windows onto social life, so students can see clearly the vital effects of group membership on their lives. Although few students will get into what Peter Berger calls "the passion of sociology," we at least can provide them the opportunity.

Sociology is like a huge jigsaw puzzle. Only gradually do the intricate pieces start to fit together. As they do so, our perspective changes as we shift our eyes from the many small, disjointed pieces onto the whole that is being formed. Although this analogy is imperfect, it indicates a fascinating process of sociological discovery. Of all the endeavors we could have entered, we chose sociology because of the ways in which it joins together the "pieces" of society and the challenges it poses to "ordinary" thinking. To share the sociological perspective with students is our privilege.

As instructors of sociology, we have set ambitious goals for ourselves: to teach both social structure and social interaction and to introduce students to the main sociological literature—both the classic theorists and contemporary research. And we would like to accomplish this in ways that enliven the classroom, encourage critical thinking, and stimulate our students' sociological imagination. Although formidable, these goals are attainable. This book, based on many years of frontline (classroom) experience, is designed to help you reach these goals. Its subtitle, *A Down-to-Earth Approach,* is not proposed lightly. My goal is to share the fascination of sociology with students and thereby make your teaching more rewarding.

Over the years, I have found the introductory course especially enjoyable. It is singularly satisfying to see students' faces light up as they begin to see how separate pieces of their world fit together. It is a pleasure to watch them gain insight into how their social experiences give shape to even their innermost desires. This is precisely what this text is designed to do—to stimulate your students' sociological imagination so that they can better perceive how the "pieces" of society fit together—and what this means for their own lives.

Filled with examples from around the world as well as from our own society, this text helps to make today's multicultural, global society come alive for students. From learning how the international elite carves up global markets to studying the intimacy of friendship and marriage, students can see how sociology is the key to explaining contemporary life—and their own place in it.

In short, this text is designed to make your teaching easier. There simply is no justification for students to have to wade through cumbersome approaches to sociology. I am firmly convinced that the introduction to sociology should be enjoyable, and that the introductory textbook can be an essential tool in sharing the discovery of sociology with students.

The Organization of this Text

The opening chapter introduces students to the sociological perspective and how sociologists do research. We then look at how culture influences us in Chapter 2, examine the deep impact of socialization in Chapter 3, and compare the macrosociological and microsociological approaches to studying social life in Chapter 4. In Chapter 5, we first analyze how broad historical changes in the structure of society affect our orientations to life and then examine the far-reaching influence of groups on how we feel, think, and act. In Chapter 6, we focus on how groups "keep us in line" and sanction those who violate their norms. In Chapter 7, we turn our focus on how social inequality pervades society and how those inequalities have an impact on our own lives. In this chapter, we begin with a global focus on social stratification and move to an analysis of social class in the United States. After establishing this broader context of social inequality, in Chapter 8 we examine gender, the most global of the inequalities. Then in Chapter 9, we focus on the pervasive inequalities of race-ethnicity. In the final chapter, as we examine the influences of the family on our lives, we look at how this social institution is changing and how its changes, in turn, influence our orientations and decisions.

Throughout this text runs a focus on social change—and its implications for our own lives. As we analyze the topics of this text, we look at the cutting edge of the vital changes that are engulfing us all. This is an exciting time to be experiencing social life—and sociology is a fascinating way of perceiving our experiences.

Themes and Features

In addition to social change, six themes run throughout this text: down-to-earth sociology, globalization, cultural diversity, critical thinking, sociology and the new technology, and the mass media in social life. Let's look at these themes.

Down-to-Earth Sociology

As many years of teaching have shown me, all too often textbooks are written to appeal to the adopters of texts rather than to the students who must learn from them. To me, this is backwards. Therefore, a central concern in writing this book has been to present sociology in a way that not only facilitates understanding but also shares its excitement. During the course of writing other texts, I often have been told that my explanations and writing style are "down-to-earth," or accessible and inviting to students—so much so that I chose this phrase as the book's subtitle. The term is also featured in my introductory reader, *Down to Earth Sociology,* 14th edition (New York: Free Press, 2007).

This first theme is highlighted by a series of boxed features that explore sociological processes that underlie everyday life. In these **Down-to-Earth Sociology** boxes, we consider such topics as feminism in the 1800s, racism during the same period, and improper and fraudulent social research (Chapter 1); the relationship between heredity and environment (Chapter 3); beauty and success and how football explains social structure (Chapter 4); making friends by facebooking (Chapter 5); serial killers in our midst and urban residents' ambivalence about gangs (Chapter 6); how hitting it big in the lottery changes people's lives and the lifestyles of the super-rich (Chapter 7); the gender gap in math and science and how sexism actually kills women (Chapter 8); voice and racial discrimination in the rental market, the mind of the Neo-Nazis, the "invisible knapsack" that whites carry, and even how a plane ride can change someone's race (Chapter 9); cohabitation, finding a mate, figuring your chances for divorce, the children of divorce, and why abused women don't pack up and leave (Chapter 10).

This first theme is actually a hallmark of the text, as my goal is to make sociology "down to earth." To help students grasp the fascination of sociology, I continually stress sociology's relevance to their lives. To reinforce this theme, I avoid unnecessary jargon and use concise explanations and clear and simple (but not reductive) language. I often use student-relevant examples to illustrate key concepts, and I have based some of the chapters' opening vignettes on my own experiences in exploring social life. That this goal of sharing sociology's fascination is being reached is evident from the many comments I receive from instructors and students alike that these materials help to make sociology "come alive."

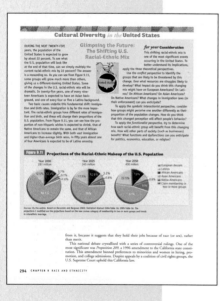

Globalization

The second theme, globalization, explores the impact of global issues. The new global economy, for example, which has intertwined the fates of nations, vitally affects our lives. The globalization of capitalism influences the kinds of skills and knowledge we need, the types of work available to us, the costs of the goods and services we consume, and even whether our country is at war or in a time of peace. In addition to this strong emphasis on global issues that runs throughout this text, Chapter 7 features systems of global stratification. What occurs in Russia, Japan, and China, as well as in much smaller nations such as Afghanistan and Iraq, has direct and far-reaching effects on our own lives. Consequently, in addition to the global focus that appears throughout the text, we continue this emphasis in the next theme, cultural diversity.

Cultural Diversity in the United States and Around the World

The third theme, cultural diversity, has two primary emphases. The first is cultural diversity around the world. Gaining an understanding of how social life is "done" in other parts of the world often challenges our taken-for-granted assumptions about social life. At times, learning about other cultures gives us an appreciation for the life of other peoples; at other times, we may be shocked or even disgusted at some aspect of another group's way of life (such as female circumcision) and come away with a renewed appreciation of our own customs.

To highlight this subtheme, I have written a series of boxes called **Cultural Diversity Around the World.** These boxes, as well as the other types I have written for this text, are one of my favorite features of the book. They are especially valuable for introducing the provocative and controversial materials that make sociology such a lively activity. The boxes that present cultural diversity around the world feature food customs that will likely test the limits of our cultural relativity and the Hmong experience of culture shock (Chapter 2); how Easterners and Westerners don't see the same thing even when they are looking at the same object (Chapter 3); human sexuality in Mexico and Kenya, and prison life in Greenland (Chapter 6); selling brides in China and circumcising girls in Africa (Chapter 8); illegal immigration (Chapter 9); love and arranged marriage in India (Chapter 10).

In the second subtheme, **Cultural Diversity in the United States,** we turn our focus on the fascinating array of people who compose U.S. society. Among the boxes that I have written with this subtheme are the significance of language: Spanish and English in Miami and the terms people choose for their own racial-ethnic self-identification (Chapter 2); the dilemma that Latinos face as they confront two cultures (Chapter 3); how the Amish resist social change (Chapter 4); how our own social networks perpetuate social inequality (Chapter 5); the upward social mobility of African Americans, how Tiger Woods represents a significant change in U.S. racial-ethnic identity, discrimination against immigrants, and our shifting racial-ethnic mix (Chapter 9).

Looking at cultural diversity—whether it be in the United States or in other regions of the world—often challenges our own orientations to life. Seeing that there are so many varieties of "doing" social life highlights the arbitrariness of our own customs—and our taken-for-granted ways of thinking. These contrasts help students to develop their sociological imagination. They are better able to see connections among key sociological concepts such as culture, socialization, norms, race-ethnicity, gender, and social class. As their sociological imagination grows, your students can attain a new perspective on their own experiences—and a better understanding of the social structure of U.S. society.

Critical Thinking

The fourth theme, critical thinking, can enliven your classroom with a vibrant exchange of ideas. Titled **Thinking Critically,** these sections focus on controversial social issues. As with the controversial materials presented in the boxed features, in these sections I present objective, fair portrayals of positions and do not take a side. In the questions that close each of the topics, however, I occasionally play the "devil's advocate."

Among the issues addressed in the Thinking Critically sections are the extent to which genes control human behavior (Chapter 2); our tendency to conform to evil authority, as uncovered by the Milgram experiments (Chapter 5); a culture clash on rape and marriage, threestakes laws, and hate crimes (Chapter 6); bounties paid to kill homeless children in Brazil, *maquiladoras* on the U.S. Mexican border, and the welfare debate (Chapter 7); biology or culture as a cause of human behavior (Chapter 8); reparations for slavery (Chapter 9); and marital tensions that arise from the inequitable sharing of housework (Chapter 10). Because the Thinking Critically sections are based on controversial social issues that either affect the student's own life or are something that he or she is vitally interested in, they stimulate critical thinking and lively class discussion. They also lend themselves especially well to debates and small-group discussions.

Sociology and the New Technology

The fifth theme, sociology and the new technology, explores an aspect of social life that has come to be central to our existence. We welcome these new tools, for they help us to be more efficient at making a living, doing our everyday tasks, and even communicating with people on the other side of the globe. The significance of the new technology, however, goes far beyond the tools and the ease and efficiency that they bring to our lives. The new technology also reshapes social organizations, which has profound effects on how we relate to one another. This technology also penetrates our "inner" life: It shapes our thinking and perception, leading to changed ways of viewing life and even the self. We are in the midst of a social revolution that will leave few aspects of our lives untouched.

This theme is introduced in Chapter 2, where technology is defined and presented as a major aspect of culture. To highlight this theme, I have written a series of boxes called **Sociology and the New Technology.** The focus of this boxed feature is on how technology is changing society and affecting our lives. In these boxes, we discuss how cloning will lead to strange relationships (Chapter 5) and how high-tech reproduction is stretching and outpacing common sense (Chapter 10).

The Mass Media and Social Life

In the sixth theme, we examine how the mass media influence our behavior and permeate our thinking. We consider how the media penetrate our consciousness to such a degree that they even influence how we perceive our own bodies. As your students are introduced to this theme, they should begin to see the mass media in a different light, which, in turn, should further stimulate their sociological imagination.

Although this theme is highlighted at appropriate points throughout the text, I have also written a series of boxed features called **Mass Media in Social Life** to make it more prominent for students, In these boxes, we explore why Native Americans like Western novels and movies even though Indians are usually portrayed as victims (Chapter 2); the influence of computer games on images of gender (Chapter 3); the worship of thinness—and how this affects our own body images (Chapter 4); the issue of censoring high-tech pornography (Chapter 6); and slavery in today's world (Chapter 7).

New Topics

Among the new topics are *anime* in the socialization of children (Chapter 3); the Hmong's cultural shock when they arrived in the United States (Chapter 2); cultural diversity in smiling, training of airport personnel as applied body language, and the promotion of women executives through the use of impression management (Chapter 4); torture warrants and the acceptance of torture by U.S. officials (Chapter 5); surprising cross-cultural differences in prisons, data on the age of rape victims, and online shaming sites (Chapter 6); education and birth to single mothers (Chapter 7); data on age of rape victims and the relationship of rapists to victims (Chapter 8); Proposition 2 of the Michigan state constitution (Chapter 9); finding brides for dead sons in China, and a new study on housework, child care, and paid labor (Chapter 10).

Visual Presentations of Sociology

Some of the most interesting—and even fascinating—topics in sociology are effectively presented in visual form. Here is a brief overview of some of the visual presentations in this text.

Through the Author's Lens   I have prepared a series of photo essays called *Through the Author's Lens.* Using this format, students are able to look over my shoulder as I experience other cultures or explore aspects of this one. Doing the research presented in this feature expanded my own sociological imagination, and I hope that these reports do the same for your students. The four photo essays in this series should open your students' minds to other ways of social life, as well as stimulate insightful class discussion.

When a Tornado Strikes: Social Organization Following a Natural Disaster   When a tornado hit a small town just hours from where I live, I drove there to see the aftermath of the disaster. The police let me in to view the neighborhood where the tornado had struck, destroying homes and killing several people. I was impressed by how quickly people were putting their lives back together, the topic of this photo essay (Chapter 4).

Small Town USA: Struggling to Survive   To take the photos for this essay, I wandered off the beaten path. On a road trip from California to Florida, instead of traveling the interstates, I followed those "little black lines" on the map. They took me to out-of-the-way places that our national transportation system has bypassed. Many of these little towns are putting on a valiant face as they struggle to survive, but as the photos show, the struggle is apparent, and, in some cases, so are the scars (Chapter 5).

The Dump People of Phnom Penh, Cambodia   Among the culture shocks I experienced in Cambodia was not to discover that people scavenge at Phnom Penh's huge city dump—this I knew about—but that they also live there. With the aid of an interpreter, I was able to interview these people, as well as photograph them as they went about their everyday lives. An entire community lives in the city dump, complete with restaurants amidst the huge piles of garbage. This photo essay reveals not just these people's activities but also their social organization (Chapter 7).

Work and Gender: Women at Work in India   As I traveled in India, I took photos of women at work in public places. The more I traveled in this country and the more photos I took, the more insight I gained into gender relations. Despite the general submissiveness of women to men in India, women's worlds are far from limited to family and home. Women are found at work throughout the society. What is even more remarkable is how vastly different "women's work" in India is compared to that in the United States. This, too, is an intellectually provocative photo essay (Chapter 8).

Photo Essay on Subcultures   To help students better understand subcultures, I have retained the photo essay in Chapter 2. Because this photo essay consists of photos taken by others, it is not a part of the series, *Through the Author's Lens.* The variety of subcultures featured in this photo essay, however, should be instructive to your students.

Photo Collages   Because sociology lends itself so well to photographic illustration, this text also includes photo collages. In Chapter 2 (page 43), students can catch a glimpse of the fascinating variety that goes into the cultural relativity of beauty. The collage in Chapter 5 (page 136) illustrates categories, aggregates, and primary and secondary groups, concepts that students sometimes wrestle to distinguish. In Chapter 8 (page 229), students can see how differently gender is portrayed in different cultures.

Other Photos by the Author   Sprinkled throughout this edition are photos that I took during travels to India and Cambodia. These photos illustrate sociological principles and topics better than photos available from commercial sources. As an example, the possibility of photographing and interviewing a feral child was one of the reasons that I went to Cambodia. While in the United States, I was told about a feral child who had been discovered living with monkeys and who had been taken to an orphanage in Cambodia. That particular photo is on page 67. Another of my favorites is on page 154.

Other Special Pedagogical Features

In addition to chapter summaries and reviews, key terms, and a comprehensive glossary, I have included several special features to aid students in learning sociology. **In Sum** section help students review important points within the chapter before going on to new sections. I have also developed a series of **Social Maps,** which illustrate how social conditions vary by geography. At the end of each chapter is **ContentSelect™**, a listing of search terms that facilitate chapter-related online research. ContentSelect™ gives students access to a huge online collection of professional journals.

Chapter-opening vignettes   feature down-to-earth illustrations of a major aspect of each chapter's content. Some of these are based on my own experiences. A couple of them come from my research with the homeless, from the time I spent with them on the streets and slept in their shelters (Chapters 1 and 7). Others recount the culture shock that I experienced in Africa (Chapters 2 and 8). I also share my experiences when I spent a night with street people at Dupont Circle in Washington, D.C. (Chapter 4). One vignette is based on an historical event (Chapter 9), and two summarize classic studies in the social sciences (Chapters 3 and 6). One summarizes an event from a novel (Chapter 5), and one is fictional (Chapter 10). Many students have told their instructors that they find these vignettes compelling, that they stimulate their interest in the chapter.

Thinking Critically About the Chapters   I close each chapter with three critical thinking questions. Each question focuses on a major feature of the chapter, asking students to reflect on and consider some issue. Many of the questions ask the students to apply sociological findings and principles to their own lives.

On Sources   Sociological data are found in a wide variety of sources, and this text reflects that variety. Cited throughout this text are standard journals such as the *American Journal Sociology, Social Problems, American Sociological Review, and Journal of Marriage and the Family,* as well as more esoteric journals such as the *Bulletin of the History of Medicine, Chronobilogy International,* and *Western Journal of Black Studies.* I have also drawn heavily from standard news sources, especially the *New York Times* and *Wall Street Journal,* as well as more unusual sources such as *El Pais.* In addition, I cite unpublished papers by sociologists, such as the study in Chapter 9 on job discrimination among applicants who have "white-sounding" and "black-sounding" names.

On Terms   Although some people still use the terms *First World, Second World,* and *Third World,* these terms are biased. Even though unintentional, to say "First World" inevitably connotes superiority of some sort—an implication of coming in first place, with other nations trailing in lesser, inferior positions. Because the collapse of the Soviet Union's system of socialism communism made these terms outmoded , some have replaced them with *Most Developed Countries, Less Developed Countries, and Least Developed Countries.* These terms, however, carry the same ethnocentric burden. They indicate that our economic state is superior: *We* are "developed ," but *they* are not—but maybe they'll be fortunate enough to become like us some day.

To overcome these problems of ethnocentric bias and misplaced cultural smugness, I have chosen neutrally descriptive terms: *Most Industrialized Nations, Industrializing Nations,* and *Least Industrialized Nations.* These terms do not carry an ethnocentric value burden, for they indicate only that a nation's amount of industrialization is measurable and relative, without a connotation that industrialization is desirable.

Acknowledgments

The gratifying response to earlier editions indicates that my efforts at making sociology down to earth have succeeded. The years that have gone into writing this text are a culmination of the many more years that preceded its writing—from graduate school to that equally demanding endeavor known as classroom teaching. No text, of course, comes solely from its author. Although I am responsible for the final words on the printed page, I have received excellent feedback from instructors who have taught from the editions of the larger text on which *Core Concepts* is based. I am especially grateful to these reviewers:

Francis O. Adeola, *University of New Orleans*

Brian W. Agnitsch, *Marshalltown Community College*

Sandra L. Albrecht, *The University of Kansas*

Richard Alman, *Sierra College*

Gabriel C. Alvarez, *Duquesne University*

Christina Alexander, *Linfield College*

Kenneth Ambrose, *Marshall University*

Alberto Arroyo, *Baldwin–Wallace College*

Karren Baird-Olsen, *Kansas State University*

Rafael Balderrama, *University of Texas—Pan American*

Linda Barbera-Stein, *The University of Illinois*

Brenda Blackburn, *California State University. Fullerton*

Ronnie J. Booxbaum, *Greenfield Community College*

Cecil D. Bradfield, *James Madison University*

Karen Bradley, *Central Missouri State University*

Francis Broouer, *Worcester State College*

Valerie S. Brown, *Cuyahoga Community College*

Sandi Brunette-Hill, *Carrol College*

Richard Brunk, *Francis Marion University*

Karen Bullock, *Salem State College*

Allison Camelot, *Saddleback College*

Allison R. Camelot, *California State University at Fullerton*

Paul Ciccantell, *Kansas State University*

Mary Jean Cravens, *College of DuPage*

John K. Cochran, *The University of Oklahoma*

James M. Cook, *Duke University*

Joan Cook-Zimmern, *College of Saint Mary*

Larry Curiel, *Cypress College*

Russell L. Curtis, *University of Houston*

John Darling, *University of Pittsburgh—Johnstown*

Ray Darville, *Stephen F. Austin State University*

Jim David, *Butler County Community College*

Nanette J. Davis, *Portland State University*

Vincent Davis, *Mt. Hood Community College*

Lynda Dodgen, *North Harris Community College*

Terry Dougherty, *Portland State University*

Marlese Durr, *Wright State University*

Helen R. Ebaugh, *University of Houston*

Obi N. Ebbe, *State University of New York—Brockport*

Cy Edwards, Chair, *Cypress Community College*

John Ehle, *Northern Virginia Community College*

Morten Ender, *U.S. Military Academy*

Rebecca Susan Fahrlander, *Bellevue University*

Louis J. Finkle, *Horry-Georgetown Technical College*

Nicole T. Flynn, *University of South Alabama*

Lorna E. Forster, *Clinton Community College*

David O. Friedrichs, *University of Scranton*

Bruce Friesen, *Kent State University—Stark*

Lada Gibson-Shreve, *Stark State College*

Norman Goodman, *State University of New York—Stony Brook*

Rosalind Gottfried, *San Joaquin Delta College*

G. Kathleen Grant, *The University of Findlay*

Bill Grisby, *University of Northern Colorado*

Ramon Guerra, *University of Texas—Pan American*

Remi Hajjar, *U.S. Military Academy*

Donald W. Hastings, *The University of Tennessee—Knoxville*

Terrell Hayes, *High Point University*

Lillian O. Holloman, *Prince George's Community College*

Michael Hoover, *Missouri Western State College*

Howard R. Housen, *Broward Community College*

James H. Huber, *Bloomsburg University*

Erwin Hummel, *Portland State University*

Charles E. Hurst, *The College of Wooster*

Nita Jackson, *Butler County Community College*

Jennifer A. Johnson, *Germanna Community College*

Kathleen R. Johnson, *Keene State College*

Tammy Jolley, *University of Arkansas Community College at Batesville*

David Jones, *Plymouth State College*

Arunas Juska, *East Carolina University*

Ali Kamali, *Missouri Western State College*

Irwin Kantor, *Middlesex County College*

Mark Kassop, *Bergen Community College*

Myles Kelleher, *Bucks County Community College*

Mary E. Kelly, *Central Missouri State University*

Alice Abel Kemp, *University of New Orleans*

Diana Kendall, *Austin Community College*

Gary Kiger, *Utah State University*

Gene W. Kilpatrick, *University of Maine—Presque Isle*

Jerome R. Koch, *Texas Tech University*

Joseph A. Kotarba, *University of Houston*

Michele Lee Kozimor-King, *Pennsylvania State University*

Darina Lepadatu, *Kennesaw State University*

Abraham Levine, *El Camino Community College*

Diane Levy, *The University of North Carolina, Wilmington*

Stephen Mabry, *Cedar Valley College*

Lori Maida, *Westchester Community College*

David Maines, *Oakland University*

Ron Matson, *Wichita State University*

Armaund L. Mauss, *Washington State University*

Cynthia McCoy, *Holmes Community College*

Evelyn Mercer, *Southwest Baptist University*

Robert Meyer, *Arkansas State University*

Michael V. Miller, *University of Texas—San Antonio*

John Mitrano, *Central Connecticut State University*

W. Lawrence Neuman, *University of Wisconsin—Whitewater*

Charles Norman, *Indiana State University*

Patricia H. O'Brien, *Elgin Community College*

Robert Ostrow, *Wayne State*

Laura O'Toole, *University of Delaware*

Mike K. Pate, *Western Oklahoma State College*

Lawrence Peck, *Erie Community College*

Ruth Pigott, *University of Nebraska—Kearney*

Phil Piket, *Joliet Junior College*

Trevor Pinch, *Cornell University*

Daniel Polak, *Hudson Valley Community College*

James Pond, *Butler Community College*

Karen Potter, *Eastern Kentucky University*

Deedy Ramo, *Del Mar College*

Adrian Rapp, *North Harris Community College*

Ray Rich, *Community College of Southern Nevada*

Barbara Richardson, *Eastern Michigan University*

Salvador Rivera, *State University of New York—Cobleskill*

Howard Robboy, *Trenton State College*

Paulina X. Ruf, *University of Tampa*

Michael Samano, *Portland Community College*

Michael L. Sanow, *Community College of Baltimore County*

Mary C. Sengstock, *Wayne State University*

Ben Shirley, *Alamance Community College*

Walt Shirley, *Sinclair Community College*

Marc Silver, *Hofstra University*

Lynn Skaggs, *Central Texas College*

Roberto E. Socas, *Essex County College*

Mark Sperling, *Ivy Tech Community College*

Susan Sprecher, *Illinois State University*

Mariella Rose Squire, *University of Maine at Fort Kent*

Randolph G. Ston, *Oakland Community College*

Rachel Stehle, *Cuyahoga Community College*

Marios Stephanides, *University of Tampa*

Vickie Holland Taylor, *Danville Community College*

Maria Jose Tenuto, *College of Lake County*

Gary Tiederman, *Oregon State University*

Kathleen Tiemann, *University of North Dakota*

Judy Turchetta, *Johnson & Wales University*

Charlotte Twombly, *Montgomery College*

Stephen L. Vassar, *Minnesota State University, Mankato*

William J. Wattendorf, *Adirondack Community College*

Jay Weinstein, *Eastern Michigan University*

Larry Weiss, *University of Alaska*

Douglas White, *Henry Ford Community College*

Stephen R. Wilson, *Temple University*

Anthony T. Woart, *Bluefield State College*

Stuart Wright, *Lamar University*

Mary Lou Wylie, *James Madison University*

Diane Kholos Wysocki, *University of Nebraska—Kearney*

Stacey G. H. Yap, *Plymouth State College*

William Yoels, *University of Alabama Birmingham*

I couldn't ask for a more outstanding team than the one that I have the pleasure to work with at Allyn and Bacon. I want to thank Jeff Lasser, whose counsel continues to be excellent; Jenn Albanese, whose willingness to pursue leads in research has been an ongoing help in this formidable task; Judy Fiske, for constantly hovering over the many details—and for wholeheartedly supporting my many suggestions; Kathy Smith, for continuing her creative copy editing; Kate Cebik, for her creativity in photo research—and for her willingness to "keep on looking"; and Dusty Friedman, who while so capably overseeing both the routine and the urgent manages to exhibit an exemplary attitude.

I do so appreciate this team. It is difficult to heap too much praise on such fine, capable, and creative people. Often going "beyond the call of duty" as we faced non-stop deadlines, their untiring efforts coalesced with mine to produce this text. Students, whom we constantly kept in mind as we prepared this edition, are the beneficiaries of this intricate teamwork.

Since this text is based on the contributions of many, I would count it a privilege if you would share with me your teaching experiences with this book, including any suggestions for improving it. Both positive and negative comments are welcome. It is in this way that I learn.

I wish you the very best in your teaching. It is my sincere desire that *Sociology: A Down-to-Earth Approach, Core Concepts* contributes to that success.

Jim Henslin

James M. Henslin
Department of Sociology
Southern Illinois University, Edwardsville

I welcome your correspondence. E-mail is the best way to reach me: henslin@aol.com

A NOTE FROM THE PUBLISHER ON SUPPLEMENTS

Instructor's Supplements

Unless otherwise noted, instructor's supplements are available at no charge to adopters and available in printed or duplicated formats, as well as electronically through Allyn & Bacon/ Longman's Instructor's Resource Center (www.ablongman.com/irc).

Instructor's Manual *Jessica Herrmeyer, Hawkeye Community College*

For each chapter in the text, the Instructor's Manual provides a list of key changes to the new edition, chapter summaries and outlines, learning objectives, key terms and people, classroom activities, discussion topics, recommended films, Web sites, and additional references.

Test Bank *Anthony W. Zumpetta, West Chester University*

The Test Bank contains approximately 150 questions per chapter in multiple-choice, true-false, short answer, essay, vocabulary matching, and open-book formats. A recent addition is a section that challenges students to look beyond words and answer questions based on the text's figures, tables, and maps. All questions are labeled and scaled according to Bloom's Taxonomy.

Computerized Test Bank

The printed Test Bank is also available through Allyn and Bacon's computerized testing system, TestGen EQ. This fully networkable test-generating software is available online at www.ablongman.com/irc (access code required). The user-friendly interface allows you to view, edit, and add questions, transfer questions to tests, and print tests in a variety of fonts. Search and sort features allow you to locate questions quickly and to arrange them in whatever order you prefer.

PowerPoint Presentation *Dan Cavanaugh*

These PowerPoint slides on a CD, created especially for the Third Edition, feature lecture outlines for every chapter and many of the tables, charts, and maps from the text. PowerPoint software is not required, as a PowerPoint viewer is included.

Transparencies to Accompany Introductory Sociology, by James Henslin

This package, updated for 2008 includes over 125 color acetates featuring illustrations from Henslin's introductory sociology texts.

Allyn and Bacon/ABC News Sociology Videos

This series of videos contains news footage and documentary-style programs from *Nightline, World News Tonight,* and *20/20* that illustrate sociological themes. Each video has an accompanying User's Guide (available electronically through Allyn and Bacon's Instructor's Resource Center). Available titles are *Poverty and Stratification, Race and Ethnicity, Gender, Deviance,* and *Aging.*

Sociology Video Library

Third-party videos are available on every major topic in sociology. Some of the videos are from Films for the Humanities and Sciences and Annenberg/CPB. Some restrictions apply. Contact your Pearson representative for details.

The Video Professor: Applying Lessons in Sociology to Classic and Modern Films *Anthony W. Zumpetta, West Chester University*

This manual describes hundreds of commercially available videos that represent nineteen of the most important topics in Introductory Sociology textbooks. Each topic lists a number of movies, along with specific assignments and suggestions for class use. Available in print, and also electronically through the Allyn & Bacon/Longman Instructor's Resource Center.

InterWrite PRS (Personal Response System)

Assess your students' progress with the Personal Response System — an easy-to-use wireless polling system that enables you to pose questions, record results, and display those results instantly in your classroom. Designed by teachers, for teachers, PRS is easy to integrate into your lectures:

- Each student uses a cell-phone-sized transmitter which they bring to class.

- You ask multiple-choice, numerical-answer, or matching questions during class; students simply click their answer into their transmitter.

- A classroom receiver (portable or mounted) connected to your computer tabulates all answers and displays them graphically in class.

- Results can be recorded for grading, attendance, or simply used as a discussion point.

Our partnership with PRS allows us to offer student rebate cards bundled with any Allyn and Bacon/Longman text. The rebate card is a direct value of $20.00 and can be redeemed with the purchase a new PRS student transmitter. In addition, institutions that order 40 or more new textbook + rebate card bundles will receive the classroom receiver—a $250 value—software and support at no additional cost. We also offer sets of questions for introductory sociology designed to be used with Personal Response Systems. Contact your Pearson representative or visit http://www.ablongman.com/prs for more information.

Student Supplements

Society: Readings to Accompany Sociology: A Down-to-Earth Approach: Core Concepts, Third Edition *James M. Henslin*

This brief reader, revised for this edition, contains two articles for each chapter of the text, each chosen and introduced by Jim Henslin. The reader can be purchased separately at full price or packaged with this text for an additional $5 net to the bookstore. An instructor's manual for the reader is available electronically through the Allyn and Bacon/Longman Instructor's Resource Center.

Study Guide Plus *Jessica Herrmeyer, Hawkeye Community College*

For every chapter in the text, the Study Guide Plus contains a chapter summary; a list of learning objectives; a detailed chapter outline; a list of key terms and people; 3–5 student projects; and a practice test with 30 multiple-choice, 20 true/false, 15 short answer, 10 matching, and 5 essay questions. An answer key is provided for all questions. The Study Guide Plus also includes a section on successful study strategies. Available separately for student purchase, or packaged with the text at a discount.

Study Card for Introduction to Sociology

Compact, efficient, and laminated for durability, the Allyn and Bacon Study Card for Introductory Sociology condenses course information down to the basics, helping students quickly master fundamental facts and concepts or prepare for an exam. Packaged on request with this text at no additional charge.

Online Course Management

MySocLab

MySocLab is a state-of-the-art interactive and instructive solution for introductory sociology, delivered within CourseCompass, Allyn and Bacon's course management system (powered by Blackboard and hosted nationally on our server). MySocLab is designed to be used as a supplement to a traditional lecture course, or to completely administer an online course. Built around a complete e-book version of the text, MySocLab enables students to explore important sociological concepts by listening to interviews with prominent researchers and social scientists; listening to stories from the National Public Radio archives; reading current newspaper articles; completing activities based on maps and graphs in the text; and performing other hands-on activities. Self-scoring practice tests (in English and Spanish) help students prepare for quizzes and exams, and create a customized study plan for them. MySocLab also includes access to Research Navigator™ (see below), and a tutorial on Writing About Sociology. Customize your course or use the materials as presented. Available at no additional charge when the text is packaged with a *MySocLab Student Access Code Card*.

MySocLab, Website Version

Provides virtually the same online content and interactivity as MySocLab, without any of the course management features or requirements. Available at no additional charge when the text is packaged with a *MySocLab Student Access Code Card*.

WebCT™ and Blackboard Test Banks

For colleges and universities with **WebCT™** and **Blackboard** licenses, we have converted the complete Test Bank into these popular course management platforms. Adopters can request a copy on CD or download the electronic file by logging in to our Instructor Resource Center.

Research Navigator™

Students receive a free six-month subscription to this valuable research database when the text is packaged with the *ResearchNavigator.com Guide for Sociology* (see below). Research Navigator's powerful search engines provide access to thousands of full-text articles from scholarly social science journals and popular magazines and newspapers, including a one-year archive of the complete *New York Times*.

Additional Supplements

New! The Allyn and Bacon Social Atlas of the United States *William H. Frey, University of Michigan, with Amy Beth Anspach, and John Paul DeWitt.*

This brief and accessible atlas uses colorful maps, graphs, and some of the best social science data available to survey the leading social, economic, and political indicators of American society. Available for purchase separately, or packaged with this text at a significant discount.

ResearchNavigator.com Guide: Sociology *Joseph E. Jacoby, Bowling Green State University.*

This manual contains a student access code for the Research Navigator™ database (www .researchnavigator.com), offering students unlimited access to a collection of more than 25,000 discipline-specific articles from leading academic publications and peer-reviewed journals, as well as the *New York Times* and other magazines and newspapers. It also includes tips for searching for articles on the site, a list of journals useful for research in their discipline, and information on how to correctly cite research. Packaged on request with this text at no additional charge.

Building Bridges: The Allyn and Bacon Guide to Service Learning   *Doris Hamner*

This manual offers practical advice for students who must complete a service-learning project as part of their required course work. Packaged on request with this text at no additional charge.

Careers in Sociology, Third Edition   *W. Richard Stephens, Eastern Nazarene College*

This supplement explains how sociology can help students prepare for careers in such fields as law, gerontology, social work, business, and computers. It also examines how sociologists entered the field. Packaged on request with this text at no additional charge.

Breaking the Ice: A Guide to Understanding People From Other Cultures, Third Edition   *Akiiki Daisy Kabagarama, Montgomery College*

Breaking the Ice helps students better understand and interact with people from other cultures, encouraging them to react and draw on their experiences. The concept of culture is discussed fully, and both its unifying and divisive elements are examined. Exercises found both throughout the text and at the end of each chapter are aimed at helping readers discover their own biases. Packaged on request with this text at no additional charge.

College and Society: An Introduction to the Sociological Imagination   *Stephen Sweet, Ithaca College*

This supplemental text uses examples from familiar surroundings—the patterns of interaction, social structures, and expectations of conduct on a typical college campus—to help students see the ways in which the larger society also operates. Available for purchase separately or packaged with this text at a special discount.

About the Author

JAMES M. HENSLIN, who was born in Minnesota, graduated from high school and junior college in California and from college in Indiana. Awarded scholarships, he earned his Master's and doctorate degrees in sociology at Washington University in St. Louis, Missouri. After this, he won a postdoctoral fellowship from the National Institute of Mental Health, and spent a year studying how people adjust to the suicide of a family member. His primary interests in sociology are the sociology of everyday life, deviance, and international relations. Among his many books is *Down to Earth Sociology: Introductory Readings* (Free Press), now in its fourteenth edition. He has also published widely in sociology journals, including *Social Problems* and *American Journal of Sociology*.

While a graduate student, Jim taught at the University of Missouri at St. Louis. After completing his doctorate, he joined the faculty at Southern Illinois University, Edwardsville, where he is Professor Emeritus of Sociology. He says, "I've always found the introductory course enjoyable to teach. I love to see students' faces light up when they first glimpse the sociological perspective and begin to see how society has become an essential part of how they view the world."

Jim enjoys reading and fishing, and he also does a bit of kayaking. His two favorite activities are writing and traveling. He especially enjoys visiting and living in other cultures, for this brings him face to face with behaviors and ways of thinking that challenge his perspectives and "make sociological principles come alive." A special pleasure has been the preparation of the photo essays that appear in this text.

Jim is currently immersed in Eastern Europe, where he is observing first-hand the transition to capitalism of former Soviet-dominated countries.

The Sociological Perspective

Diana Ong, *Rainy Day Crowd*, 1999

Even from the glow of the faded red-and-white exit sign, its faint light barely illuminating the upper bunk, I could see that the sheet was filthy. Resigned to another night of fitful sleep, I reluctantly crawled into bed.

The next morning, I joined the long line of disheveled men leaning against the chain-link fence. Their faces were as downcast as their clothes were dirty. Not a glimmer of hope among them.

No one spoke as the line slowly inched forward. When my turn came, I was handed a cup of coffee, a white plastic spoon, and a bowl of semi-liquid that I couldn't identify. It didn't look like any food I had seen before. Nor did it taste like anything I had ever eaten.

My stomach fought the foul taste, every spoonful a battle. But I was determined. "I will experience what they experience," I kept telling myself. My stomach reluctantly gave in and accepted its morning nourishment.

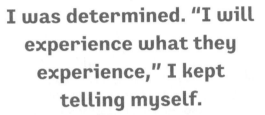

I was determined. "I will experience what they experience," I kept telling myself.

The room was eerily silent. Hundreds of men were eating, each immersed in his own private hell, his head awash with disappointment, remorse, bitterness.

As I stared at the Styrofoam cup that held my coffee, grateful for at least this small pleasure, I noticed what looked like tooth marks. I shrugged off the thought, telling myself that my long weeks as a sociological observer of the homeless were finally getting to me. "This must be some sort of crease from handling," I concluded.

I joined the silent ranks of men turning in their bowls and cups. When I saw the man behind the counter swishing out Styrofoam cups in a washtub of murky water, I began to feel sick to my stomach. I knew then that the jagged marks on my cup really had come from a previous user's mouth.

How much longer did this research have to last? I felt a deep longing to return to my family—to a welcome world of clean sheets, healthy food, and "normal" conversations.

The Sociological Perspective

Why were these men so silent? Why did they receive such despicable treatment? What was I doing in that homeless shelter? After all, I hold a respectable, professional position, and I have a home and family.

Sociology offers a perspective, a view of the world. The *sociological perspective* (or imagination) opens a window onto unfamiliar worlds and offers a fresh look at familiar worlds. In this text you will find yourself in the midst of Nazis in Germany, warriors in South America, and even the people I visited who live in a city dump in Cambodia. But you also will find yourself looking at your own world in a different light. As you view other worlds—or your own—the sociological perspective will enable you to gain a new vision of social life. In fact, this is what many find appealing about sociology.

Sociologists move beyond **common sense**—the prevailing ideas in a society, the things that "everyone knows" are true. "Everyone" can be misguided today just as easily as when common sense dictated that the world was flat or that no human could ever walk on the moon. As sociologists examine people's assumptions about the world, their findings may contradict commonsense notions about social life. To test your own "common sense," take the fun quiz on page 20.

The sociological perspective has been a motivating force in my own life. Ever since I took my introductory course in sociology, I have been enchanted by the perspective that sociology offers. I have thoroughly enjoyed both observing other groups and questioning my own assumptions about life. I sincerely hope the same happens to you.

Examining the broad social context in which people live is essential to the *sociological perspective,* for this context shapes our beliefs and attitudes and sets guidelines for what we do. From this photo, you can see how distinctive those guidelines are for the Yanomamö Indians who live on the border of Brazil and Venezuela. How has this Yanomamö man been influenced by his group? How have groups influenced your views and behavior?

Seeing the Broader Social Context

The **sociological perspective** stresses the social contexts in which people live. It examines how these contexts influence people's lives. At the center of the sociological perspective is the question of how groups influence people, especially how people are influenced by their **society**—a group of people who share a culture and a territory.

To find out why people do what they do, sociologists look at **social location,** the corners in life that people occupy because of where they are located in a society. Sociologists look at how jobs, income, education, gender, age, and race–ethnicity affect people's ideas and behavior. Consider, for example, how being identified with a group called *females* or with a group called *males* when we are growing up shapes our ideas of who we are and what we should attain in life. Growing up as a male or a female influences not only our goals in life but also how we feel about ourselves. It also affects the way we relate to others in dating and marriage and at work.

common sense those things that "everyone knows" are true

sociological perspective understanding human behavior by placing it within its broader social context

society people who share a culture and a territory

social location the group memberships that people have because of their location in history and society

Sociologist C. Wright Mills (1959) put it this way: "The sociological imagination [or perspective] enables us to grasp the connection between history and biography." By *history,* Mills meant that each society is located in a broad stream of events. Because of this, each society has specific characteristics—such as its ideas about the proper roles of men and women. By *biography,* Mills referred to the individual's specific experiences. In short, people don't do what they do because of inherited internal mechanisms, such as instincts. Rather, *external* influences—our experiences—become part of our thinking and motivations. The society in which we grow up and our particular location in that society lie at the center of what we do and what we think.

Consider a newborn baby. If we were to take the baby away from its U.S. parents and place it with a Yanomamö Indian tribe in the jungles of South America, you know that when the child begins to speak, his or her words will not be in English. You also know that the child will not think like an American. He or she will not grow up wanting credit cards, for example, or designer jeans, a car, a cell phone, an iPod, and the latest video game. Equally, the child will unquestioningly take his or her place in Yanomamö society—perhaps as a food gatherer, a hunter, or a warrior—and he or she will not even know about the world left behind at birth. And whether male or female, the child will grow up assuming that it is natural to want many children, not debating whether to have one, two, or three children.

This brings us to *you*—to how *your* social groups have shaped *your* ideas and desires. Over and over in this text, you will see that the way you look at the world is the result of your exposure to specific human groups. I think you will enjoy the process of self-discovery that sociology offers.

Origins of Sociology

Tradition Versus Science

Just how did sociology begin? In some ways, it is difficult to answer this question. Even ancient peoples tried to figure out social life. They, too, asked questions about why war exists, why some people become more powerful than others, and why some are rich, but others are poor. However, they often based their answers on superstition, myth, or even the position of the stars and did not *test* their assumptions.

Science, *in contrast, requires the development of theories that can be tested by research.* Measured by this standard, sociology only recently appeared on the human scene. It emerged about the middle of the 1800s, when social observers began to use scientific methods to test their ideas.

Sociology grew out of social upheaval. The Industrial Revolution had just begun, and masses of people were moving to cities in search of work. Their ties to the land—and to a culture that had provided them with ready answers to the difficult questions of life—were broken. The cities greeted them with horrible working conditions: low pay; long, exhausting hours; dangerous work. For families to survive, even children had to work in these conditions; some children were even chained to factory machines to make certain they could not run away. Life no longer looked the same, and tradition, which had provided the answers to social life, no longer could be counted on.

Tradition suffered further blows. The success of the American and French revolutions encouraged people to rethink social life. New ideas arose, including the conviction that individuals possess inalienable rights. As this new idea caught fire, many traditional Western monarchies gave way to more democratic forms of government. People found the ready answers of tradition inadequate.

About this same time, the *scientific method*—using objective, systematic observations to test theories—was being tried out in chemistry and physics. Many secrets that had been concealed in nature were being uncovered. With tradition no longer providing the answers to questions about social life, the logical step was to apply the scientific method to these questions. The result was the birth of sociology.

Auguste Comte and Positivism

This idea of applying the scientific method to the social world, known as **positivism,** apparently was first proposed by Auguste Comte (1798–1857). With the French Revolution still fresh in his mind, Comte left the small, conservative town in which he had grown up and moved to Paris. The changes he experienced in this move, combined with

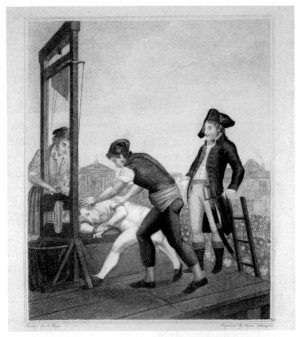

The French Revolution of 1789 not only overthrew the aristocracy but also upset the entire social order. This extensive change removed the past as a sure guide to the present. The events of this period stimulated Auguste Comte to analyze how societies change. His writings are often taken as the origin of sociology. This engraving depicts the 1794 execution of Maximilien Robespierre, a leader of the Revolution.

Auguste Comte (1798–1857), who is credited as the founder of sociology, began to analyze the bases of the social order. Although he stressed that the scientific method should be applied to the study of society, he did not apply it himself.

science the application of systematic methods to obtain knowledge and the knowledge obtained by those methods

positivism the application of the scientific approach to the social world

those France underwent in the revolution, led Comte to become interested in what holds society together. What creates social order, he wondered, instead of anarchy or chaos? And then, once society does become set on a particular course, what causes it to change?

As Comte considered these questions, he concluded that the right way to answer them was to apply the scientific method to social life. Just as this method had revealed the law of gravity, so, too, it would uncover the laws that underlie society. Comte called this new science **sociology,** "the study of society" (from the Greek *logos,* "study of," and the Latin *socius,* "companion" or "being with others"). Comte stressed that this new science not only would discover social principles but also would apply them to social reform. Sociologists would reform the entire society, making it a better place to live.

To Comte, however, applying the scientific method to social life meant practicing what we might call "armchair philosophy"—drawing conclusions from informal observations of social life. He did not do what today's sociologists would call research, and his conclusions have been abandoned. Nevertheless, Comte's insistence that we must observe and classify human activities to uncover society's fundamental laws is well taken. Because he developed this idea and coined the term *sociology,* Comte often is credited with being the founder of sociology.

Herbert Spencer and Social Darwinism

Herbert Spencer (1820–1903), who grew up in England, is sometimes called the second founder of sociology. Spencer disagreed profoundly with Comte that sociology should guide social reform. He was convinced that no one should intervene in the evolution of society. Spencer thought that societies evolve from lower ("barbarian") to higher ("civilized") forms. As generations pass, the most capable and intelligent ("the fittest") members of the society survive, while the less capable die out. Thus, over time, societies improve. If you help the lower classes, you interfere with this natural process. The fittest members will produce a more advanced society—unless misguided do-gooders get in the way and help those who are less fit to survive.

Spencer called this principle "the survival of the fittest." Although Spencer coined this phrase, it usually is attributed to his contemporary, Charles Darwin, who proposed that organisms evolve over time as they adapt to their environment. Because they are so similar to Darwin's ideas, Spencer's views of the evolution of societies became known as *social Darwinism.*

Like Comte, Spencer was more of a social philosopher than a sociologist. Also like Comte, Spencer did not conduct scientific studies. He simply developed ideas about society. After gaining a wide following in England and the United States, Spencer's ideas about social Darwinism were discarded.

Karl Marx and Class Conflict

Karl Marx (1818–1883) not only influenced sociology but also left his mark on world history. Marx's influence has been so great that even the *Wall Street Journal,* that staunch advocate of capitalism, has called him one of the three greatest modern thinkers (the other two being Sigmund Freud and Albert Einstein).

Marx, who came to England after being exiled from his native Germany for proposing revolution, believed that the engine of human history is **class conflict.** He said that the *bourgeoisie* (boor-zhwa-ZEE) (the *capitalists,* those who own the means to produce wealth—capital, land, factories, and machines) are locked in conflict with the *proletariat* (the exploited class, the mass of workers who do not own the means of production). This bitter struggle can end only when the workers unite in revolution and throw off their chains of bondage. The result will be a classless society, one free of exploitation, in which people will work according to their abilities and receive goods and services according to their needs (Marx and Engels 1848/1967).

Marxism is not the same as communism. Although Marx supported revolution as the only way that the workers could gain control of society, he did not develop the political system called *communism.* This is a later application of his ideas. Indeed, Marx felt

Herbert Spencer (1820–1903), sometimes called the second founder of sociology, coined the term "survival of the fittest." Spencer thought that helping the poor was wrong, that this merely helped the "less fit" survive.

Karl Marx (1818–1883) believed that the roots of human misery lay in class conflict, the exploitation of workers by those who own the means of production. Social change, in the form of the overthrow of the capitalists by the workers (proletariat), was inevitable from Marx's perspective. Although Marx did not consider himself a sociologist, his ideas have influenced many sociologists, particularly conflict theorists.

disgusted when he heard debates about his insights into social life. After listening to some of the positions attributed to him, he shook his head and said, "I am not a Marxist" (Dobriner 1969b:222; Gitlin 1997:89).

Emile Durkheim and Social Integration

The primary professional goal of Emile Durkheim (1858–1917), who grew up in France, was to get sociology recognized as a separate academic discipline (Coser 1977). Up to this time, sociology had been viewed as a part of the study of history and economics. Durkheim achieved this goal when he received the first academic appointment in sociology at the University of Bordeaux in 1887.

Durkheim also had another goal: to show how social forces affect people's behavior. To accomplish this, he conducted rigorous research. Comparing the suicide rates of several European countries, Durkheim (1897/1966) found that each country had a different suicide rate, and that these rates remained about the same year after year. He also found that different groups within a country had different suicide rates and that these, too, remained stable from year to year. For example, Protestants, males, and the unmarried killed themselves at a higher rate than did Catholics, Jews, females, and the married. From this, Durkheim drew the insightful conclusion that suicide is not simply a matter of individuals here and there deciding to take their lives for personal reasons. Rather, *social factors underlie suicide,* and this is what keeps a group's rates fairly constant year after year.

Durkheim identified **social integration,** the degree to which people are tied to their social group, as a key social factor in suicide. He concluded that people who have weaker social ties are more likely to commit suicide. This factor, he said, explained why Protestants, males, and the unmarried have higher suicide rates. This is how it works, Durkheim said: Protestantism encourages greater freedom of thought and action, males are more independent than females, and the unmarried lack the connections and responsibilities that come with marriage. In other words, because their social integration is weaker, members of these groups have fewer of the social ties that keep people from committing suicide. In Durkheim's term, they have less social integration.

Over a hundred years later, Durkheim's work is still quoted. His research was so thorough that the principle he uncovered still applies: People who are less socially integrated have higher rates of suicide. Even today, those same groups that Durkheim identified—Protestants, males, and the unmarried—are more likely to kill themselves.

From Durkheim's study of suicide, we see the principle that was central in his research: *Human behavior cannot be understood simply in individualistic terms; we must always examine the social forces that affect people's lives.* Suicide, for example, appears at first to be such an intensely individual act that psychologists should study it, not sociologists. Yet, as Durkheim illustrated, if we look at human behavior (such as suicide) only in individualistic terms, we miss its *social* basis.

Max Weber and the Protestant Ethic

Max Weber (Mahx VAY-ber) (1864–1920), a German sociologist and a contemporary of Durkheim, also held professorships in the new academic discipline of sociology. Like Durkheim and Marx, Weber is one of the most influential of all sociologists, and you will come across his writings and theories in the coming chapters. Let's consider an issue Weber raised that remains controversial today.

Religion and the Origin of Capitalism   Weber disagreed with Marx's claim that economics is the central force in social change. That role, he said, belongs to religion. Weber (1904/1958) theorized that the Roman Catholic belief system encouraged its followers to hold onto traditional ways of life, while the Protestant belief system encouraged its members to embrace change. Protestantism, he said, undermined people's spiritual security. Roman Catholics believed that they were on the road to heaven because they were baptized and were church members. Protestants, however, did not share this belief. Protestants of the Calvinist tradition were told that they wouldn't

The French sociologist Emile Durkheim (1858–1917) contributed many important concepts to sociology. His comparison of the suicide rates of several counties revealed an underlying social factor: People are more likely to commit suicide if their ties to others in their communities are weak. Durkheim's identification of the key role of social integration in social life remains central to sociology today.

Max Weber (1864–1920) was another early sociologist who left a profound impression on sociology. He used cross-cultural and historical materials to trace the cause of social change and to determine how social groups affect people's orientations to life.

know if they were saved until Judgment Day. Uncomfortable with this, they began to look for "signs" that they were in God's will. Eventually, they concluded that financial success was the major sign that God was on their side. To bring about this "sign" and receive spiritual comfort, they began to live frugal lives, saving their money and investing the surplus in order to make even more. This, said Weber, brought about the birth of capitalism.

Weber called this self-denying approach to life the *Protestant ethic*. He termed the readiness to invest capital in order to make more money the *spirit of capitalism*. To test his theory, Weber compared the extent of capitalism in Roman Catholic and Protestant countries. In line with his theory, he found that capitalism was more likely to flourish in Protestant countries. Weber's conclusion that religion was the key factor in the rise of capitalism was controversial when he made it, and it continues to be debated today (Wade 2007).

Sexism in Early Sociology

Attitudes of the Time

As you may have noticed, we have discussed only male sociologists. In the 1800s, sex roles were rigidly defined, with women assigned the roles of wife and mother. In the classic German phrase, women were expected to devote themselves to the four K's: *Kirche, Küchen, Kinder, und Kleider* (church, cooking, children, and clothes). Women who tried to break out of this mold experienced severe social disapproval.

Few people, male or female, received any education beyond basic reading, writing, and a little math. Higher education, for the rare few who received it, was reserved for men. A handful of women from wealthy families, however, did pursue higher education. A few even managed to study sociology, although the sexism that was so deeply entrenched in the universities stopped them from obtaining advanced degrees or becoming professors. In line with the times, their research was almost entirely ignored.

Harriet Martineau and Early Social Research

A classic example is Harriet Martineau (1802–1876), who was born into a wealthy English family. When Martineau first began to analyze social life, she would hide her writing beneath her sewing when visitors arrived, for writing was considered "masculine" and sewing "feminine" (Gilman 1911:88). Martineau persisted in her interests, however, and she eventually studied social life in both Great Britain and the United States. In 1837, two or three decades before Durkheim and Weber were born, Martineau published *Society in America*, in which she reported on this new nation's customs—family, race, gender, politics, and religion. Despite her insightful examination of U.S. life, which is still worth reading today, Martineau's research met the same fate as the work of other early women sociologists and, until recently, was ignored. Instead, she is known primarily for translating Comte's ideas into English.

Interested in social reform, Harriet Martineau (1802–1876) turned to sociology, where she discovered the writings of Comte. She became on advocate for the abolition of slavery, traveled widely, and wrote extensive analyses of social life.

Sociology in North America

Early History: The Tension Between Social Reform and Sociological Analysis

Transplanted to U.S. soil in the late nineteenth century, sociology first took root at the University of Kansas in 1890; at the University of Chicago in 1892; and at Atlanta University, then an all-black school, in 1897. It was not until 1922 that McGill University gave Canada its first department of sociology. Harvard University did not open a department of sociology until 1930, and the University of California at Berkeley didn't have one until the 1950s.

Initially, the department at the University of Chicago, which was founded by Albion Small (1854–1926), dominated sociology. (Small also founded the *American Journal of Sociology* and was its editor from 1895 to 1925.) Members of this early sociology department whose ideas continue to influence today's sociologists include Robert Park (1864–1944), Ernest Burgess (1886–1966), and George Herbert Mead (1863–1931). Mead developed the symbolic interactionist perspective, which we will examine later.

Jane Addams and Social Reform

Although many North American sociologists combined the role of sociologist with that of social reformer, none was as successful as Jane Addams (1860–1935). Like Harriet Martineau, Addams came from a background of wealth and privilege. She attended the Women's Medical College of Philadelphia, but dropped out because of illness (Addams 1910/1981). During one of her many trips to Europe, Addams observed and was impressed by the work being done on behalf of London's poor. From then on, she worked tirelessly for social justice.

In 1889, Addams cofounded Hull-House, located in Chicago's notorious slums. Hull-House was open to people who needed refuge—to immigrants, the sick, the aged, the poor. Sociologists from the nearby University of Chicago were frequent visitors at Hull-House. With her piercing insights into the ways in which workers were exploited and how immigrants adjusted to city life, Addams strived to bridge the gap between the powerful and the powerless. She worked with others to win the eight-hour work day and to pass laws against child labor. Her efforts at social reform were so outstanding that in 1931 she was a cowinner of the Nobel Prize for Peace, the only sociologist to win this coveted award.

Jane Addams, 1860–1935, a recipient of the Nobel Prize for Peace, worked on behalf of poor immigrants. With Ellen G. Starr, she founded Hull-House, a center to help immigrants in Chicago. She was also a leader in women's rights (women's suffrage), as well as the peace movement of World War I.

W. E. B. Du Bois and Race Relations

Another sociologist who combined sociology and social reform is W. E. B. Du Bois (1868–1963), the first African American to earn a doctorate at Harvard. After completing his education at the University of Berlin, where he attended lectures by Max Weber, Du Bois taught Greek and Latin at Wilberforce University. He then went to Atlanta University in 1897, where he remained for most of his career.

Although Du Bois was invited to present a paper at the 1909 meetings of the American Sociological Society, he was too poor to attend. When he could afford to attend subsequent meetings, discrimination was so prevalent in the United States that hotels and restaurants would not allow him to room or eat with the white sociologists. Later in life, when Du Bois had the money to travel, the U.S. State Department feared that he would criticize the United States and at the height of the Cold War refused to give him a passport (Du Bois 1968).

Du Bois' lifetime research interest was relations between whites and African Americans, and he published a book on this subject *each* year between 1896 and 1914. The Down-to-Earth Sociology box on the next page is taken from one of his books. Du Bois' insights into race relations were heightened by personal experiences. For example, he once saw the fingers of a lynching victim on display in a Georgia butcher shop (Aptheker 1990).

At first, Du Bois was content to collect and interpret objective data. Later, frustrated at the continuing exploitation of blacks, he turned to social action. Along with Jane Addams and others from Hull-House, Du Bois founded the National Association for the Advancement of Colored People (NAACP) (Deegan 1988). Continuing to battle racism both as a sociologist and as a journalist, he eventually embraced revolutionary Marxism. At age 93, dismayed that so little improvement had been made in race relations, he moved to Ghana, where he is buried (Stark 1989).

W(illiam) E(dward) B(urghardt) Du Bois (1868–1963) spent his lifetime studying relations between African Americans and whites. Like many early North American sociologists, Du Bois combined the role of academic sociologist with that of social reformer. He was also the editor of *Crisis*, an influential journal of the time.

Early Sociology in North America: Du Bois and Race Relations

THE WRITINGS OF W. E. B. DU BOIS, who expressed sociological thought more like an accomplished novelist than a sociologist, have been neglected in sociology. To help remedy this omission, I reprint the following excerpts from pages 66–68 of *The Souls of Black Folk* (1903). In this book, Du Bois analyzes changes that occurred in the social and economic conditions of African Americans during the thirty years following the Civil War.

For two summers, while he was a student at Fisk, Du Bois taught in a segregated school housed in a log hut "way back in the hills" of rural Tennessee. The following excerpts help us understand conditions at that time.

In the 1800s, poverty was widespread in the United States. Most people were so poor that they expended their life energies on just getting enough food, fuel, and clothing to survive. Formal education beyond the first several grades was a luxury. This photo depicts the conditions of the people Du Bois worked with.

It was a hot morning late in July when the school opened. I trembled when I heard the patter of little feet down the dusty road, and saw the growing row of dark solemn faces and bright eager eyes facing me. . . . There they sat, nearly thirty of them, on the rough benches, their faces shading from a pale cream to deep brown, the little feet bare and swinging, the eyes full of expectation, with here and there a twinkle of mischief, and the hands grasping Webster's blue-black spelling-book. I loved my school, and the fine faith the children had in the wisdom of their teacher was truly marvelous. We read and spelled together, wrote a little, picked flowers, sang, and listened to stories of the world beyond the hill. . . .

On Friday nights I often went home with some of the children,—sometimes to Doc Burke's farm. He was a great, loud, thin Black, ever working, and trying to buy these seventy-five acres of hill and dale where he lived; but people said that he would surely fail and the "white folks would get it all." His wife was a magnificent Amazon, with saffron face and shiny hair, uncorseted and barefooted, and the children were strong and barefooted. They lived in a one-and-a-half-room cabin in the hollow of the farm near the spring. . . .

I liked to stay with the Dowells, for they had four rooms and plenty of good country fare. Uncle Bird had a small, rough farm, all woods and hills, miles from the big road; but he was full of tales,—he preached now and then,—and with his children, berries, horses, and wheat

he was happy and prosperous. Often, to keep the peace, I must go where life was less lovely; for instance, 'Tildy's mother was incorrigibly dirty, Reuben's larder was limited seriously, and herds of untamed insects wandered over the Eddingses' beds. Best of all I loved to go to Josie's, and sit on the porch, eating peaches, while the mother bustled and talked: how Josie had bought the sewing-machine; how Josie worked at service in winter, but that four dollars a month was "mighty little" wages; how Josie longed to go away to school, but that it "looked liked" they never could get far enough ahead to let her; how the crops failed and the well was yet unfinished; and, finally, how mean some of the white folks were.

For two summers I lived in this little world. . . . I have called my tiny community a world, and so its isolation made it; and yet there was among us but a half-awakened common consciousness, sprung from common joy and grief, at burial, birth, or wedding; from common hardship in poverty, poor land, and low wages, and, above all, from the sight of the Veil* that hung between us and Opportunity. All this caused us to think some thoughts together; but these, when ripe for speech, were spoken in various languages. Those whose eyes twenty-five and more years before had seen "the glory of the coming of the Lord," saw in every present hindrance or help a dark fatalism bound to bring all things right in His own good time. The mass of those to whom slavery was a dim recollection of childhood found the world a puzzling thing: it asked little of them, and they answered with little, and yet it ridiculed their offering.

* "The Veil" is shorthand for the Veil of Race, referring to how race colors all human relations. Du Bois' hope was that "sometime, somewhere, men will judge men by their souls and not by their skins" (p. 261).

In the 1940s, when this photo was taken, racial segregation was a taken-for-granted fact of life. Although many changes have occurred since then—and since W. E. B. Du Bois analyzed race relations—race ethnicity remains a significant factor in the lives of Americans.

FOR COLORED ONLY

Talcott Parsons and C. Wright Mills: Theory Versus Reform

During the 1940s, the emphasis shifted from social reform to social theory. Talcott Parsons (1902–1979), for example, developed abstract models of society that greatly influenced a generation of sociologists. Parsons' models of how the parts of society work together harmoniously did nothing to stimulate social activism.

C. Wright Mills (1916–1962) deplored the theoretical abstractions of this period, and he urged sociologists to get back to social reform. He warned that an imminent threat to freedom was the coalescing of interests on the part of a group he called the *power elite*—the top leaders of business, politics, and the military. Shortly after Mills' death came the turbulent late 1960s and 1970s. This precedent-shaking era sparked interest in social activism, and Mills' ideas grew popular among a new generation of sociologists.

C. Wright Mills was a controversial figure in sociology because of his analysis of the role of the power elite in U.S. society. Today, his analysis is taken for granted by many sociologists and members of the public.

The Continuing Tension and the Rise of Applied Sociology

The apparent contradiction of these two aims—analyzing society versus working toward its reform—created a tension in sociology that is still with us today. Some sociologists believe that their proper role is to analyze some aspect of society and to publish their findings in sociology journals. This is called *basic* (or *pure*) *sociology*. Others say that basic sociology is not enough: Sociologists have an obligation to use their expertise to try to make society a better place in which to live and to help bring justice to the poor.

Somewhere between these extremes lies **applied sociology,** which uses sociology to solve problems. (See Figure 1.1 on the next page, which contrasts basic and applied sociology.) One of the first attempts at applied sociology—and one of the most successful—was one I just mentioned: the founding of the National Association for the Advancement of Colored People. As illustrated in the Down-to-Earth Sociology box on the next page, today's applied sociologists work in a variety of settings. Some work for business firms to solve problems in the workplace. Others investigate social problems such as environmental

applied sociology the use of sociology to solve problems—from the micro level of family relationships to the macro level of crime and pollution

Figure 1.1 Comparing Basic and Applied Sociology

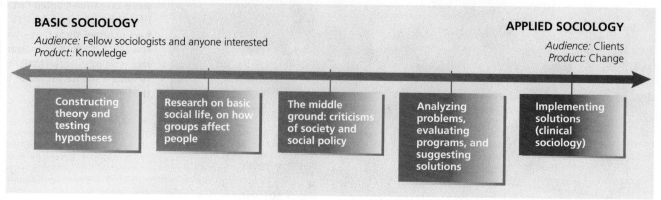

BASIC SOCIOLOGY
Audience: Fellow sociologists and anyone interested
Product: Knowledge

APPLIED SOCIOLOGY
Audience: Clients
Product: Change

- Constructing theory and testing hypotheses
- Research on basic social life, on how groups affect people
- The middle ground: criticisms of society and social policy
- Analyzing problems, evaluating programs, and suggesting solutions
- Implementing solutions (clinical sociology)

Source: By the author based on DeMartini 1982.

Down-to-Earth Sociology

Careers in Sociology: What Applied Sociologists Do

MOST SOCIOLOGISTS TEACH IN COLLEGES and universities, sharing sociological knowledge with college students, as your instructor is doing with you in this course. Applied sociologists, in contrast, work in a wide variety of areas—from counseling children to studying how diseases are transmitted. Some even make software more user-friendly. To give you an idea of this variety, let's look over the shoulders of four applied sociologists.

Leslie Green, who does marketing research at Vanderveer Group in Philadelphia, Pennsylvania, earned her bachelor's degree in sociology at Shippensburg University. She helps to develop strategies to get doctors to prescribe particular drugs. She sets up the meetings, locates moderators for the discussion groups, and arranges payments to the physicians who participate in the research. "My training in sociology," she says, "helps me in 'people skills.' It helps me to understand the needs of different groups, and to interact with them."

Stanley Capela, whose master's degree is from Fordham University, works as an applied sociologist at Heart-Share Human Services in New York. He evaluates how children's programs—such as ones that focus on housing, AIDS, group homes, and preschool education—actually work, compared with how they are supposed to work. He spots problems and suggests solutions. One of his assignments was to find out why it was taking so long to get children adopted, even though there was a long list of eager adoptive parents. Capela pinpointed how the paperwork got bogged down as it was routed through the system and suggested ways to improve the flow to accelerate the process.

Laurie Banks, who received her master's degree in sociology from Fordham University, analyzes statistics for the New York City Health Department. As she examined death certificates, she noticed that a Polish neighborhood had a high rate of stomach cancer. She alerted the Centers for Disease Control, which conducted interviews in the neighborhood. They traced the cause to eating large amounts of sausage. In another case, Banks compared birth certificates with school records. She found that problems at birth—low birth weight, lack of prenatal care, and birth complications—were linked to low reading skills and behavior problems in school.

Daniel Knapp, who earned a doctorate from the University of Oregon, decided to apply sociology by going to the dumps. Moved by the idea that urban wastes should not simply be buried, that they could be recycled and reused, he tested this idea in a small way—by scavenging at the city dump at Berkeley, California. Starting a company called Urban Ore, Knapp did studies on how to recycle urban wastes. He also campaigned successfully for changes in waste disposal laws (Knapp 2005). Knapp became a major founder of the recycling movement in the United States, with a goal of changing human behavior, and his application of sociology continues to influence us all.

From just these few examples, you can catch a glimpse of the variety of work that applied sociologists do. Some work for corporations, some are employed by government and private agencies, and others run their own businesses. You can also see that you don't need a doctorate in order to work as an applied sociologist.

pollution, the relationship between pornography and rape, or how AIDS spreads. A new application of sociology is determining ways to disrupt terrorist groups (Ebner 2005).

Applied sociology is not the same as social reform. It is an application of sociology in some specific setting, not an attempt to rebuild society, as early sociologists envisioned. Consequently, a new tension has emerged in sociology. Sociologists who want the emphasis to be on social reform say that applied sociology doesn't even come close to this. It is an application of sociology but not an attempt to change society. Those who want the emphasis to remain on discovering knowledge say that when sociology is applied, it is no longer sociology. If sociologists use sociological principles to help teenagers escape from pimps, for example, is it still sociology?

Theoretical Perspectives in Sociology

Facts never interpret themselves. In everyday life, we interpret what we observe by using "common sense." We place our observations (our "facts") into a framework of more-or-less related ideas. Sociologists do this, too, but they place their observations in a conceptual framework called a *theory*. A **theory** is a general statement about how some parts of the world fit together and how they work. It is an explanation of how two or more "facts" are related to one another.

Sociologists use three major theories: symbolic interactionism, functional analysis, and conflict theory. Let's first examine the main elements of these theories. Then let's see how each theory helps us to understand why the divorce rate in the United States is so high. As we do so, you will see how each theory, or perspective, provides a distinctive interpretation of social life.

Symbolic Interactionism

We can trace the origins of **symbolic interactionism** to the Scottish moral philosophers of the eighteenth century, who noted that individuals evaluate their own conduct by comparing themselves with others (Stryker 1990). This perspective was brought to sociology by Charles Horton Cooley (1864–1929), William I. Thomas (1863–1947), and George Herbert Mead (1863–1931). Let's look at the main elements of this theory.

Symbols in Everyday Life   Symbolic interactionists study how people use symbols to develop their views of the world and to communicate with one another. Without symbols, our social life would be no more sophisticated than that of animals. For example, without symbols we would have no aunts or uncles, employers or teachers—or even brothers and sisters. I know that this sounds strange, but it is symbols that define for us what relationships are. There would still be reproduction, of course, but no symbols to tell us how we are related to whom. We would not know to whom we owe respect and obligations or from whom we can expect privileges—the stuff that human relationships are made of.

Look at it like this: If you think of someone as your aunt or uncle, you behave in certain ways, but if you think of that person as a boyfriend or girlfriend, you behave quite differently. It is the symbol that tells you how you are related to others—and how you should act toward them.

To make this clearer

> Suppose that you have fallen head-over-heels in love with someone and are going to marry this person tomorrow. The night before your marriage, your mother confides that she had a child before she married, a child that she gave up for adoption. She then adds that she has just discovered that the person you are going to marry is this child.
>
> You can see how the symbol will change overnight!—and your behavior, too!

Symbols allow the existence not only of relationships but also of society. Without symbols, we could not coordinate our actions with those of other people. We could not make plans for a future date, time, and place. Unable to specify times, materials, sizes, or goals, we could not build bridges and highways. Without symbols, there would be no

George Herbert Mead (1863–1931) is one of the founders of symbolic interactionism, a major theoretical perspective in sociology. He taught at the University of Chicago, where his lectures were popular. Although he wrote little, after his death students complied his lectures into an influential book, *Mind, Self, and Society.*

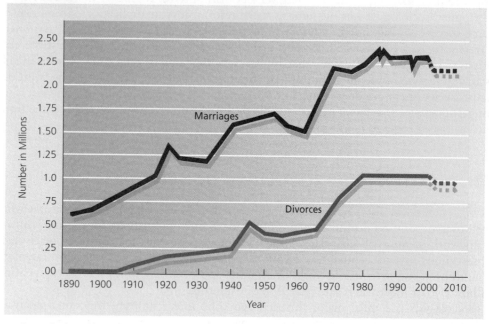

Figure 1.2 **U.S. Marriage, U.S. Divorce**

Source: By the author. Based on *Statistical Abstract of the United States* 1998:Table 92 and 2007:Table 119; earlier editions for earlier years. The broken line indicate the author's estimates.

movies or musical instruments. We would have no hospitals, no government, no religion. The class you are taking could not exist—nor could this book. On the positive side, there would be no war.

In short, symbolic interactionists analyze how our behaviors depend on the ways we define both ourselves and others. They study face-to-face interactions; they look at how people work out their relationships and how they make sense out of life and their place in it. Symbolic interactionists point out that even the self is a symbol, for it consists of the ideas we have about who we are. And the self is a changing symbol: As we interact with others, we constantly adjust our views of who we are based on how we interpret the reactions of others to us. We'll get more into this later.

Applying Symbolic Interactionism   To explain the U.S. divorce rate (see Figure 1.2 above), symbolic interactionists look at how people's ideas and behavior change as symbols change. They note that until the early 1900s, Americans thought of marriage as a sacred, lifelong commitment. Divorce was seen as an immoral, harmful action, a flagrant disregard for public opinion.

Then, slowly, the meaning of marriage began to change. In 1933, sociologist William Ogburn observed that personality was becoming more important in mate selection. In 1945, sociologists Ernest Burgess and Harvey Locke noted the growing importance of mutual affection, understanding, and compatibility in marriage. Gradually, people's views changed. No longer did they see marriage as a lifelong commitment based on duty and obligation. Instead, they began to view marriage as an arrangement, often temporary, that was based on feelings of intimacy. The meaning of divorce also changed. Formerly a symbol of failure, it became an indicator of freedom and new beginnings. Removing the stigma from divorce shattered a strong barrier that had prevented husbands and wives from breaking up.

Symbolic interactionists note that ideas about marital roles and parenthood also changed—and they point out that none of these changes strengthen marriage. For example, from tradition, newlyweds knew what they had a right to expect from each other. In contrast, with today's much vaguer guidelines, couples must figure out how to divide up responsibilities for work, home, and children. As they struggle to do so, many flounder. Although couples find it a relief not to have to conform to what they consider to be burdensome notions, those traditional expectations (or symbols) did provide a structure that made marriages last. When these symbols changed, the structure they had created was weakened, making marriage more fragile and divorce more common.

Similarly, ideas of parenthood and childhood used to be quite different. Parents had little responsibility for their children beyond providing food, clothing, shelter, and moral guidance. And this was only for a short time, for children began to contribute to the support of the family early in life. Among many people, parenthood is still like this. In Colombia, for example, children of the poor often are expected to support themselves by the age of 8 or 10. In advanced industrial societies, however, we assume that children are vulnerable beings who must depend on their parents for financial and emotional support for many years—often until they are well into their mid-twenties. That this is not the case in many cultures often comes as a surprise to Americans, who assume that their own situation is some sort of natural arrangement that is worldwide. The greater responsibilities that we assign to parenthood place heavy burdens on today's couples and, with them, more strain on marriage.

Symbolic interactionists, then, look at how changing ideas (or symbols) put pressure on married couples. No single change is *the* cause of our divorce rate, but, taken together, these changes provide a strong push toward divorce.

Functional Analysis

The central idea of **functional analysis** is that society is a whole unit; it is made up of interrelated parts that work together. Functional analysis, also known as *functionalism* and *structural functionalism,* is rooted in the origins of sociology. Auguste Comte and Herbert Spencer viewed society as a kind of living organism. Just as a person or animal has organs that function together, they wrote, so does society. Like an organism, if society is to function smoothly, its various parts must work together in harmony.

Emile Durkheim also viewed society as being composed of many parts, each with its own function. When all the parts of society fulfill their functions, society is in a "normal" state. If they do not fulfill their functions, society is in an "abnormal" or "pathological" state. To understand society, then, functionalists say that we need to look at both *structure* (how the parts of a society fit together to make the whole) and *function* (what each part does, how it contributes to society).

Robert Merton and Functionalism Robert Merton (1910–2003) dismissed the organic analogy, but he did maintain the essence of functionalism—the image of society as a whole composed of parts that work together. Merton used the term *functions* to refer to the beneficial consequences of people's actions: Functions help keep a group (society, social system) in equilibrium. In contrast, *dysfunctions* are consequences that harm society. They undermine a system's equilibrium.

Functions can be either manifest or latent. If an action is *intended* to help some part of a system, it is a *manifest function.* For example, suppose that the government becomes concerned about our low rate of childbirth. Congress offers a $10,000 bonus for every child born to a married couple. The intention, or manifest function, of the bonus is to increase childbearing. Merton pointed out that people's actions can also have *latent functions—unintended* consequences that help a system adjust. Let's suppose that the bonus works, and the birth rate jumps. As a result, the sales of diapers and baby furniture boom. Because the benefits to these businesses were not the intended consequences, they are *latent* functions of the bonus.

Of course, human actions can also hurt a system. Because such consequences usually are unintended, Merton called them *latent dysfunctions.* Let's suppose that the government has failed to specify a stopping point with regard to its bonus system. To collect the bonus, some people keep on having children. The more children they have, however, the more they need the next bonus to survive. Large families become common, and poverty increases. Welfare is reinstated, taxes jump, and the nation erupts in protest. Because these results were not intended, and because they harmed the social system, they represent latent dysfunctions of the bonus program.

functional analysis
a theoretical framework in which society is viewed as composed of various parts, each with a function that, when fulfilled, contributes to society's equilibrium; also known as *functionalism* and *structural functionalism*

Sociologists who use the *functionalist* perspective stress how industrialization and urbanization undermined the traditional *functions* of the family. Before industrialization, members of the family worked together as an economic unit, as in this painting by Leopoldo Romanch (1958–) of Havana, Cuba. As production moved away from the home, it took with it first the father and, more recently, the mother. One consequence is a major *dysfunction,* the weakening of family ties.

Applying Functional Analysis Now let's apply functional analysis to the U.S. divorce rate. Functionalists stress that industrialization and urbanization undermined the traditional functions of the family. For example, before industrialization, the family was a sort of economic team. On the farm, where most people lived, each member of the family had jobs or "chores" to do. The wife was in charge not only of household tasks but also of raising small animals, such as chickens. Milking cows, collecting eggs, and churning butter were also her responsibility—as were cooking, baking, canning, sewing, darning, washing, and cleaning. The daughters helped her. The husband was responsible for caring for large animals, such as horses and cattle, for planting and harvesting, and for maintaining buildings and tools. The sons helped him. *Together,* they formed an economic unit in which each depended on the others for survival.

The functions that bonded family members to one another also included educating the children, teaching them religion, providing home-based recreation, and caring for the sick and elderly. To see how sharply family functions have changed, look at this example from the 1800s:

> When Phil became sick, he was nursed by Ann, his wife. She cooked for him, fed him, changed the bed linen, bathed him, read to him from the Bible, and gave him his medicine. (She did this in addition to doing the housework and taking care of their six children.) Phil was also surrounded by the children, who shouldered some of his chores while he was sick.
>
> When Phil died, the male neighbors and relatives made the casket while Ann, her mother, and female friends washed and dressed the body. Phil was then "laid out" in the front parlor (the formal living room), where friends, neighbors, and relatives paid their last respects. From there, friends moved his body to the church for the final message and then to the grave they themselves had dug.

As you can see, the family used to have more functions than it does now. Families handled many aspects of life and death that we now assign to outside agencies. Similarly, economic production is no longer a cooperative, home-based effort, with husbands and wives depending on one another for their interlocking contributions to a mutual endeavor. In contrast, today's husbands and wives earn individual paychecks and function as separate components in an impersonal, multinational, and even global system. When outside agencies take over family functions, this weakens the "ties that bind." Marriages become more fragile, and divorce increases.

Conflict Theory

Conflict theory provides a third perspective on social life. Unlike the functionalists, who view society as a harmonious whole, with its parts working together, conflict theorists stress that society is composed of groups that are competing with one another for scarce resources. Although on the surface alliances or cooperation may prevail, beneath that surface is a struggle for power.

Karl Marx and Conflict Theory   Karl Marx, the founder of conflict theory, witnessed the Industrial Revolution that transformed Europe. He observed that peasants who had left the land to seek work in cities had to work for wages that provided barely enough to eat. The average worker died at age 30, the average wealthy person at age 50 (Edgerton 1992:87). Shocked by people's deep suffering and their exploitation, Marx began to analyze society and history. As he did so, he developed **conflict theory.** He concluded that the key to human history is *class conflict*. In each society, some small group controls the means of production and exploits those who are not in control. In industrialized societies, the struggle is between the *bourgeoisie,* the small group of capitalists who own the means to produce wealth, and the *proletariat,* the mass of workers who are exploited by the bourgeoisie.

When Marx made his observations, capitalism was in its infancy, and workers were at the mercy of their employers. Workers had none of what we take for granted today: minimum wages, eight-hour days, coffee breaks, five-day work weeks, paid vacations and holidays, medical benefits, sick leave, unemployment compensation, Social Security, and the right to strike. Marx's analysis reminds us that these benefits came not from generous hearts, but from workers forcing concessions from their employers.

Conflict Theory Today   Some sociologists use conflict theory in a much broader sense than Marx did. They examine how conflict permeates every layer of society—whether that be a small group, an organization, a community, or the entire society. When people in a position of authority try to enforce conformity, which their position requires them to do, this creates resentment and resistance. The result is a constant struggle throughout society to determine who has authority over what (Turner 1978; Bartos and Wehr 2002).

Sociologist Lewis Coser (1913–2003) pointed out that conflict is most likely to develop among people who are in close relationships. These people have worked out ways to distribute responsibilities and privileges, power and rewards. Any change in this arrangement can lead to hurt feelings, bitterness, and conflict. Even in intimate relationships, then, people are in a constant balancing act, with conflict lying uneasily just beneath the surface.

Feminists and Conflict Theory   Feminists stress that men and women should have equal rights. As they view relations between men and women, they see a conflict that goes back to the origins of history. Just as Marx stressed conflict between capitalists and workers, many feminists stress conflict between men and women. Feminists are not united by the conflict perspective, however. Although some focus on the oppression of women and women's struggle against that oppression, feminists tackle a variety of topics and use a variety of theories. (Feminism is discussed in Chapter 8.)

Applying Conflict Theory   To explain why the U.S. divorce rate is high, conflict theorists focus on how men's and women's relationships have changed. For millennia, men dominated women. Women had few alternatives other than accepting their exploitation. Today, however, with industrialization, women can meet their basic survival needs outside of marriage. Industrialization has also fostered a culture in which females participate in social worlds beyond the home. Consequently, today's women, refusing to bear burdens that earlier generations accepted as inevitable, are much more likely to dissolve a marriage that becomes intolerable—or even unsatisfactory.

conflict theory a theoretical framework in which society is viewed as composed of groups that are competing for scarce resources

IN SUM the dominance of men over women was once considered natural and right. As women gained education and earnings, their willingness to accept men's domination diminished, and they strived for more power. One consequence has been higher divorce rates as wives grew less inclined to put up with relationships that they defined as unfair. From the conflict perspective, then, our increase in divorce is not a sign that marriage has weakened but, rather, a sign that women are making headway in their historical struggle with men.

Levels of Analysis: Macro and Micro

macro-level analysis an examination of large-scale patterns of society

micro-level analysis an examination of small-scale patterns of society

social interaction what people do when they are in one another's presence

nonverbal interaction communication without words through gestures, use of space, silence, and so on

A major difference among these three theoretical perspectives is their level of analysis. Functionalists and conflict theorists focus on the **macro level;** that is, they examine large-scale patterns of society. In contrast, symbolic interactionists focus on the **micro level,** on **social interaction**—what people do when they are in one another's presence. These levels are summarized in Table 1.1.

To make this distinction between micro and macro levels clearer, let's return to the example of the homeless with which we opened this chapter. To study homeless people, symbolic interactionists would focus on the micro level. They would analyze what homeless people do when they are in shelters and on the streets. They would also analyze their communications, both their talk and their **nonverbal interaction** (gestures, silence, use of space, and so on). The observations I made at the beginning of this chapter about the silence in the homeless shelter, for example, would be of interest to symbolic interactionists.

Table 1.1 **Major Theoretical Perspectives in Sociology**

Perspective	Usual Level of Analysis	Focus of Analysis	Key Terms	Applying the Perspective to the U.S. Divorce Rate
Symbolic Interactionism	Microsociological-examines small-scale patterns of social interaction	Face-to face interaction, how people use symbols to create social life	Symbols Interaction Meanings Definitions	Industrialization and urbanization changed marital roles and led to a redefinition of love, marriage, children, and divorce.
Functional Analysis (also called functionalism and structural functionalism)	Macrosociological-examines large-scale patterns of society	Relationships among the parts of society; how these parts are functional (have beneficial consequences) or dysfunctional (have negative consequences)	Structure Functions (manifest and latent) Dysfunctions Equilibrium	As social change erodes the traditional functions of the family, family ties weaken, and the divorce rate increases.
Conflict Theory	Macrosociological-examines large-scale patterns of society	The struggle for scarce resources by groups in a society; how the elites use their power to control the weaker groups	Inequality Power Conflict Competition Exploitation	When men control economic life, the divorce rate is low because women find few alternatives to a bad marriage. The high divorce rate reflects a shift in the balance of power between men and women.

This micro level, however, would not interest functionalists and conflict theorists. They would focus instead on the macro level. Functionalists would examine how changes in the parts of society have increased homelessness. They might look at how changes in the family (fewer children, more divorce) and economic conditions (inflation, fewer unskilled jobs, loss of jobs overseas) cause homelessness among people who are unable to find jobs and have no family to fall back on. For their part, conflict theorists would stress the struggle between social classes, especially how the policies of the wealthy force certain groups into unemployment and homelessness. That, they point out, accounts for the disproportionate number of African Americans who are homeless.

Putting the Theoretical Perspectives Together

Which theoretical perspective should we use to study human behavior? Which level of analysis is the correct one? As you have seen, these theoretical perspectives produce contrasting pictures of human life. In the case of divorce, those interpretations are quite different from the commonsense understanding that two people are simply "incompatible." *Because each theory focuses on different features of social life, each provides a distinct interpretation. Consequently, it is necessary to use all three theoretical lenses to analyze human behavior. By combining the contributions of each, we gain a more comprehensive picture of social life.*

How Theory and Research Work Together

Theory cannot stand alone. As sociologist C. Wright Mills (1959) so forcefully argued, if theory isn't connected to research, it will be abstract and empty. It won't represent the way life really is. It is the same for research. Without theory, Mills said, research is also of little value; it is simply a collection of meaningless "facts."

Theory and research, then, go together like a hand and glove. Every theory must be tested, which requires research. And as sociologists do research, they often come up with surprising findings. Those findings must be explained, and for that, we need theory. As sociologists study social life, then, they combine research and theory.

Let's turn now to how sociologists do research.

Doing Sociological Research

Around the globe, people make assumptions about the way the world "is." Common sense, the things that "everyone knows are true," may or may not be true, however. It takes research to find out. To test your own common sense, read the Down-to-Earth Sociology box on the next page.

Regardless of the topic that we want to investigate, we need to move beyond guesswork and common sense. We want to *know* what is really going on. To find out, sociologists do research on just about every aspect of social life. Let's look at how they do their research.

A Research Model

As shown in Figure 1.3 on page 20, scientific research follows eight basic steps. This is an ideal model, however, and in the real world of research, some of these steps may run together. Some may even be omitted.

1. *Selecting a topic.* First, what do you want to know more about? Let's choose spouse abuse as our topic.
2. *Defining the problem.* The next step is to narrow the topic. Spouse abuse is too broad; we need to focus on a specific area. For example, you may want to know why men are more likely than women to be the abusers. Or perhaps you want to know what can be done to reduce domestic violence.
3. *Reviewing the literature.* You must review the literature to find out what has been published on the problem. You don't want to waste your time rediscovering what is already known.

Figure 1.3 The Research Model

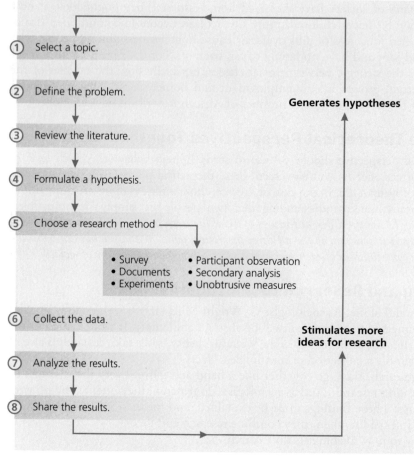

1. Select a topic.
2. Define the problem.
3. Review the literature.
4. Formulate a hypothesis.
5. Choose a research method
   - Survey
   - Documents
   - Experiments
   - Participant observation
   - Secondary analysis
   - Unobtrusive measures
6. Collect the data.
7. Analyze the results.
8. Share the results.

Generates hypotheses

Stimulates more ideas for research

Source: Modification of Figure 2.2 of Schaeffer 1989.

Down-to-Earth Sociology

Enjoying A Sociology Quiz—Sociological Findings Versus Common Sense

SOME FINDINGS OF SOCIOLOGY support commonsense understandings of social life, but others contradict them. Can you tell the difference? To enjoy this quiz, complete *all* the questions before turning the page to check your answers.

1. **True/False** More U.S. students are killed in school shootings now than ten or fifteen years ago.
2. **True/False** The earnings of U.S. women have just about caught up with those of U.S. men.
3. **True/False** It is more dangerous to walk near topless bars than fast-food restaurants.
4. **True/False** Most rapists are mentally ill.
5. **True/False** Most people on welfare are lazy and looking for a handout. They could work if they wanted to.
6. **True/False** Compared with women, men make more eye contact in face-to-face conversations.
7. **True/False** Couples who live together before marriage are usually more satisfied with their marriages than couples who do not live together before marriage.
8. **True/False** Most husbands of employed wives who themselves get laid off from work take up the slack and increase the amount of housework they do.
9. **True/False** With recent laws, bicyclists are more likely to wear helmets now than just a few years ago. Their rate of head injuries has dropped.
10. **True/False** Students in Japan are under such intense pressure to do well in school that their suicide rate is about double that of U.S. students.

Sociological Findings Versus Common Sense— Answers to the Sociology Quiz

1. **False.** More students were shot to death at U.S. schools in the early 1990s than now (National School Safety Center 2007).

2. **False.** Over the years, the wage gap has narrowed, but only slightly. On average, full-time working women earn less than 70 percent of what full-time working men earn. This low figure is actually an improvement over earlier years. See Figures 8.5 and 8.6 on pages 248 and 249.

3. **False.** The crime rate outside fast-food restaurants is considerably higher. The likely reason for this is that topless bars hire private security and parking lot attendants (Linz et al. 2004).

4. **False.** Sociologists compared the psychological profiles of prisoners convicted of rape and prisoners convicted of other crimes. Their profiles were similar. Like robbery, rape is a learned behavior (Scully and Marolla 1984/2007).

5. **False.** Most people on welfare are children, the old, the sick, the mentally and physically handicapped, or young mothers with few skills. Less than 2 percent fit the stereotype of an able-bodied man. See page 222.

6. **False.** Women make considerably more eye contact (Henley et al. 1985).

7. **False.** The opposite is true. The likely reason is that many couples who cohabit before marriage are less committed to marriage in the first place—and a key to marital success is a strong commitment to one another (Larson 1988; Dush, Cohan, and Amato 2003).

8. **False.** Most husbands who have employed wives and who themselves get laid off from work *reduce* the amount of housework they do (Hochschild 1989; Brines 1994).

9. **False.** Bicyclists today are more likely to wear helmets, but their rate of head injuries is higher. Apparently, they take more risks because the helmets make them feel safer (Barnes 2001). (Unanticipated consequences of human action are studied by functionalists. See page 15.)

10. **False.** The suicide rate of U.S. students is about double that of Japanese students (Lester 2003).

---

4. *Formulating a hypothesis.* The fourth step is to formulate a **hypothesis,** a statement of what you expect to find according to predictions that are based on a theory. A hypothesis predicts a relationship between or among **variables,** factors that vary, or change, from one person or situation to another. For example, the statement "Men who are more socially isolated are more likely to abuse their wives than are men who are more socially integrated" is a hypothesis.

Your hypothesis will need **operational definitions,** that is, precise ways to measure the variables. In this example, you would need operational definitions for three variables: social isolation, social integration, and spouse abuse.

5. *Choosing a research method.* The means by which you collect your data is called a **research method** or *research design*). Sociologists use six basic research methods, which are outlined in the next section. You will want to choose the method that will best answer your particular questions.

6. *Collecting the data.* When you gather your data, you have to take care to assure their **validity;** that is, your operational definitions must measure what they are intended to measure. In this case, you must be certain that you really are measuring social isolation, social integration, and spouse abuse—and not something else. Spouse abuse, for example, seems to be obvious. Yet what some people consider to be abuse is not considered abuse by others. Which will you choose? In other words, your operational definitions must be so precise that no one has any question about what you are measuring.

You must also be sure your data are reliable. **Reliability** means that if other researchers use your operational definitions, their findings will be consistent with yours. If your operational definitions are sloppy, husbands who have committed the same act of violence might be included in some research but excluded in other studies. You would end up with erratic results. You might show a 10 percent rate of spouse abuse, but another researcher may conclude that it is 30 percent. This would make your research unreliable.

hypothesis a statement of how variables are expected to be related to one another, often according to predictions from a theory

variable a factor thought to be significant for human behavior, which can *vary* (or change) from one case to another

operational definition the way in which a researcher measures a variable

research method (or **research design**) one of six procedures that sociologists use to collect data: surveys, participant observation, secondary analysis, documents, experiments, and unobtrusive measures

validity the extent to which an operational definition measures what it was intended to measure

reliability the extent to which research produces consistent or dependable results

Because sociologists find all human behavior to be valid research topics, their research runs from the unusual to the routines of everyday life. Their studies range from broad scale social change, such as the globalization of capitalism, to such events as exhibitions of tattooing, piercing, and body painting. Shown here is a tattooed and pierced woman at an international tattoo exposition in London, England.

7. *Analyzing the results.* You can choose from a variety of techniques to analyze the data you gathered. If a hypothesis has been part of your research, it is during this step that you will test it. (Some research, especially that done by participant observation, has no hypothesis. You may know so little about the setting you are going to research that you cannot even specify the variables in advance.)

   With today's software, in just seconds you can run tests on your data that used to take days or even weeks. Two basic programs that sociologists and many undergraduates use are Microcase and the Statistical Package for the Social Sciences (SPSS). Some software, such as the Methodologist's Toolchest, provides advice about collecting data and even about ethical issues.

8. *Sharing the results.* To wrap up your research, you will write a report to share your findings with the scientific community. You will review how you did your research, including your operational definitions. You will also show how your findings fit in with the published literature and how they support or refute the theories that apply to your topic. As Table 1.2 on the next page illustrates, sociologists often summarize their findings in tables.

   Let's look in greater detail at the fifth step and examine the research methods that sociologists use.

Research Methods

As we review the six research methods (or *research designs*) that sociologists use, we will continue our example of spouse abuse. As you will see, the method you choose will depend on the questions you want to answer. So that you can have a yardstick for comparison, you will want to know what "average" is in your study. The ways to measure average are discussed in Table 1.3 on page 24.

Surveys

Let's suppose you want to know how many wives are abused each year. Some husbands are also abused, but let's assume that you are going to focus on wives. An appropriate method would be the **survey**—asking people a series of questions. Before you begin your research, however, you must deal with practical matters that face all researchers. Let's look at these issues.

Selecting a Sample   Ideally, you might want to learn about all wives in the world. Obviously, your resources

THE FAR SIDE® BY GARY LARSON

"Anthropologists! Anthropologists!"

A major concern of sociologists and other social scientists is that their research methods do not influence their findings. Respondents often change their behavior when they know they are being studied.

Table 1.2 **How to Read a Table**

Tables summarize information. Because sociological findings are often presented in tables, it is important to understand how to read them. Tables contain six elements: title, headnote, headings, columns, rows, and source. When you understand how these elements fit together, you know how to read a table.

(1) The **title** states the topic. It is located at the top of the table. What is the title of this table? Please determine your answer before looking at the correct answer at the bottom of the page.

(2) The **headnote** is not always included in a table. When it is, it is located just below the title. Its purpose is to give more detailed information about how the data were collected or how data are presented in the table. What are the first eight words of the headnote of this table?

(3) The **headings** tell what kind of information is contained in the table. There are three headings in this table. What are they? In the second heading, what does *n* = 25 mean?

(4) The **columns** present information arranged vertically. What is the fourth number in the second column and the second number in the third column?

(5) The **rows** present information arranged horizontally. In the fourth row, which husbands are more likely to have less education than their wives?

(6) The **source** of a table, usually listed at the bottom, provides information on where the data in the table originated. Often, as in this instance, the information is specific enough for you to consult the original source. What is the source for this table?

Comparing Violent and Nonviolent Husbands

Based on interviews with 150 husbands and wives in a Midwestern city who were getting a divorce.

Husband's Achievement and Job Satisfaction	Violent Husbands *n* = 25	Nonviolent Husbands *n* = 125
He started but failed to complete high school or college.	44%	27%
He is very dissatisfied with his job.	44%	18%
His income is a source of constant conflict.	84%	24%
He has less education than his wife.	56%	14%
His job has less prestige than his father-in-law's.	37%	28%

Source: Modification of Table 1 in O'Brien 1975.

Some tables are much more complicated than this one, but all follow the same basic pattern. To apply these concepts to a table with more information, see page 284.

ANSWERS
1. Comparing Violent and Nonviolent Husbands
2. Based on interviews with 150 husbands and wives
3. Husband's Achievement and Job Satisfaction, Violent Husbands, Nonviolent Husbands. The *n* is an abbreviation for number, and *n* = 25 means that 25 violent husbands were in the sample.
4. 56%, 18%
5. Violent Husbands
6. A 1975 article by O'Brien (listed in the References section of this text).

will not permit such research, and you will have to narrow your **population,** the target group that you are going to study.

Let's assume that your resources (money, resources, time) allow you to investigate spouse abuse only on your campus. Let's also assume that your college enrollment is large, so you won't be able to survey all the married women who are enrolled. Now you must select a **sample,** individuals from among your target population. How you choose a sample is crucial, for your choice will affect the results of your study. For example, a

survey the collection of data by having people answer a series of questions

population the target group to be studied

sample the individuals intended to represent the population to be studied

Table 1.3   Three Ways to Measure "Average"

The Mean	The Median	The Mode
The term average seems clear enough. As you learned in grade school, to find the average you add a group of numbers and then divide the total by the number of cases that you added. Assume that the following numbers represent men convicted of battering their wives:	To compute the second average, the *median*, first arrange the cases in order–either from the highest to the lowest or the lowest to the highest. That arrangement will produce the following distribution.	The third measure of average, the *mode*, is simply the cases that occur the most often. In this instance the mode is 57, which is way off the mark.

The Mean	The Median	The Mode
EXAMPLE 321 229 57 289 136 57 1,795	**EXAMPLE** 57 1,795 57 321 136 289 229 **or** 229 289 136 321 57 1,795 57	**EXAMPLE** 57 57 136 229 289 321 1,795

The Mean	The Median	The Mode
The total is 2,884. Divided by 7 (the number of cases), the average is 312. Sociologists call this form of average the *mean*. The mean can be deceptive because it is strongly influenced by extreme scores, either low or high. Note that six of the seven cases are less than the mean. Two other ways to compute averages are the median and the mode.	Then look for the middle case, the one that falls halfway between the top and the bottom. That number is 229, for three numbers are lower and three numbers are higher. When there is an even number of cases, the median is the halfway mark between the two middle cases.	Because the mode is often deceptive, and only by chance comes close to either of the other two averages, sociologists seldom use it. In addition, not every distribution of cases has a mode. And if two or more numbers appear with the same frequency, you can have more than one mode.

survey of only women enrolled in introductory sociology courses, or only those in advanced physics classes, would produce skewed results.

Because you want to generalize your findings to your entire campus, you need a sample that is representative of the campus. How do you get a representative sample?

The best way is to get a **random sample.** This does not mean that you stand on some campus corner and ask questions of any woman who happens to walk by. *In a random sample, everyone in your population has the same chance of being included in the study.* In this case, because your population is every married woman enrolled in your college, all married women—whether first-year or graduate students, full- or part-time—must have an equal chance of being included in your sample.

How can you get a random sample? First, you need a list of all the married women enrolled in your college. Then you assign a number to each name on the list. Using a table of random numbers, you then determine which of these women become part of your sample. (Tables of random numbers are available in statistics books, or they can be generated by computer programs.)

A random sample represents your study's population—in this case, married women enrolled at your college. This means that you can generalize your findings to *all* the married women students on your campus, even if they were not included in your sample.

What if you want to know only about certain subgroups, such as freshmen and seniors? You could use a *stratified random sample.* You would need a list of the freshmen and senior married women. Then, using random numbers, you would select a sample from

random sample a sample in which everyone in the target population has the same chance of being included in the study

each group. This would allow you to generalize to all the freshmen and senior married women at your college, but you would not be able to draw any conclusions about the sophomores or juniors.

Asking Neutral Questions   After you have decided on your population and sample, your next task is to make certain that your questions are neutral. Your questions must allow **respondents,** the people who respond to a survey, to express their own opinions. Otherwise you will end up with biased answers, which are worthless. For example, if you were to ask, "Don't you think that men who beat their wives should go to prison?" you would be tilting the answers toward agreement with a prison sentence. The Doonesbury cartoon illustrates a more blatant example of biased questions. For examples of flawed research, see the Down-to-Earth Sociology box on page 27.

Types of Questions   You must also decide whether to use closed- or open-ended questions. **Closed-ended questions** are followed by a list of possible answers. This format would work for questions about someone's age (possible ages would be listed), but it wouldn't work for many other items. For example, how could you list all the opinions that people hold about what should be done to spouse abusers? The answers provided for closed-ended questions can miss the respondent's opinions.

As Table 1.4 on the next page illustrates, the alternative is **open-ended questions**, which allow people to answer in their own words. Although open-ended questions allow you to tap the full range of people's opinions, they make it difficult to compare answers. For example, how would you compare these answers to the question "What do you think causes men to abuse their wives?"

"They're sick."

"I think they must have had problems with their mother."

"We ought to string them up!"

Establishing Rapport   Will victims of abuse really give honest answers to strangers? The answer is yes, but first you must establish rapport ("ruh-POUR"), a feeling of trust, with your respondents. We know from studies of rape that once rapport is gained (often by first asking nonsensitive questions), victims will talk about personal, sensitive matters.

To go beyond police statistics, each year researchers interview a random sample of 100,000 Americans. They ask them whether they have been victims of burglary, robbery, and other crimes. After establishing rapport, the researchers ask about rape. They find that rape victims will talk about their experiences. The national crime victimization survey shows that the actual incidence of rape is *three* times higher than the official statistics (*Statistical Abstract* 2007: page 188).

A new technique to gather data on sensitive areas, Computer-Assisted Self-Interviewing, overcomes lingering problems of distrust. In this technique, the interviewer gives a laptop computer to the respondent, then moves aside, while the individual enters his or her own answers into the computer. In some versions of this method, the respondent listens to the questions on a headphone and answers them on the computer screen. When the

respondents people who respond to a survey, either in interviews or by self-administered questionnaires

closed-ended questions questions that are followed by a list of possible answers to be selected by the respondent

open-ended questions questions that respondents answer in their own words

Doonesbury © G. B. Trudeau. Reprinted with permission of Universal Press Syndicate. All rights reserved.

Improperly worded questions can steer respondents toward answers that are not their own, which produces invalid results.

Table 1.4 Closed- and Open-Ended Questions

A. Closed–Ended Question	B. Open–Ended Question
Which of the following best fits your idea of what should be done to someone who has been convicted of spouse abuse? 1. probation 2. jail time 3. community service 4. counseling 5. divorce 6. nothing—it's a family matter	What do you think should be done to someone who has been convicted of spouse abuse?

Spouse abuse is one of the most common forms of violence. Shown here are police pulling a woman from her bathroom window, where she had fled from her husband, who was threatening to shoot her.

participant observation (or **fieldwork**) research in which the researcher participates in a research setting while observing what is happening in that setting

secondary analysis the analysis of data that have been collected by other researchers

experiment the use of control and experimental groups and dependent and independent variables to test causation

respondent clicks the "Submit" button, the interviewer has no idea how the respondent answered any questions (Mosher et al. 2005).

Participant Observation (Fieldwork)

In **participant observation,** or **fieldwork,** the researcher *participates* in a research setting while *observing* what is happening in that setting. Obviously, this method does not mean that you would sit around and watch someone being abused. But if you wanted to learn how abuse has affected the victims' hopes and goals, their dating patterns, or their marriages, you could use participant observation.

For example, if your campus has a crisis intervention center, you may be able to observe victims of spouse abuse from the time they report the attack through their participation in counseling. With good rapport, you may even be able to spend time with them in other settings, observing other aspects of their lives. What they say and how they interact with others may help you understand how the abuse has affected their lives. This, in turn, may give you insight into how to improve college counseling services.

Secondary Analysis

If you were to analyze data that someone else has already collected, you would be doing **secondary analysis**. For example, if you were to examine the original data from a study of women who had been abused by their husbands, you would be doing secondary analysis.

Documents

Documents, or written sources, include books, newspapers, bank records, immigration records, and so on. To study spouse abuse, you might examine police reports to find out how many men in your community have been arrested for abuse. You might also use court records to find out what proportion of those men were charged, convicted, or put on probation. If you wanted to learn about the social and emotional adjustment of the victims, however, these documents would tell you nothing. Other documents, though, might provide answers. For example, a crisis intervention center might have records that contain key information—but gaining access to them is almost impossible. Perhaps an unusually cooperative center might ask victims to keep diaries that you can study later.

Experiments

A lot of people say that abusers need therapy. But no one knows whether therapy really works. Let's suppose that you want to find out. Is there a way to change a wife abuser into a loving husband? No one has made that claim, but a lot of people say that abusers need therapy. Yet no one knows if therapy really works. Let's suppose that you decide to find out. You may want to conduct an **experiment,** for experiments are useful for determining cause and effect.

Let's suppose that you propose a study to a judge. She likes your idea, and she gives you access to men who have been arrested for spouse abuse. You would randomly divide the men into two groups. (See Figure 1.4 on page 28.) This would help to ensure that

Loading the Dice: How *Not* to Do Research

THE METHODS OF SCIENCE LEND themselves to distortion, misrepresentation, and downright fraud. Consider these findings:

Americans overwhelmingly prefer Toyotas to Chryslers.
Americans overwhelmingly prefer Chryslers to Toyotas.

Obviously, these opposite conclusions cannot be true. Yet each comes from so-called scientific surveys. It turns out that *both* findings are misrepresentations. The surveys were conducted by researchers who were biased, not independent and objective.

It turns out that some consumer researchers load the dice. They are hired by firms that have a vested interest in the outcome of the research, and they deliver the results their clients are looking for.

Here are six ways to load the dice.

1. **Choose a biased sample.** If you want to "prove" that Americans prefer Chryslers over Toyotas, interview unemployed union workers who trace their job loss to Japanese imports. The answer is predictable. You'll get what you're looking for.

2. **Ask biased questions.** Even if you choose an unbiased sample, as in the *Doonesbury* cartoon on page 25, you can phrase questions in such a way that you direct people to the answer you're looking for. Suppose that you asked the question this way: "We are losing millions of jobs to workers overseas who work for just a few dollars a day. More and more Americans are being fired. Some are even homeless and hungry. Do you prefer a car that gives jobs to Americans, or one that forces our workers to lose their homes?"

This question is obviously designed to channel people's thinking toward a predetermined answer—quite contrary to the standards of scientific research.

3. **List biased choices.** Another way to load the dice is to use closed-ended questions that push people into the answers you want. Consider this finding:

U.S. college students overwhelmingly prefer Levis 501 to the jeans of any competitor.

Sound good? Before you rush out to buy Levis, note what these researchers did: In asking students which jeans would be the most popular in the coming year, their list of choices included no other jeans but Levis 501!

4. **Discard undesirable results.** Researchers can keep silent about results they find embarrassing, or they can continue to survey samples until they find one that matches what they are looking for.

The first four sources of bias are inexcusable, intentional fraud. The next two sources of bias reflect sloppi-ness, which is also inexcusable in science.

5. **Misunderstand the subjects' world.** This route can lead to errors every bit as great as those just cited. Even researchers who use good samples, word their questions properly, and offer adequate choices can end up with skewed results. They may, for example, fail to anticipate that people may be embarrassed to express an opinion that isn't "politically correct." For example, surveys show that 80 percent of Americans are environmentalists. Most Americans, however, are probably embarrassed to tell a stranger otherwise. Today, that would be like going against the flag, motherhood, and apple pie.

6. **Analyze the data incorrectly.** Even when researchers strive for objectivity, the sample is good, the wording is neutral, and the respondents answer the questions honestly, the results can still be skewed. The researchers may make a mistake in their calculations, such as entering incorrect data into computers. This, too, of course, is inexcusable in science.

Sources: Based on Crossen 1991; Goleman 1993; Barnes 1995; Resnik 2000; Armstrong 2007.

---

their individual characteristics (attitudes, number of arrests, severity of crimes, education, race-ethnicity, age, and so on) are distributed evenly between the groups. You would then arrange for the men in the **experimental group** to receive some sort of therapy. The men in the **control group** would not get therapy.

Your **independent variable,** something that causes a change in another variable, would be therapy. Your **dependent variable,** the variable that might change, would be the men's behavior: whether they abuse women after they get out of jail. To make that determination, you would need to rely on a sloppy operational definition: either reports from the wives or records indicating which men were rearrested for abuse. This is sloppy because some of the women will not report the abuse, and some of the men who are reported for abuse will not be arrested. Yet it may be the best you can do.

experimental group the group of subjects exposed to the independent variable

control group the group of subjects not exposed to the independent variable

independent variable a factor that causes a change in another variable, called the dependent variable

dependent variable a factor that is changed by an independent variable

Figure 1.4 **The Experiment**

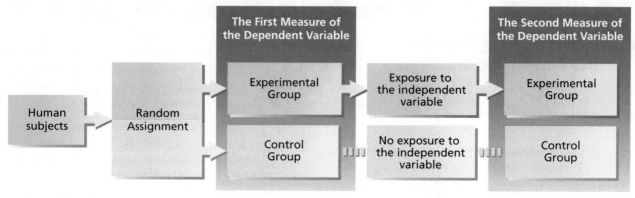

Source: By the author.

Let's assume that you choose rearrest as your operational definition. If you find that the men who received therapy are *less* likely to be rearrested for abuse, you can attribute the difference to the therapy. If you find *no difference* in rearrest rates, you can conclude that therapy was ineffective. If you find that the men who received the therapy have a *higher* rearrest rate, you can conclude that the therapy backfired.

Unobtrusive Measures

Researchers sometimes use **unobtrusive measures,** observing the behavior of people who are not aware that they are being studied. For example, social researchers studied the level of whisky consumption in a town that was legally "dry" by counting empty bottles in trashcans (Lee 2000). Billboards have been developed that can read information embedded on a chip in your car key. As you drive by, the billboard will display *your* name with a personal message (Feder 2007). The same device can *collect* information as you drive by.

It would be considered unethical to use most unobtrusive measures to research spouse abuse. You could, however, analyze 911 calls. Also, if there were a public forum held by abused or abusing spouses on the Internet, you could record and analyze the online conversations. Ethics are still a matter of dispute: To secretly record the behavior of people in public settings, such as a crowd, is generally considered acceptable, but to do so in private settings is not.

Gender in Sociological Research

You know how significant gender is in your own life, how it affects your orientations and your attitudes. You also may be aware that gender opens and closes doors to you, a topic that we will explore in Chapter 8. Because gender is also a factor in social research, researchers must take steps to prevent it from biasing their findings. For example, sociologists Diana Scully and Joseph Marolla (1984, 2007) interviewed convicted rapists in prison. They were concerned that their gender might lead to *interviewer bias*—that the prisoners might shift their answers, sharing certain experiences or opinions with Marolla, but saying something else to Scully. To prevent gender bias, each researcher interviewed half the sample.

Gender certainly can be an impediment in research. In our imagined research on spouse abuse, for example, could a man even do participant observation of women who have been beaten by their husbands? Technically, the answer is yes. But because the women have been victimized by men, they might be less likely to share their experiences and feelings with men. If so, women would be better suited to conduct this research, more likely to achieve valid results. The supposition that these victims will be

unobtrusive measures ways of observing people who do not know they are being studied

more open with women than with men, however, is just that—a supposition. Research alone will verify or refute this assumption.

Gender is significant in other ways, too. As feminist sociologists point out, it is a mistake to assume that what applies to one sex is also relevant to the other (Bird and Rieker 1999; Neuman 2006). Women's and men's lives differ significantly, and if we do research on just half of humanity, our research will be vastly incomplete. Today's huge numbers of women sociologists guarantee that women will not be ignored in social research. In the past, however, when almost all sociologists were men, women's experiences were neglected.

Gender issues can pop up in unexpected ways in sociological research. I vividly recall an incident in San Francisco.

The streets were getting dark, and I was still looking for homeless people. When I saw someone lying down, curled up in a doorway, I approached the individual. As I got close, I began my opening research line, "Hi, I'm Dr. Henslin from. . . ." The individual began to scream and started to thrash wildly. Startled by this sudden, high-pitched scream and by the rapid movements, I quickly backed away. When I later analyzed what had happened, I concluded that I had intruded into a woman's bedroom.

Of course, one can draw another lesson from this incident. Researchers do their best, but they make mistakes. Sometimes these mistakes are minor, and even humorous. The woman sleeping in the doorway wasn't frightened. It was only just getting dark, and there were many people on the street. She was just assertively marking her territory and letting me know in no uncertain terms that I was an intruder. If we make a mistake in research, we pick up and go on. As we do so, we take ethical considerations into account, which is the topic of our next section.

Ethics in Sociological Research

In addition to choosing an appropriate research method, then, we must also follow the ethics of sociology, which center on assumptions of science and morality (American Sociological Association 1999). Research ethics require openness (sharing findings with the scientific community), honesty, and truth. Ethics clearly forbid the falsification of results. They also condemn plagiarism—that is, stealing someone else's work. Another ethical guideline is that research subjects should generally be informed that they are being studied and never be harmed by the research. Ethics also require that sociologists protect the anonymity of people who provide private information. Finally, although not all sociologists agree, it generally is considered unethical for researchers to misrepresent themselves.

Sociologists take these ethical standards seriously. To illustrate the extent to which they will go to protect their respondents, consider the research conducted by Mario Brajuha.

Protecting the Subjects: The Brajuha Research

Mario Brajuha, a graduate student at the State University of New York at Stony Brook, was doing participant observation of restaurant workers. He lost his job as a waiter when the restaurant where he was working burned down—a fire of "suspicious origin," as the police said (Brajuha and Hallowell 1986). When detectives learned that Brajuha had taken field notes, they asked to see them. Because he had promised to keep his information confidential, Brajuha refused to hand them over. The district attorney subpoenaed the notes. Brajuha still refused. The district attorney then threatened to put Brajuha in jail. By this time, Brajuha's notes had become rather famous, and unsavory characters—perhaps those who had set the fire—also began to wonder what was in them. They, too, demanded to see them, accompanying their demands with threats of a different nature. Brajuha found himself between a rock and a hard place.

For two years, Brajuha refused to hand over his notes, even though he grew anxious and had to appear at several court hearings. Finally, the district attorney dropped the subpoena. When the two men under investigation for setting the fire died, so did the threats to Brajuha, his wife, and their children.

Misleading the Subjects: The Humphreys Research

Sociologists agree on the necessity to protect respondents, and they applaud the professional manner in which Brajuha handled himself. Although it is considered acceptable for sociologists to do covert participant observation (studying some situation without announcing that they are doing research), to deliberately misrepresent oneself is considered unethical. Sociologists who violate this norm can become embroiled in ethical controversy. Let's look at the case of Laud Humphreys, whose research forced sociologists to rethink and refine their ethical stance.

Laud Humphreys, a classmate of mine at Washington University in St. Louis, was an Episcopal priest who decided to become a sociologist. For his Ph.D. dissertation, Humphreys (1970, 1971, 1975) studied social interaction in "tearooms," public restrooms where some men go for quick, anonymous sex with other men.

Humphreys found that some restrooms in Forest Park, just across from our campus, were tearooms. He began a participant observation study by hanging around these restrooms. He found that in addition to the two men having sex, a third man—called a "watchqueen"—served as a lookout for police and other unwelcome strangers. Humphreys took on the role of watchqueen, not only watching for strangers but also observing what the men did. He wrote field notes after the encounters.

Humphreys decided that he wanted to know more about the regular lives of these men. For example, what was the significance of the wedding rings that many of the men wore? He came up with an ingenious technique. Many of the men parked their cars near the tearooms, and Humphreys recorded their license plate numbers. A friend in the St. Louis police department gave Humphreys each man's address. About a year later, Humphreys arranged for these men to be included in a medical survey conducted by some of the sociologists on our faculty.

Disguising himself with a different hairstyle and clothing, Humphreys visited the men's homes. He interviewed the men, supposedly for the medical study. He found that they led conventional lives. They voted, mowed their lawns, and took their kids to Little League games. Many reported that their wives were not aroused sexually or were afraid of getting pregnant because their religion did not allow them to use birth control. Humphreys concluded that heterosexual men were also using the tearooms for a form of quick sex.

This study stirred controversy among sociologists and nonsociologists alike. Many sociologists criticized Humphreys, and a national columnist even wrote a scathing denunciation of "sociological snoopers" (Von Hoffman 1970). One of our professors even tried to get Humphrey's Ph.D. revoked. As the controversy heated up and a court case loomed, Humphreys feared that his list of respondents might be subpoenaed. He gave me the list to take from Missouri to Illinois, where I had begun teaching. When he called and asked me to destroy it, I burned it in my backyard.

Was this research ethical (Galliher et al. 2004)? This question is not decided easily. Although many sociologists sided with Humphreys—and his book reporting the research won a highly acclaimed award—the criticisms continued. At first, Humphreys defended his position vigorously, but five years later, in a second edition of his book (1975), he stated that he should have identified himself as a researcher.

Values in Sociological Research

Max Weber raised an issue that remains controversial among sociologists. He said that sociology should be **value free.** By this he meant that a sociologist's **values**—beliefs

value free the view that a sociologist's personal values or biases should not influence social research

values the standards by which people define what is desirable or undesirable, good or bad, beautiful or ugly

about what is good or worthwhile in life—should not affect research. Instead, he said, we need objectivity, total neutrality, for if values influence research, sociological findings will be biased.

That bias has no place in research is not a matter of debate. All sociologists agree that no one should distort data to make them fit preconceived ideas or personal values. It is equally clear, however, that because sociologists—like everyone else—are members of a particular society at a given point in history, they, too, are infused with values of all sorts. These values inevitably play a role in the topics we choose to research. For example, values are part of the reason that one sociologist chooses to do research on the Mafia while another turns a sociological eye on kindergarten students.

Because values can lead to unintended distortions in how we interpret our findings, sociologists stress **replication,** researchers repeating a study in order to compare their results with the original findings. If an individual's values have distorted research findings, replication by other sociologists should uncover the bias and correct it.

Despite this consensus, however, values remain a hotly debated topic in sociology (Buraway 2003; Gans 2003). This debate illustrates again the tension in sociology that we discussed earlier: the goal of analyzing social life versus the goal of social reform. Some sociologists are convinced that research should be directed along paths that will help to reform society, that will alleviate poverty, racism, sexism, and so on. Other sociologists lean strongly toward *basic* or *pure sociology,* research that has no goal beyond understanding social life and testing social theories. They say that nothing but their own interests should direct sociologists to study one topic rather than another. These contrasting views are summarized in Figure 1.5.

In the midst of this controversy, sociologists study the major issues facing our society at this crucial juncture of world history. From racism and sexism to the globalization of capitalism—these are all topics that sociologists study and that we will explore in this book. Sociologists also examine face-to-face interaction—talking, touching, gestures, clothing. These, too, will be the subject of our discussions in the upcoming chapters. This beautiful variety in sociology—and the contrast of going from the larger picture to the smaller picture and back again—is part of the reason that sociology holds such fascination for me. I hope that you also find this variety appealing as you read the rest of this book.

Before we close this chapter, though, I would like you to consider two trends that are shaping sociology.

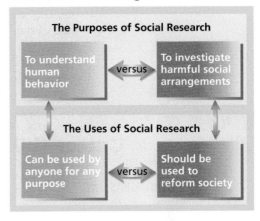

Figure 1.5 **The Debate over Values in Sociological Research**

The Purposes of Social Research

To understand human behavior **versus** To investigate harmful social arrangements

The Uses of Social Research

Can be used by anyone for any purpose **versus** Should be used to reform society

Trends Shaping the Future of Sociology

Two major trends indicate changing directions in sociology. Let's look again at the relationship of sociology to the reforming of society, and then at globalization.

Sociology Full Circle: Reform Versus Research

Reviewing the Tension in Sociology. As we have discussed, a tension between basic sociology and social reform runs through the history of sociology. When sociologists become active in social reform, they almost inevitably take the side of the poor and oppressed. As you can understand, this puts them at odds with the establishment. They experience pressure to "get off the streets and get back in the classroom"—and, in the classroom, to teach quietly. Those who continue to generate unrest are usually fired. In some instances, university administrators have taken over entire departments of sociology. The administrators replace the department chair and run the department the way they want.

Few of us want to run such risks, so most of us, even though we are convinced about what can be done to alleviate the plight of the poor, take an easier route. We do research

replication repeating a study in order to test its findings

and publish articles in what are basically obscure places, that is, journals read primarily by other sociologists.

Finding a Middle Ground: Public Sociology   Sociologists have tried to find a middle ground between social reform and rabble-rousing in a community, realizing that generating unrest brings the heavy hand of oppression slamming down on individual sociologists and departments of sociology. To find this middle ground, the American Sociological Association (ASA) is promoting *public sociology*. By this term, the ASA refers to the public—especially politicians and policy makers—becoming more aware of the sociological perspective. The ASA wants politicians and policy makers to be aware of and use data produced by sociologists. They especially want them to apply the sociological understanding of how society works as they develop social policy (American Sociological Association 2004).

Public sociology is a safe way to make strides toward social reform. Giving testimonies at hearings, serving on government committees, and submitting papers to policy makers upsets few people. If those in power find the sociologists' recommendations to their liking, they can adopt them. If they don't, they can disregard them and go on their merry way. Certainly this is a far cry from leading crowds of oppressed people to demand social change. Yet this safer, middle ground does hold the potential for social reform, as you can see from the Cultural Diversity box below. In this example of public sociology, data from basic sociological research became a stimulus for social policy.

Cultural Diversity *in the* United States

Studying Job Discrimination: A Surprising Example of Applied Sociology

SOMETIMES SOCIOLOGISTS DO basic sociology—research aimed at learning more about some behavior—and then someone else applies it.

Devah Pager was a graduate student at the University of Wisconsin in Madison. When she was doing volunteer work, homeless men told her how hard it was to find work if they had had been in prison.

Pager decided to find out just what difference a prison record made in getting a job. She sent pairs of college men to apply for 350 entry-level jobs in Milwaukee. One team was African American, and one was white. Pager prepared identical résumés for the teams, but with one difference: On each team, one of the men said he had served 18 months in prison for possession of cocaine.

Figure 1.6 shows the difference that the prison record made. Men without a prison record were two or three times as likely to be called back.

But Pager came up with another significant finding. Look at the difference that race-ethnicity made. White men with a prison record were more likely to be offered a job than African American men who had a clean record!

The application of this research? Pager didn't apply anything, but others did. After President Bush was told of these results, he announced in his State of the Union speech that he wanted Congress to fund a $300 million program to provide mentoring and other support to help former prisoners get jobs (Kroeger 2004).

As you can see, the distinction between basic sociology and applied sociology can be artificial. In some instances, as in this one, research and reform fit together well.

At this point, the prison part of the research has been applied. So far, the race-ethnicity findings have yet to be addressed by social policy.

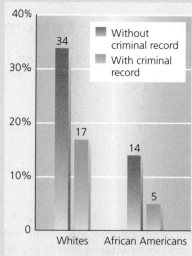

Figure 1.6   **Call-Back Rates**

Source: Courtesy of Devah Pager.

As the pendulum swings toward applying sociological knowledge, another trend is also beginning to have a profound effect on sociology. Let's look at the implications of globalization for the future of sociology.

Globalization

Globalization is the breaking down of national boundaries because of advances in communication, trade, and travel. Currently, the United States dominates sociology. As sociologists William Martin and Mark Beittel (1998) put it, U.S. sociology is the "unrivaled center of the discipline on a world scale." One consequence of this dominance is an emphasis on studying groups in the United States. We U.S. sociologists tend to look inward, concentrating on events and relationships that occur in our own country. We even base most of our findings on U.S. samples. Globalization is destined to broaden our horizons, directing us to a greater consideration of global issues. This, in turn, is likely to motivate us to try more vigorously to identify universal principles.

Globalization and Your Life   With each passing year, the world becomes smaller as we become more connected to the global village. What occurs elsewhere has a direct impact on our lives, making our welfare increasingly tied to that of people in other nations. To help broaden our horizons, in this book we will visit many cultures around the world, examining what life is like for the people who live in those cultures. Seeing how *their* society affects their behavior and orientations to life helps us to understand how *our* society influences what we do and how we feel about life.

Globalization is one of the most significant events in the entire history of the world—and you and I are living through its development. Throughout this text, I will stress the impact of globalization on your life, especially how it is likely to shape your future. We will also examine the **globalization of capitalism,** focusing on implications of the triumph of this economic system. From time to time in the following pages, you will also confront the developing new world order, which appears destined to play a significant role in your future and that of your children.

> **globalization** the growing interconnections among nations due to the expansion of capitalism
>
> **globalization of capitalism** capitalism (investing to make profits within a rational system) becoming the globe's dominant economic system

Summary *and* Review

The Sociological Perspective

What is the sociological perspective?

The **sociological perspective** stresses that people's social experiences—the groups to which they belong and their experiences within these groups—underlie their behavior. C. Wright Mills referred to this as the intersection of biography (the individual) and history (social factors that influence the individual). Pp. 4–5.

Origins of Sociology

When did sociology first appear as a separate discipline?

Sociology emerged as a separate discipline in the mid-1800s in western Europe, during the onset of the Industrial Revolution. Industrialization affected all aspects of human existence—where people lived, the nature of their work, how they viewed life, and interpersonal relationships. Early sociologists who focused on these social changes include Auguste Comte, Herbert Spencer, Karl Marx, Emile Durkheim, Max Weber, Harriet Martineau, and W. E. B. Du Bois. Pp. 5–8.

Sexism in Early Sociology

What was the position of women in early sociology?

Sociology appeared during a historical period of deep sexism. Consequently, the few women who received the education required to become sociologists were ignored. P. 8.

Sociology in North America

When was sociology established in the United States?

The earliest departments of sociology were established in the late 1800s at the universities of Kansas, Chicago, and Atlanta. During the 1940s, the University of Chicago dominated sociology. A tension between social reform and social research and theory ran through sociology, and in its early years, the contributions of women and minorities were largely overlooked. Pp. 8–11.

What is the difference between basic (or pure) and applied sociology?

U.S. sociology has experienced tension between **pure** or **basic sociology,** in which the aim is to analyze society, and attempts to use sociology to reform society. Today, these contrasting orientations exist dynamically side by side. **Applied sociology** is the use of sociology to solve problems. Pp. 11–13.

Theoretical Perspectives in Sociology

What is a theory?

A **theory** is a statement about how facts are related to one another. A theory provides a conceptual framework for interpreting facts. P. 13.

What are sociology's major theoretical perspectives?

Sociologists use three primary theoretical frameworks to interpret social life. **Symbolic interactionists** examine how people use symbols to develop and share their views of the world. Symbolic interactionists usually focus on the **micro level**—on small-scale, face-to-face interaction. **Functional analysts,** in contrast, focus on the **macro level**—on large-scale patterns of society. Functional theorists stress that a social system is made up of interrelated parts. When working properly, each part contributes to the stability of the whole, fulfilling a function that contributes to the system's equilibrium. **Conflict theorists** also focus on large-scale patterns of society. They stress that society is composed of competing groups that struggle for scarce resources. Pp. 13–19.

With each perspective focusing on select features of social life, and each providing a unique interpretation, no single theory is adequate. The combined insights of all three perspectives yield a more comprehensive picture of social life. P. 19.

What is the relationship between theory and research?

Theory and research depend on one another. Sociologists use theory to interpret the data they gather. Theory also generates questions that need to be answered by research, while research, in turn, helps to generate theory. Theory without research is not likely to represent real life, while research without theory is merely a collection of empty facts. P. 20.

Doing Sociological Research

Why do we need sociological research when we have common sense?

Common sense is unreliable. Research often shows that commonsense ideas are limited or false. Pp. 19, 20.

What are the eight basic steps in sociological research?

1. Selecting a topic 2. Defining the problem 3. Reviewing the literature 4. Formulating a **hypothesis** 5. Choosing a **research method** 6. Collecting the data 7. Analyzing the results 8. Sharing the results. These steps are explained on Pp. 19–22.

Research Methods

How do sociologists gather data?

To gather data, sociologists use six **research methods** (or **research designs**): **surveys, participant observation, secondary analysis, documents, experiments,** and **unobtrusive measures.** Pp. 22–29.

Ethics in Sociological Research

How important are ethics in sociological research?

Ethics are of fundamental concern to sociologists, who are committed to openness, honesty, truth, and protecting their subjects from harm. The Brajuha research on restaurant workers and the Humphreys research on "tearooms" illustrate ethical issues of concern to sociologists. Pp. 29–30.

What value dilemmas do sociologists face?

Max Weber stressed that social research should be **value free:** The researcher's personal beliefs must be set aside to permit objective findings. Like everyone else, however, sociologists are members of a particular society at a given point in history and are infused with **values** of all sorts. To overcome the distortions that values can cause, sociologists stress **replication,** the repetition of a study by other researchers in order to compare results. Values present a second dilemma for researchers: whether to do research solely to analyze human behavior (basic or pure sociology) or to reform harmful social arrangements. Pp. 30–31.

Trends Shaping the Future of Sociology

What trends are likely to have an impact on sociology?

The first, the renewed emphasis on applying sociology is taking sociology closer to its roots. A second major trend, **globalization,** is likely to broaden sociological horizons, refocusing research and theory away from the concentration on U.S. society. Pp. 31–33.

Thinking Critically

about Chapter 1

1. Do you think that sociologists should try to reform society or study it dispassionately?

2. Of the three theoretical perspectives, which one would you prefer to use if you were a sociologist? Why?

3. Considering the macro- and micro-level approaches in sociology, which one do you think better explains social life? Why?

Culture

Carmen Lomas Garzo, *Cakewalk*, 1987

I had never felt heat like this before. This was *northern* Africa, and I wondered what it must be like closer to the equator. Sweat poured off me as the temperature climbed past 110 degrees Fahrenheit.

As we were herded into the building—which had no air conditioning—hundreds of people lunged toward the counter at the rear of the structure. With body crushed against body, we waited as the uniformed officials behind the windows leisurely examined each passport. At times like this, I wondered what I was doing in Africa.

When I first arrived in Morocco, I found the sights that greeted me exotic—not far from the scenes in *Casablanca, Raiders of the Lost Ark,* and other movies. The men, women, and even the children really did wear those white robes that reached down to their feet. What was especially striking was that the women were almost totally covered. Despite the heat, they wore not only full-length gowns but also head coverings that reached down over their foreheads and veils that covered their faces from the nose down. All you could see was their eyes—and every eye the same shade of brown.

And how short everyone was! The Arab women looked to be, on average, 5 feet, and the men only about three or four inches taller. As the only blue-eyed, blonde, 6-foot-plus person around, and the only one who was wearing jeans and a pullover shirt, in a world of white-robed short people I stood out like a creature from another planet. Everyone stared. No matter where I went, they stared. Wherever I looked, I found brown eyes watching me intently. Even staring back at those many dark brown eyes had no effect. It was so different from home, where, if you caught someone staring at you, that person would look embarrassed and immediately glance away.

And lines? The concept apparently didn't even exist. Buying a ticket for a bus or train meant pushing and shoving toward the ticket man (always a man—no women were visible in any public position), who took the money from whichever outstretched hand he decided on.

And germs? That notion didn't seem to exist here either. Flies swarmed over the food in the restaurants and the unwrapped loaves of bread in the stores. Shopkeepers would considerately shoo off the flies before handing me a loaf. They also offered home delivery. I watched a bread vendor deliver a loaf to a woman who was standing on a second-floor balcony. She first threw her money to the bread vendor, and he then threw the unwrapped bread up to her. Only, his throw was off. The bread bounced off the wrought-iron balcony railing and landed in the street, which was filled with people, wandering dogs, and the ever-present, urinating and defecating

Everyone stared. No matter where I went, they stared.

(continued)

donkeys. The vendor simply picked up the unwrapped loaf and threw it again. This certainly wasn't his day, for he missed again. But he made it on his third attempt. The woman smiled as she turned back into her apartment, apparently to prepare the noon meal for her family.

Now, standing in the oppressive heat on the Moroccan-Algerian border, the crowd once again became unruly. Another fight had broken out. And once again, the little man in uniform appeared, shouting and knocking people aside as he forced his way to a little wooden box nailed to the floor. Climbing onto this makeshift platform, he shouted at the crowd, his arms flailing about him. The people fell silent. But just as soon as the man left, the shouting and shoving began again.

The situation had become unbearable. His body pressed against mine, the man behind me decided that this was a good time to take a nap. Determining that I made a good support, he placed his arm against my back and leaned his head against his arm. Sweat streamed down my back at the point where his arm and head touched me.

Finally, I realized that I had to abandon U.S. customs. So I pushed my way forward, forcing my frame into every square inch of vacant space that I could create. At the counter, I shouted in English. The official looked up at the sound of this strange tongue, and I thrust my long arms over the heads of three people, shoving my passport into his hand.

What Is Culture?

What is culture? The concept is sometimes easier to grasp by description than by definition. For example, suppose you meet a young woman from India who has just arrived in the United States. That her culture is different from yours is immediately evident. You first see it in her clothing, jewelry, makeup, and hairstyle. Next you hear it in her speech. It then becomes apparent by her gestures. Later, you might hear her express unfamiliar beliefs about relationships or about what is valuable in life. All of these characteristics are indicative of **culture**—the language, beliefs, values, norms, behaviors, and even material objects that are passed from one generation to the next.

In northern Africa, I was surrounded by a culture quite alien to my own. It was evident in everything I saw and heard. The **material culture**—such things as jewelry, art, buildings, weapons, machines, and even eating utensils, hairstyles, and clothing—provided a sharp contrast to what I was used to seeing. There is nothing inherently "natural" about material culture. That is, it is no more natural (or unnatural) to wear gowns on the street than it is to wear jeans.

I also found myself immersed in a contrasting **nonmaterial culture,** that is, a group's ways of thinking (its beliefs, values, and other assumptions about the world) and doing (its common patterns of behavior, including language, gestures, and other forms of interaction). North African assumptions that it is acceptable to stare at others in public and to push people aside to buy tickets are examples of nonmaterial culture. So are U.S. assumptions that it is wrong to do either of these things. Like material culture, neither custom is "right." People simply become comfortable with the customs they learn during childhood, and—as in the case of my visit to northern Africa—uncomfortable when their basic assumptions about life are challenged.

culture the language, beliefs, values, norms, behaviors, and even material objects that are passed from one generation to the next

material culture the material objects that distinguish a group of people, such as their art, buildings, weapons, utensils, machines, hairstyles, clothing, and jewelry

nonmaterial culture (also called *symbolic culture*) a group's ways of thinking (including its beliefs, values, and other assumptions about the world) and doing (its common patterns of behavior, including language and other forms of interaction)

Culture and Taken-for-Granted Orientations to Life

To develop a sociological imagination, it is essential to understand how culture affects people's lives. If we meet someone from a different culture, the encounter may make us aware of culture's pervasive influence on all aspects of a person's life. Attaining the same level of awareness regarding our own culture, however, is quite another matter. *Our* speech, *our* gestures, *our* beliefs, and *our* customs are usually taken for granted. We assume that they are "normal" or "natural," and we almost always follow them without question. As anthropologist Ralph Linton (1936) said, "The last thing a fish would ever notice would be water." So also with people: Except in unusual circumstances, most characteristics of our own culture remain imperceptible to us.

Yet culture's significance is profound; it touches almost every aspect of who and what we are. We came into this life without a language; without values and morality; with no ideas about religion, war, money, love, use of space, and so on. We possessed none of these fundamental orientations that are so essential in determining the type of people we become. Yet by this point in our lives, we all have acquired them—and take them for granted. Sociologists call this *culture within us*. These learned and shared ways of believing and of doing (another definition of culture) penetrate our beings at an early age and quickly become part of our taken-for-granted assumptions about what normal behavior is. *Culture becomes the lens through which we perceive and evaluate what is going on around us.* Seldom do we question these assumptions, for, like water to a fish, the lens through which we view life remains largely beyond our perception.

The rare instances in which these assumptions are challenged, however, can be upsetting. Although as a sociologist I should be able to look at my own culture "from the outside," my trip to Africa quickly revealed how fully I had internalized my culture. My upbringing in Western culture had given me assumptions about aspects of social life that had become deeply rooted in my being—appropriate eye contact, proper hygiene, and the use of space. But in this part of Africa these assumptions were useless in helping me navigate everyday life. No longer could I count on people to stare only surreptitiously, to take precautions against invisible microbes, or to stand in line in an orderly fashion, one behind the other.

As you can tell from the opening vignette, I found these unfamiliar behaviors upsetting, for they violated my basic expectations of "the way people *ought* to be"—and I did not even realize how firmly I held these expectations until they were challenged so abruptly. When my nonmaterial culture failed me—when it no longer enabled me to make sense out of the world—I experienced a disorientation known as **culture shock.** In the case of buying tickets, the fact that I was several inches taller than most Moroccans and thus able to outreach others helped me to adjust partially to their different ways of doing things. But I never did get used to the idea that pushing ahead of others was "right," and I always felt guilty when I used my size to receive preferential treatment.

Think of the cultural shock that people from a tribal culture would experience if they were thrust suddenly into the United States. This is the topic of the Cultural Diversity box on the next page.

An important consequence of culture within us is **ethnocentrism,** a tendency to use our own group's ways of doing things as a yardstick for judging others. All of us learn that the ways of our own group are good, right, proper, and even superior to other ways of life. As sociologist William Sumner (1906), who developed this concept, said, "One's own group is the center of everything, and all others are scaled and rated with reference to it." Ethnocentrism has both positive and negative consequences. On the positive side, it creates in-group loyalties. On the negative side, ethnocentrism can lead to discrimination against people whose ways differ from ours.

The many ways in which culture affects our lives fascinate sociologists. In this chapter, we'll examine how profoundly culture influences everything we are and do. This will serve as a basis from which you can start to analyze your own assumptions of reality. I should give you a warning at this point: You might develop a changed perspective on social life and your role in it. If so, life will never look the same.

culture shock the disorientation that people experience when they come in contact with a fundamentally different culture and can no longer depend on their taken-for-granted assumptions about life

ethnocentrism the use of one's own culture as a yardstick for judging the ways of other individuals or societies, generally leading to a negative evaluation of their values, norms, and behaviors

Cultural Diversity *in the* United States

IMAGINE THAT YOU WERE A member of a small tribal group in the mountains of Laos. Village life and the clan were all you knew. There were no schools, and you learned everything you needed to know from your relatives. U.S. agents recruited the men of your village to fight communists, and they gained a reputation as fierce fighters. When the U.S. forces were defeated in Vietnam, to prevent your people from being killed in reprisal, your people were moved to the United States.

Here is what happened. Keep in mind that you had never seen a television or a newspaper, and that you had never gone to school. Your entire world had been the village.

They put you in a big house with wings. It flew.

They give you saniwipes with other strange food on a tray. The saniwipes were hard to chew.

After the trip, you were placed in a house. This was an adventure. You had never seen locks before, as no one locked up anything in the village. Most of the village homes didn't even have doors, much less locks.

You found the bathroom perplexing. At first, you tried to wash rice in the bowl of water, which seemed to be provided for this purpose. But when you pressed the handle, the water and rice disappeared. After you learned what the toilet was for, you found it difficult not to slip off the little white round thing when you stood on it. In the village, you didn't need a white thing when you squatted to defecate.

When you threw water on the electric stove to put out the burner, it sparked and smoked. You became afraid to use the stove because it might explode.

And no one liked it when you tried to plant a vegetable garden in the park.

Your new world was so different that to help you adjust the settlement agency told you (Fadiman 1997):

Culture Shock: The Arrival of the Hmong

Children make the fastest adjustment to a new culture, although they remain caught between the old and new ones.

1. To send mail, you must use stamps.
2. The door of the refrigerator must be shut.
3. Do not stand or squat on the toilet since it may break.
4. Always ask before picking your neighbor's flowers, fruit, or vegetables.
5. In colder areas you must wear shoes, socks, and appropriate outerwear. Otherwise, you may become ill.
6. Always use a handkerchief or a tissue to blow your nose in public places or inside a public building.
7. Picking your nose or ears in public is frowned upon in the United States.
8. Never urinate in the street. This creates a smell that is offensive to Americans. They also believe that it causes disease.

To help the Hmong assimilate, U.S. officials dispersed them across the nation. This, they felt, would help them to adjust to the dominant culture and prevent a Hmong subculture from developing. The dispersal brought tremendous feelings of isolation to the clan- and village-based Hmong. As soon as they had a chance, the Hmong moved from these towns scattered across the country to the same areas, the major one being in California's Central Valley. Here they united, renewing village relationships and helping one another adjust to the society they had never desired to join.

for your Consideration

Do you think you would have reacted differently if you had been a displaced Hmong? Why did the Hmong need one another more than their American neighbors to adjust to their new life? What cultural shock do you think an American-born 19-year-old Hmong would experience if his or her parents decided to return to Laos?

IN SUM To avoid losing track of the ideas under discussion, let's pause for a moment to summarize, and in some instances clarify, the principles we have covered.

1. There is nothing "natural" about material culture. Arabs wear gowns on the street and feel that it is natural to do so. Americans do the same with jeans.
2. There is nothing "natural" about nonmaterial culture. It is just as arbitrary to stand in line as to push and shove.

3. Culture penetrates deeply into our thinking, becoming a taken-for-granted lens through which we see the world and obtain our perception of reality.
4. Culture provides implicit instructions that tell us what we ought to do and how we ought to think. It provides a fundamental basis for our decision making.
5. Culture also provides a "moral imperative"; that is, the culture that we internalize becomes the "right" way of doing things. (I, for example, believed deeply that it was wrong to push and shove to get ahead of others.)
6. Coming into contact with a radically different culture challenges our basic assumptions of life. (I experienced culture shock when I discovered that my deeply ingrained cultural ideas about hygiene and the use of personal space no longer applied.)
7. Although the particulars of culture differ from one group of people to another, culture itself is universal. That is, all people have culture, for a society cannot exist without developing shared, learned ways of dealing with the challenges of life.
8. All people are ethnocentric, which has both positive and negative consequences.

Practicing Cultural Relativism

To counter our tendency to use our own culture as the standard by which we judge other cultures, we can practice **cultural relativism;** that is, we can try to understand a culture on its own terms. This means looking at how the elements of a culture fit together, without judging those elements as superior or inferior to our own way of life.

With our own culture embedded so deeply within us, however, practicing cultural relativism can challenge our orientations to life. For example, most U.S. citizens appear to have strong feelings against raising bulls for the purpose of stabbing them to death in front of crowds that shout "Olé!" According to cultural relativism, however, bullfighting must be viewed from the perspective of the culture in which it takes place—*its* history, *its* folklore, *its* ideas of bravery, and *its* ideas of sex roles.

You may still regard bullfighting as wrong, of course, if your culture, which is deeply ingrained in you, has no history of bullfighting. We all possess culturally specific ideas about cruelty to animals, ideas that have evolved slowly and match other elements of our culture. In the United States, for example, practices that once were common in some areas—cock fighting, dog fighting, bear–dog fighting, and so on—have been gradually eliminated.

None of us can be entirely successful at practicing cultural relativism. Look at the Cultural Diversity box on the next page. My best guess is that you will evaluate these "strange" foods through the lens of your own culture. Applying cultural relativism, however, is an attempt to refocus that lens so we can appreciate other ways of life rather than simply asserting, "Our way is right." As you view the photos on page 43, try to appreciate the cultural differences in standards of beauty.

cultural relativism not judging a culture but trying to understand it on its own terms

Many Americans perceive bullfighting, which is illegal in the United States, as a cruel activity that should be abolished everywhere. To Spaniards and those who have inherited Spanish culture, however, bullfighting is a beautiful, artistic sport in which matador and bull blend into a unifying image of power, courage, and glory. *Cultural relativism* requires that we suspend our own perspectives in order to grasp the perspectives of others, something that is much easier described than attained.

You Are What You Eat? An Exploration in Cultural Relativity

HERE IS A CHANCE TO TEST your ethnocentrism and ability to practice cultural relativity. You probably know that the French like to eat snails and that in some Asian cultures, chubby dogs and cats are considered a delicacy ("Ah, lightly browned with a little doggy sauce!"). But did you know that cod sperm is a delicacy in Japan (Raisfeld and Patronite 2006)?

Marston Bates (1967), a zoologist, noted this ethnocentric reaction to food:

> I remember once, in the llanos of Colombia, sharing a dish of toasted ants at a remote farmhouse. . . . My host and I fell into conversation about the general question of what people eat or do not eat, and I remarked that in my country people eat the legs of frogs.
>
> The very thought of this filled my ant-eating friends with horror; it was as though I had mentioned some repulsive sex habit.

Then there is the experience of the production coordinator of this text, Dusty Friedman, who told me:

> When traveling in Sudan, I ate some interesting things that I wouldn't likely eat now that I'm back in our society. Raw baby camel's liver with chopped herbs was a delicacy. So was camel's milk cheese patties that had been cured in dry camel's dung.

You might be able to see yourself eating frog legs, toasted ants, perhaps cod sperm and raw camel liver, maybe even dogs and cats, but here's another test of your ethnocentrism and cultural relativity. Maxine Kingston (1975), an English professor whose parents grew up in China, wrote:

> "Do you know what people in [the Nantou region of] China eat when they have the money?" my mother began. "They buy into a monkey feast. The eaters sit around a thick wood table with a hole in the middle. Boys bring in the monkey at the end of a pole. Its neck is in a collar at the end of the pole, and it is screaming. Its hands are tied behind it. They clamp the monkey into the table; the whole table fits like another collar around its neck. Using a surgeon's saw, the cooks cut a clean line in a circle at the top of its head. To loosen the bone, they tap with a tiny hammer and wedge here and there with a silver pick. Then an old woman reaches out her hand to the monkey's face and up to its scalp, where she tufts some hairs and lifts off the lid of the skull. The eaters spoon out the brains."

What some consider food, even delicacies, can turn the stomachs of others. These little critters were for sale in a market in Laos.

for your Consideration

1. What is your opinion about eating toasted ants? About eating fried frog legs? About eating cod sperm? About eating puppies and kittens? About eating brains scooped out of a living monkey?

2. If you were reared in U.S. society, more than likely you think that eating frog legs is okay; eating ants is disgusting; and eating cod sperm, dogs, cats, and monkey brains is downright repugnant. How would you apply the concepts of ethnocentrism and cultural relativism to your perceptions of these customs?

Although employing cultural relativism helps us to avoid cultural smugness, this view has come under attack. In a provocative book, *Sick Societies* (1992), anthropologist Robert Edgerton suggests that we develop a scale for evaluating cultures on their "quality of life," much as we do for U.S. cities. He also asks why we should consider cultures that practice female circumcision, gang rape, or wife beating, or cultures that sell little girls into prostitution as morally equivalent to those that do not. Cultural values that result in exploitation, he says, are inferior to those that enhance people's lives.

Edgerton's sharp questions and incisive examples bring us to a topic that comes up repeatedly in this text: the disagreements that arise among scholars as they confront contrasting views of reality. It is such questioning of assumptions that keeps sociology interesting.

Standards of beauty vary so greatly from one culture to another that what one group finds attractive, another may not. Yet, in its *ethnocentrism,* each group thinks that its standards are the best—that the appearance reflects what beauty "really" is.

As indicated by these photos, around the world men and women aspire to their group's norms of physical attractiveness. To make themselves appealing to others, they try to make their appearance reflect those standards.

Peru

New Guinea

Thailand

China

Cameroon

Tibet

Kenya

United States

Components of Symbolic Culture

Sociologists sometimes refer to nonmaterial culture as **symbolic culture,** because its central component is the symbols that people use. A **symbol** is something to which people attach meaning and that they then use to communicate with one another. Symbols include gestures, language, values, norms, sanctions, folkways, and mores. Let's look at each of these components of symbolic culture.

Gestures

Gestures, using one's body to communicate with others, are shorthand ways to convey messages without using words. Although people in every culture of the world use gestures, a gesture's meaning may change completely from one culture to another. North Americans, for example, communicate a succinct message by raising the middle finger in a short, upward stabbing motion. I wish to stress "North Americans," for this gesture does not convey the same message in most parts of the world.

I was surprised to find that this particular gesture was not universal, having internalized it to such an extent that I thought everyone knew what it meant. When I was comparing gestures with friends in Mexico, however, this gesture drew a blank look from them. After I explained its intended meaning, they laughed and showed me their rudest gesture—placing the hand under the armpit and moving the upper arm up and down. To me, they simply looked as if they were imitating monkeys, but to them the gesture meant "Your mother is a whore"— the worst possible insult in that culture.

With the current political, military, and cultural dominance of the United States, "giving the finger" is becoming well known in other cultures. Following 9/11, the United States began to photograph and fingerprint foreign travelers. Feeling insulted, Brazil retaliated by doing the same to U.S. visitors. Angry at this, a U.S. pilot raised his middle finger while being photographed. Having become aware of the meaning of this gesture, Brazilian police arrested him. To gain his release, the pilot had to pay a fine of $13,000 ("Brazil Arrests" . . . 2004).

Gestures not only facilitate communication but also, because they differ around the world, can lead to misunderstanding, embarrassment, or worse. One time in Mexico, for example, I raised my hand to a certain height to indicate how tall a child was. My hosts began to laugh. It turned out that Mexicans use three hand gestures to indicate height: one for people, a second for animals, and yet another for plants. They were amused because I had ignorantly used the plant gesture to indicate the child's height. (See Figure 2.1.)

Figure 2.1 **Gestures to Indicate Height, Southern Mexico**

To get along in another culture, then, it is important to learn the gestures of that culture. If you don't, you will fail to achieve the simplicity of communication that gestures allow and you may overlook or misunderstand much of what is happening, run the risk of appearing foolish, and possibly offend people. In some cultures, for example, you would provoke deep offense if you were to offer food or a gift with your left hand, because the left hand is reserved for dirty tasks, such as wiping after going to the toilet. Left-handed Americans visiting Arabs, please note!

Suppose for a moment that you are visiting southern Italy. After eating one of the best meals in your life, you are so pleased that when you catch the waiter's eye, you smile broadly and use the standard U.S. "A-OK" gesture of putting your thumb and forefinger together and making a large "**O**." The waiter looks horrified, and you are struck speechless when the manager asks you to leave. What have you done? Nothing on purpose, of course, but in that culture this gesture refers to a part of the human body that is not mentioned in polite company (Ekman et al. 1984).

Is it really true that there are no universal gestures? There is some disagreement on this point. Some anthropologists claim that no gesture is universal. They point out that even nodding the head up and down to indicate "yes" is not universal, because in some parts of the world, such as areas of Turkey, nodding the head up and down means "no" (Ekman et al. 1984). However, ethologists, researchers who study biological bases of behavior, claim that expressions of anger, pouting, fear, and sadness are built into our biological makeup and are universal (Eibl-Eibesfeldt 1970:404). They point out that even infants who are born blind and deaf, who have had no chance to *learn* these gestures, express themselves in the same way.

Although this matter is not yet settled, we can note that gestures tend to vary remarkably around the world. It is also significant that certain gestures can elicit emotions; some gestures are so closely associated with emotional messages that the gestures themselves summon up emotions. For example, my introduction to Mexican gestures took place at a dinner table. It was evident that my husband-and-wife hosts were trying to hide their embarrassment at using their culture's obscene gesture at their dinner table. And I felt the same way—not about *their* gesture, of course, which meant nothing to me—but about the one I was teaching them.

Although most gestures are learned, and therefore vary from culture to culture, some gestures that represent fundamental emotions such as sadness, anger, and fear appear to be inborn. This crying child whom I photographed in India differs little from a crying child in China—or the United States or anywhere else on the globe. In a few years, however, this child will demonstrate a variety of gestures highly specific to his Hindu culture.

Language

The primary way in which people communicate with one another is through **language**—symbols that can be combined in an infinite number of ways for the purpose of communicating abstract thought. Each word is actually a symbol, a sound to which we have attached some particular meaning. Although all human groups have language, there is nothing universal about the meanings given to particular sounds. Like gestures, in different cultures the same sound may mean something entirely different—or may have no meaning at all. In German, for example, *gift* means poison, so if you give chocolate to a non-English speaking German and say, "Gift" . . .

Because *language allows culture to exist,* its significance for human life is difficult to overstate. Consider the following effects of language.

Language Allows Human Experience to Be Cumulative

By means of language, we pass ideas, knowledge, and even attitudes on to the next generation. This allows others to build on experiences in which they may never directly participate. Because of this, humans are able to modify their behavior in light of what earlier generations have learned. Hence the central sociological significance of language: *Language allows culture to develop by freeing people to move beyond their immediate experiences.*

Without language, human culture would be little more advanced than that of the lower primates. If we communicated by grunts and gestures, we would be limited to a

language a system of symbols that can be combined in an infinite number of ways and can represent not only objects but also abstract thought

short time span—to events now taking place, those that have just taken place, or those that will take place immediately—a sort of slightly extended present. You can grunt and gesture, for example, that you want a drink of water, but in the absence of language how could you share ideas concerning past or future events? There would be little or no way to communicate to others what event you had in mind, much less the greater complexities that humans communicate—ideas and feelings about events.

Language Provides a Social or Shared Past Without language, our memories would be extremely limited, for we associate experiences with words and then use words to recall the experience. Such memories as would exist in the absence of language would be highly individualized, for only rarely and incompletely could we communicate them to others, much less discuss them and agree on something. By attaching words to an event, however, and then using those words to recall it, we are able to discuss the event. As we talk about past events, we develop shared understandings about what those events mean. In short, through talk, people develop a shared past.

Language Provides a Social or Shared Future Language also extends our time horizons forward. Because language enables us to agree on times, dates, and places, it allows us to plan activities with one another. Think about it for a moment. Without language, how could you ever plan future events? How could you possibly communicate goals, times, and plans? Whatever planning could exist would be limited to rudimentary communications, perhaps to an agreement to meet at a certain place when the sun is in a certain position. But think of the difficulty, perhaps the impossibility, of conveying just a slight change in this simple arrangement, such as "I can't make it tomorrow, but my neighbor can take my place, if that's all right with you."

Language Allows Shared Perspectives Our ability to speak, then, provides us a social (or shared) past and future. This is vital for humanity. It is a watershed that distinguishes us from animals. But speech does much more than this. When we talk with one another, we are exchanging ideas about events; that is, we are sharing perspectives. Our words are the embodiment of our experiences, distilled into a readily exchangeable form, one that is mutually understandable to people who have learned that language. *Talking about events allows us to arrive at the shared understandings that form the basis of social life.* Not sharing a language while living alongside one another, however, invites miscommunication and suspicion. This risk, which comes with a diverse society, is discussed in the Cultural Diversity box on the next page.

Language is the basis of human culture around the world. The past decade has seen a major development in communication—the ease and speed with which we can "speak" to people across the globe. This development is destined to have vital effects on culture.

Miami—Language in a Changing City

Florida

WITH VAST IMMIGRATION FROM CUBA and other Spanish-speaking countries, the city of Miami has become a Latin American mecca. Nothing reflects Miami's changed character as much as its long-simmering feud over language: English versus Spanish. Half of the city's 385,000 residents have trouble speaking English. Only *one-fourth* of Miamians speak English at home.

As this chapter stresses, language is a primary means by which people learn—and communicate—their social worlds. Consequently, Miami's language differences reflect not only cultural diversity but also the separate social worlds of the city's inhabitants.

Although its ethnic stew makes Miami culturally one of the richest cities in the United States, the language gap sometimes creates misunderstandings and anger—in both directions. Anglo business owners, feeling excluded, have become fed up with people speaking Spanish. An employee at the Coral Gables Board of Realtors lost her job for speaking Spanish at the office, and a cashier at a Publix supermarket was fired for chatting with a friend in Spanish. The protests by Spanish speakers that followed these firings made headlines in Miami newspapers.

Latinos are now a majority in Miami, and many think that learning language should be a two-way street. Anglos, they feel, should try to learn at least some Spanish. Nicaraguan immigrant Pedro Falcon, for example, who is studying English, wonders why more people don't try to learn his language. "Miami is the capital of Latin America," he says. "The population speaks Spanish."

This, of course, as Anglos see it, is the problem. Miami is in the United States, not in Latin America.

This problem of the language of immigrants isn't new. The millions of Germans who immigrated to the United States in the 1800s brought their language with them. They operated schools in German, published German-language newspapers, held their religious services in German, and, of course, spoke German at home and in the taverns.

Mural from Miami.

Some of their Anglo neighbors didn't like this a bit. "Why don't those Germans assimilate?" they wondered. "Just whose side would they fight on if we had a war?" This question was answered, of course, with the participation of German Americans in two world wars.

But what happened to all this German language? The first generation of immigrants struggled with English, but spoke German almost exlusively. The second generation assimilated, learning English well, but also speaking German with their parents at home. For the most part, the third generation knew German only as "that language" that their grandparents spoke.

This is also happening with Spanish speakers. Spanish, however, is being kept alive longer because Mexico borders the United States, and there is constant traffic between the countries. In addition, the vast migration from Mexico and other Spanish-speaking countries continuously feeds the language.

If Germany had bordered the United States, there would still be a lot of German spoken here.

With the continuing immigration from Spanish-speaking countries, Miami's percentage of non-English speakers will increase further. But, as sociologist Douglas Massey says, this "doesn't mean that Miami is going to end up being a Spanish-speaking city." Instead, Massey believes that bilingualism will prevail. He says, "The people who get ahead are not monolingual English speakers or monolingual Spanish speakers. They're people who speak both languages."

In the meantime, Miami officials have tried to resolve the controversy by declaring English to be the official language of Miami. In one small way, at least, they have succeeded. When we tried to get a photograph of "Bienvenidos a Miami" for this box, we discovered that such a sign would be illegal!

Source: Based on Sharp 1992; Usdansky 1992; Kent and Lalasz 2007.

Language Allows Complex, Shared, Goal-Directed Behavior Common understandings enable us to establish a *purpose* for getting together. Let's suppose you want to go on a picnic. You use speech not only to plan the picnic but also to decide on reasons for having the picnic—which may be anything from "because it's a nice day and it shouldn't be wasted studying" to "because it's my birthday." Language permits you to blend individual activities into an integrated sequence. In other words, through discussion you decide where you will go; who will drive; who will bring the hamburgers, the potato chips, the soda; where you will meet; and so on. Only because of language can you participate in such a common yet complex event as a picnic—or build roads and bridges, or attend college classes.

IN SUM The sociological significance of language is that it takes us beyond the world of apes and allows culture to develop. Language frees us from the present, actually giving us a social past and a social future. That is, language gives us the capacity to share understandings about the past and to develop shared perceptions about the future. Language also allows us to establish underlying purposes for our activities. As in the example of planning a picnic, each individual is able to perform a small part of a larger activity, aware that others are carrying out related parts. In this way, language enables a series of separate activities to become united into a larger whole.

In short, *language is the basis of culture.* Like most aspects of culture, its linguistic base is usually invisible to us.

Language and Perception: The Sapir-Whorf Hypothesis   In the 1930s, two anthropologists, Edward Sapir and Benjamin Whorf, became intrigued when they noted that the Hopi Indians of the southwestern United States had no words to distinguish among the past, the present, and the future. English, in contrast—as well as French, Spanish, Swahili, and other languages—distinguishes carefully among these three time frames. From this observation, Sapir and Whorf began to think that words might be more than labels that people attach to things. *Eventually, they concluded that language has embedded within it ways of looking at the world.* In other words, language not only expresses our thoughts and perceptions but also shapes the way we think and perceive. When we learn a language, we learn not only words but also ways of thinking and perceiving (Sapir 1949; Whorf 1956).

The **Sapir-Whorf hypothesis** reverses common sense: It indicates that rather than objects and events forcing themselves onto our consciousness, it is our language that determines our consciousness, and hence our perception of objects and events. Sociologist Eviatar Zerubavel (1991) gives a good example. Hebrew, his native language, does not have separate words for jam and jelly. Both go by the same term, and only when Zerubavel learned English could he "see" this difference, which is "obvious" to native English speakers. Similarly, if you learn to classify students as Jocks, Goths, Stoners, Skaters, and Preps, you will perceive students in an entirely different way from someone who does not know these classifications.

Although Sapir and Whorf's observation that the Hopi do not have tenses was inaccurate (Edgerton 1992:27), they did stumble onto a major truth about social life. Learning a language means not only learning words but also acquiring the perceptions embedded in that language. In other words, language both reflects and shapes cultural experiences (Drivonikou et al. 2007). The racial-ethnic terms that our culture provides, for example, influence how we see both ourselves and others, a point that is discussed in the Cultural Diversity box on the next page.

Values, Norms, and Sanctions

To learn a culture is to learn people's **values,** their ideas of what is desirable in life. When we uncover people's values, we learn a great deal about them, for values are the standards by which people define what is good and bad, beautiful and ugly. Values underlie our preferences, guide our choices, and indicate what we hold worthwhile in life.

Every group develops expectations concerning the right way to reflect its values. Sociologists use the term **norms** to describe those expectations (or rules of behavior) that develop out of a group's values. The term **sanctions** refers to the reactions people receive for following or breaking norms. A **positive sanction** expresses approval for following a norm, and a **negative sanction** reflects disapproval for breaking a norm. Positive sanctions can be material, such as a prize, a trophy, or money, but in everyday life they usually consist of hugs, smiles, a pat on the back, or even handshakes and "high fives." Negative sanctions can also be material—being fined in court is one example—but they,

Sapir-Whorf hypothesis Edward Sapir's and Benjamin Whorf's hypothesis that language creates ways of thinking and perceiving

values the standards by which people define what is desirable or undesirable, good or bad, beautiful or ugly

norms expectations, or rules of behavior, that reflect and enforce values

sanctions expressions of approval or disapproval given to people for upholding or violating norms

positive sanction a reward or positive reaction for following norms, ranging from a smile to a prize

negative sanction an expression of disapproval for breaking a norm, ranging from a mild, informal reaction such as a frown to a formal reaction such as a prison sentence or an execution

Cultural Diversity *in the* United States

Race and Language: Searching for Self-Labels

THE GROUPS THAT DOMINATE society often determine the names that are used to refer to racial-ethnic groups. If those names become associated with oppression, they take on negative meanings. For example, the terms *Negro* and *colored people* came to be associated with submissiveness and low status. To overcome these meanings, those referred to by these terms began to identify themselves as *black* or *African American.* They infused these new terms with respect—a basic source of self-esteem that they felt the old terms denied them.

In a twist, African Americans—and to a lesser extent Latinos, Asian Americans, and Native Americans—have changed the rejected term *colored people* to *people of color.* Those who embrace this modified term are imbuing it with meanings that offer an identity of respect. The term also has political meanings. It indicates bonds that cross racial-ethnic lines, mutual ties, and a sense of identity rooted in historical oppression.

There is *always* disagreement about racial-ethnic terms, and this one is no exception. Although most rejected the term

The ethnic terms we choose—or which are given to us—are major self-identifiers. They indicate both membership in some group and a separation from other groups.

colored people, some found in it a sense of respect and claimed it for themselves. The acronym NAACP, for example, stands for the National Association for the Advancement of Colored People. The new term, *people of color,* arouses similar feelings. Some individuals whom this term would include claim that it is inappropriate. They point out that this new label still makes color the primary identifier of people. They stress that humans transcend race-ethnicity, that what we have in common as human beings goes much deeper than what you see on the surface. They stress that we should avoid terms that focus on differences in the pigmentation of our skin.

The language of self-reference in a society that is so conscious of skin color is an ongoing issue. As long as our society continues to emphasize such superficial differences, the search for adequate terms is not likely to ever be "finished." In this quest for terms that strike the right chord, the term *people of color* may become a historical footnote. If it does, it will be replaced by another term that indicates a changing self-identification in a changing historical context.

---

too, are more likely to be symbolic: harsh words, or gestures such as frowns, stares, clenched jaws, or raised fists. Getting a raise at work is a positive sanction, indicating that you have followed the norms clustering around work values. Getting fired, however, is a negative sanction, indicating that you have violated these norms. The North American finger gesture discussed earlier is, of course, a negative sanction.

Because people can find norms stifling, some cultures relieve the pressure through *moral holidays,* specified times when people are allowed to break norms. Moral holidays such as Mardi Gras often center on getting rowdy. Some activities for which people would otherwise be arrested are permitted—and expected—including public drunkenness and some nudity. The norms are never completely dropped, however—just loosened a bit. Go too far, and the police step in.

Some societies have *moral holiday places,* locations where norms are expected to be broken. Red light districts of our cities are examples. There, prostitutes are allowed to work the streets, bothered only when political pressure builds to "clean up" the area. If these same prostitutes attempt to solicit customers in adjacent areas, however, they are promptly arrested. Each year, the home town of the team that wins the Super Bowl becomes a moral holiday place—for one night.

One of the more interesting examples is "Party Cove" at Lake of the Ozarks in Missouri, a fairly straight-laced area of the country. During the summer, hundreds of boaters—from those operating cabin cruisers to jet skis—moor their vessels together in a highly publicized cove, where many get drunk, take off their clothes, and dance on the boats. In one of the more humorous incidents, boaters complained that a nude woman was riding a jet ski outside of the cove. The water patrol investigated but refused to arrest the woman because she

Many societies relax their norms during specified occasions. At these times, known as *moral holidays*, behavior that is ordinarily not permitted is allowed. From a functional standpoint, *moral holidays*, such as the Mardi Gras held at New Orleans, and spring break in Florida and Mexico, serve as safety valves, allowing a release of deviance. When the *moral holiday* is over, the usual enforcement of rules follows.

was within the law—she had sprayed shaving cream on certain parts of her body. The Missouri Water Patrol has even given a green light to Party Cove, announcing in the local newspaper that officers will not enter this cove, supposedly because "there is so much traffic that they might not be able to get out in time to handle an emergency elsewhere."

Folkways and Mores

Norms that are not strictly enforced are called **folkways.** We expect people to comply with folkways, but we are likely to shrug our shoulders and not make a big deal about it if they don't. If someone insists on passing you on the right side of the sidewalk, for example, you are unlikely to take corrective action, although if the sidewalk is crowded and you must move out of the way, you might give the person a dirty look.

Other norms, however, are taken much more seriously. We think of them as essential to our core values, and we insist on conformity. These are called **mores** (MORE-rays). A person who steals, rapes, or kills has violated some of society's most important mores. As sociologist Ian Robertson (1987:62) put it,

> A man who walks down a street wearing nothing on the upper half of his body is violating a folkway; a man who walks down the street wearing nothing on the lower half of his body is violating one of our most important mores, the requirement that people cover their genitals and buttocks in public.

It should also be noted that one group's folkways may be another group's mores. Although a man walking down the street with the upper half of his body uncovered is deviating from a folkway, a woman doing the same thing is violating the mores. In addition, the folkways and mores of a subculture (discussed in the next section) may be the opposite of mainstream culture. For example, to walk down the sidewalk in a nudist camp with the entire body uncovered would conform to that subculture's folkways.

A **taboo** refers to a norm so strongly ingrained that even the thought of its violation is greeted with revulsion. Eating human flesh and having sex with one's parents are examples of such behaviors. When someone breaks a taboo, the individual is usually judged unfit to live in the same society as others. The sanctions are severe, and may include prison, banishment, or death.

folkways norms that are not strictly enforced

mores norms that are strictly enforced because they are thought essential to core values or the well-being of the group

taboo a norm so strong that it often brings revulsion if violated

The violation of *mores* is a serious matter. In this case, it is serious enough that the police at this rugby match in Dublin, Ireland, have swung into action to protect the public from seeing a "disgraceful" sight, at least one so designated by this group.

Many Cultural Worlds

Subcultures

What common condition do you think this doctor is describing? Here is what he said:

> [It accompanies] diaphragmatic pleurisy, pneumonia, uremia, or alcoholism . . . Abdominal causes include disorders of the stomach, and esophagus, bowel diseases, pancreatitis, pregnancy, bladder irritation, hepatic metastases, or hepatitis. Thoracic and mediastinal lesions or surgery may be responsible. Posterior fossa tumors or infarcts may stimulate centers in the medulla oblongata. (Chambliss 2003:443)

My best guess is that you don't have the slightest idea what this doctor was talking about. For most of us, he might as well have been speaking Greek. Physicians who are lecturing students in medical school, however, talk like this. This doctor is describing hiccups!

Here's my favorite quote from a politician:

> There are things we know that we know. There are known unknowns; that is to say, there are things that we now know we don't know. But there are also unknown unknowns; there are things we do not know we don't know. (Dickey and Barry 2006:38)

Whatever Donald Rumsfeld, the former Secretary of Defense under George W. Bush, meant by his statement probably will remain a known unknown. (Or would it be an unknown known?)

Politicians and physicians form a **subculture,** *a world within the larger world of the dominant culture.* Subcultures consist of people whose experiences have led them to have distinctive ways of looking at life or some aspect of it. Even if we cannot understand the preceding quotes, they make us aware that the physicians' and politicians' views of life are not quite the same as ours.

U.S. society contains tens of thousands of subcultures. Some are as broad as the way of life we associate with teenagers, others as narrow as those we associate with body

subculture the values and related behaviors of a group that distinguish its members from the larger culture; a world within a world

builders—or with doctors. Some U.S. ethnic groups also form subcultures: Their values, norms, and foods set them apart. So might their religion, language, and clothing. Occupational groups also form subcultures, as anyone who has hung out with artists (McCall 1980), construction workers (Haas 1972), or undertakers (Thompson 2007) can attest. Even sociologists form a subculture. As you are learning, they also use a unique language in their efforts to understand the world.

For a visual depiction of subcultures, see the photo montage on pages 54–55.

Countercultures

Consider this quote from another subculture:

> If everyone applying for welfare had to supply a doctor's certificate of sterilization, if everyone who had committed a felony were sterilized, if anyone who had mental illness to any degree were sterilized—then our economy could easily take care of these people for the rest of their lives, giving them a decent living standard—but getting them out of the way. That way there would be no children abused, no surplus population, and, after a while, no pollution. . . .
>
> Now let's talk about stupidity. The level of intellect in this country is going down, generation after generation. The average IQ is always 100 because that is the accepted average. However, the kid with a 100 IQ today would have tested out at 70 when I was a lad. You get the concept . . . the marching morons. . . .
>
> When the . . . present world system collapses, it'll be good people like you who will be shooting people in the streets to feed their families. (Zellner 1995:58, 65)

Welcome to the world of the Survivalists, where the message is much clearer than that of physicians—and much more disturbing.

The values and norms of most subcultures blend in with mainstream society. In some cases, however, such as these survivalists, some of the group's values and norms place it at odds with the dominant culture. Sociologists use the term **counterculture** to refer to such groups. Another example would be Satanists. To better see this distinction, consider motorcycle enthusiasts and motorcycle gangs. Motorcycle enthusiasts—who emphasize personal freedom and speed *and* affirm cultural values of success through work or education—are members of a subculture. In contrast, the Hell's Angels, Pagans, and Bandidos not only stress freedom and speed but also value dirtiness and contempt toward women, work, and education. This makes them a counterculture.

Countercultures do not have to be negative, however. Back in the 1800s, the Mormons were a counterculture that challenged the dominant culture's core value of monogamy.

An assault on core values is always met with resistance. To affirm their own values, members of the mainstream culture may ridicule, isolate, or even attack members of the counterculture. The Mormons, for example, were driven out of several states before they finally settled in Utah, which was then a wilderness. Even there, the federal government would not let them practice *polygyny* (one man having more than one wife), and Utah's statehood was made conditional on its acceptance of monogamy (Anderson 1942/1966).

counterculture a group whose values, beliefs, and related behaviors place its members in opposition to the broader culture

pluralistic society a society made up of many different groups

Values in U.S. Society

An Overview of U.S. Values

As you know, the United States is a **pluralistic society,** made up of many different groups. The United States has numerous religious and racial-ethnic groups, as well as countless interest groups that focus on activities as divergent as collecting Barbie dolls and hunting deer. This state of affairs makes the job of specifying U.S. values difficult. Nonetheless, sociologists have tried to identify the underlying core values that are shared by most of the groups that make up U.S. society. Sociologist Robin Williams (1965) identified the following:

1. *Achievement and success.* Americans place a high value on personal achievement, especially outdoing others. This value includes getting ahead at work and school, and attaining wealth, power, and prestige.
2. *Individualism.* Americans cherish the ideal that an individual can rise from the bottom of society to its very top. If someone fails to "get ahead," Americans generally find fault with that individual rather than with the social system for placing roadblocks in his or her path.
3. *Activity and work.* Americans expect people to work hard and to be busy doing some activity even when not at work. This value is becoming less important.
4. *Efficiency and practicality.* Americans award high marks for getting things done efficiently. Even in everyday life, Americans consider it important to do things fast, and they seek ways to increase efficiency.
5. *Science and technology.* Americans have a passion for applied science, for using science to control nature—to tame rivers and harness winds—and to develop new technology, from iPods to Segways.
6. *Progress.* Americans expect rapid technological change. They believe that they should constantly build "more and better" gadgets that will help them move toward some vague goal called "progress."
7. *Material comfort.* Americans expect a high level of material comfort. This comfort includes not only good nutrition, medical care, and housing but also late-model cars and recreational playthings—from Land Rovers to iPhones.
8. *Humanitarianism.* Americans emphasize personal kindness, aid in mass disasters, and organized philanthropy.
9. *Freedom.* This core value pervades U.S. life. It underscored the American Revolution, and Americans pride themselves on their personal freedom. The Mass Media in Social Life box on page 56 highlights an interesting study on how this core value applies to Native Americans.
10. *Democracy.* By this term, Americans refer to majority rule, to the right of everyone to express an opinion, and to representative government.
11. *Equality.* It is impossible to understand Americans without being aware of the central role that the value of equality plays in their lives. Equality of opportunity (part of the ideal culture discussed later) has significantly influenced U.S. history and continues to mark relations among the groups that make up U.S. society.
12. *Racism and group superiority.* Although it contradicts the values of freedom, democracy, and equality, Americans regard some groups more highly than others and have done so throughout their history. The slaughter of Native Americans and the enslaving of Africans are the most notorious examples.

In an earlier publication, I updated Williams' analysis by adding these three values.

13. *Education.* Americans are expected to go as far in school as their abilities and finances allow. Over the years, the definition of an "adequate" education has changed, and today a college education is considered an appropriate goal for most Americans. Those who have an opportunity for higher education and do not take it are sometimes viewed as doing something "wrong"—not merely as making a bad choice, but as somehow being involved in an immoral act.
14. *Religiosity.* There is a feeling that "every true American ought to be religious." This does not mean that everyone is expected to join a church, synagogue, or mosque, but that everyone ought to acknowledge a belief in a Supreme Being and follow some set of matching precepts. This value is so pervasive that Americans stamp "In God We Trust" on their money and declare in their national pledge of allegiance that they are "one nation under God."
15. *Romantic love.* Americans feel that the only proper basis for marriage is romantic love. Songs, literature, mass media, and "folk beliefs" all stress this value. They especially love the theme that "love conquers all."

Looking at Subcultures

Subcultures can form around any interest or activity. Each subculture has its own values and norms that its members share, giving them a common identity. Each also has special terms that pinpoint the group's corner of life and that its members use to communicate with one another. Some of us belong to several subcultures simultaneously.

As you can see from these photos, most subcultures are compatible with the values of the dominant or mainstream culture. They represent specialized interests around which its members have chosen to build tiny worlds. Some subcultures, however, conflict with the mainstream culture. Sociologists give the name counterculture to subcultures whose values (such as those of outlaw motorcyclists) or activities and goals (such as those of terrorists) are opposed to the mainstream culture. Countercultures, however, are exceptional, and few of us belong to them.

Membership in this subculture is not easily awarded. Not only must **high-steel ironworkers** prove that they are able to work at great heights but also that they fit into the group socially. Newcomers are tested by members of the group, and they must demonstrate that they can take joking without offense.

The cabbies' subculture, centering on their occupational activities and interest, is also broken into smaller subcultures that reflect their experiences of race-ethnicity.

Participants in the rodeo subculture "advertise" their membership by wearing special clothing. The clothing symbolizes a set of values that unites its members. Among those values is the awarding of hyper-masculine status through the conquest of animals—or in this instance, the attempted conquest.

Values and interests are perhaps the two main characteristics of subcultures. What values and interests distinguish the modeling subculture?

This subculture, with its fierce traditions, used to consist of white men. The subculture's painful adjustment to changed times is evident in its name being changed from firemen to fire-fighters.

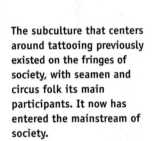

The subculture that centers around tattooing previously existed on the fringes of society, with seamen and circus folk its main participants. It now has entered the mainstream of society.

Each subculture provides its members with values and distinctive ways of viewing the world. What values and perceptions do you think are common among body builders?

People who raise champion rams belong to a small subculture, in which the norms are explicit and high conformity is expected.

Why would someone decorate themselves like this? Among the many reasons, one is to show their solidarity with the basketball subculture.

mass Media in social life

Why Do Native Americans Like Westerns?

U.S. audiences (and even German, French, and Japanese ones) devour Western movies. In the United States, it is easy to see why Anglos might like Westerns. It is they who are portrayed as heroes who tame the wilderness and defend themselves from the attacks of cruel, savage Indians who are intent on their destruction. But why would Indians like Westerns?

Sociologist JoEllen Shively, a Chippewa who grew up on Indian reservations in Montana and North Dakota, observed that Westerns are so popular that Native Americans bring bags of paperbacks into taverns to trade with one another. They even call each other "cowboy."

Intrigued, Shively decided to investigate the matter by showing a Western to adult Native Americans and Anglos in a reservation town. She matched the groups in education, age, income, and percentage of unemployment. To select the movie, Shively (1991, 1992) previewed more than seventy Westerns. She chose a John Wayne movie, *The Searchers,* because it not only focuses on conflict between Indians and cowboys but also shows the cowboys defeating the Indians. After the movie, the viewers filled out questionnaires, and Shively interviewed them.

She found something surprising: *All* Native Americans and Anglos identified with the cowboys; *none* identified with the Indians. Anglos and Native Americans, however, identified with the cowboys in different ways. Each projected a different fantasy onto the story. While Anglos saw the movie as an accurate portrayal of the Old West and a justification of their own status in society. Native Americans, in contrast, saw it as embodying a free, natural way of life. In fact, Native Americans said that they were the "real cowboys." They said, "Westerns relate to the way I wish I could live"; "He's not tied down to an eight-to-five job, day after day"; "He's his own man."

Shively adds,

> What appears to make Westerns meaningful to Indians is the fantasy of being free and independent like the cowboy. . . . Indians . . . find a fantasy in the cowboy story in which the important parts of their ways of life triumph and are morally good, validating their own cultural group in the context of a dramatically satisfying story.
>
> To express their real identity—a combination of marginality on the one hand, with a set of values which are about the land, autonomy, and being free—they

Although John Wayne often portrayed an Anglo who kills Indians, Wayne is popular among Indian men. These men tend to identify with the cowboys, who reflect their values of bravery, autonomy, and toughness.

(use) a cultural vehicle written for Anglos about Anglos, but it is one in which Indians invest a distinctive set of meanings that speak to their own experience, which they can read in a manner that affirms a way of life they value, or a fantasy they hold to.

In other words, values, not ethnicity, are the central issue. If a Native American film industry were to portray Native Americans with the same values that the Anglo movie industry projects onto cowboys, then Native Americans would identify with their own group. Thus, says Shively, Native Americans make cowboys "honorary Indians," for the cowboys express their values of bravery, autonomy, and toughness.

Value Clusters

As you can see, values are not independent units; some cluster together to form a larger whole. In the **value cluster** that surrounds success, for example, we find hard work, education, efficiency, material comfort, and individualism bound up together. Americans are expected to go far in school, to work hard afterward, to be efficient, and then to attain a high level of material comfort, which, in turn, demonstrates success. Success is attributed to the individual's efforts; lack of success is blamed on his or her faults.

Value Contradictions

value cluster values that together form a larger whole

value contradiction values that contradict one another; to follow the one means to come into conflict with the other

Not all values fall into neat, integrated packages. Some even contradict one another. The value of group superiority contradicts freedom, democracy, and equality, producing a **value contradiction.** There simply cannot be full expression of freedom, democracy, and equality along with racism and sexism. Something has to give. One way in which Americans sidestepped this contradiction in the past was to say that freedom, democracy, and equality applied only to some groups. The contradiction was bound to surface over time, however, and so it did with the Civil War and the women's liberation movement. *It is precisely at the point of value contradictions, then, that one can see a major force for social change in a society.*

Emerging Values

A value cluster of four interrelated core values—leisure, self-fulfillment, physical fitness, and youthfulness—is emerging in the United States. A fifth core value—concern for the environment—is also emerging.

1. *Leisure.* The emergence of leisure as a value is reflected in a huge recreation industry—from computer games, boats, vacation homes, and spa retreats to sports arenas, home theaters, extreme vacations, and luxury cruises.

2. *Self-fulfillment.* This value is reflected in the "human potential" movement, which emphasizes becoming "all one can be," and in magazine articles, books, and talk shows that focus on "self-help," "relating," and "personal development."

3. *Physical fitness.* Physical fitness is not a new U.S. value, but its increased emphasis is moving it into this emerging cluster. This trend is evident in the stress on nutrition and organic foods; obsessive attention to weight and diet; the growing number of joggers, cyclists, and backpackers; and the countless health clubs and physical fitness centers.

4. *Youthfulness.* Although valuing youth and disparaging old age are not new, some note a new sense of urgency. They attribute this to the huge number of aging baby boomers, who, aghast at the physical changes that accompany their advancing years, attempt to deny or at least postpone their biological fate. An extreme view is represented by a physician who claims that "aging is not a normal life event, but a disease" (Cowley 1996). It is not surprising, then, that techniques for maintaining and enhancing a youthful appearance—from cosmetic surgery to exotic creams and Botox injections—have become popular.

This emerging value cluster is a response to fundamental changes in U.S. society. Earlier generations of Americans were focused on forging a nation and fighting for economic survival. Today, millions of Americans are freed from long hours of work, and millions more are able to retire from work at an age when they anticipate decades of life ahead of them. This value cluster centers on helping people to maintain their health and vigor during their younger years and enabling them to enjoy their years of retirement.

5. *Concern for the environment.* During most of U.S. history, the environment was viewed as something to be exploited—a wilderness to be settled, forests to be cleared for farm land and lumber, rivers and lakes to be fished, and animals to be hunted. One result was the near extinction of the bison and the extinction in 1915 of the passenger pigeon, a bird previously so numerous that its annual migration would darken the skies for days. Today, Americans have developed a genuine and apparently long-term concern for the environment.

The many groups that comprise the United States contribute to its culture. With their growing numbers, Latinos are making a greater impact on U.S. art, entertainment, music, and literature. This is also true of other areas of everyday life, such as customized vehicles. These "tricked out" cars at a show at Sturgeon Bay, Wisconsin, feature bumping hydraulics and ornate paint jobs.

Values, both those held by individuals and those that represent a nation or people, can undergo deep shifts. It is difficult for many of us to grasp the pride with which earlier Americans destroyed trees that took thousands of years to grow, are located only on one tiny speck of the globe, and that we today consider part of the nation's and world's heritage. But this is a value statement, representing current views. The pride expressed on these woodcutters' faces represents another set of values entirely.

This emerging value of environmental concern is related to the current stage of U.S. economic development: People act on environmental concerns only after they have met their basic needs. At this point in their development, for example, the world's poor nations have a difficult time "affording" this value.

Culture Wars: When Values Clash

Challenges in core values are met with strong resistance by the people who hold them dear. They see changes as a threat to their way of life, an undermining of both their present and their future. Efforts to change gender roles, for example, arouse intense controversy, as does support for the marriage of homosexuals. Alarmed at such onslaughts to their values, traditionalists fiercely defend historical family relationships and the gender roles they grew up with. Today's clash in values is so severe that the term *culture wars* has been coined to refer to it. Compared with the violence directed against the Mormons, however, today's reactions to such controversies are mild.

Values as Blinders

Just as values and their supporting beliefs paint a unique picture of reality, so they also form a view of what life *ought* to be like. Americans value individualism so highly, for example, that they tend to see almost everyone as free to pursue the goal of success. This value blinds them to circumstances that keep people from reaching this goal. The dire consequences of family poverty, parents' low education, and dead-end jobs tend to drop from sight. Instead, Americans cling to the notion that everyone can make it—if they put forth enough effort. And they "know" they are right, for every day, dangling before their eyes are enticing stories of individuals who have succeeded despite huge handicaps.

"Ideal" Versus "Real" Culture

Many of the norms that surround cultural values are followed only partially. Differences always exist between a group's ideals and what its members actually do. Consequently, sociologists use the term **ideal culture** to refer to the values, norms, and goals that a group considers ideal, worth aspiring to. Success, for example, is part of ideal culture. Americans glorify academic progress, hard work, and the display of material goods as signs of individual achievement. What people actually do, however, usually falls short of the cultural ideal. Compared with their abilities, for example, most people don't work as

ideal culture the ideal values and norms of a people; the goals held out for them

hard as they could or go as far as they could in school. Sociologists call the norms and values that people actually follow **real culture.**

Cultural Universals

With the amazing variety of human cultures around the world, are there any **cultural universals**—values, norms, or other cultural traits that are found everywhere?

To answer this question, anthropologist George Murdock (1945) combed through data that anthropologists had gathered on hundreds of groups around the world. He drew up a list of customs concerning courtship, marriage, funerals, games, laws, music, myths, incest taboos, and even toilet training. He found that although such activities are present in all cultures, *the specific customs differ from one group to another.* There is no universal form of the family, no universal way of toilet training children, nor of disposing of the dead.

Even incest is defined differently from group to group. For example, the Mundugumors of New Guinea extend the incest taboo so far that for each man, seven of every eight women are ineligible marriage partners (Mead 1935/1950). Other groups go in the opposite direction and allow some men to marry their own daughters (La Barre 1954). In certain circumstances, some groups *require* that brothers and sisters marry one another (Beals and Hoijer 1965). The Burundi of Africa even insist that, in order to remove certain curses, a son must have sex with his mother (Albert 1963). Such sexual relations are usually allowed only for special people (royalty) or in extraordinary situations (such as when a lion hunter faces a dangerous hunt). No society permits generalized incest for its members.

In short, although there are universal human activities (speech, music, games, storytelling, preparing food, marrying, child rearing, disposing of the dead, and so on), there is no universally accepted way of doing any of them. Humans have no biological imperative that results in one particular form of behavior throughout the world. As indicated in the following Thinking Critically section, although a few sociologists take the position that genes significantly influence human behavior, almost all sociologists reject this view.

Thinking Critically

Are We Prisoners of Our Genes? Sociobiology and Human Behavior

A controversial view of human behavior, called **sociobiology** (also known as neo-Darwinism and evolutionary psychology), provides a sharp contrast to the perspective of this chapter, that human behavior is primarily due to culture. Sociobiologists (evolutionary psychologists, evolutionary anthropologists) believe that because of natural selection, the basic cause of human behavior is biology.

Charles Darwin (1859), who developed the idea of natural selection, pointed out that the genes of a species—the units that contain the individual's traits—are not distributed evenly among the offspring. The characteristics passed on to some members make it easier for them to survive their environment, increasing the likelihood that they will pass their genetic traits to the next generation. Over thousands of generations, the genetic traits that aid survival tend to become common in a species, while those that do not aid survival tend to disappear.

Natural selection explains not only the physical characteristics of animals but also their behavior, for over countless generations, instincts emerged. Edward Wilson (1975), an insect specialist, claims that human behavior is also the result of natural selection. Human behavior, he asserts, is no different from the behavior of cats, dogs, rats, bees, or mosquitoes—it has been bred into *Homo sapiens* through evolutionary principles.

Wilson set out to create a storm of protest, and he succeeded. He went on to claim that competition and cooperation, envy and altruism, even religion, slavery, genocide, and war and peace can be explained by sociobiology. He provocatively added that because human behavior can be explained in terms of genetic programming, sociobiology will eventually absorb sociology—as well as anthropology and psychology.

real culture the norms and values that people actually follow

cultural universal a value, norm, or other cultural trait that is found in every group

sociobiology a framework of thought that views human behavior as the result of natural selection and considers biological factors to be the fundamental cause of human behavior

Obviously, most sociologists find Wilson's position unacceptable. Not only is it a direct attack on their discipline but also it bypasses the essence of what sociologists focus on: humans developing their own cultures, their own unique ways of life. Sociologists do not deny that biology underlies human behavior—at least not in the sense that it takes a highly developed brain to develop human culture and abstract thought, and that there would be no speech if humans had no tongue or larynx.

But most sociologists find it difficult to believe that anyone would claim that genetic programming causes human behavior. Pigs act like pigs because they don't have a cerebral cortex, and instincts control their behavior. So it is for spiders, elephants, and so on (Howe et al. 1992). Humans, in contrast, possess a self and are capable of abstract thought. They discuss the reasons that underlie what they do. They develop purposes and goals. They immerse themselves in a world of symbols that allow them to consider, reflect, and make reasoned choices.

This controversy has turned into much more than simply an academic debate among scientists. Homosexuals, for example, have a personal interest in its outcome. If homosexuality is a lifestyle *choice*, then those who consider that lifestyle to be immoral will use this as a basis for excluding homosexuals from full social participation. If, however, homosexuality has a genetic basis, then choice as a reason for social exclusion is eliminated. Sociologist Peter Conrad (1997) expresses the dominant sociological position when he points out that not all homosexuals have Xq28, the so-called "gay gene," and some people who have this gene are not homosexual. This gene, then, does not determine behavior. Instead, we must look for *social* causes (Bearman and Bruckner 2002).

In short, sociobiologists and sociologists stand on opposite sides, the one looking at human behavior as determined by genetics, the other looking at human behavior as determined by social learning, by experiences in the human group. Sociologists point out that if humans were prisoners of their genes, we would not have developed such fascinatingly different ways of life around the world—we would live in a monoculture of some sort.

technology in its narrow sense, tools; its broader sense includes the skills or procedures necessary to make and use those tools

new technology the emerging technologies of an era that have a significant impact on social life

Technology in the Global Village

The New Technology

The gestures, language, values, folkways, and mores that we have discussed—all are part of symbolic or nonmaterial culture. Culture, as you recall, also has a material aspect: a group's *things,* from its houses to its toys. Central to a group's material culture is its technology. In its simplest sense, **technology** can be equated with tools. In a broader sense, technology also includes the skills or procedures necessary to make and use those tools.

We can use the term **new technology** to refer to an emerging technology that has a significant impact on social life. People develop minor technologies all the time. Most are slight modifications of existing technologies. Occasionally, however, they develop a technology that makes a major impact on human life. It is primarily to these innovations that the term *new technology* refers. For people 500 or 600 years ago, the new technology was the printing press. For us, the new technology consists of computers, satellites, and the Internet.

The sociological significance of technology goes far beyond the tool itself. *Technology sets the framework for a group's nonmaterial culture.* If a group's technology changes, so do people's ways of thinking and how they relate to one another. An example is gender relations. Through the centuries and throughout the world, it has been the custom (the nonmaterial culture of a group) for men to dominate women. Today's global communications (the material culture) make this custom more difficult to maintain. For example, when Arab women watch Western television, they observe much freer gender relations. As these women talk to other women by e-mail and telephone, their communications both convey and create discontent, as well as feelings of sisterhood. These communications motivate some of them to agitate for social change.

In today's world, the long-accepted idea that it is proper to withhold rights on the basis of someone's sex can no longer be sustained. What is usually beyond our

The adoption of new forms of communication by people who not long ago were cut off from events in the rest of the world is bound to change their *nonmaterial culture.*

How do you think the use of cell phones is changing this Buddhist monk's thinking and views of the world? (This photo was taken in Kathmandu, Nepal.)

awareness in this revolutionary change is the role of the new technology, which joins the world's nations into a global communications network.

Cultural Lag and Cultural Change

About three generations ago, sociologist William Ogburn (1922/1938), a functional analyst, coined the term **cultural lag.** By this, Ogburn meant that not all parts of a culture change at the same pace. When one part of a culture changes, other parts lag behind.

Ogburn pointed out that *a group's material culture usually changes first, with the nonmaterial culture lagging behind,* playing a game of catch-up. For example, when we get sick, we could type our symptoms into a computer and get an immediate diagnosis and a recommended course of treatment. In some tests, computers outperform physicians. Yet our customs have not caught up with our technology, and we continue to visit the doctor's office.

Sometimes nonmaterial culture never catches up. Instead, we rigorously hold onto some outmoded form—one that once was needed, but that long ago was bypassed by technology. A striking example is our nine-month school year. Have you ever wondered why it is nine months long, and why we take summers off? For most of us, this is "just the way it's always been," and we have never questioned it. But there is more to this custom than meets the eye, for it is an example of cultural lag.

In the late 1800s, when universal schooling came about, the school year matched the technology of the time, which was labor-intensive. Most parents were farmers, and for survival, they needed their children's help at the crucial times of planting and harvesting. Today, generations later, when few people farm and there is no need for the school year to be so short, we still live with this cultural lag.

Technology and Cultural Leveling

For most of human history, communication was limited and travel slow. Consequently, in their relative isolation, human groups developed highly distinctive ways of life as they responded to the particular situations they faced. The unique characteristics they developed that distinguished one culture from another tended to change little over time. The Tasmanians, who lived on a remote island off the coast of Australia, provide an extreme example. For thousands of years, they had no contact with other people. They were so isolated that they did not even know how to make clothing or fire (Edgerton 1992).

Except in such rare instances, humans have always had *some* contact with other groups. During these contacts, people learned from one another, adopting some part of the other's way of life. In this process, called **cultural diffusion,** groups are most open to changes in their technology or material culture. They usually are eager, for example, to adopt superior weapons and tools. In remote jungles in South America one can find metal cooking pots, steel axes, and even bits of clothing spun in mills in South Carolina. Although the direction of cultural diffusion today is primarily from the West to other parts of the world, cultural diffusion is not a one-way street—as bagels, woks, hammocks, and sushi in the United States attest.

With today's travel and communications, cultural diffusion is occurring rapidly. Air travel has made it possible to journey around the globe in a matter of hours. In the not-so-distant past, a trip from the United States to Africa was so unusual that only a few adventurous people made it, and newspapers would herald their feat. Today, hundreds of thousands make the trip each year.

The changes in communication are no less vast. Communication used to be limited to face-to-face speech, written messages that were passed from hand to hand, and visual signals such as smoke or light that was reflected from mirrors. Despite newspapers, people in some parts of the United States did not hear that the Civil War had ended until weeks and even months after it was over. Today's electronic communications transmit messages across the globe

COCHRAN!

"COOL! A KEYBOARD THAT WRITES WITHOUT A PRINTER."

Technological advances are now so rapid that the technology of one generation is practically unrecognizable by the next generation.

This Barbie doll, sold in Japan, is dressed in a stage costume of a Japanese singer. As objects diffuse from one culture to another, they are modified to meet the tastes of the adoptive culture. In this instance, the modification has been done intentionally as part of the globalization of capitalism.

cultural leveling the process by which cultures become similar to one another; refers especially to the process by which U.S. culture is being exported and diffused into other nations

in a matter of seconds, and we learn almost instantaneously what is happening on the other side of the world. During Gulf War II, reporters traveled with U.S. soldiers, and for the first time in history, the public was able to view live video reports of battles and deaths as they occurred.

Travel and communication unite us to such an extent that there is almost no "other side of the world" anymore. One result is **cultural leveling,** a process in which cultures become similar to one another. The globalization of capitalism is bringing both technology and Western culture to the rest of the world. Japan, for example, has adopted not only capitalism but also Western forms of dress and music. These changes have transformed Japan into a blend of Western and Eastern cultures.

Cultural leveling is occurring rapidly around the world, as is apparent to any traveler. The Golden Arches of McDonald's welcome today's visitors to Tokyo, Paris, London, Madrid, Moscow, Hong Kong, and Beijing. When I visited a jungle village in India—no electricity, no running water, and so remote that the only entrance was by a footpath—I saw a young man sporting a cap with the Nike emblem.

Although the bridging of geography and culture by electronic signals and the exportation of Western icons do not in and of themselves mark the end of traditional cultures, the inevitable result is some degree of *cultural leveling,* some blander, less distinctive way of life—U.S. culture with French, Japanese, and Brazilian accents, so to speak. Although the "cultural accent" remains, something vital is lost forever.

Summary *and* Review

What Is Culture?

All human groups possess **culture**—language, beliefs, values, norms, and material objects that are passed from one generation to the next. **Material culture** consists of objects (art, buildings, clothing, weapons, tools). **Nonmaterial** (or **symbolic**) **culture** is a group's ways of thinking and their patterns of behavior. **Ideal culture** is a group's ideal values, norms, and goals. **Real culture** is their actual behavior, which often falls short of their cultural ideals. Pp. 38–41.

What are cultural relativism and ethnocentrism?

People are naturally **ethnocentric;** that is, they use their own culture as a yardstick for judging the ways of others. In contrast, those who embrace **cultural relativism** try to understand other cultures on those cultures' own terms. Pp. 41–43.

Components of Symbolic Culture

What are the components of nonmaterial culture?

The central component is **symbols,** anything to which people attach meaning and that they use to communicate with others. Universally, the symbols of non-material culture are **gestures, language, values, norms, sanctions, folkways,** and **mores.** Pp. 44–45.

Why is language so significant to culture?

Language allows human experience to be goal-directed, cooperative, and cumulative. It also lets humans move beyond the present and share a past, future, and other common perspectives. According to the **Sapir-Whorf hypothesis,** language even shapes our thoughts and perceptions. Pp. 45–48.

How do values, norms, sanctions, folkways, and mores reflect culture?

All groups have **values**, standards by which they define what is desirable or undesirable, and **norms**, rules or expectations about behavior. Groups use **positive sanctions** to show approval of those who follow their norms, and **negative sanctions** to show disapproval of those who do not. Norms that are not strictly enforced are called **folkways**, while **mores** are norms to which groups demand conformity because they reflect core values. Pp. 48–50.

Many Cultural Worlds

How do subcultures and countercultures differ?

A **subculture** is a group whose values and related behaviors distinguish its members from the general culture. A **counterculture** holds some values that stand in opposition to those of the dominant culture. Pp. 51–52.

Values in U.S. Society

What are the core U.S. values?

Although the United States is a **pluralistic society**, made up of many groups, each with its own set of values, certain values dominate: achievement and success, individualism, activity and work, efficiency and practicality, science and technology, progress, material comfort, equality, freedom, democracy, humanitarianism, racism and group superiority, education, religiosity, and romantic love. Some values cluster together (**value clusters**) to form a larger whole. **Value contradictions** (such as equality and racism) indicate areas of tension, which are likely points of social change. Leisure, self-fulfillment, physical fitness, youthfulness, and concern for the environment are emerging core values. Core values do not change without opposition. Pp. 52–59.

Cultural Universals

Do cultural universals exist?

Cultural universals are values, norms, or other cultural traits that are found in all cultures. Although all human groups have customs concerning cooking, childbirth, funerals, and so on, because these customs vary from one culture to another, there are no cultural universals. Pp. 59–60.

Technology in the Global Village

How is technology changing culture?

William Ogburn coined the term **cultural lag** to describe how a group's nonmaterial culture lags behind its changing technology. With today's technological advances in travel and communications, **cultural diffusion** is occurring rapidly. This leads to **cultural leveling**, whereby many groups are adopting Western culture in place of their own customs. Much of the richness of the world's diverse cultures is being lost in the process. Pp. 60–62.

Thinking Critically
about Chapter 2

1. Do you favor ethnocentrism or cultural relativism? Explain your position.
2. Do you think that the language change in Miami, Florida, (discussed on page 47) is an indicator of the future of the United States? Why or why not?
3. Are you a member of any subcultures? Which one(s)? Why do you think that your group is a subculture? What is your group's relationship to the mainstream culture?

Additional Resources

What can you use MySocLab for?

 www.mysoclab.com

- **Study and Review:** Pre and Post-Tests, Practice Tests, Flash Cards, Individualized Study Plans.
- **Current Events:** *Sociology in the News,* the daily *New York Times,* and more.
- **Research and Writing:** *Research Navigator, Writing About Sociology,* and more.

Where Can I Read More on This Topic?

Suggested readings for this chapter are listed at the back of this book.

Socialization

CHAPTER **3**

OUTLINE

Simon Silva, *Orgullo de Familia (Family Pride)*, 1997

The old man was horrified when he found out. Life never had been good since his daughter lost her hearing when she was just 2 years old. She couldn't even talk—just fluttered her hands around trying to tell him things. Over the years, he had gotten used to that. But now . . . he shuddered at the thought of her being pregnant. No one would be willing to marry her; he knew that. And the neighbors, their tongues would never stop wagging. Everywhere he went, he could hear people talking behind his back.

If only his wife were still alive, maybe she could come up with something. What should he do? He couldn't just kick his daughter out into the street.

After the baby was born, the old man tried to shake his feelings, but they wouldn't let loose. Isabelle was a pretty name, but every time he looked at the baby he felt sick to his stomach.

He hated doing it, but there was no way out. His daughter and her baby would have to live in the attic.

Her behavior toward strangers, especially men, was almost that of a wild animal, manifesting much fear and hostility.

Unfortunately, this is a true story. Isabelle was discovered in Ohio in 1938 when she was about 6½ years old, living in a dark room with her deaf-mute mother. Isabelle couldn't talk, but she did use gestures to communicate with her mother. An inadequate diet and lack of sunshine had given Isabelle a disease called rickets. Her legs were so bowed that as she stood erect the soles of her shoes came nearly flat together, and she got about with a skittering gait. Her behavior toward strangers, especially men, was almost that of a wild animal, manifesting much fear and hostility. In lieu of speech she made only a strange croaking sound. (Davis 1940/ 2007:157-158)

When the newspapers reported this case, sociologist Kingsley Davis decided to find out what had happened to Isabelle after her discovery. We'll come back to that later, but first let's use the case of Isabelle to gain insight into human nature.

What Is Human Nature?

For centuries, people have been intrigued with the question of what is human about human nature. How much of people's characteristics comes from "nature" (heredity) and how much from "nurture" (the **social environment,** contact with others)? One way to answer this question is to study identical twins who were separated at birth and reared in different environments, such as those discussed in the Down-to-Earth Sociology box below. Another way is to examine children who have had little human contact. Let's consider such children.

Down-to-Earth Sociology

Heredity or Environment? The Case of Oskar and Jack, Identical Twins

IDENTICAL TWINS SHARE EXACTLY THE SAME GENETIC heredity. One fertilized egg divides to produce two embryos. If heredity determines personality—or attitudes, temperament, skills, and intelligence—then identical twins should be identical not only in their looks but also in these characteristics.

The fascinating case of Jack and Oskar helps us unravel this mystery. From their experience, we can see the far-reaching effects of the environment—how social experiences take precedence over biology.

Jack Yufe and Oskar Stohr are identical twins born in 1932 to a Jewish father and a Catholic mother. They were separated as babies after their parents divorced. Oskar was reared in Czechoslovakia by his mother's mother, who was a strict Catholic. When Oskar was a toddler, Hitler annexed this area of Czechoslovakia, and Oskar learned to love Hitler and to hate Jews. He joined the Hitler Youth (a sort of Boy Scout organization, except that this one was designed to instill the "virtues" of patriotism, loyalty, obedience—and hatred).

Jack's upbringing was a mirror image of Oskar's. Reared in Trinidad by his father, he learned loyalty to Jews and hatred of Hitler and the Nazis. After the war, Jack and his father moved to Israel. When he was 17, Jack joined a kibbutz, and later, served in the Israeli army.

In 1954, the two brothers met. It was a short meeting and Jack had been warned not to tell Oskar that they were Jews. Twenty-five years later, in 1979, when they were 47 years old, social scientists at the University of Minnesota brought them together again. These researchers figured that because Jack and Oskar had the same genes, any differences they showed would have to be the result of their environment—their different social experiences.

The question of the relative influence of heredity and the environment in human behavior has fascinated and plagued researchers. To try to answer this question, researchers have studied identical twins. Some human behaviors, such as beliefs, political and otherwise, are clearly due to the environment.

Not only did Oskar and Jack hold different attitudes toward the war, Hitler, and Jews but also their basic orientations to life were different. In their politics, Oskar was conservative, while Jack was more liberal. Oskar enjoyed leisure, while Jack was a workaholic. And, as you can predict, Jack was very proud of being a Jew. Oskar, who by this time knew that he was a Jew, wouldn't even mention it.

That would seem to settle the matter. But there was another side. The researchers also found that Oskar and Jack had both excelled at sports as children, but had difficulty with math. They also had the same rate of speech, and both liked sweet liqueur and spicy foods. Strangely, both flushed the toilet both before and after using it and enjoyed startling people by sneezing in crowded elevators.

for your Consideration

Heredity or environment? How much influence does each one have? The question is not yet settled, but at this point it seems fair to conclude that the *limits* of certain physical and mental abilities are established by heredity (such as ability at sports and aptitude for mathematics), while attitudes are the result of the environment. Basic temperament, though, seems to be inherited. Although the answer is still fuzzy, we can put it this way: For some parts of life, the blueprint is drawn by heredity; but even here the environment can redraw those lines. For other parts, the individual is a blank slate, and it is up to the environment to determine what is written on that slate.

Sources: Based on Begley 1979; Chen 1979; Wright 1995; Segal and Hershberger 2005.

Feral Children

Over the centuries, people have occasionally found children living in the forests. Supposedly, these children could not speak; they bit, scratched, growled, and walked on all fours. They drank by lapping water, ate grass, tore ravenously at raw meat, and showed an insensitivity to pain and cold. These stories of what are called **feral children** sound like exaggerations, and it is easy to dismiss them as folk myth.

Because of what happened in 1798, however, we can't be so sure. In that year, a child who walked on all fours and could not speak was found in the forests of Aveyron, France. "The wild boy of Aveyron," as this child became known, would have been simply another of those legends, except that French scientists took the child to a laboratory and studied him. Like the earlier informal reports, this child, too, gave no indication of feeling the cold. Most startling, though, the boy would growl when he saw a small animal, pounce on it, and devour it uncooked. Even today, the scientists' detailed reports make fascinating reading (Itard 1962).

Ever since I read Itard's account of this boy, I've been fascinated by feral children, especially the seemingly fantastic possibility that animals could rear human children. In 2002, I received a report from a contact in Cambodia that a feral child had been found in the jungles. When I had the opportunity the following year to visit the child and interview his caregivers, I grabbed it. The boy's photo is on this page.

If animals really have raised children, the sociological question is: If we were untouched by society, would we be like feral children? By nature, would our behavior be like that of wild animals? Unable to study feral children, sociologists have studied children like Isabelle who were reared in isolation.

Isolated Children

Reports of isolated children have been well documented. What can they tell us about human nature? We can first conclude that humans have no natural language, for Isabelle and others like her are unable to speak.

But maybe Isabelle was mentally impaired, and she simply was not able to progress through the usual stages of development. When Isabelle was given her first intelligence test, she scored practically zero. But after a few months of intensive language training, she was able to speak in short sentences. In about a year, she could write a few words, do simple addition, and retell stories after hearing them. Seven months later, she had a vocabulary of almost 2,000 words. In just two years, Isabelle reached the intellectual level that is normal for her age. She then went on to school, where she was "bright, cheerful, energetic . . . and participated in all school activities as normally as other children" (Davis 1940/2005:139).

As discussed in the previous chapter, language is the key to human development. Without language, people have no mechanism for developing and communicating thought. Unlike animals, humans have no instincts that take the place of language. If an individual lacks language, he or she lives in an isolated world—a world of internal silence, without shared ideas, lacking connections to others.

Without language, there can be no culture—no shared way of life—and culture is the key to what people become. Each of us possesses a biological heritage, but this heritage does not determine specific behaviors, attitudes, or values. It is our culture that superimposes the specifics of what we become onto our biological heritage.

Institutionalized Children

Other than language, what else is required for a child to develop into what we consider a healthy, balanced, intelligent human being? We find part of the answer in an intriguing experiment from the 1930s. Back then, parents died a lot younger, and orphanages were more common throughout the United States. Children reared in orphanages often had difficulty establishing close bonds with others—and they tended to have low IQs. "Common sense" (which we noted in Chapter 1 is unreliable) told everyone that the cause of mental retardation is biological ("They're just born that way"). Two psychologists, H. M. Skeels and H. B. Dye (1939), however, began to suspect a social cause.

One of the reasons I went to Cambodia was to interview a feral child—the boy shown here—who supposedly had been raised by monkeys. When I arrived at the remote location where the boy was living, I was disappointed to find that the story was only partially true. During its reign of terror, the Khmer Rouge had shot and killed the boy's parents, leaving him, at about the age of two, abandoned on an island. Some months later, villagers found him in the care of monkeys. They shot the female monkey that was carrying the boy. Not quite a feral child—but the closest I'll ever come to one.

feral children children assumed to have been raised by animals, in the wilderness, isolated from other humans

For background on their experiment, Skeels (1966) provides this account of a "good" orphanage in Iowa during the 1930s, where he and Dye were consultants:

Until about six months, they were cared for in the infant nursery. The babies were kept in standard hospital cribs that often had protective sheeting on the sides, thus effectively limiting visual stimulation; no toys or other objects were hung in the infants' line of vision. Human interactions were limited to busy nurses who, with the speed born of practice and necessity, changed diapers or bedding, bathed and medicated the infants, and fed them efficiently with propped bottles.

Perhaps, thought Skeels and Dye, the absence of stimulating social interaction was the problem, not some biological incapacity on the part of the children. To test their controversial idea, they selected thirteen infants whose mental retardation was so obvious that no one wanted to adopt them. They placed them in an institution for the mentally retarded. Each infant, then about 19 months old, was assigned to a separate ward of women ranging in mental age from 5 to 12 and in chronological age from 18 to 50. The women were pleased with this arrangement. Not only did they take care of the infants' physical needs—diapering, feeding, and so on—but also they loved to play with the children. They cuddled them and showered them with attention. They even competed to see which ward would have "its baby" walking or talking first. Each child had one woman who became

particularly attached to him [or her] and figuratively "adopted" him [or her]. As a consequence, an intense one-to-one adult-child relationship developed, which was supplemented by the less intense but frequent interactions with the other adults in the environment. Each child had some one person with whom he [or she] was identified and who was particularly interested in him [or her] and his [or her] achievements. (Skeels 1966)

The researchers left a control group of twelve infants at the orphanage. These infants were also thought to have low IQs, but they were considered higher in intelligence than the other thirteen. They received the usual care. Two and a half years later, Skeels and Dye tested all the children's intelligence. Their findings were startling: Those assigned to the care of women in the institution had gained an average of 28 IQ points while those who remained in the orphanage had lost 30 points.

What happened after these children were grown? Did these initial differences matter? Twenty-one years later, Skeels and Dye did a follow-up study. Those in the control group who had remained in the orphanage had, on average, less than a third-grade education. Four still lived in state institutions, while the others held low-level jobs. Only two had married. In contrast, the average level of education for the thirteen individuals in the experimental group was twelve grades (about normal for that period). Five had completed one or more years of college. One had even gone to graduate school. Eleven had married. All thirteen were self-supporting or were homemakers (Skeels 1966). Apparently, then, one characteristic that we take for granted as being a basic "human" trait—high intelligence—depends on early, close relations with other humans.

A recent experiment in India confirms the Skeels and Dye research. Many of India's orphanages are similar to the ones that Skeels and Dye studied, dismal places where unattended children lie in bed all day. When experimenters added stimulating play and interaction to the

Under Communist rule, orphans in Romania received horrible treatment. The children will carry emotional scars into adulthood. In severe cases, their treatment is likely to affect their ability to reason and to function as adults.

children's activities, the children's motor skills improved and their IQs increased (Taneja et al. 2002). The longer that children lack stimulating interaction, though, the more difficulty they have intellectually (Meese 2005).

Let's consider one other case, the story of Genie:

> **In 1970, California authorities found Genie, a 13-year-old girl who had been locked in a small room and tied to a chair since she was 20 months old. Apparently her father (70 years old when Genie was discovered) hated children, and probably had caused the death of two of Genie's siblings. Her 50-year-old mother was partially blind and frightened of her husband. Genie could not speak, did not know how to chew, was unable to stand upright, and could not straighten her hands and legs. On intelligence tests, she scored at the level of a 1-year-old. After intensive training, Genie learned to walk and use simple sentences (although they were garbled). As she grew up, her language remained primitive, she took anyone's property if it appealed to her, and she went to the bathroom wherever she wanted. At the age of 21, Genie went to live in a home for adults who cannot live alone. (Pines 1981)**

IN SUM | From Genie's pathetic story and from reports of institutionalized children, we can conclude that the basic human traits of intelligence and the ability to establish close bonds with others depend on early interaction with other humans. In addition, apparently there is a period prior to age 13 in which children must experience language and human bonding if they are to develop high intelligence and the ability to be sociable and follow social norms.

Deprived Animals

Finally, let's consider animals that have been deprived of normal interaction. In a series of experiments with rhesus monkeys, psychologists Harry and Margaret Harlow demonstrated the importance of early learning. The Harlows (1962) raised baby monkeys in isolation. They gave each monkey two artificial mothers, shown in the photo on this page. One "mother" was only a wire frame with a wooden head, but it did have a nipple from which the baby could nurse. The frame of the other "mother," which had no bottle, was covered with soft terrycloth. To obtain food, the baby monkeys nursed at the wire frame.

When the Harlows (1965) frightened the baby monkeys with a mechanical bear or dog, the babies did not run to the wire frame "mother." Instead, they would cling pathetically to their terrycloth "mother." The Harlows concluded that infant–mother bonding is not the result of feeding but, rather, of what they termed "intimate physical contact." To most of us, this phrase means cuddling.

The monkeys raised in isolation were never able to adjust to monkey life. Placed with other monkeys when they were grown, they didn't know how to participate in "monkey interaction"—to play and to engage in pretend fights—and the other monkeys rejected them. Neither did they know how to have sexual intercourse, despite futile attempts to do so. The experimenters designed a special device, which allowed some females to become pregnant. After giving birth, however, these monkeys were "ineffective, inadequate, and brutal mothers . . . [who] . . . struck their babies, kicked them, or crushed the babies against the cage floor."

In one of their many experiments, the Harlows isolated baby monkeys for different lengths of time. They found that when monkeys were isolated for shorter periods (about three months), they were able to overcome the effects of their isolation. Those isolated for six

Like humans, monkeys need interaction to thrive. Those raised in isolation are unable to interact satisfactorily with others. In this photograph, we see one of the monkeys described in the text. Purposefully frightened by the experimenter, the monkey has taken refuge in the soft terrycloth draped over an artificial "mother."

months or more, however, were unable to adjust to normal monkey life. As mentioned, they could not play or engage in pretend fights, and the other monkeys rejected them. In other words, the longer the period of isolation, the more difficult its effects are to overcome. In addition, a critical learning stage may exist: If that stage is missed, it may be impossible to compensate for what has been lost. This may have been the case with Genie.

Because humans are not monkeys, we must be careful about extrapolating from animal studies to human behavior. The Harlow experiments, however, support what we know about children who are reared in isolation.

IN SUM **Society Makes Us Human.** Apparently, babies do not develop "naturally" into human adults. Although their bodies grow, if children are reared in isolation they become little more than big animals. Without the concepts that language provides, they can't experience or even grasp relationships between people (the "connections" we call brother, sister, parent, friend, teacher, and so on). And without warm, friendly interactions, they don't become "friendly" in the accepted sense of the term, nor do they cooperate with others. In short, it is through human contact that people learn to be members of the human community. This process by which we learn the ways of society (or of particular groups), called **socialization**, is what sociologists have in mind when they say "Society makes us human."

Socialization into the Self and Mind

At birth, babies have no idea that they are separate beings. They don't even know that they are a he or she. How do we humans develop a **self,** our image of who we are? How do we develop our ability to reason? Let's see how this occurs.

Cooley and the Looking-Glass Self

About a hundred years ago, Charles Horton Cooley (1864–1929), a symbolic interactionist who taught at the University of Michigan, concluded that this unique aspect of "humanness" called the self is socially created. He said that *our sense of self develops from interaction with others.* Cooley (1902) coined the term **looking-glass self** to describe the process by which our sense of self develops. He summarized this idea in the following couplet:

> **Each to each a looking-glass**
> **Reflects the other that doth pass.**

The looking-glass self contains three elements:

1. *We imagine how we appear to those around us.* For example, we may think that others perceive us as witty or dull.
2. *We interpret others' reactions.* We come to conclusions about how others evaluate us. Do they like us for being witty? Do they dislike us for being dull?
3. *We develop a self-concept.* How we interpret others' reactions to us frames our feelings and ideas about ourselves. A favorable reflection in this *social mirror* leads to a positive self-concept; a negative reflection leads to a negative self-concept.

Note that the development of the self does *not* depend on accurate evaluations. Even if we grossly misinterpret how others think about us, those misjudgments become part of our self-concept. Note also that *although the self-concept begins in childhood, its development is an ongoing, lifelong process.* The three steps of the looking-glass self are a part of our everyday lives: As we monitor how others react to us, we continually modify the self. The self, then, is never a finished product—it is always in process, even into old age.

socialization the process by which people learn the characteristics of their group—the knowledge, skills, attitudes, values, and actions thought appropriate for them

self the unique human capacity of being able to see ourselves "from the outside"; the views we internalize of how others see us

looking-glass self a term coined by Charles Horton Cooley to refer to the process by which our self develops through internalizing others' reactions to us

Mead and Role Taking

Another symbolic interactionist, George Herbert Mead (1863–1931), who taught at the University of Chicago, added that play is crucial to the development of a self. In play, children learn to **take the role of the other,** that is, to put themselves in someone else's shoes—to understand how someone else feels and thinks and to anticipate how that person will act.

Only gradually do children attain this ability (Mead 1934; Coser 1977). Psychologist John Flavel (1968) asked 8- and 14-year-olds to explain a board game to some children who were blindfolded and to others who were not. The 14-year-olds gave more detailed instructions to those who were blindfolded, but the 8-year-olds gave the same instructions to everyone. The younger children could not yet take the role of the other, while the older children could.

As they develop this ability, at first children are able to take only the role of **significant others,** individuals who significantly influence their lives, such as parents or siblings. By assuming their roles during play, such as dressing up in their parents' clothing, children cultivate the ability to put themselves in the place of significant others.

As the self gradually develops, children internalize the expectations of more and more people. The ability to take on roles eventually extends to being able to take the role of "the group as a whole." Mead used the term **generalized other** to refer to our perception of how people in general think of us.

Taking the role of others is essential if we are to become cooperative members of human groups—whether they be our family, friends, or co-workers. This ability allows us to modify our behavior by anticipating how others will react—something Genie never learned.

Learning to take the role of the other entails three stages (see Figure 3.1):

1. *Imitation.* Children under age 3 can only mimic others. They do not yet have a sense of self separate from others, and they can only imitate people's gestures and words. (This stage is actually not role taking, but it prepares the child for it.)
2. *Play.* During the second stage, from the ages of about 3 to 6, children pretend to take the roles of specific people. They might pretend that they are a firefighter, a wrestler, a nurse, Supergirl, Spiderman, a princess, and so on. They also like costumes at this stage and enjoy dressing up in their parents' clothing, or tying a towel around their neck to "become" Spiderman or Wonder Woman.
3. *Team Games.* This third stage, organized play, or team games, begins roughly with the early school years. The significance for the self is that to play these games the individual must be able to take multiple roles. One of Mead's favorite

taking the role of the other putting oneself in someone else's shoes; understanding how someone else feels and thinks and thus anticipating how that person will act

significant other an individual who significantly influences someone else's life

generalized other the norms, values, attitudes, and expectations of people "in general"; the child's ability to take the role of the generalized other is a significant step in the development of a self

To help his students understand the term *generalized other*, Mead used baseball as an illustration. Why are team sports and organized games such excellent examples to use in explaining this concept?

Figure 3.1 **How We Learn to Take the Role of the Other: Mead's Three Stages**

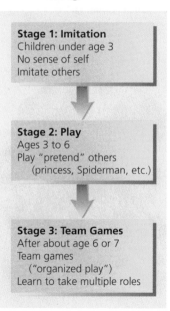

Stage 1: Imitation
Children under age 3
No sense of self
Imitate others

Stage 2: Play
Ages 3 to 6
Play "pretend" others
(princess, Spiderman, etc.)

Stage 3: Team Games
After about age 6 or 7
Team games
("organized play")
Learn to take multiple roles

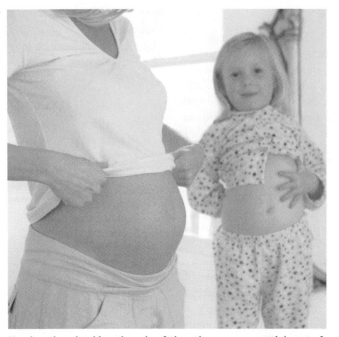

Mead analyzed *taking the role of the other* as an essential part of learning to be a full-fledged member of society. At first, we are able to take the role only of significant others, as this child is doing. Later we develop the capacity to take the role of the *generalized other*, which is essential not only for extended cooperation but also for the control of antisocial desires.

examples was that of a baseball game, in which each player must be able to take the role of all the other players. To play baseball, the child not only must know his or her own role but also must be able to anticipate who will do what when the ball is hit or thrown.

Mead also said there were two parts of the self, the "I" and the "me." The "*I*" is *the self as subject,* the active, spontaneous, creative part of the self. In contrast, the "*me*" is *the self as object.* It is made up of attitudes we internalize from our interactions with others. Mead chose these pronouns because in English "I" is the active agent, as in "I shoved him," while "me" is the object of action, as in "He shoved me." Mead stressed that we are not passive in the socialization process. We are not like robots, passively absorbing the responses of others. Rather, our "I" is active. It evaluates the reactions of others and organizes them into a unified whole. Mead added that the "I" even monitors the "me," fine-tuning our actions to help us better match what others expect of us.

Mead also drew a conclusion that some find startling: *Both the self and the human mind are social products.* Mead stressed that we cannot think without symbols. But where do these symbols come from? Only from society, which gives us our symbols by giving us language. If society did not provide the symbols, we would not be able to think, and thus would not possess what we call the mind. The mind, then, like language, is a product of society.

Piaget and the Development of Reasoning

An essential part of being human is the ability to reason. How do we learn this skill?

This question intrigued Jean Piaget (1896–1980), a Swiss psychologist who noticed that young children give similar wrong answers when they take intelligence tests. He thought that young children might be using some consistent, but incorrect, reasoning to figure out their answers. Perhaps children go through a natural process as they learn how to reason.

To find out, Piaget set up a laboratory where he could give children of different ages various problems to solve (Piaget 1950, 1954; Flavel et al. 2002). After years of testing, Piaget concluded that children go through four stages as they develop their ability to reason. (If you mentally substitute "reasoning skills" for the term *operational* in the following explanations, Piaget's findings will be easier to understand.)

Shown here is Jean Piaget with one of the children he studied in his analysis of the development of human reasoning.

1. **The sensorimotor stage** (from birth to about age 2) During this stage, understanding is limited to direct contact with the environment—sucking, touching, listening, looking. Infants do not "think" in any sense that we understand. During the first part of this stage, they do not even know that their bodies are separate from the environment. Indeed, they have yet to discover that they have toes. Neither can infants recognize cause and effect. That is, they do not know that their actions cause something to happen.
2. **The preoperational stage** (from about age 2 to age 7) During this stage, children *develop the ability to use symbols.* However, they do not yet understand common concepts such as size, speed, or causation. Although they can count, they do not really understand what numbers mean. Nor do they yet have the ability to take the role of the other. Piaget asked preoperational children to describe a clay model of a mountain range. They did just fine. But when he asked them to describe how the mountain range looked from where another child was sitting, they couldn't do it. They could only repeat what they saw from their view.

3. **The concrete operational stage** (from the age of about 7 to 12) Although reasoning abilities are more developed, they remain *concrete*. Children can now understand numbers, causation, and speed, and they are able to take the role of the other and to participate in team games. Without concrete examples, however, they are unable to talk about concepts such as truth, honesty, or justice. They can explain why Jane's answer was a lie, but they cannot describe what truth itself is.

4. **The formal operational stage** (after the age of about 12) Children are now capable of abstract thinking. They can talk about concepts, come to conclusions based on general principles, and use rules to solve abstract problems. During this stage, children are likely to become young philosophers (Kagan 1984). If shown a photo of a slave, for example, a child at the concrete operational stage might have said, "That's wrong!" However, a child at the formal operational stage is likely to add, "If our county was founded on equality, how could people have owned slaves?"

Global Aspects of the Self and Reasoning

Cooley's conclusions about the looking-glass self appear to be true for everyone around the world. So do Mead's conclusions about role taking and the mind as a social product, although researchers are finding that the self may develop earlier than Mead indicated. The stages of reasoning that Piaget identified probably also occur worldwide, although researchers have found that the stages are not as distinct as Piaget concluded and the ages at which individuals enter the stages differ from one person to another (Flavel et al. 2002). Even during the sensorimotor stage, for example, children show early signs of reasoning, which may indicate an innate ability that is wired into the brain. Although Piaget's theory is being refined, his contribution remains: *A basic structure underlies the way we develop reasoning, and children all over the world begin with the concrete and move to the abstract.*

Interestingly, some people seem to get stuck in the concreteness of the third stage and never reach the fourth stage of abstract thinking (Kohlberg and Gilligan 1971; Suizzo 2000). College, for example, nurtures the fourth stage, and most people without this experience apparently have less ability for abstract thought. Social experiences, then, can modify these stages. Also, there is much that we don't yet know about how culture influences the way we think, a topic explored in the Cultural Diversity box on the next page.

Learning Personality, Morality, and Emotions

Our personality, morality, and emotions are vital aspects of who we are. Let's look at how we learn these essential aspects of our being.

Freud and the Development of Personality

Along with the development of our mind and the self comes the development of our personality. Sigmund Freud (1856–1939) developed a theory of the origin of personality that has had a major impact on Western thought. Freud was a physician in Vienna in the early 1900s who founded *psychoanalysis,* a technique for treating emotional problems through long-term, intensive exploration of the subconscious mind. Let's look at his theory.

Freud believed that personality consists of three elements. Each child is born with the first element, an **id,** Freud's term for inborn drives that cause us to seek self-gratification. The id of the newborn is evident in its cries of hunger or pain. The pleasure-seeking id operates throughout life. It demands the immediate fulfillment of basic needs: food, safety, attention, sex, and so on.

The id's drive for immediate gratification, however, runs into a roadblock: primarily the needs of other people, especially those of the parents. To adapt to these constraints, a second component of the personality emerges, which Freud called the ego. The **ego** is

id Freud's term for our inborn basic drives

ego Freud's term for a balancing force between the id and the demands of society

Cultural Diversity *around the* World

WHICH TWO OF THESE ITEMS GO together: a panda, a monkey, and a banana? Please answer before you read further.

You probably said the panda and the monkey. Both are animals, while the banana is a fruit. This is logical.

At least this is the logic of Westerners, and it is difficult for us to see how the answer could be anything else. Someone from Japan, however, is likely to reply that the monkey and the banana go together.

Why? Whereas Westerners typically see categories (animals and fruit), Asians typically see relationships (monkeys eat bananas).

In one study, Japanese and U.S. students were shown a picture of an aquarium that contained one big, fast-moving fish and several smaller fish, along with plants, a rock, and bubbles. Later, when the students were asked what they had seen, the Japanese students were 60 percent more likely to remember background elements. They also referred more to relationships, such as the "the little pink fish was in front of the blue rock."

The students were also shown 96 objects and asked which of them had been in the picture. The Japanese students did much better at remembering when the object was

Do You See What I See? Eastern and Western Ways of Perceiving and Thinking

The World

What do you see when you look at this aquarium? Perception depends not only on biology but also on culture.

shown in its original surroundings. The U.S. students, in contrast, had not noticed the background.

Westerners pay more attention to the focal object, in this case the fish, while Asians are more attuned to the overall surroundings. The implications of this difference run deep: Easterners attribute less causation to actors and more to context, while Westerners minimize the context and place greater emphasis on individual actors.

Differences in how Westerners and Easterners perceive the world and think about it are just being uncovered. We know practically nothing about how these differences originate. *Because these initial findings indicate deep, culturally based, fundamental differences in perception and thinking,* this should prove to be a fascinating area of research.

for your Consideration

In our global village, differences in perception and thinking can have potentially devastating effects. Consider a crisis between the United States and North Korea. How might Easterners and Westerners see the matter differently? How might they attribute cause differently and, without knowing it, "talk past one another"?

Source: Based on Nisbett 2003; Davies 2007.

---

the balancing force between the id and the demands of society that suppress it. The ego also serves to balance the id and the **superego,** the third component of the personality, more commonly called the *conscience.*

The superego represents *culture within us,* the norms and values we have internalized from our social groups. As the *moral* component of the personality, the superego provokes feelings of guilt or shame when we break social rules, or pride and self-satisfaction when we follow them.

According to Freud, when the id gets out of hand, we follow our desires for pleasure and break society's norms. When the superego gets out of hand, we become overly rigid in following those norms, finding ourselves bound in a straitjacket of rules that inhibit our lives. The ego, the balancing force, tries to prevent either the superego or the id from dominating. In the emotionally healthy individual, the ego succeeds in balancing these conflicting demands of the id and the superego. In the maladjusted individual, however, the ego fails to control the inherent conflict between the id and the superego. Either the id or the superego dominates this person, leading to internal confusion and problem behaviors.

Sociological Evaluation Sociologists appreciate Freud's emphasis on socialization—that the social group into which we are born transmits norms and values that restrain our biological drives. Sociologists, however, object to the view that inborn and subconscious

superego Freud's term for the conscience, the internalized norms and values of our social groups

This photo of Freud, one of the most influential theorists of the 20th century, was taken in his office in Vienna in 1937. Most of Freud's ideas have been discarded.

motivations are the primary reasons for human behavior. *This denies the central principle of sociology:* that factors such as social class (income, education, and occupation) and people's roles in groups underlie their behavior (Epstein 1988; Bush and Simmons 1990).

Feminist sociologists have been especially critical of Freud. Although what we just summarized applies to both females and males, Freud assumed that what is "male" is "normal." He even said that females are inferior, castrated males (Chodorow 1990; Gerhard 2000). It is obvious that sociologists need to continue to research how we develop personality.

Kohlberg, Gilligan, and the Development of Morality

If you have observed young children, you know that they focus on immediate gratification and show little or no concern for others. ("Mine!" a 2-year-old will shout, as she grabs a toy from another child.) Yet, at a later age this same child will become considerate of others and concerned with moral issues. How does this change happen?

Kohlberg's Theory Psychologist Lawrence Kohlberg (1975, 1984, 1986; Walsh 2000) concluded that we go through a sequence of stages as we develop morality. Building on Piaget's work, he found that children begin in the *amoral stage* I just described. For them, there is no right or wrong, just personal needs to be satisfied. From about ages 7 to 10, children are in what Kohlberg called a *preconventional stage.* They have learned rules, and they follow them to stay out of trouble. They view right and wrong as what pleases or displeases their parents, friends, and teachers. Their concern is to avoid punishment. At about age 10, they enter the *conventional stage.* During this period, morality means following the norms and values they have learned. In the *postconventional stage,* which Kohlberg says most people don't reach, individuals reflect on abstract principles of right and wrong and judge a behavior according to these principles.

Gilligan and Gender Differences in Morality Carol Gilligan, another psychologist, grew uncomfortable with Kohlberg's conclusions, which didn't seem to match her own experience. Then she noted that Kohlberg had used only boys in his studies. By this point, more women had become social scientists, and they were questioning the assumption male researchers held that female subjects were not necessary because the results of research with boys would apply to girls as well.

Gilligan (1982, 1990) decided to find out if there were differences in how men and women looked at morality. After interviewing about 200 men and women, she concluded that women are more likely to evaluate morality in terms of *personal relationships.* Women want to know how an action affects others. They are more concerned with personal loyalties and with the harm that might come to loved ones. Men, in contrast, tend to think more along the lines of *abstract principles* that define right and wrong. As they see things, an act either matches or violates a code of ethics, and personal relationships have little to do with the matter.

Researchers tested Gilligan's conclusions. They found that *both* men and women use personal relationships and abstract principles when they make moral judgments (Wark and Krebs 1996). Although Gilligan no longer supports her original position (Brannon 1999), the matter is not yet settled. Some researchers have found differences in how men and women make moral judgments (White 1999; Jaffee and Hyde 2000). Others stress that both men and women learn cultural forms of moral reasoning (Tappan 2006).

As with personality, in this vital area of human development, sociological research is also notably absent.

Socialization into Emotions

Emotions, too, are an essential aspect of who we become. Sociologists who research this area of our "humanness" find that emotions also are not simply the results of biology. Like the mind, emotions depend on socialization (Hochschild 1975; 1983; Wang and Roberts 2006). This may sound strange. Don't all people get angry? Doesn't everyone cry? Don't we all feel guilt, shame, sadness, happiness, fear? What has socialization to do with emotions?

Global Emotions   At first, it may look as though socialization is not relevant. Paul Ekman (1980), an anthropologist, studied emotions in several countries. He concluded that everyone experiences six basic emotions: anger, disgust, fear, happiness, sadness, and surprise—and we all show the same facial expressions when we feel these emotions. A person from Zimbabwe, for example, could tell from just the look on an American's face that she is angry, disgusted, or fearful, and we could tell from the Zimbabwean's face that he is happy, sad, or surprised. Because we all show the same facial expressions when we experience these six emotions, Ekman concluded that they are built into our biology, "a product of our genes."

Expressing Emotions   The existence of universal facial expressions for these basic emotions does *not* mean that socialization has no effect on how we express them. Facial expressions are only one way in which we show emotions. Other ways vary with gender. For example, U.S. women are allowed to express their emotions more freely, while U.S. men are expected to be more reserved. To express sudden happiness, or a delighted surprise, for example, women are allowed to make "squeals of glee" in public places. Men are not. Such an expression would be a fundamental violation of their gender role.

Then there are culture, social class, and relationships. Consider culture. Two close Japanese friends who meet after a long separation don't shake hands or hug—they bow. Two Arab men will kiss. Social class is also significant, for it cuts across many other lines, even gender. Upon seeing a friend after a long absence, upper-class women and men are likely to be more reserved in expressing their delight than are lower-class women and men. Relationships also make a big difference. We express our emotions more openly if we are with close friends, more guardedly if we are at a staff meeting with the corporate CEO. A good part of childhood socialization centers on learning these "norms of emotion"—how to express our emotions in a variety of settings.

What We Feel   The matter goes deeper than this. Socialization not only leads to different ways of expressing emotions but even affects *what* we feel (Clark 1997; Shields 2002). People in one culture may even learn to experience feelings that are unknown in another culture. For example, the Ifaluk, who live on the Western Caroline Islands of Micronesia, use the word *fago* to refer to the feelings they have when they see someone

What emotions are these people expressing? Are these emotions global? Is their way of expressing them universal?

suffer. This comes close to what we call sympathy or compassion. But the Ifaluk also use this term to refer to what they feel when they are with someone who has high status, someone they highly respect or admire (Kagan 1984). To us, these are two distinct emotions, and they require separate words to express them.

Research Needed Although Ekman identified only six emotions that are universal in feeling and facial expression, I suspect that other emotions are common to people around the world—and that everyone shows similar facial expressions when they experience them. I suggest that feelings of helplessness, despair, confusion, and shock are among these universal emotions. We need cross-cultural research to find out whether this is so. We also need research into how children learn to feel and express emotions.

Society Within Us: The Self and Emotions as Social Control

Much of our socialization is intended to turn us into conforming members of society. Socialization into the self and emotions is an essential part of this process, for both the self and our emotions mold our behavior. Although we like to think that we are "free," consider for a moment just some of the factors that influence how we act: the expectations of friends and parents, or neighbors and teachers; classroom norms and college rules; city, state, and federal laws. For example, if in a moment of intense frustration, or out of a devilish desire to shock people, you wanted to tear off your clothes and run naked down the street, what would stop you?

The answer is your socialization—*society within you.* Your experiences in society have resulted in a self that thinks along certain lines and feels particular emotions. This helps to keep you in line. Thoughts such as "Would I get kicked out of school?" and "What would my friends (parents) think if they found out?" represent an awareness of the self in relationship to others. So does the desire to avoid feelings of shame and embarrassment. Our *social mirror,* then—the result of being socialized into a self and emotions—sets up effective controls over our behavior. In fact, socialization into self and emotions is so effective that some people feel embarrassed just thinking about running nude in public!

IN SUM Socialization is essential for our development as human beings. From interaction with others, we learn how to think, reason, and feel. The net result is the shaping of our behavior—including our thinking and emotions—according to cultural standards. This is what sociologists mean when they refer to "*society within us.*"

Socialization into Gender

To channel our behavior—including our thinking and emotions—along expected avenues, society also uses **gender socialization.** By expecting different attitudes and behaviors from us *because* we are male or female, the human group nudges boys and girls in separate directions in life. This foundation of contrasting attitudes and behaviors is so thorough that, as adults, most of us act, think, and even feel according to our culture's guidelines of what is appropriate for our sex.

The significance of gender is emphasized throughout this book, and we focus specifically on gender in Chapter 8. For now, though, let's briefly consider some of the "gender messages" that we get from our family and the mass media.

Gender Messages in the Family

Our parents are the first significant others who teach us our role in this fundamental symbolic division of the world. Sometimes they do so consciously, perhaps by bringing into play pink and blue, colors that have no meaning in themselves but that are now associated with gender. Our parents' own gender orientations have become embedded so firmly that they do most of this teaching without being aware of what they are doing.

This is illustrated in a classic study by psychologists Susan Goldberg and Michael Lewis (1969), whose results have been confirmed by other researchers (Fagot et al. 1985; Connors 1996).

> Goldberg and Lewis asked mothers to bring their 6-month-old infants into their laboratory, supposedly to observe the infants' development. Covertly, however, they also observed the mothers. They found that the mothers kept their daughters closer to them. They also touched their daughters more and spoke to them more frequently than they did to their sons.
>
> By the time the children were 13 months old, the girls stayed closer to their mothers during play, and they returned to their mothers sooner and more often than the boys did. When Goldberg and Lewis set up a barrier to separate the children from their mothers, who were holding toys, the girls were more likely to cry and motion for help; the boys, to try to climb over the barrier.

Goldberg and Lewis concluded that in our society mothers subconsciously reward daughters for being passive and dependent, and sons for being active and independent.

These lessons continue throughout childhood. On the basis of their sex, children are given different kinds of toys. Boys are more likely to get guns and "action figures" that destroy enemies. Girls are more likely to get dolls and jewelry. Some parents try to choose "gender neutral" toys, but kids know what is popular, and they feel left out if they don't have what the other kids have. The significance of toys in gender socialization can be summarized this way: Almost all parents would be upset if someone gave their son Barbie dolls.

gender socialization the ways in which society sets children onto different courses in life *because* they are male or female

The *gender roles* that we learn during childhood become part of our basic orientations to life. Although we refine these roles as we grow older, they remain built around the framework established during childhood.

Parents also let their preschool sons roam farther from home than their preschool daughters, and they subtly encourage the boys to participate in more rough-and-tumble play. They expect their sons to get dirtier and to be more defiant, their daughters to be daintier and more compliant (Gilman 1911/1971; Henslin 2007). In large part, they get what they expect. Such experiences in socialization lie at the heart of the sociological explanation of male–female differences.

We should note, however, that some sociologists would consider biology to be the cause, proposing that Goldberg and Lewis were simply observing innate differences in the children. In short, were the mothers creating those behaviors (the boys wanting to get down and play more, and the girls wanting to be hugged more), or were they responding to natural differences in their children? It is similarly the case with toys. In an intriguing experiment with monkeys, researchers discovered that male monkeys prefer cars and balls more than do female monkeys, who are more likely to prefer dolls and pots (Alexander and Hines 2002). We shall return to this controversial issue of nature versus nurture in Chapter 8.

The family is one of the primary ways that we learn gender. Shown here is a woman of the Chin tribe in Myanmar as she farms her field. What gender messages do you think her daughter is learning?

Gender Messages from Peers

Sociologists stress how this sorting process that begins in the family is reinforced as the child is exposed to other aspects of society. Of those other influences, one of the most powerful is the **peer group,** individuals of roughly the same age who are linked by common interests. Examples of peer groups are friends, classmates, and "the kids in the neighborhood." Consider how girls and boys teach one another what it means to be a female or a male in U.S. society.

Let's eavesdrop on a conversation between two eighth-grade girls studied by sociologist Donna Eder (2007). You can see how these girls are reinforcing images of appearance and behavior that they think are appropriate for females:

CINDY: The only thing that makes her look anything is all the makeup . . .

PENNY: She had a picture, and she's standing like this. (Poses with one hand on her hip and one by her head)

CINDY: Her face is probably this skinny, but it looks that big 'cause of all the makeup she has on it.

PENNY: She's ugly, ugly, ugly.

Boys, of course, also reinforce cultural expectations of gender (Pascoe 2003). When sociologist Melissa Milkie (1994) studied junior high school boys, she found that much of their talk centered on movies and TV programs. Of the many images they saw, the boys would single out sex and violence. They would amuse one another by repeating lines, acting out parts, and joking and laughing at what they had seen.

If you know boys in their early teens, you've probably seen behavior like this. You may have been amused, or even have shaken your head in disapproval. As a sociologist, however, Milkie peered beneath the surface. She concluded that the boys were using media images to develop their identity as males. They had gotten the message: To be a "real" male is to be obsessed with sex and violence. Not to joke and laugh about murder and promiscuous sex would have marked a boy as a "weenie," a label to be avoided at all costs.

Gender Messages in the Mass Media

Another powerful influence is the **mass media,** forms of communication that are directed to large audiences. Let's look at how images in advertising, television, and video games reinforce **gender roles,** the behaviors and attitudes considered appropriate for our sex.

Advertising Advertising bombards us so greatly that the average U.S. child watches about 25,000 commercials a year (Moore 2006). Commercials aimed at children are more likely to show girls as cooperative and boys as aggressive. They also are more likely to show girls at home and boys in other locations (Larson 2001). Girls are also more likely to be portrayed as giggly and less capable at tasks (Browne 1998). When advertising directed at adults portrays men as dominant and rugged and women as sexy and submissive, it perpetuates similar stereotypes.

The result is a spectrum of stereotypical, culturally molded images. At one end of this spectrum are cowboys who roam the wide open spaces, while at the other end are scantily clad women, whose assets are intended to sell a variety of products, from automobiles to hamburgers. The portrayal of women with unrealistic physical assets makes female viewers feel inadequate (Kilbourne 2003). This, of course, creates demand for an array of products that promise physical enhancement and romantic success.

Television Television reinforces stereotypes of the sexes. On prime-time television, male characters outnumber female characters. Male characters are also more likely to be portrayed in higher-status positions (Glascock 2001). Sports news also maintains traditional stereotypes. Sociologists who studied the content of televised sports news in Los Angeles found that women athletes receive little coverage (Messner et al. 2003). When they do, they are sometimes trivialized by men newscasters

peer group a group of individuals of roughly the same age who are linked by common interests

mass media forms of communication, such as radio, newspapers, and television that are directed to mass audiences

gender role the behaviors and attitudes considered appropriate because one is a female or a male

who focus on humorous events in women's sports or turn the woman athlete into a sexual object. Newscasters even manage to emphasize breasts and bras and to engage in locker-room humor.

Stereotype-breaking characters, in contrast, are a sign of changing times. In comedies, women are more verbally aggressive than men (Glascock 2001). The powers of the teenager *Buffy, The Vampire Slayer,* were remarkable. On *Alias,* Sydney Bristow exhibited extraordinary strength. In cartoons, Kim Possible divides her time between cheerleading practice and saving the world from evil, while, also with tongue in cheek, the Powerpuff Girls are touted as "the most elite kindergarten crime-fighting force ever assembled." This new gender portrayal continues in a variety of programs, such as *Totally Spies.*

The gender messages on these programs are mixed. Girls are powerful, but they have to be skinny and gorgeous and wear the latest fashions, too. This is almost impossible to replicate in real life.

Video Games The popularity of video games has surged. Even one-fourth of 4- to 6-year-olds play them for an average of an hour a day (Rideout and Vandewater 2003). College students, especially men, relieve stress by escaping into video games (Jones 2003).

Sports are a powerful agent of socialization. That suma wrestling teaches a form of masculinity should be apparent from this photo. What else do you think these boys are learning?

Although sociologists have begun to study how the sexes are portrayed in video games, their influence on the players' ideas of gender is still unknown (Dietz 2000; Berger 2002). Because these games are on the cutting edge of society, they sometimes also reflect cutting-edge changes in sex roles, the topic of the Mass Media in Social Life box on the next page.

Anime *Anime* is a Japanese cartoon form targeted at children. Because anime crosses boundaries of video games, television, movies, and books (comic), we shall consider it as a separate category. Perhaps the most recognizable feature of anime is the big-eyed little girls and the fighting little boys. Japanese parents are concerned about the depiction of violence and the antisocial heroes in anime, but to keep peace they reluctantly buy anime for their children (Khattak 2007). As anime becomes popular with U.S. children, it joins a scene in which targeting violence at children is taken for granted—and with its cute characters, anime is unlikely to cause a stir among Americans. Anime's depiction of active, dominant little males and submissive little females leads to the question, of course, of what gender lessons it is giving children.

IN SUM "Male" and "female" are such powerful symbols that learning them forces us to interpret the world in terms of gender. As children learn their society's symbols of gender, they learn that different behaviors and attitudes are expected of boys and girls. First transmitted by the family, these gender messages are reinforced by other social institutions. As they become integrated into our views of the world, gender messages form a picture of "how" males and females "are." Because gender serves as a primary basis for **social inequality**—giving privileges and obligations to one group of people while denying them to another—gender images are especially important to understand.

Agents of Socialization

People and groups that influence our orientations to life—our self-concept, emotions, attitudes, and behavior—are called **agents of socialization.** We have already considered how three of these agents—the family, our peers, and the

social inequality a social condition in which privileges and obligations are given to some but denied to others

agents of socialization people or groups that affect our self-concept, attitudes, behaviors, or other orientations toward life

Lara Croft, Tomb Raider: Changing Images of Women in the Mass Media

The mass media reflect women's changing role in society. Portrayals of women as passive, as subordinate, or as mere background objects remain, but a new image has broken through. Although this new image exaggerates changes, it also illustrates a fundamental change in gender relations. Lara Croft is an outstanding example of this change.

Like books and magazines, video games are made available to a mass audience. And with digital advances, they have crossed the line from what is traditionally thought of as games to something that more closely resembles interactive movies. Costing an average of $10 million to produce and another $10 million to market, video games now have intricate subplots and use celebrity voices for the characters (Nussenbaum 2004).

Sociologically, what is significant is that the *content* of video games socializes their users. As they play, gamers are exposed not only to action but also to ideas and images. The gender images of video games communicate powerful messages, just as they do in other forms of the mass media.

Lara Croft, an adventure-seeking archeologist and star of *Tomb Raider* and its many sequels, is the essence of the new gender image. Lara is smart, strong, and able to utterly vanquish foes. With both guns blazing, she is the cowboy of the twenty-first century, the term *cowboy* being purposefully chosen, as Lara breaks stereotypical gender roles and dominates what previously was the domain of men. She was the first female protagonist in a

The mass media not only reflect gender stereotypes but also they play a role in changing them. Sometimes they do both simultaneously. The images of Lara Croft not only reflect women's changing role in society, but also, by exaggerating the change, they mold new stereotypes.

field of muscle-rippling, gun-toting macho caricatures (Taylor 1999).

Yet the old remains powerfully encapsulated in the new. As the photos on this page make evident, Lara is a fantasy girl for young men of the digital generation. No matter her foe, no matter her predicament, Lara oozes sex. Her form-fitting outfits, which flatter her voluptuous physique, reflect the mental images of the men who fashioned this digital character.

Lara has caught young men's fancy to such an extent that they have bombarded corporate headquarters with questions about her personal life. Lara is the star of two movies and a comic book. There is even a Lara Croft candy bar.

for your Consideration

A sociologist who reviewed this text said, "It seems that for women to be defined as equal, we have to become symbolic males—warriors with breasts." Why is gender change mostly one-way—females adopting traditional male characteristics? To see why men get to keep their gender roles, these two questions should help: Who is moving into the traditional territory of the other? Do people prefer to imitate power or powerlessness?

Finally, consider just how far stereotypes have actually been left behind. The ultimate goal of the video game, after foes are vanquished, is to see Lara in a nightie.

mass media—influence our ideas of gender. Now we'll look more closely at how agents of socialization prepare us to take our place in society. We shall first consider the family, then the neighborhood, religion, day care, school and peers, sports, and the workplace.

The Family

Around the world, the first group to have a major impact on us is our family. Our experiences in the family are so intense that their influence is lifelong. These experiences lay down our basic sense of self, establishing our initial motivations, values, and beliefs. The family gives us ideas about who we are and what we deserve out of life. It is in the family that we begin to think of ourselves as strong or weak, smart or dumb, good-looking or ugly—or somewhere in between. And as already noted, the lifelong process of defining ourselves as female or male also begins in the family.

The Family and Social Class Middle-class and working-class families socialize their children differently, a process that has life-long consequences on children. Sociologist Melvin Kohn (1959, 1963, 1976, 1977; Kohn et al. 1986) found that working-class parents are mainly concerned that their children stay out of trouble. They also tend to use physical punishment. Middle-class parents, in contrast, focus more on developing their children's curiosity, self-expression, and self-control. They are more likely to reason with their children than to use physical punishment.

This photo captures an extreme form of family socialization. The father seems to be more emotionally involved in the goal—and in more pain—than his daughter, as he pushes her toward the finish line in the Teen Tours of America Kid's Triathlon.

These findings were a sociological puzzle. Just why would working-class and middle-class parents rear their children so differently? Kohn knew that life experiences of some sort held the key, and he found that key in the world of work. Bosses usually tell blue-collar workers exactly what to do. Since blue-collar parents expect their children's lives to be like theirs, they stress obedience. At their work, in contrast, middle-class parents take more initiative. Expecting their children to work at similar jobs, middle-class parents socialize them into the qualities they have found valuable.

Kohn was still puzzled, for some working-class parents act more like middle-class parents, and vice versa. As Kohn probed this puzzle, the pieces fell into place. The key was the parents' type of job. Middle-class office workers, for example, are closely supervised, and Kohn found that they follow the working-class pattern of child rearing, emphasizing conformity. And some blue-collar workers, such as those who do home repairs, have a good deal of freedom. These workers follow the middle-class model in rearing their children (Pearlin and Kohn 1966; Kohn and Schooler 1969).

Working-class and middle-class parents also have different views of how children develop, which has interesting consequences for children's play (Lareau 2002). Working-class parents think of children as developing naturally, while middle-class parents think that children need a lot of guidance to develop correctly. As a result, working-class parents see their job as providing food, shelter, and comfort, with the child's development taking care of itself. They set limits ("Don't go near the railroad tracks"), and let their children play as they wish. Middle-class parents, in contrast, want to structure their children's play to help them develop knowledge and social skills. For example, they may want them to play baseball, not for the enjoyment of the sport, but to help them learn how to be team players.

The Neighborhood

As all parents know, some neighborhoods are better than others for their children. Parents try to move to those neighborhoods—if they can afford them. Their commonsense evaluations are borne out by sociological research. Children from poor neighborhoods are more likely to get in trouble with the law, to become pregnant, to drop out of school, and even to have worse mental health in later life (Brooks-Gunn et al. 1997; Sampson et al. 2001; Wheaton and Clarke 2003; Yonas et al. 2006).

Sociologists have also found that the residents of more affluent neighborhoods watch out for the children more than do the residents of poor neighborhoods (Sampson et al. 1999). This isn't because the adults in poor neighborhoods care less about children. Rather, the more affluent neighborhoods have less transition, so the adults are more likely to know the local children and their parents. This better equips them to help keep the children safe and out of trouble.

Religion

By influencing values, religion becomes a key component in people's ideas of right and wrong. Religion is so important to Americans that half of them belong to a local congregation, and during a typical week, two of every five Americans report that they attend a religious service (Gallup Poll 2007; *Statistical Abstract* 2007:Tables 73, 75). Religion is significant even for people who are reared in nonreligious homes; religious ideas pervade U.S. society, providing basic ideas of morality for us all.

The influence of religion extends to many areas of our lives. For example, participation in religious services teaches us not only beliefs about the hereafter but also ideas about what kinds of dress, speech, and manners are appropriate for formal occasions.

Day Care

It is rare for social science research to make national news, but occasionally it does. This is what happened when researchers published their findings on 1,200 kindergarten children they had studied since their first month after birth. They had observed the children multiple times both at home and at day care. They had also videotaped and made detailed notes on the children's interaction with their mothers (National Institute of Child Health and Human Development 1999; Guensburg 2001). What caught the media's attention? Children who spend more time in day care have weaker bonds with their mothers and are less affectionate to them. They are also less cooperative with others and more likely to fight, to be cruel, and to be "mean." By the time they get to kindergarten, they are more likely to talk back to teachers and to disrupt the classroom. This holds true regardless of the quality of the day care, the family's social class, or whether the child is a girl or a boy (Belsky 2006). On the positive side, the children also scored higher on language tests.

Are we, then, producing a generation of "smart but mean" children? This question has come to bother many, especially since the study was designed so well and an even larger study of children in England has come up with similar findings (Belsky 2006). Some point out that the differences between children who spend a lot of time in day care and those who spend less time is slight. Others stress that with several million children in day care (*Sociological Abstract* 2007:Table 564), slight differences can be significant for society. The researchers are following these children as they continue in school. The most recent report on the children, when they were in the 6th grade, indicates that these patterns are continuing (Belsky et al. 2007).

The School

Part of the **manifest function,** or *intended* purpose, of formal education is to teach knowledge and skills, such as reading, writing, and arithmetic. The teaching of such skills is certainly part of socialization, but so are the schools' **latent functions,** their *unintended* consequences that help the social system. Let's look at this less visible aspect of education.

At home, children learn attitudes and values that match their family's situation in life. At school, they learn a broader perspective that helps prepare them to take a role in the world beyond the family. At home, for example, a child may have been the almost exclusive focus of doting parents, but in school, the child learns *universality*—that

manifest functions the intended beneficial consequences of people's actions

latent functions unintended beneficial consequences of people's actions

the same rules apply to everyone, regardless of who their parents are or how special they may be at home. The Cultural Diversity box below explores how these new values and ways of looking at the world sometimes even replace those the child learns at home.

Cultural Diversity *in the* United States

Caught Between Two Worlds

California
California

IT IS A STRUGGLE TO LEARN a new culture, for its behaviors and ways of thinking contrast with the ones already learned. This can lead to inner turmoil. One way to handle the conflict is to cut ties with your first culture. This, however, can create a sense of loss, perhaps one that is recognized only later in life.

Richard Rodriguez, a literature professor and essayist, was born to working-class Mexican immigrants. Wanting their son to be successful in their adopted land, his parents named him Richard instead of Ricardo. While his English-Spanish hybrid name indicates the parents' aspirations for their son, it was also an omen of the conflict that Richard would experience.

Like other children of Mexican immigrants, Richard's first language was Spanish—a rich mother tongue that introduced him to the world. Until the age of 5, when he began school, Richard knew only fifty words in English. He describes what happened when he began school:

> The change came gradually but early. When I was beginning grade school, I noted to myself the fact that the classroom environment was so different in its styles and assumptions from my own family environment that survival would essentially entail a choice between both worlds. When I became a student, I was literally "remade"; neither I nor my teachers considered anything I had known before as relevant. I had to forget most of what my culture had provided, because to remember it was a disadvantage. The past and its cultural values became detachable, like a piece of clothing grown heavy on a warm day and finally put away.

As happened to millions of immigrants before him, whose parents spoke German, Polish, Italian, and so on, learning English eroded family and class ties and ate away at his ethnic roots. For him, language and education were not simply devices that eased the transition to the dominant culture. Instead, they slashed at the roots that had given him life.

To face conflicting cultures is to confront a fork in the road. Some turn one way and withdraw from the new culture—a clue that helps to explain why so many Latinos drop out of

U.S. schools. Others go in the opposite direction. Cutting ties with their family and cultural roots, they wholeheartedly adopt the new culture.

Rodriguez took the second road. He excelled in his new language—so well, in fact, that he graduated from Stanford University and then became a graduate student in English at the University of California at Berkeley. He was even awarded a prestigious Fulbright fellowship to study English Renaissance literature at the British Museum.

But the past wouldn't let Rodriguez alone. Prospective employers were impressed with his knowledge of Renaissance literature. At job interviews, however, they would skip over the Renaissance training and ask him if he would teach the Mexican novel and be an adviser to Latino students. Rodriguez was also haunted by the image of his grandmother, the warmth of the culture he had left behind, and the language and thought to which he had become a stranger.

Richard Rodriguez represents millions of immigrants—not just those of Latino origin but those from other cultures, too—who want to be a part of life in the United States without betraying their past. They fear that to integrate into U.S. culture is to lose their roots. They are caught between two cultures, each beckoning, each offering rich rewards.

for your Consideration

I saw this conflict firsthand with my father, who did not learn English until after the seventh grade (his last in school). German was left behind, but broken English and awkward expressions remained for a lifetime. Then, too, there were the lingering emotional connections to old ways, as well as the suspicions, haughtiness, and slights of more assimilated Americans. His longing for security by grasping the past was combined with his wanting to succeed in the everyday reality of the new culture. Have you seen anything similar?

Sources: Based on Richard Rodriguez 1975, 1982, 1990, 1991, 1995.

Schools are one of the primary agents of socialization. One of their chief functions is to sort young people into the adult roles thought appropriate for them, and to teach them the attitudes and skills that match those roles. What sorts of attitudes and adult roles do you think this 8-year old is learning from the 15-year old cheerleader? Are these attitudes and roles functions or dysfunctions—or both?

Sociologists have also identified a *hidden curriculum* in our schools. This term refers to values that, although not explicitly taught, are part of a school's "message." For example, the stories and examples that are used to teach math and English may bring with them lessons in patriotism, democracy, justice, and honesty. There is also a *corridor curriculum,* what students teach one another outside the classroom. Unfortunately, the corridor curriculum seems to emphasize racism, sexism, illicit ways to make money, and coolness (Hemmings 1999). You can determine for yourself which of these is functional and which is dysfunctional.

Conflict theorists point out that social class separates children into different worlds. Children born to wealthy parents go to private schools, where they learn skills and values that match their higher position. Children born to middle- and lower-class parents go to public schools, which further refine the separate worlds of social class. Middle-class children learn that good jobs, even the professions, beckon, while children from blue-collar families learn that not many of "their kind" will become professionals or leaders. This is one of the many reasons that children from blue-collar families are less likely to take college prep courses or to go to college. In short, schools around the world reflect and reinforce their nation's social class, economic, and political systems.

Peer Groups

As a child's experiences with agents of socialization broaden, the influence of the family decreases. Entry into school marks only one of many steps in this transfer of allegiance. One of the most significant aspects of education is that it exposes children to peer groups that help them resist the efforts of parents and schools to socialize them.

When sociologists Patricia and Peter Adler (1998) observed children at two elementary schools in Colorado, they saw how children separate themselves by sex and develop their own worlds with unique norms. The norms that made boys popular were athletic ability, coolness, and toughness. For girls, popularity was based on family background, physical appearance (clothing and use of makeup), and the ability to attract popular boys. In this children's subculture, academic achievement pulled in opposite directions: For boys, high grades lowered their popularity, but for girls, good grades increased their standing among peers.

You know from your own experience how compelling peer groups are. It is almost impossible to go against a peer group, whose cardinal rule seems to be "conformity or rejec-

Gradeschool boys and girls often separate themselves by gender, as in this lunchroom in Schenectady, New York. They generally also prefer to play all-girl and all-boy games. The socialization that occurs during self-segregation by gender is a topic of study by sociologists.

tion." Anyone who doesn't do what the others want becomes an "outsider," a "nonmember," an "outcast." For preteens and teens just learning their way around in the world, it is not surprising that the peer group rules.

As a result, the standards of our peer groups tend to dominate our lives. If your peers, for example, listen to rap, nortec, death metal, rock and roll, country, or gospel, it is almost inevitable that you also prefer that kind of music. It is the same for clothing styles and dating standards. Peer influences also extend to behaviors that violate social norms. If your peers are college-bound and upwardly striving, that is most likely what you will be; but if they use drugs, cheat, and steal, you are likely to do so, too.

Sports and Competitive Success

Sports are another powerful socializing agent. Everyone recognizes that sports teach not only physical skills but also values. In fact, "teaching youngsters to be team players" is often given as the reason for financing organized sports.

Sports have deep effects on the self-image. Boys who are successful in sports, especially combative sports such as football, are considered to be more macho or masculine (Pascoe 2003). Boys who fail at sports have to confront negative images of being less masculine, in some cases, even of being sissies. I am sure that this doesn't surprise you. It is likely that your own experiences in social life make this seem obvious. The implications of this aspect of sports, however, are far reaching. Sociologist Michael Messner (1990) points out that deriving such emotionally gratifying rewards from success in sports encourages boys to develop *instrumental* relationships—those based on what they can get out of people. (This would also apply to other areas of competitive success, not just to sports.)

I am sure you can see how being socialized into relating instrumentally affects gender relationships. Competitive success fosters the strong motivation that boys already have to see what they can get from girls. Girls, in contrast, have traditionally been socialized to construct more of their identities around meaningful relationships, not on instrumental ones. With sports and competitive success in other areas apparently becoming more important in the formation of female identities, it will be interesting to see what effects this has on women.

The Workplace

Another agent of socialization that comes into play somewhat later in life is the workplace. Those initial jobs that we take in high school and college are much more than just a way to earn a few dollars. From the people we rub shoulders with at work, we learn not only a set of skills but also perspectives on the world.

Most of us eventually become committed to some particular line of work, often after trying out many jobs. This may involve **anticipatory socialization,** learning to play a role before entering it. Anticipatory socialization is a sort of mental rehearsal for some future activity. We may talk to people who work in a particular career, read novels about that type of work, or take a summer internship in that field. This allows us to gradually identify with the role, to become aware of what would be expected of us. Sometimes this helps people avoid committing themselves to an unrewarding career, as with some of my students who tried student teaching, found that they couldn't stand it, and then moved on to other fields more to their liking.

An intriguing aspect of work as a socializing agent is that the more you participate in a line of work, the more the work becomes a part of your self-concept. Eventually you come to think of yourself so much in terms of the job that if someone asks you to describe yourself, you are likely to include the job in your self-description. You might say, "I'm a teacher," "I'm a nurse," or "I'm a sociologist."

Resocialization

What does a woman who has just become a nun have in common with a man who has just divorced? The answer is that they both are undergoing **resocialization;** that is, they are learning new norms, values, attitudes, and behaviors to

anticipatory socialization because one anticipates a future role, one learns parts of it now

resocialization the process of learning new norms, values, attitudes, and behaviors

match their new situation in life. In its most common form, resocialization occurs each time we learn something contrary to our previous experiences. A new boss who insists on a different way of doing things is resocializing you. Most resocialization is mild—only a slight modification of things we have already learned.

Resocialization can also be intense. People who join Alcoholics Anonymous (AA), for example, are surrounded by reformed drinkers who affirm the destructive effects of excessive drinking. Some students experience an intense period of resocialization when they leave high school and start college—especially during those initially scary days before they find companions, start to fit in, and feel comfortable. To join a cult or to begin psychotherapy is even more profound, for these events expose people to ideas that conflict with their previous ways of looking at the world. If these ideas "take," not only does the individual's behavior change but also he or she learns a fundamentally different way of looking at life.

Total Institutions

Relatively few of us experience the powerful agent of socialization that sociologist Erving Goffman (1961) called the **total institution.** He coined this term to refer to a place in which people are cut off from the rest of society and where they come under almost total control of the officials who are in charge. Boot camp, prisons, concentration camps, convents, some religious cults, and some boarding schools, such as West Point, are total institutions.

A person entering a total institution is greeted with a **degradation ceremony** (Garfinkel 1956), an attempt to remake the self by stripping away the individual's current identity and stamping a new one in its place. This unwelcome greeting may involve fingerprinting, photographing, shaving the head, and banning the individual's *personal identity kit* (items such as jewelry, hairstyles, clothing, and other body decorations used to express individuality). Newcomers may be ordered to strip, undergo an examination (often in a humiliating, semipublic setting), and then to put on a uniform that designates their new status. (For prisoners, the public reading of the verdict and being led away in handcuffs by armed police are also part of the degradation ceremony.)

Total institutions are isolated from the public. The walls, bars, gates, and guards not only keep the inmates in but also keep outsiders out. Staff members closely supervise the day-to-day lives of the residents. Eating, sleeping, showering, recreation—all are standardized. Inmates learn that their previous statuses—student, worker, spouse, parent—mean nothing. The only thing that counts is their current status.

No one leaves a total institution unscathed, for the experience brands an indelible mark on the individual's self and colors the way he or she sees the world. Boot camp, as described in the Down-to-Earth Sociology box on the next page, is brutal but swift. Prison, in contrast, is brutal and prolonged. Neither recruit nor prisoner, however, has difficulty in pinpointing how the institution affected the self.

Socialization Through the Life Course

You are at a particular stage in your life now, and college is a good part of it. You know that you have more stages ahead of you as you go through life. These stages, from birth to death, are called the **life course** (Elder 1975; 1999). The sociological significance of the life course is twofold. First, as you pass through a stage, it affects your behavior and orientations. You simply don't think about life in the same way when you are 30, are married, and have a baby and a mortgage, as you do when you are 18 or 20, single, and in college. (Actually, you don't even see life the same as a freshman and as a senior.) Second, your life course differs by social location. Your social class, race-ethnicity, and gender, for example, map out distinctive worlds of experience. Consequently, the typical life course differs for males and females, the rich and the poor, and so on. To emphasize this major sociological point, in the sketch that follows I will stress the *historical* setting of people's lives. Because of your particular social location, your own life course may differ from this sketch, which is a composite of stages that others have suggested (Levinson 1978; Carr et al. 1995; Quadagno 2007).

total institution a place in which people are cut off from the rest of society and are almost totally controlled by the officials who run the place

degradation ceremony a term coined by Harold Garfinkel to describe an attempt to remake the self by stripping away an individual's current identity and stamping a new one in its place

life course the stages of our life as we go from birth to death

Boot Camp as a Total Institution

THE BUS ARRIVES AT PARRIS ISLAND, South Carolina, at 3 A.M. The early hour is no accident. The recruits are groggy, confused. Up to a few hours ago, the young men were ordinary civilians. Now, as a sergeant sneeringly calls them "maggots," their heads are buzzed (25 seconds per recruit), and they are quickly thrust into the harsh world of Marine boot camp.

Buzzing the boys' hair is just the first step in stripping away their identity so that the Marines can stamp a new one in its place. The uniform serves the same purpose. There is a ban on using the first person "I." Even a simple request must be made in precise Marine style or it will not be acknowledged. ("Sir, Recruit Jones requests permission to make a head call, Sir.")

Every intense moment of the next eleven weeks reminds the recruits that they are joining a subculture of self-discipline. Here pleasure is suspect and sacrifice is good. As they learn the Marine way of talking, walking, and thinking, they are denied the diversions they once took for granted: television, cigarettes, cars, candy, soft drinks, video games, music, alcohol, drugs, and sex.

Lessons are bestowed with fierce intensity. When Sgt. Carey checks brass belt buckles, Recruit Robert Shelton nervously blurts, "I don't have one." Sgt. Carey's face grows red as his neck cords bulge. "I?" he says, his face just inches from the recruit. With spittle flying from his mouth, he screams, " 'I' is gone!"

"Nobody's an individual" is the lesson that is driven home again and again. "You are a team, a Marine. Not a civilian. Not black or white, not Hispanic or Indian or some hyphenated American—but a Marine. You will live like a Marine, fight like a Marine, and, if necessary, die like a Marine."

Each day begins before dawn with close-order formations. The rest of the day is filled with training in hand-to-hand combat, marching, running, calisthenics, Marine history, and—always—following orders.

"An M-16 can blow someone's head off at 500 meters," Sgt. Norman says. "That's beautiful, isn't it?"

"Yes, sir!" shout the platoon's fifty-nine voices.

"Pick your nose!" Simultaneously fifty nine index fingers shoot into nostrils.

The pressure to conform is intense. Those who are sent packing for insubordination or suicidal tendencies are mocked in cadence during drills. ("Hope you like the sights you see/Parris Island casualty.") As lights go out at 9 P.M., the exhausted recruits perform the day's last task: The entire platoon, in unison, chants the virtues of the Marines.

Recruits are constantly scrutinized. Subperformance is not accepted, whether it be a dirty rifle or a loose thread on a uniform. The subperformer is shouted at, derided, humiliated. The group suffers for the individual. If a recruit is slow, the entire platoon is punished.

The system works.

One of the new Marines (until graduation, they are recruits, not Marines) says, "I feel like I've joined a new society or religion."

He has.

for your Consideration

Of what significance is the recruits' degradation ceremony? Why are recruits not allowed video games, cigarettes, or calls home? Why are the Marines so unfair as to punish an entire platoon for the failure of an individual? Use concepts in this chapter to explain why the system works.

Sources: Based on Garfinkel 1956; Goffman 1961; Ricks 1995; Dyer 2007.

Childhood (from birth to about age 12)

Consider how different your childhood would have been if you had grown up in another historical era. Historian Philippe Ariès (1965) noticed that in European paintings from about 1000 to 1800 A.D. children were always dressed in adult clothing. If they were not depicted stiffly posed, as in a family portrait, they were shown doing adult activities.

From this, Ariès drew a conclusion that sparked a debate among historians: He believed that during this era in Europe, childhood was not regarded as a special time of life. He said that adults viewed children as miniature adults, and put them to work at very early ages. At the age of 7, for example, a boy might leave home for good to learn to be a jeweler or a stonecutter. A girl, in contrast, stayed home until she married, but by the age of 7 she was expected to assume her share of the household tasks. Historians do

In contemporary Western societies such as the United States, children are viewed as innocent and in need of protection from adult responsibilities such as work and self-support. Ideas of childhood vary historically and cross-culturally. From paintings, such as this 1642 British painting by the Le Nain brothers, "A Woman and Five Children," some historians conclude that Europeans once viewed children as miniature adults who assumed adult roles at the earliest opportunity.

not deny that these were the customs of that time, but some say that Ariès' conclusion is ridiculous. They say that other evidence of that period indicates that childhood was viewed as a special time of life (Orme 2002).

Having children work like adults did not disappear with the Middle Ages. It is still common in the Least Industrialized Nations, where children still work in many jobs, from blacksmiths to waiters. They are the most visible as street peddlers, hawking everything from shoelaces to chewing gum. This reflects not just different activities but also a view of children different from the one common in the Most Industrialized Nations.

In earlier centuries, parents and teachers also considered it their moral duty to terrorize children to keep them in line. They would lock children in dark closets, frighten them with bedtime stories of death and hellfire, and force them to witness gruesome events. Consider this:

> **A common moral lesson involved taking children to visit the gibbet [an upraised post on which executed bodies were left hanging from chains], where they were forced to inspect rotting corpses hanging there as an example of what happens to bad children when they grow up. Whole classes were taken out of school to witness hangings, and parents would often whip their children afterwards to make them remember what they had seen. (DeMause 1975)**

Industrialization transformed the way we perceive children. With children having the leisure to go to school, they came to be thought of as tender and innocent, as needing more adult care, comfort, and protection. Over time, such attitudes of dependency grew, and today we view children as needing gentle guidance if they are to develop emotionally, intellectually, morally, even physically. We take our view for granted—after all, it is only "common sense." Yet, as you can see, our view is not "natural." It is, instead, rooted in geography and history.

Technology can also change the nature of childhood. When television shows images of murder, rape, war, and other violence, children of a tender age learn about a world that used to be kept hidden from them (Lee 2001).

![IN SUM] Childhood is more than biology. Everyone's childhood occurs at some point in history, and is embedded in particular social locations, especially social class and gender. *These social factors are as vital as our biology, for they determine what childhood will be like for us.* Although a child's *biological* characteristics (such as being small and dependent) are universal, the child's *social* experiences (the kind of life the child lives) are not. Because of this, sociologists say that childhood varies from culture to culture.

Adolescence (ages 13–17)

Adolescence is not a "natural" age division. It is a social invention. In earlier centuries, people simply moved from childhood into young adulthood, with no stopover in between. The Industrial Revolution brought such an abundance of material surpluses, however, that for the first time in history, millions of people in their teens were able to remain outside the labor force. At the same time, education became a more important factor in achieving success. The convergence of these two forces in industrialized societies created a gap between childhood and adulthood. In the early 1900s, the term *adolescence* was coined to indicate this new stage in life (Hall 1904), one that has become renowned for inner turmoil.

To ground the self-identity of children and mark their passage into adulthood, tribal societies hold *initiation rites*. In the industrialized world, however, adolescents must "find" themselves on their own. As they attempt to carve out an identity that is distinct from both the "younger" world being left behind and the "older" world that is still out of range, adolescents develop their own subcultures, with distinctive clothing, hairstyles, language, gestures, and music. We usually fail to realize that contemporary society, not biology, created this period of inner turmoil that we call *adolescence.*

In many societies, manhood is not bestowed upon males simply because they reach a certain age. Manhood, rather, signifies a standing in the community that must be achieved. Shown here is an initiation ceremony in Indonesia, where boys, to lay claim to the status of manhood, must jump over this barrier.

Transitional Adulthood (ages 18–29)

If society invented adolescence, can it also invent other periods of life? As Figure 3.2 on the next page illustrates, this is actually happening now. Postindustrial societies are adding a period of extended youth to the life course, which sociologists call **transitional adulthood** (also known as *adultolescence*). After high school, millions of young adults go to college, where they postpone adult responsibilities. They are mostly freed from the control of their parents, yet they don't have to support themselves. Even after college, many return home, so they can live cheaply while they establish themselves in a career—and, of course, continue to "find themselves." During this time, people are "neither psychological adolescents nor sociological adults" (Keniston 1971). At some point during this period of extended youth, young adults gradually ease into adult responsibilities. They take a full-time job, become serious about a career, engage in courtship rituals, get married—and go into debt.

transitional adulthood a term that refers to a period following high school when young adults have not yet taken on the responsibilities ordinarily associated with adulthood; also called *adultolescence*

The Middle Years (ages 30–65)

The Early Middle Years (ages 30–49)   During their early middle years, most people are more sure of themselves and of their goals in life. As with any point in the life course, however, the self can receive severe jolts. Common in this period are divorce

Figure 3.2 Transitional Adulthood: A New Stage in the Life Course

Who has completed the transition?

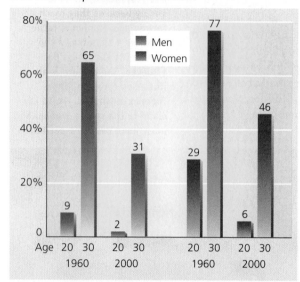

The data show the percent who have completed the transition to adulthood, as measured by leaving home, finishing school, getting married, having a child, and being financially independent.

Source: Furstenberg et al. 2004.

and losing jobs. It may take years for the self to stabilize after such ruptures.

The early middle years pose a special challenge for many U.S. women, who have been given the message, especially by the media, that they can "have it all." They can be superworkers, superwives, and supermoms—all rolled into one. The reality, however, usually consists of conflicting pressures—too little time and too many demands. Something has to give. Attempts to resolve this dilemma are often compounded by another hard reality—that during gender socialization, their husbands learned that housework and child care are not "masculine." In short, adjustments continue in this and all phases of life.

The Later Middle Years (ages 50–65) During the later middle years, health issues and mortality begin to loom large as people feel their bodies change, especially if they watch their parents become frail, fall ill, and die. The consequence is a fundamental reorientation in thinking—*from time since birth to time left to live* (Neugarten 1976). With this changed orientation, people attempt to evaluate the past and come to terms with what lies ahead. They compare what they have accomplished with what they had hoped to achieve. Many people also find themselves caring not only for their own children but also for their aging parents. Because of this set of burdens, which is often crushing, people in the later middle years sometimes are called the "sandwich generation."

Life during this stage isn't stressful for everyone. Many find late middle age to be the most comfortable period of their lives. They enjoy job security and a standard of living higher than ever before; they have a bigger house (one that may even be paid for), newer cars, and longer and more exotic vacations. The children are grown, the self is firmly planted, and fewer upheavals are likely to occur.

As they anticipate the next stage of life, however, most people do not like what they see.

The Older Years (about age 65 on)

The Early Older Years In industrialized societies, the older years begin around the mid-60s. This, too, is recent, for in agricultural societies, when most people died early, old age was thought to begin at around age 40. Industrialization brought about improved nutrition and public health, which prolonged life. Today, people in good health who are over the age of 65 often experience this period not as old age, but as an extension of the middle years. People who continue to work or to do things they enjoy are less likely to perceive themselves as old (Neugarten 1977). Although frequency of sex declines, most men and women in their 60s and 70s are sexually active (Denney and Quadagno 1992).

Because we have a self and can reason abstractly, we can contemplate death. Initially, we regard death as a vague notion, a remote possibility. But as people see their friends die and observe their own bodies no longer functioning as before, the thought of death becomes less abstract. Increasingly during this stage in the life course, people feel that "time is closing in" on them.

The Later Older Years As with the preceding periods of life except the first one, there is no precise beginning point to this last stage. For some, the 75th birthday may mark entry into this period of life. For others, that marker may be the 80th or even the 85th birthday. For most, this stage is marked by growing frailty and illness; for all who reach this stage, it is ended by death. For some, the physical decline is slow, and a rare few manage to see their 100th birthday mentally alert and in good physical health.

The Sociological Significance of the Life Course

The sociological significance of the life course is that it does not merely represent biology, things that naturally occur to all of us as we add years to our lives. Rather, *social* factors influence our life course. As you just saw, *when* you live makes a huge difference in the course that your life takes. And with today's rapid social change, the difference in historical time does not have to be vast. Being born just ten years earlier or later may mean that you experience war or peace, an expanding economy or a depression—factors that vitally affect what happens to you not just during childhood but throughout your life.

Your *social location,* such as social class, gender, and race-ethnicity is also highly significant. Your experience of society's events will be similar to that of people who share your social location, but different from that of people who do not. If you are poor, for example, you likely will feel older faster than most wealthy people for whom life is much less demanding. Individual factors—such as your health, or marrying early or entering college late—may throw your life course "out of sequence," making it atypical.

For all these reasons, this sketch of the life course may not adequately reflect your own past, present, and future. As sociologist C. Wright Mills (1959) would say, because employers are beating a path to your door, or failing to do so, you are more inclined to marry, to buy a house, and to start a family—or to postpone these life course events, perhaps indefinitely. In short, changing times change lives, steering the life course into different directions.

This January 1937 photo from Sneedville, Tennessee, shows Eunice Johns, age 9, and her husband, Charlie Johns, age 22. The groom gave his wife a doll as a wedding gift. The new husband and wife planned to build a cabin, and, as Charlie Johns phrased it, "go to housekeepin'."

This photo illustrates the cultural relativity of life stages, which we sometimes mistake as fixed. It also is interesting from a symbolic interactionist perspective—that of changing definitions. Today, such a marriage would land the husband in jail and the wife in protective custody.

Are We Prisoners of Socialization?

 From our discussion of socialization, you might conclude that sociologists think of people as robots: The socialization goes in, and the behavior comes out. People cannot help what they do, think, or feel, for everything is simply a result of their exposure to socializing agents.

Sociologists do *not* think of people in this way. Although socialization is powerful, and profoundly affects us all, we have a self. Established in childhood and continually modified by later experience, the self is dynamic. It is not a sponge that passively absorbs influences from the environment, but, rather, a vigorous, essential part of our being that allows us to act on our environment.

Indeed, it is precisely because individuals are not robots that their behavior is so hard to predict. The countless reactions of other people merge in each of us. As the self develops, each person internalizes or "puts together" these innumerable reactions, producing a unique whole called the *individual.* Each individual uses his or her own mind to reason and to make choices in life.

In this way, *each of us is actively involved in the construction of the self.* For example, although our experiences in the family lay down the basic elements of our personality, including fundamental orientations to life, we are not doomed to keep those orientations if we do not like them. We can purposely expose ourselves to groups and ideas that we prefer. Those experiences, in turn, will have their own effects on our self. In short, although socialization is powerful, we can change even the self within the limitations of the framework laid down by our social locations. And that self—along with the options available within society—is the key to our behavior.

Summary *and* Review

What Is Human Nature?

How much of our human characteristics come from "nature" (heredity) and how much from "nurture" (the social environment)?

Observations of isolated, institutionalized, and **feral children** help to answer this question, as do experiments with monkeys that were raised in isolation. Language and intimate social interaction—aspects of "nurture"—are essential to the development of what we consider to be human characteristics. Pp. 66–70.

Socialization into the Self and Mind

How do we acquire a self?

Humans are born with the *capacity* to develop a **self,** but the self must be socially constructed; that is, its contents depend on social interaction. According to Charles Horton Cooley's concept of the **looking-glass self,** our self develops as we internalize others' reactions to us. George Herbert Mead identified the ability to **take the role of the other** as essential to the development of the self. Mead concluded that even the mind is a social product. Pp. 70–72.

How do children develop reasoning skills?

Jean Piaget identified four stages that children go through as they develop the ability to reason: (1) *sensorimotor,* in which understanding is limited to sensory stimuli such as touch and sight; (2) *preoperational,* the ability to use symbols; (3) *concrete operational,* in which reasoning ability is more complex but not yet capable of complex abstractions; and (4) *formal operational,* or abstract thinking. Pp. 72–73.

Learning Personality, Morality, and Emotions

How do sociologists evaluate Freud's psychoanalytic theory of personality development?

Freud viewed personality development as the result of our **id** (inborn, self-centered desires) clashing with the demands of society. The **ego** develops to balance the id and the **superego,** the conscience. Sociologists, in contrast, do not examine inborn or subconscious motivations, but, instead, how *social* factors—social class, gender, religion, education, and so forth—underlie personality development. Pp. 73–75.

How do people develop morality?

Children are born without morality, and, according to Kohlberg, they go through four stages in learning it: amoral, preconventional, conventional, and postconventional. As they make moral decisions, both men and women use personal relationships and abstract principles. Pp. 75–76.

How does socialization influence emotions?

Socialization influences not only *how we express our emotions* but also *what emotions we feel.* Socialization into emotions is one of the means by which society produces conformity. Pp. 76–78.

Socialization into Gender

How does gender socialization affect our sense of self?

Gender socialization—sorting males and females into different roles—is a primary means of controlling human behavior. Children receive messages about gender even in infancy. A society's ideals of sex-linked behaviors are reinforced by its social institutions. Pp. 78–81.

Agents of Socialization

What are the main agents of socialization?

The **agents of socialization** include the family, neighborhood, religion, day care, school, **peer groups,** sports, the **mass media**, and the workplace. Each has its particular influences in socializing us into becoming full-fledged members of society. Pp. 81–87.

Resocialization

What is resocialization?

Resocialization is the process of learning new norms, values, attitudes, and behavior. Most resocialization is voluntary, but some, as with residents of **total institutions,** is involuntary. Pp. 87–88.

Socialization Through the Life Course

Does socialization end when we enter adulthood?

Socialization occurs throughout the life course. In industrialized societies, the **life course** can be divided into childhood, adolescence, young adulthood, the middle years, and the older years. The West is adding a new stage, transitional adulthood. Life course patterns vary by social location such as history, gender, race-ethnicity, and social class, as well as by individual experiences such as health and age at marriage. Pp. 88–93.

Are We Prisoners of Socialization?

Although socialization is powerful, we are not merely the sum of our socialization experiences. Just as socialization influences human behavior, so humans act on their environment and influence even their self concept. P. 93.

Thinking Critically

about Chapter 3

1. What two agents of socialization have influenced you the most? Can you pinpoint their influence on your attitudes, beliefs, values, or other orientations to life?

2. Summarize your views of the "proper" relationships of women and men. What in your socialization has led you to have these views?

3. What is your location in the life course? How does the text's summary of that location match your experiences? Explain the similarities and differences.

Additional Resources

What can you use MySocLab for?  www.mysoclab.com

- **Study and Review:** Pre and Post-Tests, Practice Tests, Flash Cards, Individualized Study Plans.

- **Current Events:** *Sociology in the News,* the daily *New York Times,* and more.

- **Research and Writing:** *Research Navigator, Writing About Sociology,* and more.

Where Can I Read More on This Topic?

Suggested readings for this chapter are listed at the back of this book.

Social Structure and Social Interaction

Jacob Lawrence, *Street Scene (Boy with Kite)*, 1962

My curiosity had gotten the better of me. When the sociology convention finished, I climbed aboard the first city bus that came along. I didn't know where the bus was going, and I didn't know where I would spend the night.

"Maybe I overdid it this time," I thought, as the bus began winding down streets I had never seen before. Actually, this was my first visit to Washington, D.C., so everything was unfamiliar to me. I had no destination, no plans, not even a map. I carried no billfold, just a driver's license shoved into my jeans for emergency identification, some pocket change, and a $10 bill tucked into my sock. My goal was simple: If I saw something interesting, I would get off the bus and check it out.

"Nothing but the

Suddenly one of the men jumped up, smashed the empty bottle against the sidewalk, and . . .

usual things," I mused, as we passed row after row of apartment buildings and stores. I could see myself riding buses the entire night. Then something caught my eye. Nothing spectacular—just groups of people clustered around a large circular area where several streets intersected.

I climbed off the bus and made my way to what turned out to be Dupont Circle. I took a seat on a sidewalk bench and began to observe what was going on around me. As the scene came into focus, I noticed several streetcorner men drinking and joking with one another. One of the men broke from his companions and sat down next to me. As we talked, I mostly listened.

As night fell, the men said that they wanted to get another bottle of wine. I contributed. They counted their money and asked if I wanted to go with them.

Although I felt my stomach churning—a combination of hesitation and fear—I heard a confident "Sure!" come out of my mouth. As we left the circle, the three men began to cut through an alley. "Oh, no," I thought. "This isn't what I had in mind."

I had but a split second to make a decision. I found myself continuing to walk with the men, but holding back half a step so that none of the three was behind me. As we walked, they passed around the remnants of their bottle. When my turn came, I didn't know what to do. I shuddered to think about the diseases lurking within that bottle. I made another quick decision. In the semidarkness I faked it, letting only my thumb and forefinger touch my lips and nothing enter my mouth.

When we returned to Dupont Circle, we sat on the benches, and the men passed around their new bottle of Thunderbird. I couldn't fake it in the light, so I passed, pointing at my stomach to indicate that I was having digestive problems.

Suddenly one of the men jumped up, smashed the emptied bottle against the sidewalk, and thrust the jagged neck outward in a menacing gesture. He glared straight ahead at another bench, where he had spotted someone with whom he had some sort of unfinished business. As the other men told him to cool it, I moved slightly to one side of the group—ready to flee, just in case.

Levels of Sociological Analysis

On this sociological adventure, I almost got myself in over my head. Fortunately, it turned out all right. The man's "enemy" didn't look our way, the man put the broken bottle next to the bench "just in case he needed it," and my intriguing introduction to a life that up until then I had only read about continued until dawn.

Sociologists Elliot Liebow (1967/1999), Mitchell Duneier (1999), and Elijah Anderson (1978, 1990, 2006) have written fascinating accounts about men like my companions from that evening. Although streetcorner men may appear to be disorganized—simply coming and going as they please and doing whatever feels good at the moment— sociologists have analyzed how, like us, these men are influenced by the norms and beliefs of our society. This will become more apparent as we examine the two levels of analysis that sociologists use.

Macrosociology and Microsociology

The first level, **macrosociology,** focuses on broad features of society. Conflict theorists and functionalists use this approach to analyze such things as social class and how groups are related to one another. If they were to analyze streetcorner men, for example, they would stress that these men are located at the bottom of the U.S. social class system. Their low status means that many opportunities are closed to them: The men have few job skills, little education, hardly anything to offer an employer. As "able-bodied" men, however, they are not eligible for welfare–even for a two-year limit–so they hustle to survive. As a consequence, they spend their lives on the streets.

In the second level, **microsociology,** the focus is on **social interaction,** what people do when they come together. Sociologists who use this approach are likely to focus on the men's rules or "codes" for getting along; their survival strategies ("hustles"); how they divide up money, wine, or whatever other resources they have; their relationships with girlfriends, family, and friends; where they spend their time and what they do there; their language; their pecking order; and so on. With their focus on face-to-face interaction, it is primarily symbolic interactionists who use microsociology.

Because each approach has a different focus, macrosociology and microsociology yield distinctive perspectives, and both are needed to gain a fuller understanding of social life. We cannot adequately understand streetcorner men, for example, without using

Sociologists use both macro and micro levels of analysis to study social life. Those who use *macrosociology* to analyze the homeless—or any human behavior—focus on broad aspects of society, such as the economy and social classes. Sociologists who use the *microsociological approach* analyze how people interact with one another. This photo illustrates social structure—the disparities between power and powerlessness are amply evident. It also illustrates the micro level—the interaction of these homeless men.

macrosociology. It is essential that we place the men within the broad context of how groups in U.S. society are related to one another—for, as is true for ourselves, the social class of these men helps to shape their attitudes and behavior. Nor can we adequately understand these men without *microsociology,* for their everyday situations also form a significant part of their lives—as they do for all of us.

Let's look in more detail at how these two approaches in sociology work together to help us understand social life. As we examine them more closely, you may find yourself feeling more comfortable with one approach than the other. This is what happens with sociologists. For reasons that include personal background and professional training, sociologists find themselves more comfortable with one approach and tend to use it in their research. Both approaches, however, are necessary to understand life in society.

The Macrosociological Perspective: Social Structure

Why did the street people in the opening vignette act as they did, staying up all night drinking wine, prepared to use a lethal weapon? Why don't *we* act like this? Social structure helps us answer such questions.

The Sociological Significance of Social Structure

To better understand human behavior, we need to understand *social structure,* the framework of society that was already laid out before you were born. **Social structure** refers to the typical patterns of a group, such as its usual relationships between men and women or students and teachers. *The sociological significance of social structure is that it guides our behavior.*

Because this term may seem vague, let's consider how you experience social structure in your own life. As I write this, I do not know your race-ethnicity. I do not know your religion. I do not know whether you are young or old, tall or short, male or female. I do not know whether you were reared on a farm, in the suburbs, or in the inner city. I do not know whether you went to a public high school or to an exclusive prep school. But I do know that you are in college. And this, alone, tells me a great deal about you.

From this one piece of information, I can assume that the social structure of your college is now shaping what you do. For example, let's suppose that today you felt euphoric over some great news. I can be fairly certain (not absolutely, mind you, but relatively confident) that when you entered the classroom, social structure overrode your mood. That is, instead of shouting at the top of your lungs and joyously throwing this book into the air, you entered the classroom in a fairly subdued manner and took your seat.

The same social structure influences your instructor, even if he or she, on the one hand, is facing a divorce or has a child dying of cancer, or, on the other, has just been awarded a promotion or a million-dollar grant. Your instructor may feel like either retreating into seclusion or celebrating wildly, but most likely he or she will conduct class in the usual manner. In short, social structure tends to override personal feelings and desires.

Just as social structure influences you and your instructor, so it also establishes limits for street people. They, too, find themselves in a specific location in the U.S. social structure—although it is quite different from yours or your instructor's. Consequently, they are affected in different ways. Nothing about their social location leads them to take notes or to lecture. Their behaviors, however, are as logical an outcome of where they find themselves in the social structure as are your own. In their position in the social structure, it is just as "natural" to drink wine all night as it is for you to stay up studying all night for a crucial examination. It is just as "natural" for you to nod and say, "Excuse me," when you enter a crowded classroom late and have to claim a desk on which someone has already placed books as it is for them to break off the neck of a wine bottle and glare at an enemy.

social structure the framework that surrounds us, consisting of the relationships of people and groups, which gives direction to and sets limits on behavior

In short, people learn their behaviors and attitudes because of their location in the social structure (whether they be privileged, deprived, or in between), and they act accordingly. This is equally true of street people and ourselves. *The differences in behavior and attitudes are due not to biology (race, sex, or any other supposed genetic factors), but to people's location in the social structure.* Switch places with street people and watch your behaviors and attitudes change!

To better understand social structure, read the Down-to-Earth Sociology box on football below.

Because social structure so crucially affects who we are and what we are like, let's look more closely at its major components: culture, social class, social status, roles, groups, and social institutions.

Culture

In Chapter 2, we considered culture's far-reaching effects on our lives. At this point, let's simply summarize its main impact. Sociologists use the term *culture* to refer to a group's language, beliefs, values, behaviors, and even gestures. Culture also includes the material

Down-to-Earth Sociology

College Football as Social Structure

TO GAIN A BETTER IDEA OF WHAT *social structure* is, think of college football (see Dobriner 1969a). You probably know the various positions on the team: center, guards, tackles, ends, quarterback, running backs, and the like. Each is a *status;* that is, each is a social position. For each of these statuses, there is a *role;* that is, each of these positions has certain expectations attached to it. The center is expected to snap the ball, the quarterback to pass it, the guards to block, the tackles to tackle or block, the ends to receive passes, and so on. Those role expectations guide each player's actions; that is, the players try to do what their particular role requires.

Let's suppose that football is your favorite sport and you never miss a home game at your college. Let's also suppose that you graduate, get a great job, and move across the country. Five years later, you return to your campus for a nostalgic visit. The climax of your visit is the biggest football game of the season. When you get to the game, you might be surprised to see a different coach, but you are not surprised that each playing position is occupied by people you don't know, for all the players you knew have graduated, and their places have been filled by others.

This scenario mirrors *social structure,* the framework around which a group exists. In football, that framework consists of the coaching staff and the eleven playing positions. The game does not depend on any particular individual, but, rather, on *social statuses,* the positions that the individuals occupy. When someone leaves a position, the game can go on because someone else takes over that position or status and plays the role. The game will continue even though not a single individual remains from

one period of time to the next. Notre Dame's football team endures today even though Knute Rockne, the Gipper, and his teammates are long dead.

Even though you may not play football, you nevertheless live your life within a clearly established social structure. The statuses that you occupy and the roles you play were already in place before you were born. You take your particular positions in life, others do the same, and society goes about its business. Although the specifics change with time, the game—whether of life or of football—goes on.

Figure 4.1 **Team Positions (Statuses) in Football**

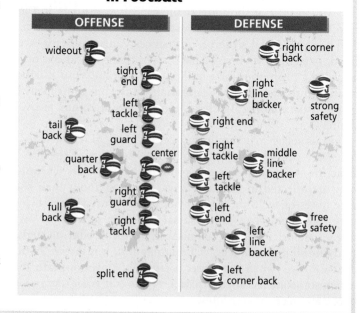

objects that a group uses. Culture is the broadest framework that determines what kind of people we become. If we are reared in Chinese, Arab, or U.S. culture, we will grow up to be like most Chinese, Arabs, or Americans. On the outside, we will look and act like them; and on the inside, we will think and feel like them.

Social Class

To understand people, we must examine the social locations that they hold in life. Especially significant is *social class,* which is based on income, education, and occupational prestige. Large numbers of people who have similar amounts of income and education and who work at jobs that are roughly comparable in prestige make up a **social class.** It is hard to overemphasize this aspect of social structure, for our social class influences not only our behaviors but even our ideas and attitudes. We have this in common, then, with the street people described in the opening vignette: We both are influenced by our location in the social class structure. Theirs may be a considerably less privileged position, but it has no less influence on their lives. Social class is so significant that we shall spend an entire chapter (Chapter 7) on this topic.

Social Status

When you hear the word *status,* you are likely to think of prestige. These two words are welded together in people's minds. As you saw in the box on football, however, sociologists use **status** in a different way—to refer to the *position* that someone occupies. That position may carry a great deal of prestige, as in the case of a judge or an astronaut, or it may bring little prestige, as in the case of a convenience store clerk or a waitress at the local truck stop. The status may also be looked down on, as in the case of a streetcorner man, an ex-convict, or a thief.

All of us occupy several positions at the same time. You may simultaneously be a son or daughter, a worker, a date, and a student. Sociologists use the term **status set** to refer to all the statuses or positions that you occupy. Obviously your status set changes as your particular statuses change. For example, if you graduate from college and take a full-time job, get married, buy a home, have children, and so on, your status set changes to include the positions of worker, spouse, homeowner, and parent.

Like other aspects of social structure, statuses are part of our basic framework of living in society. The example I gave of students and teachers who come to class and do what others expect of them despite their particular circumstances and moods illustrates how statuses affect our actions—and those of the people around us. Our statuses—whether daughter or son, worker or date—serve as guides for our behavior.

Ascribed and Achieved Statuses   An **ascribed status** is involuntary. You do not ask for it, nor can you choose it. You inherit some ascribed statuses at birth such as your race-ethnicity, sex, and the social class of your parents, as well as your statuses as female or male, daughter or son, niece or nephew. Others, such as teenager and senior citizen, are related to the life course discussed in Chapter 3, and are given to you later in life.

Achieved statuses, in contrast, are voluntary. These you earn or accomplish. As a result of your efforts you become a student, a friend, a spouse, a lawyer, or a member of the clergy. Or, for lack of effort (or for efforts that others fail to appreciate), you become a school dropout, a former friend, an ex-spouse, a debarred lawyer, or a defrocked member of the clergy. In other words, achieved statuses can be either positive or negative; both college president and bank robber are achieved statuses.

Each status provides guidelines for how we are to act and feel. Like other aspects of social structure, statuses set limits on what we can and cannot do. Because social statuses are an essential part of the social structure, they are found in all human groups.

Status Symbols   People who are pleased with their social status often want others to recognize their particular position. To elicit this recognition, they use **status symbols,** signs that identify a status. For example, people wear wedding rings to announce their marital status; uniforms, guns, and badges to proclaim that they are police officers (and not so subtly to let you know that their status gives them authority over you); and "backward" collars to declare that they are Lutheran ministers or Roman Catholic or Episcopal priests.

social class according to Weber, a large group of people who rank close to one another in wealth, prestige, and power; according to Marx, one of two groups: capitalists who own the means of production or workers who sell their labor

status the position that someone occupies in society or in a social group

status set all the statuses or positions that an individual occupies

ascribed statuses positions an individual either inherits at birth or receives involuntarily later in life

achieved statuses positions that are earned, accomplished, or involve at least some effort or activity on the individual's part

status symbols items used to identify a status

master status a status that cuts across the other statuses that an individual occupies

status inconsistency ranking high on some dimensions of social class and low on others, also called *status discrepancy*

Some social statuses are negative, and so, therefore, are their status symbols. The scarlet letter in Nathaniel Hawthorne's book by the same title is one example. Another is the CONVICTED DUI (Driving Under the Influence) bumper sticker that some U.S. courts require convicted drunk drivers to display if they wish to avoid a jail sentence.

All of us use status symbols to announce our statuses to others and to help smooth our interactions in everyday life. You might consider what your own status symbols communicate. For example, how does your clothing announce your statuses of sex, age, and college student?

Master Statuses A **master status** is one that cuts across the other statuses that you hold. Some master statuses are ascribed. An example is your sex. Whatever you do, people perceive you as a male or as a female. If you are working your way through college by flipping burgers, people see you not only as a burger flipper and a student but also as a *male* or *female* burger flipper and a *male* or *female* college student. Other master statuses are race and age.

Some master statuses are achieved. If you become very, very wealthy (and it doesn't matter whether your wealth comes from a successful invention or from winning the lottery—it is still *achieved* as far as sociologists are concerned), your wealth is likely to become a master status. For example, people might say, "She is a very rich burger flipper"—or, more likely, "She's very rich, and she used to flip burgers!"

Similarly, people who become disfigured find, to their dismay, that their condition becomes a master status. For example, a person whose face is scarred from severe burns will be viewed through this unwelcome master status regardless of his or her occupation or accomplishments. In the same way, people who are confined to wheelchairs can attest to how their handicap overrides all their other statuses and influences others' perceptions of everything they do.

Although our statuses usually fit together fairly well, some people have a contradiction or mismatch between their statuses. This is known as **status inconsistency** (or discrepancy). A 14-year-old college student is an example. So is a 40-year-old married woman who is dating a 19-year-old college sophomore.

These examples reveal an essential aspect of social statuses: Like other components of social structure, they come with built-in *norms* (that is, expectations) that guide our behavior. When statuses mesh well, as they usually do, we know what to expect of people. This helps social interaction to unfold smoothly. Status inconsistency, however, upsets our expectations. In the preceding examples, how are you supposed to act? Are you

Master statuses are those that overshadow our other statuses. Shown here is Stephen Hawking, who is severely disabled by Lou Gehrig's disease. For some, his *master status* is that of a person with disabilities. Because Hawking is one of the greatest physicists who has ever lived, however, his outstanding achievements have given him another *master status*, that of world-class physicist in the ranking of Einstein.

supposed to treat the 14-year-old as you would a young teenager, or as you would your college classmate? Do you react to the married woman as you would to the mother of your friend, or as you would to a classmate's date?

Roles

> All the world's a stage
> And all the men and women merely players.
> They have their exits and their entrances;
> And one man in his time plays many parts . . .
> (William Shakespeare, *As You Like It*, Act II, Scene 7)

Like Shakespeare, sociologists see roles as essential to social life. When you were born, **roles**—the behaviors, obligations, and privileges attached to a status—were already set up for you. Society was waiting with outstretched arms to teach you how it expected you to act as a boy or a girl. And whether you were born poor, rich, or somewhere in between, that, too, attached certain behaviors, obligations, and privileges to your statuses.

The difference between role and status is that you *occupy* a status, but you *play* a role (Linton 1936). For example, being a son or daughter is your status, but your expectations of receiving food and shelter from your parents—as well as their expectations that you show respect to them—are part of your role. Or, again, your status is student, but your role is to attend class, take notes, do homework, and take tests.

Roles are like a fence. They allow us a certain amount of freedom, but for most of us that freedom doesn't go very far. Suppose that a woman decides that she is not going to wear dresses—or a man that he will not wear suits and ties—regardless of what anyone says. In most situations, they'll stick to their decision. When a formal occasion comes along, however, such as a family wedding or a funeral, they are likely to cave in to norms that they find overwhelming. Almost all of us follow the guidelines for what is "appropriate" for our roles. Few of us are bothered by such constraints, for our socialization is so thorough that we usually *want* to do what our roles indicate is appropriate.

The sociological significance of roles is that they lay out what is expected of people. As individuals throughout society perform their roles, those roles mesh together to form this thing called *society*. As Shakespeare put it, people's roles provide "their exits and their entrances" on the stage of life. In short, roles are remarkably effective at keeping people in line—telling them when they should "enter" and when they should "exit," as well as what to do in between.

Groups

A **group** consists of people who regularly interact with one another. Ordinarily, the members of a group share similar values, norms, and expectations. Just as social class, statuses, and roles influence our actions, so, too, the groups to which we belong are powerful forces in our lives. In fact, *to belong to a group is to yield to others the right to make certain decisions about our behavior.* If we belong to a group, we assume an obligation to act according to the expectations of other members of that group.

Although this principle holds true for all groups, some groups wield influence over only small segments of our behavior. For example, if you belong to a stamp collector's club, the group's influence may center on your display of knowledge about stamps, and perhaps fairness in trading them. Other groups, in contrast, such as the family, control many aspects of our behavior. When parents say to their 15-year-old daughter, "As long as you are living under my roof, you had better be home by midnight," they show their expectation that their daughter, as a member of the family, will conform to their ideas about many aspects of life, including their views on curfew. They are saying that as long as the daughter wants to remain a member of the household, her behavior must conform to their expectations.

Let's look in greater detail at the next component of social structure, social institutions.

role the behaviors, obligations, and privileges attached to a status

group people who have something in common and who believe that what they have in common is significant; also called a *social group*

Social Institutions

At first glance, the term *social institution* may seem to have little relevance to your life. The term seems so cold and abstract. In fact, however, **social institutions**—the ways that each society develops to meet its basic needs—vitally affect your life. By weaving the fabric of society, social institutions shape our behavior. They even color our thoughts. How can this be? Look at what social institutions are: the family, religion, education, economics, medicine, politics, law, science, the military, and the mass media.

In industrialized societies, social institutions tend to be more formal; in tribal societies, they are more informal. Education in industrialized societies, for example, is highly structured, while in tribal societies it usually consists of children informally learning what adults do. Figure 4.2 on the next page summarizes the basic social institutions. Note that each institution has its own groups, statuses, values, and norms. Social institutions are so significant that Part IV of this book focuses on them.

The Sociological Significance of Social Institutions

To understand social institutions is to realize how profoundly social structure affects our lives. Much of the influence of social institutions lies beyond our ordinary awareness. For example, because of our economic institution, it is common to work eight hours a day for five days every week. There is nothing normal or natural about this pattern, however. This rhythm is only an arbitrary arrangement for dividing work and leisure. Yet this one aspect of a single social institution has far-reaching effects. Not only does it dictate how people divide up their days, but it also lays out a structure for their interaction with family and friends and for how they meet their personal needs.

Each of the other social institutions also has far-reaching effects on our lives. They establish the context in which we live, shaping our behavior and coloring our thoughts. Social institutions are so significant that if they were different, we would be different people. We certainly could not remain the same, for social institutions influence our orientations to the social world, and even to life itself.

An Example: The Mass Media as an Emerging Social Institution

Far beyond serving simply as sources of information, the mass media influence our attitudes toward social issues, the ways that we view other people, and even our self-concept. Because the media significantly shape public opinion, all governments attempt to influence them. Totalitarian governments try to control them.

The mass media are relatively new in human history, owing their origins to the invention of the printing press in the 1400s. This invention had profound consequences on all social institutions. The printing of the Bible altered religion, for instance, while the publication of political broadsides and newspapers altered politics. From these beginnings, a series of inventions—from radio and movies to television and the microchip—has made the media an increasingly powerful force.

One of the most significant questions we can ask about this social institution is: Who controls it? That control, which in totalitarian countries is obvious, is much less visible in democratic nations. Functionalists might conclude that the media in a democratic nation represent the varied interests of the many groups that make up that nation. Conflict theorists, in contrast, see the matter quite differently: The mass media—at least a country's most influential newspapers and television stations—represent the interests of the political elite. They give coverage to mildly dissenting opinions, but they

The mass media are a major influence in contemporary life. Until 1436, when Johann Gutenberg invented movable type, printing was a slow process, and printed materials were expensive. Today, printed materials are common and often cheap. "Cheap" has a double meaning, with its second meaning illustrated in this photo.

Social Institution	Basic Needs	Some Groups or Organizations	Some Statuses	Some Values	Some Norms
Family	Regulate reproduction, socialize and protect children	Relatives, kinship groups	Daughter, son, father, mother, brother, sister, aunt, uncle, grandparent	Sexual fidelity, providing for your family, keeping a clean house, respect for parents	Have only as many children as you can afford, be faithful to your spouse
Religion	Concerns about life after death, the meaning of suffering and loss; desire to connect with the Creator	Congregation, synagogue, mosque, denomination, charity; clergy associations	Priest, minister, rabbi, imam, worshipper, teacher, disciple, missionary, prophet, convert	Reading and adhering to holy texts such as the Bible, the Torah, and the Koran, honoring God	Attend worship services, contribute money, follow the teachings
Education	Transmit knowledge and skills across generations	School, college, student senate, sports team, PTA, teachers' union	Teacher, student, dean, principal, football player, cheerleader	Academic honesty, good grades, being "cool"	Do homework, prepare lectures, don't snitch on classmates
Economy	Produce and distribute goods and services	Credit unions, banks, credit card companies, buying clubs	Worker, boss, buyer, seller, creditor, debtor, advertiser	Making money, paying bills on time, producing efficiently	Maximize profits, "the customer is always right," work hard
Medicine	Heal the sick and injured, care for the dying	AMA, hospitals, pharmacies, insurance companies, HMOs	Doctor, nurse, patient, pharmacist, medical insurer	Hippocratic oath, staying in good health, following doctor's orders	Don't exploit patients, give best medical care available
Politics	Allocate power, determine authority, prevent chaos	Political party, congress, parliament, monarchy	President, senator, lobbyist, voter, candidate, spin doctor	Majority rule, the right to vote as a privilege and a sacred trust	One vote per person, be informed about candidates
Law	Maintain social order	Police, courts, prisons	Judge, police officer, lawyer, defendant, prison guard	Trial by one's peers, innocence until proven guilty	Give true testimony, follow the rules of evidence
Science	Master the environment	Local, state, regional, national, and international associations	Scientist, researcher, technician, administrator, journal editor	Unbiased research, open dissemination of research findings, originality	Follow scientific method, be objective, disclose findings, don't plagiarize
Military	Protection from enemies, support of national interests	Army, navy, air force, marines, coast guard, national guard	Soldier, recruit, enlisted person, officer, veteran, prisoner, spy	To die for one's country is an honor, obedience unto death	Follow orders, be ready to go to war, sacrifice for your buddies
Mass Media (an emerging institution)	Disseminate information, mold public opinion, report events	TV networks, radio stations, publishers, association of bloggers	Journalist, newscaster, author, editor, publisher, blogger	Timeliness, accuracy, large audiences, freedom of the press	Be accurate, fair, timely, and profitable

stand solidly behind the government. The most obvious example is the positive treatment that the media give to the inauguration of a president.

Since the mass media are so influential in our lives today, the answer to this question of who controls the media is of more than passing interest. This matter is vital to our understanding of contemporary society.

Comparing Functionalist and Conflict Perspectives

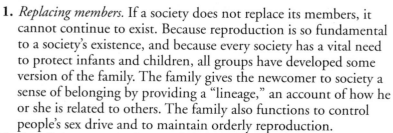

Just as the functionalist and conflict perspectives of the mass media differ, so do their views of the nature of social institutions. Let's compare these views.

The Functionalist Perspective Functionalists stress that social institutions perform such vital functions for human survival that no society is without them. A group may be too small to have people who specialize in education, but it will have its own established ways of teaching skills and ideas to the young. It may be too small to have a military, but it will have some mechanism of self-defense. To survive, every society must meet its basic needs (or **functional requisites**). According to functionalists, that is the purpose of social institutions.

What are those basic needs? Functionalists identify five *functional requisites* that each society must fulfill if it is to survive (Aberle et al. 1950; Mack and Bradford 1979).

Functionalist theorists have identified five *functional requisites* for the survival of a society. One, providing a sense of purpose, is often met through religious groups. To most people, snake handling, as in this church service in Kingston, Georgia, is nonsensical. From a functionalist perspective, however, it makes a great deal of sense. Can you identify its sociological meanings?

1. *Replacing members.* If a society does not replace its members, it cannot continue to exist. Because reproduction is so fundamental to a society's existence, and because every society has a vital need to protect infants and children, all groups have developed some version of the family. The family gives the newcomer to society a sense of belonging by providing a "lineage," an account of how he or she is related to others. The family also functions to control people's sex drive and to maintain orderly reproduction.

2. *Socializing new members.* Each baby must be taught what it means to be a member of the group into which it is born. To accomplish this, each human group develops devices to ensure that its newcomers learn the group's basic expectations. As the primary "bearer of culture," the family is essential to this process, but other social institutions, such as religion and education, also help meet this basic need.

3. *Producing and distributing goods and services.* Every society must produce and distribute basic resources, from food and clothing to shelter and education. Consequently, every society establishes an *economic* institution, a means of producing goods and services along with routine ways of distributing them.

4. *Preserving order.* Societies face two threats of disorder: one internal, the potential for chaos, and the other external, the possibility of attack. To defend themselves against external conquest, they develop a means of defense, some form of the military. To protect themselves from internal threat, they develop a system of policing themselves, ranging from formal organizations of armed groups to informal systems of gossip.

5. *Providing a sense of purpose.* Every society must get people to yield self-interest in favor of the needs of the group. To convince people to sacrifice personal gains, societies instill a sense of purpose. Human groups develop many ways to implant such beliefs, but a primary one is religion, which attempts to answer questions about ultimate meaning. Actually, all of a society's institutions are involved in meeting this functional requisite; the family provides one set of answers about the sense of purpose, the school another, and so on.

The Conflict Perspective Although conflict theorists agree that social institutions were designed originally to meet basic survival needs, they do not view social institutions as working harmoniously for the common good. On the contrary, conflict theorists stress that powerful groups control society's institutions, manipulating them in order to maintain their own privileged position of wealth and power (Useem 1984; Domhoff 1999a, b, 2006).

Conflict theorists point out that a fairly small group of people has garnered the lion's share of the nation's wealth. Members of this elite sit on the boards of both the major corporations and the country's most prestigious universities. They make strategic campaign contributions to influence (or control) the nation's lawmakers, and it is they who make the major decisions in this society: to go to war or to refrain from war; to increase or to decrease taxes; to raise or to lower interest rates; and to pass laws that favor or impede moving capital, technology, and jobs out of the country.

Feminist sociologists (both women and men) have used conflict theory to gain a better understanding of how social institutions affect gender relations. Their basic insight is that gender is also an element of social structure, not simply a characteristic of individuals. In other words, throughout the world, social institutions divide males and females into separate groups, each with unequal access to society's resources.

IN SUM Functionalists view social institutions as working together to meet universal human needs. Conflict theorists, in contrast, regard social institutions as having a single primary purpose—to preserve the social order. For them, this means safeguarding the wealthy and powerful in their positions of privilege.

Changes in Social Structure

As you can see, this enveloping system that we call social structure powerfully affects our lives. This means that as social structure changes, so, too, do our orientations to life. Our culture is not static. It is continuously evolving as it responds to changing values, to new technology, and to contact with cultures around the world. As our culture changes, so do we. Similarly, as our economy responds to globalization, it either grows or stagnates. This opens or closes opportunities, changing our lives, sometimes brutally so. New groups such as the Department of Homeland Security come into being, wielding extraordinary power over us. In short, the corner in life that we occupy, though small and seemingly private, is not closed off; rather, it is pushed and pulled and stretched in different directions as our social structure changes.

What Holds Society Together?

With its many, often conflicting, groups and its extensive social change, how can a society manage to hold together? Let's examine two answers that sociologists have proposed.

Mechanical and Organic Solidarity Sociologist Emile Durkheim (1893/1933) found the key to **social integration**—the degree to which members of a society are united by shared values and other social bonds—in what he called **mechanical solidarity**. By this term, Durkheim meant that people who perform similar tasks develop a shared consciousness. Think of a farming community in which everyone is involved in planting, cultivating, and harvesting. Members of this group have so much in common that they know how almost everyone else in the community feels about life. Societies with mechanical solidarity tolerate little diversity in thinking and attitudes, for their unity depends on similar thinking.

As societies get larger, their **division of labor** (how they divide up work) becomes more specialized. Some people mine gold, others turn it into jewelry, while still others sell it. This division of labor makes people depend on one another—for the work of each person contributes to the well-being of the whole group.

Durkheim called this new form of solidarity based on interdependence **organic solidarity.** To see why he used this term, think about how you depend on your teacher to guide you through this introductory course in sociology. At the same time, your teacher needs you and other students in order to have a job. You and your teacher are *like organs in the same body.* (The "body" in this case is the college or university.) Although each of you performs different tasks, you depend on one another. This creates a form of unity.

The change to organic solidarity produced a new basis for solidarity—not similar views, but separate activities that contribute to the overall welfare of the group. As a result, modern societies can encompass many differences among people and still manage to work as a whole. Both past and present societies are based on social solidarity, but the types of solidarity differ remarkably.

social integration the degree to which members of a group or a society feel united by shared values and other social bonds; also known as social cohesion

mechanical solidarity Durkheim's term for the unity (a shared consciousness) that people feel as a result of performing the same or similar tasks

division of labor the splitting of a group's or a society's tasks into specialties

organic solidarity Durkheim's term for the interdependence that results from the division of labor; people depending on others to fulfill their jobs

Gemeinschaft and Gesellschaft Ferdinand Tönnies (1887/1988) also analyzed this fundamental shift in relationships. He used the term **Gemeinschaft** (Guh-MINE-shoft), or "intimate community," to describe village life, the type of society in which everyone knows everyone else. He noted that in the society that was emerging, the personal ties, kinship connections, and lifelong friendships that marked village life were being crowded out by short-term relationships, individual accomplishments, and self-interest. Tönnies called this new type of society **Gesellschaft** (Guh-ZELL-shoft), or "impersonal association." He did not mean that we no longer have intimate ties to family and friends, but, rather, that our lives no longer center on them. Few of us take jobs in a family business, for example, and contracts replace handshakes. Much of our time is spent with strangers and short-term acquaintances.

How Relevant Are These Concepts Today? I know that *Gemeinschaft, Gesellschaft,* and *mechanical* and *organic solidarity* are strange terms and that Durkheim's and Tönnies' observations must seem like a dead issue. The concern these sociologists expressed, however—that their world was changing from a community in which people are united by close ties and shared ideas and feelings to an anonymous association built around impersonal, short-term contacts—is still very real. In large part, this same concern explains the rise of Islamic fundamentalism (Volti 1995). Islamic leaders fear that Western values will uproot their traditional culture, that cold rationality will replace the informal personal relationships among families and clans. They fear, rightly so, that this will change even their views on life and morality. Although the terms may sound strange, even obscure, you can see that the ideas remain a vital part of today's world.

IN SUM Whether the terms are *Gemeinschaft* and *Gesellschaft* or *mechanical solidarity* and *organic solidarity,* they indicate that as societies change, so do people's orientations to life. *The sociological point is that social structure sets the context for what we do, feel, and think, and ultimately, then, for the kind of people we become.* As you read the Cultural Diversity box on the next page, which describes one of the few remaining *Gemeinschaft* societies in the United States, think of how fundamentally different you would be had you been reared in an Amish family.

The warm, more intimate relationships of *Gemeinschaft* society are apparent in this restaurant in Salzburg, Austria. The more impersonal relationships of *Gesellschaft* society are evident in this café in Bangkok, Thailand, where, ignoring one another, the customers engage in electronic interactions.

The Amish: *Gemeinschaft* Community in a *Gesellschaft* Society

FERDINAND TÖNNIES' TERM, *Gesellschaft*, certainly applies to the United States. Impersonal associations pervade our everyday life. Local, state, and federal governments regulate many of our activities. Corporations hire and fire people not on the basis of personal relationships, but on the basis of the bottom line. And, perhaps even more significantly, millions of Americans do not even know their neighbors.

Within the United States, a handful of small communities exhibits characteristics that are distinct from those of the mainstream society. One such community is the Old Order Amish, followers of a sect that broke away from the Swiss-German Mennonite church in the 1600s, and settled in Pennsylvania around 1727. Today, about 150,000 Old Order Amish live in the United States. About 75 percent live in just three states: Pennsylvania, Ohio, and Indiana. The largest concentration, about 22,000, reside in Lancaster County, Pennsylvania. The Amish, who believe that birth control is wrong, have doubled in population in just the past two decades.

Because Amish farmers use horses instead of tractors, most of their farms are one hundred acres or less. To the five million tourists who pass through Lancaster County each year, the rolling green pastures, white farmhouses, simple barns, horse-drawn buggies, and clotheslines hung with somber-colored garments convey a sense of peace and innocence reminiscent of another era. Although just sixty-five miles from Philadelphia, "Amish country" is a world away.

Amish life is based on separation from the world—an idea taken from Christ's Sermon on the Mount—and obedience to the church's teachings and leaders. This rejection of worldly concerns, writes sociologist Donald Kraybill in *The Riddle of Amish Culture* (2002), "provides the foundation of such Amish values as humility, faithfulness, thrift, tradition, communal goals, joy of work, a slow-paced life, and trust in divine providence."

The *Gemeinschaft* of village life that has been largely lost to industrialization remains a vibrant part of Amish life. The Amish make their decisions in weekly meetings, where, by consensus, they follow a set of rules, or *Ordnung*, to guide their behavior. Religion and discipline are the glue that holds the Amish together. Brotherly love and the welfare of the community are paramount values. In times of birth,

sickness, and death, neighbors pitch in with the chores. In these ways, they maintain the bonds of intimate community.

The Amish are bound by other ties, including language (a dialect of German known as Pennsylvania Dutch), plain clothing—often black, whose style has remained unchanged for almost 300 years–and church-sponsored schools. Nearly all Amish marry, and divorce is forbidden. The family is a vital ingredient in Amish life; all major events take place in the home, including weddings, births, funerals, and church services. Amish children attend church schools, but only until the age of 13. (In 1972, the Supreme Court ruled that Amish parents had the right to take their children out of school after the eighth grade.) To go to school beyond the eighth grade would expose them to values and "worldly concerns" that would drive a wedge between the children and their community. The Amish believe that violence is bad, even personal self-defense, and they register as conscientious objectors during times of war. They pay no Social Security, and they receive no government benefits.

The Amish cannot resist all change, of course. Instead, they try to adapt to change in ways that will least disrupt their core values. Because urban sprawl has driven up the price of farmland, about half of Amish men work at jobs other than farming, most in farm-related businesses or in woodcrafts. They go to great lengths to avoid leaving the home. The Amish believe that when a husband works away from home, all aspects of life change—from the marital relationship to the care of the children—certainly an astute sociological insight. They also believe that if a man receives a paycheck, he will think that his work is of more value than his wife's. For the Amish, intimate, or *Gemeinschaft*, society is essential for maintaining their way of life.

Perhaps this is the most poignant illustration of how the Amish approach to life differs from the dominant culture: When in 2006 a non-Amish man shot several girls at a one-room school, the Amish community raised money not only for the families of the dead children but also for the family of the killer.

Sources: Hostetler 1980; Aeppel 1996; Kephart and Zellner 2001; Kraybill 1989, 2002; Dawley 2003; Johnson-Weiner 2007.

stereotype assumptions of what people are like, whether true or false

The Microsociological Perspective: Social Interaction in Everyday Life

Whereas the macrosociological approach stresses the broad features of society, the microsociological approach has a narrower focus. Microsociologists examine *face-to-face interaction*—what people do when they are in one another's presence. Let's examine some of the areas of social life that microsociologists study.

Symbolic Interaction

For symbolic interactionists, the most significant part of life in society is social interaction. Symbolic interactionists are especially interested in the symbols that people use. They want to know how people look at things and how this, in turn, affects their behavior and orientations to life. Of the many areas of social life that microsociologists study, let's look at stereotyping, personal space, touching, eye contact, and smiling.

Stereotypes in Everyday Life You are familiar with how strong first impressions are and the way they set the tone for interaction. When you first meet someone, you cannot help but notice certain features, especially the person's sex, race-ethnicity, age, and clothing. Despite your best intentions, your assumptions about these characteristics shape your first impressions. They also affect how you act toward that person—and, in turn, how that person acts toward you. These fascinating aspects of our social interaction are discussed in the Down-to-Earth Sociology box on the next page.

Personal Space We all surround ourselves with a "personal bubble" that we go to great lengths to protect. We open the bubble to intimates—to our friends, children, parents, and so on—but we're careful to keep most people out of this space. In a crowded hallway between classes, we might walk with our books clasped in front of us (a strategy often chosen by females). When we stand in line, we make certain there is enough space so that we don't touch the person in front of us and aren't touched by the person behind us.

At times, we extend our personal space. In the library, for example, you may place your coat on the chair next to you—claiming that space for yourself even though you aren't using it. If you want to really extend your space, you might even spread books in front of the other chairs, keeping the whole table to yourself by giving the impression that others have just stepped away.

The amount of space that people prefer varies from one culture to another. South Americans, for example, like to be closer when they speak to others than do people reared in the United States. Anthropologist Edward Hall (1959; Hall and Hall 2007) recounts a conversation with a man from South America who had attended one of his lectures.

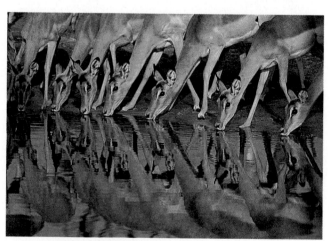

Social space is one of the many aspects of social life studied by sociologists who have a microsociological focus. What do you see in common in these two photos?

Beauty May Be Only Skin Deep, But Its Effects Go On Forever: Stereotypes in Everyday Life

MARK SNYDER, A PSYCHOLOGIST, wondered whether **stereotypes**—our assumptions of what people are like—might be self-fulfilling. He came up with an ingenious way to test this idea. He (1993) gave college men a Polaroid snapshot of a woman (supposedly taken just moments before) and told them that he would introduce them to her after they talked with her on the telephone. Actually, the photographs—showing either a pretty or a homely woman—had been prepared before the experiment began. The photo was not of the woman the men would talk to.

Stereotypes came into play immediately. As Snyder gave each man the photograph, he asked him what he thought the woman would be like. The men who saw the photograph of the attractive woman said that they expected to meet a poised, humorous, outgoing woman. The men who had been given a photo of the unattractive woman described her as awkward, serious, and unsociable.

The men's stereotypes influenced the way they spoke to the women on the telephone, who did not know about the photographs. The men who had seen the photograph of a pretty woman were warm, friendly, and humorous. This, in turn, affected the women they spoke to, for they responded in a warm, friendly, outgoing manner. And the men who had seen the photograph of a homely woman? On the phone, they were cold, reserved, and humorless, and the women they spoke to became cool, reserved, and humorless. Keep in mind that the women did not know that their looks had been

evaluated—and that the photographs were not even of them. In short, stereotypes tend to produce behaviors that match the stereotype. This principle is illustrated in Figure 4.3.

Although beauty might be only skin deep, its consequences permeate our lives (Katz 2007). Not only does beauty bestow an advantage in everyday interaction, but people who are physically attractive are likely to make more money. Researchers in both Holland and the United States found that advertising firms with better-looking executives have higher revenues (Bosman et al. 1997; Pfann et al. 2000). The reason? The researchers suggest that people are more willing to associate with individuals whom they perceive as good-looking.

for your Consideration

Stereotypes have no single, inevitable effect. They are not magical. People can resist stereotypes and change outcomes. However, these studies do illustrate that stereotypes deeply influence how we react to one another.

Instead of beauty, consider gender and race-ethnicity. How do they affect those who do the stereotyping and those who are stereotyped?

Physical attractiveness underlies much of our social interaction in everyday life. The experiment reviewed in this box illustrates how college men modified their interactions on the basis of attractiveness. How do you think men would modify their interactions if they were to meet the two women in these photographs? How about women? Would they change their interactions in the same way?

Figure 4.3 **How Self-Fulfilling Stereotypes Work**

We see features of the person, or hear things about the person.

↓

We fit what we see or hear into stereotypes, and then expect the person to act in certain ways.

↓

How we expect the person to act shapes our attitudes and actions.

↓

From how we act, the person gets ideas of how we perceive him or her.

↓

The behaviors of the person change to match our expectations, thus confirming the stereotype.

He came to the front of the class at the end of the lecture. . . . We started out facing each other, and as he talked I became dimly aware that he was standing a little too close and that I was beginning to back up. Fortunately I was able to suppress my first impulse and remain stationary because there was nothing to communicate aggression in his behavior except the conversational distance. . . .

By experimenting I was able to observe that as I moved away slightly, there was an associated shift in the pattern of interaction. He had more trouble expressing himself. If I shifted to where I felt comfortable (about twenty-one inches), he looked somewhat puzzled and hurt, almost as though he was saying, "Why is he acting that way? Here I am doing everything I can to talk to him in a friendly manner and he suddenly withdraws. Have I done anything wrong? Said something I shouldn't?" Having ascertained that distance had a direct effect on his conversation, I stood my ground, letting him set the distance.

As you can see, despite Hall's extensive knowledge of other cultures, he still felt uncomfortable in this conversation. He first interpreted the invasion of his personal space as possible aggression, for people get close (and jut out their chins and chests) when they are hostile. But when he realized that this was not the case, Hall resisted his impulse to move.

After Hall (1969; Hall and Hall 2007) analyzed situations like this, he observed that North Americans use four different "distance zones."

1. *Intimate distance.* This is the zone that the South American unwittingly invaded. It extends to about 18 inches from our bodies. We reserve this space for comforting, protecting, hugging, intimate touching, and lovemaking.
2. *Personal distance.* This zone extends from 18 inches to 4 feet. We reserve it for friends and acquaintances and ordinary conversations. This is the zone in which Hall would have preferred speaking with the South American.
3. *Social distance.* This zone, extending out from us about 4 to 12 feet, marks impersonal or formal relationships. We use this zone for such things as job interviews.
4. *Public distance.* This zone, extending beyond 12 feet, marks even more formal relationships. It is used to separate dignitaries and public speakers from the general public.

Touching   Not only does frequency of touching differ across cultures, but so does the meaning of touching within a culture. In general, higher-status individuals do more touching. Thus you are much more likely to see teachers touch students and bosses touch secretaries than the other way around. Apparently it is considered unseemly for lower-status individuals to put their hands on superiors.

An experiment with surgery patients illustrates how touching can have different meanings. The nurse, whose job it was to tell patients about their upcoming surgery, purposely touched the patients twice, once briefly on the arm when she introduced herself, and then for a full minute on the arm during the instruction period. When she left, she also shook the patient's hand (Thayer 1988).

Men and women reacted differently. Touching soothed the women patients. It lowered their blood pressure both before the surgery and for more than an hour afterward. The men's blood pressure increased, however. The experimenters suggest that the men found it harder to acknowledge dependency and fear. Instead of a comfort, the touch was a threatening reminder of their vulnerability. Perhaps. But the answer could be much simpler: Being touched by a pretty nurse aroused the men sexually, which increased their blood pressure. We don't know the reason. For this, we need more research.

Eye Contact   One way that we protect our personal bubble is by controlling eye contact. Letting someone gaze into our eyes—unless the person is our eye doctor—can be taken as a sign that we are attracted to that person, and even as an invitation to intimacy. Wanting to become "the friendliest store in town," a chain of supermarkets in Illinois ordered their checkout clerks to make direct eye contact with each customer. Women clerks complained that men customers were taking their eye contact the wrong way, as an invitation to intimacy. Management said they were exaggerating. The clerks' reply

"Eye encounters" are a fascinating aspect of everyday life. We use fleeting eye contact for most of our interactions, such as those with clerks or people we pass in the hall between classes. Just as we reserve our close personal space for intimates, so, too, we reserve lingering eye contact for them.

was, "We know the kind of looks we're getting back from men," and they refused to make direct eye contact with them.

Smiling   In the United States, we take it for granted that clerks will smile as they wait on us. But it isn't this way in all cultures. Apparently, Germans aren't used to smiling clerks, and when Wal-Mart expanded into Germany, it brought its American ways with it. The company ordered its German clerks to smile at their customers. They did—and the customers complained. The German customers interpreted the smiles as flirting (Samor et al. 2006).

Applied Body Language   The ways we use our bodies to give messages to others—from our facial expressions to our posture—are called **body language.** We all learn to interpret body language as part of our childhood lessons in culture, and we use this learning to help us get through everyday life. But now interpreting body language has become a tool in the government's fight against terrorism. Because many of the messages we give with our bodies lie beneath our consciousness, airport personnel and interrogators are being trained to look for tell-tale facial signs—from a quick downturn of the mouth to rapid blinking—that might indicate nervousness or that the individual is telling a lie (Davis et al. 2002).

Let's now turn to dramaturgy, a special area of symbolic interactionism.

Dramaturgy: The Presentation of Self in Everyday Life

It was their big day, two years in the making. Jennifer Mackey wore a white wedding gown adorned with an 11-foot train and 24,000 seed pearls that she and her mother had sewn onto the dress. Next to her at the altar in Lexington, Kentucky, stood her intended, Jeffrey Degler, in black tie. They said their vows, then turned to gaze for a moment at the four hundred guests.

That's when groomsman Daniel Mackey collapsed. As the shocked organist struggled to play Mendelssohn's "Wedding March," Mr. Mackey's unconscious body was dragged away, his feet striking—loudly—every step of the altar stairs.

"I couldn't believe he would die at my wedding," the bride said. (Hughes 1990)

Sociologist Erving Goffman (1922–1982) added a new twist to microsociology when he developed **dramaturgy** (or dramaturgical analysis). By this term he meant that social life is like a drama or a stage play: Birth ushers us onto the stage of everyday life, and our socialization consists of learning to perform on that stage. The self that we studied in the previous chapter lies at the center of our performances. We have ideas of how we want others to think of us, and we use our roles in everyday life to communicate those ideas. Goffman called these efforts to manage the impressions that others receive of us **impression management.**

Stages   Everyday life, said Goffman, involves playing our assigned roles. We have **front stages** on which to perform them, as did Jennifer and Jeffrey. (By the way, Daniel Mackey didn't really die—he had just fainted.) But we don't have to look at weddings to find front stages. Everyday life is filled with them. Where your teacher lectures is a front stage. And if you make an announcement at the dinner table, you are using a front stage. In fact, you spend most of your time on front stages, for a front stage is wherever you deliver your lines. We also have **back stages,** places where we can retreat and let our hair

body language the ways in which people use their bodies to give messages to others, much of which is done subconsciously

dramaturgy an approach, pioneered by Erving Goffman, in which social life is analyzed in terms of drama or the stage; also called dramaturgical analysis

impression management people's efforts to control the impressions that others receive of them

front stage where performances are given

back stage where people rest from their performances, discuss their presentations, and plan future performances

In *dramaturgy*, a specialty within sociology, social life is viewed as similar to the theater. In our everyday lives, we all are actors like those in this cast of *The George Lopez Show*. We, too, perform roles, use props, and deliver lines to fellow actors—who, in turn, do the same.

down. When you close the bathroom or bedroom door for privacy, for example, you are entering a back stage.

The same setting can serve as both a back and a front stage. For example, when you get into your car and look over your hair in the mirror or check your makeup, you are using the car as a back stage. But when you wave at friends or if you give that familiar gesture to someone who has just cut in front of you in traffic, you are using your car as a front stage.

Role Performance, Conflict, and Strain   Everyday life brings with it many roles. As discussed earlier, the same person may be a student, a teenager, a shopper, a worker, and a date, as well as a daughter or a son. Although a role lays down the basic outline for a performance, it also allows a great deal of flexibility. The particular emphasis or interpretation that we give a role, our "style," is known as **role performance.** Consider your role as son or daughter. You may play the role of ideal daughter or son—being respectful, coming home at the hours your parents set, and so forth. Or this description may not even come close to your particular role performance.

Ordinarily, our statuses are sufficiently separated that we find minimal conflict between them. Occasionally, however, what is expected of us in one status (our role) is incompatible with what is expected of us in another status. This problem, known as **role conflict,** is illustrated in Figure 4.4 on the next page, in which family, friendship, student, and work roles come crashing together. Usually, however, we manage to avoid role conflict by segregating our statuses, which in some instances requires an intense juggling act.

Sometimes the *same* status contains incompatible roles, a conflict known as **role strain.** Suppose that you are exceptionally well prepared for a particular class assignment. Although the instructor asks an unusually difficult question, you find yourself knowing the answer when no one else does. If you want to raise your hand, yet don't want to make your fellow students look bad, you will experience role strain. As illustrated in Figure 4.4, the difference between role conflict and role strain is that role conflict is conflict *between roles,* while role strain is conflict *within* a role.

role performance the ways in which someone performs a role, showing a particular "style" or "personality"

role conflict conflicts that someone feels *between* roles because the expectations attached to one role are incompatible with the expectations of another role

role strain conflicts that someone feels *within* a role

Figure 4.4 **Role Strain and Role Conflict**

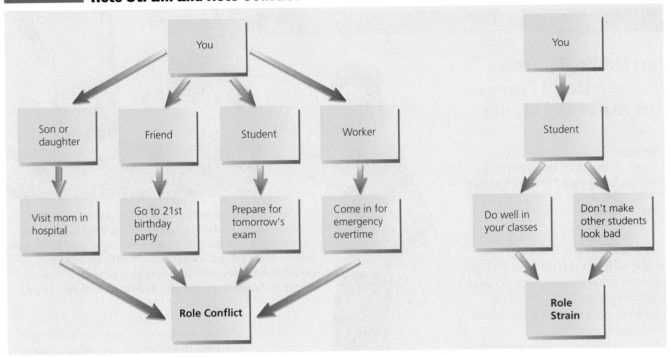

Source: By the author.

Sign-Vehicles To communicate information about the self, we use three types of **sign-vehicles:** the social setting, our appearance, and our manner. The *social setting* is the place where the action unfolds. This is where the curtain goes up on your performance, where you find yourself on stage playing parts and delivering lines. A social setting might be an office, dorm, living room, church, gym, or bar. It is wherever you interact with others. Your social setting includes *scenery*, the furnishings you use to communicate messages, such as desks, blackboards, scoreboards, couches, and so on.

The second sign-vehicle is *appearance*, or how we look when we play our roles. Appearance includes *props*, which are like scenery except that they decorate the person rather than the setting. The teacher has books, lecture notes, and chalk, while the football player wears a costume called a uniform. Although few of us carry around a football, we all use makeup, hairstyles, and clothing to communicate messages about ourselves. Props and other aspects of appearance give us cues that help us navigate everyday life: By letting us know what to expect from others, props tell us how we should react. Think of the messages that props communicate. Some people use clothing to say they are college students, others to say they are older adults. Some use clothing to say they are clergy, others to say they are prostitutes. Similarly, people choose brands of cigarettes, liquor, and automobiles to convey messages about the self.

Our body is an especially important sign-vehicle, its shape proclaiming messages about the self. The messages that are attached to various shapes change over time, but, as explored in the Mass Media box on the next page, thinness currently screams desirability.

The third sign-vehicle is *manner*, the attitudes we show as we play our roles. We use manner to communicate information about our feelings and moods. If we show anger or indifference, sincerity or good humor, for example, we indicate to others what they can expect of us as we play our roles.

Teamwork Being a good role player brings positive recognition from others, something we all covet. To accomplish this, we often use **teamwork**—two or more people working together to make certain that a performance goes off as planned. When a performance doesn't come off quite right, however, it may require **face-saving behavior.**

sign-vehicles the term used by Goffman to refer to how people use social setting, appearance, and manner to communicate information about the self

teamwork the collaboration of two or more people to manage impressions jointly

face-saving behavior techniques used to salvage a performance that is going sour

You Can't Be Thin Enough: Body Images and the Mass Media

An ad for Kellogg's Special K cereal shows an 18-month-old girl wearing nothing but a diaper. She has a worried look on her face. A bubble caption over her head has her asking, "Do I look fat?" (Krane et al. 2001)

When you stand before a mirror, do you like what you see? To make your body more attractive, do you watch your weight or work out? You have ideas about what you should look like. Where did you get them?

TV and magazine ads keep pounding home the message that our bodies aren't good enough, that we've got to improve them. The way to improve them, of course, is to buy the advertised products: hair extensions for women, hairpieces for men, hair transplants, padded bras, diet programs, anti-aging products, and exercise equipment. Muscular hulks show off machines that magically produce "six-pack abs" and incredible biceps—in just a few minutes a day. Female movie stars effortlessly go through their own tough workouts without even breaking into a sweat. Women and men get the feeling that attractive members of the opposite sex will flock to them if they purchase that wonder-working workout machine.

Although we try to shrug off such messages, knowing that they are designed to sell products, the messages still get our attention. They penetrate our thinking and feelings, helping to shape ideal images of

All of us contrast the reality we see when we look in the mirror with our culture's ideal body types. Mischa Barton represents an ideal body type that has developed in some parts of Western culture. These cultural images make it difficult for larger people to maintain positive images of their bodies. These women in Florida have struggled against cultural stereotypes.

how we "ought" to look. Those models so attractively clothed and coiffed as they walk down the runway, could they be any thinner? For women, the message is clear: You can't be thin enough. The men's message is also clear: You can't be muscular enough.

Woman or man, your body isn't good enough. It sags where it should be firm. It bulges where it should be smooth. It sticks out where it shouldn't, and it doesn't stick out enough where it should.

And—no matter what your weight is—it's too much. You've got to be thinner.

Exercise takes time, and getting in shape is painful. Once you do get in shape, if you slack off it seems to take only a few days for your body to sag into its previous slothful, drab appearance. You

We may, for example, ignore flaws in someone's performance, which Goffman defines as *tact*.

Suppose your teacher is about to make an important point. Suppose also that her lecturing has been outstanding and the class is hanging on every word. Just as she pauses for emphasis, her stomach lets out a loud growl. She might then use a *face-saving technique* by remarking, "I was so busy preparing for class that I didn't get breakfast this morning." It is more likely, however, that both class and teacher will simply ignore the sound, giving the impression that no one heard a thing—a face-saving technique called *studied nonobservance*. This allows the teacher to make the point, or as Goffman would say, it allows the performance to go on.

Becoming the Roles We Play   We become so used to the roles we play in everyday life that we tend to think we are "just doing" things, not that we are like actors on a stage

can't let up, you can't exercise enough, and you can't diet enough.

But who can continue at such a torrid pace, striving for what are unrealistic cultural ideals? A few people, of course, but not many. So liposuction is appealing. Just lie there, put up with a little discomfort, and the doctor will vacuum the fat right out of your body. Surgeons can transform flat breasts into super breasts overnight. They can lower receding hairlines and smooth furrowed brows. They remove lumps with their magical tummy tucks, and can take off a decade with their rejuvenating skin peels, face lifts, and Botox injections.

With impossibly shaped models at *Victoria's Secret* and skinny models showing off the latest fashions in *Vogue* and *Seventeen*, half of U.S. adolescent girls feel fat and count calories (Hill 2006). Some teens even call the plastic surgeon. Anxious lest their child violate peer ideals and trail behind in her race for popularity, parents foot the bill. Some parents pay $25,000 just to give their daughters a flatter tummy (Gross 1998).

With peer pressure to alter the body already intense, surgeons keep stoking the fire. A sample ad: "No Ifs, Ands or Butts. You Can Change Your Bottom Line in Hours!" Some surgeons even offer gift certificates—so you can give your loved ones liposuction or botox injections along with their greeting card (Dowd 2002).

The thinness craze has moved to the East. Glossy magazines in Japan and China are filled with skinny models and crammed with ads touting diet pills and diet teas. In China, where famine used to abound, a little extra padding was valued as a sign of good health. Today, the obsession is thinness (Rosenthal 1999; Prystay and Fowler 2003). Not-so-subtle ads scream that fat is bad. Some teas come with a package of diet pills. Weight-loss machines, with electrodes attached to acupuncture pressure points, not only reduce fat but also build breasts—or so the advertisers claim.

Not limited by our rules, advertisers in Japan and China push a soap that supposedly "sucks up fat through the skin's pores" (Marshall 1995). What a dream product! After all, even though our TV models smile as they go through their paces, those exercise machines do look like a lot of hard work.

Then there is the other bottom line: Attractiveness does pay off. U.S. economists studied physical attractiveness and earnings. The result? "Good-looking" men and women earn the most, "average-looking" men and women earn more than "plain" people, and the "ugly" earn the least (Hamermesh and Biddle 1994). In Europe, too, the more attractive workers earn more (Brunello and D'Hombres 2007). Then there is that potent cash advantage that "attractive" women have: They attract and marry higher-earning men (Kanasawa and Kovar 2004).

More popularity *and* more money? Maybe you can't be thin enough after all. Maybe those exercise machines are a good investment. If only we could catch up with the Japanese and develop a soap that would suck the fat right out of our pores. You can practically hear the jingle now.

for your Consideration

What image do you have of your body? How do cultural expectations of "ideal" bodies underlie your image? Can you recall any advertisement or television program that has affected your body image?

What is considered ideal body size differs with historical periods and from one ethnic group to another. The women who posed for 16th century European sculptors and painters, for example, were much "thicker" than the so-called "ideal" young women of today. (As I was looking at a painting in the Vatican, I heard a woman remark,"Look at those rolls of fat!") Why do you think that this difference exists?

Most advertising and television programs that focus on weight are directed at women. Women are more concerned than men about weight, more likely to have eating disorders, and more likely to be dissatisfied with their bodies (Honeycutt 1995; Hill 2006). Do you think that the targeting of women in advertising creates these attitudes and behaviors? Or do you think that these attitudes and behaviors would exist even if there were no such ads? Why?

who manage impressions. Yet every time we dress for school, or for any other activity, we are preparing for impression management. Have you ever noticed how some clothing simply doesn't "feel" right for certain occasions? Have you ever changed your mind about something you were wearing and decided to change your clothing? Or maybe just switch shirts or add a necklace? That is fine-tuning the impressions you want to make. Similarly, you may have noticed that when teenagers want to impress the opposite sex, they stand before a mirror for hours as they comb and restyle their hair, and then change and adjust their clothing as they try to "get it just right."

Although roles might be uncomfortable at first, after we get used to them *we tend to become the roles we play.* That is, roles become incorporated into the self-concept, especially roles for which we prepare long and hard and that become part of our everyday lives. When sociologist Helen Ebaugh (1988), who had been a nun, studied *role exit,* she interviewed people who had left marriages, police work, the military, medicine, and

Both individuals and organizations do *impression management,* **trying to communicate messages about the self (or organization) that best meets their goals. At times, these efforts fail.**

religious vocations. She found that the role had become so intertwined with the individual's self-concept that leaving it threatened the person's identity. The question these people struggled with was "Who am I, now that I am not a nun (or wife, police officer, colonel, physician, and so on)?" Even years after leaving these roles, many continue to perform them in their dreams.

A statement by one of my respondents illustrates how roles become part of the person and linger even after the individual leaves them:

> After I left the ministry, I felt like a fish out of water. Wearing that backward collar had become a part of me. It was especially strange on Sunday mornings when I'd listen to someone else give the sermon. I knew that I should be up there preaching. I felt as though I had left God.

Applying Impression Management   I can just hear someone saying, "Impression management is interesting, but is it really significant?" In fact, it is so significant that the right impression management can make a vital difference in your career. To be promoted, you must be perceived as someone who *should* be promoted. You must appear dominant. You certainly cannot go unnoticed. But how you manage this impression is crucial. If an executive woman tries to appear dominant by wearing loud clothing, using garish makeup, and cursing, this will get her noticed—but it will not put her on the path to promotion. How, then, can she exhibit dominance in the right way? To help women walk this fine line between femininity and dominance, career counselors advise women on fine details of impression management. Here are two things they recommend—that women place their hands on the table during executive sessions, not in their lap, and that they carry a purse that looks more like a briefcase (Needham 2006).

Ethnomethodology: Uncovering Background Assumptions

Certainly one of the strangest words in sociology is *ethnomethodology.* To better understand this term, consider the word's three basic components. *Ethno* means "folk" or "people"; *method* means how people do something; *ology* means "the study of." Putting them together, then, *ethno/method/ology* means "the study of how people do things." Specifically, **ethnomethodology** is the study of how people use commonsense understandings to make sense of life.

Let's suppose that during a routine office visit, your doctor remarks that your hair is rather long, then takes out a pair of scissors and starts to give you a haircut. You would feel strange about this, for your doctor would be violating **background assumptions**—your ideas about the way life is and the way things ought to work. These assumptions, which lie at the root of everyday life, are so deeply embedded in our consciousness that we are seldom aware of them, and most of us fulfill them unquestioningly. Thus, your doctor does not offer you a haircut, even if he or she is good at cutting hair and you need one!

The founder of ethnomethodology, sociologist Harold Garfinkel, conducted some interesting exercises designed to reveal our background assumptions. Garfinkel (1967) asked his students to act as though they did not understand the basic rules of social life. Some tried to bargain with supermarket clerks; others would inch close to people and stare directly at them. They were met with surprise, bewilderment, even anger. In one exercise Garfinkel

ethnomethodology the study of how people use background assumptions to make sense out of life

background assumptions deeply embedded common understandings of how the world operates and of how people ought to act

asked students to act as though they were boarders in their own homes. They addressed their parents as "Mr." and "Mrs.," asked permission to use the bathroom, sat stiffly, were courteous, and spoke only when spoken to. As you can imagine, the other family members didn't know what to make of this (Garfinkel 1967):

> They vigorously sought to make the strange actions intelligible and to restore the situation to normal appearances. Reports (by the students) were filled with accounts of astonishment, bewilderment, shock, anxiety, embarrassment, and anger, and with charges by various family members that the student was mean, inconsiderate, selfish, nasty, or impolite. Family members demanded explanations: What's the matter? What's gotten into you? . . . Are you sick? . . . Are you out of your mind or are you just stupid?

In another exercise, Garfinkel asked students to take words and phrases literally. When a student asked his girlfriend what she meant when she said that she had a flat tire, she said:

> What do you mean, "What do you mean?"? A flat tire is a flat tire. That is what I meant. Nothing special. What a crazy question!

Another conversation went like this:

ACQUAINTANCE: How are you?

STUDENT: How am I in regard to what? My health, my finances, my schoolwork, my peace of mind, my . . . ?

ACQUAINTANCE: (red in the face): Look! I was just trying to be polite. Frankly, I don't give a damn how you are.

Students who are asked to break background assumptions can be highly creative. The young children of one of my students were surprised one morning when they came down for breakfast to find a sheet spread across the living room floor. On it were dishes, silverware, lit candles—and bowls of ice cream. They, too, wondered what was going on, but they dug eagerly into the ice cream before their mother could change her mind.

This is a risky assignment to give students, however, for breaking some background assumptions can make people suspicious. When a colleague of mine gave this assignment, a couple of his students began to wash dollar bills in a laundromat. By the time they put the bills in the dryer, the police had arrived.

All of us have *background assumptions*, deeply ingrained assumptions of how the world operates. How do you think the background assumptions of this Londoner differ from this Ecuadoran shaman, who is performing a healing ceremony to rid London of its evil spirits?

IN SUM Ethnomethodologists explore *background assumptions*, the taken-for-granted ideas about the world that underlie our behavior. Most of these assumptions, or basic rules of social life, are unstated. We learn them as we learn our culture, and we violate them only with risk. Deeply embedded in our minds, they give us basic directions for living everyday life.

The Social Construction of Reality

Symbolic interactionists stress how our ideas help determine our reality. In what has become known as *the definition of the situation,* or the **Thomas theorem,** sociologists W. I. and Dorothy S. Thomas said "If people define situations as real, they are real in their consequences." Consider the following incident:

> On a visit to Morocco, in northern Africa, I decided to buy a watermelon. When I indicated to the street vendor that the knife he was going to use to cut the watermelon was dirty (encrusted with filth would be more apt), he was very obliging. He immediately

Thomas theorem William I. and Dorothy S. Thomas' classic formulation of the definition of the situation: "If people define situations as real, they are real in their consequences."

bent down and began to swish the knife in a puddle on the street. I shuddered as I looked at the passing burros that were urinating and defecating as they went by. Quickly, I indicated by gesture that I preferred my melon uncut after all.

For that vendor, germs did not exist. For me, they did. And each of us acted according to our definition of the situation. My perception and behavior did not come from the fact that germs are real but *because I grew up in a society that teaches they are real.* Microbes, of course, *objectively* exist, and whether or not germs are part of our thought world makes no difference as to whether we are infected by them. Our behavior, however, does not depend on the *objective* existence of something but, rather, on our *subjective interpretation,* on what sociologists call our *definition of reality.* In other words, it is not the reality of microbes that impresses itself on us, but society that impresses the reality of microbes on us.

Let's consider another example. Do you remember the identical twins, Oskar and Jack, who grew up so differently? As discussed on page 66, Jack was reared in Trinidad and learned to hate Hitler, while Oskar was reared in Germany and learned to love Hitler. Thus what Hitler meant to Oskar and Jack (and what he means to us) depends not on Hitler's acts, but, rather, on how we view his acts—that is, on our definition of the situation.

This is the **social construction of reality.** Our society, or the social groups to which we belong, holds particular views of life. From our groups (the *social* part of this process), we learn ways of looking at life—whether that be our view of Hitler or Osama bin Laden (they're good, they're evil), germs (they exist, they don't exist), or *anything else in life.* In short, through our interaction with others, we *construct reality;* that is, we learn ways of interpreting our experiences in life.

Gynecological Examinations To better understand the social construction of reality, let's consider an extended example.

To do research on vaginal examinations, I interviewed a gynecological nurse who had been present at about 14,000 examinations. I focused on how doctors construct social reality in order to define this examination as nonsexual (Henslin and Biggs 1971/2007). It became apparent that the pelvic examination unfolds much as a stage play does. I will use "he" to refer to the physician because only male physicians were part of this study. Perhaps the results would be different with women gynecologists.

Scene 1 (the patient as person) In this scene, the doctor maintains eye contact with his patient, calls her by name, and discusses her problems in a professional manner. If he decides that a vaginal examination is necessary, he tells a nurse, "Pelvic in room 1." By this statement, he is announcing that a major change will occur in the next scene.

Scene 2 (from person to pelvic) This scene is the depersonalizing stage. In line with the doctor's announcement, the patient begins the transition from a "person" to a "pelvic." The doctor leaves the room, and a female nurse enters to help the patient make the transition. The nurse prepares the "props" for the coming examination and answers any questions the woman might have.

What occurs at this point is essential for the social construction of reality, for *the doctor's absence removes even the suggestion of sexuality.* To undress in front of him could suggest either a striptease or intimacy, thus undermining the reality so carefully being defined: that of nonsexuality.

The patient also wants to remove any hint of sexuality, and during this scene she may express concern about what to do with her panties. Some mutter to the nurse, "I don't want him to see these." Most women solve the problem by either slipping their panties under their other clothes or placing them in their purse.

Scene 3 (the person as pelvic) This scene opens when the doctor enters the room. Before him is a woman lying on a table, her feet in stirrups, her knees tightly together, and her body covered by a drape sheet. The doctor seats himself on a low stool before the woman and says, "Let your knees fall apart" (rather than the sexually loaded "Spread your legs"), and begins the examination.

social construction of reality the use of background assumptions and life experiences to define what is real

The drape sheet is crucial in this process of desexualization, for it *dissociates the pelvic area from the person:* Leaning forward and with the drape sheet above his head, the physician can see only the vagina, not the patient's face. Thus dissociated from the individual, the vagina is dramaturgically transformed into an object of analysis. If the doctor examines the patient's breasts, he also dissociates them from her person by examining them one at a time, with a towel covering the unexamined breast. Like the vagina, each breast becomes an isolated item dissociated from the person.

In this third scene, the patient cooperates in being an object, becoming, for all practical purposes, a pelvis to be examined. She withdraws eye contact from the doctor, and usually from the nurse, is likely to stare at the wall or at the ceiling, and avoids initiating conversation.

Scene 4 (from pelvic to person) In this scene, the patient becomes "repersonalized." The doctor has left the examining room; the patient dresses and fixes her hair and makeup. Her reemergence as a person is indicated by such statements to the nurse as, "My dress isn't too wrinkled, is it?" indicating a need for reassurance that the metamorphosis from "pelvic" back to "person" has been completed satisfactorily.

Scene 5 (the patient as person) In this final scene, the patient is once again treated as a person rather than as an object. The doctor makes eye contact with her and addresses her by name. She, too, makes eye contact with the doctor, and the usual middle-class interaction patterns are followed. She has been fully restored.

IN SUM To an outsider to our culture, the custom of women going to a male stranger for a vaginal examination might seem bizarre. But not to us. We learn that pelvic examinations are nonsexual. To sustain this definition requires teamwork—patients, doctors, and nurses working together to *socially construct reality.*

It is not just pelvic examinations or our views of microbes that make up our definitions of reality. Rather, *our behavior depends on how we define reality.* Our definitions (or constructions) provide the basis for what we do and how we feel about life. To understand human behavior, then, we must know how people define reality.

The Need for Both Macrosociology and Microsociology

As was noted earlier, both microsociology and macrosociology make vital contributions to our understanding of human behavior. Our understanding of social life would be vastly incomplete without one or the other. The photo essay on the next two pages should help to make clear why we need *both* perspectives.

To illustrate this point, let's consider two groups of high school boys studied by sociologist William Chambliss (1973/2007). Both groups attended Hanibal High School. In one group were eight middle-class boys who came from "good" families and were perceived by the community as "going somewhere." Chambliss calls this group the "Saints." The other group consisted of six lower-class boys who were seen as headed down a dead-end road. Chambliss calls this group the "Roughnecks."

Boys in both groups skipped school, got drunk, and did a lot of fighting and vandalism. The Saints were actually somewhat more delinquent, for they were truant more often and engaged in more vandalism. Yet the Saints had a good reputation, while the Roughnecks were seen by teachers, the police, and the general community as no good and headed for trouble.

The boys' reputations set them on distinct paths. Seven of the eight Saints went on to graduate from college. Three studied for advanced degrees: One finished law school and became active in state politics, one finished medical school, and one went on to earn a Ph.D. The four other college graduates entered managerial or executive training programs with large firms. After his parents divorced, one Saint failed to graduate from high school on time and had to repeat his senior year. Although this boy tried to go to

When a **Tornado Strikes:**
Social Organization Following a Natural Disaster

as I was watching television on March 20, 2003, I heard a report that a tornado had hit Camilla, Georgia. "Like a big lawn mower," the report said, it had cut a path of destruction through this little town. In its fury, the tornado had left behind six dead and about 200 injured.

From sociological studies of natural disasters, I knew that immediately after the initial shock the survivors of natural disasters work together to try to restore order to their disrupted lives. I wanted to see this restructuring process first hand. The next morning, I took off for Georgia.

These photos, taken the day after the tornado struck, tell the story of people who are in the midst of trying to put their lives back together. I was impressed at how little time people spend commiserating about their misfortune and how quickly they take practical steps to restore their lives.

As you look at these photos, try to determine why you need both microsociology and macrosociology to understand what occurs after a natural disaster.

After making sure that their loved ones are safe, one of the next steps people take is to recover their possessions. The cooperation that emerges among people, as documented in the sociological literature on natural disasters, is illustrated here.

© James M. Henslin, all photos

▲ In addition to the inquiring sociologist, television news teams also were interviewing survivors and photographing the damage. This was the second time in just three years that a tornado had hit this neighborhood.

◄ The owners of this house invited me inside to see what the tornado had done to their home. In what had been her dining room, this woman is trying to salvage whatever she can from the rubble. She and her family survived by taking refuge in the bathroom. They had been there only five seconds, she said, when the tornado struck.

Just the night before, members of this church had held evening worship service. After the tornado, someone mounted a U.S. flag on top of the cross, symbolic of the church members' patriotism and religiosity—and of their enduring hope.

Personal relationships are essential in putting lives together. Consequently, reminders of these relationships are one of the main possessions that people attempt to salvage. This young man, having just recovered the family photo album, is eagerly reviewing the photos.

Formal organizations also help the survivors of natural disasters recover. In this neighborhood, I saw representatives of insurance companies, the police, the fire department, and an electrical co-op. The Salvation Army brought meals to the neighborhood.

For children, family photos are not as important as toys. This girl has managed to salvage a favorite toy, which will help anchor her to her previous life.

A sign of the times. Like electricity and gas, cable television also has to be re-stored as soon as possible.

college by attending night school, he never finished. He was unemployed the last time Chambliss saw him.

In contrast, only four of the Roughnecks finished high school. Two of these boys did exceptionally well in sports and were awarded athletic scholarships to college. They both graduated from college and became high school coaches. Of the two others who graduated from high school, one became a small-time gambler and the other disappeared "up north," where he was last reported to be driving a truck. The two who did not complete high school were convicted of separate murders and sent to prison.

To understand what happened to the Saints and the Roughnecks, we need to grasp *both* social structure and social interaction. Using *macrosociology,* we can place these boys within the larger framework of the U.S. social class system. This reveals how opportunities open or close to people depending on their social class and how people learn different goals as they grow up in different groups. We can then use *microsociology* to follow their everyday lives. We can see how the Saints manipulated their "good" reputations to skip classes and how their access to automobiles allowed them to protect those reputations by transferring their troublemaking to different communities. In contrast, the Roughnecks, who did not have cars, were highly visible. Their lawbreaking, which was limited to a small area, readily came to the attention of the community. Microsociology also reveals how their respective reputations opened doors of opportunity to the first group of boys while closing them to the other.

It is clear that we need both kinds of sociology, and both are stressed in the following chapters.

Summary *and* Review

Levels of Sociological Analysis

What two levels of analysis do sociologists use?

Sociologists use macrosociological and microsociological levels of analysis. In **macrosociology,** the focus is placed on large-scale features of social life, while in **microsociology,** the focus is on **social interaction.** Functionalists and conflict theorists tend to use a macrosociological approach, while symbolic interactionists are more likely to use a microsociological approach. Pp. 98–99.

The Macrosociological Perspective: Social Structure

How does social structure influence our behavior?

The term **social structure** refers to the social envelope that surrounds us and establishes limits on our behavior. Social structure consists of culture, social class, social statuses, roles, groups, and social institutions. Our location in the social structure underlies our perceptions, attitudes, and behaviors.

Culture lays the broadest framework, while **social class** divides people according to income, education, and occupational prestige. Each of us receives **ascribed statuses** at birth; later we add **achieved statuses.** Our behaviors and orientations are further influenced by the **roles** we play, the **groups** to which we belong, and our experiences with social institutions. These components of society work together to help maintain social order. Pp. 99–103.

Social Institutions

What are social institutions?

Social institutions are the standard ways that a society develops to meet its basic needs. As summarized in Figure 4.2 (page 105), industrial and postindustrial societies have ten social institutions—the family, religion, education, economics, medicine, politics, law, science, the military, and the mass media. From the functionalist perspective, social institutions meet universal group needs, or **functional requisites.** Conflict theorists stress how society's elites use social institutions to maintain their privileged positions. Pp. 104–107.

What holds society together?

According to Emile Durkheim, in agricultural societies people are united by **mechanical solidarity** (having similar views and feelings). With industrialization comes **organic solidarity** (people depend on one another to do their more specialized jobs). Ferdinand Tönnies pointed out that the informal means of control of *Gemeinschaft* (small, intimate) societies are replaced by formal mechanisms in *Gesellschaft* (larger, more impersonal) societies. Pp. 107–109.

The Microsociological Perspective: Social Interaction in Everyday Life

What is the focus of symbolic interactionism?

In contrast to functionalists and conflict theorists, who as macrosociologists focus on the "big picture," symbolic interactionists tend to be microsociologists who focus on face-to-face social interaction. Symbolic interactionists analyze how people define their worlds, and how their definitions, in turn, influence their behavior. P. 110.

How do stereotypes affect social interaction?

Stereotypes are assumptions of what people are like. When we first meet people, we classify them according to our perceptions of their visible characteristics. Our ideas about those characteristics guide our behavior toward them. Our behavior, in turn, may influence them to behave in ways that reinforce our stereotypes. Pp. 110–111.

Do all human groups share a similar sense of personal space?

In examining how people use physical space, symbolic interactionists stress that we surround ourselves with a "personal bubble" that we carefully protect. People from different cultures use "personal bubbles" of varying sizes, so the answer to the question is no. Americans typically use four different "distance zones": intimate, personal, social, and public. Pp. 110, 112.

What is dramaturgy?

Erving Goffman developed **dramaturgy** (or dramaturgical analysis), in which everyday life is analyzed in terms of the stage. At the core of this analysis is **impression management,** our attempts to control the impressions we make on others. For this, we use the **sign-vehicles** of setting, appearance, and manner. Our performances often call for **teamwork** and **face-saving behavior.** Pp. 113–118.

What is the social construction of reality?

The phrase **the social construction of reality** refers to how we construct our views of the world, which, in turn, underlie our actions. **Ethnomethodology** is the study of how people make sense of everyday life. Ethnomethodologists try to uncover **background assumptions,** our basic ideas about the way life is. Pp. 118–121.

The Need for Both Macrosociology and Microsociology

Why are both levels of analysis necessary?

Because each focuses on different aspects of the human experience, both microsociology and macrosociology are necessary for us to understand social life. Pp. 121–124.

Thinking Critically
about Chapter 4

1. The major components of social structure are culture, social class, social status, roles, groups, and social institutions. Use social structure to explain why Native Americans have such a low rate of college graduation. (See Table 9.2 on page 284.)

2. Dramaturgy is a form of microsociology. Use dramaturgy to analyze a situation with which you are intimately familiar (such as interaction with your family or friends, or in one of your college classes).

3. To illustrate why we need both macrosociology and microsociology to understand social life, consider a student getting kicked out of college as an example.

Additional Resources

What can you use MySocLab for?

 www.mysoclab.com

- **Study and Review:** Pre- and Post-Tests, Practice Tests, Flash Cards, Individualized Study Plans.

- **Current Events:** *Sociology in the News,* the daily *New York Times,* and more.

- **Research and Writing:** *Research Navigator, Writing About Sociology,* and more.

Where Can I Read More on This Topic?

Suggested readings for this chapter are listed at the back of this book.

Societies to Social Networks

Bharati Chaudhuri, *Unity*

When Kody Scott joined the L.A. Crips, his initiation had two parts. Here's the first:

"How old is you now anyway?"

"Eleven, but I'll be twelve in November."

I never saw the blow to my head come from Huck. Bam! And I was on all fours . . . Kicked in the stomach, I was on my back counting stars in the blackness. Grabbed by the collar, I was made to stand again. A solid blow to my chest exploded pain on the blank screen that had now become my mind. Bam! Another, then another. Blows rained on me from every direction . . .

Up until this point not a word had been spoken. . . . Then I just started swinging, with no style or finesse, just anger and the instinct to survive. . . . (This) reflected my ability to represent the set [gang] in hand-to-hand combat. The blows stopped abruptly . . . My ear was bleeding, and my neck and face were deep red . . .

Scott's beating was followed immediately by the second part of his initiation. For this, he received the name *Monster,* which he carried proudly:

"Give Kody the pump" [12-gauge pump action shotgun] . . . Tray Ball spoke with the calm of a football coach. "Tonight we gonna rock they world." . . . Hand slaps were passed around the room . . . "Kody, you got eight shots, you don't come back to the car unless they all are gone."

Kody, you got eight shots, you don't come back to the car unless they all are gone.

"Righteous," I said, eager to show my worth . . . .

Hanging close to buildings, houses, and bushes, we made our way, one after the other, to within spitting distance of the Bloods. . . . Huck and Fly stepped from the shadows simultaneously and were never noticed until it was too late. Boom! Boom! Heavy bodies hitting the ground, confusion, yells of dismay, running, . . . By my sixth shot I had advanced past the first fallen bodies and into the street in pursuit of those who had sought refuge behind cars and trees. . . .

Back in the shack we smoked more pot and drank more beer. I was the center of attention for my acts of aggression. . . .

Tray Ball said. "You got potential, 'cause you eager to learn. Bangin' [being a gang member] ain't no part-time thang, it's full-time, it's a career. It's bein' down when ain't nobody else down with you. It's gettin' caught and not tellin'. Killin' and not caring, and dyin' without fear. It's love for your set and hate for the enemy. You hear what I'm sayin'?"

Kody adds this insightful remark:

Though never verbally stated, death was looked upon as a sort of reward, a badge of honor, especially if one died in some heroic capacity for the hood . . . The supreme sacrifice was to "take a

(continued)

bullet for a homie" [fellow gang member]. The set functioned as a religion. Nothing held a light to the power of the set. If you died on the trigger you surely were smiled upon by the Crip God.

Excerpts from Scott 1994:8–13, 103.

Excerpts from Scott 1994:8–13, 103.

group people who have something in common and who believe that what they have in common is significant; also called a social group

society people who share a culture and a territory

Groups are the essence of life in society. We become who we are because of our membership in human groups. As we saw in Chapter 3, even our minds are a product of society, or, more specifically phrased, of the groups to which we belong.

In this chapter, we'll consider how groups influence our lives—and examine the power that groups wield over us. Although none of us wants to think that we could participate in killings such as those recounted in our opening vignette, don't bet on it. You are going to read some surprising things about groups in this chapter.

Societies and Their Transformation

To better understand **groups**—people who interact with one another and who think of themselves as belonging together—let's first look at the big picture. The largest and most complex group that sociologists study is **society,** which consists of people who share a culture and a territory. Society, which surrounds us, sets the stage for our life experiences. Not only does it lay the broad framework for our behavior but also it influences the ways we think and feel. Its effect is so significant that if you had grown up in a different society, you would be a different type of person.

As society—the largest and most complex type of group—changes, so, too, do the groups, activities, and, ultimately, the type of people who form that society. This photo of Russian and Austrian wrestlers in the Olympics at Greece captures some of the changes occurring in Western societies. What social changes can you identify from this photo?

To see how our society developed, look at Figure 5.1. You can see that technology is the key to understanding the broad, sweeping changes that produced our society. As we summarize these changes, picture yourself as a member of each society. Consider how your life—even your thoughts and values—would be different in each society.

Hunting and Gathering Societies

Societies with the fewest social divisions are called **hunting and gathering societies.** As the name implies, in order to survive, these groups depend on hunting animals and gathering plants. In some groups, the men do the hunting, and the women the gathering. In others, both men and women (and children) gather plants, the men hunt large animals, and both men and women hunt small animals. Beyond this basic division of labor by sex, there are few social divisions. The groups usually have a **shaman,** an individual thought to be able to influence spiritual forces, but shamans, too, must help obtain food. Although these groups give greater prestige to the men, whose hunting supplies the major source of meat, the women gatherers contribute more food to the group, perhaps even four-fifths of their total food supply (Bernard 1992).

Because a region cannot support a large number of people who hunt animals and gather plants (group members do not plant—they only gather what is already there), hunting and gathering societies are small. They usually consist of only twenty-five to forty people. These groups are nomadic. As their food supply dwindles in one area, they move to another location. They place high value on sharing food, which is essential to their survival. Because of disease, drought, and pestilence, children have only about a fifty-fifty chance of surviving to adulthood (Lenski and Lenski 1987).

Of all societies, hunters and gatherers are the most egalitarian. Because what they hunt and gather is perishable, the people accumulate few personal possessions. Consequently, no one becomes wealthier than anyone else. There are no rulers, and most decisions are arrived at through discussion. Because their needs are basic and they do not work to store up material possessions, hunters and gatherers have the most leisure of all human groups (Sahlins 1972; Lorber 1994; Volti 1995).

All human groups were once hunters and gatherers, and until several hundred years ago such societies were common. Their demise came when other groups took over the regions in which they moved about in their search for food. Today, fewer than 300 hunter-gatherer groups remain; they include the pygmies of central Africa, the aborigines of Australia, and groups in South America represented by the photo on the next page (Stiles 2003). These groups seem doomed to a similar fate, and it is likely that their way of life will soon disappear from the human scene (Lenski and Lenski 1987).

Pastoral and Horticultural Societies

About ten thousand years ago, some groups found that they could tame and breed some of the animals they hunted—primarily goats, sheep, cattle, and camels. Others discovered that they could cultivate plants. As a result, hunting and gathering societies branched into two directions, each with different means of acquiring food.

The key to understanding the first branching is the word *pasture;* **pastoral** (or herding) **societies** are based on the *pasturing of animals.* Pastoral societies developed in

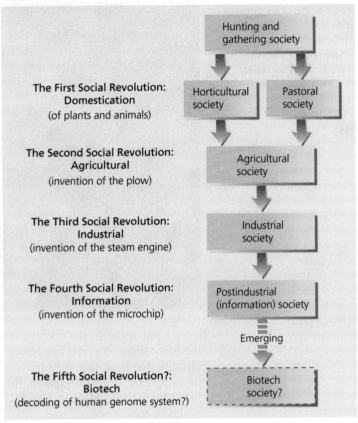

Figure 5.1 **The Social Transformations of Society**

Hunting and gathering society

The First Social Revolution: Domestication (of plants and animals) → Horticultural society, Pastoral society

The Second Social Revolution: Agricultural (invention of the plow) → Agricultural society

The Third Social Revolution: Industrial (invention of the steam engine) → Industrial society

The Fourth Social Revolution: Information (invention of the microchip) → Postindustrial (information) society

Emerging

The Fifth Social Revolution?: Biotech (decoding of human genome system?) → Biotech society?

Source: By the author.

hunting and gathering society a human group that depends on hunting and gathering for its survival

shaman the healing specialist of a tribe who attempts to control the spirits thought to cause a disease or injury; commonly called a witch doctor

pastoral society a society based on the pasturing of animals

The simplest forms of societies are called *hunting and gathering societies.* Members of these societies have adapted well to their environments, and they have more leisure than the members of other societies, Shown here are tribal members in the rainforest of Paraguay. What cultural diffusion do you see?

regions where low rainfall made it impractical to build life around growing crops. Groups that took this turn remained nomadic, for they followed their animals to fresh pasture. The key to understanding the second branching is the word *horticulture,* or plant cultivation. **Horticultural** (or gardening) **societies** are based on the *cultivation of plants by the use of hand tools.* Because they no longer had to abandon an area as the food supply gave out, these groups developed permanent settlements.

We can call the domestication of animals and plants the *first social revolution.* As shown in Figure 5.2, it transformed society. Although the **domestication revolution** was gradual, occurring over thousands of years, it represented a fundamental break with the past and it changed human history. The more dependable food supply ushered in changes that touched almost every aspect of human life. Groups became larger because the more dependable food supply supported more people. With more food available than was needed for survival, no longer was it necessary for everyone to work at providing food. This allowed groups to develop a *division of labor.* Some people began to make jewelry, others tools, others weapons, and so on. This led to a surplus of objects, which, in turn, stimulated trade. With trading, groups began to accumulate objects they prized, such as gold, jewelry, and utensils.

Figure 5.2 illustrates how these changes set the stage for *social inequality.* Some families (or clans) acquired more goods than others. This led to feuds and war, for groups now possessed animals, pastures, croplands, jewelry, and other material goods to fight about. War, in turn, opened the door to slavery, for people found it convenient to let captives do their drudge work. Social inequality remained limited, however, for the surplus itself was limited. As individuals passed their possessions on to their descendants, wealth grew more concentrated. So did power, and for the first time, some individuals became chiefs.

Note the primary pattern that runs through this transformation of group life: the change *from fewer to more possessions and from greater to lesser equality.* Where people were located *within* the hierarchy of a society became vital for determining what happened to them in life. Again, Figure 5.2 summarizes how these changes led to social inequality.

Agricultural Societies

When the plow was invented about five or six thousand years ago, social life was once again changed forever. Compared with hoes and digging sticks, the use of animals to pull plows was immensely efficient. As the earth was plowed, more nutrients were returned to

horticultural society a society based on cultivating plants by the use of hand tools

domestication revolution the first social revolution, based on the domestication of plants and animals, which led to pastoral and horticultural societies

agricultural revolution the second social revolution, based on the invention of the plow, which led to agricultural societies

agricultural society a society based on large-scale agriculture; plows drawn by animals are the source of food production

Industrial Revolution the third social revolution, occurring when machines powered by fuels replaced most animal and human power

industrial society a society based on the harnessing of machines powered by fuels

the soil, making the land more productive. The food surplus of the **agricultural revolution** was unlike anything ever seen in human history. It allowed even more people to engage in activities other than farming. In this new **agricultural society,** people developed cities and what is popularly known as "culture," such as philosophy, art, music, literature, and architecture. Accompanied by the inventions of the wheel, writing, and numbers, the changes were so profound that this period is sometimes referred to as "the dawn of civilization."

The tendency toward social inequality of previous societies was only a forerunner of what was to come. *Inequality became a fundamental feature of life in society.* Some people managed to gain control of the growing surplus of resources. To protect their expanding privileges and power, this elite surrounded itself with armed men. They even levied taxes on others, who now had become their "subjects." As conflict theorists point out, this concentration of resources and power—along with the oppression of people not in power—was the forerunner of the state.

No one knows exactly how it happened, but during this period females also became subject to males. Sociologist Elise Boulding (1976) theorizes that this change occurred because men were in charge of plowing and the cows. She suggests that when metals were developed, men took on the new job of attaching the metal as tips to the wooden plows and doing the plowing. As a result,

> the shift of the status of the woman farmer may have happened quite rapidly, once there were two male specializations relating to agriculture: plowing and the care of cattle. This situation left women with all the subsidiary tasks, including weeding and carrying water to the fields. The new fields were larger, so women had to work just as many hours as they did before, but now they worked at more secondary tasks. . . . This would contribute further to the erosion of the status of women.

This explanation, however, creates more questions than it answers. Why, for example, did men take over metal work and plowing? Why didn't women? It also does not account for why men control societies in which women are in charge of the cattle. In short, we are left in the dark as to why and how men became dominant, a reason likely to remain lost in human history.

Industrial Societies

The *third* social invention also turned society upside down. The **Industrial Revolution** began in Great Britain in 1765 when the steam engine was first used to run machinery. Before this, a few machines (such as windmills and water wheels) had been used to harness nature, but most machines depended on human and animal power. The resulting **industrial society** is defined by sociologist Herbert Blumer (1990) as one in which goods are produced by machines powered by fuels, instead of by the brute force of humans or animals.

The steam engine was followed by another leap in social inequality. This new technology was far more efficient than anything that preceded it. Just as its surplus was greater, so also were its effects on social life. Those who first used the steam engine accumulated such wealth that in some instances their riches outran the imagination of royalty. Gaining an early position in the markets, the early industrialists were able not only to control the means of production (factories, machinery, tools) but also to dictate people's working conditions. The breakdown of feudal society also helped them to control the workers. Masses of people were thrown off the lands that their ancestors had farmed as tenants for centuries. Having become homeless, these landless peasants moved to the cities. There they faced the choice of stealing, starving, or working for wages barely sufficient to sustain life (the equivalent of a loaf of bread for a day's work).

Workers had no legal right to safe working conditions, nor the right to unionize. Employment was a private contract between the employer and the individual worker. If workers banded together to protest or to ask for higher wages, they were

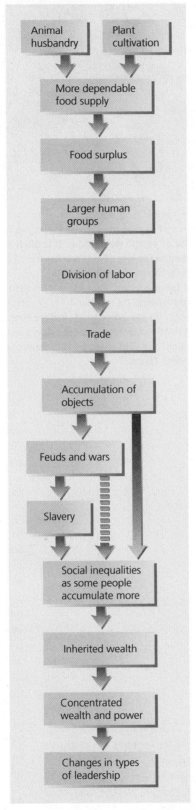

Figure 5.2 Consequences of Animal Domestication and Plant Cultivation

- Animal husbandry
- Plant cultivation
- More dependable food supply
- Food surplus
- Larger human groups
- Division of labor
- Trade
- Accumulation of objects
- Feuds and wars
- Slavery
- Social inequalities as some people accumulate more
- Inherited wealth
- Concentrated wealth and power
- Changes in types of leadership

Source: By the author.

The sociological significance of the social revolutions discussed in the text is that the type of society in which we live determines the kind of people we become. It is obvious, for example, that the orientations to life of this worker would differ markedly from the people in the photo on page 130.

The machinery that ushered in industrial society was met with ambivalence. On one hand, it brought a multitude of welcomed goods. On the other hand, factory time clocks and the incessant production line made people slaves to the very machines they built, a condition illustrated by this classic scene of Charlie Chaplin's in *Modern Times*.

fired. If they returned to the factory, they were arrested for trespassing on private property. Strikes were illegal, and strikers were beaten savagely by the employer's private security force. On some occasions during the early 1900s, U.S. strikers were shot by private police, and even by the National Guard. Against these odds, workers gradually won their fight for better working conditions.

As industrialization continued, more goods were produced, more money circulated, and wealth spread to larger segments of society. As a result, the earlier pattern of growing inequality was reversed. Home ownership became common, as did the ownership of automobiles and an incredible variety of consumer goods. Today's typical worker enjoys a high standard of living in terms of health care, longevity, material possessions, and access to libraries and education. On an even broader level are the abolition of slavery, the shift from monarchies to more representative political systems, greater rights for women and minorities, the rights to a jury trial, to cross-examine witnesses, to vote, and to travel. A recent extension of these equalities is the right to set up your own Internet blog where you can bemoan life in your school or criticize the President.

It is difficult to overstate the sociological principle that the type of society we live in is the fundamental reason for why we become who we are. To see how industrial society affects your life, note that you would not be taking this course if it were not for industrialization. Clearly you would not have a computer, car, cell phone, television, iPod, or your type of clothing or home. You wouldn't even have electric lights. And on a much deeper level, you would not feel the same about life, or have your particular aspirations for the future. Actually, no aspect of your life would be the same; you would be locked into the attitudes and views that come with an agricultural or horticultural way of life.

Postindustrial (Information) Societies

If you were to choose one word that characterizes our society, what would it be? Of the many candidates, the word *change* would have to rank high among them. The primary source of the sweeping changes that are transforming our lives is the technology centering around the microchip. The change is so vast that sociologists say that a new type of society has emerged. They call it the **postindustrial** (or **information**) **society.**

What are the main characteristics of this new society? Unlike the industrial society, its hallmark is not raw materials and manufacturing. Rather, its basic component is *information*. Teachers pass on knowledge to students, while lawyers, physicians, bankers, pilots, and interior decorators sell their specialized knowledge of law, the body, money, aerodynamics, and color schemes to clients. Unlike the factory workers of an industrial society, these individuals don't *produce* anything. Rather, they transmit or use information to provide services that others are willing to pay for.

The United States was the first country to have more than 50 percent of its workforce in service industries such as education, health, research, the government, counseling, banking, investments, insurance, sales, law, and the mass media. Australia, New Zealand, western Europe, and Japan soon followed. This trend away from manufacturing and toward selling information and services shows no sign of letting up.

The changes have been so profound that they have led to a *fourth social revolution*. The microchip is transforming established ways of life, uprooting old perspectives and replacing them with new ones. This new technology allows us to work at home, and while we ride in cars, trucks, and airplanes, to talk to others in distant cities and even to people on the other side of the globe. This tiny device lets us examine the surface of

postindustrial (information) society a society based on information, services, and high technology, rather than on raw materials and manufacturing

Mars and to probe other remote regions of space. It is changing our shopping patterns as we spend billions of dollars on Internet purchases. And because of it, millions of children spend countless hours battling virtual video villains.

Biotech Societies: Is a New Type of Society Emerging?

Can you believe these new products?

- Tobacco that fights cancer. ("Yes, smoke your way to health!")
- Corn that fights herpes and is a contraceptive. ("Corn flakes in the morning—and safe sex all day!")
- Goats whose milk contains spider silk (to make fishing lines and body armor) ("Got milk? The best bulletproofing.")
- Animals that are part human: Human genes have been inserted into animal genes, so they produce medicines for humans. ("Ah, those liver secretions. Good for what ails you.")
- No-Sneeze kitties—hypoallergenic cats at $4,000 each (you can write your own jingle for this one).

I know that this sounds like science fiction, but we *already* have the goats that make spider silk and the part-human animals that produce medicine (Elias 2001; Kristoff 2002; Osborne 2002). The no-sneeze cats are for sale—and there is a waiting list (Rosenthal 2006). Some suggest that the changes in which we are immersed are revolutionary, that we are entering another new type of society. In this new **biotech society,** the economy will center on applying and altering genetic structures—both plant and animal—to produce food, medicine, and materials.

If there is a new society, then when did it begin? There are no firm edges to new societies, for each new one overlaps the one it is replacing. The biotech society could have begun in 1953, when Francis Crick and James Watson identified the double-helix structure of DNA. Or perhaps historians will trace the date to the decoding of the human genome in 2001.

Whether the changes that are swirling around us are part of a new type of society is not the main point. *The sociological significance of these changes is that just as the larger group called society always profoundly affects people's thinking and behavior, so, too, these recent developments will do the same for us.* As society is transformed, we will be swept along with it. The changes will be so extensive that they will transform even the ways we think about the self and life.

Projecting a new type of society so soon after the arrival of the information society is risky. The wedding of genetics and economics could turn out to be simply another aspect of our information society—or we really may have just stepped into a new type of society. In either case, we can anticipate revolutionary changes in health care (prevention, instead of treating disease) and, with cloning and bioengineering, perhaps even changes in the human species. The Sociology and the New Technology box on the next page examines implications of cloning.

IN SUM Our society sets boundaries around our lives. By laying out a framework of statuses, roles, groups, and social institutions, society establishes the values and beliefs that prevail. It also determines the type and extent of social inequality. These factors, in turn, set the stage for relationships between men and women, the young and the elderly, racial–ethnic groups, the rich and the poor, and so on.

It is difficult to overstate the sociological principle that the type of society in which we live is the fundamental reason why we become who we are—why we feel about things the way we do, and even why we think our particular thoughts. On the obvious level, if you lived in a hunting and gathering society you would not be listening to your favorite music, watching TV programs, or playing video games. On a deeper level, you would not feel the same about life or hold your particular aspirations for the future.

Finally, we should note that not all the world's societies will go through the transformations shown in Figure 5.1 (page 129). Whether any hunting and gathering societies will

biotech society a society whose economy increasingly centers around the application of genetics—human genetics for medicine, and plant and animal genetics for the production of food and materials

"So, You Want to Be Yourself?" Cloning in the Coming Biotech Society

NO TYPE OF SOCIETY ENDS ABRUPTLY. The edges are fuzzy, and the new one often overlaps the old. As the information society matures, it looks as though it is being overtaken by a biotech society. Let's try to peer over the edge of our current society to glimpse the one that may be coming. What will life be like? There are many issues we could examine, but since space is limited, let's consider just one: cloning.

Consider this scenario:

Your four-year-old daughter has drowned, and you can't get over your sorrow. You go to the regional cloning clinic, where you have stored DNA from all members of your family. You pay the standard fee, and the director hires a surrogate mother to bring your daughter back as a newborn.

Will cloning humans become a reality? Since human embryos already have been cloned, it seems inevitable that some group somewhere will complete the process. If cloning humans becomes routine—well, consider these scenarios:

Suppose that a couple can't have children. Testing shows that the husband is sterile. The couple talk about their dilemma, and the wife agrees to have her husband's genetic material implanted into one of her eggs. Would this woman, in effect, be rearing her husband as a little boy?

Or suppose that you love your mother dearly, and she is dying. With her permission, you decide to clone her. Who is the clone? Would you be rearing your own mother?

What if a woman gave birth to her own clone? Would the clone be her daughter or her sister?

When genetic duplicates appear, the questions of what humans are, what their relationship is to their "parents," and indeed what "parents" and children" are, will be brought up at every kitchen table.

for your Consideration

As these scenarios show, the issue of cloning provokes profound questions. Perhaps the most weighty concerns the future of society. Let's suppose that mass cloning becomes possible.

Many people object that cloning is immoral, but some will argue the opposite. They will ask why we should leave human reproduction to people who have inferior traits—genetic diseases, low IQs, perhaps even the propensity for crime and violence. They will suggest that we select people with the finer characteristics—high creative ability, high intelligence, compassion, and a propensity for peace.

Let's assume that scientists have traced these characteristics—along with the ability to appreciate and create beautiful poetry, music, and architecture; to excel in mathematics, science, and other intellectual pursuits; and to be successful in love—to genetics. Do you think that it should be our moral obligation to populate society with people like this? To try to build a society that is better for all—one without terrorism, war, violence, and greed? Could this perhaps even be our evolutionary destiny?

Source: Based on Kaebnick 2000; McGee 2000; Bjerklie et al. 2001; Davis 2001; Weiss 2004; Regalado 2005.

---

survive, however, remains to be seen. Perhaps a few will, maybe kept on "small reserves" that will be off limits to developers—but open to guided "ethnotours" at a hefty fee.

Now that we have reviewed the major historical shifts in societies, let's turn to groups within society. Just how do they affect our lives?

Groups Within Society

Sociologist Emile Durkheim (1893/1933) wondered what could be done to prevent *anomie* (AN-uh-mee), that bewildering sense of not fitting in, of not belonging. Durkheim found the answer in small groups. He said that small groups stand as a buffer between the individual and the larger society. If it weren't for these groups, we would feel oppressed by that huge, amorphous entity known as society. By providing intimate relationships, small groups give us a sense of meaning and purpose, helping to prevent anomie.

Before we examine groups in more detail, we should distinguish some terms. Two terms sometimes confused with "group" are *aggregate* and *category*. An **aggregate** consists of individuals who temporarily share the same physical space but who do not see themselves as belonging together. People standing in a checkout line or drivers waiting at a red light are an aggregate. A **category** is a statistic. It consists of people who share similar characteristics, such as all college women who wear glasses or all men over 6 feet tall. Unlike groups, the individuals who make up a category neither interact with one another nor take one another into account. The members of a *group,* in contrast, think of themselves as belonging together, and they interact with one another. These concepts are illustrated in the photos on the next page.

Primary Groups

Our first group, the family, gives us our basic orientations to life. Later, among friends, we find more intimacy and an additional sense of belonging. These groups are what sociologist Charles Cooley called **primary groups.** By providing intimate, face-to-face interaction, they give us an identity, a feeling of who we are. As Cooley (1909) put it,

> By primary groups I mean those characterized by intimate face-to-face association and co-operation. They are primary in several senses, but chiefly in that they are fundamental in forming the social nature and ideals of the individual.

Producing a Mirror Within   Cooley called primary groups the "springs of life." By this, he means that primary groups, such as family and friends, are essential to our emotional well-being. As humans, we have an intense need for face-to-face interaction that generates feelings of self-esteem. By offering a sense of belonging and a feeling of being appreciated—and sometimes even loved—primary groups are uniquely equipped to meet this basic need. From our opening vignette, you can see that gangs are also primary groups.

Primary groups are also significant because their values and attitudes become fused into our identity. We internalize their views, which then become the lenses through which we view life. Even as adults—no matter how far we move away from our childhood roots—early primary groups remain "inside" us. There, they continue to form part of the perspective from which we look out onto the world. Ultimately, then, it is difficult, if not impossible, for us to separate the self from our primary groups, for the self and our groups merge into a "we."

Secondary Groups

Compared with primary groups, **secondary groups** are larger, more anonymous, more formal, and more impersonal. Secondary groups are based on some common interest or activity, and their members are likely to interact on the basis of specific statuses, such as president, manager, worker, or student. Examples are a college class, the American Sociological Association, and the Democratic Party. Contemporary society could not function without secondary groups. They are part of the way we get our education, make our living, spend our money, and use our leisure time.

As necessary as secondary groups are for contemporary life, they often fail to satisfy our deep needs for intimate association. Consequently, *secondary groups tend to break down into primary groups.* At school and work, we form friendships. Our interaction with our friends is so important that we sometimes feel that if it weren't for them, school or work "would drive us crazy." The primary groups that we form within secondary groups, then, serve as a buffer between ourselves and the demands that secondary groups place on us.

In-Groups and Out-Groups

Groups toward which we feel loyalty are called **in-groups;** those toward which we feel antagonism are called **out-groups.** For Monster Kody in our opening vignette, the Crips

aggregate individuals who temporarily share the same physical space but who do not see themselves as belonging together

category people who have similar characteristics

primary group a group characterized by intimate, long-term, face-to-face association and cooperation

secondary group compared with a primary group, a larger, relatively temporary, more anonymous, formal, and impersonal group based on some interest or activity. Its members are likely to interact on the basis of specific statuses

in-groups groups toward which we feel loyalty

out-groups groups toward which we feel antagonism

Categories, Aggregates, Primary and Secondary Groups

Groups have a deep impact on our views and attitudes, even what we feel and think about life. Yet, as illustrated by these photos, not everything that appears to be a group is actually a group in the sociological sense.

Secondary groups are larger and more anonymous, formal, and impersonal than primary groups. Why is this photo of a political convention an example of a secondary group?

Aggregates are simply people who happen to be in the same place at the same time.

Primary groups such as the family play a key role in the development of the self. As a small group, the family also serves as a buffer from the often-threatening larger group known as society. The family has been of primary significance in forming the basic orientations of this couple, as it will be for their daughter.

The outstanding trait that these three people have in common does not make them a group, but a **category.**

were an in-group, while the Bloods were an out-group. That the Crips—and we—make such a fundamental division of the world has far-reaching consequences for our lives.

Producing Loyalty, a Sense of Superiority, and Rivalries Identification with a group often generates not only a sense of belonging, but also loyalty and feelings of superiority. These, in turn, often produce rivalries. Usually the rivalries are mild, such as sports rivalries among neighboring towns, in which the most extreme act is likely to be the furtive invasion of the out-group's territory to steal a mascot, paint a rock, or uproot a goal post. The consequences of in-group membership can also be discrimination, hatred, and, as we saw in our opening vignette, even participation in murder.

Implications for a Socially Diverse Society The strong identifications with members of our in-groups are the basis of many gender and racial-ethnic divisions. As sociologist Robert Merton (1968) observed, our favoritism leads to biased perception. Following a fascinating double standard, we tend to view the traits of our in-group as virtues, while we see those *same* traits as vices in out-groups. Men may perceive an aggressive man as assertive but an aggressive woman as pushy. They may think that a male employee who doesn't speak up "knows when to keep his mouth shut," while they consider a quiet woman as too timid to make it in the business world.

To divide the world into "we" and "they" poses a danger for a pluralistic society. For the Nazis, the Jews were an out-group that came to symbolize evil. One consequence of biased perception is that harming others can come to be viewed as justifiable. The Nazis weren't alone in their views; many ordinary, "good" Germans defended the Holocaust as "dirty work" that someone had to do (Hughes 1962/2005). This principle might seem to pertain only to the past, but it continues today—and likely always will. Consider what happened following the terrorist attacks of 9/11. Viewing Arabs as sinister, bloodthirsty villains, top U.S. officials approved "cruel, inhuman, and degrading" treatment of prisoners—as long as they didn't call it torture (Gonzales 2002). A prominent civil libertarian at Harvard Law School went further, suggesting that judges should be able to issue "torture warrants" (Shulz 2002). This would give torture a legal standing, making it a tidy matter. Cruel interrogation and torture—for the sake of the lives they might save—quickly became "dirty work" that someone had to do.

Economic downturns are especially perilous in this regard. The Nazis took power during a depression so severe that it was wiping out the middle classes. If such a depression were to occur in the United States, immigrants would be transformed from "nice people who do jobs that Americans think are beneath them" to "sneaky people who steal jobs from friends and family." A national anti-immigration policy would follow, accompanied by a resurgence of hate groups such as the neo-Nazis, the Ku Klux Klan, and skinheads.

In short, to divide the world into in-groups and out-groups is a natural part of social life. But in addition to bringing functional consequences, it can bring dysfunctional ones.

"So long, Bill. This is my club. You can't come in."

How our participation in social groups shapes our self-concept is a focus of symbolic interactionists. In this process, knowing who we are *not* is as significant as knowing who we are.

Reference Groups

Suppose you have just been offered a good job. It pays double what you hope to make even after you graduate from college. You have only two days to make up your mind. If you accept it, you will have to drop out of college. As you consider the matter, thoughts like this may go through your mind: "My friends will say I'm a fool if I don't take the job . . . but Dad and Mom will practically go crazy. They've made sacrifices for me, and

All of us have *reference groups*—the groups we use as standards to evaluate ourselves. How do you think the reference groups of these members of the KKK who are demonstrating in Jaspar, Texas, differ from those of the police officer who is protecting their right of free speech? Although the KKK and this police officer use different groups to evaluate their attitudes and behaviors, the process is the same.

they'll be crushed if I don't finish college. They've always said I've got to get my education first, that good jobs will always be there. . . . But, then, I'd like to see the look on the faces of those neighbors who said I'd never amount to much!"

This is an example of how people use **reference groups,** the groups we use as standards to evaluate ourselves. Your reference groups may include your family, neighbors, teachers, classmates, co-workers, and the Scouts or the members of a church, synagogue, or mosque. If you were like Monster Kody in our opening vignette, the "set" would be your main reference group. Even a group you don't belong to can be a reference group. For example, if you are thinking about going to graduate school, graduate students or members of the profession you want to join may form a reference group. You would consider their standards as you evaluate your grades or writing skills.

Providing Standards to Evaluate Ourselves

Reference groups exert tremendous influence over our lives. For example, if you want to become a corporate executive, you might start to dress more formally, try to improve your vocabulary, read the *Wall Street Journal,* and change your major to business or law. In contrast, if you want to become a rock musician, you might wear jewelry in several places where you have pierced your body, get elaborate tattoos, dress in ways your parents and many of your peers consider extreme, read *Rolling Stone,* drop out of college, and hang around clubs and rock groups.

Exposure to Contradictory Standards in a Socially Diverse Society From these examples, you can see how we use reference groups to evaluate our behavior. When we see ourselves as measuring up to a reference group's standards, we feel no conflict. If our behavior—or even aspirations—does not match the group's standards, however, the mismatch can lead to inner turmoil. For example, to want to become a corporate executive would create no inner turmoil for most of us. It would, however, if you had grown up in an Amish home, for the Amish strongly disapprove of such aspirations for their children. They ban high school and college education, three-piece suits, and corporate employment. Similarly, if you wanted to become a soldier and your parents were dedicated pacifists, you likely would feel deep conflict, as your parents would hold quite different aspirations for you.

Given the social diversity of our society and our social mobility, as we grow up, many of us are exposed to contradictory ideas and standards from the groups that become significant to us. The "internal recordings" that play contradictory messages from these reference groups, then, are one price we pay for our social mobility.

Social Networks

Although we live in a huge and diverse society, we don't experience social life as a sea of nameless, strange faces. Instead, we interact within social networks. The term **social network** refers to people who are linked to one another. Your social network includes your family, friends, acquaintances, people at work and school, and even your "friends of friends." Think of your social network as lines that extend outward from yourself, gradually encompassing more and more people.

If you are a member of a large group, you probably associate regularly with a few people within that group. In a sociology class I was teaching at a commuter campus, six women who didn't know one another ended up working together on a project. They got along well, and they began to sit together. Eventually they planned a Christmas

reference group a group that we use as a standard to evaluate ourselves

social network the social ties radiating outward from the self that link people together

We all use *reference groups* to evaluate our accomplishments, failures, values, and attitudes. We compare what we see in ourselves with what we perceive as normative in our reference groups. As is evident in these two photos, the reference groups these youths are using are not likely to lead them to the same social destination.

party at one of their homes. This type of social network, the clusters within a group, or its internal factions, is called a **clique** (cleek).

The analysis of social networks has moved from theory and laboratory study to the practical world. On a more personal level, a fascinating development in social networks is *facebooking*, the topic of the Sociology and the New Technology box on the next page.

The Small World Phenomenon Social scientists have wondered just how extensive the connections are between social networks. If you list everyone you know, each of those individuals lists everyone he or she knows, and you keep doing this, would almost everyone in the United States eventually be included on those lists?

It would be too cumbersome to test this hypothesis by drawing up such lists, but psychologist Stanley Milgram (1933–1984) came up with an interesting idea. In a classic study known as "the small world phenomenon," Milgram (1967) addressed a letter to "targets": the wife of a divinity student in Cambridge and a stockbroker in Boston. He sent the letter to "starters," who did not know these people. He asked them to send the letter to someone they knew on a first-name basis, someone they thought might know the "target." The recipients, in turn, were asked to mail the letter to someone they knew who might know the "target," and so on. The question was: Would the letters ever reach the "target"? If so, how long would the chain be?

Think of yourself as part of this study. What would you do if you were a "starter," but the "target" lived in a state in which you knew no one? You would send the letter to someone you know who might know someone in that state. This, Milgram reported, is just what happened. Although none of the senders knew the targets, the letters reached the designated individual in an average of just six jumps.

Milgram's study caught the public's fancy, leading to the phrase, "six degrees of separation." This expression means that, on average, everyone in the United States is separated by just six individuals. Milgram's conclusions have become so popular that a game, "Six Degrees of Kevin Bacon," was built around it.

Is the Small World Phenomenon an Academic Myth? Unfortunately, things are not this simple. There is a problem with Milgram's research, as psychologist Judith Kleinfeld (2002a, 2002b) discovered when she decided to replicate Milgram's study.

clique a cluster of people within a larger group who choose to interact with one another; an internal faction

> SOCIOLOGY and the NEW TECHNOLOGY

Facebooking: Social Networks Online

MAKING NEW FRIENDS AND MAINTAINING friendships can take effort. You have to clean up, put on clothes, leave your room, and engage in conversations. The talk can turn in directions that don't interest you, and people can drop into your group that you don't particularly care for. Situations can arise that make you feel awkward or embarrassed. Maybe you would like to disengage for a few minutes—to take a little power nap or to read a book. You can't do this without offending someone.

Not so with facebooking. You are in charge. Talk with people when you want. Stop when you want.

This is part of the allure of facebooking. The facebook is like an ever-changing, online yearbook. To find people with similar interests, just type in that interest. Your favorite book is Kerouac's *On The Road*? *The DaVinci Code*? *Pride and Prejudice*? Your favorite movie is *Fight Club*? *Barbarella*? *Reefer Madness*? You enjoy *J. Crew* or *Wheezer*? Your favorite activity is making out? Fiddling with guns? Looking at pink shoes? And you want to find people who share your interest? Just a mouse-click away.

You can even form your own group—and invite others to join it. The group can be as esoteric as you prefer. Some actual groups: "Ann Coulter Fan Club." "Republican Princesses." "Preppy Since Conception." "Cancer Corner" (for students who love to smoke). "I Want to Be a Trophy Wife and You Can't Stop Me." There is even an "anti-group" group.

You see a cute guy or girl in class. Back in your room, with one click you learn not only their e-mail address but also the other classes they are taking and their interests. This will give you good pick-up info. That person won't even know they've been cyberstalked.

One woman who contacted a man after reading his profile said, "We had all the same interests. Books. Movies. Everything. It was a little weird, though—like dating a website."

Facebooking is free. If you have a school e-mail address, just answer a few questions, post your picture—and start making friends. You can do a search of your own campus or even locate old friends who might be attending college somewhere else.

A photo blinks onto your computer screen, and someone asks to be listed as part of your social network. You consider it for a couple of seconds, faintly recalling the individual from high school, and you click yes. You have just "friended" him.

You have control. You can set the privacy settings to determine who can view which parts of your profile: the contact information, personal information, courses you are taking, and a list of your friends.

Many students find the allure of facebooking irresistible, a new form of creative procrastination. And in college, there is so much to procrastinate from.

"The Wall" is a favorite facebooking site. On this virtual "wall" friends scrawl messages, some fanciful ("Meathead was here") and some private ("My love for you grows with each passing minute. I can hardly wait until I'm in your arms again.") In our new online world, private messages are proudly made public.

Change your mind about someone? Just click the "de-friend" button. But this is risky. It's a slap in the face.

Not only do you see a list of your friends but also you can track your social network—the friends of friends, the people you can reach in three or fewer steps. In just three steps, your network could balloon to several thousand.

Facebooking has a touch of whimsy. The poke option lets you "poke" others. No one knows what the "poke" really means, but it seems to be, "Hey! How ya doin'?" The poke can be a conversation starter, like "zup" ("What's up?"), a tap on the shoulder as it were.

The usual popularity contest has reared its head, of course. Who has the most friends listed? Some students even contact members they've never met just to ask to be "friended." Larger numbers give them bragging rights. Pathetic, but true.

There is something strange about groups that exist only in cyberspace, profiles that might be faked, and friends you may not even know. But life itself is strange.

Facebooking's implications extend beyond dates and popularity. Employers have used facebooking to check out some well-dressed, serious job applicants. There they discovered their prospective employees bragging about getting drunk, getting laid, and smoking substances other than tobacco . . .

Source: Based on Copeland 2004; Sales 2004; Schackner 2004; Coughlan 2006.

When she went to the archives at Yale University Library to get more details, she found that Milgram had stacked the deck in favor of finding a small world. The "starters" came from mailing lists of people who were likely to have higher incomes and therefore were not representative of average people. In addition, one of the "targets" was a stockbroker, and that person's "starters" were investors in blue-chip stocks. Kleinfeld also found another discrepancy: On average, only 30 percent of the letters reached their "target." In one of Milgram's studies, the success rate was just 5 percent.

Since most letters did *not* reach their targets, even with the deck stacked in favor of success, we can draw the *opposite* conclusion from the one that Milgram reported: People who don't know one another are dramatically separated by social barriers. How great the barriers are is illustrated by another attempt to replicate Milgram's study, this one using e-mail. Only 384 of 24,000 chains reached their targets (Dodds et al. 2003).

As Kleinfeld says, "Rather than living in a small world, we may live in a world that looks a lot like a bowl of lumpy oatmeal, with many small worlds loosely connected and perhaps some small worlds not connected at all." Somehow, I don't think that the phrase, "lumpy oatmeal phenomenon," will become standard, but the criticism of Milgram's research is valid.

Implications for a Socially Diverse Society   Besides geography, the barriers that separate us into many small worlds are primarily those of social class, gender, and race-ethnicity. Overcoming these social barriers is difficult because even our own social networks contribute to social inequality, a topic that we explore in the Cultural Diversity box on the next page.

Implications for Science   Kleinfeld's revelations of Milgram's research reinforce the need of replication, a topic discussed in the Chapter 1. For our knowledge of social life, we cannot depend on single studies—there may be problems of generalizability on the one hand, or those of negligence or even fraud on the other. Replication by objective researchers is essential to build and advance solid social knowledge.

A New Group: Electronic Communities

In the 1990s, a new type of human group, the **electronic community,** made its appearance. People "meet" online in chat rooms to talk about almost any conceivable topic, from donkey racing and bird-watching to sociology and quantum physics. Most news groups are simply a way of communicating. Some, however, meet our definition of *group,* people who interact with one another and who think of themselves as belonging together. They pride themselves on the distinctive nature of their interest and knowledge—factors that give them a common identity and bind them together

Group Dynamics

As you know from personal experience, the lively interaction *within* groups—who does what with whom—has profound consequences for how you adjust to life. Sociologists use the term **group dynamics** to refer to how groups influence us and how we affect groups. Let's consider how the size of a group makes a difference, and then examine leadership, conformity, and decision making.

Before doing this, we should see how sociologists define the term *small group.* In a **small group,** there are few enough members that each one can interact directly with all the other members. Small groups can be either primary or secondary. A wife, husband, and children make up a primary small group, as do workers who take their breaks together, while bidders at an auction and students in an introductory sociology class are secondary small groups.

Effects of Group Size on Stability and Intimacy

Writing in the early 1900s, sociologist Georg Simmel (1858–1918) noted the significance of group size. He used the term **dyad** for the smallest possible group, which consists of two people. Dyads, which include marriages, love affairs, and close friendships, show two distinct qualities. First, they are the most intense or intimate of human groups. Because only two people are involved, the interaction is focused on them. Second, because dyads require that both members participate and be committed, it takes

electronic community individuals who regularly interact with one another on the Internet and who think of themselves as belonging together

group dynamics the ways in which individuals affect groups and the ways in which groups influence individuals

small group a group small enough for everyone to interact directly with all the other members

dyad the smallest possible group, consisting of two persons

How Our Own Social Networks Perpetuate Social Inequality

CONSIDER SOME OF THE PRINCIPLES we have reviewed. People tend to form in-groups with which they identify; they use reference groups to evaluate their attitudes and behavior; and they interact in social networks. Our in-groups, reference groups, and social networks are likely to consist of people whose backgrounds are similar to our own. This means that, for most of us, just as social inequality is built into society, so it is built into our own relationships. One consequence is that we tend to perpetuate social inequality.

To see why, suppose that an outstanding job—great pay, interesting work, opportunity for advancement—has just opened up where you work. Who are you going to tell? Most likely it will be someone you know, a friend or at least someone to whom you owe a favor. And most likely your social network is made up of people who look much like yourself—especially their race-ethnicity, age, social class, and probably also, gender. This tends to keep good jobs moving in the direction of people whose characteristics are similar to those of the people already in an organization. You can see how our social networks both reflect the inequality that characterizes our society and help to perpetuate it.

Consider a network of white men who are established in an organization. As they learn of opportunities (jobs, investments, real estate, and so on), they share this information with their networks. Opportunities and good jobs flow to people who have characteristics similar to their own. Those who benefit from this information, in turn, reciprocate with similar information when they learn of it. This bypasses people who have different characteristics, in this ex-

Social networks, **which open and close doors of opportunity, are important for careers. Despite the official program of sociology conventions, much of the "real" business centers around renewing and extending social networks.**

ample women and minorities, while it perpetuates the "good old boy'" network. No intentional discrimination need be involved.

To overcome this barrier, women and minorities do **networking.** They try to meet people who can help advance their careers. Like the "good old boys," they go to parties and join clubs, churches, synagogues, mosques, and political parties. African American leaders, for example, cultivate a network of African American leaders. As a result, the network of African American leaders is so tight that one-fifth of the entire national African American leadership are personal acquaintances. Add some "friends of a friend," and *three-fourths* of the entire leadership belong to the same network (Taylor 1992).

Similarly, women cultivate a network of women. As a result, some women who reach top positions end up in a circle so tight that the term "new girl" network is being used, especially in the field of law. Remembering those who helped them and sympathetic to those who are trying to get ahead, these women tend to steer business to other women. Like the "good old boys" who preceded them, the new insiders have a ready set of reasons to justify their exclusionary practice (Jacobs 1997).

for your Consideration

The perpetuation of social inequality does not require intentional discrimination. Just as social inequality is built into society, so is it built into our personal relationships. How do you think your own social network helps to perpetuate social inequality? How do you think we can break this cycle? (The key must center on creating diversity in social networks.)

---

just one member to lose interest for the dyad to collapse. In larger groups, by contrast, even if one member withdraws, the group can continue, for its existence does not depend on any single member (Simmel 1950).

A **triad** is a group of three people. As Simmel noted, the addition of a third person fundamentally changes the group. With three people, interaction between the first two decreases. This can create strain. For example, with the birth of a child, hardly any aspect of a couple's relationship goes untouched. Attention focuses on the baby, and interaction between the husband and wife diminishes. Despite the difficulty that this presents—including in many instances the husband's jealousy that he is getting less attention from his wife—the marriage usually becomes stronger. Although the intensity of

networking using one's social networks for some gain

triad a group of three people

Japanese who work for the same firm think of themselves more as a group or team, Americans perceive themselves more as individuals. Japanese corporations use many techniques to encourage group identity, such as making group exercise a part of the work day. Similarity of appearance and activity helps to fuse group identity and company loyalty.

interaction is less in triads, they are inherently stronger and give greater stability to a relationship.

Yet, as Simmel noted, triads, too, are inherently unstable. They tend to form **coalitions**—some group members aligning themselves against others. In a triad, it is not uncommon for two members to feel a strong bond and to prefer one another. This leaves the third person feeling hurt and excluded. Another characteristic of triads is that they often produce an arbitrator or mediator, someone who tries to settle disagreements between the other two. In one-child families, you can often observe both of these characteristics of triads—coalitions and arbitration.

The general principle is this: *As a small group grows larger, it becomes more stable, but its intensity, or intimacy, decreases.* To see why, look at Figure 5.3. As each new person comes into a group, the connections among people multiply. In a dyad, there is only 1 relationship; in a triad, there are 3; in a group of four, 6; in a group of five, 10. If we expand the group to six, we have 15 relationships, while a group of seven yields 21 relationships. If we continue adding members, we soon are unable to follow the connections: A group of eight has 28 possible relationships; a group of nine, 36 relationships; a group of ten, 45; and so on.

It is not only the number of relationships that makes larger groups more stable. As groups grow, they also tend to develop a more formal structure to accomplish their goals. For example, leaders emerge and more specialized roles come into play. This often results in such familiar offices as president, secretary, and treasurer. This structure provides a framework that helps the group survive over time.

coalition the alignment of some members of a group against others

Effects of Group Size on Attitudes and Behavior

Imagine that your social psychology professors have asked you to join a few students to discuss your adjustment to college life. When you arrive, they tell you that to make the discussion anonymous they

Figure 5.3 **The Effects of Group Size on Relationships**

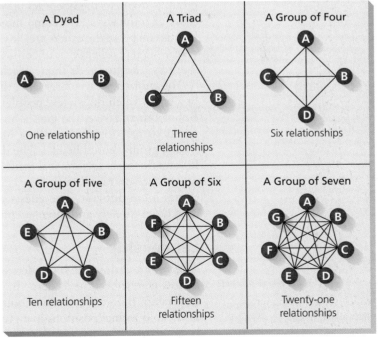

A Dyad — One relationship

A Triad — Three relationships

A Group of Four — Six relationships

A Group of Five — Ten relationships

A Group of Six — Fifteen relationships

A Group of Seven — Twenty-one relationships

Group size has a significant influence on how people interact. When a group changes from a dyad (two people) to a triad (three people), the relationships among the participants undergo a shift. How do you think the birth of this child affected the relationship between the mother and father?

want you to sit unseen in a booth. You will participate in the discussion over an intercom, talking when your microphone comes on. The professors say that they will not listen to the conversation, and they leave.

You find the format somewhat strange, to say the least, but you go along with it. You have not seen the other students in their booths, but when they talk about their experiences, you find yourself becoming wrapped up in the problems that they begin to share. One student even mentions how frightening he has found college because of his history of epileptic seizures. Later, you hear this individual breathe heavily into the microphone. Then he stammers and cries for help. A crashing noise follows, and you imagine him lying helpless on the floor.

Nothing but an eerie silence follows. What do you do?

Your professors, John Darley and Bibb Latané (1968), staged the whole thing, but you don't know this. No one had a seizure. In fact, no one was even in the other booths. Everything, except your comments, was on tape.

Some participants were told that they would be discussing the topic with just one other student, others with two, others with three, and so on. Darley and Latané found that all students who thought they were part of a dyad rushed out to help. If they thought they were part of a triad, only 80 percent went to help—and they were slower in leaving the booth. In six-person groups, only 60 percent went to see what was wrong—and they were even slower.

This experiment demonstrates how deeply group size influences our attitudes and behavior: It even affects our willingness to help one another. Students in the dyad knew that it was up to them to help the other student. The professor was gone, and if they didn't help there was no one else. In the larger groups, including the triad, students felt *a diffusion of responsibility:* Giving help was no more their responsibility than anyone else's.

You probably have observed the second consequence of group size firsthand. When a group is small, its members act informally, but as the group grows, the members lose their sense of intimacy and become more formal with one another. No longer can the members assume that the others are "insiders" in sympathy with what they say. Now they must take a "larger audience" into consideration, and instead of merely "talking," they begin to "address" the group. As their speech becomes more formal, their body language stiffens.

You probably have observed a third aspect of group dynamics, too. In the early stages of a party, when only a few people are present, almost everyone talks with everyone else. But as others arrive, the guests break into smaller groups. Some hosts, who want their guests to mix together, make a nuisance of themselves trying to achieve *their* idea of what a group should be like. The division into small groups is inevitable, however, for it follows the basic sociological principles that we have just reviewed. Because the addition of each person rapidly increases connections (in this case, "talk lines"), conversation becomes more difficult. The guests break into smaller groups in which they can look at each other directly and interact comfortably with one another.

Leadership

All of us are influenced by leaders, so it is important to understand leadership. Let's look at how people become leaders, the types of leaders there are, and their different styles of leadership. Before we do this, though, it is important to clarify that leaders don't necessarily hold formal positions in a group. **Leaders** are simply people who influence the behaviors, opinions, or attitudes of others. Even a group of friends has leaders.

leader someone who influences other people

Adolf Hitler, shown here in Nuremberg in 1933, was one of the most influential—and evil—persons of the twentieth century. Why did so many people follow Hitler? This question stimulated the research by Stanley Milgram (discussed on pages 147–149).

Who Becomes a Leader?   Are leaders born with characteristics that propel them to the forefront of a group? No sociologist would agree with such an idea. In general, people who become leaders are perceived by group members as strongly representing their values, or as able to lead a group out of a crisis (Trice and Beyer 1991). Leaders also tend to be more talkative and to express determination and self-confidence.

These findings may not be surprising, as such traits appear to be related to leadership. Researchers, however, have also discovered traits that seem to have no bearing on the ability to lead. For example, taller people and those who are judged better looking are more likely to become leaders (Stodgill 1974; Judge and Cable 2004). The taller and more attractive are also likely to earn more, but that is another story (Deck 1968; Feldman 1972; Case and Paxson 2006; Katz 2007).

Many other factors underlie people's choice of leaders, most of which are quite subtle. A simple experiment performed by social psychologists Lloyd Howells and Selwyn Becker (1962) uncovered one of these factors. They formed groups of five people who did not know one another, seating them at a rectangular table, three on one side and two on the other. After discussing a topic for a set period of time, each group chose a leader. The findings are startling: Although only 40 percent of the people sat on the two-person side, 70 percent of the leaders emerged from that side. The explanation is that we tend to direct more interactions to people facing us than to people to the side of us.

Types of Leaders   Groups have two types of leaders (Bales 1950, 1953; Cartwright and Zander 1968). The first is easy to recognize. This person, called an **instrumental leader** (or *task-oriented leader*), tries to keep the group moving toward its goals. These leaders try to keep group members from getting sidetracked, reminding them of what they are trying to accomplish. The **expressive leader** (or *socioemotional leader*), in contrast, usually is not recognized as a leader, but he or she certainly is one. This person is likely to crack jokes, to offer sympathy, or to do other things that help to lift the group's morale. Both types of leadership are essential: the one to keep the group on track, the other to increase harmony and minimize conflicts.

It is difficult for the same person to be both an instrumental and an expressive leader, for these roles contradict one another. Because instrumental leaders are task oriented, they sometimes create friction as they prod the group to get on with the job. Their actions often cost them popularity. Expressive leaders, in contrast, who stimulate personal bonds and reduce friction, are usually more popular (Olmsted and Hare 1978).

instrumental leader an individual who tries to keep the group moving toward its goals; also known as a *task-oriented leader*

expressive leader an individual who increases harmony and minimizes conflict in a group; also known as a *socioemotional leader*

leadership styles ways in
which people express their
leadership

authoritarian leader an individual who leads by giving
orders

democratic leader an individual who leads by trying to
reach a consensus

laissez-faire leader an individual who leads by being
highly permissive

Leadership Styles   Let's suppose that the president of your college has asked you to head a task force to determine how the college can improve race relations on campus. Although this position requires you to be an instrumental leader, you can adopt a number of **leadership styles,** or ways of expressing yourself as a leader. The three basic styles are those of **authoritarian leader,** one who gives orders; **democratic leader,** one who tries to gain a consensus; and **laissez-faire leader,** one who is highly permissive. Which style should you choose?

Social psychologists Ronald Lippitt and Ralph White (1958) carried out a classic study of these leadership styles. Boys who were matched for IQ, popularity, physical energy, and leadership were assigned to "craft clubs" made up of five boys each. The experimenters trained adult men in the three leadership styles. As the researchers peered through peep-holes, taking notes and making movies, each adult rotated among the clubs, playing all three styles to control possible influences of their individual personalities.

The *authoritarian* leaders assigned tasks to the boys and told them exactly what to do. They also praised or condemned the boys' work arbitrarily, giving no explanation for why they judged it good or bad. The *democratic* leaders held discussions with the boys, outlining the steps that would help them reach their goals. They also suggested alternative approaches and let the boys work at their own pace. When they evaluated the projects, they gave "facts" as the bases for their decisions. The *laissez-faire* leaders were passive. They gave the boys almost total freedom to do as they wished. They offered help when asked, but made few suggestions. They did not evaluate the boys' projects, either positively or negatively.

The results? The boys who had authoritarian leaders grew dependent on their leader and showed a high degree of internal solidarity. They also became either aggressive or apathetic, with the aggressive boys growing hostile toward their leader. In contrast, the boys who had democratic leaders were friendlier, and looked to one another for mutual approval. They did less scapegoating, and when the leader left the room they continued to work at a steadier pace. The boys with laissez-faire leaders asked more questions, but they made fewer decisions. They were notable for their lack of achievement. The researchers concluded that the democratic style of leadership works best. Their conclusion, however, may have been biased, as the researchers favored a democratic style of leadership in the first place (Olmsted and Hare 1978). Apparently, this same bias in studies of leadership continues (Cassel 1999).

You may have noticed that only boys and men were involved in this experiment. It is interesting to speculate how the results might differ if we were to repeat the experiment with all-girl groups and with mixed groups of girls and boys—and if we used both men and women as leaders. Perhaps you will become the sociologist to study such variations of this classic experiment.

Leadership Styles in Changing Situations   Different situations require different styles of leadership. Suppose, for example, that you are leading a dozen backpackers in the Sierra Madre mountains north of Los Angeles, and it is time to make dinner. A laissez-faire style would be appropriate if the backpackers had brought their own food, or perhaps a democratic style if everyone were supposed to pitch in. Authoritarian leadership—you telling the hikers how to prepare their meals—would create resentment. This, in turn, would likely interfere with meeting the primary goal of the group, which in this case is to have a good time while enjoying nature.

Now assume the same group but a different situation: One of your party is lost, and a blizzard is on its way. This situation calls for you to take charge and be authoritarian. To simply shrug your shoulders and say, "You figure it out," would invite disaster—and probably a lawsuit.

The Power of Peer Pressure: The Asch Experiment

How influential are groups in our lives? To answer this, let's look first at *conformity* in the sense of going along with our peers. Our peers have no authority over us, only the influence that we allow.

Imagine that you are taking a course in social psychology with Dr. Solomon Asch and you have agreed to participate in an experiment. As you enter his laboratory, you see seven chairs, five of them already filled by other students. You are given the sixth. Soon the seventh person arrives. Dr. Asch stands at the front of the room next to a covered easel. He explains that he will first show a large card with a vertical line on it, then another card with three vertical lines. Each of you is to tell him which of the three lines matches the line on the first card (see Figure 5.4).

Dr. Asch then uncovers the first card with the single line and the comparison card with the three lines. The correct answer is easy, for two of the lines are obviously wrong, and one is exactly right. Each person, in order, states his or her answer aloud. You all answer correctly. The second trial is just as easy, and you begin to wonder why you are there.

Then on the third trial, something unexpected happens. Just as before, it is easy to tell which lines match. The first student, however, gives a wrong answer. The second gives the same incorrect answer. So do the third and the fourth. By now, you are wondering what is wrong. How will the person next to you answer? You can hardly believe it when he, too, gives the same wrong answer. Then it is your turn, and you give what you know is the right answer. The seventh person also gives the same wrong answer.

On the next trial, the same thing happens. You know that the choice of the other six is wrong. They are giving what to you are obviously wrong answers. You don't know what to think. Why aren't they seeing things the same way you are? Sometimes they do, but in twelve trials they don't. Something is seriously wrong, and you are no longer sure what to do.

When the eighteenth trial is finished, you heave a sigh of relief. The experiment is finally over, and you are ready to bolt for the door. Dr. Asch walks over to you with a big smile on his face, and thanks you for participating in the experiment. He explains that you were the only real subject in the experiment! "The other six were stooges. I paid them to give those answers," he says. Now you feel real relief. Your eyes weren't playing tricks on you after all.

What were the results? Asch (1952) tested fifty people. One-third (33 percent) gave in to the group half the time, giving what they knew to be wrong answers. Another two out of five (40 percent) gave wrong answers, but not as often. One out of four (25 percent) stuck to their guns and always gave the right answer. I don't know how I would do on this test (if I knew nothing about it in advance), but I like to think that I would be part of the 25 percent. You probably feel the same way about yourself. But why should we feel that we wouldn't be like *most* people?

The results are disturbing, and researchers are still replicating Asch's experiment (Bond 2005). In our "land of individualism," the group is so powerful that most people are willing to say things that they know are not true. And this was a group of strangers! How much more conformity can we expect when our group consists of friends, people we value highly and depend on for getting along in life? Again, maybe you will become the sociologist to run that variation of Asch's experiment, perhaps using female subjects.

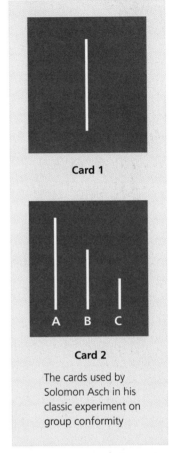

Figure 5.4 Asch's Cards

Card 1

Card 2

The cards used by Solomon Asch in his classic experiment on group conformity

Source: Asch 1952:452–453.

The Power of Authority: The Milgram Experiment

Even more disturbing are the results of the experiment described in the following Thinking Critically section.

Thinking Critically

If Hitler Asked You to Execute a Stranger, Would You? The Milgram Experiment

Imagine that you are taking a course with Dr. Stanley Milgram (1963, 1965), a former student of Dr. Asch. Assume that you do not know about the Asch experiment and have no reason to be wary. You arrive at the laboratory to participate in a study on punishment and learning. You and a second student draw lots for the roles of "teacher" and "learner." You are to be the teacher.

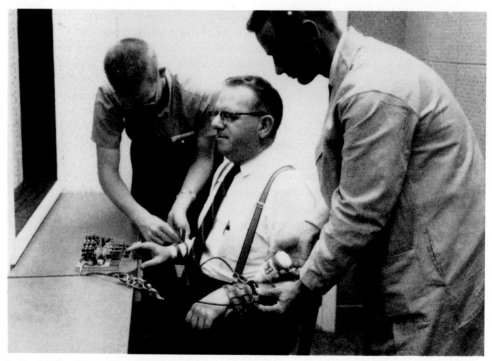

In the 1960s, U.S. social psychologists ran a series of creative but controversial experiments. Among these were Stanley Milgram's experiments. From this photo of the "learner" being prepared for the experiment, you can get an idea of how convincing the situation would be for the "teacher."

When you see that the learner's chair has protruding electrodes, you are glad that you are the teacher. Dr. Milgram shows you the machine you will run. You see that one side of the control panel is marked "Mild Shock, 15 volts," while the center says "Intense Shock, 350 Volts," and the far right side reads "DANGER: SEVERE SHOCK."

"As the teacher, you will read aloud a pair of words," explains Dr. Milgram. "Then you will repeat the first word, and the learner will reply with the second word. If the learner can't remember the word, you press this lever on the shock generator. The shock will serve as punishment, and we can then determine if punishment improves memory." You nod, now very relieved that you haven't been designated the learner.

"Every time the learner makes an error, increase the punishment by 15 volts," instructs Dr. Milgram. Then, seeing the look on your face, he adds, "The shocks can be extremely painful, but they won't cause any permanent tissue damage." He pauses, and then says, "I want you to see." You then follow him to the "electric chair," and Dr. Milgram gives you a shock of 45 volts. "There. That wasn't too bad, was it?" "No," you mumble.

The experiment begins. You hope for the learner's sake that he is bright, but unfortunately he turns out to be rather dull. He gets some answers right, but you have to keep turning up the dial. Each turn makes you more and more uncomfortable. You find yourself hoping that the learner won't miss another answer. But he does. When he received the first shocks, he let out some moans and groans, but now he is screaming in agony. He even protests that he suffers from a heart condition.

How far do you turn that dial?

By now, you probably have guessed that there was no electricity attached to the electrodes and that the "learner" was a stooge who only pretended to feel pain. The purpose of the experiment was to find out at what point people refuse to participate. Does anyone actually turn the lever all the way to "DANGER: SEVERE SHOCK"?

Milgram wanted the answer because millions of ordinary people did nothing to stop the Nazi slaughter of Jews, gypsies, Slavs, homosexuals, people with disabilities, and others whom the Nazis designated as "inferior." That seeming compliance in the face of all of these deaths seemed bizarre, and Milgram wanted to see how ordinary, intelligent Americans might react in an analogous situation.

Milgram was upset by what he found. Many "teachers" broke into a sweat and protested to the experimenter that this was inhuman and should be stopped. But when the experimenter calmly replied that the experiment must go on, this assurance from an "authority" ("scientist, white coat, university laboratory") was enough for most "teachers" to continue, even though the "learner" screamed in agony. Even "teachers" who were "reduced to twitching, stuttering wrecks" continued to follow orders.

Milgram varied the experiments (Nestar and Gregory 2005). He used both men and women. In some experiments, he put the "teachers" and "learners" in the same room, so the "teacher" could clearly see the suffering. In others, he put the "learners" in a separate room, and had them pound and kick the wall during the first shocks and then go silent. The results varied. When there was no verbal feedback from the "learner," 65 percent of the "teachers" pushed the lever all the way to 450 volts. Of those who could see the "learner," 40 percent turned the lever all the way. When Milgram added a second "teacher," a stooge who refused to go along with the experiment, only 5 percent of the "teachers" turned the lever all the way, a result that bears out some of Asch's findings.

A stormy discussion about research ethics erupted. Not only were researchers surprised and disturbed by what Milgram found but also they were alarmed at his methods. Universities began to require that subjects be informed of the nature and purpose of social research. Researchers agreed that to reduce subjects to "twitching, stuttering wrecks" was unethical, and almost all deception was banned.

for your Consideration

What is the connection between Milgram's experiment and the actions of Monster Kody in our opening vignette? Taking into account how significant these findings are, do you think that the scientific community overreacted to Milgram's experiments? Should we allow such research? Consider both the Asch and Milgram experiments, and use symbolic interactionism, functionalism, and conflict theory to explain why groups have such influence over us.

Global Consequences of Group Dynamics: Groupthink

Suppose you are a member of the President's inner circle. It is midnight, and the President has just called an emergency meeting to deal with a terrorist attack. At first, several options are presented. Eventually, these are narrowed to only a couple of choices, and at some point, everyone seems to agree on what now appears to be "the only possible course of action." To express doubts at that juncture will bring you into conflict with all the other important people in the room. To criticize will mark you as not being a "team player." So you keep your mouth shut, with the result that each step commits you—and them—more and more to the "only" course of action.

From the Milgram and Asch experiments, we can see the power of authority and the influence of peers. Under some circumstances, as in this example, this can lead to **groupthink.** Sociologist Irving Janis (1972, 1982) coined this term to refer to the collective tunnel vision that group members sometimes develop. As they begin to think alike, they become convinced that there is only one "right" viewpoint and a single course of action to follow. They take any suggestion of alternatives as a sign of disloyalty. With their perspective narrowed and fully convinced that they are right, they may even put aside moral judgments and disregard risk (Hart 1991; Flippen 1999).

Groupthink can bring serious consequences. Consider the *Columbia* space shuttle disaster of 2003.

Foam broke loose during launch, and engineers were concerned that it might have damaged tiles on the nose cone. Because this would make reentry dangerous, they sent e-mails to NASA officials, warning them about the risk. One engineer even suggested that the crew do a "space walk" to examine the tiles (Vartabedian and Gold 2003). The team in charge of the Columbia shuttle, however, disregarded the warnings. Convinced that a piece of foam weighing less than two pounds could not seriously harm the shuttle, they refused to even consider the possibility (Wald and Schwartz 2003). The fiery results of their mental closure were transmitted around the globe.

groupthink a narrowing of thought by a group of people, leading to the perception that there is only one correct answer; to even suggest alternatives becomes a sign of disloyalty

The consequences of groupthink can be even greater than this. In 1941, President Franklin D. Roosevelt and his chiefs of staff had evidence that the Japanese were preparing to attack Pearl Harbor. They simply refused to believe it and decided to continue naval operations as usual. The destruction of the U.S. naval fleet ushered the United States into World War II. In the war with Vietnam, U.S. officials had evidence of the strength and determination of the North Vietnamese military. They arrogantly threw such evidence aside, refusing to believe that "little, uneducated, barefoot people in pajamas" could defeat the U.S. military.

In each of these cases, options closed as officials committed themselves to a single course of action. Questioning the decisions would have indicated disloyalty and disregard for "team playing." Those in power plunged ahead, unable to see alternative perspectives. No longer did they try to objectively weigh evidence as it came in; instead, they interpreted everything as supporting their one "correct" decision.

Groupthink knows few bounds. Consider the aftermath of 9/11, when government officials defended torture as moral, "the lesser of two evils." Groupthink narrowed thought to the point that the U.S. Justice Department ruled that the United States was not bound by the Geneva Convention that prohibits torture. Facing protests, the Justice Department backed down (Lewis 2005).

The U.S. military involvement in Iraq appears to be a similar example. Top leaders, convinced that they made the right decision to go to war and that they were being successful in building a new Iraqi society, continuously interpreted even disconfirming evidence as favorable. Opinions and debate that contradicted their mindset were written off as signs of ignorance and disloyalty. Despite mounting casualties and growing negative public sentiment and political opposition to the war, the President and his advisors seem to have been blinded by groupthink.

Preventing Groupthink Groupthink is a danger that faces government leaders, who tend to surround themselves with an inner circle that closely reflects their own views. In "briefings," written summaries, and "talking points," this inner circle spoon feeds the leaders carefully selected information. The result is that top leaders, such as the President, become cut off from information that does not support their own opinions.

Perhaps the key to preventing the mental captivity and intellectual paralysis known as groupthink is the widest possible circulation—especially among a nation's top government officials—of research that has been conducted by social scientists independent of the government and information that has been gathered freely by media reporters. If this conclusion comes across as an unabashed plug for sociological research and the free exchange of ideas, it is. Giving free rein to diverse opinions can curb groupthink, which—if not prevented—can lead to the destruction of a society and, in today's world of nuclear, chemical, and biological weapons, the obliteration of Earth's inhabitants.

Summary *and* Review

Social Groups and Societies

What is a group?

Sociologists use many definitions of groups, but, in general, **groups** consist of people who interact with one another and think of themselves as belonging together. **Societies** are the largest and most complex group that sociologists study. P. 128.

Societies and Their Transformation

How is technology linked to the change from one type of society to another?

On their way to postindustrial society, humans passed through four types of societies. Each emerged from a social revolution that was linked to new technology. The **domestication revolution,** which brought the pasturing of animals and the cultivation of plants, transformed **hunting and gathering societies** into **pastoral** and **horticultural societies.** Then the invention of the plow ushered in the **agricultural society,** while the **Industrial Revolution,** brought about by machines that were powered by fuels, led to the **industrial society.** The computer chip ushered in a new type of society called **postindustrial** (or **information**) **society.** Another new type of society, the **bioetech society,** may be emerging. Pp. 128–133.

How is social inequality linked to the transformation of societies?

Social equality was greatest in hunting and gathering societies, but over time social inequality grew. The root of the transition to social inequality was the accumulation of a food surplus, made possible through the domestication revolution. This surplus stimulated the division of labor, trade, accumulation of material goods, the subordination of females by males, the emergence of leaders, and the development of the state. Pp. 128–133.

Groups Within Society

How do sociologists classify groups?

Sociologists divide groups into primary groups, secondary groups, in-groups, out-groups, reference groups, and networks. The cooperative, intimate, long-term, face-to-face relationships provided by **primary groups** are fundamental to our sense of self. **Secondary groups** are larger, relatively temporary, and more anonymous, formal, and impersonal than primary groups. **In-groups** provide members with a strong sense of identity and belonging. **Out-groups** also foster identity by showing in-group members what they are *not*. **Reference groups** are groups whose standards we refer to as we evaluate ourselves. **Social networks** consist of social ties that link people together. The new technology has given birth to a new type of group, the **electronic community.** Pp. 134–141.

Group Dynamics

How does a group's size affect its dynamics?

The term **group dynamics** refers to how individuals affect groups and how groups influence individuals. In a **small group,** everyone can interact directly with everyone else. As a group grows larger, its intensity decreases but its stability increases. A **dyad,** consisting of two people, is the most unstable of human groups, but it provides the most intense or intimate relationships. The addition of a third person, forming a **triad,** fundamentally alters relationships. Triads are unstable, as **coalitions** (the alignment of some members of a group against others) tend to form. Pp. 141–144.

What characterizes a leader?

A **leader** is someone who influences others. **Instrumental leaders** try to keep a group moving toward its goals, even though this causes friction and they lose popularity. **Expressive leaders** focus on creating harmony and raising group morale. Both types are essential to the functioning of groups. P. 145.

What are the three main leadership styles?

Authoritarian leaders give orders, **democratic leaders** try to lead by consensus, and **laissez-faire leaders** are highly permissive. An authoritarian style appears to be more effective in emergency situations, a democratic style works best for most situations, and a laissez-faire style is usually ineffective. P. 146.

How do groups encourage conformity?

The Asch experiment was cited to illustrate the power of peer pressure, the Milgram experiment to illustrate the influence of authority. Both experiments demonstrate how easily we can succumb to **groupthink,** a kind of collective tunnel vision. Preventing groupthink requires the free circulation of contrasting ideas. Pp. 146–150.

Thinking Critically
about Chapter 5

1. How would your orientations to life (your ideas, attitudes, values, goals) be different if you had been reared in an agricultural society?
2. Identify your in-groups and your out-groups. How have your in-groups influenced the way you see the world?
3. Milgram's and Asch's experiments illustrate the power of peer pressure. How has peer pressure operated in your life? Think about something that you did not want to do but did anyway because of peer pressure.

Deviance and Social Control

Vincent Van Gogh, *Prisoners Exercising*, 1890

In just a few moments I was to meet my first Yanomamö, my first primitive man. What would it be like? . . . I looked up (from my canoe) and gasped when I saw a dozen burly, naked, filthy, hideous men staring at us down the shafts of their drawn arrows. Immense wads of green tobacco were stuck between their lower teeth and lips, making them look even more hideous, and strands of dark-green slime dripped or hung from their noses. We arrived at the village while the men were blowing a hallucinogenic drug up their noses. One of the side effects of the drug is a runny nose. The mucus is always saturated with the green powder, and the Indians usually let it run freely from their nostrils. . . . I just sat there holding my notebook, helpless and pathetic . . .

The whole situation was depressing, and I wondered why I ever decided to switch from civil engineering to anthropology in the first place. . . . (Soon) I was covered with red pigment, the result of a dozen or so complete examinations. . . . These examinations capped an otherwise grim day. The Indians would blow their noses into their hands, flick as much of the mucus off that would separate in a snap of the wrist, wipe the residue into their hair, and then carefully examine my face, arms, legs, hair, and the contents of my pockets. I said (in their language), "Your hands are dirty"; my comments were met by the Indians in the following way: they would "clean" their hands by spitting a quantity of slimy tobacco juice into them, rub them together, and then proceed with the examination.

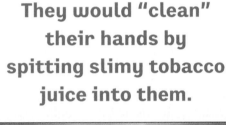

They would "clean" their hands by spitting slimy tobacco juice into them.

This is how Napoleon Chagnon describes the cultural shock he felt when he met the Yanomamö tribe of the rain forests of Brazil. His ensuing months of fieldwork continued to bring surprise after surprise, and often Chagnon (1977) could hardly believe his eyes—or his nose.

If you were to list the deviant behaviors of the Yanomamö, what would you include? The way they appear naked in public? Use hallucinogenic drugs? Let mucus hang from their noses? Or the way they rub hands filled with mucus, spittle, and tobacco juice over a frightened stranger who doesn't dare to protest? Perhaps. But it isn't this simple, for as we shall see, deviance is relative.

What Is Deviance?

Sociologists use the term **deviance** to refer to any violation of norms, whether the infraction is as minor as driving over the speed limit, as serious as murder, or as humorous as Chagnon's encounter with the Yanomamö. This deceptively simple definition takes us to the heart of the sociological perspective on deviance, which sociologist Howard S. Becker (1966) described this way: *It is not the act itself, but the reactions to the act, that make something deviant.* What Chagnon saw disturbed him, but to the Yanomamö those same behaviors represented normal, everyday life. What was deviant to Chagnon was *conformist* to the Yanomamö. From their viewpoint, you *should* check out strangers the way they did, and nakedness is good, as are hallucinogenic drugs and letting mucus be "natural."

Chagnon's abrupt introduction to the Yanomamö allows us to see the *relativity of deviance*, a major point made by symbolic interactionists. Because different groups have different norms, *what is deviant to some is not deviant to others.* (See the photo on this page.) This principle holds both *within* a society as well as across cultures. Thus, acts that are acceptable in one culture—or in one group within a society—may be considered deviant in another culture, or by another group within the same society. This idea is explored in the Cultural Diversity box on the next page.

This principle also applies to a specific form of deviance known as **crime,** the violation of rules that have been written into law. In the extreme, an act that is applauded by one group may be so despised by another group that it is punishable by death. Making a huge profit on business deals is one example. Americans who do this are admired. Like Donald Trump, Jack Welch, and Warren Buffet, they may even write books about their exploits. In China, however, until recently this same act was considered a crime called *profiteering.* Anyone who was found guilty was hanged in a public square as a lesson to all.

Unlike the general public, sociologists use the term *deviance* nonjudgmentally, to refer to any act to which people respond negatively. When sociologists use this term, it does not mean that they agree that an act is bad, just that people judge it negatively. To sociologists, then, *all* of us are deviants of one sort or another, for we all violate norms from time to time.

To be considered deviant, a person does not even have to *do* anything. Sociologist Erving Goffman (1963) used the term **stigma** to refer to characteristics that discredit people. These include violations of norms of ability (blindness, deafness, mental handicaps) and norms of appearance (a facial birthmark, obesity). They also include involuntary memberships, such as being a victim of AIDS or the brother of a rapist. The stigma can become a person's master status, defining him or her as deviant. Recall from Chapter 4 that a master status cuts across all other statuses that a person occupies.

I took this photo on the outskirts of Hyderabad, India. Is this man deviant? If this were a U.S. street, he would be. But here? No houses have running water in his neighborhood, and the men, women, and children bathe at the neighborhood water pump. This man, then, would not be deviant in his culture. And yet, he is actually mugging for my camera, making the three bystanders laugh. Does this additional factor make this a scene of deviance?

How Norms Make Social Life Possible

No human group can exist without norms, for *norms make social life possible by making behavior predictable.* What would life be like if you could not predict what others would do? Imagine for a moment that you have gone to a store to purchase milk:

> Suppose the clerk says, "I won't sell you any milk. We're overstocked with soda, and I'm not going to sell anyone milk until our soda inventory is reduced."

Human Sexuality in Cross-Cultural Perspective

HUMAN SEXUALITY ILLUSTRATES how a group's *definition* of an act, not the act itself, determines whether it will be considered deviant. Let's look at some examples reported by anthropologist Robert Edgerton (1976).

Norms of sexual behavior vary so widely around the world that what is considered normal in one society may be considered deviant in another. In Kenya, a group called the Pokot place high emphasis on sexual pleasure, and they expect that both a husband and wife will reach orgasm. If a husband does not satisfy his wife, he is in trouble—especially if she thinks that his failure is because of adultery. If this is so, the wife and her female friends will sneak up on her husband when he is asleep. The women will tie him up, shout obscenities at him, beat him, and then urinate on him. As a final gesture of their contempt, before releasing him, they will slaughter and eat his favorite ox. The husband's hours of painful humiliation are intended to make him more dutiful concerning his wife's conjugal rights.

Pokot married man, northern Kenya

People can also become deviants for failing to understand that the group's ideal norms may not be its real norms. As with many groups, the Zapotec Indians of Mexico profess that sexual relations should take place exclusively between husband and wife. Yet the *only* person in one Zapotec community who had not had any extramarital affairs was considered deviant. Evidently, these people have an unspoken understanding that married couples will engage in affairs, but be discreet about them. When a wife learns that her husband is having an affair, she usually has one, too.

One Zapotec wife did not follow this covert norm. Instead, she would praise her own virtue to her husband—and then voice the familiar "headache" excuse. She also told other wives the names of the women their husbands were sleeping with. As a result, this virtuous woman was condemned by everyone in the village. Clearly, real norms can conflict with ideal norms—another illustration of the gap between ideal and real culture.

for your Consideration

How do the behaviors of the Pokot wife and husband look from the perspective of U.S. norms? Are there U.S. norms in the first place? How about the Zapotec woman? The rest of the Zapotec community? How does cultural relativity apply? (We discussed this concept in Chapter 2, pages 41–42.)

You don't like it, but you decide to buy a case of soda. At the checkout, the clerk says, "I hope you don't mind, but there's a $5 service charge on every fifteenth customer." You, of course, are the fifteenth.

Just as you start to leave, another clerk stops you and says, "We're not working any more. We decided to have a party." Suddenly a CD player begins to blast, and everyone in the store begins to dance. "Oh, good, you've brought the soda," says a different clerk, who takes your package and passes sodas all around.

Life is not like this, of course. You can depend on grocery clerks to sell you milk. You can also depend on paying the same price as everyone else, and not being forced to attend a party in the store. Why can you depend on this? Because we are socialized to follow norms, to play the basic roles that society assigns to us.

Without norms, we would have social chaos. Norms lay out the basic guidelines for how we should play our roles and interact with others. In short, norms bring about **social order,** a group's customary social arrangements. Our lives are based on these arrangements, which is why deviance often is perceived as threatening: Deviance undermines predictability, the foundation of social life. Consequently, human groups develop a system of **social control**—formal and informal means of enforcing norms.

social order a group's usual and customary social arrangements, on which its members depend and on which they base their lives

social control a group's formal and informal means of enforcing its norms

There is no norm that says, "Do not hang in the air, suspended by flesh hooks," as this woman is doing at a tattoo festival in Woodstock, New York. What sanctions might come into play if she did this at work during her lunch hour? Why the difference?

negative sanction an expression of disapproval for breaking a norm, ranging from a mild, informal reaction such as a frown to a formal reaction such as a prison sentence or an execution

positive sanction a reward or positive reaction for following norms, ranging from a smile to a prize

degradation ceremony a term coined by Harold Garfinkel to describe rituals designed to remake the self by stripping away an individual's particular social identity and stamping a new one in its place

Sanctions

As we discussed in Chapter 2, people do not enforce folkways strictly, but they become upset when people break mores (MORE-rays). Expressions of disapproval of deviance, called **negative sanctions,** range from frowns and gossip for breaking folkways to imprisonment and capital punishment for breaking mores. In general, the more seriously the group takes a norm, the harsher the penalty for violating it. In contrast, **positive sanctions**—from smiles to formal awards—are used to reward people for conforming to norms. Getting a raise is a positive sanction; being fired is a negative sanction. Getting an *A* in intro to sociology is a positive sanction; getting an *F* is a negative one.

Most negative sanctions are informal. You might stare if you observe someone dressed in what you consider to be inappropriate clothing, or you might gossip if a married person you know spends the night with someone other than his or her spouse. Whether you consider the breaking of a norm merely an amusing matter that warrants no severe sanction or a serious infraction that does, however, depends on your perspective. If a woman appears at your college graduation ceremonies in a bikini, you may stare and laugh, but if this is *your* mother, you are likely to feel that different sanctions are appropriate. Similarly, if it is *your* father who spends the night with an 18-year-old college freshman, you are likely to do more than gossip.

Shaming and Degradation Ceremonies

Shaming is another sanction. Shaming is especially effective when members of a primary group use it. For this reason, parents sometimes use it to keep children in line. Shaming is also effective in small communities, where the individual's reputation is at stake. As our society grew large and urban, its sense of community diminished, and shaming lost its effectiveness. Shaming seems to be making a comeback. One Arizona sheriff makes the men in his jail wear pink underwear (Boxer 2001). Digital cameras and camera cell phones have encouraged online shaming sites. They feature bad drivers, older men who leer at teenaged girls, and dog walkers who don't pick up their dog's poop (Saranow 2007). Some sites include photos of the offenders, as well as their addresses and phone numbers.

In small communities, shaming can be the centerpiece of the enforcement of norms, with the violator marked as a deviant and held up for all the world to see. In Nathaniel Hawthorne's *The Scarlet Letter*, town officials forced Hester Prynne to wear a scarlet A sewn on her dress. The A stood for *adulteress.* Wherever she went, Prynne had to wear this badge of shame, and the community expected her to wear it every day for the rest of her life.

Sociologist Harold Garfinkel (1956) gave the name **degradation ceremony** to formal attempts to brand someone as an outsider. The individual is called to account before the group, witnesses denounce him or her, the offender is pronounced guilty, and steps are taken to strip the individual of his or her identity as a group member. In some court martials, officers who are found guilty stand at attention before their peers while the insignia of rank are ripped from their uniforms. This procedure dramatizes that the individual is no longer a member of the group. Although Hester Prynne was not banished from the group physically, she was banished morally; her degradation ceremony proclaimed her a *moral* outcast from the community. The scarlet A marked her as "not one" of them.

Although we don't use scarlet A's today, informal degradation ceremonies still occur. Consider what happened to Joseph Gray (Chivers 2001):

Joseph Gray, a fifteen-year veteran of the New York City police force, was involved in a fatal accident. The *New York Times* and New York television stations reported that Gray had spent the afternoon drinking in a topless bar before plowing his car into a vehicle carrying a pregnant woman, her son, and her sister. All three died. Gray was accused of manslaughter and drunk driving. (He was later convicted on both counts.)

The news media kept hammering this story to the public. Three weeks later, as Gray left police headquarters after resigning from his job, an angry crowd gathered around him. Gray hung his head in public disgrace as Victor Manuel Herrera, whose wife and son were killed in the crash, followed him, shouting, "You're a murderer!"

IN SUM In sociology, the term *deviance* refers to all violations of social rules, regardless of their seriousness. The term is not a judgment about the behavior. Deviance is relative, for what is deviant in one group may be conformist in another. Consequently, we must consider deviance from *within* a group's own framework, for it is *their* meanings that underlie their behavior. The following Thinking Critically section focuses on this issue.

Thinking Critically

Is It Rape, Or Is It Marriage? A Study in Culture Clash

Surrounded by cornfields, Lincoln, Nebraska, is about as provincial as a state capital gets. Most of its residents have little experience dealing with people who come from different ways of life. Their baptism into cultural diversity came as a shock.

The wedding was traditional and followed millennia-old Islamic practices (Annin and Hamilton 1996). A 39-year-old immigrant from Iraq had arranged for his two eldest daughters, ages 13 and 14, to marry two fellow Iraqi immigrants, ages 28 and 34. A Muslim cleric flew in from Ohio to perform the ceremony.

Nebraska went into shock. So did the immigrants. What is marriage in Iraq is rape in Nebraska. The husbands were charged with rape, the girls' father with child abuse, and their mother with contributing to the delinquency of minors.

The event made front page news in Saudi Arabia, where people shook their heads in amazement at Americans. Nebraskans shook their heads in amazement, too.

In Fresno, California, a young Hmong immigrant took a group of friends to a local college campus. There, they picked up the Hmong girl whom he had selected to be his wife (Sherman 1988; Lacayo 1993b). The young men brought her to his house, where he had sex with her. The young woman, however, was not in agreement with this plan.

The Hmong call this *zij poj niam*, "marriage by capture." For them, this is an acceptable form of mate selection, one that mirrors Hmong courtship ideals of strong men and virtuous, resistant women. The Fresno District Attorney, however, called it kidnapping and rape.

Degradation ceremonies are intended to humiliate norm violators and mark them as "not members" of the group. This photo was taken by the U.S. army in 1945 after U.S. troops liberated Cherbourg, France. Members of the French resistance shaved the heads of these women, who had "collaborated" (had sex with) the occupying Nazis. They then marched the shamed women down the streets of the city, while the public shouted insults and spat on them.

Culture conflict centered around parents giving girls like this in marriage to men 15 to 20 years older.

As migration intensifies, other countries are experiencing similar culture shock. Germans awoke one morning to the news that a 28-year-old Turkish man had taken his 11-year-old wife to the registry office in Dusseldorf to get her an ID card. The shocked officials detained the girl and shipped her back to Turkey (Stephens 2006).

In Bishkek, Kyrgystan, a former republic of the Soviet Union, one father said that he wouldn't mind if a man kidnapped his daugher to marry her. "After all," he said, "that's how I got my wife" (Smith 2005).

for your Consideration

To apply *symbolic interactionism* to these real-life dramas, ask how the perspectives of the people involved explain why they did what they did. To apply *functionalism*, ask how the U.S. laws that were violated are "functional" (that is, what are their benefits, and to whom?). To apply *conflict theory*, ask what groups are in conflict in these examples. (Do not focus on the individuals involved, but on the groups to which they belong.)

Understanding events in terms of different theoretical perspectives does not tell us which reaction is "right" when cultures clash. Science can analyze causes and consequences, but it cannot answer questions of what is "right" or moral. Any "ought" that you feel about these cases comes from your values, which brings us, once again, to the initial issue: the relativity of deviance.

Competing Explanations of Deviance: Sociology, Sociobiology, and Psychology

If social life is to exist, norms are essential. So why do people violate them? To better understand the reasons, it is useful to know how sociological explanations differ from biological and psychological ones.

Sociobiologists explain deviance by looking for answers *within* individuals. They assume that **genetic predispositions** lead people to such deviances as juvenile delinquency and crime (Lombroso 1911; Wilson and Herrnstein 1985; Goozen et al. 2007). Among their explanations are the following three theories: (1) intelligence—low intelligence leads to crime; (2) the "XYY" theory—an extra Y chromosome in males leads to crime; and (3) body type—people with "squarish, muscular" bodies are more likely to commit **street crime**—acts such as mugging, rape, and burglary.

How have these theories held up? We should first note that most people who have these supposedly "causal" characteristics do not become criminals. Regarding intelligence, you already know that some criminals are very intelligent, and that most people of low intelligence do not commit crimes. Regarding the extra Y chromosome, most men who commit crimes have the normal XY chromosome combination, and most men with the XYY combination do not become criminals. No women have this combination of genes, so this explanation can't even be applied to female criminals. Regarding body type, criminals exhibit the full range of body types, and most people with "squarish, muscular" bodies do not become street criminals.

Psychologists also focus on abnormalities *within* the individual. They examine what are called **personality disorders.** Their supposition is that deviating individuals have deviating personalities (Barnes 2001; Mayer 2007), and that subconscious motives drive people to deviance. No specific childhood experience, however, is invariably linked with deviance. For example, children who had "bad toilet training," "suffocating mothers," or "emotionally aloof fathers" may become embezzling bookkeepers—or good accountants. Just as college students, teachers, and police officers represent a variety of bad—and good—childhood experiences, so do deviants. Similarly, people with "suppressed anger" can become freeway snipers or military heroes—or anything else. In short, there is no inevitable outcome of any childhood experience. Deviance is not associated with any particular personality.

In contrast with both sociobiologists and psychologists, *sociologists* search for factors *outside* the individual. They look for social influences that "recruit" people to break norms. To account for why people commit crimes, for example, sociologists examine such external influences as socialization, membership in subcultures, and social class.

genetic predisposition inborn tendencies; in this context, to commit deviant acts

street crime crimes such as mugging, rape, and burglary

personality disorders the view that a personality disturbance of some sort causes an individual to violate social norms

Social class, a concept that we will discuss in depth in Chapter 7 refers to people's relative standing in terms of education, occupation, and especially income and wealth.

The point stressed earlier, that deviance is relative, leads sociologists to ask a crucial question: Why should we expect to find something constant within people to account for a behavior that is conforming in one society and deviant in another?

To see how sociologists explain deviance, let's contrast the three sociological perspectives—symbolic interactionism, functionalism, and conflict theory.

The Symbolic Interactionist Perspective

As we examine symbolic interactionism, it will become more evident why sociologists are not satisfied with explanations that are rooted in biology or personality. A basic principle of symbolic interactionism is this: We act according to our interpretations of situations, not according to blind predisposition. Let's consider how our membership in groups influences our views of life and thus affects our behavior.

Differential Association Theory

The Theory Contrary to theories built around biology and personality, sociologists stress that people *learn* deviance. Edwin Sutherland coined the term **differential association** to indicate that we learn to deviate from or conform to society's norms primarily from the *different* groups we *associate* with (Sutherland 1924, 1947; Sutherland et al. 1992). On the most obvious level, some boys and girls join street gangs, while others join the Scouts. As sociologists have repeatedly demonstrated, what we learn influences us toward or away from deviance (Deflem 2006; Chambliss 1973/2007).

Sutherland's theory is actually more complicated than this, but he basically said that deviance is learned. This goes directly against the view that deviance is due to biology or personality. Sutherland stressed that the different groups with which we associate (our "*different*ial association") give us messages about conformity and deviance. We may receive mixed messages, but we end up with more of one than the other (an "excess of definitions," as Sutherland put it). The end result is an imbalance—attitudes that tilt us more toward one direction than another. Consequently, either we conform or we deviate.

Families Since our family is so important for teaching us attitudes, it probably is obvious to you that the family makes a big difference in whether we learn deviance or conformity. Researchers have confirmed this informal observation. They have found that delinquents are more likely to come from families that get in trouble with the law. Of the many studies that show this, one stands out: Of all jail inmates across the United States, almost *half* have a father, mother, brother, sister, or spouse who has served time in prison (*Sourcebook of Criminal Justice Statistics* 2003:Table 6.0011). In short, families that are involved in crime tend to set their children on a lawbreaking path.

Friends, Neighborhoods, and Subcultures Most people don't know the term *differential association,* but they do know how it works. Most parents want to move out of "bad" neighborhoods because they know that if their kids have delinquent friends, they are likely to become delinquent, too. Sociological research supports this common observation (Miller 1958; Chung and Steinberg 2006; Yonas et al. 2006). Some neighborhoods even develop a subculture of violence. In these places, even a teasing remark can mean instant death. If the neighbors feel that a victim deserved to be killed, they refuse to testify because "he got what was coming to him" (Kubrin and Weitzer 2003).

differential association Edwin Sutherland's term to indicate that associating with some groups results in learning an "excess of definitions" of deviance, and, by extension, in a greater likelihood that one will become deviant

To experience a sense of belonging is a basic human need. Membership in groups, especially peer groups, is a primary way that people meet this need. Regardless of the orientation of the group— whether to conformity or to deviance—the process is the same. These members of a street gang in Cali, Colombia, are showing off their homemade guns.

control theory the idea that two control systems—inner controls and outer controls—work against our tendencies to deviate

Some neighborhoods even develop subcultures in which killing is considered an honorable act:

Sociologist Ruth Horowitz (1983, 2005), who did participant observation in a lower-class Chicano neighborhood in Chicago, discovered how associating with people who have a certain concept of "honor" propels young men to deviance. The formula is simple. "A real man has honor. An insult is a threat to one's honor. Therefore, not to stand up to someone is to be less than a real man."

Now suppose you are a young man growing up in this neighborhood. You likely would do a fair amount of fighting, for you would interpret many things as attacks on your honor. You might even carry a knife or a gun, for words and fists wouldn't always be sufficient. Along with members of your group, you would define fighting, knifing, and shooting quite differently from the way most people do.

Members of the Mafia also intertwine ideas of manliness with violence. For them, *to kill is a measure of their manhood.* Not all killings are accorded the same respect, however, for "the more awesome and potent the victim, the more worthy and meritorious the killer" (Arlacchi 1980). Some killings are done to enforce norms. A member of the Mafia who gives information to the police, for example, has violated *omertá* (the Mafia's vow of secrecy). This offense can never be tolerated, for it threatens the very existence of the group. Mafia killings further illustrate just how relative deviance is. Although killing is deviant to mainstream society, for members of the Mafia, *not* to kill after certain rules are broken—such as when someone "squeals" to the cops—is the deviant act.

Prison or Freedom? As was mentioned in Chapter 3, an issue that comes up over and over again in sociology is whether we are prisoners of socialization. Symbolic interactionists stress that we are not mere pawns in the hands of others. We are not destined to think and act as our group memberships dictate. Rather, we *help to produce our own orientations to life.* By joining one group rather than another (differential association), for example, we help to shape the self. For instance, one college student may join a feminist group that is trying to change the treatment of women in college; another may associate with a group of women who shoplift on weekends. Their choice of groups points them in different directions. The one who associates with shoplifters may become even more oriented toward criminal activities, while the one who joins the feminist group may develop an even greater interest in producing social change.

Control Theory

Inside most of us, it seems, are desires to do things that would get us in trouble—inner drives, temptations, urges, hostilities, and so on. Yet most of the time we stifle these desires. Why?

The Theory Sociologist Walter Reckless (1973), who developed **control theory,** stresses that two control systems work against our motivations to deviate. Our *inner controls* include our internalized morality—conscience, religious principles, ideas of right and wrong. Inner controls also include fears of punishment, feelings of integrity, and the desire to be a "good" person (Hirschi 1969; Rogers 1977; McShane and Williams 2007). Our *outer controls* consist of people—such as family, friends, and the police—who influence us not to deviate.

The stronger our bonds are with society, the more effective our inner controls are (Hirschi 1969). Bonds are based on *attachments* (feeling affection and respect for people who

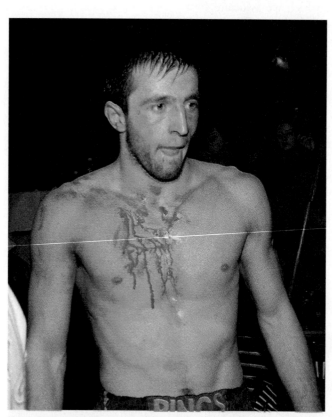

The social control of deviance takes many forms, some rather subtle. With its mayhem, "cage fighting" might look like the opposite of social control, but it is a way to channel aggressive impulses in a way that leaves no vendetta, feud, or "score to settle."

conform to mainstream norms), *commitments* (having a stake in society that you don't want to risk, such as a respected place in your family, a good standing at college, a good job), *involvements* (putting time and energy into approved activities), and *beliefs* (believing that certain actions are morally wrong).

This theory can be summarized as *self*-control, says sociologist Travis Hirschi. The key to learning high self-control is socialization, especially in childhood. Parents help their children to develop self-control by supervising them and punishing their deviant acts (Gottfredson and Hirschi 1990).

Applying the Theory

Suppose that some friends have invited you to a night club. When you get there, you notice that everyone seems unusually happy—almost giddy would be a better word. They seem to be euphoric in their animated conversations and dancing. Your friends tell you that almost everyone here has taken the drug Ecstasy, and they invite you to take some with them.

What do you do? Let's not explore the question of whether taking Ecstasy in this setting is a deviant or a conforming act. That is a separate issue. Instead, concentrate on the pushes and pulls you would feel. The pushes toward taking the drug: your friends, the setting, and your curiosity. Then there are the inner controls: the inner voices of your conscience and your parents, perhaps of your teachers, as well as your fears of arrest and of the dangers of illegal drugs. There are also the outer controls—perhaps the uniformed security guard looking in your direction.

So, what *did* you decide? Which was stronger: your inner and outer controls or the pushes and pulls toward taking the drug? It is you who can best weigh these forces, for they differ with each of us.

Labeling Theory

Symbolic interactionists have developed **labeling theory,** which focuses on the significance of the labels (names, reputations) that we are given. Labels tend to become a part of our self-concept, and help to set us on paths that either propel us into or divert us from deviance. Let's look at how people react to society's labels—from "whore" and "pervert" to "cheat" and "slob."

Rejecting Labels: How People Neutralize Deviance

Most people resist the negative labels that others try to pin on them. Some are so successful that even though they persist in deviance, they still consider themselves conformists. For example, even though they beat up people and vandalize property, some delinquents consider themselves to be conforming members of society. How do they do it?

Sociologists Gresham Sykes and David Matza (1957/1988) studied boys like this. They found that the boys used five **techniques of neutralization** to deflect society's norms.

Denial of Responsibility Some boys said, "I'm not responsible for what happened because . . ." and then they were quite creative about the "becauses." Some said that what happened was an "accident." Other boys saw themselves as "victims" of society. What else could you expect? They were like billiard balls shot around the pool table of life.

Denial of Injury Another favorite explanation of the boys was "What I did wasn't wrong because no one got hurt." They would define vandalism as "mischief," gang fights as a "private quarrel," and stealing cars as "borrowing." They might acknowledge that what they did was illegal, but claim that they were "just having a little fun."

Denial of a Victim Some boys thought of themselves as avengers. Vandalizing a teacher's car was done to get revenge

Jerry Springer guides people to publicly reveal their deviances. As Springer parades deviants before the public, the shock and surprise wear off, making the deviance seem "more" normal. What is occurring is the *mainstreaming of deviance*—disapproved behaviors moving into the mainstream, or becoming more socially acceptable.

for an unfair grade, while shoplifting was a way to even the score with "crooked" store owners. In short, even if the boys did accept responsibility and admit that someone had gotten hurt, they protected their self-concept by claiming that the people "deserved what they got."

Condemnation of the Condemners Another technique the boys used was to deny that others had the right to judge them. They might accuse people who pointed their fingers at them of being "a bunch of hypocrites": The police were "on the take," teachers had "pets," and parents cheated on their taxes. In short, they said, "Who are *they* to accuse *me* of something?"

Appeal to Higher Loyalties A final technique the boys used to justify antisocial activities was to consider loyalty to the gang more important than following the norms of society. They might say, "I had to help my friends. That's why I got in the fight." Not incidentally, the boy may have shot two members of a rival group, as well as a bystander!

In sum: These five techniques of neutralization have implications far beyond this group of boys, for it is not only delinquents who try to neutralize the norms of mainstream society. Look again at these five techniques—don't they sound familiar? (1) "I couldn't help myself"; (2) "Who really got hurt?"; (3) "Don't you think she deserved that, after what *she* did?"; (4) "Who are *you* to talk?"; and (5) "I had to help my friends—wouldn't you have done the same thing?" All of us attempt to neutralize the moral demands of society, for neutralization helps us to sleep at night.

Embracing Labels: The Example of Outlaw Bikers
Although most of us resist attempts to label us as deviant, some people revel in a deviant identity. Some teenagers, for example, make certain by their clothing, choice of music, hairstyles, and "body art" that no one misses their rejection of adult norms. Their status among fellow members of a subculture—within which they are almost obsessive conformists—is vastly more important than any status outside it.

One of the best examples of a group that embraces deviance is motorcycle gangs. Sociologist Mark Watson (1980/2006) did participant observation with outlaw bikers. He rebuilt Harleys with them, hung around their bars and homes, and went on "runs" (trips) with them. He concluded that outlaw bikers see the world as "hostile, weak, and effeminate." They pride themselves on looking "dirty, mean, and generally undesirable" and take pleasure in provoking shocked reactions to their appearance and behavior. Holding the conventional world in contempt, they also pride themselves on getting into trouble, laughing at death, and treating women as lesser beings whose primary value is to provide them with services—especially sex. Outlaw bikers also regard themselves as losers, a factor that becomes woven into their unusual embrace of deviance.

The Power of Labels: The Saints and the Roughnecks
We can see how powerful labeling is by referring back to the study of the "Saints" and the "Roughnecks" that was cited in Chapter 4 (page 121). As you recall, both groups of high school boys were "constantly occupied with truancy, drinking, wild parties, petty theft, and vandalism." Yet their teachers looked on the Saints as "headed for success" and the Roughnecks as "headed for trouble." By the time they finished high school, not one Saint had been arrested, while the Roughnecks had been in constant trouble with the police.

Why did the members of the community perceive these boys so differently? Chambliss (1973/2007) concluded that this split vision was due to *social class*. As symbolic interactionists emphasize, social class vitally affects our perceptions and behavior. The Saints came from respectable, middle-class families, while the Roughnecks were from less respectable, working-class families. These backgrounds led teachers and the authorities to expect good behavior from the Saints but trouble from the Roughnecks. And, like the rest of us, teachers and police saw what they expected to see.

The boys' social class also affected their visibility. The Saints had automobiles, and they did their drinking and vandalism outside of town. Without cars, the Roughnecks hung around their own street corners, where their drinking and boisterous behavior drew the attention of police and confirmed the negative impressions that the community already had of them.

The boys' social class also equipped them with distinct *styles of interaction*. When police or teachers questioned them, the Saints were apologetic. Their show of respect for authority elicited a positive reaction from teachers and police, allowing the Saints to escape school and legal problems. The Roughnecks, said Chambliss, were "almost the polar opposite." When questioned, they were hostile. Even when they tried to assume a respectful attitude, everyone could see through it. Consequently, while teachers and police let the Saints off with warnings, they came down hard on the Roughnecks.

Although what happens in life is not determined by labels alone, the Saints and the Roughnecks did live up to the labels that the community gave them. As you may recall, all but one of the Saints went on to college. One earned a Ph.D., one became a lawyer, one a doctor, and the others business managers. In contrast, only two of the Roughnecks went to college. They earned athletic scholarships and became coaches. The other Roughnecks did not fare so well. Two of them dropped out of high school, later became involved in separate killings, and were sent to prison. One became a local bookie, and no one knows the whereabouts of the other.

How do labels work? Although the matter is complex, because it involves the self-concept and reactions that vary from one individual to another, we can note that labels open and close doors of opportunity. Unlike its meaning in sociology, the term *deviant* in everyday usage is emotionally charged with a judgment of some sort. This label can lock people out of conforming groups and push them into almost exclusive contact with people who have been similarly labeled.

IN SUM Symbolic interactionists examine how people's definitions of the situation underlie their deviating from or conforming to social norms. They focus on group membership (differential association), how people balance pressures to conform and to deviate (control theory), and the significance of the labels that are given to people (labeling theory).

The label *deviant* involves competing definitions and reactions to the same behavior. This central point of symbolic interactionism is explored in the Mass Media box on the next page.

The Functionalist Perspective

When we think of deviance, its dysfunctions are likely to come to mind. Functionalists, in contrast, are as likely to stress the functions of deviance as they are to emphasize its dysfunctions.

Can Deviance Really Be Functional for Society?

Most of us are upset by deviance, especially crime, and assume that society would be better off without it. The classic functionalist theorist Emile Durkheim (1893/1933, 1895/1964), however, came to a surprising conclusion. Deviance, he said—including crime—is functional for society, for it contributes to the social order. Its three main functions are:

1. *Deviance clarifies moral boundaries and affirms norms.* A group's ideas about how people should think and act mark its *moral boundaries*. Deviant acts challenge those boundaries. To call a member into account is to say, in effect, "You broke an important rule, and we cannot tolerate that." Punishing deviants affirms the group's norms and clarifies what it means to be a member of the group.
2. *Deviance promotes social unity.* To affirm the group's moral boundaries by punishing deviants fosters a "we" feeling among the group's members. In saying, "You can't get away with that," the group collectively affirms the rightness of its own ways.

Pornography on the Internet: Freedom Versus Censorship

Pornography vividly illustrates one of the sociological principles discussed in this chapter: the relativity of deviance. It is not the act, but reactions to the act, that make something deviant. Consider one of today's major issues, pornography on the Internet.

Web surfers have such a wide choice of pornography that some sites are indexed by race-ethnicity, hair color, body type, heterosexual or gay, single or group, teenagers, cheerleaders, and older women who "still think they have it." Some offer only photographs, others video. There also are live sites. After signing in and agreeing to the hefty per-minute charges, you can command your "model" to do anything your heart desires. The Internet sex industry even has an annual trade show, Internext. Predictions at Internext are that hotels will soon offer not just sex videos on demand but also live images of people having sex (Johnston 2007).

What is the problem? Why can't people exchange nude photos electronically if they want to? Or watch others having sex online, if someone offers that service?

Although some people object to any kind of sex site, what disturbs many are the sites that feature bondage, torture, rape, bestiality (humans having sex with animals), and sex with children.

The Internet abounds with chat rooms, where people "meet" online to discuss some topic. No one is bothered by the chat rooms where the topic is Roman architecture or rap music or sports. But those whose focus is how to torture women are another matter. So are those that offer lessons on how to seduce grade school children—or that extol the delights of having sex with three-year-olds.

The state and federal governments have passed laws against child pornography, and the police seize computers and search them for illegal pictures. The penalties can be severe. When photos of children in sex acts were found on an Arizona man's computer, he was sentenced to 200 years in prison (Greenhouse 2007). When he appealed his sentence as unconstitutional, his sentence was upheld. To exchange pictures of tortured and sexually abused women, however, remains legal.

for your Consideration

Some people feel that no matter how much they may disagree with a point of view or find it repugnant, communications about it (including photos and videos) must be allowed. They believe that if we let the government censor the Internet in any way, it will censor other communications. Do you think it should be legal to exchange photos of women being sexually abused or tortured? Should it be legal to discuss ways to seduce children? If not, on what basis should they be banned? If we make these activities illegal, then what other communications should we prohibit? On what basis?

Finally, can you disprove the central point of the symbolic interactionists—that an activity is deviant only because people decide that it is deviant? You may use examples cited in this box, or any others that you wish. You cannot invoke God or moral absolutes in your argument, however, as they are outside the field of sociology. Sociology cannot decide moral issues, even in extreme cases.

---

3. *Deviance promotes social change.* Groups do not always agree on what to do with people who push beyond their accepted ways of doing things. Some group members may even approve of the rule-breaking behavior. Boundary violations that gain enough support become new, acceptable behaviors. Thus, deviance may force a group to rethink and redefine its moral boundaries, helping groups—and whole societies—to change their customary ways.

Strain Theory: How Social Values Produce Deviance

Functionalists argue that crime is a *natural* part of society, not an aberration or some alien element in our midst. Indeed, they say, some mainstream values actually generate crime. To understand what they mean, consider what sociologists Richard Cloward and Lloyd Ohlin (1960) identified as the crucial problem of the industrialized world: the need to locate and train the most talented people of every generation—whether they were born into wealth or into poverty—so that they can take over the key technical jobs of society. When children are born, no one knows which ones will have the ability to become dentists, nuclear physicists, or engineers. To get the most talented people to compete with one another, society tries to motivate *everyone* to strive for success. It does this by arousing discontent—making people feel dissatisfied with what they have so that they will try to "better" themselves.

Most people, then, end up with strong desires to reach **cultural goals** such as wealth or high status, or to achieve whatever other objectives society holds out for them. However, not everyone has equal access to society's **institutionalized means,** the legitimate ways of achieving success. Some people find their path to education and good jobs blocked. These people experience *strain* or frustration, which may motivate them to take a deviant path.

This perspective, known as **strain theory,** was developed by sociologist Robert Merton (1956, 1968). People who experience strain, he said, are likely to feel *anomie,* a sense of normlessness. Because mainstream norms (such as working hard or pursuing higher education) don't seem to be getting them anywhere, people who experience strain find it difficult to identify with these norms. They may even feel wronged by the system, and its rules may seem illegitimate.

Table 6.1 compares people's reactions to cultural goals and institutionalized means. The first reaction, which Merton said is the most common, is *conformity,* using socially acceptable means to try to reach cultural goals. In industrialized societies most people try to get good jobs, a good education, and so on. If well-paid jobs are unavailable, they take less desirable jobs. If they are denied access to Harvard or Stanford, they go to a state university. Others take night classes and go to vocational schools. In short, most people take the socially acceptable road.

Four Deviant Paths   The remaining four responses, which are deviant, represent reactions to strain. Let's look at each. *Innovators* are people who accept the goals of society but use illegitimate means to try to reach them. Crack dealers, for instance, accept the goal of achieving wealth, but they reject the legitimate avenues for doing so. Other examples are embezzlers, robbers, and con artists.

The second deviant path is taken by people who become discouraged and give up on achieving cultural goals. Yet they still cling to conventional rules of conduct. Merton called this response *ritualism.* Although ritualists have given up on getting ahead at work, they survive by following the rules of their job. Teachers whose idealism is shattered (who are said to suffer from "burnout"), for example, remain in the classroom, where they teach without enthusiasm. Their response is considered deviant because they cling to the job even though they have abandoned the goal, which may have been to stimulate young minds or to make the world a better place.

People who choose the third deviant path, *retreatism,* reject both the cultural goals and the institutionalized means of achieving them. Those who drop out of the pursuit of success by way of alcohol or drugs are retreatists. Although their withdrawal takes them on a different path, women who enter a convent or men a monastery are also retreatists.

cultural goals the legitimate objectives held out to the members of a society

institutionalized means approved ways of reaching cultural goals

strain theory Robert Merton's term for the strain engendered when a society socializes large numbers of people to desire a cultural goal (such as success), but withholds from many the approved means of reaching that goal; one adaptation to the strain is crime, the choice of an innovative means (one outside the approved system) to attain the cultural goal

Table 6.1   How People Match Their Goals to Their Means

Do They Feel the Strain That Leads to Anomie?	Mode of Adaptation	Cultural Goals	Institutionalized Means
No	Conformity	Accept	Accept
Yes	**Deviant Paths:**		
	1. Innovation	Accept	Reject
	2. Ritualism	Reject	Accept
	3. Retreatism	Reject	Reject
	4. Rebellion	Reject/Replace	Reject/Replace

Source: Based on Merton 1968.

The final type of deviant response is *rebellion*. Convinced that their society is corrupt, rebels, like retreatists, reject both society's goals and its institutionalized means. Unlike retreatists, however, rebels seek to give society new goals. Revolutionaries are the most committed type of rebels.

In sum: Strain theory underscores the sociological principle that deviants are the product of society. Mainstream social values (cultural goals and institutionalized means to reach those goals) can produce strain (frustration, dissatisfaction). People who feel this strain are more likely than others to take the deviant (nonconforming) paths summarized in Table 6.1.

Illegitimate Opportunity Structures: Social Class and Crime

One of the more interesting sociological findings in the study of deviance is that the social classes have distinct styles of crime. Let's see how unequal access to the institutionalized means to success helps to explain this.

Street Crime Functionalists point out that industrialized societies have no trouble socializing the poor into wanting to own things. Like others, the poor are bombarded with messages urging them to buy everything from X boxes and iPods to designer jeans and new cars. Television and movies show images of middle-class people enjoying luxurious lives. These images reinforce the myth that all full-fledged Americans can afford society's many goods and services.

In contrast, the school system, the most common route to success, often fails the poor. The middle class runs it, and there the children of the poor confront a bewildering world, one that is at odds with their background. Their speech, with its nonstandard grammar, is often sprinkled with what the middle class considers obscenities. Their ideas of punctuality, as well as their poor preparation in paper-and-pencil skills, are also a mismatch with their new environment. Facing such barriers, the poor are more likely than their more privileged counterparts to drop out of school. Educational failure, in turn, closes the door on many legitimate avenues to financial success.

Not infrequently, however, a different door opens to the poor, one that Cloward and Ohlin (1960) called **illegitimate opportunity structures.** Woven into the texture of life in urban slums, for example, are robbery, burglary, drug dealing, prostitution, pimping, gambling, and other crimes, commonly called "hustles" (Liebow 1967/1999; Sanchez-Jankowski 2003; Anderson 1978, 1990/2006). For many of the poor, the "hustler" is a role model—glamorous, in control, the image of "easy money," one of the few people in the area who comes close to attaining the cultural goal of success. For such reasons, then, these activities attract disproportionate numbers of the poor. As is discussed in the Down-to-Earth Sociology box on the next page, gangs are one way that the illegitimate opportunity structure beckons disadvantaged youth.

White-Collar Crime The more privileged social classes are not crime-free, of course, but for them different illegitimate opportunities beckon. They find *other forms* of crime to be functional. Physicians, for example, don't hold up cabbies, but many do cheat Medicare. You've heard about bookkeepers who embezzle from their employers and corporate officers who manipulate stock prices. In other words, rather than mugging, pimping, and committing burglary, the more privileged encounter "opportunities" for evading income tax, bribing public officials, embezzling, and so on. Sociologist Edwin Sutherland (1949) coined the term **white-collar crime** to refer to crimes that people of respectable and high social status commit in the course of their occupations.

A special form of white-collar crime is **corporate crime,** crimes committed by executives in order to benefit their corporation. For example, to increase corporate profits, Sears executives defrauded the poor of over $100 million. Their victims were so poor that they had filed for bankruptcy. To avoid a

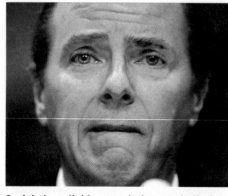

Social class divides people into such distinct ways of life that even crimes differ by social class. Jeffrey Skilling, former CEO of Enron Corporation, was convicted of 19 counts of fraud, conspiracy, and insider trading. The poor have neither the opportunity to commit these types of crimes nor the chance to make the huge profits they offer. In addition to his sentence of 24 years in prison, Skilling also had to pay back $45 million to victims of his crimes.

Islands in the Street: Urban Gangs in the United States

FOR MORE THAN TEN YEARS, sociologist Martín Sánchez Jankowski (1991) did participant observation of thirty-seven African American, Chicano, Dominican, Irish, Jamaican, and Puerto Rican gangs in Boston, Los Angeles, and New York City. The gangs earned money through gambling, arson, mugging, armed robbery, and selling moonshine, drugs, guns, stolen car parts, and protection. Jankowski ate, slept, and sometimes fought with the gangs, but by mutual agreement he did not participate in drug dealing or other illegal activities. He was seriously injured twice during the study.

Contrary to stereotypes, Jankowski did not find that the motive for joining was to escape a broken home (there were as many members from intact families as from broken homes) or to seek a substitute family (the same number of boys said they were close to their families as those that said they were not). Rather, the boys joined to gain access to money, to have recreation (including girls and drugs), to maintain anonymity in committing crimes, to get protection, and to help the community. This last reason may seem surprising, but in some neighborhoods, gangs protect residents from outsiders and spearhead political change (Kontos et al. 2003). The boys also saw the gang as an alternative to the dead-end—and deadening—jobs held by their parents.

Neighborhood residents are ambivalent about gangs. On the one hand, they fear the violence. On the other hand, many of the adults once belonged to gangs, some gangs provide better protection than the police, and gang members are the children of people who live in the neighborhood.

Particular gangs will come and go, but gangs will likely always remain part of the city. As functionalists point out, gangs fulfill needs of poor youth who live on the margins of society.

for your Consideration

What are the functions that gangs fulfill (the needs they meet)? Suppose that you have been hired as an urban planner by the City of Los Angeles. How could you arrange to meet the needs that gangs fulfill in ways that minimize violence and encourage youth to follow mainstream norms?

---

criminal trial, Sears pleaded guilty. This frightened the parent companies of Macy's and Bloomingdales, which had similar deceptive practices, and they settled with their debtors out of court (McCormick 1999). Similarly, Citigroup had to pay $70 million for preying on the poor (O'Brien 2004). None of the corporate thieves at Sears, Macy's, Bloomingdales, or Citigroup spent a day in jail.

Seldom is corporate crime taken seriously, even when it results in death. One of the most notorious corporate crimes involved the decision by Firestone executives to allow faulty tires to remain on U.S. vehicles—even though they were recalling the tires in Saudi Arabia and Venezuela. These tires cost the lives of about 200 Americans (White et al. 2001). No Firestone executive went to jail.

Consider this: Under federal law, causing the death of a worker by willfully violating safety rules is a misdemeanor punishable by up to six months in prison. Yet harassing a wild burro on federal lands is punishable by a year in prison (Barstow and Bergman 2003).

At $400 billion a year (Reiman 2004), "crime in the suites" actually costs more than "crime in the streets." This refers only to dollar costs. No one has yet figured out a way to compare, for example, the suffering experienced by a rape victim with the pain felt by an elderly couple who have lost their life savings to white-collar fraud.

The greatest concern of Americans, however, is street crime. They fear the violent stranger who will change their life forever. As the Social Map on the next page shows, the chances of such an encounter depend on where you live. From this map, you can see that entire regions are safer or more dangerous than others. In general, the northern states are the safest, and the southern states the most dangerous.

Figure 6.1 Some States Are Safer: Violent Crime in the United States

Violent crimes are murder, rape, robbery, and aggravated assault. As this figure illustrates, violent crime varies widely among the states. The chances of becoming a victim of these crimes are ten times higher in South Carolina, the most dangerous state, than in North Dakota, the safest state. Washington, D.C., not a state, is in a class by itself. Its rate of 1,371 is three times the national average and over 17 times North Dakota's rate.

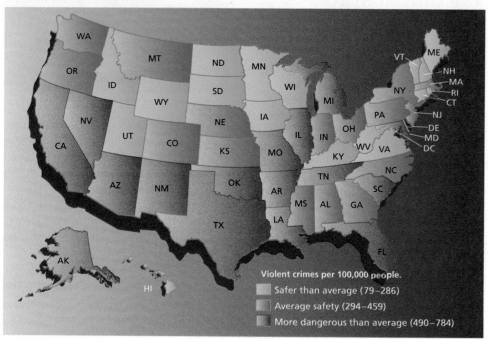

Violent crimes per 100,000 people.
- Safer than average (79–286)
- Average safety (294–459)
- More dangerous than average (490–784)

Source: By the author. Based on *Statistical Abstract of the United States* 2007:Table 297.

Gender and Crime   A major change in the nature of crime is the growing number of female offenders. As Table 6.2 shows, women are committing a larger proportion of crime—from car theft to possession of illegal weapons. The basic reason for this increase is women's changed social location. As more women work in factories, corporations, and

Table 6.2 Women and Crime: What a Difference a Dozen Years Make

Of all those arrested, what percentage are women?

Crime	1992	2004	Change
Car Theft	10.8%	17.1%	+58%
Burglary	9.2%	14.2%	+54%
Stolen Property	12.5%	18.6%	+49%
Aggravated Assault	14.8%	20.6%	+39%
Drunken Driving	13.8%	18.6%	+35%
Robbery	8.5%	11.0%	+29%
Arson	13.4%	16.2%	+21%
Larceny/Theft	32.1%	38.2%	+19%
Illegal Drugs	16.4%	18.9%	+15%
Forgery and Counterfeiting	34.7%	39.7%	+14%
Illegal Weapons	7.5%	8.2%	+9%
Fraud	42.1%	45.0%	+7%

Source: By the author. Based on *Statistical Abstract of the United States* 2007:Table 317.

the professions, their opportunities for crime increase. Like men, women are also enticed by illegitimate opportunities.

IN SUM Functionalists conclude that much street crime is the consequence of socializing everyone into equating success with owning material possessions, while denying many in the lower social classes the legitimate means to attain that success. People from higher social classes encounter different opportunities to commit crimes. The growing crime rates of women illustrate how changing gender roles are giving more women access to illegitimate opportunities.

The Conflict Perspective

Class, Crime, and the Criminal Justice System

Two leading U.S. aerospace companies, Hughes Electronics and Boeing Satellite Systems, were accused of illegally exporting missile technology to China. The technology places the United States at risk, for it allowed China to improve its delivery system for nuclear weapons. The two companies pleaded guilty and paid fines. No executives went to jail. (Gerth 2003)

Contrast this corporate crime—which places you in danger—with stories in newspapers about people who are sentenced to several years in prison for stealing cars. How can a legal system that is supposed to provide "justice for all" be so inconsistent? According to conflict theorists, this question is central to the analysis of crime and the **criminal justice system**—the police, courts, and prisons that deal with people who are accused of having committed crimes. Let's see what conflict theorists have to say about this.

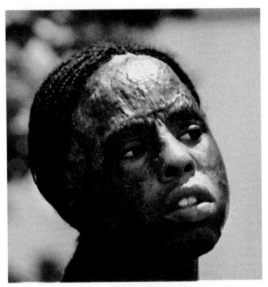

Most white-collar crime is a harmless nuisance, but some brings horrible costs. Shown here is Alisha Parker, who, with three siblings, was burned when the gas tank of her 1979 Chevrolet Malibu exploded after a rear-end collision. Although General Motors executives knew about the problem with the Malibu gas tanks, they had ignored it. Outraged at the callousness of GM's conduct, the jury awarded these victims the staggering sum of $4.9 billion.

This 1871 wood engraving depicts children as they are being paid for their day's work in a London brickyard. In early capitalism, most street criminals came from the *marginal working class*, as did these children. It is the same today.

criminal justice system the system of police, courts, and prisons set up to deal with people who are accused of having committed a crime

"If you want justice, it's two hundred dollars an hour. Obstruction of justice runs a bit more."

The cartoonist's hyperbole makes an excellent commentary on the social class disparity of our criminal justic system. Not only are the crimes of the wealthy not as likely to come to the attention of authorities as are the crimes of the poor, but when they do, the wealthy can afford legal expertise that the poor cannot.

Power and Inequality

Conflict theorists regard power and social inequality as the main characteristics of society. They stress that the power elite that runs society also controls the criminal justice system. This group makes certain that laws are passed that will protect its position in society. Other norms, such as those that govern informal behavior (chewing with a closed mouth, appearing in public with combed hair, and so on), may come from other sources, but they are not as important. Such norms influence our everyday behavior, but they do not determine who has power or who gets sent to prison.

Conflict theorists see the most fundamental division in capitalist society as that between the few who own the means of production and the many who sell their labor. Those who buy labor, and thereby control workers, make up the **capitalist class;** those who sell their labor form the **working class.** Toward the most depressed end of the working class is the **marginal working class:** people who have few skills, who are subject to layoffs, and whose jobs are low paying, part time, or seasonal. This class is marked by unemployment and poverty. From its ranks come most of the prison inmates in the United States. Desperate, these people commit street crimes, and because their crimes threaten the social order that keeps the elite in power, they are punished severely.

The Law as an Instrument of Oppression

According to conflict theorists, the idea that the law operates impartially and administers a code that is shared by all is a cultural myth promoted by the capitalist class. These theorists see the law as an instrument of oppression, a tool designed by the powerful to maintain their privileged position (Spitzer 1975; Reiman 2004; Chambliss 2000, 2007). Because the working class has the potential to rebel and overthrow the current social order, when its members get out of line, the law comes down hard on them.

For this reason, the criminal justice system does not focus on the owners of corporations and the harm they do through manufacturing unsafe products, creating pollution, and manipulating prices—or the crimes of Hughes and Boeing mentioned on the previous page. Instead, it directs its energies against violations by the working class. The violations of the capitalist class cannot be ignored totally, however, for if they become too outrageous or oppressive, the working class might rise up and revolt. To prevent this, a flagrant violation by a member of the capitalist class is occasionally prosecuted. The publicity given to the case helps to stabilize the social system by providing evidence of the "fairness" of the criminal justice system.

Usually, however, the powerful are able to bypass the courts altogether, appearing instead before an agency that has no power to imprison (such as the Federal Trade Commission). People from wealthy backgrounds who sympathize with the intricacies of the corporate world direct these agencies. It is they who oversee most cases of manipulating the price of stocks, insider trading, violating fiduciary duty, and so on. Is it surprising, then, that the typical sanction for corporate crime is a token fine?

When groups that have been denied access to power gain that access, we can expect to see changes in the legal system. This is precisely what is occurring now. Racial-ethnic minorities and homosexuals, for example, have more political power today than ever before. In line with conflict theory, a new category called *hate crime* has been formulated. We analyze this change in a different context on pages 178–179.

capitalist class the wealthy who own the means of production and buy the labor of the working class

working class those people who sell their labor to the capitalist class

marginal working class the most desperate members of the working class, who have few skills, little job security, and are often unemployed

IN SUM From the perspective of conflict theory, the small penalties that are imposed for crimes committed by the powerful are typical of a legal system that has been designed by the elite (capitalists) to keep themselves in power, to control workers, and, ultimately, to stabilize the social order. From this perspective, law enforcement is a cultural device through which the capitalist class carries out self-protective and repressive policies.

Reactions to Deviance

Whether it involves cheating on a sociology quiz or holding up a liquor store, any violation of norms invites reaction. Reactions, though, vary with culture. Before we examine reactions in the United States, let's take a little side trip to Greenland, an island nation three times the size of Texas located between Canada and Denmark. I think you'll enjoy this little excursion in cultural diversity.

Cultural Diversity *around the* World

"What Kind of Prison Is This?"

THE PRISON IN NUUK, the capital of Greenland, has no wall around it. It has no fence. It doesn't even have bars.

The other day, Meeraq Lendenhann, a convicted rapist, walked out of prison. He didn't run or hide. He just walked out. Meeraq went to a store he likes to shop at, bought a CD of his favorite group, U2, and then walked back to the prison.

If Meeraq tires of listening to music, he can send e-mail and play games on a computer. Like other prisoners, he also has a personal TV with satellite hookup.

The prison holds 60 prisoners—the country's killers, rapists, and a few thieves. The prisoners leave the prison to work at regular jobs, where they average $28,000 or so a year. But they have to return to the prison after work. And they are locked into their rooms at 9:30.

The prisoners have to work, because the prison charges them $150 a week for room and board. The extra money goes into their savings accounts, or to help support their families.

And, of course, the prisoners can have guns. At least during the summer. A major summer sport for Greenlanders is hunting reindeer and seals. Prisoners don't want to miss out on the fun, so if they ask, they are given shotguns.

But gun use isn't as easy as it sounds. Judges have set a severe requirement: The prisoners have to be accompanied by armed guards. If that isn't bad enough, the judges have added another requirement—that the prisoners not get drunk while they hunt.

One woman prisoner who said she was going to a beauty salon got sidetracked and went to a bar instead. When it got late and she was quite drunk, she called the prison and asked somone to come and get her.

If someone from another culture asks about the prisoners running away, the head of the prison says, "Where would they run? It's warm inside, and cold outside."

Then, of course, the prisoners probably wouldn't want to miss breakfast—a buffet of five kinds of imported cheese, various breads, marmalade, honey, coffee, and tea.

—Based on Naik 2004.

for your Consideration

Greenland's unique approach arose out of its history of hunting and fishing for a living. If men were locked up, they wouldn't be able to hunt or fish, and their families would suffer. From this history has come the main goal of Greenland's prison—to integrate offenders into society. This treatment helps prisoners slip back into village life after they have served their sentence. The incorrigibles, those who remain dangerous, about 20 men—are sent to a prison in Copenhagen, Denmark. Meeraq, the rapist, is given injections of androcur, a testosterone-reducing drug that lowers his sex drive. Alcoholics are given antabuse, a drug that triggers nasty reactions if someone drinks alcohol.

How do you think we could apply Greenland's approach to the United States?

Street Crime and Prisons

Let's turn back to the United States. Figure 6.2 illustrates the remarkable growth in the U.S. prison population. The number of prisoners is actually higher than the total shown in this figure. If we add jail inmates, the total comes to over two million people—one out of every 143 citizens. Not only does the United States have more prisoners than any other nation, but it also has a larger percentage of its population in prison as well. The number of prisoners has grown so fast that the states have had to hire private companies to operate jails for them. About 110,000 prisoners are in these "private" jails (*Sourcebook of Criminal Justice Statistics* 2006:Table 6.32).

To better understand U.S. prisoners, let's compare them with the U.S. population. As you look at Table 6.3 on the next page, several things may strike you. Almost all prisoners (87 percent) are ages 18 to 44, and almost all of them are men. Then there is this remarkable statistic: Although African Americans make up just 12.8 percent of the U.S. population, close to half of all prisoners are African Americans. On any given day, about

Figure 6.2 **How Much Is Enough? The Explosion in the Number of U.S. Prisoners**

To better understand how remarkable this change is, compare the increase in U.S. prisoners with the increase in the U.S. population. Between 1970 and 2004, the U.S. population increased 43 percent, while the number of prisoners increased 764 percent, *18 times greater*. If the number of prisoners had grown at the same rate as the U.S. population, there would be about 280,000 prisoners, only 13 percent of today's total. (Or, if the U.S. population had increased at the same rate as that of U.S. prisoners, the U.S. population would be 3,650,000,000—more than the population of China, India, Canada, Mexico, and all of Europe combined.)

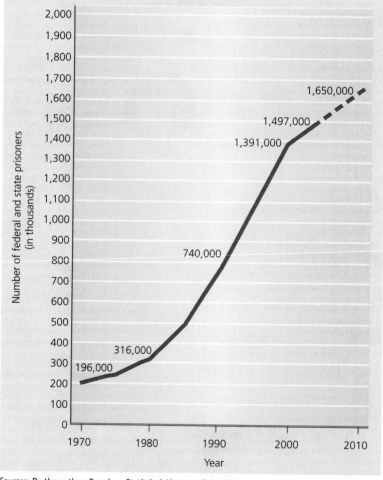

Sources: By the author. Based on *Statistical Abstract of the United States* 1995:Table 349; 2007:Table 334. The broken line is the author's estimate.

Table 6.3 **Inmates in U.S. State Prisons**

Characteristics	Percentage of Prisoners with These Characteristics	Percentage of U.S. Population with These Characteristics
Age		
18–24	26.4%	9.9%
25–34	35.4%	13.5%
35–44	25.2%	14.8%
45–54	10.4%	14.3%
55 and older	1.0%	22.7%
Race-Ethnicity		
African American	47.3%	12.8%
White	36.9%	66.9%
Latino	14.2%	14.4%
Asian Americans	0.6%	4.3%
Native Americans	0.9%	1.0%
Sex		
Male	93.4%	49.3%
Female	6.3%	50.7%
Marital Status		
Never Married	59.8%	28.2%
Divorced	15.5%	10.2%
Married	17.3%	58.6%
Widowed	1.1%	6.4%
Education		
Less than high school	39.7%	14.8%
High school graduate	49.0%	32.2%
Some college	9.0%	25.4%
College graduate (BA or higher)	2.4%	27.6%

Source: By the author. Based on *Sourcebook of Criminal Justice Statisitcs* 2003:Tables 6.000b, 6.28; 2006:Tables 6.34, 6.45; *Statistical Abstract of the United States* 2007:Tables 12, 14, 23, 55, 216.

one out of eight African American men ages 20 to 34 is in jail or prison (Butterfield 2003). Finally, note how marriage and education—two of the major techniques society has of "anchoring" us—provide protection from prison.

As I mentioned earlier, social class funnels some people into the criminal justice system and diverts others away from it. This table illuminates the power of education, a major component of social class. You can see how people who drop out of high school have a high chance of ending up in prison—and how unlikely it is for a college graduate to have this unwelcome destination in life.

For about the past 20 years or so, the United States has followed a "get tough" policy. "Three strikes and you're out" laws upon conviction for a third felony have become common. When someone is convicted of a third felony, judges are required to give a mandatory sentence, sometimes life imprisonment. While few of us would feel sympathy if a man convicted of a third brutal rape or a third murder were sent to prison for life, these laws have had unanticipated consequences, as you will see in the following Thinking Critically section.

Thinking Critically

"Three Strikes and You're Out!" Unintended Consequences of Well-Intended Laws

In the 1980s, the violent crime rate soared. Americans grew fearful, and they demanded that their lawmakers do something. Politicians heard the message, and they responded by passing the

recidivism rate the proportion of released convicts who are rearrested

"three strikes" law. Anyone who is convicted of a third felony receives an automatic mandatory sentence. Judges are not allowed to consider the circumstances. Some mandatory sentences carry life imprisonment.

In their haste to appease the public, the politicians did not limit the three-strike laws to *violent* crimes. And they did not consider that some minor crimes are considered felonies. As the functionalists would say, this has led to unanticipated consequences.

Here are some actual cases:

- In Los Angeles, a 27-year-old man was sentenced to 25 years for stealing a pizza (Cloud 1998).
- In New York City, a man who was about to be sentenced for selling crack said to the judge, "I'm only 19. This is terrible." He then hurled himself out of a courtroom window, plunging to his death sixteen stories below (Cloud 1998).
- In Sacramento, a man who passed himself off as Tiger Woods to go on a $17,000 shopping spree was sentenced to 200 years in prison (Reuters 2001).
- In California, a man who stole 9 videotapes from Kmart was sentenced to 50 years in prison without parole. He appealed to the U.S. Supreme Court, which upheld his sentence (Greenhouse 2003).
- In Utah, a 25-year-old was sentenced to 55 years in prison for selling small bags of marijuana to a police informant. The judge who sentenced the man said the sentence was unjust (Madigan 2004).

for your Consideration

Apply the symbolic interactionist, functionalist, and conflict perspectives to mandatory sentencing. For *symbolic interactionism*, what do these laws represent to the public? How does your answer differ depending on what part of "the public" you are referring to? For *functionalism*, who benefits from these laws? What are some of their dysfunctions? For the *conflict perspective*, what groups are in conflict? Who has the power to enforce their will on others?

The Decline in Violent Crime

As you saw in Figure 6.2, judges have put more and more people in prison. In addition, legislators passed the three-strikes laws and reduced early releases of prisoners. As these changes occurred, the crime rate dropped sharply, which has led to a controversy in sociology. Some sociologists conclude that getting tough on criminals was the main reason for the drop in violent crime (Conklin 2003). Others point to higher employment, a drop in drug use, and even abortion (Rosenfeld 2002; Reiman 2004; Blumstein and Wallman 2006). This matter is not yet settled, but both tough sentencing and the economy seem to be important factors.

Recidivism

A major problem with prisons is that they fail to teach their clients to stay away from crime. Our **recidivism rate**—the percentage of former prisoners who are rearrested—is high. For those who are sentenced to prison for crimes of violence, within just three

Beneath the humor of this cartoon lies a serious point about the high recidivism of U.S. prisoners.

Figure 6.3 Recidivism of U.S. Prisoners

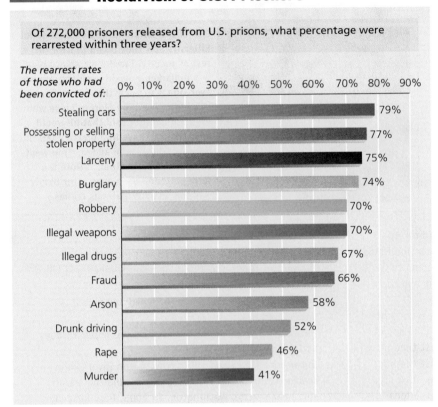

Of 272,000 prisoners released from U.S. prisons, what percentage were rearrested within three years?

The rearrest rates of those who had been convicted of:

Stealing cars	79%
Possessing or selling stolen property	77%
Larceny	75%
Burglary	74%
Robbery	70%
Illegal weapons	70%
Illegal drugs	67%
Fraud	66%
Arson	58%
Drunk driving	52%
Rape	46%
Murder	41%

Note: The individuals were not necessarily rearrested for the same crime for which they had originally been imprisoned.

Source: By the author. Based on *Sourcebook of Criminal Justice Statistics* 2003:Table 6.50.

years of their release, two out of three (62 percent) are rearrested, and half (52 percent) are back in prison (*Sourcebook of Criminal Justice Statistics* 2003:Table 6.52). Figure 6.3 shows recidivism by type of crime. It is safe to conclude that if—and this is a big if—the purpose of prisons is to teach people that crime doesn't pay, they are colossal failures.

The Death Penalty and Bias

Capital punishment, the death penalty, is the most extreme measure the state takes. The death penalty is mired in controversy, arousing impassioned opposition and support on both moral and philosophical grounds. Advances in DNA testing have given opponents of the death penalty a strong argument: Innocent people have been sent to death row, and some have been executed. Others are passionate about retaining the death penalty, pointing to such crimes as those of the serial killers discussed in the Down-to-Earth Sociology box on the next page.

Apart from anyone's personal position on the death penalty, it certainly is clear that the death penalty is not administered evenly. Consider geography: The Social Map on page 177 shows that where people commit murder greatly affects their chances of being put to death.

The death penalty also shows social class bias. As you know from news reports on murder and sentencing, it is rare for a rich person to be sentenced to death. Although the government does not collect statistics on social class and the death penalty, this common observation is borne out by the average education of the prisoners on death row. *Most* prisoners on death row (51 percent) have not finished high school (*Sourcebook of Criminal Justice Statistics* 2006:Table 6.81).

Figure 6.5 on page 178 shows gender bias in the death penalty. It is almost unheard of for a woman to be sentenced to death. Although women commit 9.6 percent of the

capital punishment the death penalty

Down-to-Earth Sociology

The Killer Next Door: Serial Murderers in Our Midst

I WAS STUNNED BY THE IMAGES. Television cameras showed the Houston police digging up dozens of bodies from under a boat storage shed. Fascinated, I waited impatiently for spring break. A few days later, I drove from Illinois to Houston, where 33-year-old Dean Corll had befriended Elmer Wayne Henley and David Brooks, two teenagers from broken homes. Together, they had killed 27 boys. Elmer and David would pick up young hitchhikers and deliver them to Corll to rape and kill. Sometimes they even brought him their high school classmates.

I talked to one of Elmer's neighbors, as he was painting his front porch. His 15-year-old son had gone to get a haircut one Saturday morning; it was the last time he had seen his son alive. The police insisted that the boy had run away, and they refused to investigate. On a city map, I plotted the locations of the homes of the local murder victims. Many clustered around the homes of the teenage killers.

I was going to spend my coming sabbatical writing a novel on this case, but, to be frank, I became frightened and didn't write the book. I didn't know if I could recover psychologically if I were to immerse myself in grisly details day after day for months on end. One of these details was a piece of plywood, with a hole in each of its four corners. Corll and the boys would spreadeagle their victims handcuffed to the plywood. There, they would torture the boys (no girl victims) for hours. Sometimes, they would even pause to order pizza.

My interviews confirmed what has since become common knowledge about serial killers: They lead double lives so successfully that their friends and family are unaware of their criminal activities. Henley's mother swore to me that her son was a good boy and couldn't possibly be guilty. Some of his high school friends told me the same thing. They stressed that Elmer couldn't be involved in homosexual rape and murder because he was interested only in girls. I conducted my interviews in Henley's bedroom, and for proof of what they told me, his friends pointed to a pair of girls' panties that were draped across a lamp shade.

Serial murder is the killing of several victims in three or more separate events. The murders may occur over several days, weeks, or years. The elapsed time between murders distinguishes serial killers from *mass murderers*, who do their killing all at once. Here are some infamous examples:

One of the striking traits of most serial killers is how they blend in with the rest of society. Ted Bundy, shown here, was remarkable in this respect. Almost everyone who knew this law student liked him. Even the Florida judge who found him guilty said that he would have liked to have him practice law in his court, but, as he added, "You went the wrong way, partner." (Note the term partner—used even after Bundy was convicted of heinous crimes.)

- Between 1962 and 1964, Albert De Salvo ("the Boston Strangler") raped and killed 13 women.
- During the 1960s and 1970s, Ted Bundy raped and killed dozens of women in four states.
- In the 1970s, John Wayne Gacy raped and killed 33 young men in Chicago.
- Between 1979 and 1981, Wayne Williams killed 28 boys and young men in Atlanta.
- During the 1980s and 1990s, the "Green River" killer scattered the bodies of prostitutes around the countryside near Seattle, Washington. In 2003, Gary Ridgway was convicted of the crimes and given 48 consecutive life sentences for killing 48 women.
- In 2005, in Wichita, Kansas, Dennis Rader pleaded guilty as the BTK (Bind, Torture, and Kill) strangler, a name he had proudly given himself. His 10 killings spanned 1974 to 1991.
- The serial killer with the most victims appears to be Harold Shipman of Manchester, England. From 1977 to 2000, this quiet, unassuming physician killed 230 to 275 of his elderly women patients. While making housecalls, he gave the women lethal injections.
- One of the most bizarre serial killers was Jeffrey Dahmer of Milwaukee. Dahmer fried and ate parts of his victims. When he did, he felt a "unity" with the victim.

Almost all serial killers are men, but an occasional woman joins this list of infamy:

- In North Carolina, Blanche Taylor Moore used arsenic to kill her father, her first husband, and a boyfriend. She was tripped up in 1986 when she tried to poison her current husband.
- In 1987 and 1988, Dorothea Montalvo Puente, who operated a boarding house in Sacramento, killed 7 of her boarders. Her motive was to collect their Social Security checks.
- In Missouri, from 1986 to 1989, Faye Copeland and her husband killed 5 transient men.
- In the late 1980s and early 1990s, Aileen Wuornos, hitchhiking along Florida's freeways, killed 7 men after having sex with them.

Many serial killers are motivated by lust and are sexually aroused by killing, so the FBI sometimes uses the term "lust murder." As with Ted Bundy and Jeffrey Dahmer, some have sex with their dead victims. Bundy returned day after day to the countryside to copulate with the corpses of his victims. Other serial killers, however, are more "garden variety," motivated by greed, like Dorothea Puente, who killed for money.

Is serial murder more common now than it used to be? Not likely. In the past, police departments had little communication with one another. When killings occurred in different jurisdictions, seldom did anyone connect them.

Today's more efficient communications, investigative techniques, and DNA matching make it easier for the police to conclude that a serial killer is operating in an area. Part of the perception that there are more serial killers today is also due to ignorance of our history: In our frontier past, serial killers went from ranch to ranch. Some would say that mass murderers wiped out entire villages of Native Americans.

for your Consideration

Do you think that serial killers should be given the death penalty? Why or why not? How do your social locations influence your opinion?

murders, they make up only 1.6 percent of death row inmates (*Sourcebook of Criminal Justice Statistics* 2006:Table 3.129). It is possible that this statistic reflects not only gender bias but also the relative brutality of the women's murders. We need research to determine this.

Bias used to be so flagrant that it once put a stop to the death penalty. Donald Partington (1965), a lawyer in Virginia, was shocked by the bias he saw in the courtroom, and he decided to document it. He found that 2,798 men had been convicted for rape and attempted rape in Virginia between 1908 and 1963—56 percent whites and 44 percent blacks. For attempted rape, 13 had been executed. For rape, 41 men had been executed. *All those executed were black.* Not one of the whites was executed.

After listening to evidence like this, in 1972 the Supreme Court ruled in *Furman* v. *Georgia* that the death penalty, was applied, was unconstitutional. The execution of prisoners stopped—but not for long. The states wrote new laws, and in 1977 they again began to execute prisoners. Since then, 67 percent of those put to death have been white and 33 percent African American (*Statistical Abstract* 2007:Table 340). (Latinos are evidently counted as whites in this statistic.) Table 6.4 on the next page shows the race-ethnicity of the prisoners who are on death row.

serial murder the killing of several victims in three or more separate events

Figure 6.4   Executions in the United States

Executions since 1977, when the death penalty was reinstated.

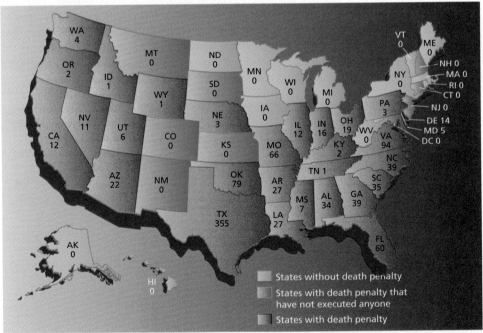

States without death penalty

States with death penalty that have not executed anyone

States with death penalty

Source: By the author. Based on *Statistical Abstract of the United States* 2007:Table 341.

Figure 6.5 Women and Men on Death Row

98.4%

Men

1.6%

Women

Source: By the author. Based on
Sourcebook of Criminal Justice Statistics
2006:Table 6.81.

Table 6.4 The Racial-Ethnicity of the 3,486 Prisoners on Death Row

	Percentage	
	on Death Row	in U.S. Population
Whites	45%	68%
African Americans	42%	12%
Latinos	11%	14%
Asian Americans	1%	4%
Native Americans	1%	1%

Source: By the author. Based on Sourcebook of Criminal Justice Statistics 2007:Table 6.80 and Figure 9.5 of this text.

Legal Change

Did you know that it is a crime in Saudi Arabia for a woman to drive a car (Fattah 2007)? A crime in Florida to sell alcohol before 1 p.m. on Sundays? Or illegal in Wells, Maine, to advertise on tombstones? As has been stressed in this chapter, deviance, including the form called *crime,* is relative. It varies from one society to another, and from group to group within a society. Crime also varies from one time period to another, as opinions change or as different groups gain access to power.

Hate crimes are an example of legal change, the topic of the next Thinking Critically Section.

Thinking Critically

Changing Views: Making Hate a Crime

Because crime consists of whatever acts authorities decide to assign that label, new crimes emerge from time to time. A prime example is juvenile delinquency, which Illinois lawmakers designated a separate type of crime in 1899. Juveniles committed crimes before this time, of course, but youths were not considered to be a separate type of lawbreaker. They were just young people who committed crimes, and they were treated the same as adults who committed the same crime. Sometimes new technology leads to new crimes. Motor vehicle theft, a separate crime in the United States, obviously did not exist before the automobile was invented.

Hate crimes, which range from murder and injury to defacing property with symbols of hatred, include arson, the suspected cause of the fire at this synagogue.

In the 1980s, another new crime was born when state governments developed the classification **hate crime.** This is a crime that is motivated by *bias* (dislike, hatred) against someone's race-ethnicity, religion, sexual orientation, disability, or national origin. Before this, of course, people attacked others or destroyed their property out of these same motivations, but in those cases the motivation was not the issue. If someone injured or killed another person because of that person's race-ethnicity, religion, sexual orientation, national origin, or disability, he or she was charged with assault or murder. Today, motivation has become a central issue, and hate crimes carry more severe sentences than do the same acts that do not have hatred as their motive. Table 6.5 summarizes the victims of hate crimes.

We can be certain that the "evolution" of crime is not yet complete. As society changes and as different groups gain access to power, we can expect the definitions of crime to change accordingly.

Table 6.5 Hate Crimes	
Directed Against	**Number of Victims**
Race-Ethnicity	
African Americans	3,494
Whites	1,027
Latinos	646
Asian Americans	272
Native Americans	102
Religion	
Jews	1,086
Muslims	202
Catholics	68
Protestants	48
Sexual Orientation	
Male Homosexual	902
Homosexual (general)	314
Female Homosexual	213
Heterosexual	32
Bisexual	18
Disabilities	
Mental	49
Physical	24

Source: Statistical Abstract of the United States 2007:Table 308.

for your **Consideration**

Why should we have a separate classification called hate crime? Why aren't the crimes of assault, robbery, and murder adequate? As one analyst (Sullivan 1999) said: "Was the brutal murder of gay college student Matthew Shepard [a hate crime] in Laramie, Wyoming, in 1998 worse than the abduction, rape, and murder of an eight-year-old Laramie girl [not a hate crime] by a pedophile that same year?"

How do you think your social location (race-ethnicity, gender, social class, sexual orientation, or physical ability) affects your opinion?

The Trouble with Official Statistics

Both the findings of symbolic interactionists (that stereotypes operate when authorities deal with groups such as the Saints and the Roughnecks) and the conclusion of conflict theorists (that the criminal justice system exists to serve the ruling elite) demonstrate the need for caution in interpreting official statistics. Crime statistics do not have an objective, independent existence. They are not like oranges that you pick out in a grocery store. Rather, crime statistics are a human creation. One major element in producing them is the particular laws that exist. Another is how those laws are enforced. Still another is how officials report their statistics. Change these factors, and the statistics also change.

Consider this: According to official statistics, working-class boys are clearly more delinquent than middle-class boys. Yet, as we have seen, who actually gets arrested for what is influenced by social class, a point that has far-reaching implications. As symbolic interactionists point out, the police follow a symbolic system as they enforce the law. Their ideas of "typical criminals" and "typical good citizens," for example, permeate their work. The more a suspect matches their stereotypes (which they call "criminal profiles"), the more likely that person is to be arrested. **Police discretion,** the decision of whether to arrest someone or even to ignore a matter, is a routine part of police work. Consequently, official crime statistics always reflect these and many other biases.

hate crime crimes to which more severe penalties are attached because they are motivated by hatred (dislike, animosity) of someone's race-ethnicity, religion, sexual orientation, disability, or national origin

police discretion the practice of the police, in the normal course of their duties, to either arrest or ticket someone for an offense or to overlook the matter

Reactions to deviants vary from such mild sanctions as frowns and stares to such severe responses as imprisonment and death. Some sanctions are formal—court hearings, for example—but most are informal, as when friends refuse to talk to each other. One sanction is to label someone a deviant, which can have powerful consequences for the person's life, especially if the label closes off conforming activities and opens deviant ones. The degradation ceremony, in which someone is publicly labeled "not one of us," is a powerful sanction. So is imprisonment. Official statistics must be viewed with caution, for they reflect biases.

The Medicalization of Deviance: Mental Illness

Another way in which society deals with deviance is to "medicalize" it. Let's look at what this entails.

Neither Mental Nor Illness?

medicalization of deviance to make deviance a medical matter, a symptom of some underlying illness that needs to be treated by physicians

To *medicalize* something is to make it a medical matter, to classify it as a form of illness that properly belongs in the care of physicians. For the past hundred years or so, especially since the time of Sigmund Freud (1856–1939), the Viennese physician who founded psychoanalysis, there has been a growing tendency toward the **medicalization of deviance.** In this view, deviance, including crime, is a sign of mental sickness. Rape, murder, stealing, cheating, and so on are external symptoms of internal disorders, consequences of a confused or tortured mind.

Thomas Szasz (1986, 1996, 1998), a renegade in his profession of psychiatry, argues that *mental illnesses are neither mental nor illnesses. They are simply problem behaviors.* Some forms of so-called mental illnesses have organic causes; that is, they are *physical* illnesses that result in unusual perceptions or behavior. Some depression, for example, is caused by a chemical imbalance in the brain, which can be treated by drugs. The depression, however, may appear in the forms of crying, long-term sadness, and lack of interest in family, work, school, or one's appearance. When someone becomes deviant in ways that disturb others, *and* when these others cannot find a satisfying explanation for why the person is "like that," a "sickness in the head" is often taken as the cause of the unacceptable behavior.

Attention deficit disorder (ADD) is an excellent example. As Szasz says, "No one explains where this disease came from, why it didn't exist 50 years ago. No one is able to diagnose it with objective tests." It is diagnosed by a teacher or a parent complaining about a child misbehaving. Misbehaving children have been a problem throughout history, but now their problem behavior has become a sign of mental illness.

All of us have troubles. Some of us face a constant barrage of problems as we go through life. Most of us continue the struggle, perhaps encouraged by relatives and friends and motivated by job, family responsibilities, religious faith, and life goals. Even when the odds seem hopeless, we carry on, not perfectly, but as best we can.

People whose behaviors violate norms often are called mentally ill. "Why else would they do such things?" is a common response to deviant behaviors that we don't understand. Mental illness is a label that contains the assumption that there is something wrong "within" people that "causes" their disapproved behavior. The surprise with this man, who changed his legal name to "Scary Guy," is that he speaks at schools across the country, where he promotes acceptance, awareness, love, and understanding.

Some people, however, fail to cope well with life's challenges. Overwhelmed, they become depressed, uncooperative, or hostile. Some strike out at others, while some, in Merton's terms, become retreatists and withdraw into their apartments or homes, not wanting to come out. These are *behaviors, not mental illnesses*, stresses Szasz. They may be inappropriate coping devices, but they are coping devices nevertheless, not mental illnesses. Thus, Szasz concludes that "mental illness" is a myth foisted on a naive public by a medical profession that uses pseudoscientific jargon in order to expand its area of control and force nonconforming people to accept society's definitions of "normal."

Szasz's extreme claim forces us to look anew at the forms of deviance that we usually refer to as mental illness. To explain behavior that people find bizarre, he directs our attention not to causes hidden deep within the "subconscious," but, instead, to how people learn such behaviors. To ask, "What is the origin of someone's inappropriate or bizarre behavior?" then becomes similar to asking "Why do some women steal?" "Why do some men rape?" "Why do some teenagers cuss their parents and stalk out of the room, slamming the door?" *The answers depend on those people's particular experiences in life, not on an illness in their mind.* In short, some sociologists find Szasz's renegade analysis refreshing because it indicates that *social experiences*, not some illness of the mind, underlie bizarre behaviors—as well as deviance in general.

The Homeless Mentally Ill

Jamie was sitting on a low wall surrounding the landscaped courtyard of an exclusive restaurant. She appeared unaware of the stares that were elicited by her layers of mismatched clothing, her matted hair and dirty face, and the shopping cart that overflowed with her meager possessions.

When I saw Jamie point to the street and concentrate, slowly moving her finger horizontally. I asked her what she was doing.

"I'm directing traffic," she replied. "I control where the cars go. Look, that one turned right there," she said, now withdrawing her finger.

"Really?" I said.

After a while she confided that her cart talked to her.

"Really?" I said again.

"Yes," she replied. "You can hear it, too." At that, she pushed the shopping cart a bit. "Did you hear that?" she asked.

When I shook my head, she demonstrated again. Then it hit me. She was referring to the squeaking wheels!

I nodded.

When I left, Jamie was pointing to the sky, for, as she told me, she also controlled the flight of airplanes.

To most of us, Jamie's behavior and thinking are bizarre. They simply do not match any reality we know. Could you or I become like Jamie?

Suppose for a bitter moment that you are homeless and have to live on the streets. You have no money, no place to sleep, no bathroom. You do not know *if* you are going to eat, much less where. You have no friends or anyone you can trust, and you live in constant fear of rape and other violence. Do you think this might be enough to drive you over the edge?

Consider just the problems involved in not having a place to bathe. (Shelters are often so dangerous that many homeless people prefer to sleep in public settings.) At first, you try to wash in the rest rooms of gas stations, bars, the bus station, or a shopping center. But you are dirty, and people stare when you enter and call the management when they see you wash your feet in the sink. You are thrown out and told in no uncertain terms never to come back. So you get dirtier and dirtier. Eventually, you come to think of being dirty as a fact of life. Soon, maybe, you don't even care. The stares no longer bother you—at least not as much.

Mental illness is common among the homeless. This man, who hangs out near Boston Common in Boston, Massachusetts, has been homeless for 44 years. This gives you an idea of the depth of the problem of rehabilitation.

No one will talk to you, and you withdraw more and more into yourself. You begin to build a fantasy life. You talk openly to yourself. People stare, but so what? They stare anyway. Besides, they are no longer important to you.

Jamie might be mentally ill. Some organic problem, such as a chemical imbalance in her brain, might underlie her behavior. But perhaps not. How long would it take you to exhibit bizarre behaviors if you were homeless—and hopeless? The point is that *just being on the streets can cause mental illness*—or whatever we want to label socially inappropriate behaviors that we find difficult to classify. *Homelessness and mental illness are reciprocal:* Just as "mental illness" can cause homelessness, so the trials of being homeless, of living on cold, hostile streets, can lead to unusual thinking and behaviors.

The Need for a More Humane Approach

As Durkheim (1895/1964:68) pointed out, deviance is inevitable—even in a group of saints.

> Imagine a society of saints, a perfect cloister of exemplary individuals. Crimes, properly so called, will there be unknown; but faults which appear [invisible] to the layman will create there the same scandal that the ordinary offense does in ordinary [society].

With deviance inevitable, one measure of a society is how it treats its deviants. Our prisons certainly don't say much good about U.S. society. Filled with the poor, they are warehouses of the unwanted. They reflect patterns of broad discrimination in our larger society. White-collar criminals continue to get by with a slap on the wrist while street criminals are punished severely. Some deviants, who fail to meet current standards of admission to either prison or mental hospital, take refuge in shelters, as well as in cardboard boxes tucked away in urban recesses. Although no one has *the* answer, it does not take much reflection to see that there are more humane approaches than these.

Because deviance is inevitable, the larger issues are to find ways to protect people from deviant behaviors that are harmful to themselves or others, to tolerate those behaviors that are not harmful, and to develop systems of fairer treatment for deviants. In the absence of fundamental changes that would bring about a truly equitable social system, most efforts are, unfortunately, like putting a Band Aid on a gunshot wound. What we need is a more humane social system, one that would prevent the social inequalities that are the focus of the next four chapters.

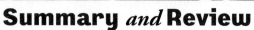

Summary *and* Review

What Is Deviance?

From a sociological perspective, **deviance** (the violation of norms) is relative. What people consider deviant varies from one culture to another and from group to group within the same society. As symbolic interactionists stress, it is not the act, but the reactions to the act, that make something deviant. All groups develop systems of **social control** to punish **deviants**—those who violate their norms. Pp. 154–158.

How do sociological and individualistic explanations of deviance differ?

To explain why people deviate, sociobiologists and psychologists look for reasons *within* the individual, such as **genetic predispositions** or **personality disorders.** Sociologists, in contrast, look for explanations *outside* the individual, in social experiences. Pp. 158–159.

The Symbolic Interactionist Perspective

How do symbolic interactionists explain deviance?

Symbolic interactionists have developed several theories to explain deviance such as **crime** (the violation of norms that are written into law). According to **differential association theory,** people learn to deviate by associating with others. According to **control theory,** each of us is propelled toward deviance, but most of us conform because of an effecti ve system of inner and outer controls. People who have less effective controls deviate. Pp. 159–161.

Labeling theory focuses on how labels (names, reputations) help to funnel people into or divert them away from deviance. People who commit deviant acts often use techniques of neutralization to continue to think of themselves as conformists. Pp. 161–163.

The Functionalist Perspective

How do functionalists explain deviance?

Functionalists point out that deviance, including criminal acts, is functional for society. Functions include affirming norms and promoting social unity and social change. According to **strain theory,** societies socialize their members into desiring **cultural goals.** Many people are unable to achieve these goals in socially acceptable ways—that is, by **institutionalized means.** *Deviants,* then, are people who either give up on the goals or use deviant means to attain them. Merton identified five types of responses to cultural goals and institutionalized means: conformity, innovation, ritualism, retreatism, and rebellion. **Illegitimate opportunity theory** stresses that some people have easier access to illegal means of achieving goals. Pp. 163–169.

The Conflict Perspective

How do conflict theorists explain deviance?

Conflict theorists take the position that the group in power (the **capitalist class**) imposes its definitions of deviance on other groups (the **working class** and the **marginal working class**). From the conflict perspective, the law is an instrument of oppression used to maintain the power and privilege of the few over the many. The marginal working class has little income, is desperate, and commits highly visible property crimes. The ruling class directs the **criminal justice system,** using it to punish the crimes of the poor while diverting its own criminal activities away from this punitive system. Pp. 169–171.

Reactions to Deviance

What are common reactions to deviance in the United States?

In following a "get-tough" policy, the United States has imprisoned millions of people. African Americans and Latinos make up a disproportionate percentage of U.S. prisoners. The death penalty shows biases by geography, social class, race–ethnicity, and gender. In line with conflict theory, as groups gain political power, their views are reflected in the criminal code. **Hate crime** legislation was considered in this context. Pp. 171–179.

Are official statistics on crime reliable?

The conclusions of both symbolic interactionists (that the police operate with a large measure of discretion) and conflict theorists (that the capitalist class controls the legal system) indicate that we must be cautious when using crime statistics. P. 179.

What is the medicalization of deviance?

The medical profession has attempted to **medicalize** many forms of **deviance,** claiming that they represent mental illnesses. Thomas Szasz disagrees, asserting that they are problem behaviors, not mental illnesses. Research on homeless people illustrates how problems in living can lead to bizarre behavior and thinking. Pp. 180–181.

What is a more humane approach?

Deviance is inevitable, so the larger issues are to find ways to protect people from deviance that harms themselves and others, to tolerate deviance that is not harmful, and to develop systems of fairer treatment for deviants. P. 181.

Thinking Critically
about Chapter 6

1. Select some deviance with which you are personally familiar. (It does not have to be your own—it can be something that someone you know did.) Choose one of the three theoretical perspectives to explain what happened.

2. As is explained in the text, deviance can be mild. Recall some instance in which you broke a social rule in dress, etiquette, or speech. What was the reaction? Why do you think people reacted like that? What was your response to their reactions?

3. What do you think should be done about the U.S. crime problem? What sociological theories support your view?

Additional Resources

What can you use MySocLab for?  www.mysoclab.com

- **Study and Review:** Pre- and Post-Tests, Practice Tests, Flash Cards, Individualized Study Plans.

- **Current Events:** *Sociology in the News,* the daily *New York Times,* and more.

- **Research and Writing:** *Research Navigator, Writing About Sociology,* and more.

Where Can I Read More on This Topic?

Suggested readings for this chapter are listed at the back of this book.

Social Stratification

Frank Freed, *Have and Have Not* 1970

Ah, New Orleans, that fabled city on the Mississippi Delta. Images from its rich past floated through my head—pirates, treasure, intrigue. Memories from a pleasant vacation stirred my thoughts—the exotic French Quarter with its enticing aroma of Creole food and sounds of earthy jazz drifting through the air.

The shelter for the homeless, however, forced me back to an unwelcome reality. The shelter was the same as those I had visited in the North, West, and East—only dirtier. The dirt, in fact, was the worst that I had encountered during my research, and this shelter was the only one to insist on payment in exchange for sleeping in one of its filthy beds.

The men looked the same—disheveled and haggard, wearing that unmistakable expression of despair—just like the homeless anywhere in the country. Except for the accent, you wouldn't know what region you were in. Poverty wears the same tired face wherever you are, I realized. The accent may differ, but the look remains the same.

I was startled by a sight so out of step with the misery and despair I had just experienced that I stopped in midtrack.

I had grown used to the sights and smells of abject poverty. Those no longer surprised me. But after my fitful sleep with the homeless, I saw something that did. Just a block or so from the shelter, I was startled by a sight so out of step with the misery and despair I had just experienced that I stopped in midtrack.

Indignation swelled within me. Confronting me were life-size, full-color photos mounted on the transparent plexiglass shelter of a bus stop. Staring back at me were images of finely dressed men and women proudly strutting about as they modeled elegant suits, dresses, diamonds, and furs.

A wave of disgust swept over me. "Something is cockeyed in this society," I thought, my mind refusing to stop juxtaposing these images of extravagance with the suffering I had just witnessed. Occasionally, the reality of social class hits home with brute force. This was one of those moments.

social stratification the division of large numbers of people into layers according to their relative power, property, and prestige; applies to both nations and to people within a nation, society, or other group

slavery a form of social stratification in which some people own other people

The disjunction that I felt in New Orleans was triggered by the ads, but it was not the first time that I had experienced this sensation. Whenever my research abruptly transported me from the world of the homeless to one of another social class, I experienced a sense of disjointed unreality. Each social class has its own way of being, and because these fundamental orientations to the world contrast so sharply, the classes do not mix well.

An Overview of Social Stratification

Some of the world's nations are wealthy, others poor, and some in between. This layering of nations—and of groups of people within a nation—is called **social stratification.** This term refers to a system in which groups of people are divided into layers according to their relative property, prestige, and power. Social stratification is one of the most significant topics we discuss in this book, for it affects our life chances—from our access to material possessions to the age at which we die.

Every society stratifies its members. Some societies have greater inequality than others, but social stratification is universal. In addition, in every society of the world, *gender* is a basis for stratifying people. On the basis of their gender, people are either allowed or denied access to the good things offered by their society.

Let's consider three systems of social stratification: slavery, caste, and class.

Slavery

Slavery, whose essential characteristic is that *some individuals own other people,* has been common throughout world history. The Old Testament even lays out rules for how owners should treat their slaves. So does the Koran. The Romans also had slaves, as did the Africans and Greeks. In classical Greece and Rome, slaves did the work, freeing citizens to engage in politics and the arts. Slavery was most widespread in agricultural societies and least common among nomads, especially hunters and gatherers (Landtman 1938/1968). As we examine the major causes and conditions of slavery, you will see how remarkably slavery has varied around the world.

Causes of Slavery   Contrary to popular assumption, slavery was usually based not on racism but on one of three other factors. The first was *debt.* In some societies, creditors would enslave people who could not pay their debts. The second was *crime.* Instead of being killed, a murderer or thief might be enslaved by the victim's family as compensation for their loss. The third was *war.* When one group of people conquered another, they often enslaved some of the vanquished. Historian Gerda Lerner (1986) notes that women were the first people enslaved through warfare. When tribal men raided another group, they killed the men, raped the women, and then brought the women back as slaves. The women were valued for sexual purposes, for reproduction, and for their labor.

Roughly twenty-five hundred years ago, when Greece was but a collection of city-states, slavery was common. A city that became powerful and conquered another city would enslave some of the vanquished. Both slaves and slaveholders were Greek. Similarly, when Rome became the supreme power of the Mediterranean area about two thousand years ago, following the custom of the time, the Romans enslaved some of the Greeks they had conquered. More educated than their conquerors, some of these slaves served as tutors in Roman homes. Slavery, then, was a sign of debt, of crime, or of defeat in battle. It was not a sign that the slave was inherently inferior.

Conditions of Slavery   The conditions of slavery have varied widely around the world. *In some places, slavery was temporary.* Slaves of the Israelites were set free in the year of jubilee, which occurred every fifty years. Roman slaves ordinarily had the right to buy themselves out of slavery.

Negroes for Sale.

A Cargo of very fine stout Men and Women, in good order and fit for immediate service, just imported from the Windward Coast of Africa, in the Ship Two Brothers.—
Conditions are one half Cash or Produce, the other half payable the first of January next, giving Bond and Security if required.
   The Sale to be opened at 10 o'Clock each Day, in Mr. Bourdeaux's Yard, at No. 48, on the Bay.
   May 19, 1784.   JOHN MITCHELL.

Under slavery, humans are sold like a commodity. This 1784 announcement reveals that slaves could be bought for cash or exchanged for produce (crops).

They knew what their purchase price was, and some were able to meet this price by striking a bargain with their owner and selling their services to others. In most instances, however, slavery was a lifelong condition. Some criminals, for example, became slaves when they were given life sentences as oarsmen on Roman war ships. There they served until death, which often came quickly to those in this exhausting service.

Slavery was not necessarily inheritable. In most places, the children of slaves were automatically slaves themselves. But in some instances, the child of a slave who served a rich family might even be adopted by that family, becoming an heir who bore the family name along with the other sons or daughters of the household. In ancient Mexico, the children of slaves were always free (Landtman 1938/1968:271).

Slaves were not necessarily powerless and poor. In almost all instances, slaves owned no property and had no power. Among some groups, however, slaves could accumulate property and even rise to high positions in the community. Occasionally, a slave might even become wealthy, loan money to the master, and, while still a slave, own slaves himself or herself (Landtman 1938/1968). This, however, was rare.

Slavery in the New World A gray area between a contract and slavery is **bonded labor,** also called **indentured service.** Many people who wanted to start a new life in the American colonies were unable to pay their passage across the ocean. Ship captains would transport them on credit, and colonists would "buy their paper" when they arrived. This arrangement provided passage for the penniless, payment for the ship's captain, and, for wealthier colonists, servants for a set number of years. During that specified period, the servants were required by law to serve their master. If they ran away, they became outlaws who were hunted down and forcibly returned. At the end of the period of indenture, they became full citizens, able to live where they chose and free to sell their labor (Main 1965; Elkins 1968).

When there were not enough indentured servants to meet their growing need for labor, some colonists tried to enslave Native Americans. This attempt failed miserably. One reason was that when Indians escaped, they knew how to survive in the wilderness and were able to make their way back to their tribe. The colonists then turned to Africans, who were being brought to North and South America by the Dutch, English, Portuguese, and Spanish.

Because slavery has a broad range of causes, some analysts conclude that racism didn't lead to slavery, but, rather, slavery led to racism. Finding it profitable to make people slaves for life, U.S. slave owners developed an **ideology,** beliefs that justify social arrangements. Ideology leads to a perception of the world that makes current social arrangements seem inevitable, necessary, and fair. The colonists developed the view that their slaves were inferior. Some even said that they were not fully human. In short, the colonists wove elaborate justifications for slavery, built on the presumed superiority of their own group.

To make slavery even more profitable, slave states passed laws that made slavery *inheritable;* that is, the babies born to slaves became the property of the slave owners (Stampp 1956). These children could be sold, bartered, or traded. To strengthen their control, slave states passed laws making it illegal for slaves to hold meetings or to be away from the master's premises without carrying a pass (Lerner 1972). As sociologist W. E. B. Du Bois (1935/1992:12) noted, "gradually the entire white South became an armed camp to keep Negroes in slavery and to kill the black rebel."

The Civil War did not end legal discrimination. For example, until 1954 the states operated two separate school systems. Even until the 1950s, in order to keep the races from "mixing," it was illegal in Mississippi for a white and an African American to sit together on the same seat of a car! The reason there was no outright ban on blacks and whites being in the same car was to allow whites to employ African American chauffeurs.

Slavery Today Slavery has again reared its ugly head in several parts of the world. The Ivory Coast, Mauritania, Niger, and Sudan have a long history of slavery, and not until the 1980s was slavery made illegal in Mauritania and Sudan (Ayittey 1998). It took until 2004 for slavery to be banned in Niger (Andersson 2005). Although officially abolished, slavery in this region continues, the topic of the Mass Media box on the next page.

bonded labor, or **indentured service** a contractual system in which someone sells his or her body (services) for a specified period of time in an arrangement very close to slavery, except that it is voluntarily entered into

ideology beliefs about the way things ought to be that justify social arrangements

mass Media in social life

What Price Freedom? Slavery Today

Children of the Dinka tribe in rural Sudan don't go to school. They work. Their families depend on them to tend the cattle that are essential to their way of life.

> On the morning of the raid, ten-year-old Adhieu had been watching the cattle. "We were very happy because we would soon leave the cattle camps and return home to our parents. But in the morning, there was shooting. There was yelling and crying everywhere. My uncle grabbed me by the hand, and we ran. We swam across the river. I saw some children drowning. We hid behind a rock."

By morning's end, 500 children were either dead or enslaved. Their attackers were their fellow countrymen—Arabs from northern Sudan. The children who were captured were forced to march hundreds of miles north. Some escaped on the way. Others tried to—and were shot (Akol 1998).

Tens of thousands of Dinkas were killed or enslaved after civil war broke out in Sudan in the 1980s. Yet the Arab-led government—the National Islamic Front—insisted that slavery did not exist. It claimed that foreign politicians and Christian humanitarians who didn't like the Sudanese government invented the slavery. Then the hostile foreign media publicized the nonexistent slavery (Akol 1998).

That was quite a creative defense. But the slavery did exist. There were too many witnesses and too much documentation by human rights groups. Journalists also provided devastating accounts: In the United States, public television (PBS) ran film footage of captive children in chains. And escaped slaves recounted their ordeal in horrifying detail (Salopek 2003; Mende and Lewis 2005).

The United States bombed Kosovo (in Serbia) into submission for its crimes against humanity, yet it remained largely silent in the face of the outrage in Sudan. A cynic might say that Kosovo was located at a politically strategic spot in Europe, whereas Sudan occupies an area of Africa in which the U.S. and European powers have had little interest. A cynic might add that these powers fear Arab retaliation, which might take the form of oil embargoes and terrorism. A cynic might also suggest that outrages against black Africans are not as significant to these powers as those against white Europeans. Finally, a cynic might add that this will change as Sudan's oil reserves become more strategic to Western interests.

When the world's most powerful governments didn't act on behalf of the slaves, private groups stepped in. One was Christian Solidarity International (CSI), based in Zurich, Switzerland. CSI sent Arab "retrievers" to northern Sudan, where they either bought or abducted slaves. Walking by night and hiding by day, the retrievers eluded security forces and brought the slaves south. There, CSI paid the retrievers $50 per slave (Mabry 1999).

> As CBS news cameras rolled, the rescuer paid the slave trader $50,000 in Sudanese pounds. At $50 per person, the bundle of bills was enough to free 1,000 slaves. The liberated slaves, mostly women and children, were then free to return to their villages. (Jacobs 1999)

These payments brought harsh criticism from those who claimed that buying slaves, even to free them, encourages slavery. Critics said that the money provided motivation to enslave people in order to turn around and sell them. Certainly $50 is a lot of money in Sudan, where people are lucky to make $50 a month *(Sociological Abstract* 2007:Table 1324).

In this photo, a representative of the Liason Agency Network (on the left) is buying the freedom of the Sudanese slaves (in the background).

CSI said that this was a bogus argument. What is intolerable, they said, is to leave women and children in slavery where they are deprived of their freedom and families, and beaten and raped by brutal masters.

for your Consideration

What do you think about buying the freedom of slaves? Can you suggest a workable alternative in such a situation? Why do you think the U.S. government remained largely silent about this issue, when it invaded other countries such as Serbia and Haiti for human rights abuses? Do you think that, perhaps, political motivations outweigh human rights motivations? If not, why the silence in the face of slavery?

The media coverage of this issue motivated many Americans to become active in freeing slaves. Some high schools—and even grade schools—raised money to participate in slave buyback programs. If you were a school principal, would you encourage this practice? Why or why not?

The enslavement of children for work and sex is a problem in Africa, Asia, and South America (LaFraniere 2006). A unique form of child slavery occurs in Kuwait, Qatar, and the United Arab Emirates. There, little boys are held in captivity because they are prized as jockeys in camel races (Brinkley 2005). It is thought that their screams make the camels run faster.

Caste

The second system of social stratification is caste. In a **caste system,** status is determined by birth and is lifelong. Someone who is born into a low-status group will always have low status, no matter how much that person may accomplish in life. In sociological terms, a caste system is built on ascribed status (discussed on page 101). Achieved status cannot change an individual's place in this system.

Societies with this form of stratification try to make certain that the boundaries between castes remain firm. They practice **endogamy,** marriage within their own group, and prohibit intermarriage. To reduce contact between castes, they even develop elaborate rules about *ritual pollution,* teaching that contact with inferior castes contaminates the superior caste.

India's Religious Castes India provides the best example of a caste system. Based not on race but on religion, India's caste system has existed for almost three thousand years (Chandra 1993a; Jaffrelot 2006). India's four main castes are depicted in Table 7.1 on the next page. These four castes are subdivided into about three thousand subcastes, or *jati.* Each *jati* specializes in a particular occupation. For example, one subcaste washes clothes, another sharpens knives, and yet another repairs shoes.

The lowest group listed in Table 7.1, the Dalit, make up India's "untouchables." If a Dalit touches someone of a higher caste, that person becomes unclean. Even the shadow of an untouchable can contaminate. Early morning and late afternoons are especially risky, for the long shadows of these periods pose a danger to everyone higher up the caste system. Consequently, Dalits are not allowed in some villages during these times. Anyone who becomes contaminated must follow *ablution,* or washing rituals, to restore purity.

During my research in India, I interviewed this 8-year-old girl. Mahashury is a *bonded laborer* who was exchanged by her parents for a 2,000 rupee loan (about $14). To repay the loan, Mahashury must do construction work for one year. She will receive one meal a day and one set of clothing for the year. Because this centuries-old practice is now illegal, the master bribes Indian officials, who inform him when they are going to inspect the construction site. He then hides his bonded laborers. I was able to interview and photograph Mahashury because her master was absent the day I visited the construction site.

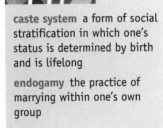

caste system a form of social stratification in which one's status is determined by birth and is lifelong

endogamy the practice of marrying within one's own group

In a *caste system*, status is determined by birth and is lifelong. At birth, these women received not only membership in a lower caste but also, because of their gender, a predetermined position in that caste. When I photographed these women, they were carrying sand to the second floor of a house being constructed in Andhra Pradesh, India.

Table 7.1 India's Caste System	
Caste	**Occupation**
Brahman	Priests and teachers
Kshatriya	Rulers and soldiers
Vaishya	Merchants and traders
Shudra	Peasants and laborers
Dalit (untouchables)	The outcastes; degrading or polluting labor

Although the Indian government formally abolished the caste system in 1949, centuries-old practices cannot be eliminated so easily, and the caste system remains part of everyday life in India. The ceremonies people follow at births, marriages, and deaths, for example, are dictated by caste (Chandra 1993a). The upper castes dread the upward mobility of the untouchables, sometimes resisting it even with violence and ritual suicide (Crossette 1996; Deliege 2001; Jaffrelot 2006). From personal observations in India, I can add that in some villages, Dalit children are not allowed in the government schools. If they try to enroll, they are beaten.

A U.S. Racial Caste System Before leaving the subject of caste, we should note that when slavery ended in the United States, it was replaced by a *racial caste system.* From the moment of birth, everyone was marked for life (Berger 1963/2007). In this system, *all* whites, even if they were poor and uneducated, considered themselves to have a higher status than *all* African Americans. As in India and South Africa, the upper caste, fearing pollution from the lower caste, prohibited intermarriage, and insisted on separate schools, hotels, restaurants, and even toilets and drinking fountains in public facilities. When any white met any African American on a Southern sidewalk, the African American had to move aside—which the untouchables of India still must do when they meet someone of a higher caste (Deliege 2001).

Social Class

class system a form of social stratification based primarily on the possession of money or material possessions

social mobility movement up or down the social class ladder

As we have seen, stratification systems based on slavery, caste, and estate are rigid. The lines drawn between people are firm, and there is little or no movement from one group to another. A **class system,** in contrast, is much more open, for it is based primarily on money or material possessions, which can be acquired. This system, too, is in place at birth, when children are ascribed the status of their parents, but, unlike the other systems, individuals can change their social class by what they achieve (or fail to achieve) in life. In addition, no laws specify people's occupations on the basis of birth or prohibit marriage between the classes.

A major characteristic of the class system, then, is its relatively fluid boundaries. A class system allows **social mobility,** movement up or down the class ladder. The potential for improving one's life—or for falling down the class ladder—is a major force that drives people to go far in school and to work hard. In the extreme, the family background that a child inherits at birth may present such obstacles that he or she has little chance of climbing very far—or it may provide such privileges that it makes it almost impossible to fall down the class ladder.

Global Stratification and the Status of Females

In *every* society of the world, gender is a basis for social stratification. In no society is gender the sole basis for stratifying people, but gender cuts across *all* systems of social stratification—whether slavery, caste, estate, or class (Huber 1990). In all these systems, on the basis of their gender, people are sorted into categories and given different access to the good things available in their society.

Apparently these distinctions always favor males. It is remarkable, for example, that in *every* society of the world men's earnings are higher than women's. Men's dominance is even more evident when we consider female circumcision

Sisters Venus and Serena Williams have dominated the women's tennis world for over a decade. To determine the social class of athletes as highly successful as the Williams sisters presents a sociological puzzle. With their fame and growing wealth, what do you think their social class is? Why?

(see the box in the next chapter, page 241). That most of the world's illiterate are females also drives home women's relative position in society. Of the several hundred million adults who cannot read, about two-thirds are women (UNESCO 2006). Because gender is such a significant factor in what happens to us in life, we shall focus on it more closely in Chapter 8.

Global Stratification: Three Worlds

As was noted at the beginning of this chapter, just as the people within a nation are stratified by power, prestige, and property, so are the world's nations. Until recently, a simple model consisting of First, Second, and Third Worlds was used to depict global stratification. *First World* referred to the industrialized capitalist nations, *Second World* to the communist (or socialist) countries, and *Third World* to any nation that did not fit into the first two categories. The breakup of the Soviet Union in 1989 made these terms outdated. In addition, although *first, second,* and *third* did not mean "best," "better," and "worst," they implied it. An alternative classification that some now use—developed, developing, and undeveloped nations—has the same drawback. By calling ourselves "developed," it sounds as though we are mature and the "undeveloped" nations are somehow retarded.

To try to solve this problem, I use more neutral, descriptive terms: *Most Industrialized, Industrializing,* and *Least Industrialized* nations. We can measure industrialization with no judgment implied as to whether a nation's industrialization represents "development," ranks it "first," or is even desirable at all. The intention is to depict on a global level the three primary dimensions of social stratification: property, power, and prestige. The Most Industrialized Nations have much greater property (wealth), prestige (they are looked up to as world leaders), and power (they usually get their way in international relations).

The Most Industrialized Nations

The Most Industrialized Nations are the United States and Canada in North America; Great Britain, France, Germany, Switzerland, and the other industrialized countries of western Europe; Japan in Asia; and Australia and New Zealand in the area of the world known as Oceania. Although there are variations in their economic systems, these nations are capitalistic. As Table 7.2 shows, although these nations have only 16 percent of the world's people, they possess 31 percent of the earth's land. Their wealth is so enormous that even their poor live better and longer lives than do the average citizens of the Least Industrialized Nations. The Social Map on pages 192–193 shows the tremendous disparities in income among the world's nations.

The Industrializing Nations

The Industrializing Nations include most of the nations of the former Soviet Union and its former satellites in eastern Europe. As Table 7.2 shows, these nations account for 20 percent of the earth's land and 16 percent of its people.

The dividing points between the three "worlds" are soft, making it difficult to know how to classify some nations. This is especially the case with the Industrializing Nations. Exactly how much industrialization must a nation have to be in this category? Although soft, these categories do pinpoint essential differences among nations. Most people who live in the Industrializing Nations have much lower incomes and standards of living than those who live in the Most Industrialized Nations. The majority, however, are better off than those who live in the Least Industrialized Nations. For example, on such measures as access to electricity, indoor plumbing, automobiles, telephones, and

Table 7.2 **Distribution of the World's Land and Population**

	Land	Population
Most Industrialized Nations	31%	16%
Industrializing Nations	20%	16%
Least Industrialized Nations	49%	68%

Sources: Computed from Kurian 1990, 1991, 1992.

Figure 7.1 **Global Stratification: Income[1] of the World's Nations**

The Most Industrialized Nations

	Nation	Income per Person
1	Luxembourg	$58,900
2	United States	$39,820
3	Norway	$38,680
4	Switzerland	$35,660
5	Ireland	$32,930
6	Iceland	$31,900
7	Austria	$31,800
8	Denmark	$31,770
9	Hong Kong (a part of China)	$31,560
10	Belgium	$31,530
11	United Kingdom	$31,430
12	Netherlands	$31,360
13	Canada	$30,760
14	Sweden	$29,880
15	Japan	$29,810
16	Finland	$29,800
17	France	$29,460
18	Australia	$29,340
19	Germany	$28,170
20	Italy	$28,020
21	Singapore	$27,370
22	Taiwan	$25,300
23	Israel	$23,770
24	New Zealand	$22,260

The Industrializing Nations

	Nation	Income per Person
25	Spain	$24,750
26	Greece	$22,230
27	Slovenia	$20,830
28	Korea, South	$20,530
29	Portugal	$19,240
30	Czech Republic	$18,420
31	Hungary	$15,800
32	Slovakia	$14,480
33	Saudi Arabia	$13,810
34	Estonia	$13,630
35	Poland	$12,730
36	Lithuania	$12,690
37	Argentina	$12,530
38	Croatia	$11,920
39	Latvia	$11,820
40	South Africa	$10,960
41	Chile	$10,610
42	Malaysia	$9,720
43	Russia	$9,680
44	Mexico	$9,640
45	Costa Rica	$9,220
46	Uruguay	$9,030
47	Romania	$8,330
48	Brazil	$7,940
49	Bulgaria	$7,940
50	Thailand	$7,930
51	Bosnia	$7,230
52	Colombia	$6,940
53	Venezuela	$5,830

The Least Industrialized Nations

	Nation	Income per Person		Nation	Income per Person
54	Botswana[3]	$9,580	70	Lebanon	$5,550
55	Turkey	$7,720	71	Peru	$5,400
56	Namibia	$7,520	72	Albania	$5,070
57	Tunisia	$7,430	73	Philippines	$4,950
58	Belarus	$6,970	74	El Salvador	$4,890
59	Kazakhstan	$6,930	75	Paraguay	$4,820
60	Dominican Republic	$6,860	76	Jordan	$4,770
61	Panama	$6,730	77	Suriname	$4,300
62	Macedonia	$6,560	78	Guatemala	$4,260
63	Belize	$6,500	79	Morocco	$4,250
64	Ukraine	$6,330	80	Sri Lanka	$4,210
65	Algeria	$6,320	81	Egypt	$4,200
66	China	$5,890	82	Armenia	$4,160
67	Gabon	$5,700	83	Jamaica	$3,950
68	Turkmenistan	$5,700	84	Azerbaijan	$3,810
69	Swaziland	$5,650	85	Guyana	$3,800
			86	Ecuador	$3,770

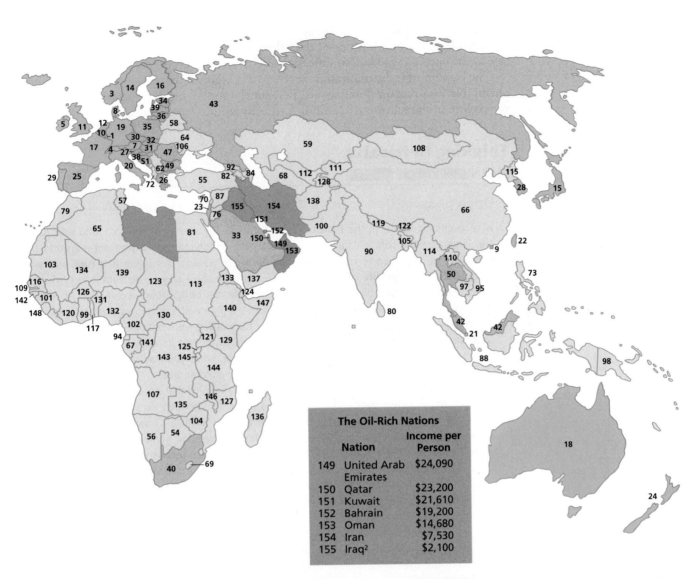

The Oil-Rich Nations

	Nation	Income per Person
149	United Arab Emirates	$24,090
150	Qatar	$23,200
151	Kuwait	$21,610
152	Bahrain	$19,200
153	Oman	$14,680
154	Iran	$7,530
155	Iraq[2]	$2,100

The Least Industrialized Nations

Nation	Income per Person	Nation	Income per Person	Nation	Income per Person	Nation	Income per Person
87 Syria	$3,500	102 Cameroon	$2,120	119 Nepal	$1,480	135 Zambia	$890
88 Indonesia	$3,480	103 Mauritania	$2,050	120 Cote d'Ivoire	$1,470	136 Madagascar	$840
89 Nicaragua	$3,480	104 Zimbabwe	$2,040	121 Uganda	$1,450	137 Yemen	$810
90 India	$3,120	105 Bangladesh	$1,970	122 Bhutan	$1,400	138 Afghanistan	$800
91 Cuba	$3,000	106 Moldova	$1,950	123 Chad	$1,340	139 Niger	$780
92 Georgia	$2,900	107 Angola	$1,930	124 Djibouti	$1,300	140 Ethiopia	$750
93 Honduras	$2,760	108 Mongolia	$1,900	125 Rwanda	$1,240	141 Congo	$740
94 Equatorial Guinea	$2,700	109 Gambia	$1,890	126 Burkina Faso	$1,170	142 Guinea-Bissau	$690
95 Vietnam	$2,700	110 Laos	$1,880	127 Mozambique	$1,170	143 Congo, Democratic Republic	$680
96 Bolivia	$2,600	111 Krygyzstan	$1,860	128 Tajikistan	$1,160	144 Tanzania	$670
97 Cambodia	$2,310	112 Uzbekistan	$1,860	129 Kenya	$1,130	145 Burundi	$660
98 Papua-New Guinea	$2,280	113 Sudan	$1,810	130 Central African Republic	$1,100	146 Malawi	$630
99 Ghana	$2,220	114 Burma	$1,700	131 Benin	$1,090	147 Somalia	$600
100 Pakistan	$2,170	115 Korea, North	$1,700	132 Nigeria	$970	148 Sierra Leone	$550
101 Guinea	$2,160	116 Senegal	$1,660	133 Eritrea	$960		
		117 Togo	$1,510	134 Mali	$950		
		118 Haiti	$1,500				

[1]Income is a country's purchasing power parity based on its per capita gross domestic product measured in U.S. dollars. Since some totals vary widely from year to year, they must be taken as approximate. [2]Iraq's oil has been disrupted by war. [3]Botswana's relative wealth is based on its diamond mines.

Sources: By the author. Based on *Statistical Abstract of the United States* 2007:Table 1324, with a few missing countries taken from the CIA's latest *World Factbook*.

even food, most citizens of the Industrializing Nations rank lower than those in the Most Industrialized Nations, but higher than those in the Least Industrialized Nations. As you saw in the opening vignette, stratification affects even life expectancy.

The benefits of industrialization are uneven. Large numbers of people in the Industrializing Nations remain illiterate and desperately poor. Conditions can be gruesome, as we explore in the following Thinking Critically section.

Thinking Critically

Open Season: Children As Prey

What is childhood like in the Industrializing Nations? The answer depends on who your parents are. If you are the son or daughter of rich parents, childhood can be pleasant—a world filled with luxuries, and even servants. If you are born into poverty, but living in a rural area where there is plenty to eat, life can still be good—although there may be no books, television, and little education. If you live in a slum, however, life can be horrible—worse even than in the slums of the Most Industrialized Nations. Let's take a glance at a notorious slum of Brazil.

There is not enough food—this you can take for granted—and wife abuse, broken homes, alcoholism, and drug abuse, along with a lot of crime. From your knowledge of slums in the Most Industrialized Nations, you would expect these things. What you may not expect, however, are the brutal conditions in which Brazilian slum *(favela)* children live.

Sociologist Martha Huggins (Huggins et al. 2002) reports that poverty is so deep that children and adults swarm over garbage dumps to try to find enough decaying food to keep them alive. You might also be surprised to discover that the owners of some of these dumps hire armed guards to keep the poor out—so that they can sell the garbage for pig food. And you might be shocked to learn that the Brazilian police and death squads murder some of these children. Some shop owners even hire hit men and auction designated victims off to the lowest bidder! The going rate is half a month's salary—figured at the low Brazilian minimum wage.

Life is cheap in the poor nations—but death squads for children? To understand this, we must first note that Brazil has a long history of violence. Brazil also has a high rate of poverty, has only a tiny middle class, and is controlled by a small group of families who, under a veneer of democracy, make the country's major decisions. Hordes of homeless children, with no schools or jobs, roam the streets. To survive, they wash windshields, shine shoes, beg, and steal (Huggins and Rodrigues 2004).

The "respectable" classes see these children as nothing but trouble. They hurt business, for customers feel intimidated when they see begging children—especially teenaged males–clustered in front of stores. Some shoplift; others dare to sell items that place them in competition with the stores. With no effective social institutions to care for these children, one solution is to kill them. As Huggins notes, murder sends a clear message—especially if it is accompanied by ritual torture: gouging out the eyes, ripping open the chest, cutting off the genitals, raping the girls, and burning the victim's body.

Not all life is bad in the Industrializing Nations, but this is about as bad as it gets.

for your Consideration

Do you think there is anything the Most Industrialized Nations can do about this situation? Or is it any of their business? Is it, though unfortunate, just an "internal" affair that is up to the Brazilians to handle as they wish?

The Least Industrialized Nations

In the Least Industrialized Nations, most people live on small farms or in villages, have large families, and barely survive. These nations account for 49 percent of the Earth's land and 68 percent of the world's people.

Poverty plagues these nations to such an extent that some families actually *live* in the city dump. This is hard to believe, but look at the photos on pages 196–197, which I took in Phnom Penh, the capital of Cambodia. Although wealthy nations have their pockets of poverty, *most* people in the Least Industrialized nations are poor. *Most* of them have no running water, indoor plumbing, or access to trained teachers or physicians. And it is in these nations that most of the world's population growth occurs, placing even greater burdens on their limited resources and causing them to fall farther behind each year.

Homeless people sleeping on the streets is a common sight in India's cities. I took this photo in Chennai (formerly Madrás).

How Did the World's Nations Become Stratified?

How did the globe become stratified into such distinct worlds? The commonsense answer is that the poorer nations have fewer resources than the richer nations. As with many commonsense answers, however, this one, too, falls short. Many of the Industrializing and Least Industrialized Nations are rich in natural resources, while one Most Industrialized Nation, Japan, has few. Three theories explain how global stratification came about.

Colonialism

The first theory, **colonialism,** stresses that the countries that industrialized first got the jump on the rest of the world. Beginning in Great Britain about 1750, industrialization spread throughout western Europe. Plowing some of their immense profits into powerful armaments and fast ships, these countries invaded weaker nations, making colonies out of them (Harrison 1993). After subduing these weaker nations, the more powerful countries left behind a controlling force in order to exploit the nations' labor and natural resources. At one point, there was even a free-for-all among the industrialized European countries as they rushed to divide up an entire continent. As they sliced Africa into pieces, even tiny Belgium got into the act and acquired the Congo, which was *seventy-five* times larger than itself.

The purpose of colonialism was to establish *economic colonies*—to exploit the nation's people and resources for the benefit of the "mother" country. The more powerful European countries would plant their national flags in a colony and send their representatives to run the government, but the United States usually chose to plant corporate flags in a colony and let these corporations dominate the territory's government. Central and South America are prime examples. There were exceptions, such as the conquest of the Philippines, which President McKinley said was motivated by the desire "to educate the Filipinos, and uplift and civilize and Christianize them" (Krugman 2002).

Colonialism, then, shaped many of the Least Industrialized Nations. In some instances, the Most Industrialized Nations were so powerful that when dividing their spoils, they drew lines across a map, creating new states without regard for tribal or cultural considerations (Kifner 1999). Britain and France did just this as they divided up North Africa and parts of the Middle East—which is why the national boundaries of Libya, Saudi Arabia, Kuwait, and other countries are so straight. This legacy of European conquests is a background factor in much of today's racial-ethnic and tribal violence: Groups with no history of national identity were incorporated arbitrarily into the same political boundaries.

World System Theory

The second explanation of how global stratification came about was proposed by Immanuel Wallerstein (1974, 1979, 1990). According to **world system theory,** industrialization led to four groups of nations. The first group is the *core nations,* the countries

colonialism the process by which one nation takes over another nation, usually for the purpose of exploiting its labor and natural resources

world system theory the idea that the world's nations became stratified based on their relationship to industrialization

The Dump People:
Working and Living and Playing in the City Dump of Phnom Penh, Cambodia

went to Cambodia to inspect orphanages, to see how well the children were being cared for. While in Phnom Penh, Cambodia's capital, I was told about people who live in the city dump. *Live* there? I could hardly believe my ears. I knew that people made their living by picking scraps from the city dump, but I didn't know they actually lived among the garbage. This I had to see for myself.

I did. And there I found a highly developed social organization—an intricate support system. Because words are inadequate to depict the abject poverty of the Least Industrialized Nations, these photos can provide more insight into these people's lives than anything I could say.

This is a typical sight—family and friends working together. The trash, which is constantly burning, contains harmful chemicals. Why do people work under such conditions? Because they have few options. It is either this or starve.

The people live at the edge of the dump, in homemade huts (visible in the background). This woman, who was on her way home after a day's work, put down her sack of salvaged items to let me take her picture.

After the garbage arrives by truck, people stream around it, struggling to be the first to discover something of value. To sift through the trash, the workers use metal picks, like the one this child is holding. Note that children work alongside the adults.

The children who live in the dump also play there. These children are riding bicycles on a "road," a packed, leveled area of garbage that leads to their huts. The huge stacks in the background are piled trash. Note the ubiquitous Nike.

One of my many surprises was to find food stands in the dump. Although this one primarily offers drinks and snacks, others serve more substantial food. One even has chairs for its customers.

I was surprised to learn that ice is delivered to the dump. This woman is using a hand grinder to crush ice for drinks for her customers. The customers, of course, are other people who also live in the dump.

At the day's end, the workers wash at the community pump. This hand pump serves all their water needs—drinking, washing, and cooking. There is no indoor plumbing. The weeds in the background serve that purpose.

Not too many visitors to Phnom Penh tell a cab driver to take them to the city dump. The cabbie looked a bit perplexed, but he did as I asked. Two cabs are shown here because my friends insisted on accompanying me.

I know they were curious themselves, but my friends had also discovered that the destinations I want to visit are usually not in the tourist guides, and they wanted to protect me.

© James M. Henslin, all photos

globalization of capitalism
capitalism (investing to make profits within a rational system) becoming the globe's dominant economic system

that industrialized first (Britain, France, Holland, and later Germany), which grew rich and powerful. The second group is the *semiperiphery*. The economies of these nations, located around the Mediterranean, stagnated because they grew dependent on trade with the core nations. The economies of the third group, the *periphery,* or fringe nations, developed even less. These are the eastern European countries, which sold cash crops to the core nations. The fourth group of nations includes most of Africa and Asia. Called the *external area,* these nations were left out of the development of capitalism altogether. The current expansion of capitalism has changed the relationships among these groups. Most notably, Asia is no longer left out of capitalism.

The **globalization of capitalism**—the adoption of capitalism around the world—has created extensive ties among the world's nations. Production and trade are now so interconnected that events around the globe affect us all. Sometimes this is immediate, as happens when a civil war disrupts the flow of oil, or—perish the thought—as would be the case if terrorists managed to get their hands on nuclear or biological weapons. At other times, the effects are like a slow ripple, as when a government adopts some policy that gradually impedes its ability to compete in world markets. All of today's societies, then, no matter where they are located, are part of a *world system.*

The interconnections are most evident among nations that do extensive trading with one another. The following Thinking Critically section explores implications of Mexico's *maquiladoras.*

Thinking Critically

When Globalization Comes Home: *Maquiladoras* South of the Border

When Humberto drives his truck among Ciudad Juarez's shanties—patched together from packing crates, discarded tires, and cardboard—women and children flock around him. Humberto is the water man, and his truckload of water means life.

Two hundred thousand Mexicans rush to Juarez each year, fleeing the hopelessness of the rural areas in pursuit of a better life. They didn't have running water or plumbing in the country anyway, and here they have the possibility of a job, a weekly check to buy food for the kids.

The pay is $10 a day.

This may not sound like much, but it is more than twice the minimum daily wage in Mexico.

A photo taken inside a *maquiladora* in Matamoros, Mexico. The steering wheels are for U.S. auto makers.

This is where the workers live.

Assembly-for-export plants, known as *maquiladoras,* dot the Mexican border (Wise and Cypher 2007). The North American Free Trade Agreement (NAFTA) allows U.S. companies to import materials to Mexico without paying tax and to then export the finished products into the United States, again without tax. It's a sweet deal: few taxes and $10 a day for workers starved for jobs. Some companies get an even sweeter deal. They pay their workers Mexico's minimum wage of $4—for 10-hour days with a 30-minute break (Darweesh 2000).

That these workers live in shacks, with no running water or sewage disposal is not the employers' concern.

Nor is the pollution. The stinking air doesn't stay on the Mexican side of the border. Neither does the garbage. Heavy rains wash torrents of untreated sewage and industrial wastes into the Rio Grande (Lacey 2007).

There is also the loss of jobs for U.S. workers. Six of the fifteen poorest cities in the United States are located along the sewage-infested Rio Grande. NAFTA didn't bring poverty to these cities. They were poor before this treaty, but residents resent the jobs they've seen move across the border (Thompson 2001).

What if the *maquiladora* workers organize and demand better pay? Farther south, even cheaper labor beckons. Guatemala and Honduras will gladly take the *maquiladoras.* So will China, where workers make $1 a day. Mexico has already lost many of its *maquiladora* jobs to places where people even more desperate will work for even less (Luhnow 2004).

Many Mexican politicians would say that this presentation is one-sided. "Sure there are problems," they would say, "but that is always how it is when a country industrializes. Don't you realize that the *maquiladoras* bring jobs to people who have no work? They also bring roads, telephone lines, and electricity to undeveloped areas." "In fact," said Vicente Fox, when he was the president of Mexico, "workers at the *maquiladoras* make more than the average salary in Mexico—and that's what we call fair wages" (Fraser 2001).

for your Consideration

Let's apply our three theoretical perspectives to see where reality lies. Conflict theorists say that capitalists try to weaken the bargaining power of workers by exploiting divisions among them. In what is known as the *split labor market,* capitalists pit one group of workers against another to lower the cost of labor. How do you think that *maquiladoras* fit this conflict perspective?

When functionalists analyze a situation, they identify its functions and dysfunctions. What functions and dysfunctions of *maquiladoras* do you see?

Do *maquiladoras* represent exploitation or opportunity? As symbolic interactionists point out, reality is a perspective based on one's experience. What multiple realities do you see here?

Culture of Poverty

The third explanation of global stratification is quite unlike the other two. Economist John Kenneth Galbraith (1979) claimed that the cultures of the Least Industrialized Nations hold them back. Building on the ideas of anthropologist Oscar Lewis (1966a, 1966b), Galbraith argued that some nations are crippled by a **culture of poverty,** a way of life that perpetuates poverty from one generation to the next. He explained it this way: Most of the world's poor people are farmers who live on little plots of land. They barely produce enough food to survive. Living so close to the edge of starvation, they have little room for risk—so they stick closely to tried-and-true, traditional ways. To experiment with new farming techniques could bring disaster, for failure would lead to hunger and death.

Their religion also encourages them to accept their situation, for it teaches fatalism: the belief that an individual's position in life is God's will. For example, in India, the Dalits are taught that they must have done very bad things in a previous life to suffer so. They are supposed to submit to their situation—and in the next life maybe they'll come back in a more desirable state.

Evaluating the Theories

Most sociologists prefer colonialism and world system theory. To them, an explanation based on a culture of poverty places blame on the victim—the poor nations themselves. It points to characteristics of the poor nations, rather than to international political arrangements that benefit the Most Industrialized Nations at the expense of the poor nations. But even taken together, these theories yield only part of the picture. None of these theories, for example, would have led anyone to expect that after World War II, Japan would become an economic powerhouse: Japan had a religion that stressed fatalism, two of its major cities had been destroyed by atomic bombs, and it been stripped of its colonies.

Each theory, then, yields but a partial explanation, and the grand theorist who will put the many pieces of this puzzle together has yet to appear.

Why Is Social Stratification Universal?

What is it about social life that makes all societies stratified? We shall first consider the explanation proposed by functionalists, which has aroused much controversy in sociology, and then explanations proposed by conflict theorists.

The Functionalist Perspective: Motivating Qualified People

Functionalists take the position that the patterns of behavior that characterize a society exist because they are functional for that society. Because social inequality is universal, inequality must help societies survive. But how?

Davis and Moore's Explanation   Two functionalists, Kingsley Davis and Wilbert Moore (1945, 1953), wrestled with this question. They concluded that stratification of society is inevitable because:

1. Society must make certain that its positions are filled.
2. Some positions are more important than others.
3. The more important positions must be filled by the more qualified people.
4. To motivate the more qualified people to fill these positions, society must offer them greater rewards.

To flesh out this functionalist argument, consider college presidents and military generals. The position of college president is more important than that of student because the president's decisions affect a large number of people, including many students. College presidents are also accountable for their performance to boards of trustees. It is the same with generals. Their decisions affect many people, and can determine life and death. Generals are accountable to superior generals and to the country's leader.

Why do people accept such high-pressure positions? Why don't they just take less demanding jobs? The answer, said Davis and Moore, is that society offers greater rewards—prestige, pay, and benefits—for its more demanding and accountable positions. To get highly qualified people to compete with one another, some positions offer a salary of $2 million a year, country club membership, a private jet and pilot, and a chauffeured limousine. For less demanding positions, a $30,000 salary without fringe benefits is enough to get hundreds of people to compete. If a job requires rigorous training, it, too, must offer more salary and benefits. If you can get the same pay with a high school diploma, why suffer through the many tests and term papers that college requires?

Tumin's Critique of Davis and Moore Davis and Moore tried to explain *why* social stratification is universal, not justify social inequality. Nevertheless, their view makes many sociologists uncomfortable, for they see it as coming close to justifying the inequalities in society. Its bottom line seems to be: The people who contribute more to society are paid more, while those who contribute less are paid less.

Melvin Tumin (1953) was the first sociologist to point out what he saw as major flaws in the functionalist position. Here are three of his arguments.

First, how do we know that the positions that offer the higher rewards are more important? A heart surgeon, for example, saves lives and earns much more than a garbage collector, but this doesn't mean that garbage collectors are less important to society. By helping to prevent contagious diseases, garbage collectors save thousands of lives. We need independent methods of measuring importance, and we don't have them.

Second, if stratification worked as Davis and Moore described it, society would be a **meritocracy**; that is, positions would be awarded on the basis of merit. But is this what we have? The best predictor of who goes to college, for example, is not ability but income: The more a family earns, the more likely their children are to go to college (Carnevale and Rose 2003). This has nothing to do with merit. It is simply another form of the inequality that is built into society. In short, people's positions in society are based on many reasons other than merit.

Third, if social stratification is so functional, it ought to benefit almost everyone. Yet social stratification is *dysfunctional* for many. Think of the people who could have made valuable contributions to society had they not been born in slums, dropped out of school, and taken menial jobs to help support their families. Then there are the many who, born female, are assigned "women's work," thus ensuring that they do not maximize their mental abilities.

IN SUM Functionalists argue that society works better if its most qualified people hold its most important positions. Therefore, those positions offer higher rewards. For example, to get highly talented people to become surgeons—to undergo years of rigorous training and then cope with life-and-death situations, as well as malpractice suits—society must provide a high payoff.

The Conflict Perspective: Class Conflict and Scarce Resources

Conflict theorists don't just criticize details of the functionalist argument. Rather, they go for the throat and attack its basic premise. Conflict, not function, they stress, is the reason that we have social stratification. Let's look at the major arguments.

Marx's Position If he were alive to hear the functionalist argument, Karl Marx would be enraged. From his point of view, the people in power are not there because of superior traits, as the functionalists would have us believe. This view is simply an ideology that members of the elite use to justify their being at the top—and to seduce the

meritocracy a form of social stratification in which all positions are awarded on the basis of merit

oppressed into believing that their welfare depends on keeping society stable. Human history is the chronicle of class struggle, of those in power using society's resources to benefit themselves and to oppress those beneath them—and of oppressed groups trying to overcome domination.

Marx predicted that the workers would revolt. The day will come, he said, when class consciousness will overcome the ideology that now blinds workers. When they realize their common oppression, workers will rebel against the capitalists. The struggle to control the means of production may be covert at first, taking the form of work slowdowns or industrial sabotage. Ultimately, however, resistance will break out into the open. The revolution will not be easy, for the bourgeoisie control the police, the military, and even the educational system, where they implant false class consciousness in the minds of the workers' children.

Current Applications of Conflict Theory   Just as Marx focused on overarching historic events—the accumulation of capital and power and the struggle between workers and capitalists—some of today's conflict sociologists are doing the same. Their focus is on the current capitalist triumph on a global level (Sklair 2001). They analyze both the use of armed forces to keep capitalist nations dominant and the exploitation of workers as capital is moved from the Most Industrialized Nations to the Least Industrialized Nations.

Some conflict sociologists, in contrast, examine conflict wherever it is found, not just as it relates to capitalists and workers. They examine how groups *within the same class* compete with one another for a larger slice of the pie (Schellenberg 1996; Collins 1988, 1999). Even within the same industry, for example, union will fight against union for higher salaries, shorter hours, and more power. A special focus has been conflict between racial–ethnic groups as they compete for education, housing, and even prestige—whatever benefits society has to offer. Another focus has been relations between women and men, which conflict theorists say are best understood as a conflict over power—over who controls society's resources. Unlike functionalists, conflict theorists hold that just beneath the surface of what may appear to be a tranquil society lies conflict that is barely held in check.

IN SUM Conflict theorists stress that in every society groups struggle with one another to gain a larger share of their society's resources. Whenever a group gains power, it uses that power to extract what it can from the groups beneath it. This elite group also uses the social institutions to keep itself in power.

What Determines Social Class?

Because social class is the social stratification system of the United States, let's look at social class in greater detail. In the early days of sociology, a disagreement arose about the meaning of social class. Let's compare how Marx and Weber analyzed the issue.

Karl Marx: The Means of Production

As was discussed in Chapter 1, the breakup of the feudal system displaced masses of peasants from their traditional lands and occupations. Fleeing to cities, they competed for the few available jobs. Offered only a pittance for their labor, they wore rags, went hungry, and slept under bridges and in shacks. In contrast, the factory owners built mansions, hired servants, and lived in the lap of luxury. Seeing this great disparity between owners and workers, Karl Marx (1818–1883) concluded that social class depends on a single factor: people's

Taken at the end of the 1800s, these photos illustrate the contrasting worlds of *social classes* produced by capitalism. The sleeping boys shown in this classic 1890 photo by Jacob Riis sold newspapers in London. They did not go to school, and they had no home. The children on the left, Cornelius and Gladys Vanderbilt, are shown in front of their parents' estate. They went to school and did not work. You can see how the social locations illustrated in these photos would have produced different orientations to life and, therefore, politics, ideas about marriage, values, and so on—the stuff of which life is made.

relationship to the **means of production**—the tools, factories, land, and investment capital used to produce wealth (Marx 1844/1964; Marx and Engels 1848/1967).

Marx argued that the distinctions people often make among themselves—such as clothing, speech, education, paycheck, the neighborhood they live in, even the car they drive—are superficial matters. These things camouflage the only dividing line that counts. There are just two classes of people, said Marx: the **bourgeoisie** (*capitalists*), those who own the means of production, and the **proletariat** (*workers*), those who work for the owners. In short, people's relationship to the means of production determines their social class.

Marx did recognize other groups: farmers and peasants; a *lumpenproletariat* (people living on the margin of society, such as beggars, vagrants, and criminals); and a middle group of self-employed professionals. Marx did not consider these groups social classes, however, for they lack **class consciousness**—a shared identity based on their position in the means of production. In other words, they did not perceive themselves as exploited workers whose plight could be solved by collective action. Consequently, Marx thought of these groups as insignificant in the future he foresaw—a workers' revolution that was destined to overthrow capitalism.

The capitalists will grow even wealthier, Marx said, and the hostilities will increase. When workers come to realize that capitalists are the source of their oppression, they will unite and throw off the chains of their oppressors. In a bloody revolution, they will seize the means of production and usher in a classless society, in which no longer will the few grow rich at the expense of the many. What holds back the workers' unity and their revolution is **false class consciousness,** workers mistakenly thinking of themselves as capitalists. For example, workers with a few dollars in the bank may forget that they are workers and instead see themselves as investors, or as capitalists who are about to launch a successful business.

The only distinction worth mentioning, then, is whether a person is an owner or a worker. This decides everything else, Marx stressed, for property determines people's lifestyles, establishes their relationships with one another, and even shapes their ideas.

Max Weber: Property, Prestige, and Power

Max Weber (1864–1920) was an outspoken critic of Marx. Weber argued that property is only part of the picture. *Social class,* he said, has three components: property, prestige, and power (Gerth and Mills 1958; Weber 1922/1968). Some call these the three P's of social class. (Although Weber used the terms *class, status,* and *power,* some sociologists find *property, prestige,* and *power* to be clearer terms. To make them even clearer, you may wish to substitute *wealth* for *property.*)

means of production the tools, factories, land, and investment capital used to produce wealth

bourgeoisie Marx's term for capitalists, those who own the means of production

proletariat Marx's term for the exploited class, the mass of workers who do not own the means of production

class consciousness Marx's term for awareness of a common identity based on one's position in the means of production

false class consciousness Marx's term to refer to workers identifying with the interests of capitalists

Figure 7.2 Weber's Three Components of Social Class

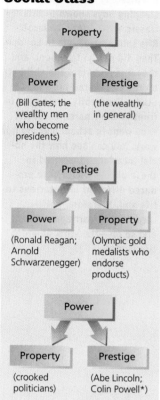

Property

Power | **Prestige**

(Bill Gates; the wealthy men who become presidents) | (the wealthy in general)

Prestige

Power | **Property**

(Ronald Reagan; Arnold Schwarzenegger) | (Olympic gold medalists who endorse products)

Power

Property | **Prestige**

(crooked politicians) | (Abe Lincoln; Colin Powell*)

*Colin Powell illustrates the circularity of these components. Powell's power as Chairman of the Joint Chiefs of Staff led to prestige. Powell's prestige, in turn, led to power when he was called from retirement to serve as Secretary of State in George W. Bush's first administration.

Property (or wealth), said Weber, is certainly significant in determining a person's standing in society. On that point he agreed with Marx. But, added Weber, ownership is not the only significant aspect of property. For example, some powerful people, such as managers of corporations, *control* the means of production even though they do not *own* them. If managers can control property for their own benefit—awarding themselves huge bonuses and magnificent perks—it makes no practical difference that they do not own the property that they use so generously for their own benefit.

Prestige, the second element in Weber's analysis, is often derived from property, for people tend to admire the wealthy. Prestige, however, can be based on other factors. Olympic gold medalists, for example, might not own property, yet they have high prestige. Some are even able to exchange their prestige for property—such as those who are paid a small fortune for endorsing a certain brand of sportswear or for claiming that they start their day with "the breakfast of champions." In other words, property and prestige are not one-way streets: Although property can bring prestige, prestige can also bring property.

Power, the third element of social class, is the ability to control others, even over their objections. Weber agreed with Marx that property is a major source of power, but he added that it is not the only source. For example, prestige can be turned into power. Two well-known examples are actors Arnold Schwarzeneggar, who became governor of California, and Ronald Reagan, who became president of the United States. Figure 7.2 shows how property, prestige, and power are interrelated.

IN SUM For Marx, social class was based solely on a person's relationship to the means of production. One is a member of either the bourgeoisie or the proletariat. Weber argued that social class is a combination of property, prestige, and power.

Social Class in the United States

If you ask most Americans about their country's social class system, you are likely to get a blank look. If you press the matter, you are likely to get an answer like this: "There are the poor and the rich—and then there are you and I, neither poor nor rich." This is just about as far as most Americans' consciousness of social class goes. Let's try to flesh out this idea.

Our task is made somewhat difficult because sociologists have no clear-cut, agreed-on definition of social class. Conflict sociologists (of the Marxist orientation) see only two social classes: those who own the means of production and those who do not. The problem with this view, say most sociologists, is that it lumps too many people together. Teenage "order takers" at McDonald's who work for $15,000 a year are lumped together with that company's executives who make $500,000 a year—because they both are workers at McDonald's, not owners.,

Most sociologists agree with Weber that there is more to social class than just a person's relationship to the means of production. Consequently, most sociologists use the components Weber identified and define **social class** as a large group of people who rank closely to one another in property, prestige, and power. These three elements separate people into different lifestyles, give them different chances in life, and provide them with distinct ways of looking at the self and the world.

Let's look at how sociologists measure these three components of social class.

Property

Property comes in many forms, such as buildings, land, animals, machinery, cars, stocks, bonds, businesses, furniture, and bank accounts. When you add up the value of someone's property and subtract that person's debts, you have what sociologists call **wealth.** This

social class according to Marx, one of two groups: capitalists who own the means of production or workers who sell their labor according to Weber, a large group of people who rank close to one another in wealth, power, and prestige

wealth the total value of everything someone owns, minus the debts

term can be misleading, as some of us have little wealth—especially most college students. Nevertheless, if your net total comes to $10, then that is your wealth. (Obviously, wealth as a sociological term does not equal wealthy.)

Distinguishing Between Wealth and Income   Wealth and income are sometimes confused, but they are not the same. Where *wealth* is a person's net worth, **income** is a flow of money. Income can come from a number of sources: usually a business or wages, but also from rent, interest, or royalties, even from alimony, an allowance, or gambling. Some people have much wealth and little income. For example, a farmer may own much land (a form of wealth), but bad weather, combined with the high cost of fertilizers and machinery, can cause the income to dry up. Others have much income and little wealth. An executive with a $250,000 annual income may be debt-ridden. Below the surface prosperity—the exotic vacations, country club membership, private schools for the children, sports cars, and an elegant home—the credit cards may be maxed out, the sports cars in danger of being repossessed, and the mortgage payments "past due." Typically, however, wealth and income go together.

Distribution of Property   Who owns the property in the United States? One answer, of course, is "everyone." Although this statement has some merit, it overlooks how the nation's property is divided among "everyone."

Overall, Americans are worth a hefty sum, about $38 trillion (*Statistical Abstract* 2007:Table 704). This includes all real estate, stocks, bonds, and business assets in the entire country. Figure 7.3 shows how highly concentrated this wealth is. Most wealth, 70 percent, is owned by only *10 percent* of the nation's families. As you can also see from this figure, 1 percent of Americans own one third of all the U.S. assets.

Distribution of Income   How is income distributed in the United States? Economist Paul Samuelson (Samuelson and Nordhaus 2005) put it this way: "If we made an income pyramid out of a child's blocks, with each layer portraying $500 of income, the peak would be far higher than Mount Everest, but most people would be within a few feet of the ground."

Actually, if each block were 1-½ inches tall, the typical American would be just 9 *feet off the ground,* for the average per capita income in the United States is about $35,000 per year. (This average income includes every American, even children.) The typical family climbs a little higher, for most families have more than one worker, and together they average about $54,000 a year. Compared with the few families who are on the mountain's peak, the average U.S. family would find itself only 14 feet off the ground (*Statistical Abstract* 2007:Tables 660, 677). Figure 7.4 on the next page portrays these differences.

The fact that some Americans enjoy the peaks of Mount Everest while most—despite their efforts—make it only 9 to 14 feet up the slope presents a striking image of income inequality in the United States. Another picture emerges if we divide the U.S. population into five equal groups and rank them from highest to lowest income. As Figure 7.5 on page 207 shows, the top 20 percent of the population receives *almost half* (47.9 percent) of all income in the United States. In contrast, the bottom 20 percent of Americans receives only 4.0 percent of the nation's income.

Two features of Figure 7.5 are outstanding. First, notice how little change there has been in the distribution of income through the years. Second, look at how income inequality decreased from 1935 to 1970. *Since 1970, the richest 20 percent of U.S. families have grown richer, while the poorest 20 percent have grown poorer.* Despite numerous government antipoverty programs, the poorest 20 percent of Americans receive *less* of the nation's income today than they did a

income   money received, usually from a job, business, or assets

Figure 7.3   **Distribution of the Property of Americans**

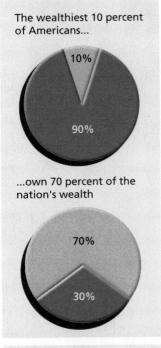

The wealthiest 10 percent of Americans...

10%

90%

...own 70 percent of the nation's wealth

70%

30%

The wealthiest 1 percent of Americans...

1%

99%

...owns 33 percent of the nation's wealth

33%

67%

Source: By the author. Based on Beeghley 2008.

Figure 7.4 **Distribution of the Income of Americans**

Some U.S. families have incomes that exceed the height of Mt. Everest, 29,028 feet

Average U.S. family income $54,000 or 14 feet

Average U.S. individual income $35,000 or 9 feet

If a 1 1/2 inch child's block equals $500 of income, the average individual's annual income of $35,000 would represent a height of 9 feet, and the average family's annual income of $54,000 would represent a height of 14 feet. The income of some families, in contrast, would represent a height greater than that of Mt. Everest.

Source: By the author.

generation ago. The richest 20 percent, in contrast, are receiving more, but not as much as they did in 1935.

The chief executive officers (CEOs) of the nation's largest corporations are especially affluent. The *Wall Street Journal* surveyed the 350 largest U.S. companies to find out what they paid their CEOs ("The Boss's Pay" 2007). Their median compensation (including salaries, bonuses, and stock options) came to $6,549,000 a year. (Median means that half received more than this amount, and half less.)

The CEOs' income—which does *not* include their income from interest, dividends, or rents, or the value of company-paid limousines and chauffeurs, airplanes and pilots, and private boxes at the symphony and sporting events—is *166 times* higher than the average pay of U.S. workers (*Statistical Abstract* 2007:Table 629). To really see the disparity consider this: The average U.S. worker would have to work *1,475 years* to earn the amount received by the highest-paid executive listed in Table 7.3.

Imagine how you could live with an income like this. And this is precisely the point. Beyond cold numbers lies a dynamic reality that profoundly affects people's lives. The difference in wealth between those at the top and those at the bottom of the U.S. class structure means that these individuals experience vastly different lifestyles. For example, a colleague of mine who was teaching at an exclusive Eastern university piqued his students' curiosity when he lectured on poverty in Latin America. That weekend, one of the students borrowed his parents' corporate jet and pilot, and in class on Monday, he and his friends related their personal observations on poverty in Latin America. Americans who are at the low end of the income ladder, in contrast, lack the funds to travel even to a neighboring town for the weekend. For young parents, choices may revolve around whether to spend the little they have at the laundromat or on milk for the baby. The elderly might have to choose between purchasing the medicines they need or buying food. In short, divisions of wealth represent not "mere" numbers, but choices that make vital differences in people's lives, a topic that we explore in the Down-to-Earth Sociology box on page 208.

Power

Like many people, you may have said to yourself, "Sure, I can vote, but somehow the big decisions are always made despite what I might think. Certainly *I* don't make the decision to send soldiers to Afghanistan or Iraq. *I* don't launch missiles against Kosovo or Baghdad. *I* don't decide to raise taxes or lower interest rates. It isn't *I* who decides to change Social Security or Medicare benefits."

And then another part of you may say, "But I do participate in these decisions through my representatives in Congress, and by voting for president." True enough—as far as it goes. The trouble is, it just doesn't go far enough. Such views of being a participant in the nation's "big" decisions are a playback of the ideology we learn at an early age—an ideology that Marx said is promoted by the elites to both legitimate and perpetuate their power. Sociologists Daniel Hellinger and Dennis Judd (1991) call this the "democratic facade" that conceals the real source of power in the United States.

Table 7.3 **The 5 Highest-Paid CEOs**

Executive	Company	Compensation
1. Lloyd Blankfein	Goldman Sachs Group	$55 million
2. Stanley O'Neal	Merrill Lynch	$50 million
3. Ray Irani	Occidental Petroleum	$48 million
4. John Mack	Morgan Stanley	$40 million
5. Lawrence Ellison	Oracle	$39 million

Note: Compensation includes salary, bonuses, and stock options.

Source: "The Boss's Pay" 2007.

Figure 7.5 The More Things Change, the More They Stay the Same: The Percentage of the Nation's Income Received by Each Fifth of U.S. Families

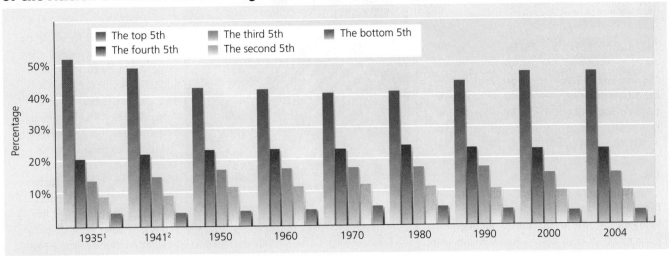

[1]Earliest year available.
[2]No data for 1940.

Source: By the author. Based on *Statistical Abstract* 1960:Table 417; 1970:Table 489; 2007:Table 678.

Back in the 1950s, sociologist C. Wright Mills (1956) was criticized for insisting that **power**—the ability to carry out your will despite resistance—was concentrated in the hands of a few, for his analysis contradicted the dominant ideology of equality. To refer to those who make the big decisions in U.S. society, Mills coined the term **power elite**.

Mills and others have stressed how wealth and power coalesce in a group of like-minded individuals who share ideologies and values. These individuals belong to the same private clubs, vacation at the same exclusive resorts, and even hire the same

power the ability to carry out your will, even over the resistance of others

power elite C. Wright Mills' term for the top people in U.S. corporations, military, and politics who make the nation's major decisions

A mere one-half of 1 percent of Americans owns over a quarter of the entire nation's wealth. Very few minorities are numbered among this 0.5 percent. An exception is Oprah Winfrey, who has had an ultra-successful career in entertainment and investing. Worth $1.3 billion, she is the 215th richest person in the United States. Winfrey, who has given millions of dollars to help minority children, is shown here as she is interviewed by David Letterman.

How the Super-Rich Live

IT'S GOOD TO SEE how other people live. It gives us a different perspective on life. Let's take a glimpse at the life of John Castle (his real name). After earning a degree in physics at MIT and an MBA at Harvard, John went into banking and securities, where he made more than $100 million (Lublin 1999).

Wanting to be connected to someone famous, John bought President John F. Kennedy's "Winter White House," an ocean-front estate in Palm Beach, Florida. John spent $11 million to remodel the 13,000-square-foot house so that it would be more to his liking. Among those changes: adding bathrooms numbers 14 and 15. He likes to show off John F. Kennedy's bed and also the dresser that has the drawer labeled "black underwear," carefully hand-lettered by Rose Kennedy.

At his beachfront estate, John gives what he calls "refined feasts" to the glitterati ("On History . . . " 1999). If he gets tired of such activities—or weary of swimming in the Olympic-size pool where JFK swam the weekend before his assassination—he entertains himself by riding one of his thoroughbred horses at his nearby 10-acre ranch. If this fails to ease his boredom, he can relax aboard his custom-built 42-foot Hinckley yacht.

The yacht is a real source of diversion. John once boarded it for an around-the-world trip. He didn't stay on board, though—just joined the cruise from time to time. A captain and crew kept the vessel on course, and whenever

How do the super-rich live? This photo helps give you an idea of how different their lifestyles are from most of us. Shown here is Wayne Huizenga, who is featured in this box, with one of his vintage automobiles.

John felt like it he would fly in and stay a few days. Then he would fly back to the States to direct his business. He did this about a dozen times, flying perhaps 150,000 miles. An interesting way to go around the world.

How much does a custom-built Hinckley yacht cost? John can't tell you. As he says, "I don't want to know what anything costs. When you've got enough money, price doesn't make a difference. That's part of the freedom of being rich."

Right. And for John, being rich also means paying $1,000,000 to charter a private jet to fly Spot, his Appaloosa horse, back and forth to the vet. John didn't want Spot to have to endure a long trailer ride. Oh, and of course, there was the cost of Spot's medical treatment, another $500,000.

Other wealthy people put John to shame. Wayne Huizenga, the founder of Blockbuster, wanted more elbow room for his estate at Nantucket, so he added the house next door for $2.5 million (Fabrikant 2005). He also bought a 2,000-acre country club, complete with an 18-hole golf course, a 55,000-square-foot-clubhouse, and 68 slips for visiting vessels. The club is so exclusive that its only members are Wayne and his wife.

---

bands for their daughters' debutante balls. Their shared backgrounds and vested interests reinforce their view of both the world and their special place in it (Domhoff 1999a, 2006). This elite wields extraordinary power in U.S. society. Although there are exceptions, *most* U.S. presidents have come from this group—millionaire white men from families with "old money" (Baltzell and Schneiderman 1988).

Continuing in the tradition of Mills, sociologist William Domhoff (1990, 2006) argues that this group is so powerful that no major decision of the U.S. government is made without its approval. He analyzed how this group works behind the scenes with elected officials to determine both the nation's foreign and domestic policy—from setting Social Security taxes to imposing trade tariffs. Although Domhoff's conclusions are controversial—and alarming—they certainly follow logically from the principle that wealth brings power, and extreme wealth brings extreme power.

Prestige

Occupations and Prestige What are you thinking about doing after college? Chances are, you don't have the option of lolling under palm trees at the beach. Almost

prestige respect or regard

status consistency ranking high or low on all three dimensions of social class

status inconsistency ranking high on some dimensions of social class and low on others, also called *status discrepancy*

status the position that someone occupies in society or a social group

all of us have to choose an occupation and go to work. Look at Table 7.4 to see how the career you are considering stacks up in terms of **prestige** (respect or regard). Because we are moving toward a global society, this table also shows how the rankings given by Americans compare with those of the residents of sixty other countries.

Why do people give more prestige to some jobs than to others? If you look at Table 7.4, you will notice that the jobs at the top share four features:

1. They pay more.
2. They require more education.
3. They entail more abstract thought.
4. They offer greater autonomy (independence, or self-direction).

If you look at the bottom of the list, you can see that people give less prestige to jobs with the opposite characteristics: These jobs are low-paying, require less preparation or education, involve more physical labor, and are closely supervised. In short, the professions and the white-collar jobs are at the top of the list, the blue-collar jobs at the bottom.

One of the more interesting aspects of these rankings is how consistent they are across countries and over time. For example, people in every country rank college professors higher than nurses, nurses higher than social workers, and social workers higher than janitors. Similarly, the occupations that were ranked high 25 years ago still rank high today—and likely will rank high in the years to come.

Status Inconsistency

Ordinarily a person has a similar rank on all three dimensions of social class—property, power, and prestige. The homeless men in the opening vignette are an example. Such people are **status consistent.** Sometimes that match is not there, however, and someone has a mixture of high and low ranks, a condition called **status inconsistency.** This leads to some interesting situations.

Sociologist Gerhard Lenski (1954, 1966) pointed out that each of us tries to maximize our **status,** our social ranking. Thus individuals who rank high on one dimension of social class but lower on others want people to judge them on the basis of their highest status. Others, however, who are trying to maximize their own position, may respond to status inconsistent individuals according to their lowest ranking.

A classic study of status inconsistency was done by sociologist Ray Gold (1952). He found that after apartment-house janitors unionized, they made more money than some of the tenants whose garbage they carried out. Tenants became upset when they saw their janitors driving more expen-

Table 7.4	Occupational Prestige: How the United States Compares with 60 Countries	
Occupation	**United States**	**Average of 60 Countries**
Physician	86	78
Supreme court judge	85	82
College president	81	86
Astronaut	80	80
Lawyer	75	73
College professor	74	78
Airline pilot	73	66
Architect	73	72
Biologist	73	69
Dentist	72	70
Civil engineer	69	70
Clergy	69	60
Psychologist	69	66
Pharmacist	68	64
High school teacher	66	64
Registered nurse	66	54
Professional athlete	65	48
Electrical engineer	64	65
Author	63	62
Banker	63	67
Veterinarian	62	61
Police officer	61	40
Sociologist	61	67
Journalist	60	55
Classical musician	59	56
Actor or actress	58	52
Chiropractor	57	62
Athletic coach	53	50
Social worker	52	56
Electrician	51	44
Undertaker	49	34
Jazz musician	48	38
Real estate agent	48	49
Mail carrier	47	33
Secretary	46	53
Plumber	45	34
Carpenter	43	37
Farmer	40	47
Barber	36	30
Store sales clerk	36	34
Truck driver	30	33
Cab driver	28	28
Garbage collector	28	13
Waiter or waitress	28	23
Bartender	25	23
Lives on public aid	25	16
Bill collector	24	27
Factory worker	24	29
Janitor	22	21
Shoe shiner	17	12
Street sweeper	11	13

Note: For five occupations not located in the 1994 source, the 1991 ratings were used: Supreme Court judge, astronaut, athletic coach, lives on public aid, and street sweeper.

Sources: Treiman 1977, Appendices A and D; Nakao and Treas 1991; 1994: Appendix D.

Display of prestige and social position varies over time and from one culture to another. Shown here is Elizabeth I, Queen of England and Ireland. Elizabeth became queen in 1558 at the age of 25 and ruled for 45 years, until 1603. This painting hangs in the National Portrait Gallery.

sive cars than they did. Some attempted to "put the janitor in his place" by making "snotty" remarks to him. For their part, the janitors took delight in knowing "dirty" secrets about the tenants, gleaned from their garbage.

Individuals with status inconsistency, then, are likely to confront one frustrating situation after another (Heames et al. 2006). They claim the higher status, but are handed the lower one. The significance of this condition, said Lenski (1954), is that such people tend to be more politically radical. An example is college professors. Their prestige is very high, as we saw in Table 7.4, but their incomes are relatively low. Hardly anyone in U.S. society is more educated, and yet college professors don't even come close to the top of the income pyramid. In line with Lenski's prediction, the politics of most college professors are left of center. This hypothesis may also hold true among academic departments; that is, the higher a department's average pay, the less radical are the members' politics. Teachers in departments of business and medicine, for example, are among the most highly paid in the university—and they also are the most politically conservative.

Instant wealth, the topic of the Down-to-Earth Sociology box on the next page, provides an interesting case of status inconsistency.

A Model of Social Class

Sociologists Joseph Kahl and Dennis Gilbert (Gilbert and Kahl 1998; Gilbert 2003) developed a six-tier model to portray the class structure of the United States and other capitalist countries. Think of this model, illustrated in Figure 7.6 on page 212, as a ladder. Our discussion starts with the highest rung and moves downward. In line with Weber, on each lower rung you find less property (wealth), less power, and less prestige. Note that in this model education is also a primary measure of class.

The Capitalist Class

Sitting on the top rung of the class ladder is a powerful elite that consists of just 1 percent of the U.S. population. As you saw in Figure 7.3 on page 205, this capitalist class is so wealthy that it owns one–third of all U.S. assets. *This tiny 1 percent is worth more than the entire bottom 90 percent of the country* (Beeghley 2008).

Power and influence cling to this small elite. They have direct access to top politicians, and their decisions open or close job opportunities for millions of people. They even help to shape the consciousness of the nation: They own our major media and entertainment outlets—newspapers, magazines, radio and television stations, and sports franchises. They also control the boards of directors of our most influential colleges and universities. The super-rich perpetuate themselves in privilege by passing on their assets and social networks to their children.

The capitalist class can be divided into "old" and "new" money. The longer that wealth has been in a family, the more it adds to the family's prestige. The children of "old"

Down-to-Earth Sociology

The Big Win: Life After the Lottery

"IF I JUST WIN THE LOTTERY, life will be good. These problems I've got, they'll be gone. I can just see myself now."

So goes the dream. And many Americans shell out megabucks every week, with the glimmering hope that "Maybe this week, I'll hit it big."

Most are lucky to get $10, or maybe just win another scratch-off ticket.

But there are the big hits. What happens to these winners? Are their lives all wine, roses, and chocolate afterward?

Unfortunately, we don't yet have any systematic studies of the big winners, so I can't tell you what life is like for the average winner. But several themes are apparent from reporters' interviews.

The most common consequence of hitting it big is that life becomes topsy-turvy (Ross 2004). All of us are rooted somewhere. We have connections with others that provide the basis for our orientations to life and how we feel about the world. Sudden wealth can rip these moorings apart, and the resulting *status inconsistency* can lead to a condition sociologists call **anomie.**

First comes the shock. As Mary Sanderson, a telephone operator in Dover, New Hampshire, who won $66 million, said, "I was afraid to believe it was real, and afraid to believe it wasn't." Mary says that she never slept worse than her first night as a multimillionaire. "I spent the whole time crying—and throwing up" (Tresniowski 1999).

Reporters and TV camera operators appear on your doorstep. "What are you going to do with all that money?" they demand. You haven't the slightest idea, but in a daze you mumble something.

Then come the calls. Some are welcome. Your Mom and Dad call to congratulate you. But long-forgotten friends and distant relatives suddenly remember how close they really are to you—and strangely enough, they all have emergencies that your money can solve. You even get calls from strangers who have ailing mothers, terminally ill kids, sick dogs . . .

You have to unplug the phone and get an unlisted number.

Some lottery winners are flooded with marriage proposals. These individuals certainly didn't become more attractive or sexy overnight—or did they? Maybe money makes people sexy.

You can no longer trust people. You don't know what their real motives are. Before, no one could be after your money because you didn't have any. You may even fear kidnappers. Before, this wasn't a problem—unless some kidnapper wanted the ransom of a seven-year-old car.

The normal becomes abnormal. Even picking out a wedding gift is a problem. If you give the usual toaster, everyone will think you're stingy. But should you write a check for $25,000? If you do, you'll be invited to every wedding in town—and everyone will expect the same.

Status inconsistency is common for lottery winners, whose new wealth is vastly greater than their education and occupational status. Shown here are John and Sandy Jarrell of Chicago, after they learned that they were one of 13 families to share a $295 million jackpot. How do you think their $22 million will affect their lives?

Here is what happened to some lottery winners:

As a tip, a customer gave a lottery ticket to Tonda Dickerson, a waitress at the Waffle House in Grand Bay, Alabama. She won $10 million. (Yes, just like the Nicholas Cage movie, *It Could Happen to You.*) Her coworkers sued her, saying that they had always agreed to split such winnings ("House Divided" 1999).

Then there is Michael Klinebiel of Rahway, New Jersey. When he won $2 million, his mother, Phyllis, said that they had pooled $20 a month for years to play the lottery. He said that was true, but his winning ticket wasn't from their pool. He had bought this one on his own. Phyllis sued her son ("Sticky Ticket" 1998).

Frank Capaci, a retired electrician in Streamwood, Illinois, who won $195 million, is no longer welcome at his old neighborhood bar. Two bartenders had collected $5 from customers and driven an hour to Wisconsin to buy tickets. When Frank won, he gave $10,000 to each of them. They said that he promised them more. Also, his former friends say that Capaci started to act "like a big shot," buying rounds of drinks but saying, "Except him," while pointing to someone he didn't like (Annin 1999).

Mack Metcalf of Corbin, Kentucky, wasn't as fortunate as Frank Capaci. After Mark hit the jackpot for $34 million, he built a beautiful home—but his former wife sued him, his current wife divorced him, his new girlfriend got $500,000 while he was drunk, and within three years of his good fortune he had drunk himself to death (Dao 2005).

Winners who avoid *anomie* seem to be people who don't make sudden changes in their lifestyle or their behavior. They hold onto their old friends, routines, and other anchors in life that give them identity and a sense of belonging. Some even keep their old jobs—not for the money, of course, but because working anchors them to an identity with which they are familiar and comfortable.

Sudden wealth, in other words, poses a threat that has to be guarded against.

And I can just hear you say, "I'll take the risk!"

Figure 7.6 The U.S. Social Class Ladder

Social Class	Education	Occupation	Income	Percentage of Population
Capitalist	Prestigious university	Investors and heirs, a few top executives	$1,000,000+	1%
Upper Middle	College or university, often with postgraduate study	Professionals and upper managers	$125,000+	15%
Lower Middle	High school or college; often apprenticeship	Semiprofessionals and lower managers, craftspeople, foremen	About $60,000	34%
Working	High school	Factory workers, clerical workers, low-paid retail sales, and craftspeople	About $35,000	30%
Working Poor	Some high school	Laborers, service workers, low-paid salespeople	About $17,000	16%
Underclass	Some high school	Unemployed and part-time, on welfare	Under $10,000	4%

Source: Based on Gilbert and Kahl 1998 and Gilbert 2003; income estimates are modified from Duff 1995.

money seldom mingle with "common" folk. Instead, they attend exclusive private schools where they learn views of life that support their privileged position. They don't work for wages; instead, many study business or enter the field of law so that they can manage the family fortune. These old-money capitalists (also called "blue-bloods") wield vast power as they use their extensive political connections to protect their economic empires (Sklair 2001; Domhoff 1990, 1999b, 2006).

At the lower end of the capitalist class are the *nouveau riche,* those who have "new money." Although they have made fortunes in business, the stock market, inventions, entertainment, or sports, they are outsiders to this upper class. They have not attended the "right" schools, and they don't share the social networks that come with old money.

With a fortune of $48 billion, Bill Gates, a cofounder of Microsoft Corporation, is the second wealthiest person in the world. His 40,000-square-foot home (sometimes called a "technopalace") in Seattle, Washington, was appraised at $110 million.

Gates has given more money to the poor and minorities than any individual in history. His foundation is now focusing on fighting infectious diseases, developing vaccines, and improving schools.

Not blue-bloods, they aren't trusted to have the right orientations to life (Burris 2000). Even their "taste" in clothing and status symbols is suspect (Fabricant 2005). Donald Trump, whose money is "new," is not listed in the *Social Register,* the "White Pages" of the blue-bloods that lists the most prestigious and wealthy one-tenth of 1 percent of the U.S. population. Trump says he "doesn't care," but he reveals his true feelings by adding that his heirs will be in it (Kaufman 1996). He is probably right, for the children of the new-moneyed can ascend into the top part of the capitalist class—if they go to the right schools *and* marry old money.

Many in the capitalist class are philanthropic. They establish foundations and give huge sums to "causes." Their motivations vary. Some feel guilty because they have so much while others have so little. Others seek prestige, acclaim, or fame. Still others feel a responsibility—even a sense of fate or purpose—to use their money for doing good. Bill Gates, who has given more money to the poor than any other person, seems to fall into this latter category.

The Upper Middle Class

Of all the classes, the upper middle class is the one most shaped by education. Almost all members of this class have at least a bachelor's degree, and many have postgraduate degrees in business, management, law, or medicine. These people manage the corporations owned by the capitalist class or else operate their own business or profession. As Gilbert and Kahl (1998) say, these positions

may not grant prestige equivalent to a title of nobility in the Germany of Max Weber, but they certainly represent the sign of having "made it" in contemporary America. . . . Their

Johnny Depp

LeBron James

Penelope Cruz

Sandra Oh

Sociologists use income, education, and occupational prestige to measure social class. For most people, this classification works well, but not for everyone. Entertainers sometimes are difficult to fit in. To what social class do Depp, Cruz, Oh, and James belong? Johnny Depp makes $10 million a year, Penelope Cruz $1 to 2 million, and Sandra Oh around $200,000. When Lebron James got out of high school, he signed more than $100 million in endorsement contracts, as well as a $4 million contract to play basketball for the Cleveland Cavaliers.

underclass a group of people for whom poverty persists year after year and across generations

income is sufficient to purchase houses and cars and travel that become public symbols for all to see and for advertisers to portray with words and pictures that connote success, glamour, and high style.

Consequently, parents and teachers push children to prepare for upper-middle-class jobs. About 15 percent of the population belong to this class.

The Lower Middle Class

About 34 percent of the population belong to the lower middle class. Members of this class have jobs that call for them to follow orders given by those who have upper-middle-class credentials. With their technical and lower-level management positions, they can afford a mainstream lifestyle, and many anticipate being able to move up the social class ladder. Feelings of insecurity are common, however, with the threat of taxes, inflation, and job insecuirty bringing a nagging sense that they might fall down the class ladder (Kefalas 2007).

The distinctions between the lower middle class and the working class on the next rung below are more blurred than those between other classes. In general, however, members of the lower middle class work at jobs that have slightly more prestige, and their incomes are generally higher.

The Working Class

About 30 percent of the U.S. population belong to this class of relatively unskilled blue-collar and white-collar workers. Compared with the lower middle class, they have less education and lower incomes. Their jobs are also less secure, more routine, and more closely supervised. One of their greatest fears is that of being laid off during a recession. With only a high school diploma, the average member of the working class has little hope of climbing up the class ladder. Job changes usually bring "more of the same," so most concentrate on getting ahead by achieving seniority on the job rather than by changing their type of work. They tend to think of themselves as having "real jobs," and regard the "suits" above them as paper pushers who have no practical experience (Morris and Grimes 2005).

The Working Poor

Members of this class, about 16 percent of the population, work at unskilled, low-paying, temporary and seasonal jobs, such as sharecropping, migrant farm work, housecleaning, and day labor. Most are high school dropouts. Many are functionally illiterate, finding it difficult to read even the want ads. They are not likely to vote (Gilbert and Kahl 1998; Beeghley 2008), for they believe that no matter what party is elected to office, their situation won't change.

Although they work full time, millions of the working poor depend on help such as food stamps and donations from local food pantries to survive on their meager incomes (O'Hare 1996b). It is easy to see how you can work full time and still be poor. Suppose that you are married and have a baby 3 months old and another child 3 years old. Your spouse stays home to care for them, so earning the income is up to you. But as a high-school dropout, all you can get is a minimum wage job. At $5.15 an hour, you earn $206 for 40 hours. In a year, this comes to $10,712—before deductions. Your nagging fear—and daily nightmare—is of ending up "on the streets."

The Underclass

On the lowest rung, and with next to no chance of climbing anywhere, is the **underclass.** Concentrated in the inner city, this group has little or no connection with the job market. Those who are employed—and some are—do menial, low-paying, temporary work. Welfare, if it is available, along with food stamps and food pantries, is their main support. Most members of other classes consider these people the "ne'er-do-wells" of society. Life is the toughest in this class, and it is filled with despair. About 4 percent of the population fall into this class.

The homeless men described in the opening vignette of this chapter, and the women and children like them, are part of the underclass. These are the people whom most Americans wish would just go away. Their presence on our city streets bothers passersby from the more privileged social classes—which includes just about everyone. "What are those obnoxious, dirty, foul-smelling people doing here, cluttering up my city?" appears to be a common response. Some people react with sympathy and a desire to do something. But what? Almost all of us just shrug our shoulders and look the other way, despairing of a solution and somewhat intimidated by their presence.

The homeless are the "fallout" of our postindustrial economy. In another era, they would have had plenty of work. They would have tended horses, worked on farms, dug ditches, shoveled coal, and run the factory looms. Some would have explored and settled the West. Others would have been lured to California, Alaska, and Australia by the prospect of gold. Today, however, with no frontiers to settle, factory jobs scarce, and farms that are becoming technological marvels, we have little need for unskilled labor.

Consequences of Social Class

Each social class can be thought of as a broad subculture with distinct approaches to life. Social class affects people's health, family life, and education. It also influences their religion and politics, and even their experiences with crime and the criminal justice system. Let's look at these consequences of social class, as well as how the new technology is related to social class.

Physical Health

If you want to get a sense of how social class affects health, take a ride on Washington's Metro system. Start in the blighted Southeast section of downtown D.C. For every mile you travel to where the wealthy live in Montgomery County in Maryland, life expectancy rises about a year and a half. By the time you get off, you will find a twenty-year gap between the poor blacks where you started your trip and the rich whites where you ended it. (Cohen 2004) (The foldout at the front of the book illustrates these effects of social class.)

The effects of social class on physical health are startling. The principle is simple: The lower a person's social class, the more likely that individual is to die before the expected age. This principle holds true at all ages. Infants born to the poor are more likely than other infants to die before their first birthday. In old age—whether 75 or 95—a larger proportion of the poor die each year than do the wealthy.

How can social class have such dramatic effects? A fundamental reason is that health care in the United States is not a citizens' right but a commodity for sale. This gives us a two-tier system of medical care: superior care for those who can afford the cost and inferior care for those who cannot (Budrys 2003). Unlike the middle and upper classes, few poor people have a personal physician, and they often spend hours waiting in crowded public health clinics. After waiting most of a day, some don't even get to see a doctor. Instead, they are told to come back the next day. And when the poor are hospitalized, they are likely to find themselves in understaffed and underfunded public hospitals, treated by rotating interns who do not know them and cannot follow up on their progress.

A second reason is lifestyles, which are shaped by social class. People in the lower social classes are more likely to smoke, eat a lot of fats, be overweight, abuse drugs and alcohol, get little or no exercise, and practice unsafe sex (Chin et al. 2000; Navarro 2002; Liu 2007). This, to understate the matter, does not improve people's health.

There is a third reason, too. Life is hard on the poor. The persistent stresses they face cause their bodies to wear out faster (Spector 2007). The rich find life better. They have fewer problems and more resources to deal with the ones they have. This gives them a sense of control over their lives, a source of both physical and mental health.

Mental Health

From the 1930s until now, sociologists have found that the mental health of the lower classes is worse than that of the higher classes (Faris and Dunham 1939; Srole et al. 1978; Pratt et al. 2007). Greater mental problems are part of the higher stress that accompanies poverty. Compared with middle- and upper-class Americans, the poor have less job security and lower wages. They are more likely to divorce, to be the victims of crime, and to have more physical illnesses. Couple these conditions with bill collectors and the threat of eviction, and you can see how they can deal severe blows to people's emotional well-being.

People higher up the social class ladder experience stress in daily life, of course, but their stress is generally less, and their coping resources are greater. Not only can they afford vacations, psychiatrists, and counselors but also *their class position gives them greater control over their lives, a key to good mental health.*

As indicated in the following thinking critically section, social class is also significant for mental health care.

Thinking Critically

Mental Illness and Inequality in Health Care

Standing among the police, I watched as the elderly nude man, looking confused, struggled to put on his clothing. The man had ripped the wires out of the homeless shelter's main electrical box and then led the police on a merry chase as he ran from room to room.

I asked the officers where they were going to take the man, and the replied, "To Malcolm Bliss" (the state mental hospital). When I commented, "I guess he'll be in there for a quite a while," they replied, "Probably just a day or two. We picked him up last week—he was crawling under cars stopped at a traffic light—and they let him out in two days."

The police explained that a person must be a danger to others or to oneself to be admitted as a long-term patient. Visualizing this old man crawling under cars in traffic and the possibility of electrocuting himself by ripping out electrical wires with his bare hands, I marveled at the definition of "danger" that the hospital psychiatrists must be using.

Stripped of its veil, the two-tier system of medical care is readily visible. The poor—such as this confused naked man—find it difficult to get into mental hospitals. If they are admitted, they are sent to the dreaded state hospitals. In contrast, private hospitals serve the wealthy and those who have good insurance. The rich are likely to be treated with "talk therapy" (forms of psychotherapy), the poor with "drug therapy" (tranquilizers to make them docile, sometimes known as "medicinal straitjackets").

For your consideration

How can we improve the treatment of the mentally ill poor? Take into consideration that the public does not want higher taxes. What about the broader, more fundamental issue: that of inequality in health care? Should medical care be a commodity that is sold to those who can afford it? Or do all citizens possess some fundamental right that should guarantee them high-quality health care? If so, what is the basis of that right?

Family Life

Social class also plays a significant role in family life. It even affects our choice of spouse, our chances of getting divorced, and how we rear our children.

Choice of Husband or Wife   Members of the capitalist class place strong emphasis on family tradition. They stress the family's ancestors, history, and even a sense of purpose or destiny in life (Baltzell 1979; Aldrich 1989). Children of this class learn that their choice of husband or wife affects not just themselves but also the entire family, that their spouse will have an impact on the "family line." Because of these background expectations, the field of "eligible" marriage partners is much narrower than it is for the children of any other social class. As a result, parents in this class play a strong role in their children's mate selection.

Divorce   The more difficult life of the lower social classes, especially the many tensions that come from insecure jobs and inadequate incomes, leads to higher marital friction and a greater likelihood of divorce. Consequently, children of the poor are more likely to grow up in broken homes.

Education

As we saw in Figure 7.6 on page 212, education increases as one goes up the social class ladder. It is not just the amount of education that changes, but also the type of education. Children of the capitalist class bypass public schools. They attend exclusive private schools where they are trained to take a commanding role in society. Prep schools such as Phillips Exeter Academy, Groton School, and Woodberry Forest School teach upper-class values and prepare their students for prestigious universities (Cookson and Persell 2005; Beeghley 2008).

Keenly aware that private schools can be a key to social mobility, some upper middle class parents do their best to get their children into the prestigious preschools that feed into these exclusive prep schools. Although some preschools cost $23,000 a year, they have a waiting list (Rohwedder 2007). Parents even elicit letters of recommendation for their 2- and 3-year-olds. Such parental expectations and resources are major

How much difference does social class make in our lives? Shown here are actress Jillian Barberie in the walk-in closet of her home in Los Angeles, California, and Paulina Rodriguez in the living room of her home in Rio Grande Valley, Texas. Can you see why these women are likely to see the world in highly distinctive ways, and why even their politics and aspirations in life are likely to differ?

reasons why children from the more privileged classes are more likely to enter and to graduate from college.

Religion

One area of social life that we might think would be unaffected by social class is religion. ("People are just religious, or they are not. What does social class have to do with it?") Social class, however, is a significant sorter of people in all areas of social life, and religion is no exception to this principle. The classes tend to cluster in different denominations. Episcopalians, for example, are more likely to attract the middle and upper classes, while Baptists draw heavily from the lower classes. Patterns of worship also follow class lines: The lower classes are attracted to more expressive worship services and louder music, while the middle and upper classes prefer more "subdued" worship.

Politics

As has been stressed throughout this text, symbolic interactionists emphasize that people perceive events from their own corner in life. Political views are no exception to this principle, and the rich and the poor walk different political paths. The higher that people are on the social class ladder, the more likely they are to vote for Republicans (Burris 2005). In contrast, most members of the working class believe that the government should intervene in the economy to provide jobs and to make citizens financially secure. They are more likely to vote for Democrats. Although the working class is more liberal on *economic* issues (policies that increase government spending), it is more conservative on *social* issues (such as opposing abortion and the Equal Rights Amendment) (Lipset 1959; Houtman 1995). People toward the bottom of the class structure are also less likely to be politically active—to campaign for candidates or even to vote (Soss 1999; Gilbert 2003; Beeghley 2008).

Social Mobility

No aspect of life, then—from marriage to politics—goes untouched by social class. Because life is so much more satisfying in the more privileged classes, people strive to climb the social class ladder. What affects their chances?

Three Types of Social Mobility

There are three basic types of social mobility: intergenerational, structural, and exchange. **Intergenerational mobility** refers to a change that occurs between genera-

The term *structural mobility* refers to changes in society that push large numbers of people either up or down the social class ladder. A remarkable example was the stock market crash of 1929, when tens of thousands of people suddenly lost immense amounts of wealth. People who once "had it made" found themselves standing on street corners selling apples or, as depicted here, selling their possessions at fire-sale prices.

Social Class and the Upward Social Mobility of African Americans

THE OVERVIEW OF SOCIAL CLASS presented in this chapter doesn't apply equally to all the groups that make up U.S. society. Consider geography: What constitutes the upper class of a town of 5,000 people will be quite different from that of a city of a million. The extremes of wealth and the diversity and prestige of occupations will be less in the small town, where family background is likely to play a more significant role.

So, too, there are differences within racial-ethnic groups. While all racial-ethnic groups are marked by divisions of social class, what constitutes a particular social class will differ from one group to another—as well as from one historical period to another. Consider social class among African Americans (Cole and Omari 2003).

The earliest class divisions can be traced to slavery—to slaves who worked in the fields and those who worked in the "big house." Those who worked in the plantation home were exposed to more "genteel" manners and forms of speech. Their more privileged position—which brought with it better food, clothing, and lighter work—was often based on skin color. Mulattos, lighter-skinned slaves, were often chosen for this more desirable work. One result was the development of a "mulatto elite," a segment of the slave population that, proud of its distinctiveness, distanced itself from the other slaves. At this time, there also were free blacks. Not only were they able to own property but some of them even owned black slaves.

After the War Between the States (as the Civil War is known in the South), these two groups, the mulatto elite and the free blacks, became the basis of an upper class. Proud of their earlier status, they distanced themselves from other blacks. From these groups came most of the black professionals.

After World War II, just as with whites, the expansion of the black middle class opened access to a wider range of occupations and residential neighborhoods. Beginning about 1960, the numbers of African Americans who were middle class surged. Today, more than half of all African American adults work at white-collar jobs, with twenty-two percent working at the professional or managerial level (Beeghley 2008). As with members of other racial-ethnic groups, African Americans who move up the social class ladder experience a hidden cost: They feel an uncomfortable distancing from their roots, a separation from significant others—parents, siblings, and childhood friends (hooks 2000). The upwardly mobile individual has entered a world unknown to those left behind.

The cost of upward mobility that comes with trying to straddle two worlds is common to individuals from all groups. What appears to be different for African Americans, however, is a sense of leaving one's racial-ethnic group, of the necessity—if one is to succeed in the new world—of conforming to a dominant culture. This includes appearance and speech, but also something much deeper—values, aspirations, and ways of evaluating the self. In addition, the increased contact with whites that comes with social mobility often brings a greater sense of deprivation. Whites become a primary reference group, yet racism, mostly subtle and beneath the surface, continues. Awareness that they are not fully accepted in their new world engenders frustration, dissatisfaction, and cynicism.

for your Consideration

If you review the box on upward social mobility on page 85, you will find that Latinos face a similar situation. Why do you think this is? What connections do you see among upward mobility, frustration, and strong racial-ethnic identity? How do you think that the upward mobility of whites is different? Why?

tions—when grown-up children end up on a different rung of the social class ladder from the one occupied by their parents. If the child of someone who sells used cars graduates from college and buys a Saturn dealership, that person experiences **upward social mobility.** Conversely, if a child of the dealership's owner parties too much, drops out of college, and ends up selling cars, he or she experiences **downward social mobility.**

downward social mobility movement down the social class ladder

structural mobility move-
ment up or down the social
class ladder because of
changes in the structure of society, not to individual efforts

exchange mobility about the
same numbers of people moving up and down the social
class ladder, such that, on
balance, the social class system shows little change

As discussed in the Cultural Diversity box on the previous page, social mobility
comes at a cost.

We like to think that individual efforts are the reason people move up the class ladder—
and their faults the reason they move down. In these examples, we can identify hard work,
sacrifice, and ambition on the one hand, versus indolence and substance abuse on the
other. Although individual factors such as these do underlie social mobility, sociologists
consider **structural mobility** to be the crucial factor. This second basic type of mobility
refers to changes in society that cause large numbers of people to move up or down the
class ladder.

To better understand structural mobility, think of how opportunities opened when
computers were invented. New types of jobs appeared overnight. Huge numbers of
people attended workshops and took crash courses, switching from blue-collar to
white-collar work. Although individual effort certainly was involved—for some seized
the opportunity while others did not—the underlying cause was a change in the
structure of work. Consider the opposite—how opportunities disappear during a depression, which forces millions of people downward on the class ladder. In this instance, too, their changed status is due less to individual behavior than to *structural*
changes in society.

The third type of social mobility, **exchange mobility,** occurs when large numbers of
people move up and down the social class ladder, but, on balance, the proportions of the
social classes remain about the same. Suppose that a million or so working-class people
are trained in some new technology, and they move up the class ladder. Suppose also
that because of a surge in imports, about a million skilled workers have to take lower-
status jobs. Although millions of people change their social class, there is, in effect, an
exchange among them. The net result more or less balances out, and the class system remains basically untouched.

Women in Studies of Social Mobility

In classic studies, sociologists concluded that about half of sons passed their fathers on
the social class ladder; about one-third stayed at the same level, and about one-sixth
moved down (Blau and Duncan 1967; Featherman and Hauser 1978; Featherman
1979).

Feminists objected that it wasn't good science to focus on sons and ignore daughters
(Davis and Robinson 1988). They also pointed out that it was wrong to assume that
women had no social class position of their own, that it was not valid to assign wives to
the class of their husbands. The defense made by male sociologists of the time was that
too few women were in the labor force to make a difference.

With huge numbers of women now working for pay, more recent studies include
women (Gofen 2007; Beeghley 2008). Sociologists Elizabeth Higginbotham and Lynn
Weber (1992), for example, studied 200 women from working-class backgrounds who
became professionals, managers, and administrators in Memphis. They found that almost
without exception, the women's parents had encouraged them while they were still little
girls to postpone marriage and get an education. This study confirms how important the
family is in the socialization process. It also supports the observation that the primary
entry to the upper middle class is a college education. At the same time, if there had not
been a *structural* change in society, the millions of new positions that women occupy
would not exist.

Poverty

Many Americans find that the "limitless possibilities" on which the
American dream is based are really quite elusive. As is illustrated in Figure 7.6 on page
212, the working poor and underclass together form about one-fifth of the U.S. population. This translates into a huge number, about 60 million people. Who are these
people?

WIZARD OF ID

THE KING WILL NOW OUTLINE HIS PLAN TO ELIMINATE POVERTY

IN THE FUTURE, THERE WILL BE NO MONETARY AMOUNT USED TO DEFINE POVERTY

GEE, I FEEL RICHER ALREADY!

By permission of Johnny Hart and Creators Syndicate

This cartoon pinpoints the arbitrary nature of the poverty line. This makes me almost think that the creators of the Wizard of Id have been studying sociology.

Drawing the Poverty Line

To determine who is poor, the U.S. government draws a **poverty line.** This measure was set in the 1960s, when poor people were thought to spend about one-third of their incomes on food. On the basis of this assumption, each year the government computes a low-cost food budget and multiplies it by 3. Families whose incomes are less than this amount are classified as poor; those whose incomes are higher—even by a dollar—are determined to be "not poor."

This official measure of poverty is grossly inadequate. Poor people actually spend only about 20 percent of their incomes on food, so to determine a poverty line, we really ought to multiply their food budget by 5 instead of 3 (Uchitelle 2001). No political party in power wants to do this, as redrawing the line in this way would make it appear that poverty increased under their watch. Another problem with the poverty line is that some mothers work outside the home and have to pay for child care, but they are treated the same as mothers who don't have this expense. The poverty line is also the same for everyone across the nation, even though the cost of living is much higher in New York than in Alabama. In addition, the government does not count food stamps as income.

That a change in the poverty line would instantly make millions of people poor—or take away their poverty—would be a laughable matter, if it weren't so serious. (The absurdity has not been lost on Parker and Hart, as you can see from their sarcastic cartoon.) Although this line is arbitrary, it is the official measure of poverty, and the government uses it to decide who will receive help and who will not. On the basis of this line, let's see who in the United States is poor. Before we do this, though, compare your ideas of the poor with the myths explored in the Down-to-Earth Sociology box on the next page.

Race-Ethnicity   One of the strongest factors in poverty is race-ethnicity. As Figure 7.7 on the next page shows, only 10 percent of Asian Americans and 11 percent of whites are poor, but 22 percent of Latinos and 25 percent of African Americans live in poverty. The stereotype that most poor people are African Americans and Latinos is untrue. Because there are so many more whites in U.S. society, their much lower rate of poverty translates into larger numbers. As a result, most poor people are white.

Children of Poverty

Children are more likely to live in poverty than are adults or the elderly. That millions of U.S. children are reared in poverty is shocking when one considers the wealth of this country and the supposed concern for the well-being of children. This tragic aspect of poverty is the topic of the following Thinking Critically section on page 223.

poverty line the official measure of poverty; calculated to include incomes that are less than three times a low-cost food budget

Down-to-Earth Sociology

Exploring Myths About the Poor

Myth 1 Most poor people are lazy. They are poor because they do not want to work. Half of the poor are either too old or too young to work: About 40 percent are under age 18, and another 10 percent are age 65 or older. About 30 percent of the working-age poor work at least half the year.

Myth 2 Poor people are trapped in a cycle of poverty that few escape. Long-term poverty is rare. Most poverty lasts less than a year (Lichter and Crowley 2002). Only 12 percent remain in poverty for five or more consecutive years (O'Hare 1996a). Most children who are born in poverty are *not* poor as adults (Ruggles 1989; Corcoron 2001).

Myth 3 Most of the poor are African Americans and Latinos. As shown in 7.7, the poverty rates of African Americans and Latinos are much higher than that of whites. Because there are so many more whites in the U.S. population, however, *most of the poor are white.* Of the 37 million U.S. poor, about 57 percent are white, 20 percent African American, 20 percent Latino, and 3 percent Asian American (*Statistical Abstract* 2007:Table 694).

Myth 4 Most of the poor are single mothers and their children. Although about 38 percent of the poor match this stereotype, 34 percent of the poor live in married-couple families, 22 percent live alone or with nonrelatives, and 6 percent live in other settings.

Myth 5 Most of the poor live in the inner city. This one is close to fact, as about 42 percent do live in the inner city. But 36 percent live in the suburbs, and 22 percent live in small towns and rural areas.

Myth 6 The poor live on welfare. About half of the income of poor adults comes from wages and pensions, about 25 percent from welfare, and about 22 percent from Social Security.

Sources: Primarily O'Hare 1996a, 1996b, with other sources as indicated.

Figure 7.7 **Poverty in the United States, by Age and Race-Ethnicity**

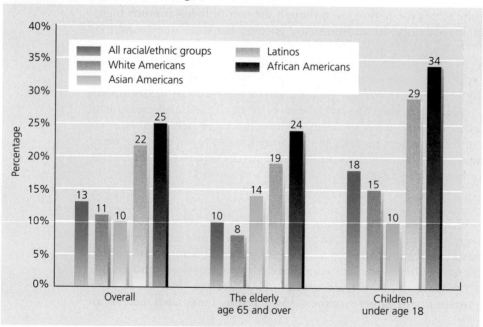

Note: Only these groups are listed in the source. The poverty line on which this figure is based is $19,307 for a family of four.

Source: By the author. Based on *Statistical Abstract* 2007:Table 694.

Thinking Critically

The Nation's Shame: Children in Poverty

One of the most startling statistics in sociology is shown in Figure 7.7 on page 222. Look at the rate of childhood poverty: For Asian Americans, one of ten children is poor; for whites, one of seven; for Latinos, one of three or four; and for African Americans, an astounding one of three. These percentages translate into incredible numbers—approximately *16 million* children live in poverty: 8 million white children, 4 million Latino children, 4 million African American children, and 300,000 Asian American children.

Why do so many U.S. children live in poverty? The main reason, said sociologist and former U.S. Senator Daniel Moynihan (1991), is an increase in births outside marriage. In 1960, one of twenty U.S. children was born to a single woman. Today that total is about *seven times higher,* and single women now account for one of three (36 percent) of all U.S. births (*Statistical Abstract* 2007:Table 84). Sociologists Lee Rainwater and Timothy Smeeding (2003), who note that *the poverty rate of U.S. children is the highest in the industrialized world,* point to another cause: the lack of government support to children.

Births to single women follow patterns that are significant for their children's welfare. The less education a woman has, the more likely she is to bear children when she is not married. As you can see from Figure 7.8, births to single women drop with each gain in education. Because people with lower education earn less, this means that the single women who can least afford children are those most likely to give birth. Their children are likely to live in poverty and to face the suffering and obstacles to a satisfying life that poverty entails. They are more likely to die in infancy, to go hungry, to be malnourished, to develop more slowly, and to have more health problems. They also are more likely to drop out of school, to become involved in criminal activities, and to have children while still in their teens—thus perpetuating the cycle of poverty.

Figure 7.8 **Births to Single Mothers**

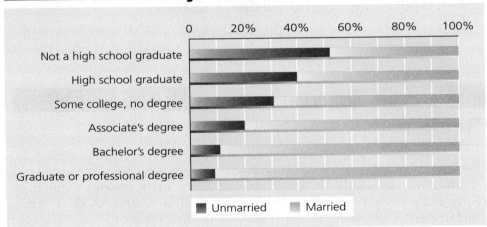

Note: Based on a national U.S. sample of all births in the preceding 12 months.

Source: Dye 2005.

for your Consideration

With education so important to obtain jobs that pay better, in light of Figure 7.8, what programs would you suggest for helping women attain more education? Be specific and practical.

A society's dominant ideologies are reinforced throughout the society, including its literature. Horatio Alger provided inspirational heroes for thousands of boys. The central theme of these many novels, immensely popular in their time, was rags to riches. Through rugged determination and self-sacrifice, a boy could overcome seemingly insurmountable obstacles to reach the pinnacle of success. (Girls did not strive for financial success, but were dependent on fathers and husbands.)

Where Is Horatio Alger? The Social Functions of a Myth

In the late 1800s, Horatio Alger was one of the country's most talked-about authors. The rags-to-riches exploits of his fictional boy heroes and their amazing successes in overcoming severe odds motivated thousands of boys of that period. Although Alger's characters have disappeared from U.S. literature, they remain alive and well in the psyche of Americans. From real-life examples of people of humble origin who climbed the social class ladder, Americans know that anyone can get ahead if they really try. In fact, they believe that most Americans, including minorities and the working poor, have an average or better-than-average chance of getting ahead—obviously a statistical impossibility (Kluegel and Smith 1986).

The accuracy of the **Horatio Alger myth** is less important than the belief that limitless possibilities exist for everyone. Functionalists would stress that this belief is functional for society. On the one hand, it encourages people to compete for higher positions, or, as the song says, "to reach for the highest star." On the other hand, it places blame for failure squarely on the individual. If you don't make it—in the face of ample opportunities to get ahead—the fault must be your own. The Horatio Alger myth helps to stabilize society: Since the fault is viewed as the individual's, not society's, current social arrangements can be regarded as satisfactory. This reduces pressures to change the system.

As Marx and Weber pointed out, social class penetrates our consciousness, shaping our ideas of life and our "proper" place in society. When the rich look at the world around them, they sense superiority and anticipate control over their own destiny. When the poor look around them, they are more likely to sense defeat, and to anticipate that unpredictable forces will batter their lives. Both rich and poor know the dominant ideology, that their particular niche in life is due to their own efforts, that the reasons for success—or failure—lie solely with the self. Like fish that don't notice the water, people tend not to perceive the effects of social class on their own lives.

Horatio Alger myth the belief that due to limitless possibilities anyone can get ahead if he or she tries hard enough

Summary *and* Review

What is social stratification?

Social stratification refers to a hierarchy of relative privilege based on power, property, and prestige. Every society stratifies its members, and in every society men as a group are placed above women as a group. P. 186.

What are three major systems of social stratification?

Four major stratification systems are slavery, caste, estate, and class. The essential characteristic of **slavery** is that some people own other people. Initially, slavery was based not on race but on debt, punishment, or defeat in battle. Slavery could be temporary or permanent, and was not necessarily passed on to one's children. North American slaves had no legal rights, and the system was gradually buttressed by a racist **ideology.** In a **caste system,** status is determined by birth and is lifelong. A **class system** is much more open than these other systems, for it is based primarily on money or material possessions. Industrialization encourages the formation of class systems. Gender cuts across all forms of social stratification. Pp. 186–195.

How Did the World's Nations Become Stratified?

Why are some nations rich and others poor?

The main theories that seek to account for global stratification are **colonialism, world system theory,** and the **culture of poverty.** Pp. 195, 198.

Why Is Social Stratification Universal?

To explain why stratification is universal, functionalists Kingsley Davis and Wilbert Moore argued that to attract the most capable people to fill its important positions, society must offer them greater rewards. Melvin Tumin said that if this view were correct, society would be a **meritocracy**, with all positions awarded on the basis of merit. Gaetano Mosca argued that stratification is inevitable because every society must have leadership, which by definition means inequality. Conflict theorists argue that stratification came about because resources are limited, and an elite emerges as groups struggle for them. Pp. 200–202.

What Determines Social Class?

Karl Marx argued that a single factor determines social class: If you own the means of production, you belong to the **bourgeoisie;** if you do not, you are one of the **proletariat.** Max Weber argued that three elements determine social class: *property, prestige,* and *power.* Pp. 202–204.

What changes are occurring in social class?

The distribution of **wealth** in the United States has changed little since World War II, but the changes that have occurred have been toward greater inequality. People's rankings of occupational prestige are similar from country to country. Globally, the occupations that bring greater prestige are those that pay more, require more education and abstract thought and offer greater independence. Pp 204–209.

What is meant by the term status inconsistency?

Status is social ranking. Most people are **status consistent;** that is, they rank high or low on all three dimensions of social class. People who rank higher on some dimensions than on others are status inconsistent. The frustrations of **status inconsistency** tend to produce political radicalism. Pp. 209–210.

What six-class model portrays the social classes?

Kahl and Gilbert developed a six-class model based on Weber. At the top is the capitalist class. In descending order are the upper middle class, the lower middle class, the working class, the working poor, and the **underclass.** Pp. 210–215.

How does social class affect people's lives?

Social class leaves no aspect of life untouched. It affects our chances of benefiting from the new technology, dying early, becoming ill, receiving good health care, and getting divorced. Social class membership also affects child rearing, educational attainment, religious affiliation, political participation, and contact with the criminal justice system. Pp. 215–218.

What are three types of social mobility?

The term **intergenerational mobility** refers to changes in social class from one generation to the next. **Structural mobility** refers to changes in society that lead large numbers of people to change their social class. **Exchange mobility** is the movement of large numbers of people from one class to another, with the net result that the relative proportions of the population in the classes remain about the same. Pp. 218–220.

Poverty

Who are the poor?

Poverty is unequally distributed in the United States. Racial–ethnic minorities (except Asian Americans), children, women-headed households, and rural Americans are more likely than others to be poor. The poverty rate of the elderly is less than that of the general population. Pp. 220–223.

How is the Horatio Alger myth functional for society?

The **Horatio Alger myth**—the belief that anyone can get ahead if only he or she tries hard enough—encourages people to strive to get ahead. It also deflects blame for failure from society to the individual. P. 224.

Thinking Critically
about Chapter 7

1. How do slavery, caste, and class systems of social stratification differ?
2. The belief that the United States is the land of opportunity draws millions of legal and illegal immigrants to the United States each year. How do the materials in this chapter support or undermine this belief?
3. What social mobility has your own family experienced? In what ways has this affected your life?

Sex and Gender

Pacita Abad, *Women in Burkah* 1979

In Tunis, the capital of Tunisia, on Africa's northern coast, I met some U.S. college students, and spent a couple of days with them. They wanted to see the city's red light district, but I wondered whether it would be worth the trip. I already had seen other red light districts, including the unusual one in Amsterdam where the state licenses the women, requires that they have medical checkups (certificates must be posted so that customers can check them), sets their prices, and pays them social security benefits upon retirement. The prostitutes sit behind lighted picture windows while customers stroll along the canal side streets and browse from the outside.

I decided to go with them. We ended up on a wharf that extended into the Mediterranean. Each side was lined with a row of one-room wooden shacks, crowded one against the next. In front of each open door stood a young woman. Peering from outside into the dark interiors, I could see that each door led to a tiny room with a well-worn bed.

The wharf was crowded with men who were eyeing the women. Many of the men wore sailor uniforms from countries that I couldn't identify.

As I looked more closely, I could see that some of the women had runny sores on their legs. Incredibly, with such visible evidence of their disease, customers still sought them out. Evidently, the $2 price was too low to resist.

With a sick feeling in my stomach and the desire to vomit, I kept a good distance between the beckoning women and myself. One tour of the two-block area was more than sufficient.

Somewhere nearby, out of sight, I knew that there were men whose wealth derived from exploiting these women who were condemned to live short lives punctuated by fear and misery.

In front of each open door stood a young woman. I could see . . . a well-worn bed.

In this chapter, we examine **gender stratification**—males' and females' unequal access to property, power, and prestige. Gender is especially significant because it is a *master status;* that is, it cuts across *all* aspects of social life. No matter what we attain in life, we carry the label *male* or *female.* These labels convey images and expectations about how we should act. They not only guide our behavior but also serve as a basis of power and privilege.

In this chapter's fascinating journey, we shall look at inequality between the sexes both around the world and in the United States. We shall explore whether it is biology or culture that makes us the way we are, and review sexual harassment, unequal pay, and violence against women. This excursion will provide a good context for understanding the power differences between men and women that lead to situations such as the one described in our opening vignette. It should also give you insight into your own experiences with gender.

Issues of Sex and Gender

When we consider how females and males differ, the first thing that usually comes to mind is **sex,** the *biological characteristics* that distinguish males and females. *Primary sex characteristics* consist of a vagina or a penis and other organs related to reproduction. *Secondary sex characteristics* are the physical distinctions between males and females that are not directly connected with reproduction. These characteristics become clearly evident at puberty when males develop more muscles and a lower voice, and gain more body hair and height, while females develop breasts and form more fatty tissue and broader hips.

Gender, in contrast, is a *social,* not a biological characteristic. **Gender** consists of whatever behaviors and attitudes a group considers proper for its males and females. Consequently, gender varies from one society to another. Whereas *sex* refers to male or female, *gender* refers to masculinity or femininity. In short, you inherit your sex, but you learn your gender as you are socialized into the behaviors and attitudes your culture asserts are appropriate for your sex.

As the photo montage on the next page illustrates, these expectations differ around the world. They vary so greatly that some sociologists suggest that we replace the terms *masculinity* and *femininity* with *masculinities* and *femininities.*

The sociological significance of gender is that it is a device by which society controls its members. Gender sorts us, on the basis of sex, into different life experiences. It opens and closes doors to property, power, and even prestige. Like social class, gender is a structural feature of society.

Before examining inequalities of gender, let's consider why the behaviors of men and women differ.

Gender Differences in Behavior: Biology or Culture?

Why are most males more aggressive than most females? Why do women enter "nurturing" occupations such as teaching young children and nursing in far greater numbers than men? To answer such questions, many people respond with some variation of "They're just born that way."

Is this the correct answer? Certainly biology plays a significant role in our lives. Each of us begins as a fertilized egg. The egg, or ovum, is contributed by our mother, the sperm that fertilizes the egg by our father. At the very moment the egg is fertilized, our sex is determined. Each of us receives twenty-three pairs of chromosomes from the ovum and twenty-three pairs from the sperm. The egg has an X chromosome. If the sperm that fertilizes the egg also has an X chromosome, we become a girl (XX). If the sperm has a Y chromosome, we become a boy (XY).

That's the biology. Now, the sociological question is: Does this biological difference control our behavior? Does it, for example, make females more nurturing and submissive and males more aggressive and domineering? Almost all sociologists take the side of "nurture" in this "nature versus nurture" controversy, but a few do not, as you can see from the following Thinking Critically section.

gender stratification males' and females' unequal access to power, prestige, and property on the basis of their sex

sex biological characteristics that distinguish females and males, consisting of primary and secondary sex characteristics

gender the behaviors and attitudes that a society considers proper for its males and females; masculinity or femininity

Merida, Mexico

Madaba, Jordan

Standards of Gender

Each human group determines its ideas of "maleness" and "femaleness." As you can see from these photos of four women and four men, standards of gender are arbitrary and vary from one culture to another. Yet, in its ethnocentrism, each group thinks that its preferences reflect what gender "really" is. As indicated here, around the world men and women try to make themselves appealing by aspiring to their group's standards of gender.

Altamira, Brazil

India

Moran, Kenya

Sichuan Province, Tibet

Chile

Turmi, Ethiopia

Cynthia Fuchs Epstein, whose position in the ongoing "nature versus nurture" debate is summarized here.

Thinking Critically

Biology Versus Culture—Culture Is the Answer

Sociologist Cynthia Fuchs Epstein (1988, 1999, 2007) stresses that differences between the behavior of males and females are solely the result of social factors—specifically, socialization and social control. Her argument is as follows:

1. The anthropological record shows greater equality between the sexes in the past than we had thought. In earlier societies, women, as well as men, hunted small game, made tools, and gathered food. In hunting and gathering societies, the roles of both women and men are less rigid than those created by stereotypes. For example, the Agta and Mbuti are egalitarian. This proves that hunting and gathering societies exist in which women are not subordinate to men. Anthropologists claim that in these societies women have a separate but equal status.

2. The types of work that men and women do in each society are determined not by biology but by social arrangements. Few people can escape these arrangements, and almost everyone works within his or her assigned narrow range. This gender division of work serves the interests of men, and both informal customs and formal laws enforce it. When these socially constructed barriers are removed, women's work habits are similar to those of men.

3. Biology "causes" some human behaviors, but they are related to reproduction or differences in body structure. These differences are relevant for only a few activities, such as playing basketball or "crawling through a small space."

4. Female crime rates are rising in many parts of the world. This indicates that aggression, which is often considered a biologically dictated male behavior, is related instead to social factors. When social conditions permit, such as when women become lawyers, they, too, become "adversarial, assertive, and dominant." Not incidentally, another form of this "dominant behavior" is the challenges that women make in scholarly journals to the biased views about human nature proposed by men.

In short, rather than "women's incompetence or inability to read a legal brief, perform brain surgery, [or] to predict a bull market," social factors—socialization, gender discrimination, and other forms of social control—create gender differences in behavior. Arguments that assign "an evolutionary and genetic basis" to explain differences in the behaviors of women and men are simplistic. They "rest on a dubious structure of inappropriate, highly selective, and poor data, oversimplification in logic and in inappropriate inferences by use of analogy."

The Dominant Position in Sociology

The dominant sociological position is that social factors, not biology, are the reasons we behave the way we do. Our visible differences of sex do not come with meanings built into them. Rather, each human group makes its own interpretation of these physical differences and on this basis assigns males and females to separate groups. In these groups, people learn what is expected of them and are given different access to property, power, prestige, and other privileges available in their society.

Most sociologists find compelling the argument that if biology were the principal factor in human behavior, all around the world we would find women behaving in one way and men in another. In fact, however, ideas of gender vary greatly from one culture to another—and, as a result, so do male–female behaviors.

Opening the Door to Biology

The matter of "nature" versus "nurture" is not so easily settled, however, and some sociologists acknowledge that biological factors are involved in some human behavior other than reproduction and childbearing (Udry 2000). Alice Rossi, a feminist sociologist and former president of the American Sociological Association, has suggested that women are better prepared biologically for "mothering" than are men. Rossi (1977, 1984) says

Thinking Critically

Biology Versus Culture—Biology Is the Answer

Sociologist Steven Goldberg (1974, 1986, 1993, 2003) finds it astonishing that anyone should doubt "the presence of core-deep differences in males and females, differences of temperament and emotion we call masculinity and femininity." Goldberg's argument—that it is not environment but inborn differences that "give masculine and feminine direction to the emotions and behaviors of men and women"—is as follows:

1. The anthropological record shows that all societies for which evidence exists are (or were) **patriarchies** (societies in which men dominate women). Stories about long-lost **matriarchies** (societies in which women dominate men) are myths.

2. In all societies, past and present, the highest statuses are associated with men. In every society, politics is ruled by "hierarchies overwhelmingly dominated by men."

3. Men dominate societies because they "have a lower threshold for the elicitation of dominance behavior . . . a greater tendency to exhibit whatever behavior is necessary in any environment to attain dominance in hierarchies and male-female encounters and relationships." Men are more willing "to sacrifice the rewards of other motivations—the desire for affection, health, family life, safety, relaxation, vacation and the like—in order to attain dominance and status."

4. Just as a 6-foot woman does not prove the social basis of height, so exceptional individuals, such as highly achieving and dominant women, do not refute "the physiological roots of behavior."

In short, there is only one valid interpretation of why every society from that of the Pygmy to that of the Swede associates dominance and attainment with men. Male dominance of society is "an inevitable resolution of the psychophysiological reality." Socialization and social institutions merely *reflect*—and sometimes exaggerate—inborn tendencies. Any interpretation other than inborn differences is "wrongheaded, ignorant, tendentious, internally illogical, discordant with the evidence, and implausible in the extreme." The argument that males are more aggressive because they have been socialized that way is equivalent to the claim that men can grow moustaches because boys have been socialized that way.

To acknowledge this reality is *not* to defend discrimination against women. Approval or disapproval of what societies have done with these basic biological differences is not the issue. The point is that biology leads males and females to different behaviors and attitudes—regardless of how we feel about this or whether we wish it were different.

Steven Goldberg, whose position in the ongoing "nature versus nurture" debate is summarized here.

that women are more sensitive to the infant's soft skin and to their nonverbal communications. She stresses that the issue is not either biology or society. Instead, nature provides biological predispositions, which are then overlaid with culture.

To see why the door to biology is opening just slightly in sociology, let's consider a medical accident and a study of Vietnam veterans.

A Medical Accident   The drama began in 1963, when 7-month-old identical twin boys were taken to a doctor for a routine circumcision (Money and Ehrhardt 1972). The inept physician, who was using a heated needle, turned the electric current too high and accidentally burned off the penis of one of the boys. You can imagine the parents' disbelief—and then their horror—as the truth sank in.

What can be done in a situation like this? The damage was irreversible. The parents were told that their boy could never have sexual relations. After months of soul-searching and tearful consultations with experts, the parents decided that their son should have a sex change operation. When he was 22 months old, surgeons castrated the boy, using the skin to construct a vagina. The parents then gave the child a new name, Brenda, dressed him in frilly clothing, let his hair grow long, and began to treat him as a girl. Later, physicians gave Brenda female steroids to promote female pubertal growth (Colapinto 2001).

patriarchy a society in which men as a group dominate women as a group; authority is vested in males

matriarchy a society in which women as a group dominate men as a group; authority is vested in females

At first, the results were promising. When the twins were 4 years old, the mother said (remember that the children are biologically identical):

> One thing that really amazes me is that she is so feminine. I've never seen a little girl so neat and tidy. . . . She likes for me to wipe her face. She doesn't like to be dirty, and yet my son is quite different. I can't wash his face for anything. . . . She is very proud of herself, when she puts on a new dress, or I set her hair. . . . She seems to be daintier. (Money and Ehrhardt 1972)

About a year later, the mother described how their daughter imitated her while their son copied his father:

> I found that my son, he chose very masculine things like a fireman or a policeman. . . . He wanted to do what daddy does, work where daddy does, and carry a lunch kit. . . . [My daughter] didn't want any of those things. She wants to be a doctor or a teacher. . . . But none of the things that she ever wanted to be were like a policeman or a fireman, and that sort of thing never appealed to her. (Money and Ehrhardt 1972)

If the matter were this clear-cut, we could use this case to conclude that gender is entirely up to nurture. Seldom are things in life so simple, however, and a twist occurs in this story. Despite this promising start and her parents' coaching, Brenda did not adapt well to femininity. She preferred to mimic her father shaving, rather than her mother putting on makeup. She rejected dolls, favoring guns and her brother's toys. She liked rough and tumble games and insisted on urinating standing up. Classmates teased her and called her a "cavewoman" because she walked like a boy. At age 14, she was expelled from school for beating up a girl who teased her. Despite estrogen treatment, she was not attracted to boys, and at age 14, in despair over her inner turmoil, she was thinking of suicide. In a tearful confrontation, her father told her about the accident and her sex change.

"All of a sudden everything clicked. For the first time, things made sense, and I understood who and what I was," the twin said of this revelation. David (his new name) then had testosterone shots and, later, surgery to partially reconstruct a penis. At age 25, he married a woman and adopted her children (Diamond and Sigmundson 1997; Colapinto 2001). There is an unfortunate end to this story, however. In 2004, David committed suicide.

The Vietnam Veterans Study   Time after time, researchers have found that boys and men who have higher levels of testosterone tend to be more aggressive. In one study, researchers compared the testosterone levels of college men in a "rowdy" fraternity with those of men in a fraternity that had a reputation for academic achievement and social responsibility. Men in the "rowdy" fraternity had higher levels of testosterone (Dabbs et al. 1996). In another study, researchers found that prisoners who had committed sex crimes and acts of violence against people had higher levels of testosterone than those who had committed property crimes (Dabbs et al. 1995). The samples that the researchers used were small, however, leaving the nagging uncertainty that these findings might be due to chance.

Then in 1985, the U.S. government began a health study of Vietnam veterans. To be certain that the study was representative, the researchers chose a random sample of 4,462 men. Among the data they collected was a measurement of testosterone. This gave sociologists a large random sample to analyze, one that is still providing surprising clues about human behavior.

This sample supports earlier studies showing that men who have higher levels of testosterone tend to be more aggressive and to have more problems as a consequence. When the veterans with higher testosterone levels were boys, they were more likely to get in trouble with parents and teachers and to become delinquents. As adults, they were more likely to use hard drugs, to get into fights, to end up in lower-status jobs, and to have more sexual partners. Knowing this, you probably won't be surprised to learn that they also were less likely to marry—certainly their low-paying jobs and trouble with the police made them less appealing candidates for marriage. Those who did marry were

Sociologists stress the social factors that underlie human behavior, the experiences that mold us, funneling us into different directions in life. The study of Vietnam veterans discussed in the text is one indication of how the sociological door is opening slowly to also consider biological factors in human behavior. Using a shirt as a stretcher, these soldiers are carrying a wounded buddy from the jungle after heavy fighting near the Cambodian border in Tay Ninh, South Vietnam, on April 6, 1967.

more likely to have affairs, to hit their wives, and, it follows, to get divorced (Dabbs and Morris 1990; Booth and Dabbs 1993).

Fortunately, the Vietnam veterans study does not leave us sociologists with biology as the sole basis for behavior. Not all men with high testosterone get in trouble with the law, do poorly in school, or mistreat their wives. A chief difference, in fact, is social class. High-testosterone men from higher social classes are less likely to be involved in antisocial behaviors than are high-testosterone men from lower social classes (Dabbs and Morris 1990). *Social* factors such as socialization, life goals, and self-definitions, then, also play a part. The matter becomes even more complicated, for in some instances men with higher testosterone have better marriages (Booth, Johnson, and Granger 2004). Discovering how social factors work in combination with testosterone level is of great interest to sociologists.

IN SUM The findings are preliminary, but significant and provocative. They indicate that human behavior is not a matter of either nature or nurture, but of the two working together. Some behavior that we sociologists usually assume to be due entirely to socialization is apparently influenced by biology. In the years to come, this should prove to be an exciting—and controversial—area of sociological research. One level of research will be to determine if any behaviors are due only to biology. The second level will be to discover the ways that social factors modify biology. The third level will be, in sociologist Janet Chafetz's (1990:30) phrase, to determine how "different" becomes translated into "unequal."

"Nature or nurture?" The matter continues to be controversial. In the Down-to-Earth Sociology box on the next page, we see that gender differences have even become the focus of national attention.

Gender Inequality in Global Perspective

Around the world, gender is *the* primary division between people. Every society sets up barriers to provide unequal access to property, power, and prestige on the basis of sex. The barriers *always* favor men-as-a-group. After reviewing the historical record, historian and feminist Gerda Lerner (1986) concluded that "there is not a single society known where women-as-a-group have decision-making power over men (as a group)." Consequently, sociologists classify females as a *minority group*. Because females

Down-to-Earth Sociology

The Gender Gap in Math and Science: A National Debate

OVERWHELMINGLY, ENGINEERS AND SCIENTISTS are men. Why? A national debate erupted in 2005 when Larry Summers, president of Harvard University at that time, suggested that the reason might be innate differences between men and women. In essence, he was suggesting that women's inborn characteristics might make them less qualified to succeed in these endeavors.

Larry Summers, president of Harvard University, after the faculty gave him a vote of no confidence.

Summers' statement landed him squarely on editorial pages throughout the nation. Harvard's Arts and Sciences faculty, which was already upset over what they called his authoritarian manner, took his statement as a "last straw." The faculty met and gave Summers a "no confidence" vote, the equivalent of saying that he should resign. This was the first such repudiation of a president since Harvard was founded in 1636 (Finer 2005). In the face of such opposition, Summers resigned from the presidency of Harvard.

Summers' suggestion that biology *might* be the reason why men dominate science and engineering indicated that he had touched a sore spot in academia. Among the many who weighed in with replies to Summers was the Council of the American Sociological Association ("ASA Council . . ." 2005). The council replied that research gives us clear and compelling evidence that social factors, not genetics, are the reason that women have not done as well as men in science and engineering. To support its position, the council made this compelling argument:

Gender differences in test results in math and science abilities have changed over time. There are now hardly any differences in test scores among male and female U.S. students. In Great Britain, girls now outperform boys on these tests. Biology didn't change—but social factors did: more access to courses in school, changed attitudes of school counselors, and more role models for women.

The council added that women's interests change as opportunities open to them. This, too, is social, not biological. As a result, we can expect many more women to enter the fields of science and engineering. These women, unfortunately, will have to struggle against negative stereotypes about their abilities, as their predecessors have.

Anthropologist George Murdock surveyed 324 traditional societies worldwide. In all of them, some work was considered "men's work," while other tasks were considered "women's work." He found that hunting is almost universally considered "men's work." These men, who live on the steppes of Mongolia, ride reindeer when they go hunting.

outnumber males, you may find this strange. The term *minority group* applies, however, because it refers to people who are discriminated against on the basis of physical or cultural characteristics, regardless of their numbers (Hacker 1951). For an overview of gender discrimination in a changing society, see the Cultural Diversity box on the next page.

How Females Became a Minority Group

Have females always been a minority group? Some analysts speculate that in hunting and gathering societies, women and men were social equals (Leacock 1981; Hendrix 1994) and that horticultural societies also had less gender discrimination than is common today (Collins et al. 1993). In these societies, women may have contributed about 60 percent of the group's total food. Yet, around the world, gender is the basis for discrimination. How, then, did it happen that women became a minority group? Let's consider the primary theory that has been proposed.

"Pssst. You Wanna Buy a Bride?" China in Transition

NGUYEN THI HOAN, AGE 22, thanked her lucky stars. A Vietnamese country girl, she had just arrived in Hanoi to look for work, and while she was still at the bus station a woman offered her a job in a candy factory.

It was a trap. After Nguyen had loaded a few sacks of sugar, the woman took her into the country to "get supplies." There some men took her to China, which was only 100 miles away. Nguyen was put up for auction, along with a 16-year-old Vietnamese girl. Each brought $350. Nguyen was traded from one bride dealer to another until she was taken to a Chinese village. There she was introduced to her new husband, who had paid $700 for her (Marshall 1999).

Why are tens of thousands of women kidnapped and sold as brides in China each year (Rosenthal 2001b)? First, parts of China have a centuries-old tradition of bride selling. Second, China has a shortage of women. The government enforces a "one couple–one child" policy. Since sons are preferred, female infanticide has become common. One result is a shortage of women of marriageable age. In some provinces, for every 100 women there are over 120 men. Yet all the men are expected to marry and produce heirs (Rosenthal 2001b).

Actually, Nguyen was lucky. Some kidnapped women are sold as prostitutes.

Bride selling and forced prostitution are ancient practices. But China is also entering a new era, which is bringing with it new pressures for Chinese women. Ideas of beauty are changing, and blonde, blue-eyed women are becoming a fetish. As a consequence, Chinese women feel a pressure to "Westernize" their bodies. Surgeons promise to give them bigger breasts and Western-looking eyes. A Western style of advertising is gaining ground, too: Ads now show scantily clad women perched on top of sports cars (Chen 1995; Johansson 1999; Yat-ming Sin and Honming Yau 2001).

China in transition . . . It is continuing the old—bride selling—while moving toward the new, Western ideas of beauty and advertising. In both the old and new, women are commodities for the consumption of men.

The Origins of Patriarchy

The major theory of the origin of *patriarchy*—men dominating society—points to social consequences of human reproduction (Lerner 1986; Friedl 1990). In early human history, life was short. To balance the high death rate and maintain the population, women had to give birth to many children. This brought severe consequences for women. Because only females get pregnant, carry a child for nine months, give birth, and nurse, women were limited in their activities for a considerable part of their lives. To survive, an infant needed a nursing mother. With a child at her breast or in her uterus, or one carried on her hip or on her back, women were physically encumbered. Consequently, around the world women assumed tasks that were associated with the home and child care, while men took over the hunting of large animals and other tasks that required both greater speed and longer absences from the base camp (Huber 1990).

As a result, men became dominant. It was the men who left camp to hunt animals, who made contact with other tribes, who traded with these other groups, and who quarreled and waged war with them. It was also the men who made and controlled the instruments of death, the weapons that were used for hunting and warfare. It was

Throughout history, women have been denied the right to pursue various occupations on the basis of presumed biological characteristics. As society—and sex roles—have changed, women have increasingly entered occupations traditionally reserved for men. This woman is "hot tarring" a roof.

they who accumulated possessions in trade and gained prestige by returning to the camp triumphantly, leading captured prisoners or bringing large animals they had killed to feed the tribe. In contrast, little prestige was given to the routine, taken-for-granted activities of women—who were not perceived as risking their lives for the group. Eventually, men took over society. Their sources of power were their weapons, items of trade, and knowledge gained from contact with other groups. Women became second-class citizens, subject to men's decisions.

Is this theory correct? Remember that the answer lies buried in human history, and there is no way of testing it. Male dominance may be the result of some entirely different cause. For example, anthropologist Marvin Harris (1977) proposed that because most men are stronger than most women and hand-to-hand combat was necessary in tribal groups, men became the warriors, and women became the reward that enticed men to risk their lives in battle. Frederick Engels proposed that patriarchy came with the development of private property (Lerner 1986; Mezentseva 2001). He could not explain why private property should have produced male dominance, however. Gerda Lerner (1986) suggests that patriarchy may even have had different origins in different places.

Whatever its origins, a circular system of thought evolved. Men came to think of themselves as inherently superior—based on the evidence that they dominated society. They shrouded many of their activities with secrecy, and constructed elaborate rules and rituals to avoid "contamination" by females, whom they openly deemed inferior by that time. Even today, patriarchy is always accompanied by cultural supports designed to justify male dominance—such as designating certain activities as "not appropriate" for women.

As tribal societies developed into larger groups, men, who enjoyed their power and privileges, maintained their dominance. Long after hunting and hand-to-hand combat ceased to be routine, and even after large numbers of children were no longer needed to maintain the population, men held on to their power. Male dominance in contemporary societies, then, is a continuation of a millennia-old pattern whose origin is lost in history.

A theory of how *patriarchy* originated centers on childbirth. Because only women give birth, they assumed tasks associated with home and child care, while men hunted and performed other survival tasks that required greater strength, speed, and absence from home. This woman farmer in Burma, Myanmar, also takes care of her child—just as her female ancestors have done for centuries.

Sex Typing of Work

Anthropologist George Murdock (1937) analyzed data that researchers had reported on 324 societies around the world. He found that in all of them, activities are *sex typed*. In other words, every society associates certain activities with one sex or the other. He also found that activities that are considered "female" in one society may be considered "male" in another. In some groups, for example, taking care of cattle is women's work, while other groups assign this task to men.

The exception was metalworking, which was considered men's work in all of the societies that Murdock examined. Three other pursuits—making weapons, pursuing sea mammals, and hunting—also were almost universally the domain of men. In a few societies, however, women participated in these activities. Although Murdock found no specific work that was universally assigned only to women, he did find that making clothing, cooking, carrying water, and grinding grain were almost always female tasks. In a few societies, however, such activities were regarded as men's work.

From Murdock's cross-cultural survey, we can conclude that nothing about biology requires men and women to be assigned different work. Anatomy does not have to equal destiny when it comes to occupations, for as we have seen, pursuits that are considered feminine in one society may be deemed masculine in another, and vice versa. On pages 238–239 is a photo essay on women at work in India that underscores this point.

Gender and the Prestige of Work

You might ask whether this division of labor really illustrates social inequality. Does it perhaps simply represent arbitrary ways of dividing up labor, not gender discrimination?

This could be the case, except for this finding: *Universally, greater prestige is given to male activities—regardless of what those activities are* (Linton 1936; Rosaldo 1974). If taking care of goats is men's work, then the care of goats is considered important and carries high prestige, but if it is women's work, it is considered less important and given less prestige. Or, to take an example closer to home, when delivering babies was "women's work" and was done by midwives, it was given low prestige. But when men took over this task, they became "baby doctors" with high prestige (Ehrenreich and English 1973). In short, it is not the work that provides the prestige, but the sex with which the work is associated.

Other Areas of Global Discrimination

Let's briefly consider four additional aspects of global gender discrimination. Later, when we focus on the United States, we shall examine these topics in greater detail.

The Global Gap in Education   Almost 1 billion adults around the world cannot read; two-thirds are women (UNESCO 2006). Table 8.1 lists the countries in which less than half the women can read and write, illustrating this point further. In *every* one of these countries, a higher percentage of men are literate. This table also shows how illiteracy is clustered, for 22 of these 32 countries are in Africa.

The Global Gap in Politics   Around the world, women lack equal access to national decision making. Except for Rwanda (at 49 percent), no national legislature of any country has as many women as men. In some countries, such as Kuwait and Papua New Guinea, the total is only 1 percent. In the United Arab Emirates, women still can't vote, but, then, neither can men. In most nations, women hold about 15 percent of the seats in parliaments and congress ("Women in Politics" 2006).

The Global Gap in Pay   In every nation, women average less pay than men. In the United States, full-time working women average only 70 percent of what men make (see Figure 8.8 on page 250). In some countries, women make much less than this.

Violence Against Women   A global human rights issue is violence against women. Historical examples are foot binding in China, witch burning in Europe, and *suttee* (burning the living widow with the body of her

Foot binding was practiced in China until about 1900. Tiny feet were a status symbol. Making it difficult for a woman to walk, small feet indicated that a woman's husband did not need his wife's labor. To make the feet even smaller, sometimes the baby's feet were broken and wrapped tightly. Some baby's toes were cut off. This photo was taken in Hubei Province, China. The woman getting the pedicure is reportedly 105 years old.

Table 8.1   Countries Where Half or More Men and Women Cannot Read and Write

Country	CANNOT READ	
	Women	Men
Niger	92%	76%
Burkina Faso	86%	66%
Guinea-Bissau	81%	40%
Pakistan	79%	40%
Afghanistan	78%	48%
Sierra Leone	77%	49%
Nepal	76%	41%
Benin	75%	43%
Yemen	75%	32%
Senegal	72%	53%
Mozambique	71%	40%
Bangladesh	70%	48%
Mauritania	68%	47%
Ethiopia	67%	56%
Laos	67%	36%
Mali	66%	51%
Chad	66%	48%
Bhutan	66%	39%
Libya	64%	38%
Morocco	64%	38%
Liberia	62%	30%
Cote d'Ivoire	61%	45%
Burundi	59%	43%
Togo	59%	25%
Egypt	56%	33%
Central African Republic	55%	40%
Eritrea	55%	33%
India	55%	32%
Iraq	54%	34%
Sudan	54%	30%
Malawi	53%	25%
Haiti	52%	48%

Source: "Women of Our World" 2002.

Work and Gender:
Women at Work in India

traveling through India was both a pleasant and an eye-opening experience. The country is incredibly diverse, the people friendly, and the land culturally rich. For this photo essay, wherever I went—whether city, village, or countryside—I took photos of women at work.

From these photos, you can see that Indian women work in a wide variety of occupations. Some of their jobs match traditional Western expectations, and some diverge sharply from our gender stereotypes. Although women in India remain subservient to men—with the women's movement hardly able to break the cultural surface—women's occupations are hardly limited to the home. I was surprised at some of the hard, heavy labor that Indian women do.

Indian women are highly visible in public places. A storekeeper is as likely to be a woman as a man. This woman is selling glasses of water at a beach on the Bay of Bengal. The structure on which her glasses rest is built of sand.

The villages of India have no indoor plumbing. Instead, each village has a well with a hand pump, and it is the women's job to fetch the water. This is backbreaking work, for, after pumping the water, the women wrestle the heavy buckets onto their heads and carry them home. This was one of the few occupations I saw that was limited to women.

Women also take care of livestock. It looks as though this woman dressed up and posed for her photo, but this is what she was wearing and doing when I saw her in the field and stopped to talk to her. While the sheep are feeding, her job is primarily to "be" there, to make certain the sheep don't wander off or that no one steals them.

Sweeping the house is traditional work for Western women. So it is in India, but the sweeping has been extended to areas outside the home. These women are sweeping a major intersection in Chennai. When the traffic light changes here, the women will continue sweeping, with the drivers swerving around them. This was one of the few occupations that seems to be limited to women.

As in the West, food preparation in India is traditional women's work. Here, however, food preparation takes an unexpected twist. Having poured rice from the 60-pound sack onto the floor, these women in Chittoor search for pebbles or other foreign objects that might be in the rice.

I visited quarries in different parts of India, where I found men, women, and children hard at work in the tropical sun. This woman works 8 1/2 hours a day, six days a week. She earns 40 rupees a day (about ninety cents). Men make 60 rupees a day (about $1.35). Like many quarry workers, this woman is a bonded laborer. She must give half of her wages to her master.

When I saw this unusual sight, I had to stop and talk to the workers. From historical pictures, I knew that belt-driven machines were common on U.S. farms 100 years ago. This one in Tamil Nadu processes sugar cane. The woman feeds sugar cane into the machine, which disgorges the stalks on one side and sugar cane juice on the other.

This woman belongs to the Dhobi subcaste, whose occupation is washing clothes. She stands waist deep at this same spot doing the same thing day after day. The banks of this canal in Hyderabad are lined with men and women of her caste, who are washing linens for hotels and clothing for more well-to-do families.

A common sight in India is women working on construction crews. As they work on buildings and on highways, they mix cement, unload trucks, carry rubble, and, following Indian culture, carry loads of bricks atop their heads. This photo was taken in Raipur, Chhattisgarh.

dead husband) in India. Today we have rape, wife beating, female infanticide, and forced prostitution, which was probably the case in our opening vignette. One of today's most notorious examples is female circumcision, the topic of the Cultural Diversity box on the next page.

"Honor killings" are another form of violence against women (Werbner 2007). In some societies, such as Pakistan, Jordan, and Kurdistan, a woman who is thought to have brought disgrace on her family is killed by a male relative—usually a brother or husband, but sometimes her father or uncles. What threat to the family's honor can be so severe that the men kill a daughter, wife, or sister? The usual reason is sex outside of marriage. In Iraq, even a woman who has been raped is in danger of becoming the victim of an honor killing (Banerjee 2003). Killing the girl or woman removes the "stain" she has brought to the family, and restores their honor in the community. Sharing this perspective, the police in these countries generally ignore honor killings, viewing them as private family matters.

The women's struggle for equal rights has been long and hard. Shown here is a 1919 photo from the first wave of the U.S. women's movement. Only against enormous opposition from men did U.S. women win the right to vote. Women first voted in national elections in 1920.

Gender Inequality in the United States

Gender inequality is not some accidental, hit-or-miss affair. Rather, the institutions of each society work together to maintain the group's particular forms of inequality. Customs, often venerated throughout history, both justify and maintain these arrangements. Let's take a brief look at how change in this vital area of social life came about in the United States.

Fighting Back: The Rise of Feminism

To see how far we have come, it is useful to see where we used to be. In early U.S. society, the second-class status of women was taken for granted. A husband and wife were legally one person—him (Chafetz and Dworkin 1986). Women could not vote, buy property in their own name, make legal contracts, or serve on juries. How could things have changed so much in the last century that these examples sound like fiction?

A central lesson of conflict theory is that power yields privilege; like a magnet, power draws society's best resources to the elite. Because men tenaciously held onto their privileges and used social institutions to maintain their position, basic rights for women came only through prolonged and bitter struggle.

Feminism—the view that biology is not destiny and that stratification by gender is wrong and should be resisted—met with strong opposition, both by men who had privilege to lose and by women who accepted their status as morally correct. In 1894, for example, Jeannette Gilder said that women should not have the right to vote because "Politics is too public, too wearing, and too unfitted to the nature of women" (Crossen 2003).

Feminists, then known as suffragists, struggled against such views. In 1916, they founded the National Women's Party, and in 1917 they began to picket the White House. After picketing for six months, the women were arrested. Hundreds were sent to prison, including Lucy Burns, a leader of the National Women's Party. The extent to which these women had threatened male privilege is demonstrated by how they were treated in prison.

> Two men brought in Dorothy Day [the editor of a periodical that promoted women's rights], twisting her arms above her head. Suddenly they lifted her and brought her body down twice over the back of an iron bench. . . . They had been there a few minutes when Mrs. Lewis, all doubled over like a sack of flour, was thrown in. Her head struck the iron bed and she fell to the floor senseless. As for

feminism the philosophy that men and women should be politically, economically, and socially equal; organized activities on behalf of this principle

Female Circumcision

"LIE DOWN THERE," the excisor suddenly said to me [when I was 12], pointing to a mat on the ground. No sooner had I laid down than I felt my frail, thin legs grasped by heavy hands and pulled wide apart. . . . Two women on each side of me pinned me to the ground . . . I underwent the ablation of the labia minor and then of the clitoris. The operation seemed to go on forever. I was in the throes of agony, torn apart both physically and psychologically. It was the rule that girls of my age did not weep in this situation. I broke the rule. I cried and screamed with pain. . . !

Afterwards they forced me, not only to walk back to join the other girls who had already been excised, but to dance with them. I was doing my best, but then I fainted. . . . It was a month before I was completely healed. When I was better, everyone mocked me, as I hadn't been brave, they said. (Walker and Parmar 1993:107–108)

Female circumcision is common in parts of Muslim Africa and in some parts of Malaysia and Indonesia. Often called female genital cutting by Westerners, this practice is also known as clitoral excision, clitoridectomy, infibulation, and labiadectomy, depending on how much of the tissue is removed. Worldwide, between 100 million and 200 million females have been circumcised. In Egypt, 97 percent of the women have been circumcised (Boyle et al. 2001; Douglas 2005).

In some cultures, only the girl's clitoris is cut off; in others, more is removed. In Sudan, the Nubia cut away most of the girl's genitalia, then sew together the remaining outer edges. They bind the girl's legs from her ankles to her waist for several weeks while scar tissue closes up the vagina. They leave a small opening the diameter of a pencil for the passage of urine and menstrual fluids.

Among most groups, the surgery takes place between the ages of 4 and 8. In some cultures, it occurs seven to ten days after birth. In others, it is not performed until girls reach adolescence. Because the surgery is usually done without anesthesia, the pain is so excruciating that adults must hold the girl down. In urban areas, physicians sometimes perform the operation; in rural areas, a neighborhood woman usually does it.

Shock, bleeding, infection, infertility, and death are among the risks. Common side-effects are vaginal spasms, painful intercourse, and lack of orgasms. Urinary tract infec-

This poster is used in Sudan to try to get parents to stop circumcising their daughters.

tions also occur as urine and menstrual flow build up behind the tiny opening.

When a woman marries, the opening is cut wider to permit sexual intercourse. In some groups, this is the husband's responsibility. Before a woman gives birth, the opening is enlarged further. After birth, the vagina is again sutured shut; this cycle of surgically closing and opening begins anew with each birth.

What are the reasons for this custom? Some groups believe that it reduces female sexual desire, making it more likely that a woman will be a virgin at marriage, and, afterward, remain faithful to her husband. Others think that women can't bear children if they aren't circumcised.

Feminists call female circumcision a form of ritual torture to control female sexuality. They point out that men dominate the societies that practice it. Mothers cooperate with the surgery because in these societies an uncircumcised woman is considered impure and is not allowed to marry. Grandmothers insist that the custom continue out of concern that their granddaughters marry well.

The growing opposition to female circumcision has created intense controversy in Africa, perhaps nowhere demonstrated more forcefully than this contrast: On the one hand, fourteen African countries have banned female circumcision (the laws, however, are seldom enforced). On the other hand, to drum up votes for her husband, the wife of the president of Sierra Leone personally sponsored the circumcision of 1,500 girls (Douglas 2005; "Sierra Leone" 2005).

for your Consideration

Do you think that the United States should try to make other nations stop this custom? Or would this be ethnocentric, the imposition of Western values on other cultures? As one Somali woman said, "The Somali woman doesn't need an alien woman telling her how to treat her private parts." Do you think that it is ever legitimate for members of one culture to interfere with another?

How would you respond to those who oppose male circumcision, also a growing movement? How would you respond to those who point out that female circumcision was a custom of Victorian England (Silverman 2004)?

Sources: As cited, and Lightfoot-Klein 1989; Merwine 1993; Chalkley 1997; Collymore 2000; "Ethiopia" 2005; Tuhus-Dubrow 2007.

Lucy Burns, they handcuffed her wrists and fastened the handcuffs over [her] head to the cell door. (Cowley 1969)

This *first wave* of the women's movement had a radical branch that wanted to reform all the institutions of society and a conservative branch whose concern was to win the vote for women (Freedman 2001). The conservative branch dominated, and after the right to vote was won in 1920, the movement basically dissolved.

The *second wave* began in the 1960s. Sociologist Janet Chafetz (1990) points out that up to this time most women thought of work as a temporary activity intended to fill the time between completing school and getting married. To see how children's books reinforced such thinking, see Figure 8.1. As more women took jobs and began to regard them as careers, however, they began to compare their working conditions with those of men. This shift in their reference group changed the way women viewed their conditions at work. The result was a second wave of protest against gender inequalities. The goals of this second wave (which continues today) are broad, ranging from raising women's pay to changing policies on violence against women.

A *third wave* of feminism is emerging. Three main aspects are apparent. The first is a greater focus on the problems of women in the Least Industrialized Nations (Spivak 2000; Hamid 2006). The second is a criticism of the values that dominate work and society. Some feminists argue that competition, toughness, calloused emotions, and independence represent "male" qualities and need to be replaced with cooperation, connection, openness, and interdependence (England 2000). A third aspect is the removal of impediments to women's love and sexual pleasure (Gilligan 2002). As this third wave develops, we can assume that it, too, will have its liberal and conservative branches.

Figure 8.1 Teaching Gender

By looking at the past, we get an idea of how far we have come. This illustration from a 1970s children's book shows the mind-set of the day. You can see how children who grew up during this period were taught to view gender and work.

Boys are pilots.

Girls are stewardesses.

Boys are presidents.

Girls are First Ladies.

Boys are doctors.

Girls are nurses.

Boys build houses.

Girls keep houses.

Source: From a 1970's children's book.

Although women enjoy fundamental rights today, gender inequality continues to play a central role in social life. Let's look at gender relations in health care, education, and everyday life, and then, in greater detail, at discrimination in the world of work.

Gender Inequality in Health Care

Medical researchers were perplexed. Reports were coming in from all over the country: Women were twice as likely as men to die after coronary bypass surgery. Researchers at Cedars-Sinai Medical Center in Los Angeles checked their own records. They found that of 2,300 coronary bypass patients, 4.6 percent of the women died as a result of the surgery, compared with 2.6 percent of the men.

These findings presented a sociological puzzle. To solve it, researchers first turned to biology (Bishop 1990). In coronary bypass surgery, a blood vessel is taken from one part of the body and stitched to an artery on the surface of the heart. Perhaps this operation was more difficult to perform on women because they have smaller arteries. To find out, researchers measured the amount of time that surgeons kept patients on the heart-lung machine while they operated. They were surprised to learn that women spent *less* time on the machine than men. This indicated that the operation was not more difficult to perform on women.

As the researchers probed, a surprising answer unfolded: unintended sexual discrimination. Physicians had not taken the chest pains of their women patients as seriously as they took the complaints of their men patients. The physicians were *ten* times more likely to give men exercise stress tests and radioactive heart scans. They also sent men to surgery on the basis of abnormal stress tests but waited until women showed clear-cut symptoms of heart disease before sending them to surgery. Patients who have surgery after the disease is more advanced are less likely to survive.

As more women become physicians, perhaps such subconscious discrimination will change. Women doctors are more likely to order Pap smears and mammograms (Lurie et al. 1993). They also offer more encouragement to patients and engage them more in making decisions about their care, so it is likely that they will be more responsive to the health problems of women (Levinson and Lurie 2004).

In the Down-to-Earth Sociology box on the next page, we look at a more blatant form of sexism in medicine.

Gender Inequality in Education

In education, too, a glimpse of the past sheds light on the present. Until 1832, women were not allowed to attend college with men. When women were admitted—first at Oberlin College in Ohio—they had to remain silent at public assemblies, do the men students' laundry, clean their rooms, and serve them their meals (Flexner 1971/1999). Educators thought that women were less qualified for higher education because their female organs dominated their minds. Referring to menstruation, Dr. Edward Clarke, of Harvard University, expressed the dominant sentiment this way:

> **A girl upon whom Nature, for a limited period and for a definite purpose, imposes so great a physiological task, will not have as much power left for the tasks of school, as the boy of whom Nature requires less at the corresponding epoch. (Andersen 1988)**

Because women were so much weaker, Clarke urged them to study only one-third as much as young men—and not to study at all during menstruation.

Like out-of-fashion clothing, such ideas were discarded, and women entered college in growing numbers. As Figure 8.2 on the next page shows, by 1900, one third of college students were women. The change has been so extensive that 57 percent of today's college students are women. Women also earn 57 percent of all bachelor's degrees and 59 percent of all master's degrees (*Statistical Abstract* 2007:Table 288). Because men are now lagging behind, some have begun to call for *affirmative action for men* (Kleinfeld 2002a). To see why, look at Figure 8.3 on page 245.

Down-to-Earth Sociology

Cold-Hearted Surgeons and Their Women Victims

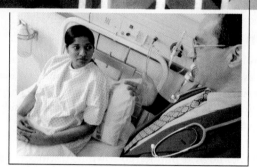

SOCIOLOGIST SUE FISHER (1986), who did participant observation in a hospital, was surprised to hear surgeons recommend total hysterectomy (removal of both the uterus and the ovaries) *when no cancer was present*. When she asked why, the men doctors explained that the uterus and ovaries are "potentially disease producing." They also said that these organs are unnecessary after the childbearing years, so why not remove them? Doctors who reviewed hysterectomies confirmed this bias: They found that three out of four of these surgeries were, in their term, inappropriate (Broder et al. 2000).

Greed is a powerful motivator in life, and it certainly shows up in surgical sexism. Surgeons perform hysterectomies to make money, but they have to "sell" this operation, since women, to understate the matter, are reluctant to part with these organs. Here is how one resident explained the "hard sell" to sociologist Diana Scully (1994):

> You have to look for your surgical procedures; you have to go after patients. Because no one is crazy enough to come and say, "Hey, here I am. I want you to operate on me." You have to sometimes convince the patient that she

is really sick—if she is, of course [laughs], and that she is better off with a surgical procedure.

To "convince" a woman to have this surgery, the doctor puts on a serious face and tells her that the examination has turned up fibroids in her uterus—and they *might* turn into cancer. This statement is often sufficient, for it frightens women, who picture themselves dying from cancer. To clinch the sale, the surgeon withholds the rest of the truth—that fibroids are common, that they most likely will *not* turn into cancer, and that the patient has several nonsurgical alternatives.

I wonder how men would feel if surgeons systematically suggested to them that they be castrated when they get older—since "that organ is no longer necessary, and it might cause disease."

for your Consideration

Hysterectomies have become so common that one of three U.S. women eventually has her uterus surgically removed (Elson 2004). Why do you think that surgeons are so quick to operate? How can women find nonsurgical alternatives?

Figure 8.2　Changes in College Enrollment, by Sex

What percentages of U.S. college students are female and male?

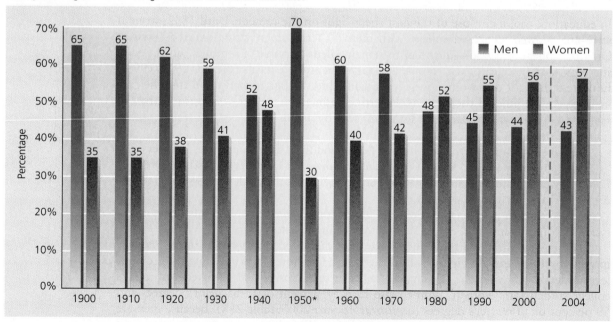

Note: This sharp drop in female enrollment is probably due to the large numbers of male soldiers returning from World War II who attended college under the new GI Bill of Rights.

Source: By the author. Based on *Statistical Abstract* 1938:Table 114; 1959:Table 158; 1991:Table 261; 2007:Table 268.

Figure 8.3

College Students, by Sex and Race-Ethnicity

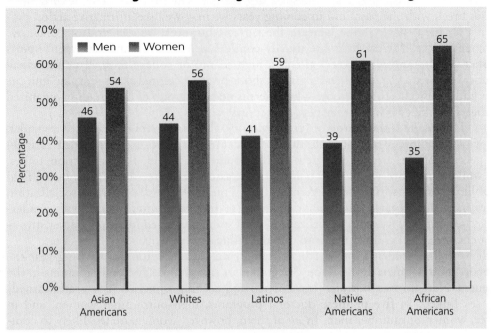

Note: This figure can be confusing. To read it, ask: What percentage of the group in college are men or women? (For example, what percentage of Asian American college students are men or women?)

Source: By the author. Based on *Statistical Abstract* 2007:Table 268.

Figure 8.4 illustrates another major change. From this figure, you can see how women have increased their share of professional degrees. The greatest change is in dentistry: In 1970, across the entire United States, only 34 women earned degrees in dentistry. Today, about 1,800 women become dentists each year. The change is so extensive that about as many women as men now graduate from U.S. law schools.

Figure 8.4 **Gender Changes in Professional Degrees**

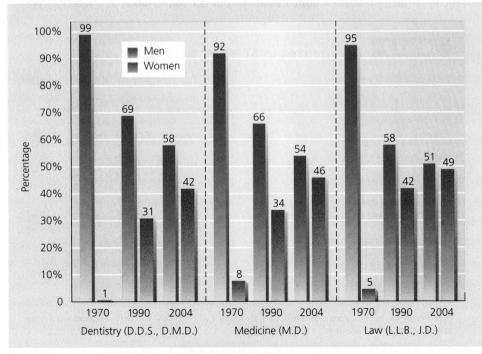

Source: By the author. Based on *Statistical Abstract* 2007:Table 293.

From grade school through college, male sports have been emphasized, and women's sports underfunded. Due to federal laws (*Title IX*), the funding gap has closed considerably, and there is an increasing emphasis on women's accomplishments in sports. Shown here is Mia Hamm, who played forward on the U.S. Women's National Soccer team.

That men have fallen behind women in college enrollment and need to catch up with them in bachelor's and master's degrees is a new situation. This is certainly a major break with the past, and in coming years we may well see affirmative action programs for men. If we probe beneath the surface, however, we still find old practices. Women's sports, for example, are usually considered less important than men's sports (Fisher 2002). And whenever I attend a high school or college football or basketball game, I still see a group of slender girls in short, brightly colored skirts jumping into the air and wildly cheering the boys—but there is no such group of boys leading organized cheers for the girls when they play *their* sports.

Then there is the matter of *gender tracking;* that is, degrees tend to follow gender, which reinforces male–female distinctions. Here are two extremes: Men earn 94 percent of the associate degrees in the "masculine" field of construction trades, while women are awarded 89 percent of the associate degrees in the "feminine" field of library science (*Statistical Abstract* 2007:Table 290). Because gender socialization gives men and women different orientations to life, they enter college with gender-linked aspirations. It is their socialization—not some presumed innate characteristics—that channels men and women into different educational paths.

If we follow students into graduate school, we see that with each passing year the proportion of women drops. Table 8.2 gives us a snapshot of doctoral programs in the sciences. Note how aspirations (enrollment) and accomplishments (doctorates earned) are sex linked. In five of these doctoral programs, men outnumber women, and in three, women outnumber men. In *all* of them, however, women are less likely to complete the doctorate.

If we follow those who earn doctoral degrees to their teaching careers at colleges and universities, we find gender stratification in rank and pay. Throughout the United States, women are less likely to become full professors, the highest-paying and most prestigious rank. In both private and public colleges, professors average more than twice the salary of instructors (*Statistical Abstract* 2007:Table 284). Even when women do become full professors, their average pay is less than that of men who are full professors (AAUP 2007:Table 5).

Beyond the pay gap lies more subtle and invasive discrimination. Women professors are not taken as seriously as men (Epstein 2007). As Barbara Grosz, a professor at Harvard, put it (Zernike 2001):

The first time you're mistaken for a secretary is funny. The 99th time is not. The first time the guys [men professors] don't include you in the conversation at a meeting, you

Table 8.2 Doctorates in Science, By Sex

Field	STUDENTS ENROLLED		DOCTORATES CONFERRED		COMPLETION RATIO* (HIGHER OR LOWER THAN EXPECTED)	
	Women	Men	Women	Men	Women	Men
Mathematics	36%	64%	28%	72%	−22	+13
Computer sciences	27%	73%	21%	79%	−22	+8
Social sciences	53%	47%	44%	56%	−17	+19
Biological sciences	55%	45%	46%	54%	−16	+20
Agriculture	45%	55%	38%	62%	−16	+13
Physical sciences	31%	69%	26%	74%	−16	+7
Engineering	21%	79%	18%	82%	−14	+4
Psychology	74%	26%	67%	33%	−9	+27

*The formula for the completion ratio is X minus Y divided by Y, where X is the doctorates conferred and Y is the proportion enrolled in a program.

Source: By the author. Based on *Statistical Abstract* 2007:Tables 785, 789.

think, "I'm not interested anyway." But a whole year of these conversations—there's this kind of constant erosion.

Gender Inequality in Everyday Life

Of the many aspects of gender discrimination in everyday life that we could examine, we have space to look only at two: the general devaluation of femininity in U.S. society, and male dominance of conversation.

General Devaluation of Things Feminine

Leaning against the water cooler, two men—both minor executives—are nursing their cups of coffee, discussing last Sunday's Giants game, postponing for as long as possible the moment when work must finally be faced.

A [male] vice president walks by and hears them talking about sports. Does he stop and send them back to their desks? Does he frown? Probably not. Being a man, he is far more likely to pause and join in the conversation, anxious to prove that he, too, is "one of the boys," feigning an interest in football that he may very well not share at all. These men—all the men in the office—are his troops, his comrades-in-arms.

Now, let's assume that two women are standing by the water cooler discussing whatever you please: women's liberation, clothes, work, any subject—except football, of course. The vice president walks by, sees them, and moves down the hall in a fury, cursing and wondering whether it is worth the trouble to complain—but to whom?—about all those bitches standing around gabbing when they should be working. "Don't they know," he will ask, in the words of a million men, "that this is an office?" (Korda 1973:20–21)

As indicated in this scenario, women often have a difficult time being taken seriously by men. In general, a higher value is placed on things considered masculine, for masculinity symbolizes strength and success. In contrast, femininity is devalued, for it is perceived as representing weakness and lack of accomplishment.

Sociologist Samuel Stouffer headed a research team that produced *The American Soldier* (1949), a classic study of World War II combat soldiers. To motivate their men, officers used feminine terms as insults. If a man showed less-than-expected courage or endurance, an officer might say, "Whatsa matter, Bud—got lace on your drawers?" A generation later, as they trained soldiers to fight in Vietnam, officers still used accusations of femininity to motivate their men. Drill sergeants would mock their troops by saying, "Can't hack it, little girls?" (Eisenhart 1975). The practice continues. Male soldiers who show hesitation during maneuvers are mocked by others, who call them girls (Miller 1997/2007).

In sports, we see the same thing. Anthropologist Douglas Foley (1990/2006) notes that football coaches insult boys who don't play well by saying that they are "wearing skirts." In her research, sociologist Donna Eder (1995) heard junior high boys call one another "girl" when they didn't hit hard enough in football. When they play basketball, boys of this age also call one another a "woman" when they miss a basket (Stockard and Johnson 1980). In professional hockey, if players are not rough enough on the ice, their teammates call them "girls" (Gallmeier 1988:227).

These insults roll so easily off the tongues of men in sports and war that it is easy to lose sight of their significance: They represent a devaluation of females. As Stockard and Johnson (1980:12) point out, "There is no comparable phenomenon among women, for young girls do not insult each other by calling each other 'man.'"

Gender and Conversation   You may have noticed that men are more likely than women to interrupt conversations. Some sociologists note that talk between a man and a woman is often more like talk between a boss and an employee than between social equals (West and Garcia 1988; Smith-Lovin and Brody 1989; Tannen 1990, 2007). A tally of who makes topic switches in conversations, however, indicates that men and women are about equally as likely to do so (Okamoto and Smith-Lovin 2001). Perhaps more significant than gender is the relative status of the speakers, with higher status people exerting greater control over conversations. As sociologists do more research, we should be able to resolve this question.

The inequality of gender in everyday life is related to a structural inequality that runs throughout society. Let's look at this structural feature in the workplace.

Gender Inequality in the Workplace

 To examine the work setting is to make visible basic relations between men and women. Let's begin with one of the most remarkable areas of gender inequality at work, the pay gap.

The Pay Gap

One of the chief characteristics of the U.S. workforce is a steady growth in the numbers of women who work for wages outside the home. Figure 8.5 shows that in 1890 about one of every five paid workers was a woman. By 1940, this ratio had grown to one of four; by 1960 to one of three; and today it is almost one of two. As shown on this figure, the projections are that the ratio will remain 55 percent men and 45 percent women for the next few years.

Women who work for wages are not evenly distributed throughout the United States. From the Social Map on the next page, you can see that where a woman lives makes a difference in how likely she is to work outside the home. Why is there such a clustering among the states? The geographical patterns evident in this map reflect regional-subcultural differences about which we currently have little understanding.

After college, you might like to take a few years off, travel around Europe, sail the oceans, or maybe sit on a beach in some South American paradise and drink piña coladas. But chances are, you are going to go to work instead. Since you have to work, how would you like to earn an extra $1,100,000 on your job? If this sounds appealing, read on. I'm going to reveal how you can make an extra $2,300 a month between the ages of 25 and 65.

Figure 8.5 **Women's and Men's Proportion of the U.S. Labor Force**

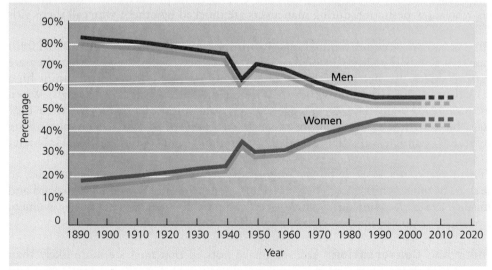

Note: Pre-1940 totals include women 14 and over; totals for 1940 and after are for women 16 and over. Broken lines are the author's projections.

Sources: By the author. Based on 1969 *Handbook on Women Workers,* 1969:10; *Manpower Report to the President,* 1971:203, 205; Mills and Palumbo, 1980:6, 45; *Statistical Abstract* 2007:Table 574.

Figure 8.6 **Women in the Workforce**

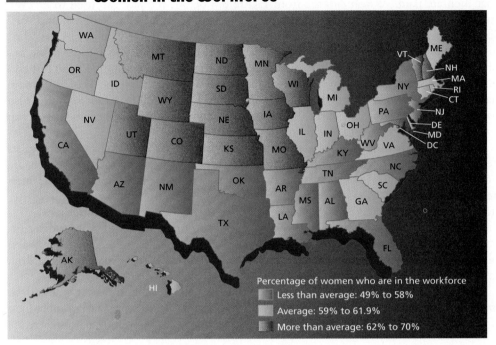

Note: At 49.1%, West Virginia has the lowest rate of women in the workforce, while South Dakota, at 69.4%, has the highest.

Source: By the author. Based on *Statistical Abstract* 2007:Table 579.

Is this hard to do? Actually, it is simple for some, but impossible for others. As Figure 8.7 shows, all you have to do is be born a male and graduate from college. If we compare full-time workers, based on current differences in earnings this is how much more money the *average male* college graduate can expect to earn over the course of his career. Hardly any single factor pinpoints gender discrimination better than this total. As you can see, the pay gap shows up at *all* levels of education.

Figure 8.7 **The Gender Pay Gap, by Education**[1]

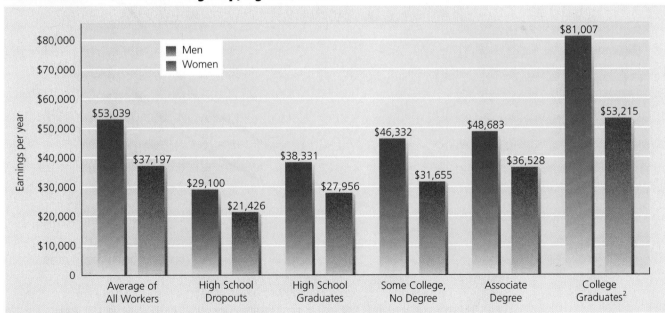

[1]Full-time workers in all fields.
[2]Bachelor's and all higher degrees, including professional degrees.

Source: By the author. Based on *Statistical Abstract* 2007:Table 684.

The pay gap is so great that U.S. women who work full time average *only 70 percent* of what men are paid. As you can see from Figure 8.8 below, the pay gap used to be even worse. The gender gap in pay occurs not only in the United States but also in *all* industrialized nations.

If $1,100,000 additional earnings aren't enough, how would you like to make another $166,000 extra at work? If so, just make sure that you are not only a man but also a *tall* man. Over their lifetimes, men who are over 6 feet tall average $166,000 more than men who are 5 feet 5 inches or less (Judge and Cable 2004). Taller women also make more than shorter women. But even when it comes to height, the gender pay gap persists, and tall men make more than tall women.

What logic can underlie the gender pay gap? Earlier we saw that college degrees are gender linked, so perhaps this gap is due to career choices. Maybe women are more likely to choose lower-paying jobs, such as teaching grade school, while men are more likely to go into better-paying fields, such as business and engineering. Actually, this is true, and researchers have found that about *half* of the gender pay gap is due to such factors. And the balance? It consists of a combination of gender discrimination (Jacobs 2003; Roth 2003) and what is called the "child penalty"—women missing out on work experience and opportunities while they care for children (Hundley 2001; Chaker and Stout 2004).

For college students, the gender gap in pay begins with the first job after graduation. You might know of a particular woman who was offered a higher salary than most men in her class, but she would be an exception. On average, men enjoy a "testosterone

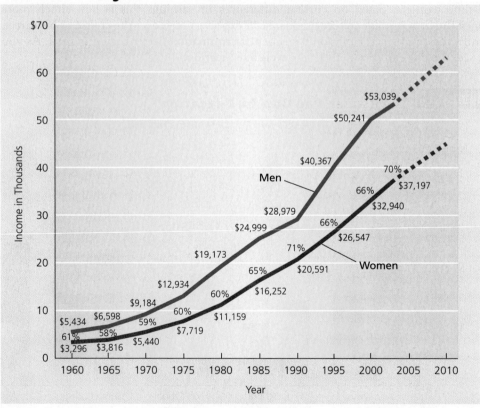

Figure 8.8 **The Gender Pay Gap Over Time: What Percentage of Men's Income Do Women Earn?**

Note: The income jump from 1990 to 1995 could be due to a statistical procedure. The 1995 source (for 1990 income) uses "median income," while the 1997 source (for 1995 income) merely says "average earnings." How the "average" is computed is not stated. The last year for which the source has data is 2003. Broken lines indicate the author's estimates.

Source: By the author. Based on *Statistical Abstract* 1995:Table 739; 2002:Table 666; 2007:Table 684, and earlier years.

bonus," and employers start them out at higher salaries than women (Fuller and Schoenberger 1991; Harris et al. 2005). Depending on your sex, then, you will either benefit from the pay gap or be victimized by it.

As a final indication of the extent of the U.S. gender pay gap, consider this. Of the nation's top 500 corporations (the so-called "Fortune 500"), only 10 are headed by women (Fuhrmans and Hymowitz 2007). And 10 is a record-breaking number! I examined the names of the CEOs of the 350 largest U.S. corporations, and I found that your best chance to reach the top is to be named (in this order) John, Robert, James, William, or Charles. Edward, Lawrence, and Richard are also advantageous names. Amber, Katherine, Leticia, and Maria, however, apparently draw a severe penalty. Naming your baby girl John or Robert might seem a little severe, but it could help her reach the top. (I say this only slightly tongue-in-cheek. One of the few women to head a Fortune 500 company—before she was fired and given $21 million severance pay—had a man's first name: Carleton Fiorina of Hewlett-Packard.)

The Cracking Glass Ceiling

What keeps women from breaking through the **glass ceiling,** the mostly invisible barrier that prevents women from reaching the executive suite? Researchers have identified a "pipeline" that leads to the top: the marketing, sales, and production positions that directly affect the corporate bottom line (Hymowitz 2004; DeCrow 2005). Men, who dominate the executive suite, stereotype women as being less capable of leadership than they are (Heilman 2001). Viewing women as good at "support," they steer women into human resources or public relations. There, successful projects are not appreciated in the same way as those that bring corporate profits—and bonuses for their managers.

Another reason the glass ceiling is so powerful is that women lack mentors—successful executives who take an interest in them and teach them the ropes. Lack of a mentor is no trivial matter, for mentors can provide opportunities to develop leadership skills that open the door to the executive suite (Heilman 2001; Hymowitz 2007).

The glass ceiling is cracking, however (Solomon 2000; Hymowitz 2004). A look at women who have broken through reveals highly motivated individuals with a fierce competitive spirit who are willing to give up sleep and recreation for the sake of career advancement. They also learn to play by "men's rules," developing a style that makes men comfortable. Most of these women also have supportive husbands who share household duties and adapt their careers to accommodate the needs of their executive wives (Lublin 1996). In addition, women who began their careers 20 to 30 years ago are running many major divisions within the largest companies (Hymowitz 2004). With this background, some of these women have begun to emerge as the new top CEOs.

Then there is the *glass escalator*. Sociologist Christine Williams (1995) interviewed men and women who worked in traditionally female jobs—as nurses, elementary school teachers, librarians, and social workers. Instead of bumping their heads against a glass ceiling, the men

glass ceiling the mostly invisible barrier that keeps women from advancing to the top levels at work

Dilbert

One of the frustrations felt by many women in the labor force is that no matter what they do, they hit a glass ceiling. Another is that to succeed they feel forced to abandon characteristics they feel are essential to their self.

in these occupations found themselves aboard a **glass escalator.** They were given higher-level positions, more desirable work assignments, and higher salaries. The motor that drives the glass escalator is gender—the stereotype that because someone is male he is more capable.

Gender and the Control of Workers

Conflict theorists analyze how capitalists exploit gender divisions among workers in order to control them. This does not come in an overt form, such as "Men, if you don't agree to what we are proposing, we'll hire women to take your place." Rather, owners and managers divide workers in subtle ways. For example, a Silicon Valley manufacturing firm specifies the color of the smocks that it requires its workers to wear. The color of the men's smocks depends on the particular job they do, but all the women wear the same color, regardless of their jobs.

Why should management have such a policy? According to sociologist Karen Hossfeld (2000), who studied these workers, the underlying message is: No matter what your job is, you are primarily a woman. Encouraging the women to think of themselves not as workers, but as *women* workers, makes them easier to control. For example, Hossfeld found that when their bosses flirted with them, the women were less inclined to file grievances.

This same company has a "Ladies' Corner" in its newsletter, but it has no "Men's Corner." The subtle message: It is the men's newsletter, with a little corner devoted to women. In other words, men are the *real* workers, but women are there, too.

Sexual Harassment—and Worse

Sexual harassment—unwelcome sexual attention at work or at school, which may affect a person's job or school performance or create a hostile environment—was not recognized as a problem until the 1970s. Before this, women considered unwanted sexual comments, touches, looks, and pressure to have sex to be a personal matter.

With the prodding of feminists, women began to perceive unwanted sexual advances at work and school as part of a *structural* problem. That is, they began to realize that the issue was more than a man here or there doing obnoxious things because he was attracted to a woman; rather, it was men abusing their positions of authority in order to force unwanted sexual activities on women. Now that women have moved into positions of authority, they, too, have become sexual harassers (Wayne et al. 2001). With most authority vested in men, however, the majority of sexual harassers are men.

As symbolic interactionists stress, labels affect our perception. Because we have the term *sexual harassment,* we perceive actions in a different light than did our predecessors. The meaning of sexual harassment is vague and shifting, however, and court cases constantly change what this term does and does not include. Originally sexual desire was an element of sexual harassment, but it no longer is. This changed when the U.S. Supreme Court considered the lawsuit of a homosexual who had been tormented by his supervisors and fellow workers. The Court ruled that sexual desire is not necessary—that sexual harassment laws also apply to homosexuals who are harassed by heterosexuals while on the job (Felsenthal 1998). By extension, the law applies to heterosexuals who are sexually harassed by homosexuals.

Central to sexual harassment is the abuse of power, a topic that is explored in the following Thinking Critically section.

Thinking Critically

Sexual Harassment and Rape of Women in the Military

Women raped at West Point! Other women raped at the U.S. Air Force Academy!

So shrieked the headlines and the TV news teasers. For once, the facts turned out to be just as startling. Women cadets, who were studying to become officers in the U.S. military, had been sexually assaulted by their fellow cadets.

glass escalator the mostly invisible accelerators that push men into higher-level positions, more desirable work assignments, and higher salaries

sexual harassment the abuse of one's position of authority to force unwanted sexual demands on someone

And when the women reported the attacks, *they* were the ones who were punished. The women found themselves charged with drinking alcohol and socializing with upperclassmen. For the most part, the women's charges against the men were ignored. The one man who faced a court martial was acquitted (Schemo 2003a).

This got the attention of Congress. Hearings were held, and the commander of the Air Force Academy was replaced.

A few years earlier, several male Army sergeants at Aberdeen Proving Ground in Maryland had been accused of forcing sex on unwilling female recruits (McIntyre 1997). The drill sergeants, who claimed that the sex was consensual, were found guilty of rape. One married sergeant, who had pleaded guilty to having consensual sex with 11 trainees (adultery is a crime in the Army), was convicted of raping another 6 trainees a total of 18 times and was sentenced to 25 years in prison.

The Army appointed a blue-ribbon panel to investigate sexual harassment in its ranks. When Sgt. Major Gene McKinney, the highest-ranking of the Army's 410,000 noncommissioned officers, was appointed to this committee, former subordinates accused him of sexual harassment (Shenon 1997). McKinney was relieved of his duties and court-martialed. Found not guilty of sexual harassment, but guilty of obstruction of justice, McKinney was reprimanded and demoted. His embittered accusers claimed the Army had sacrificed them for McKinney.

Rape in the military is not an isolated event. Researchers who interviewed a random sample of women veterans found that 4 of 5 had experienced sexual harassment during their military service, and 30 percent had been victims of attempted or completed rape. Three-fourths of the women who had been raped did not report their assault (Sadler et al. 2003). A study of women graduates of the Air Force Academy showed that 12 percent had been victims of rape or attempted rape (Schemo 2003b). In light of such findings, the military appointed a coordinator of sexual assault at every military base (Stout 2005), and apparently, more sexual assaults are being reported (Associated Press 2007; Gleason 2007).

After the U.S. military was sent to Iraq and Afghanistan, the headlines again screamed rape, this time in the Persian Gulf. Again, the headlines were right. And once again, Congress held hearings (Schmitt 2004). We'll have to see how long this cycle of rape followed by hearings repeats itself before adequate reforms are put in place.

With the publicity about rape scarring our military schools, accusations are being taken more seriously. Shown here is a Navy Midshipman being escorted from his court martial after being sentenced to two years for sexual assault.

for your Consideration

How can we set up a structure to minimize sexual harassment and rape in the military? Can we do this and still train men and women together? Can we do this and still have men and women sleep in the same barracks and on the same ships? Be specific about the structure you would establish.

Gender and Violence

One of the consistent characteristics of violence in the United States—and the world—is its gender inequality. That is, females are much more likely to be the victims of males, not the other way around. Let's briefly review this almost one-way street in gender violence as it applies to the United States.

Violence Against Women

In the Thinking Critically section above, we considered rape in the military; on pages 237 and 240, we examined violence against women in other cultures; on page 244, we reviewed a form of surgical violence; and in Chapter 10 we shall review violence in the home. Here, due to space limitations, we can review only briefly some primary features of violence.

Forcible Rape Being raped is a common fear of U.S. women, a fear that is far from groundless. According to FBI statistics, each year 8 of every 10,000 females age 12 and older are raped. From the National Crime Victimization Survey, however, we know that only one third of rape victims report this crime to the police (*Statistical Abstract* 2007:Table 311). A more accurate total, then, is *three* times the official rate, or about 24 victims per 10,000 rather than 8. Despite these high numbers, women are safer now than they were 10 and 20 years ago, as the rape rate has been declining.

Although any woman can be a victim of sexual assault—and victims included babies and elderly women—the typical victim is 12 to 34 years old. As you can see from Table 8.3, sexual assault drops sharply for women older than 34 and continues to decline with age.

Women's most common fear seems to be that of strangers—who appear as if from nowhere, catch them unprepared, and abduct and rape them. Contrary to the stereotypes that underlie these fears, however, most victims know their attacker. As you can see from Table 8.4, about one of three rapes is committed by strangers.

An aspect of rape that is usually overlooked is the rape of men in prison. With prison officials reluctant to let the public know about the horrible conditions behind bars, our studies are far from perfect. Those we have, however, indicate that about 15 to 20 percent of men in prison are raped. From court cases, we know that some guards even punish prisoners by placing them in cells with sexual predators (Donaldson 1993; Lewin 2001b).

Date (Acquaintance) Rape What has shocked so many about date rape (also known as *acquaintance rape*) are studies showing that it does not consist of a few isolated events (Collymore 2000; Goode 2001). Some researchers even report that most women students experience unwanted, forced, or coerced sex (Kalof 2000). Others report much smaller numbers. Researchers who used a representative sample of courses to survey the students at Marietta College, a private school in Ohio, found that 2.5 percent of the women had been physically forced to have sex (Felton et al. 2001). About as many men (23 percent) as women (24 percent) had given in to pressure to have sex when they didn't want to, but—and this is no surprise—none of the men had been physically forced to have sex.

Most date rapes go unreported. A primary reason is that the victim feels partially responsible because she knows the person and was with him voluntarily. However, as a physician who treats victims of date rape said, "Would you feel responsible if someone hit you over the head with a shovel—just because you knew the person?" (Carpenito 1999).

Murder All over the world, men are more likely than women to be killers. Figure 8.9 on the next page illustrates this gender pattern in U.S. murders. Note that although females make up about 51 percent of the U.S. population, they don't even come close to making up 51 percent of the nation's killers. As you can see from this figure, when women are murdered, about eight or nine times out of ten the killer is a man.

Table 8.3 Rape Victims	
Age	**Rate per 1,000 Females**
12–15	1.2
16–19	1.3
20–24	1.7
25–34	1.6
35–49	0.6
50–64	0.4
65 and Older	0.1

Source: By the author. Based on *Statistical Abstract* 2007:Table 311.

Table 8.4 Relationship of Rapists to Victims	
Relationship	**Percentage**
Relative	3.6%
Known Well	27.1%
Casual Acquaintance	26.1%
Stranger	33.5%
Not Reported	9.7%

Source: By the Author. Based on *Statistical Abstract* 2007:Table 315.

Figure 8.9 — Killers and Their Victims

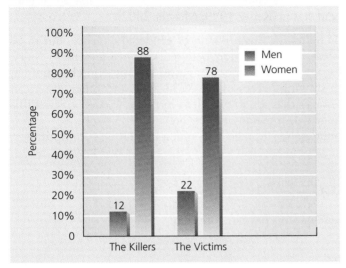

Source: By the author. Based on *Statistical Abstract* 2007:Tables 300, 317.

Violence in the Home   Women are also the typical victims of family violence. Spouse battering, marital rape, and incest are discussed in Chapter 10, pages 329–331. A particular form of violence against women, genital circumcision, is the focus of the Cultural Diversity box on page 241.

Women in the Criminal Justice System   There is another side to gender and violence. Although women are much less likely to kill, when they do kill, judges tend to be more lenient with them. As Table 8.5 shows, women are more likely to be given probation for murder (as well as for robbery, burglary, and all crimes listed on this table). Sexual stereotypes probably underlie these decisions—such as the idea that women are less of a menace than men and should be given another chance. It is also possible that women defendants have less of a criminal history ("rap sheet") when they are charged with crimes. We need research on this topic.

Feminism and Gendered Violence   Feminist sociologists have been especially effective in bringing violence against women to the public's attention. Some use symbolic interactionism, pointing out that to associate strength and virility with violence—as is

Table 8.5 — Going Easier on Women

When Men and Women Are Convicted of the Same Crime, Who Gets Off Easier?*				
	PRISON		PROBATION	
Crime	Men	Women	Men	Women
Murder	97%	89%	1%	5%
Robbery	78%	67%	9%	13%
Burglary	55%	43%	19%	23%
Aggravated Assault	54%	30%	18%	26%
Drug Dealing	50%	37%	20%	26%
Weapons	49%	28%	22%	30%
Larceny	42%	28%	24%	34%
Fraud	39%	31%	28%	41%

*This table examines the extremes of sentencing; totals do not add to 100 percent because of jail sentences and the source's unspecified "other" dispositions.

Source: Sourcebook of Criminal Justice Statistics 1997:Table 5.50. (Table dropped in later editions.)

done in many cultures—is to promote violence. Others use conflict theory. They argue that men are losing power, and that some men turn violently against women as a way to reassert their declining power and status (Reiser 1999; Meltzer 2002).

Solutions   There is no magic bullet for this problem of gendered violence, but to be effective, any solution must break the connection between violence and masculinity. This would require an educational program that encompasses schools, churches, homes, and the media. Given the gun-slinging heroes of the Wild West and other American icons, as well as the violent messages that are so prevalent in the mass media, it is difficult to be optimistic that a change will come any time soon.

Our next topic, women in politics, however, gives us much more reason for optimism.

The Changing Face of Politics

What do these nations have in common?

Africa: Liberia and Rwanda

Asia: Indonesia and the Philippines

Europe: Great Britain, Finland, France, Germany, Ireland, Latvia, Portugal, Poland, Switzerland, and Turkey

Middle East: Israel

North America: Canada and Haiti

South and Central America: Argentina, Bolivia, Chile, Ecuador, Guyana, Nicaragua, and Panama

The Subcontinent: Bangladesh, India, Pakistan, and Sri Lanka

The answer is that all have had a woman president or prime minister ("Women in Politics" 2006).

Although women are underrepresented severely in U.S. politics, the situation is changing, at least gradually. The two highest profile women as this edition was being written are Nancy Pelosi, the first woman minority and majority leader, and Hillary Clinton, U.S. Senator and contender for the U.S. presidency.

Then why not the United States? Why don't women, who outnumber men, take political control of the nation? Eight million more women than men are of voting age, and more women than men vote in U.S. national elections. As Table 8.6 shows, however, men greatly outnumber women in political office. Despite the gains women have made in recent elections, since 1789 over 1,800 men have served in the U.S. Senate, but only 35 women have served, including 16 current senators. Not until 1992 was the first African American woman (Carol Moseley-Braun) elected to the U.S. Senate. No Latina or Asian American woman has yet been elected to the Senate (National Women's Political Caucus 1998; *Statistical Abstract* 2007:Table 395).

Why are women underrepresented in U.S. politics? First, women are still underrepresented in law and business, the careers from which most politicians emerge. Most women also find that the irregular hours kept by those who run for office are incompatible with their role as mother. Fathers, in contrast, whose traditional roles are more likely to take them away from home, are less likely to feel this conflict. Women are also not as likely to have a supportive spouse who is willing to play an unassuming background role while providing solace, encouragement, child care, and voter appeal. Finally, preferring to hold on to their positions of power, men have been reluctant to incorporate women into centers of decision making or to present them as viable candidates.

These conditions are changing. Watershed events occurred when Nancy Pelosi was elected by her colleagues in

Table 8.6 U.S. Women in Political Office

	Percentage of Offices Held by Women	Number of Offices Held by Women
National Office		
U.S. Senate	16%	16
U.S. House of Representatives	16%	71
State Office		
Governors	18%	9
Lt. Governors	22%	11
Attorneys General	8%	4
Secretaries of State	24%	12
Treasurers	22%	11
State Auditors	12%	6
State Legislators	24%	1,734

Source: Center for American Women and Politics 2007.

2002 as the first woman minority leader, and then in 2007 as the first woman Speaker of the House. These posts made her the most powerful woman ever in the House of Representatives. We can also note that more women are becoming corporate executives, and, as indicated in Figure 8.4 (on page 245), more women are also becoming lawyers. In these positions, women are doing more traveling and making statewide and national contacts. Another change is that child care is increasingly seen as a responsibility of both mother and father. This generation, then, is likely to mark a fundamental change in women's political participation, and it appears to be only a matter of time until a woman occupies the Oval Office.

Glimpsing the Future—with Hope

Women's fuller participation in the decision-making processes of our social institutions has shattered stereotypes that tended to limit females to "feminine" activities and push males into "masculine" ones. As structural barriers continue to fall and more activities are degendered, both males and females will have greater freedom to pursue activities that are more compatible with their abilities and desires as individuals.

In the midst of this change, what may be developing are new ideas of what males and females are. As stereotypes continue to be broken, new role models develop, and socialization of children changes, males and females will gain new perceptions of themselves and of one another. As sociologists Janet Chafetz (1974), Janet Giele (1978), Judith Lorber (1994), and others have pointed out, this will allow men and women to express needs and emotions that traditional social arrangements denied them. Women and girls will likely perceive themselves as more in control of their environment, become more assertive, and strive more for positions of leadership. Men and boys will likely feel and express more emotional sensitivity—becoming warmer, more affectionate and tender, and giving greater expression to anxieties and stresses that their gender has forced them to suppress.

As females and males develop a new consciousness both of their capacities and of their potential, relationships will change. Distinctions between the sexes will not disappear, but there is no reason for biological differences to be translated into social inequalities. If current trends continue, we may see a growing appreciation of sexual differences coupled with greater equality of opportunity—which has the potential of transforming society (Gilman 1911/1971; Offen 1990). If this happens, as sociologist Alison Jaggar (1990) observed, gender equality can become less a goal than a background condition for living in society.

Summary *and* Review

Issues of Sex and Gender

What is gender stratification?

The term **gender stratification** refers to unequal access to property, power, and prestige on the basis of sex. Each society establishes a structure that, on the basis of sex and gender, opens and closes doors to its privileges. P. 228.

How do sex and gender differ?

Sex refers to biological distinctions between males and females. It consists of both primary and secondary sex characteristics. **Gender,** in contrast, is what a society considers proper behaviors and attitudes for its male and female members. Sex physically distinguishes males from females; gender defines what is "masculine" and "feminine." P. 228.

Why do the behaviors of males and females differ?

The "nature versus nurture" debate refers to whether differences in the behaviors of males and females are caused by inherited (biological) or learned (cultural) characteristics. Almost all sociologists take the side of nurture. In recent years, however, sociologists have begun to cautiously open the door to biology. Pp. 229–233.

Gender Inequality in Global Perspective

Is gender stratification universal?

George Murdock surveyed information on tribal societies and found that all of them have sex-linked activities and give greater prestige to male activities. **Patriarchy,** or male dominance, appears to be universal. Besides work, other areas of discrimination include education, politics, and violence. Pp. 233–234.

How did females become a minority group?

The origin of discrimination against females is lost in history, but the primary theory of how females became a minority group in their own societies focuses on the physical limitations imposed by childbirth. Pp. 234–240.

Gender Inequality in the United States

Is the feminist movement new?

In what is called the "first wave," feminists made political demands for change in the early 1900s—and were met with hostility, and even violence. The "second wave" began in the 1960s and continues today. A "third wave" is emerging. Pp. 240–243.

What forms do gender discrimination in health care and gender stratification in education take?

Physicians don't take women's health complaints as seriously as those of men. Hysterectomies are a special case of discrimination. In education, more women than men attend college, but each tends to select fields that are categorized as "feminine" or "masculine." Women are less likely to complete the doctoral programs in science. Fundamental change is indicated by the growing numbers of women in law and medicine. Pp. 243–247.

Is there gender inequality in everyday life?

An indication of gender inequality in everyday life is the devaluation of femininity. The question of male dominance of conversation needs more research. Pp. 247–248.

Gender Inequality in the Workplace

How does gender inequality show up in the workplace?

All occupations show a gender gap in pay. For college graduates, the lifetime pay gap runs over a million dollars in favor of men. **Sexual harassment** also continues to be a reality of the workplace. Pp. 248–253.

Gender and Violence

What is the relationship between gender and violence?

Overwhelmingly, the victims of rape and murder are females. Female circumcision is a special case of violence against females. Conflict theorists point out that men use violence to maintain their power and privilege. Pp. 253–256.

The Changing Face of Politics

What is the trend in gender inequality in politics?

A traditional division of gender roles—women as child care providers and homemakers, men as workers outside the home—used to keep women out of politics. Women continue to be underrepresented in politics, but the trend toward greater political equality is firmly in place. Pp. 256–257.

Glimpsing the Future—with Hope

How might changes in gender roles and stereotypes affect our lives?

In the United States, women are more involved in the decision-making processes of our social institutions. Men, too, are reexamining their traditional roles. New gender expectations may be developing, ones that allow both males and females to pursue more individual, less stereotypical interests. P. 257.

Thinking Critically

about Chapter 8

1. What is your position on the "nature versus nurture" (biology or culture) debate? What materials in this chapter support your position?
2. Why do you think that the gender gap in pay exists all over the world?
3. What do you think can be done to reduce gender inequality?

Additional Resources

What can you use MySocLab for?  www.mysoclab.com

- **Study and Review:** Pre- and Post-Tests, Practice Tests, Flash Cards, Individualized Study Plans.
- **Current Events:** *Sociology in the News,* the daily *New York Times,* and more.

- **Research and Writing:** *Research Navigator, Writing About Sociology,* and more.

Where Can I Read More on This Topic?

Suggested readings for this chapter are listed at the back of this book.

Race
and Ethnicity

Ron Waddams, *All Human Beings Are Born Free and Equal in Dignity and Human Rights,* 1998

Imagine that you are an African American man living in Macon County, Alabama, during the Great Depression of the 1930s. Your home is a little country shack with a dirt floor. You have no electricity or running water. You never finished grade school, and you make a living, such as it is, by doing odd jobs. You haven't been feeling too good lately, but you can't afford a doctor.

Then you hear the fantastic news. You rub your eyes in disbelief. It is just like winning the lottery! If you join *Miss Rivers' Lodge* (and it is free to join), you will get free physical examinations at Tuskegee University. You will even get free rides to and from the clinic, hot meals on examination days, and free treatment for minor ailments.

You eagerly join *Miss Rivers' Lodge*.

After your first physical examination, the doctor gives you the bad news. "You've got bad blood," he says. "That's why you've been feeling bad. Miss Rivers will give you some medicine and schedule you for your next exam. I've got to warn you, though. If you

You have just become part of one of the most callous experiments of all time.

go to another doctor, there's no more free exams or medicine."

You can't afford another doctor anyway. You take your medicine and look forward to the next trip to the university.

What has really happened? You have just become part of what is surely slated to go down in history as one of the most callous experiments of all time, outside of the infamous World War II Nazi and Japanese experiments. With heartless disregard for human life, the U.S. Public Health Service told 399 African American men that they had joined a social club and burial society called "Miss Rivers' Lodge." What the men were *not* told was that they had syphilis. For forty years, the "Public Health Service" allowed these men to go without treatment for their syphilis—just "to see what would happen." There was even a control group of 201 men who were free of the disease (Jones 1993).

By the way, you do get one further benefit: a free autopsy to determine the ravages of syphilis on your body.

Laying the Sociological Foundation

As unlikely as it seems, this is a true story. It really did happen. Seldom do race and ethnic relations degenerate to this point, but troubled race relations are no stranger to us. Today's newspapers and TV news shows regularly report on racial problems. Sociology can contribute greatly to our understanding of this aspect of social life—and this chapter may be an eye-opener for you. To begin, let's consider to what extent race itself is a myth.

Race: Myth and Reality

With its more than 6.5 billion people, the world offers a fascinating variety of human shapes and colors. People see one another as black, white, red, yellow, and brown. Eyes come in shades of blue, brown, and green. Lips are thick and thin. Hair is straight, curly, kinky, black, blonde, and red—and, of course, all shades of brown.

Humans show such remarkable diversity that, as the text explains, there are no pure races. Shown here are Verne Troyer, who weighs about 45 pounds and is 2 feet 8 inches short, and Yao Ming, who weighs 296 pounds and is 7 feet 5 inches tall.

As humans spread throughout the world, their adaptations to diverse climates and other living conditions resulted in this profusion of complexions, hair textures and colors, eye hues, and other physical variations. Genetic mutations added distinct characteristics to the peoples of the globe. In this sense, the concept of **race**—a group of people with inherited physical characteristics that distinguish it from another group—is a reality. Humans do, indeed, come in a variety of colors and shapes.

In two senses, however, race is a myth, a fabrication of the human mind. The *first* myth is the idea that any race is superior to others. All races have their geniuses—and their idiots. As with language, no race is superior to another.

Ideas of racial superiority abound, however. They are not only false but also dangerous. Adolf Hitler, for example, believed that the Aryans were a superior race, responsible for the cultural achievements of Europe. The Aryans, he said, were destined to establish a superior culture and usher in a new world order. This destiny required them to avoid the "racial contamination" that would come from breeding with inferior races; therefore, it was necessary to isolate or destroy races that threatened Aryan purity and culture.

Put into practice, Hitler's views left an appalling legacy—the Nazi slaughter of those they deemed inferior: Jews, Slavs, gypsies, homosexuals, and people with mental and physical disabilities. Horrific images of gas ovens and emaciated bodies stacked like cordwood haunted the world's nations. At Nuremberg, the Allies, flush with victory, put the top Nazis on trial, exposing their heinous deeds to a shocked world. Their public executions, everyone assumed, marked the end of such grisly acts.

Obviously, they didn't. In the summer of 1994 in Rwanda, Hutus slaughtered about 800,000 Tutsis—mostly with machetes (Cowell 2006). A few years later, the Serbs in Bosnia massacred Muslims, giving us the new term "ethnic cleansing." As these events sadly attest, **genocide,** the attempt to destroy a group of people because of their presumed race or ethnicity, remains alive and well. Although more recent killings are not accompanied by swastikas and gas ovens, the perpetrators' goal is the same.

The *second* myth is that "pure" races exist. Humans show such a mixture of physical characteristics—in skin color, hair texture, nose shape, head shape, eye color, and so on—that there are no "pure" races. Instead of falling into distinct types that are clearly separate from one another, human characteristics flow endlessly together. The mapping of the human genome system shows that humans are strikingly homogenous, that so-called racial groups differ from one another only once in a thousand subunits of the genome (Angler 2000). Humans, then, vary from one another in only

race physical characteristics that distinguish one group from another

genocide the systematic annihilation or attempted annihilation of a people because of their presumed race or ethnic group

The reason I selected these photos is to illustrate how seriously we must take all preaching of hatred and of racial supremacy, even though it seems to come from harmless or even humorous sources. The strange-looking person on the left, who is wearing lederhosen, traditional clothing of Bavaria, Germany, is Adolf Hitler. He caused the horrific scene on the right, which greeted the British army when it liberated the concentration camp in Buchenwald, Germany: Thousands of people were dying of starvation and diseases amidst piles of rotting corpses awaiting mass burial.

very slight ways. As you can see from the example of Tiger Woods, discussed in the Cultural Diversity box on the next page, these minute gradations make any attempt to draw lines of race purely arbitrary.

Although large groupings of people can be classified by blood type and gene frequencies, even these classifications do not uncover "race." Rather, race is so arbitrary that biologists and anthropologists cannot even agree on how many "races" there are. They have drawn up many lists, each containing a different number. Ashley Montagu (1964, 1999), a physical anthropologist, pointed out that some scientists have classified humans into only two "races," while others have found as many as two thousand. Montagu (1960) himself classified humans into forty "racial" groups. As the Down-to-Earth Sociology box on page 265 illustrates, even a plane ride can change someone's race!

The *idea* of race, of course, is far from a myth. Firmly embedded in our culture, it is a powerful force in our everyday lives. That no race is superior and that even biologists cannot decide how people should be classified into races is not what counts. "I know what I see, and you can't tell me any different" seems to be the common attitude. As was noted in Chapter 4, sociologists W. I. and D. S. Thomas (1928) observed that "If people define situations as real, they are real in their consequences." In other words, people act on beliefs, not facts. As a result, we will always have people like Hitler and, as illustrated in our opening vignette, officials like those in the U.S. Public Health Service who thought that it was fine to experiment with people whom they deemed inferior. While few people hold such extreme views, most people appear to be ethnocentric enough to believe that their own race is—at least just a little—superior to others.

IN SUM Race, then, lies in the eye of the beholder. Humans show such a mixture of physical characteristics—in skin color, hair texture, nose shape, head shape, eye color, and so on—that there is no inevitable, much less universal, way to classify our many biological differences. Instead of falling into distinct types clearly separate from one another, human characteristics flow endlessly together. Because racial classifications are arbitrary, the categories people use differ from one society to another, and the categories are fluid, changing over time. In this sense, then, the concept of race and its accompanying notions of racial superiority are myths.

Ethnic Groups

Whereas people use the term *race* to refer to supposed biological characteristics that distinguish one group of people from another, **ethnicity** and **ethnic** apply to cultural

ethnicity (and **ethnic**) having distinctive cultural characteristics

Tiger Woods and the Emerging Multiracial Identity: Mapping New Ethnic Terrain

TIGER WOODS, PERHAPS THE TOP golfer of all time, calls himself Cablinasian. Woods invented this term as a boy to try to explain to himself just who he was—a combination of Caucasian, Black, Indian, and Asian (Leland and Beals 1997; Hall 2001). Woods wants to embrace both sides of his family. To be known by a racial-ethnic identity that applies to just one of his parents is to deny the other parent.

Like many of us, Tiger Woods' heritage is difficult to specify. Analysts who like to quantify ethnic heritage put Woods at one-quarter Thai, one-quarter Chinese, one-quarter white, an eighth Native American, and an eighth African American. From this chapter, you know how ridiculous such computations are, but the sociological question is why many people consider Tiger Woods an African American. The U.S. racial scene is indeed complex, but a good part of the reason is simply that this is the label the media placed on him. "Everyone has to fit somewhere" seems to be our attitude. If they don't, we grow uncomfortable. And for Tiger Woods, the media chose African American.

The United States once had a firm "color line"—barriers between racial-ethnic groups that you didn't dare cross, especially in dating or marriage. This invisible barrier has broken down, and today such marriages are common (*Statistical Abstract* 2007:Table 58). Several campuses have interracial student organizations. Harvard has two, one just for students who have one African American parent (Leland and Beals 1997).

As we march into unfamiliar ethnic terrain, our classifications are bursting at the seams. Consider how Kwame Anthony Appiah, of Harvard's Philosophy and Afro-American Studies Departments, described his situation:

> "My mother is English; my father is Ghanaian. My sisters are married to a Nigerian and a Norwegian. I have nephews who range from blond-haired kids to very black kids. They are all first cousins. Now according to the American scheme of things, they're all black—even the guy with blond hair who skis in Oslo" (Wright 1994).

I marvel at what racial experts the U.S. census takers once were. When they took the census, which is done every ten years, they looked at people and assigned them a race. At various points, the census contained these categories:

Tiger Woods as he answers questions at a news conference.

mulatto, quadroon, octoroon, Negro, black, Mexican, white, Indian, Filipino, Japanese, Chinese, and Hindu. Quadroon (one-fourth black and three-fourths white) and octoroon (one-eighth black and seven-eighths white) proved too difficult to "measure," and these categories were used only in 1890. Mulatto appeared in the 1850 census, but disappeared in 1930. The Mexican government complained about Mexicans being treated as a race, and this category was used only in 1930. I don't know whose strange idea it was to make Hindu a race, but it lasted for three censuses, from 1920 to 1940 (Bean et al. 2004; Tafoya, Johnson, and Hill 2005).

Today people are able to choose their own categories—and they have a lot of choices. In the 2000 census, everyone first declared that they were or were not "Spanish/Hispanic/Latino." Then they marked "one or more races" that they "consider themselves to be." They could choose from White; Black, African American, or Negro; American Indian or Alaska Native; Asian Indian, Chinese, Filipino, Japanese, Korean, Vietnamese, Native Hawaiian, Guamanian or Chamorro, Samoan, and other Pacific Islander. If these didn't do it, they could check a box called "Some Other Race" and then write whatever they wanted.

Perhaps the census should list Cablinasian, after all. There should also be ANGEL for African-Norwegian-German-English-Latino Americans, DEVIL for those of Danish-English-Vietnamese-Italian-Lebanese descent, and STUDY for the Swedish-Turkish-Uruguayan-Djibouti-Yugoslavian Americans. As you read farther in this chapter, you will see why these terms make as much sense as the categories we currently use.

for your Consideration

Just why do we count people by "race" anyway? Why not eliminate race from the U.S. census? (Race became a factor in 1790 during the first census when, for purposes of taxation and determining the number of representatives from each state, slaves were counted as three-fifths of whites!) Why is race so important to some people? Perhaps you can use the materials in this chapter to answer these questions.

Can a Plane Ride Change Your Race?

AT THE BEGINNING OF this text (pages 21–22), I mentioned that common sense and sociology often differ. This is especially so when it comes to race. According to common sense, our racial classifications represent biological differences between people. Sociologists, in contrast, stress that what we call races are *social* classifications, not biological categories.

Sociologists point out that *our "race" depends more on the society in which we live than on our biological characteristics.* For example, the racial categories common in the United States are merely one of *numerous* ways by which people around the world classify physical appearances. Although various groups use different categories, each group assumes that its categories are natural, merely a response to visible biology.

To better understand this essential sociological point—that race is more social than it is biological—consider this: In the United States, children born to the same parents are all of the same race. "What could be more natural?" Americans assume. But in Brazil, children born to the same parents may be of different races—if their appearances differ. "What could be more natural?" assume Brazilians.

Consider how Americans usually classify a child born to a "black" mother and a "white" father. Why do they usually say that the child is "black"? Wouldn't it be equally as logical to classify the child as "white"? Similarly, if a child has one grandmother who is "black," but all her other ancestors are "white," the child is often considered "black." Yet she has much more "white blood" than "black blood." Why, then, is she considered "black"? Certainly not because of biology. Rather, such thinking is a legacy of slavery. In an attempt to preserve the "purity" of their "race" in the face of numerous children whose fathers were white slave masters and mothers were black slaves, whites classified anyone

What "race" are these two Brazilians? Is the child of a different "race" than the mother? The text explains why "race" is such an unreliable concept that it changes even with geography.

with even a "drop of black blood" as black. This was actually known as the "one-drop" rule.

Even a plane trip can change a person's race. In the city of Salvador in Brazil, people classify one another by color of skin and eyes, breadth of nose and lips, and color and curliness of hair. They use at least seven terms for what we call white and black. Consider again a U.S. child who has "white" and "black" parents. If she flies to Brazil, she is no longer "black"; she now belongs to one of their several "whiter" categories (Fish 1995).

If the girl makes such a flight, would her "race" actually change? Our common sense revolts at this, I know, but it actually would. We want to argue that because her biological characteristics remain unchanged, her race remains unchanged. This is because we think of race as biological, when *race is actually a label we use to describe perceived biological characteristics.* Simply put, the race we "are" depends on our social location—on who is doing the classifying.

"Racial" classifications are also fluid, not fixed. You can see change occurring even now in the classifications that are used in the United States. The category "multiracial," for example, indicates changing thought and perception.

for your Consideration

How would you explain to "Joe and Suzie Six-Pack" that race is more a social classification than a biological one? Can you come up with any arguments to refute it? How do you think our racial-ethnic categories will change in the future?

characteristics. Derived from the word *ethnos* (a Greek word meaning "people" or "nation"), ethnicity and ethnic refer to people who identify with one another on the basis of common ancestry and cultural heritage. Their sense of belonging may center on their nation of origin, distinctive foods, clothing, language, music, religion, or family names and relationships.

People often confuse the terms *race* and *ethnic group.* For example, many people, including many Jews, consider Jews a race. Jews, however, are more properly considered an ethnic group, for it is their cultural characteristics, especially their religion, that bind them together. Wherever Jews have lived in the world, they have intermarried. Consequently,

Because ideas of *race and ethnicity* are such a significant part of society, all of us are classified according to those ideas. This photo illustrates the difficulty such assumptions posed for Israel. The Ethiopians, shown here as they arrived in Israel, although claiming to be Jews, looked so different from other Jews that it took several years for Israeli authorities to acknowledge this group's "true Jewishness."

Jews in China may have Chinese features, while some Swedish Jews are blue-eyed blonds. This matter is strikingly illustrated in the photo on this page. Ethiopian Jews look so different from European Jews that when they immigrated to Israel many European Jews felt that the Ethiopians could not be *real* Jews.

Minority Groups and Dominant Groups

Sociologist Louis Wirth (1945) defined a **minority group** as people who are singled out for unequal treatment and who regard themselves as objects of collective discrimination. Worldwide, minorities share several conditions: Their physical or cultural traits are held in low esteem by the dominant group, which treats them unfairly, and they tend to marry within their own group (Wagley and Harris 1958). These conditions tend to create a sense of identity among minorities (a feeling of "we-ness"). In many instances, a sense of common destiny emerges (Chandra 1993b).

Surprisingly, a minority group is not necessarily a *numerical* minority. For example, before India's independence in 1947, a handful of British colonial rulers discriminated against tens of millions of Indians. Similarly, when South Africa practiced apartheid, a smaller group of Dutch discriminated against a much larger number of blacks. And all over the world, females are a minority group. Accordingly, sociologists usually refer to those who do the discriminating not as the *majority*, but, rather, as the **dominant group**, for they have the greater power, privileges, and social status.

Possessing political power and unified by shared physical and cultural traits, the dominant group uses its position to discriminate against those with different—and supposedly inferior—traits. The dominant group considers its privileged position to be the result of its own innate superiority.

Emergence of Minority Groups   A group becomes a minority in one of two ways. The *first* is through the expansion of political boundaries. With the exception of females, tribal societies contain no minority groups. Everyone shares the same culture, including the same language, and belongs to the same group. When a group expands its political boundaries, however, it produces minority groups if it incorporates people with different customs, languages, values, and physical characteristics into the same political

minority group people who are singled out for unequal treatment and who regard themselves as objects of collective discrimination

dominant group the group with most power, greatest privileges, and highest social status

entity and discriminates against them. For example, after defeating Mexico in war in 1848, the United States took over the Southwest. The Mexicans living there, who had been the dominant group prior to the war, were transformed into a minority group, a master status that has influenced their lives ever since. Referring to his ancestors, one Latino said, "We didn't move across the border—the border moved across us."

A *second* way in which a group becomes a minority is by migration. This can be voluntary, as with the millions of people who have chosen to move from Mexico to the United States, or involuntary, as with the millions of Africans who were brought in chains to the United States. (The way females became a minority group represents a third way, but, as discussed in the previous chapter, no one knows just how this occurred.)

How People Construct Their Racial-Ethnic Identity

Some of us have a greater sense of ethnicity than others. Some of us feel firm boundaries between "us" and "them." Others have assimilated so extensively into the mainstream culture that they are only vaguely aware of their ethnic origins. With interethnic marrying common, some do not even know the countries from which their families originated—nor do they care. If asked to identify themselves ethnically, they respond with something like "I'm Heinz 57—German and Irish, with a little Italian and French thrown in—and I think someone said something about being one-sixteenth Indian, too."

Why do some people feel an intense sense of ethnic identity, while others feel hardly any? Figure 9.1 portrays four factors, identified by sociologist Ashley Doane, that heighten or reduce our sense of ethnic identity. From this figure, you can see that the keys are relative size, power, appearance, and discrimination. If your group is relatively small, has little power, looks different from most people in society, and is an object of discrimination, you will have a heightened sense of ethnic identity. In contrast, if you belong to the dominant group that holds most of the power, look like most people in the society, and feel no discrimination, you are likely to experience a sense of "belonging"—and to wonder why ethnic identity is such a big deal.

We can use the term **ethnic work** to refer to the way people construct their ethnicity. For people who have a strong ethnic identity, this term refers to how they enhance and maintain their group's distinctions—from clothing, food, and language to religious practices and holidays. For people whose ethnic identity is not as firm, it refers to attempts to recover their ethnic heritage, such as trying to trace family lines or visiting the country or region of their family's origin. Millions of Americans are engaged in ethnic work, which has confounded the experts who thought that the United States would be a **melting pot,** with most of its groups blending into a sort of ethnic stew. Because so many Americans have become fascinated with their "roots," some analysts have suggested that "tossed salad" is a more appropriate term than "melting pot."

Figure 9.1 A Sense of Ethnicity

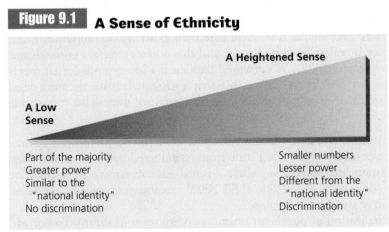

A Heightened Sense

A Low Sense

Part of the majority	Smaller numbers
Greater power	Lesser power
Similar to the "national identity"	Different from the "national identity"
No discrimination	Discrimination

Source: By the author. Based on Doane 1997.

ethnic work activities designed to discover, enhance, or maintain ethnic and racial identification

melting pot the view that Americans of various backgrounds would blend into a sort of ethnic stew

Prejudice and Discrimination

With prejudice and discrimination so significant in social life, let's consider the origin of prejudice and the extent of discrimination.

Learning Prejudice

Distinguishing Between Prejudice and Discrimination Prejudice and discrimination are common throughout the world. In Mexico, Hispanic Mexicans discriminate against Native American Mexicans; in Israel, Ashkenazi Jews, primarily of European descent, discriminate against Sephardi Jews from the Muslim world. In some places, the elderly discriminate against the young; in others, the young discriminate against the elderly. And all around the world, men discriminate against women.

Discrimination is an *action*—unfair treatment directed against someone. Discrimination can be based on many characteristics: age, sex, height, weight, clothing, income, education, marital status, sexual orientation, disease, disability, religion, and politics. When the basis of discrimination is someone's perception of race, it is known as **racism.** Discrimination is often the result of an *attitude* called **prejudice**—a prejudging of some sort, usually in a negative way. There is also *positive prejudice*, which exaggerates the virtues of a group, as when people think that some group (usually their own) is more capable than others. Most prejudice, however, is negative and involves prejudging a group as inferior.

Learning from Association As with our other attitudes, we are not born with prejudice. Rather, we learn prejudice from the people around us. In a fascinating study, sociologist Kathleen Blee (2005) interviewed women who were members of the KKK and Aryan Nations. Her first finding is of the "ho hum" variety: Most women were recruited by someone who already belonged to the group. Blee's second finding, however, holds a surprise: Some women learned to be racists *after* they joined the group. They were attracted to the group not because it matched their racist beliefs but because someone they liked belonged to it. Blee found that their racism was not the *cause* of their joining but, rather, the *result* of their membership.

The Far-Reaching Nature of Prejudice It is amazing how much prejudice people can learn. In a classic article, psychologist Eugene Hartley (1946) asked people how they felt about several racial and ethnic groups. Besides blacks, Jews, and so on, he included the Wallonians, Pireneans, and Danireans—names he had made up. Most people who expressed dislike for Jews and blacks also expressed dislike for these three fictitious groups.

Hartley's study shows that prejudice does not depend on negative experiences with others. It also reveals that people who are prejudiced against one racial or ethnic group also tend to be prejudiced against other groups. People can be, and are, prejudiced against people they have never met—and even against groups that do not exist!

The neo-Nazis and the Ku Klux Klan base their existence on prejudice. These groups believe that race is real, that white is best, and that society's surface conceals underlying conspiracies (Ezekiel 2002). What would happen if a Jew attended their meetings? Would he or she survive? In the Down-to-Earth Sociology box on the next page, sociologist Raphael Ezekiel reveals some of the insights he gained during his remarkable study of these groups.

Internalizing Dominant Norms People can even learn to be prejudiced against their *own* group. A national survey of black Americans conducted by black interviewers found that African Americans think that lighter-skinned African American women are more attractive than those with darker skin (Hill 2002). Sociologists call this *the internalization of the norms of the dominant group.*

To study the internalization of dominant norms, psychologists Mahzarin Banaji and Anthony Greenwald created the "Implicit Association Test." In one version of this test,

In the early 1900s, the Ku Klux Klan was a powerful political force. By the 1950s when this photo was taken in Montgomery, Alabama, the Klan possessed only a shadow of its former power. Today's Klan gets a headline here and there, but few are listening to its message. The group continues to have followers, however.

discrimination an act of unfair treatment directed against an individual or a group

racism prejudice and discrimination on the basis of race

prejudice an attitude or prejudging, usually in a negative way

Down-to-Earth Sociology

The Racist Mind

SOCIOLOGIST RAPHAEL EZEKIEL WANTED to get a close look at the racist mind. The best way to study racism from the inside is to do participant observation (see page 136). But Ezekiel is a Jew. Could he study these groups by participant observation? To find out, Ezekiel told Ku Klux Klan and neo-Nazi leaders that he wanted to interview them and attend their meetings. He also told them that he was a Jew. Surprisingly, they agreed. Ezekiel published his path-breaking research in a book, *The Racist Mind* (1995). Here are some of the insights he gained during his fascinating sociological adventure:

> [The leader] builds on mass anxiety about economic insecurity and on popular tendencies to see an Establishment as the cause of economic threat; he hopes to teach people to identify that Establishment as the puppets of a conspiracy of Jews. [He has a] belief in exclusive categories. For the white racist leader, it is profoundly true . . . that the socially defined collections we call races represent fundamental categories. A man is black or a man is white; there are no in-betweens. Every human belongs to a racial category, and all the members of one category are radically different from all the members of other categories. Moreover, race represents the essence of the person. A truck is a truck, a car is a car, a cat is a cat, a dog is a dog, a black is a black, a white is a white. . . . These axioms have a rock-hard quality in the leaders' minds; the world is made up of racial groups. That is what exists for them.
>
> Two further beliefs play a major role in the minds of leaders. First, life is war. The world is made of distinct racial groups; life is about the war between these groups. Second, events have secret causes, are never what they seem superficially. . . . Any myth is plausible, as long as it involves intricate plotting. . . . It does not matter to him what others say. . . . He lives in his ideas and in the little world he has created where they are

taken seriously. . . . Gold can be made from the tongues of frogs; Yahweh's call can be heard in the flapping swastika banner. (pp. 66–67)

Who is attracted to the neo-Nazis and Ku Klux Klan? Here is what Ezekiel discovered:

> [There is a] ready pool of whites who will respond to the racist signal. . . . This population [is] always hungry for activity—or for the talk of activity—that promises dignity and meaning to lives that are working poorly in a highly competitive world. . . . Much as I don't want to believe it, [this] movement brings a sense of meaning—at least for a while—to some of the discontented. To struggle in a cause that transcends the individual lends meaning to life, no matter how ill-founded or narrowing the cause. For the young men in the neo-Nazi group . . . membership was an alternative to atomization and drift; within the group they worked for a cause and took direct risks in the company of comrades. . . .
>
> When interviewing the young neo-Nazis in Detroit, I often found myself driving with them past the closed factories, the idled plants of our shrinking manufacturing base. The fewer and fewer plants that remain can demand better educated and more highly skilled workers. These fatherless Nazi youths, these high-school dropouts, will find little place in the emerging economy . . . a permanently underemployed white underclass is taking its place alongside the permanent black underclass. The struggle over race merely diverts youth from confronting the real issues of their lives. Not many seats are left on the train, and the train is leaving the station. (pp. 32–33)

for your Consideration

Use functionalism, conflict theory, and symbolic interaction to explain how the leaders and followers of these hate groups view the world. Use these same perspectives to explain why some people are attracted to the message of hate.

---

good and bad words are flashed on a screen along with photos of African Americans and whites. Most subjects are quicker to associate positive words (such as "love," "peace," and "baby") with whites and negative words (such as "cancer," "bomb," and "devil") with blacks. Here's the clincher: This is true for *both* white and black subjects (Dasgupta et al. 2000; Greenwald and Krieger 2006). Apparently, we all learn the *ethnic maps* of our culture, and, along with them, their route to biased perception.

Individual and Institutional Discrimination

Sociologists stress that we need to move beyond thinking in terms of **individual discrimination,** the negative treatment of one person by another. Although such behavior creates problems, it is primarily an issue between individuals. With their focus on the broader picture, sociologists encourage us to examine **institutional discrimination,** that is, to see how discrimination is woven into the fabric of society. Let's look at two examples.

individual discrimination the negative treatment of one person by another on the basis of that person's perceived characteristics

institutional discrimination the negative treatment of a minority group that is built into a society's institutions; also called *systemic discrimination*

Home Mortgages and Car Loans Bank lending provides an excellent illustration of institutional discrimination. As shown in Figure 9.2, race-ethnicity is a significant factor in getting a mortgage. When bankers looked at the statistics shown in this figure, they cried foul. It might *look* like discrimination, they said, but the truth is that whites have better credit histories. To see if this were true, researchers went over the data again, comparing the credit histories of the applicants. The lending gap did narrow a bit, but the bottom line was that even when applicants were identical in all these areas, African Americans and Latinos were *60 percent* more likely than whites to be rejected (Thomas 1992; Passell 1996). African Americans are also likely to be charged more than whites for their mortgages (Avery et al. 2005) and for car loans ("Judge Rules . . ." 2005; Peters and Hakim 2005). In short, it is not a matter of a banker here or there discriminating according to personal prejudices; rather, discrimination is built into the country's financial institutions.

Health Care Discrimination does not have to be deliberate. It can occur without the awareness of both those doing the discriminating and those being discriminated against. White patients, for example, are more likely than either Latino or African American patients to receive knee replacements (Skinner et al. 2003) and coronary bypass surgery (Smedley et al. 2003). Treatment after a heart attack follows a similar pattern. A study of 40,000 patients shows that whites are more likely than blacks to be given cardiac catheterization, a test to detect blockage of blood vessels. This study holds a surprise: Both black *and* white doctors are more likely to give this preventive care to whites (Stolberg 2001).

Researchers do not know why race-ethnicity is a factor in medical decisions. With both white and black doctors involved, we can be certain that physicians *do not intend* to discriminate. In ways we do not yet understand—but which could be related to the implicit bias that apparently comes with the internalization of dominant norms—discrimination is built into the medical delivery system. Race seems to work like gender: Just as women's higher death rates in coronary bypass surgery can be traced to implicit attitudes about gender (see page 243), so also race-ethnicity becomes a subconscious motivation for giving or denying access to advanced medical procedures.

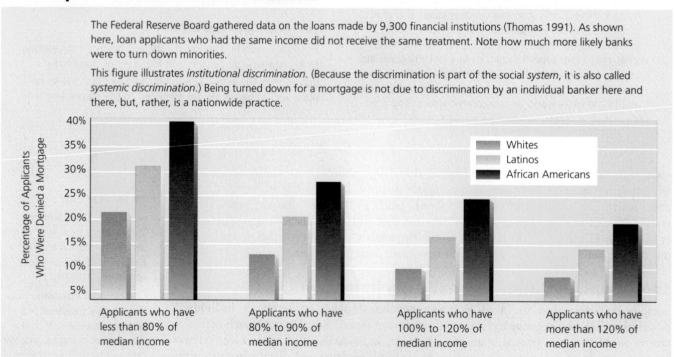

Figure 9.2 Race-Ethnicity and Mortgages: An Example of Institutional Discrimination

The Federal Reserve Board gathered data on the loans made by 9,300 financial institutions (Thomas 1991). As shown here, loan applicants who had the same income did not receive the same treatment. Note how much more likely banks were to turn down minorities.

This figure illustrates *institutional discrimination*. (Because the discrimination is part of the social *system*, it is also called *systemic discrimination*.) Being turned down for a mortgage is not due to discrimination by an individual banker here and there, but, rather, is a nationwide practice.

Source: By the author. Based on Thomas 1991.

Theories of Prejudice

Social scientists have developed several theories to explain prejudice. Let's first look at psychological explanations, then sociological ones.

Psychological Perspectives

Frustration and Scapegoats   In 1939, psychologist John Dollard suggested that prejudice is the result of frustration. People who are unable to strike out at the real source of their frustration (such as unemployment) look for someone to blame. They unfairly attribute their troubles to a **scapegoat**—often a racial, ethnic, or religious minority—and this person or group becomes a target on which they vent their frustrations. Gender and age also provide common bases for scapegoating.

Even mild frustration can increase prejudice. A team of psychologists led by Emory Cowen (1959) measured the prejudice of a sample of students. They then gave the students two puzzles to solve, making sure the students did not have enough time to solve them. After the students had worked furiously on the puzzles, the experimenters shook their heads in disgust and said that they couldn't believe the students hadn't finished such a simple task. They then retested the students and found that their scores on prejudice had increased. The students had directed their frustrations outward, transferring them to people who had nothing to do with the contempt that the experimenters had directed toward them.

The Authoritarian Personality   Have you ever wondered whether personality is a cause of prejudice? Maybe some people are more inclined to be prejudiced, and others more fair-minded. For psychologist Theodor Adorno, who had fled from the Nazis, this was no idle speculation. With the horrors he had observed still fresh in his mind, Adorno wondered whether there might be a certain type of person who is more likely to fall for the racist spewings of people like Hitler, Mussolini, and those in the Ku Klux Klan.

To find out, Adorno (1950) tested about two thousand people, ranging from college professors to prison inmates. To measure their ethnocentrism, anti-Semitism (bias against Jews), and support for strong, authoritarian leaders, he gave them three tests. Adorno found that people who scored high on one test also scored high on the other two. For example, people who agreed with anti-Semitic statements also said that governments should be authoritarian and that foreign ways of life pose a threat to the "American" way.

Adorno concluded that highly prejudiced people are insecure conformists. They have deep respect for authority and are submissive to superiors. He termed this the **authoritarian personality.** These people believe that things are either right or wrong. Ambiguity disturbs them, especially in matters of religion or sex. They become anxious when they confront norms and values that vary from their own. To view people who differ from themselves as inferior assures them that their own positions are right.

Adorno's research stirred the scientific community, stimulating more than a thousand research studies. In general, the researchers found that people who are older, less educated, less intelligent, and from a lower social class are more likely to be authoritarian. Critics say that this doesn't indicate a particular personality, just that the less educated are more prejudiced—which we already knew (Yinger 1965; Ray 1991). Nevertheless, researchers continue to study this concept (Stenner 2005).

Sociological Perspectives

Sociologists find psychological explanations inadequate. They stress that the key to understanding prejudice cannot be found by looking *inside* people, but rather by examining conditions *outside* them. Therefore, sociologists focus on how social environments influence prejudice. With this background, let's compare functionalist, conflict, and symbolic interactionist perspectives on prejudice.

Functionalism   In a telling scene from a television documentary, journalist Bill Moyers interviewed Fritz Hipler, a Nazi intellectual who at age 29 was put in charge of the entire German film industry. Hipler said that when Hitler came to power the Germans were

scapegoat an individual or group unfairly blamed for someone else's troubles

authoritarian personality Theodor Adorno's term for people who are prejudiced and rank high on scales of conformity, intolerance, insecurity, respect for authority, and submissiveness to superiors

no more anti-Semitic than the French, and probably less so. He was told to create anti-Semitism. Obediently, Hipler produced movies that contained vivid scenes comparing Jews to rats—with their breeding threatening to infest the population.

Why was Hipler told to create hatred? Prejudice and discrimination were functional for the Nazis. Germany was on its knees at this time. It had been defeated in World War I and was being economically devastated by war reparations. The middle class was being destroyed by runaway inflation. The Jews provided a scapegoat, a common enemy against which the Nazis could unite Germany. In addition, the Jews owned businesses, bank accounts, fine art, and other property that the Nazis could confiscate. Jews also held key positions (as university professors, reporters, judges, and so on), into which the Nazis could place their own flunkies. In the end, hatred also showed its dysfunctional side, as the Nazi officials who were hanged at Nuremberg discovered.

Prejudice becomes practically irresistible when state machinery is harnessed to advance the cause of hatred. To produce prejudice, the Nazis exploited government agencies, the schools, police, courts, and mass media. The results were devastating. Recall the identical twins featured in the Down-to-Earth Sociology box on page 66. Oskar and Jack had been separated as babies. Jack was brought up as a Jew in Trinidad, while Oskar was reared as a Catholic in Czechoslovakia. Under the Nazi regime, Oskar learned to hate Jews, unaware that he himself was a Jew.

That prejudice is functional and is shaped by the social environment was demonstrated by psychologists Muzafer and Carolyn Sherif (1953). In a boys' summer camp, they assigned friends to different cabins and then had the cabin groups compete in sports. In just a few days, strong in-groups had formed, and even former lifelong friends were calling one another "crybaby" and "sissy," and showing intense dislike for one another.

The Sherif study teaches us several important lessons about social life. Note how it is possible to arrange the social environment to generate either positive or negative feelings about people, and how prejudice arises if we pit groups against one another in an "I win, you lose" situation. You can also see that prejudice is functional, how it creates in-group solidarity. And, of course, it is obvious how dysfunctional prejudice is, when you observe the way it destroys human relationships.

Conflict Theory   Conflict theorists also analyze how groups are pitted against one another, but they focus on how this arrangement benefits those with power. They begin by noting that workers want better food, health care, housing, and education. To attain these goals, workers need good jobs. If workers are united, they can demand higher wages and better working conditions, but if capitalists can keep workers divided, they can hold wages down. To do this, capitalists use two main tactics.

The first tactic is to keep workers insecure. Fear of unemployment works especially well. The unemployed serve as a **reserve labor force** for capitalists. The capitalists draw on the unemployed to expand production during economic booms, and when the economy contracts, they release these workers to rejoin the ranks of the unemployed. The lesson is not lost on workers who have jobs. They fear eviction and worry about having their cars and furniture repossessed. Many know they are just one paycheck away from ending up "on the streets." This helps to keep workers docile.

The second tactic is encouraging and exploiting racial-ethnic divisions (Patterson 2007). Pitting worker against worker weakens labor's bargaining power. When white workers went on strike in California in the 1800s, owners of factories replaced them with Chinese workers. To break strikes by Japanese workers on plantations in Hawaii, owners used to hire Koreans (Xie and Goyette 2004). This division of workers along racial-ethnic and gender lines is known as a **split labor market** (Du Bois 1935/1992; Roediger 2002). Although today's exploitation is more subtle, fear and suspicion continue to split workers. Whites are aware that other groups are ready to take their jobs, African Americans often perceive Latinos as competitors, and men know that women are eager to get promoted. All of this helps to make workers more docile.

The consequences are devastating, say conflict theorists. It is just like the boys in the Sherif experiment. African Americans, Latinos, whites, and others see themselves as able to make gains only at the expense of members of the other groups. This rivalry shows up

reserve labor force the unemployed; unemployed workers are thought of as being "in reserve"—capitalists take them "out of reserve" (put them back to work) during times of high production and then lay them off (put them back in reserve) when they are no longer needed

split labor market workers split along racial, ethnic, gender, age, or any other lines; this split is exploited by owners to weaken the bargaining power of workers along even finer racial-ethnic lines, such as that in Miami between Haitians and African Americans, who distrust each other as competitors. Divisions among workers deflect anger and hostility away from the power elite and direct these powerful emotions toward other racial and ethnic groups. Instead of recognizing their common class interests and working for their mutual welfare, workers learn to fear and distrust one another.

selective perception seeing certain features of an object or situation, but remaining blind to others

Symbolic Interactionism   While conflict theorists focus on the role of the capitalist class in exploiting racial and ethnic divisions, symbolic interactionists examine how labels affect perception and create prejudice.

How Labels Create Prejudice   Symbolic interactionists stress that *the labels we learn affect the way we see people.* Labels cause **selective perception;** that is, they lead us to see certain things while they blind us to others. If we apply a label to a group, we tend to perceive its members as all alike. We shake off evidence that doesn't fit (Simpson and Yinger 1972). Racial and ethnic labels are especially powerful. They are shorthand for emotionally charged stereotypes. The term *nigger*, for example, is not neutral. Nor are *honky, cracker, spic, mick, kike, limey, kraut, dago, guinea,* or any of the other scornful words people use to belittle ethnic groups. Such words overpower us with emotions, blocking out rational thought about the people to whom they refer (Allport 1954).

Labels and the Self-Fulfilling Prophecy   Some stereotypes not only justify prejudice and discrimination but even produce the behavior depicted in the stereotype. Let's consider Group X. Negative stereotypes characterize the members of Group X as lazy, so they don't deserve good jobs. ("They are lazy and undependable and wouldn't do well.") This attitude creates a *self-fulfilling prophecy.* Because they are denied jobs that require high dedication and energy, most members of Group X are limited to doing "dirty work," the kind of employment thought appropriate for "that kind" of people. Since much "dirty work" is sporadic, members of Group X are often seen "on the streets." The sight of their idleness reinforces the original stereotype of laziness. The discrimination that created the "laziness" in the first place passes unnoticed.

To apply these three theoretical perspectives and catch a glimpse of how amazingly different things were in the past, read the Down-to-Earth Sociology box on the next page.

Global Patterns of Intergroup Relations

Sociologists have studied racial-ethnic relations around the world. They have found six basic patterns that characterize the relationship of dominant groups and minorities. These patterns are shown in Figure 9.3. Let's look at each.

Figure 9.3   **Global Patterns of Intergroup Relations: A Continuum**

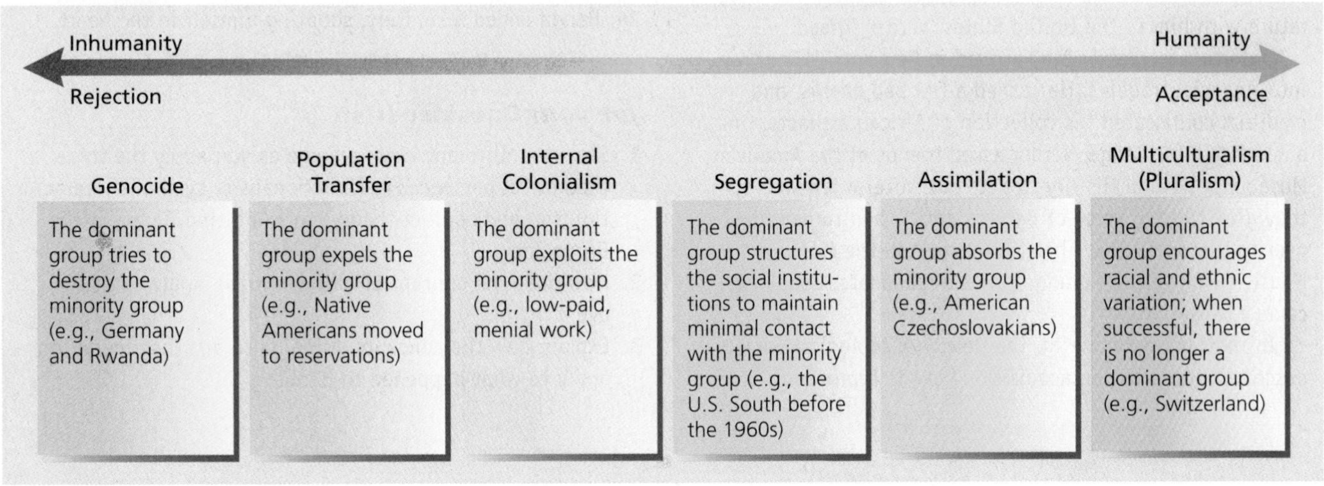

Inhumanity ←					Humanity →
Rejection					Acceptance
Genocide	**Population Transfer**	**Internal Colonialism**	**Segregation**	**Assimilation**	**Multiculturalism (Pluralism)**
The dominant group tries to destroy the minority group (e.g., Germany and Rwanda)	The dominant group expels the minority group (e.g., Native Americans moved to reservations)	The dominant group exploits the minority group (e.g., low-paid, menial work)	The dominant group structures the social institutions to maintain minimal contact with the minority group (e.g., the U.S. South before the 1960s)	The dominant group absorbs the minority group (e.g., American Czechoslovakians)	The dominant group encourages racial and ethnic variation; when successful, there is no longer a dominant group (e.g., Switzerland)

Down-to-Earth Sociology

The Man in the Zoo

YOU ARE GOING TO THINK I'm kidding, but listen to this:

> The Bronx Zoo in New York City used to keep a 22-year-old pygmy in the Monkey House. The man—and the orangutan he lived with—became the most popular exhibit at the zoo. Thousands of visitors would arrive daily, and head straight for the Monkey House. Eyewitnesses to what they thought was a lower form of human in the long chain of evolution, the visitors were fascinated by the pygmy, especially by his sharpened teeth.
>
> To make the exhibit even more alluring, the zoo director ordered that animal bones be scattered in front of the man.

Ota Benga, 1906, on exhibit in the Bronx Zoo.

© Wildlife Conservation Society

I know it sounds as though I must have made this up. Could this really have happened? Actually, this is a true story, and here's the background on it.

The World's Fair was going to be held in St. Louis in 1904, and the Department of Anthropology wanted to show genuine villages from different cultures. They asked Samuel Verner, an explorer familiar with Africa, if he could get some pygmies to come to St. Louis to serve as live exhibits for a few months. Verner agreed, and on his next trip to Africa, in the Belgian Congo he came across Ota Benga (or Otabenga), a pygmy who had been enslaved by another tribe. Benga, then about age 20, said he was willing to go to St. Louis. After Verner bought Benga's freedom for a few yards of cloth, Benga recruited another half dozen pygmies to go with them.

As promised, after the World's Fair, Verner took the pygmies back to Africa. In his absence, however, a hostile tribe had wiped out Benga's village and killed his family. With few alternatives before him, Benga asked Verner if he could return with him to the United States. Verner agreed.

Unfortunately, after they arrived in New York, Verner ran into financial troubles. He cashed a few bad checks, and creditors confiscated his collection of African artifacts. Unable to care for Benga, Verner asked friends at the American Museum of Natural History to help out. After a few weeks, they grew tired of some of Benga's antics, and turned him over to the Bronx Zoo. There, on exhibit in the Monkey House, living with an orangutan as a roommate, Benga became a sensation.

In their official bulletin, the New York Zoological Society described Benga as "an acquisition" of the Bronx Zoo.

An article in the New York Times said that it was fortunate that Benga couldn't think very deeply, or else he might be bothered by living with monkeys.

When African American ministers protested, saying that the zoo's exhibit was degrading, zoo officials defended themselves. They said that they were "taking excellent care of the little fellow." To further make their case, they added that "he has one of the best rooms at the primate house."

As the protest of members of the Colored Baptist Ministers' Conference grew louder and more insistent, zoo officials finally gave in. They decided to let Benga out of his cage. They put a white shirt on him and let him walk around the zoo wherever he wanted. Benga returned at night to sleep in the monkey house.

This limited freedom made life even more miserable for Benga. Now zoo visitors followed him around, howling, jeering, laughing, and poking at him. One day, Benga found a knife in the feeding room of the Monkey House and flourished it at the visitors. Zoo officials took the knife away.

Benga then made a little bow and some arrows and began shooting at the obnoxious visitors. At that point, all the fun was over for the zoo officials. Not liking this turn of events, they decided that Benga had to leave.

After living in several orphanages for African American children, Benga ended up working as a laborer in a tobacco factory in Lynchburg, Virginia.

Benga remained desperately lonely, never fitting in, always being treated as a freak, and in despair that he had no home or family to return to in Africa. In 1916, at the age of 26, Benga ended his misery, shooting himself in the heart.

—Based on Bradford and Blume 1992; Crossen 2006; Richman 2006.

for your Consideration

1. See what different views emerge as you apply the three theoretical perspectives (functionalism, symbolic interactionism, and conflict theory) to exhibiting Benga at the Bronx Zoo.
2. How does the concept of ethnocentrism apply to this event?
3. Explain how the concepts of prejudice and discrimination apply to what happened to Benga.

Genocide

Last century's two most notorious examples of genocide occurred in Europe and Africa. In Germany during the 1930s and 1940s, Hitler and the Nazis attempted to destroy all Jews. In the 1990s, in Rwanda, the Hutus tried to destroy all Tutsis. One of the horrifying aspects of these slaughters was that those who participated did not crawl out from under a rock someplace. Rather, they were ordinary citizens whose participation was facilitated by labels that singled out the victims as enemies who deserved to die (Huttenbach 1991; Browning 1993; Gross 2001).

To better understand how ordinary people can participate in genocide, let's look at an example from the United States. To call the Native Americans "savages," as U.S. officials and white settlers did, was to label them as inferior, as somehow less than human. This identification made it easier to justify killing the Native Americans in order to take over their resources.

> When gold was discovered in northern California in 1849, the fabled "Forty-Niners" rushed in. With the region already inhabited by 150,000 Native Americans, the white government put a bounty on the heads of Native Americans. It even reimbursed the whites for their bullets. The result was the slaughter of 120,000 Native American men, women, and children. (Schaefer 2004)

Most Native Americans, however, died not from bullets but from diseases that the whites brought with them. The Native Americans had no immunity against diseases such as measles, smallpox, and the flu (Dobyns 1983; Schaefer 2004). The settlers also ruthlessly destroyed the Native Americans' food supply (buffalos, crops). As a result, about *95 percent* of Native Americans died (Thornton 1987; Churchill 1997).

The same thing was happening in other places. In South Africa, the Boers, or Dutch settlers, viewed the native Hottentots as jungle animals and totally wiped them out. In Tasmania, the British settlers stalked the local aboriginal population, hunting them for sport and sometimes even for dog food.

Labels are powerful forces in human life. Labels that dehumanize others help people to **compartmentalize**—to separate their acts from their sense of being good and moral people. To regard members of a particular group as inferior or even less than human means that it is okay to treat them inhumanely. Thus people can kill—and still retain a good self-concept (Bernard et al. 1971). In short, *labeling the targeted group as inferior or even less than fully human facilitates genocide.*

compartmentalize to separate acts from feelings or attitudes

population transfer forcing a minority group to move

Population Transfer

There are two types of **population transfer:** indirect and direct. *Indirect transfer* is achieved by making life so unbearable for members of a minority that they leave "voluntarily." Under the bitter conditions of czarist Russia, for example, millions of Jews made this "choice." *Direct transfer* occurs when a dominant group expels a minority. Examples include the U.S. government relocating Native Americans to reservations and transferring Americans of Japanese descent to internment camps during World War II.

In the 1990s, a combination of genocide and population transfer occurred in Bosnia and Kosovo, parts of the former Yugoslavia. A hatred nurtured for centuries had been kept under wraps by Tito's iron-fisted rule

Amid fears that Japanese Americans were "enemies within" who would sabotage industrial and military installations on the West Coast, in the early days of World War II Japanese Americans were transferred to "relocation camps." Many returned home after the war to find that their property had been confiscated or vandalized.

from 1944 to 1980. After Tito's death, these suppressed, smoldering hostilities soared to the surface, and Yugoslavia split into warring factions. When the Serbs gained power, Muslims rebelled and began guerilla warfare. The Serbs vented their hatred by what they termed **ethnic cleansing:** They terrorized villages with killing and rape, forcing survivors to flee in fear.

Internal Colonialism

In Chapter 7, the term *colonialism* was used to refer to one way that the Most Industrialized Nations exploit the Least Industrialized Nations (p. 195). Conflict theorists use the term **internal colonialism** to describe the way in which a country's dominant group exploits minority groups for its economic advantage. The dominant group manipulates the social institutions to suppress minorities and deny them full access to their society's benefits. Slavery, reviewed in Chapter 7, is an extreme example of internal colonialism, as was the South African system of *apartheid.* Although the dominant Afrikaners despised the minority, they found its presence necessary. As Simpson and Yinger (1972) put it, who else would do the hard work?

Segregation

Internal colonialism is often accompanied by **segregation**—the separation of racial or ethnic groups. Segregation allows the dominant group to maintain social distance from the minority and yet to exploit their labor as cooks, cleaners, chauffeurs, housekeepers, nannies, factory workers, and so on. In the U.S. South until the 1960s, by law, African Americans and whites had to use separate public facilities such as hotels, schools, swimming pools, bathrooms, and even drinking fountains. In thirty-eight states, laws prohibited marriage between blacks and whites. Violators could be sent to prison (Mahoney and Kooistra 1995; Crossen 2004). The last law of this type was repealed in 1967 (Spickard 1989). In the villages of India, an ethnic group, the Dalits (untouchables), is forbidden to use the village pump. Dalit women must walk long distances to streams or pumps outside of the village to fetch their water (author's notes).

Racial-ethnic segregation in housing is still a fact of life for most Americans. In the Cultural Diversity box on the next page, you can see how residential segregation is related to internal colonialism.

Assimilation

Assimilation is the process by which a minority group is absorbed into the mainstream culture. There are two types. In *forced assimilation,* the dominant group refuses to allow the minority to practice its religion, to speak its language, or to follow its customs. Before the fall of the Soviet Union, for example, the dominant group, the Russians, required that Armenian children attend schools where they were taught in Russian. Armenians could celebrate only Russian holidays, not Armenian ones. *Permissible assimilation,* in contrast, allows the minority to adopt the dominant group's patterns in its own way and at its own speed.

Multiculturalism (Pluralism)

A policy of **multiculturalism,** also called **pluralism,** permits or even encourages racial and ethnic variation. The minority groups are able to maintain their separate identities, yet participate freely in the country's social institutions, from education to politics. Switzerland provides an outstanding example of multiculturalism. The Swiss population includes four ethnic groups: French, Italians, Germans, and Romansh. These groups have kept their own languages, and they live peacefully in political and economic unity. Multiculturalism has been so successful that none of these groups can properly be called a minority.

ethnic cleansing a policy of population elimination, including forcible expulsion and genocide

internal colonialism the policy of economically exploiting minority groups

segregation the policy of keeping racial-ethnic groups apart

assimilation the process of being absorbed into the mainstream culture

multiculturalism (also called **pluralism**) a philosophy or political policy that permits or encourages ethnic difference

Cultural Diversity *in the* United States

"You Can Work for Us, But You Can't Live Near Us"

NEVER BEFORE HAD SO MANY people crowded into the city hall in Glen Cove, Long Island. What drew them was nothing less than the future of their community, which had become an ethnic and social class crucible. At the front sat the well-groomed Long Islanders in their designer clothing. At the back were men in soiled jeans and work boots whose calloused hands bespoke their occupations as landscape laborers and construction workers. Most of them had fled the civil war in El Salvador, seeking safety and jobs in the United States.

The meeting was called to order by the town mayor, the son of Italian immigrants, who had launched a campaign to rid the town of a day labor shape-up area. He had asked the Immigration and Naturalization Service to raid the area where men gathered on the sidewalks in the early mornings to look for day jobs. This evening he proposed an ordinance making it illegal for groups of five or more to assemble on city streets for the purpose of seeking

Day laborers soliciting work in Farmingville, New York.

work. City residents testified that the men made cat calls at women and urinated in public. They called the shape-up area an eyesore. Representatives of the immigrants countered by affirming the immigrants' constitutional right to freedom of assembly and argued that they were not loitering in the streets but waiting peacefully on the sidewalks.

The larger issue that haunted the Long Islanders, one that they were reluctant to acknowledge publicly but that a few individuals admitted to me privately, was the fear that the immigrants gave the impression that the town was in decline. Such a perception in suburbia jeopardizes real estate values—the bedrock of U.S. middle-class security. Even

the hint of racial or ethnic turnover frightens homeowners and potential buyers. In Glen Cove, this fear led to the campaign to get rid of the "shape-up," the single most vivid image of the ethnically distinct people residing in the community.

In the town meeting the point was made that the immigrants had been attracted to the area precisely because the suburbanites desired their inexpensive labor. Almost all the landscapers on Long Island are now Salvadoran, and many families depend on immigrant women to clean their houses and take care of their children and elderly. Immigrants, especially from El Salvador and other Latin American countries, toil in the island's restaurants, factories, and laundries, and, at night, in office buildings. They do the jobs that U.S. workers do not want to do or cannot afford to do because the jobs pay too little to support their families.

When the Salvadorans and other immigrants arrived on Long Island, seeking their futures, they first lived in communities with high minority populations. But as the immigrants moved closer to their jobs, their numbers swelled in more traditional bedroom communities like Glen Cove. These other towns also began to adopt "not in my backyard" policies by passing new ordinances or enforcing old ones, even refusing to let undocumented immigrant children attend their public schools. Old-timers felt that such measures could stem the decline in their way of life. What they overlooked was how the immigrant labor is preserving their standard of living.

Source: Sarah Maher, University of Vermont, *Salvadorans in Suburbia.*

Race and Ethnic Relations in the United States

To write on race-ethnicity is like stepping onto a minefield: One never knows where to expect the next explosion. Even basic terms are controversial. The term African American, for example, is rejected by those who ask why this term doesn't include white immigrants from South Africa. Some people classified as African Americans also reject this term because they identify themselves as blacks. Similarly, some Latinos prefer the term *Hispanic American,* but others reject it, saying that it ignores the Indian side of their heritage. Some would limit the term *Chicanos*—commonly used to

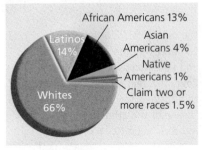

Figure 9.4 **Race-Ethnicity of the U.S. Population**

African Americans 13%

Latinos 14%

Asian Americans 4%

Native Americans 1%

Claim two or more races 1.5%

Whites 66%

Source: By the author. See Figure 9.5.

refer to Americans from Mexico—to those who have a sense of oppression and ethnic unity; they say that it does not apply to those who have assimilated.

No term that I use here, then, will satisfy everyone. Racial-ethnic identity is fluid, constantly changing, and all terms carry a risk as they take on politically charged meanings. Nevertheless, as part of everyday life, we classify ourselves and one another as belonging to distinct racial-ethnic groups. As Figures 9.4 and 9.5 show, on the basis of these self-identities, whites make up 66 percent of the U.S. population, minorities (African Americans, Asian Americans, Latinos, and Native Americans) 32 percent. Between 1 and 2 percent claim membership in two or more racial-ethnic groups.

As you can see from the Social Map on the next page, the distribution of dominant and minority groups among the states seldom comes close to the national average. This is because minority groups tend to be clustered in regions. The extreme distributions are represented by Maine and Vermont, each of which has only 4 percent minority, and by Hawaii, where minorities outnumber whites 77 percent to 23 percent. With this as background, let's review the major groups in the United States, going from the largest to the smallest.

Figure 9.5 **U.S. Racial-Ethnic Groups**

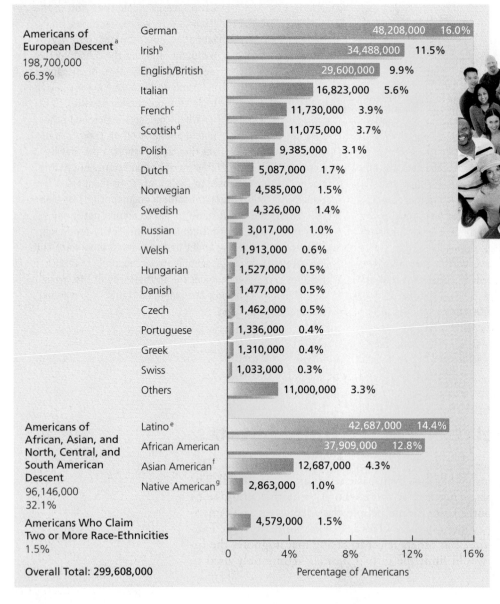

Americans of European Descent[a] 198,700,000 66.3%		
German	48,208,000	16.0%
Irish[b]	34,488,000	11.5%
English/British	29,600,000	9.9%
Italian	16,823,000	5.6%
French[c]	11,730,000	3.9%
Scottish[d]	11,075,000	3.7%
Polish	9,385,000	3.1%
Dutch	5,087,000	1.7%
Norwegian	4,585,000	1.5%
Swedish	4,326,000	1.4%
Russian	3,017,000	1.0%
Welsh	1,913,000	0.6%
Hungarian	1,527,000	0.5%
Danish	1,477,000	0.5%
Czech	1,462,000	0.5%
Portuguese	1,336,000	0.4%
Greek	1,310,000	0.4%
Swiss	1,033,000	0.3%
Others	11,000,000	3.3%

Americans of African, Asian, and North, Central, and South American Descent 96,146,000 32.1%		
Latino[e]	42,687,000	14.4%
African American	37,909,000	12.8%
Asian American[f]	12,687,000	4.3%
Native American[g]	2,863,000	1.0%

Americans Who Claim Two or More Race-Ethnicities 1.5%

4,579,000   1.5%

Overall Total: 299,608,000

Percentage of Americans
0   4%   8%   12%   16%

USA—the land of diversity

Notes:

[a]The totals in this figure should be taken as broadly accurate only. The totals for groups and even for the U.S. population vary from table to table in the source. Because the total of the individual white ethnic groups listed in the source is 10 percent above the total of whites, I arbitrarily reduced each white ethnic group by 10 percent.

[b]Interestingly, this total is *six* times higher than all the Irish who live in Ireland.

[c]Includes French Canadian.

[d]Includes "Scottish-Irish."

[e]Most Latinos trace at least part of their ancestry to Europe.

[f]In descending order, the largest groups of Asian Americans are from China, the Philippines, India, Korea, Vietnam, and Japan. See Figure 9.10 on page 361. Also includes those who identify themselves as Native Hawaiian or Pacific Islander.

[g]Includes Native American, Inuit, and Aleut.

Source: By the author. Based on *Statistical Abstract* 2007:Table 50.

Figure 9.6 The Distribution of Dominant and Minority Groups

This social map indicates how unevenly distributed U.S. minority groups are. The extremes are Hawaii with 77 percent minority and Maine and Vermont with 4 percent minority.

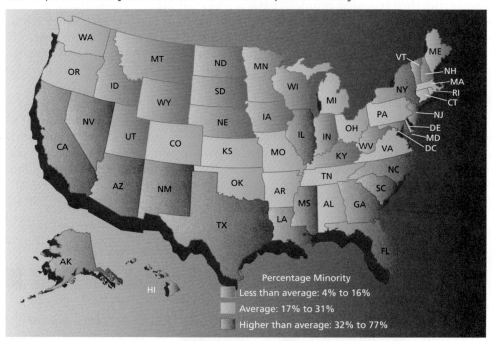

Percentage Minority
- Less than average: 4% to 16%
- Average: 17% to 31%
- Higher than average: 32% to 77%

Source: By the author. Based on *Statistical Abstract* 2007:Table 23.

European Americans

Perhaps the event that best crystallizes the racial view of the nation's founders occurred at the first Continental Congress of the United States. There they passed the Naturalization Act of 1790, declaring that only white immigrants could apply for citizenship. The sense of superiority and privilege of **WASPs** (white Anglo-Saxon Protestants) was not limited to their views of race. They also viewed as inferior white Europeans from countries other than England. They greeted **white ethnics**—immigrants from Europe whose language and other customs differed from theirs—with disdain and negative stereotypes. They especially despised the Irish, viewing them as dirty, lazy drunkards, but they also painted Germans, Poles, Jews, Italians, and others with similarly broad disparaging brush strokes.

To get an idea of how intense these feelings were, consider this statement by Benjamin Franklin regarding immigrants from Germany:

> Why should the Palatine boors be suffered to swarm into our settlements and by herding together establish their language and manners to the exclusion of ours? Why should Pennsylvania, founded by the English, become a colony of aliens, who will shortly be so numerous as to germanize us instead of our anglifying them? (In Alba and Nee 2003:17)

The cultural and political dominance of the WASPs placed pressure on immigrants to assimilate into the mainstream culture. The children of most immigrants embraced the new way of life and quickly came to think of themselves as Americans rather than as Germans, French, Hungarians, and so on. They dropped their distinctive customs, especially their language, often viewing them as symbols of shame. This second generation of immigrants was sandwiched between two worlds: "the old country" of their parents and their new home. Their children, the third generation, had an easier adjustment, for they had fewer customs to discard. As immigrants from other parts of Europe assimilated into this Anglo culture, the meaning of WASP expanded to include people of this descent.

WASP White Anglo-Saxon Protestant; narrowly, an American

white ethnics white immigrants to the United States whose cultures differ from that of WASPs

IN SUM Because Protestant English immigrants settled the colonies, they established the culture—from the dominant language to the dominant religion. Highly ethnocentric, they regarded as inferior the customs of other groups. Because white Europeans took power, they determined the national agenda to which other ethnic groups had to react and conform. Their institutional and cultural dominance still sets the stage for current ethnic relations, a topic that is explored in the Down-to-Earth Sociology box below.

Latinos (Hispanics)

A Note on Terms. Before reviewing major characteristics of Latinos, it is important to stress that *Latino* and *Hispanic* refer not to a race but to ethnic groups. Latinos may identify themselves racially as black, white, or Native American. With changing self-identifications, some Latinos who have an African heritage refer to themselves as Afro-Latinos (Navarro 2003).

Down-to-Earth Sociology

Unpacking the Invisible Knapsack: Exploring Cultural Privilege

OVERT RACISM IN THE United States has dropped sharply, but doors still open and close on the basis of the color of our skin. Whites have a difficult time grasping the idea that good things come their way because they are white. They usually fail to perceive how "whiteness" operates in their own lives.

Peggy McIntosh, of Irish descent, began to wonder why she was so seldom aware of her race-ethnicity, while her African American friends were so conscious of theirs. She realized that people are not highly aware of things that they take for granted—and that "whiteness" is a "taken-for-granted" background assumption of U.S. society. To explore this, she drew up a list of things that she can take for granted because of her "whiteness," what she calls her "invisible knapsack."

What is in this "knapsack"? That is, what taken-for-granted privileges can most white people in U.S. society assume? Because she is white, McIntosh (1988) says:

1. If I don't do well as a leader, I can be sure people won't say that it is because of my race.
2. When I go shopping, store detectives won't follow me.
3. When I watch television or look at the front page of the paper, I see people of my race positively presented.
4. When I study our national heritage, I see people of my color and am taught that they made our country great.

One of the cultural privileges of being white in the United States is less suspicion of wrongdoing.

5. When I cash a check or use a credit card, my skin color does not make the clerk think that I may be financially irresponsible.
6. To protect my children, I do not have to teach them to be aware of racism.
7. I can talk with my mouth full and not have people put this down to my color.
8. I can speak at a public meeting without putting my race on trial.
9. I can achieve at something and not be "a credit to my race."
10. I am never asked to speak for all the people of my race.
11. If a traffic cop pulls me over, I can be sure that it isn't because I'm white.
9. I can be late to a meeting without people thinking I was late because "That's how *they* are."

for your Consideration

Can you think of other "unearned privileges" of everyday life that come to whites because of their skin color? (McIntosh's list contains 46 items.) Why are whites seldom aware that they carry this invisible knapsack?

Numbers, Origins, and Location. When birds still nested in the trees that would be used to build the *Mayflower*, Latinos had already established settlements in Florida and New Mexico (Bretos 1994). Today, Latinos are the largest minority group in the United States. As shown in Figure 9.7, about 28 million people trace their origin to Mexico, 3 to 4 million to Puerto Rico, 1 to 2 million to Cuba, and about 7 million to Central or South America.

Although Latinos are officially tallied at 42 million, another 7 million Latinos are living here illegally, 5 million from Mexico and 2 million from Central and South America (*Statistical Abstract* 2006:Table 7). Most Latinos are legal residents, but each year more than *1 million* Mexicans are apprehended at the border or at points inland and are returned to Mexico (*Statistical Abstract* 2007:Table 518). Several hundred thousand others manage to enter the United States each year. With this vast migration, there are millions more Latinos in the United States than there are Canadians in Canada (33 million). As Figure 9.8 shows, two-thirds live in just four states: California, Texas, Florida, and New York.

The migration of Mexicans across the U.S. border became a major social issue. As public concern grew, it led to an emotionally charged debate in the U.S. Congress. One response was to tighten the border, and, despite protests from the Mexican government, U.S. officials built a wall at various points on the U.S. side of the border. Helping to shape the international debate was the arrival of volunteers, calling themselves Minutemen, organized through the Internet to patrol the border. Their arrival in Arizona spread fear among Mexicans and upset U.S. officials, who worried that there would be bloody clashes between the volunteers and the "coyotes" who were smuggling migrants (Peña 2005; Ramos 2005; Rotstein 2005). The violence didn't happen, and the unwelcome unofficial patrolling of the border continued. So did the migration. Despite walls, patrols, and attempts at political compromises in immigration bills, as long as there is a need for unskilled labor and so many Mexicans live in poverty, this flow of undocumented workers will continue. To gain insight into why, see the Cultural Diversity box on the next page.

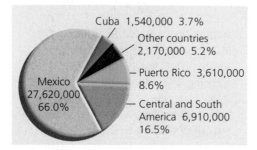

Figure 9.7 **Geographical Origin of U.S. Latinos**

Cuba 1,540,000 3.7%
Other countries 2,170,000 5.2%
Puerto Rico 3,610,000 8.6%
Central and South America 6,910,000 16.5%
Mexico 27,620,000 66.0%

Source: By the author. Based on *Statistical Abstract* 2007:Table 44.

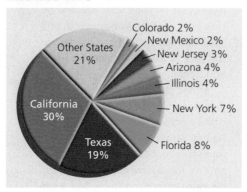

Figure 9.8 **Where U.S. Latinos Live**

Colorado 2%
New Mexico 2%
New Jersey 3%
Arizona 4%
Illinois 4%
New York 7%
Florida 8%
Other States 21%
California 30%
Texas 19%

Source: By the author. Based on *Statistical Abstract* 2007:Table 23.

The illegal migration of Mexicans into the United States has become a major social issue. For political reasons, especially that of relations with Mexico, U.S. officials have hesitated to close the border. The appearance of citizen patrols proved an embarrassment to the official U.S. Border Patrol, as well as a threat to international relations.

Cultural Diversity *in the* United States

The Illegal Travel Guide

MANUEL WAS A DRINKING BUDDY of Jose, a man I had met in Colima, Mexico. At 45, Manuel was friendly, outgoing, and enterprising.

Manuel, who had lived in the United States for seven years, spoke fluent English. Preferring to live in his home town in Colima, where he palled around with his childhood friends, Manuel always seemed to have money and free time.

When Manuel invited me to go on a business trip with him, I accepted. I never could figure out what he did for a living or how he could afford a car, a luxury that none of his friends had. As we traveled from one remote village to another, Manuel would sell used clothing that he had heaped in the back of his older-model Ford station wagon.

At one stop, Manuel took me into a dirt-floored, thatched-roof hut. While chickens ran in and out, Manuel whispered to a slender man who was about 23 years old. The poverty was overwhelming. Juan, as his name turned out to be, had a partial grade school education. He also had a wife, four hungry children under the age of 5, and two pigs—his main food supply. Although eager to work, Juan had no job, for there was simply no work available in this remote village.

As we were drinking a Coke, which seems to be the national beverage of Mexico's poor, Manuel explained to me that he was not only selling clothing—he was also lining up migrants to the United States. For $200 he would take a man to the border and introduce him to a "wolf," who would help him make a night crossing into the promised land.

Mexicans crossing the Rio Grande. Photo taken from the Mexican side of the border, near Nuevo Laredo.

When I saw the hope in Juan's face, I knew nothing would stop him. He was borrowing every cent he could from every friend and relative to scrape the money together. Although he risked losing everything if apprehended and he would be facing unknown risks, Juan would make the trip, for wealth beckoned on the other side. He knew people who had been to the United States and spoke glowingly of its opportunities. Manuel, of course, stoked the fires of hope.

Looking up from the children playing on the dirt floor with the chickens pecking about them, I saw a man who loved his family. In order to make the desperate bid for a better life, he would suffer an enforced absence, as well as the uncertainties of a foreign culture whose language he did not know.

Juan opened his billfold, took something out, and slowly handed it to me. I looked at it curiously. I felt tears as I saw the tenderness with which he handled this piece of paper. It was his passport to the land of opportunity: a Social Security card made out in his name, sent by a friend who had already made the trip and who was waiting for Juan on the other side of the border.

It was then that I realized that the thousands of Manuels scurrying about Mexico and the millions of Juans they were transporting could never be stopped, for only the United States could fulfill their dream of a better life.

for your Consideration

The vast stream of immigrants crossing illegally across the Mexican-U.S. border has become a national issue. What do you think is the best way to deal with this issue? Why?

Spanish Language The Spanish language distinguishes most Latinos from other U.S. ethnic groups. With 31 million people speaking Spanish at home, the United States has become one of the largest Spanish-speaking nations in the world (*Statistical Abstract* 2007:Table 51). Because about half of Latinos are unable to speak English, or can do so only with difficulty, many millions face a major obstacle to getting good jobs.

The growing use of Spanish has become a matter of controversy. Perceiving the prevalence of Spanish as a threat, Senator S. I. Hayakawa of California initiated an "English-only" movement in 1981. The constitutional amendment that he sponsored never got off the ground, but 26 states have passed laws that declare English their official language (Schaefer 2004).

Diversity   For Latinos, country of origin is highly significant. Those from Puerto Rico, for example, feel that they have little in common with people from Mexico, Venezuela, or El Salvador—just as earlier immigrants from Germany, Sweden, and England felt they had little in common with one another. A sign of these divisions is that many refer to themselves in terms of their country of origin, such as puertorriqueños or cubanos, rather than as Latino or Hispanic.

As with other ethnic groups, Latinos are separated by social class. The half-million Cubans who fled Castro's rise to power in 1959, for example, were mostly well-educated, well-to-do professionals or businesspeople. In contrast, the "boat people" who fled later were mostly lower-class refugees, people with whom the earlier arrivals would not have associated in Cuba. The earlier arrivals, who are firmly established in Florida and who control many businesses and financial institutions, distance themselves from the more recent immigrants.

These divisions of national origin and social class are a major obstacle to political unity. One consequence is a severe underrepresentation in politics. Because Latinos make up 14.4 percent of the U.S. population, we might expect 14 or 15 U.S. Senators to be Latino. How many are there? *Two.* In addition, Latinos hold only 5 percent of the seats in the U.S. House of Representatives (*Statistical Abstract* 2007:Table 395).

The potential political power of Latinos, however, is remarkable, and in coming years we will see more of this potential realized. As Latinos have become more visible in U.S. society and more vocal in their demands for equality, they have come face to face with African Americans who fear that Latino gains in employment and at the ballot box will come at their expense (Cose 2006). Together, Latinos and African Americans make up more than one-fourth of the U.S. population. If these two groups were to join together, their unity would produce an unstoppable political force.

When the U.S. government took control of what is now the southwestern United States, Mexicans living there were transformed from the dominant group into a minority group. To try to maintain their culture, *Chicanos,* Americans of Mexican origin, do *ethnic work,* such as this dance by Danza Teocalt at a Cinco de Mayo celebration in Los Angeles. (The Cinco de Mayo—Fifth of May—holiday marks the Mexican army's 1862 defeat of French troops at the city of Puebla.)

Comparative Conditions   To see howLatinos are doing on some major indicators of well-being, look at Table 9.2 on the next page. As you can see, compared with white Americans and Asian Americans, Latinos have less income, higher unemployment, and more poverty. They are also less likely to own their homes. Now look at how closely Latinos rank with African Americans and Native Americans. From this table, you can see how significant country of origin is. People from Cuba score higher on all these indicators of well-being, while those from Puerto Rico score lower.

The significance of country or region of origin is also underscored by Table 9.2. You can see that people from Cuba attain considerably more education than do those who come from other areas. You can also see that two of every five Latinos do not complete high school, and only 12 percent graduate from college. In a postindustrial society that increasingly requires advanced skills, these totals indicate that huge numbers of Latinos will be left behind.

African Americans

After slavery was abolished, the Southern states passed legislation (*Jim Crow* laws) to segregate blacks and whites. In 1896, the U.S. Supreme Court ruled in *Plessy v. Ferguson* that state laws requiring "separate but equal" accommodations for blacks were a reasonable use of state power. Whites used this ruling to strip blacks of the political power they had gained after the Civil War. One way they did this was to prohibit blacks from voting in "white" primaries. It was not until 1944 that the Supreme Court ruled that African Americans could vote in Southern primaries, and not until 1954 that they had the legal

Table 9.1 Race-Ethnicity and Comparative Well-Being[1]

Racial-Ethnic Group	INCOME		UNEMPLOYMENT		POVERTY		HOME OWNERSHIP	
	Median Family Income	Compared to Whites	Percentage Unemployed	Compared to Whites	Percentage Below Poverty Line	Compared to Whites	Percentage Who Own Their Homes	Compared to Whites
Whites	$59,907	—	3.5%	—	7.7%	—	76.3%	—
Latinos	$36,820	39% lower	4.8%	37% higher	21.9%	184% higher	49.4%	35% lower
Country or Area of Origin								
Cuba	NA[2]	NA	2.0%	57% lower	14.5%	88% higher	61.3%	20% lower
Central and South America	NA	NA	NA	NA	17.8%	131% higher	39.2%	49% lower
Mexico	NA	NA	4.2%	20% higher	23.8%	209% higher	51.4%	33% lower
Puerto Rico	NA	NA	4.7%	34% higher	22.9%	197% higher	39.7%	48% lower
African Americans	$34,851	42% lower	7.5%	114% higher	24.5%	218% higher	49.5%	35% lower
Asian Americans[3]	$65,132	9% higher	3.5%	The same	11.7%	52% higher	57.6%	25% lower
Native Americans	$35,981	40% lower	NA	NA	24.6%	219% higher	55.5%	27% lower

[1]Data are from 2004 and 2005.
[2]Not Available
[3]Includes Pacific Islanders

Source: By the author. Based on *Statistical Abstract* 2007:Tables 40, 41, 44, 613, 677.

Table 9.2 Race-Ethnicity and Education

Racial-Ethnic Group	EDUCATION COMPLETED				DOCTORATES		
	Less than High School	High School	Some College	College (BA or Higher)	Number Awarded	Percentage of all U.S. Doctorates[1]	Percentage of U.S. Population
Whites	9.7%	33.4%	28.0%	28.9%	28,214	81.0%	66.3%
Latinos	41.1%	27.3%	19.6%	12.1%	1,662	4.7%	14.4%
Country or Area of Origin							
Cuba	26.5%	30.4%	18.4%	24.7%	NA	NA	
Puerto Rico	27.8%	33.7%	24.7%	13.8%	NA	NA	
Central and South America	37.6%	25.6%	18.3%	18.5%	NA	NA	
Mexico	47.7%	26.6%	17.4%	8.3%	NA	NA	
African Americans	19.4%	36.0%	27.0%	17.6%	2,900	8.1%	12.8%
Asian Americans	15.1%	17.2%	19.3%	48.2%	2,632	7.4%	4.3%
Native Americans	23.3%	31.3%	31.1%	14.1%	217	0.6%	1.0%

[1]Percentage after the doctorates awarded to nonresidents are deducted from the total.

Source: By the author. Based on *Statistical Abstract* 2007:Tables 41, 44, 289 and Figure 9.5 of this text.

right to attend the same public schools as whites (Schaefer 2004). Well into the 1960s, the South was still openly—and legally—practicing segregation.

The Struggle for Civil Rights

It was 1955, in Montgomery, Alabama. As specified by law, whites took the front seats of the bus, and blacks went to the back. As the bus filled up, blacks had to give up their seats to whites.

When Rosa Parks, a 42-year-old African American woman and secretary of the Montgomery NAACP, was told that she would have to stand so that white folks could sit, she refused (Bray 1995). She stubbornly sat there while the bus driver raged and whites felt insulted. Her arrest touched off mass demonstrations, led 50,000 blacks to boycott the city's buses for a year, and thrust an otherwise unknown preacher into a historic role.

Reverend Martin Luther King, Jr., who had majored in sociology at Morehouse College in Atlanta, Georgia, took control. He organized car pools and preached nonviolence. Incensed at this radical organizer and at the stirrings in the normally compliant black community, segregationists also put their beliefs into practice—by bombing the homes of blacks and dynamiting their churches.

Rising Expectations and Civil Strife The barriers came down, but they came down slowly. Not until 1964 did Congress pass the Civil Rights Act, making it illegal to discriminate on the basis of race. African Americans were finally allowed in "white" restaurants, hotels, theaters, and other public places. Then in 1965, Congress passed the Voting Rights Act, banning the fraudulent literacy tests that the Southern states had used to keep African Americans from voting.

Encouraged by these gains, African Americans experienced what sociologists call **rising expectations;** that is, they believed that better conditions would soon follow. The lives of the poor among them, however, changed little, if at all. Frustrations built, finally exploding in Watts in 1965, when people living in that African American ghetto of central Los Angeles took to the streets in the first of what were termed "urban revolts." When King was assassinated by a white supremacist on April 4, 1968, inner cities across the nation erupted in fiery violence. Under threat of the destruction of U.S. cities, Congress passed the sweeping Civil Rights Act of 1968.

Until the 1960s, the South's public facilities were segregated. Some were reserved for whites only, others for blacks only. This *apartheid* was broken by blacks and whites who worked together and risked their lives to bring about a fairer society. Shown here is a 1963 sit-in at a Woolworth's lunch counter in Jackson, Mississippi. Sugar, ketchup, and mustard are being poured over the heads of the demonstrators.

Continued Gains Since then, African Americans have made remarkable gains in politics, education, and jobs. At 10 percent, the number of African Americans in the U.S. House of Representatives is almost *three times* what it was a generation ago (*Statistical Abstract* 1989:Table 423; 2007:Table 395). As college enrollments increased, the middle class expanded, and today half of all African American families make more than $35,000 a year. One in three makes more than $50,000 a year, and one in six earns more than $75,000 (*Statistical Abstract* 2007:Table 675). Contrary to stereotypes, the average African American family is *not* poor.

The extent of African American political prominence was highlighted when Jesse Jackson (another sociology major) competed for the Democratic presidential nomination in 1984 and 1988. Political progress was further confirmed in 1989 when L. Douglas Wilder was elected governor of Virginia and again in 2006 when Deval Patrick became governor of Massachusetts. The most publicized African American political candidate has been Barack Obama, who was elected Senator from Illinois in 2004 and ran for the Democratic nomination for president in 2007.

Current Losses Despite these gains, African Americans continue to lag behind in politics, economics, and education. Only *one* U.S. Senator is African American, but on the basis of the percentage of African Americans in the U.S. population we would expect about 13. As Tables 9.1 and 9.2 on page 284 show, African Americans average only 58 percent of white income, have much more unemployment and poverty, and are less likely to own their home or to have a college education. That half of African American families have incomes over $35,000 is only part of the story. Table 9.3 shows the other part—how much more likely white and Asian American families are to have the higher incomes and that one of every five families makes less than $15,000 a year.

These changes have created two worlds of African American experience—one educated and affluent, the other uneducated and poor. Concentrated among the poor are those with the least hope, the highest despair, and the violence that so often dominates the evening news. Although homicide rates have dropped to their lowest point in 30 years, African Americans are *six* times as likely to be murdered as are whites (*Statistical Abstract* 2007:Table 302). Compared with whites,

Table 9.3 **Race-Ethnicity and Income Extremes**

	Less than $15,000	Over $75,000
Asian Americans	6.3%	53.2%
Whites	6.7%	38.6%
African Americans	21.1%	17.7%
Latinos	15.8%	16.6%

Note: These are family incomes. Only these groups are listed in the source.

Source: By the author: Based on *Statistical Abstract* 2007:Table 675.

African Americans are severely underrepresented in Congress. In 2004, Barack Obama became the first African American man to be elected to the U.S. Senate since the period immediately following the Civil War. This photo was taken of Obama working a crowd in Austin, Texas, after he announced that he was running for president.

African Americans are also *eleven* times more likely to die from AIDS (*Statistical Abstract* 2007:Table 117).

Race or Social Class? A Sociological Debate   This division of African Americans into "haves" and "have-nots" has fueled a sociological controversy. Sociologist William Julius Wilson (1978, 1987, 2000) argues that social class has become more important than race in determining the life chances of African Americans. Before civil rights legislation, he says, the African American experience was dominated by race. Throughout the United States, African Americans were excluded from avenues of economic advancement: good schools and good jobs. When civil rights legislation opened new opportunities, African Americans seized them. Just as legislation began to open doors to African Americans, however, manufacturing jobs dried up, and many blue-collar jobs were moved to the suburbs. As better-educated African Americans obtained middle-class, white-collar jobs and moved out of the inner city, they left behind the African Americans with poor education and few skills.

Sociologists disagree about the relative significance of race and social class in determining social and economic conditions of African Americans. William Julius Wilson, shown here, is an avid proponent of the social class side of this debate.

Wilson stresses the significance of these two worlds of African American experience. The group that is stuck in the inner city lives in poverty, attends poor schools, and faces dead-end jobs or welfare. This group is filled with hopelessness and despair, combined with apathy or hostility. In contrast, those who have moved up the social class ladder live in comfortable homes in secure neighborhoods. They work at jobs that provide decent incomes, and they send their children to good schools. Their middle-class experiences and lifestyle have changed their views on life, and their aspirations and values have little in common with those of African Americans who remain poor. According to Wilson, then, social class—not race—has become the most significant factor in the lives of African Americans.

Some sociologists reply that this analysis overlooks the discrimination that continues to underlie the African American experience. They note that even when African Americans do the same work as whites they average less pay (Willie 1991; Herring 2002). This, they argue, points to racial discrimination, not to social class.

What is the answer to this debate? Wilson would reply that it is not an either-or question. My book is titled *The **Declining** Significance of Race,* he would say, not *The **Absence** of Race.* Certainly racism is still alive, he would add, but today social class is more central to the African American experience than is racial discrimination. He stresses that for the poor in the inner city, we need to provide jobs—for work provides an anchor to a responsible life (Wilson 1996, 2000).

Racism as an Everyday Burden   Today, racism is more subtle than it used to be, but it still walks among us (Feagin and McKinney 2003; Perry 2006). To study discrimination in the job market, researchers sent out 5,000 resumes in response to help wanted ads in the Boston and Chicago Sunday papers (Bertrand and Mullainathan 2002). The resumes were identical, except for the names of the job applicants. Some applicants had white-sounding names, such as Emily and Brandon, while other had black-sounding names, such as Lakisha and Jamal. Although the qualifications of the supposed job applicants were identical, the white-sounding names elicited *50 percent* more callbacks than the black-sounding names. The Down-to-Earth Sociology box on the next page presents another study of subtle racism.

African Americans who occupy higher statuses enjoy greater opportunities, and they also face less discrimination. The discrimination that they encounter, however, is no less painful. Unlike whites of the same social class, they feel discrimination constantly hovering over them. Here is how an African American professor described it:

> [One problem with] being black in America is that you have to spend so much time thinking about stuff that most white people just don't even have to think about. I worry when I get pulled over by a cop. . . . I worry what some white cop is going to think when he walks over to our car, because he's holding on to a gun. And I'm very aware of how many black folks accidentally get shot by cops. I worry when I walk into a store, that someone's going to think I'm in there shoplifting. . . . And I get resentful that I have to think about things that a lot of people, even my very close white friends whose politics are similar to mine, simply don't have to worry about. (Feagin 1999:398)

Down-to-Earth Sociology

Stealth Racism in the Rental Market: What You Reveal by Your Voice

BLATANT DISCRIMINATION HAS BECOME a thing of the past. There was a time when whites could burn crosses with impunity at the homes of blacks. Some whites even lynched African Americans and Asian Americans without fear of the law. Today, cross burning and lynching will make the national news and the perpetrators will be investigated and prosecuted. If local officials don't make an arrest, the FBI will step in. Similarly, discrimination in public accommodations was once standard—and legal. With today's changed laws and the vigilance of groups such as the NAACP, no hotel, restaurant, or gas station would refuse service on the basis of race-ethnicity.

Racism, however, is not a thing of the past. Although overt racism has been relegated to the back shelves of social life, stealth racism is alive and well, as sociologists have demonstrated (Pager 2003; Farley and Squires 2005). At the University of Pennsylvania, for example, Douglas Massey and the students in his undergraduate course in research methods discussed how Americans often identify one another racially by their speech. In Massey's class were whites who spoke what is called White Middle Class English, African Americans who spoke a dialect known as Black English Vernacular, and other African Americans who spoke middle-class English with a black accent.

The discussion stimulated Massey and his students to investigate how voice is used to discriminate in the housing market. They designed standard identities for the class members who spoke these variants of English, assigning them similar incomes, jobs, and education. They also developed a standard script and translated it into Black English Vernacular. The students called on 79 apartments that were advertised for rent in newspapers. The study was done blindly, with the white and black students not knowing how the others were being treated.

What did they find? Compared with whites, African Americans were less likely to get to talk to rental agents, who often used answering machines to screen calls. When they did get through, they were less likely to be told that an apartment was available, more likely to have to pay an application fee, and more likely to be asked about their credit history. Students who posed as lower-class blacks (speakers of Black English Vernacular) had the least access to apartments. Figure 9.9 summarizes the percentages of callers who were told an apartment was available.

As you can see from this figure, although both men and women were discriminated against, the discrimination was worse for the women. Sociologists refer to this as the *double bind* that African American women experience: being discriminated against both because they are African American and because they are women.

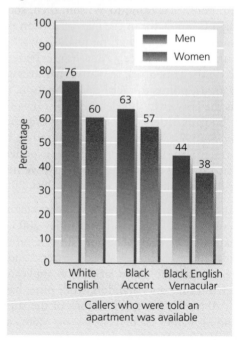

Figure 9.9 Cloaked Discrimination in Apartment Rentals

Callers who were told an apartment was available

Source: Massey and Lundy 2001.

Asian Americans

I have stressed in this chapter that our racial-ethnic categories are based more on social considerations than on biological ones. This point is again obvious when we examine the category Asian American. As Figure 9.10 shows, those who are called Asian Americans came to the United States from many nations. With no unifying culture or "race," why should they ever be clustered together in a single category—except that others perceive them as a unit? Think about it. What culture or race-ethnicity do Samoans and Vietnamese have in common? Or Laotians and Pakistanis? Or Native Hawaiians and Chinese? Or people from India and those from Guam? Yet all these groups—and more—are lumped together and called Asian Americans. Apparently, the U.S. government is not satisfied until it is able to pigeonhole everyone into a racial-ethnic category.

Since *Asian American* is a standard term, however, let's look at the characteristics of the 13 million people who are lumped together and assigned this label.

A Background of Discrimination From their first arrival in the United States, Asian Americans confronted discrimination. Lured by gold strikes in the West and an urgent need for unskilled workers to build the railroads, 200,000 Chinese immigrated between 1850 and 1880. When the famous golden spike was driven at Promontory, Utah, in 1869 to mark the completion of the railroad to the West Coast, white workers prevented Chinese workers from being in the photo—even though Chinese made up 90 percent of Central Pacific Railroad's labor force (Hsu 1971).

After the railroad was complete, the Chinese took other jobs. Feeling threatened by their cheap labor, Anglos formed vigilante groups to intimidate them. They also used the law. California's 1850 Foreign Miner's Act required Chinese (and Latinos) to pay a fee of $20 a month in order to work—when wages were a dollar a day. The California Supreme Court ruled that Chinese could not testify against whites (Carlson and Colburn 1972). In 1882, Congress passed the Chinese Exclusion Act, suspending all Chinese immigration for ten years. Four years later, the Statue of Liberty was dedicated. The tired, the poor, and the huddled masses it was intended to welcome were obviously not Chinese.

When immigrants from Japan arrived, they encountered *spillover bigotry,* a stereotype that lumped Asians together, depicting them as sneaky, lazy, and untrustworthy. After Japan attacked Pearl Harbor in 1941, conditions grew worse for the 110,000 Japanese Americans who called the United States their home. U.S. authorities feared that Japan would invade the United States and that the Japanese Americans would fight on Japan's side. They also feared that Japanese Americans would sabotage military installations on the West Coast. Although no Japanese American had been involved in even a single act of sabotage, on February 19, 1942, President Franklin D. Roosevelt ordered that everyone who was *one-eighth Japanese or more* be confined in detention centers (called "internment camps"). These people were charged with no crime, and they had no trials. Japanese ancestry was sufficient cause for being imprisoned.

Diversity As you can see from Table 9.1 on page 284, the annual income of Asian Americans has outstripped that of whites. This has led to an assumption that all Asian Americans are successful, a stereotype that masks huge differences. With a poverty rate that is actually 50 percent higher than that of whites, between one and two million Asian Americans live in poverty. Like Latinos, country of origin is significant: Poverty is unusual among Chinese and Japanese Americans, but it clusters among Americans from Southeast Asia.

Reasons for Success As you can see from Table 9.1, the average income of Asian Americans is high. This can be traced to three major factors: family life, educational achievement, and assimilation into mainstream culture.

Of all ethnic groups, including whites, Asian American children are the most likely to grow up with two parents and the least likely to be born to a single mother (*Statistical Abstract* 2007:Tables 53, 64). Most grow up in close-knit families that stress self-discipline, thrift, and

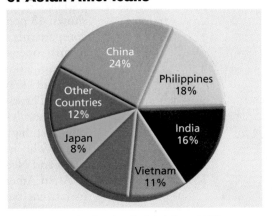

Figure 9.10 **The Country of Origin of Asian Americans**

China 24%
Philippines 18%
Other Countries 12%
India 16%
Japan 8%
Vietnam 11%

Source: By the author. Based on *Statistical Abstract* 2006: Table 24.

Of the racial-ethnic groups in the United States, Asian Americans have the highest rate of intermarriage.

hard work (Suzuki 1985; Bell 1991). This early socialization provides strong impetus for the other two factors.

The second factor is their high rate of college graduation. As Table 9.2 on page 284 shows, 48 percent of Asian Americans complete college. To realize how stunning this is, compare this with the other groups shown on this table. This educational achievement, in turn, opens doors to economic success.

Assimilation, the third factor, is indicated by housing and marriage. Asian Americans are more likely than other racial-ethnic groups to live in integrated neighborhoods (Lee 1998). Those who trace their descent from Japan and China—who are the most successful financially—are also the most assimilated. The intermarriage rate of Japanese Americans is so high that two of every three children born to a Japanese American have one parent who is not of Japanese descent (Schaefer 2004). The Chinese are close behind (Alba and Nee 2003).

Asian Americans are becoming more prominent in politics. With more than half of its citizens being Asian American, Hawaii has elected Asian American governors and sent several Asian American senators to Washington, including the two now serving there (Lee 1998, *Statistical Abstract* 2007:Table 395). The first Asian American governor outside of Hawaii is Gary Locke, who in 1996 was elected governor of Washington, a state in which Asian Americans make up less than 6 percent of the population.

Native Americans

"I don't go so far as to think that the only good Indians are dead Indians, but I believe nine out of ten are—and I shouldn't inquire too closely in the case of the tenth. The most vicious cowboy has more moral principle than the average Indian."

—Teddy Roosevelt, 1886 President of the United States, 1901–1909

Diversity of Groups   This quote from Teddy Roosevelt provides insight into the rampant racism of earlier generations. Yet, even today, thanks to countless grade B Westerns, some Americans view the original inhabitants of what became the United States as wild, uncivilized savages, a single group of people subdivided into separate tribes. The European immigrants to the colonies, however, encountered diverse groups of people with a variety of cultures—from nomadic hunters and gatherers to people who lived in wooden houses in settled agricultural communities. Altogether, they spoke over 700 languages (Schaefer 2004). Each group had its own norms and values—and the usual ethnocentric pride in its own culture. Consider what happened in 1744 when the colonists of Virginia offered college scholarships for "savage lads." The Iroquois replied:

"Several of our young people were formerly brought up at the colleges of Northern Provinces. They were instructed in all your sciences. But when they came back to us, they were bad runners, ignorant of every means of living in the woods, unable to bear either cold or hunger, knew neither how to build a cabin, take a deer, or kill an enemy. . . . They were totally good for nothing."

They added, "If the English gentlemen would send a dozen or two of their children to Onondaga, the great Council would take care of their education, bring them up in really what was the best manner and make men of them." (Nash 1974; in McLemore 1994)

Native Americans, who numbered about 10 million, had no immunity to the diseases the Europeans brought with them. With deaths due to disease—and warfare, a much lesser cause—their population plummeted. The low point came in 1890, when the census reported only 250,000 Native Americans. If the census and the estimate of the original population are accurate, Native Americans had been reduced to about *one-fortieth* their original size. The population has never recovered, but Native Americans now number almost 3 million (see Figure 9.5 on page 278). Native Americans, who today speak 150 different languages, do not think of themselves as a single people who fit neatly within a single label (McLemore 1994).

From Treaties to Genocide and Population Transfer At first, the Native Americans tried to accommodate the strangers, as there was plenty of land for both the few newcomers and themselves. Soon, however, the settlers began to raid Indian villages and pillage their food supplies (Horn 2006). As wave after wave of settlers arrived, Pontiac, an Ottawa chief, saw the future—and didn't like it. He convinced several tribes to unite in an effort to push the Europeans into the sea. He almost succeeded, but failed when the English were reinforced by fresh troops (McLemore 1994).

A pattern of deception evolved. The U.S. government would make treaties to buy some of a tribe's land, with the promise to honor forever the tribe's right to what it had not sold. European immigrants, who continued to pour into the United States, would then disregard these boundaries. The tribes would resist, with death tolls on both sides. The U.S. government would then intervene—not to enforce the treaty, but to force the tribe off its lands. In its relentless drive westward, the U.S. government embarked on a policy of genocide. It assigned the U.S. cavalry the task of "pacification," which translated into slaughtering Native Americans who "stood in the way" of this territorial expansion.

The acts of cruelty perpetrated by the Europeans against Native Americans appear endless, but two are especially notable. The first is the Trail of Tears. In the winter of 1838–1839, the U.S. Army rounded up 15,000 Cherokees and forced them to walk a thousand miles from the Carolinas and Georgia to Oklahoma. Coming from the South, many of the Cherokees wore only light clothing. Conditions were so inhumane that about 4,000 of those who were forced on this midwinter march died before they reached Oklahoma. About 50 years later came the symbolic end to Native American resistance to the European expansion. In 1890, at Wounded Knee, South Dakota, the U.S. cavalry gunned down 300 men, women, and children. After the massacre, the soldiers threw the bodies of the Dakota Sioux into a mass grave (Thornton 1987; Lind 1995; DiSilvestro 2006). These acts took place after the U.S. government had begun a policy called *Indian Removal,* forcefully confining Native Americans to specified areas called *reservations.*

The Native Americans stood in the way of the U.S. government's westward expansion. To seize their lands, the government followed a policy of *genocide,* later replaced by *population transfer.* This depiction of Apache shepherds being attacked by the U.S. Cavalry is by Rufus Zogbaum, a popular U.S. illustrator of the 1880s.

The Invisible Minority and Self-Determination Native Americans can truly be called the invisible minority. Because about half live in rural areas and one-third in just three states—Oklahoma, California, and Arizona—most other Americans are hardly aware of a Native American presence in the United States. The isolation of about half of Native Americans on reservations further reduces their visibility (Schaefer 2004).

The systematic attempts of European Americans to destroy the Native Americans' way of life and their forced resettlement onto reservations continue to have deleterious effects. The rate of suicide of Native Americans is the highest of any racial-ethnic group, and their life expectancy is lower than that of the nation as a whole (Murray et al. 2006; Centers for Disease Control 2007b). Table 9.2 on page 284 shows that their education also lags behind most groups: Only 14 percent graduate from college.

Native Americans are experiencing major changes. In the 1800s, U.S. courts ruled that Native Americans did not own the land on which they had been settled and determined that they had no right to develop its resources. Native Americans were made wards of the state and treated like children by the Bureau of Indian Affairs (Mohawk 1991; Schaefer 2004). Then, in the 1960s, Native Americans won a series of legal victories that gave them control over reservation lands. As a result, many Native American tribes have opened businesses—ranging from industrial parks serving metropolitan areas to fish canneries. The Skywalk, opened by the Hualapai, which offers breathtaking views of the Grand Canyon, gives an idea of the varieties of businesses to come.

It is the casinos, though, that have attracted the most attention. In 1988, the federal government passed a law that allowed Native Americans to operate gambling establishments on reservations. Now over 200 tribes operate casinos. *They bring in about $25 billion a year, twice as much as all the casinos in Las Vegas* (Werner 2007). The Oneida tribe of New York, which has only 1,000 members, runs a casino that nets $232,000 a year for each man, woman, and child (Peterson 2003). This huge amount, however, pales in comparison with that of the Pequot of Connecticut. With only 310 members, they bring in more than $2 million a day (Zielbauer 2000). Incredibly, one tribe has only *one* member: She has her own casino (Barlett and Steele 2002).

A highly controversial issue is *separatism.* Because Native Americans were independent peoples when the Europeans arrived and they never willingly joined the United States, many tribes maintain the right to remain separate from the U.S. government and U.S. society. The chief of the Onondaga tribe in New York, a member of the Iroquois Federation, summarized the issue this way:

> **For the whole history of the Iroquois, we have maintained that we are a separate nation. We have never lost a war. Our government still operates. We have refused the U.S. government's reorganization plans for us. We have kept our language and our traditions, and when we fly to Geneva to UN meetings, we carry Hau de no sau nee passports. We made some treaties that lost some land, but that also confirmed our separate-nation status. That the U.S. denies all this doesn't make it any less the case. (Mander 1992)**

One of the most significant changes is **pan-Indianism.** This emphasis on common elements that run through Native American cultures is an attempt to develop an identity that goes beyond the tribe. Pan-Indianism ("We are all Indians") is a remarkable example of the plasticity of ethnicity. The label "Indian"—originally imposed by whites—is embraced and substituted for individual tribal identities. As sociologist Irwin Deutscher (2002:61) puts it, "The peoples who have accepted the larger definition of who they are, have, in fact, little else in common with each other than the stereotypes of the dominant group which labels them."

Native Americans say that they must be the ones to determine whether they want to establish a common identity and work together as in pan-Indianism or to stress separatism and identify solely with their own tribe; to assimilate into the dominant culture or to remain apart from it; to move to cities or to remain on reservations; or to operate casinos or to engage only in traditional activities. "Such decisions must be ours," say the Native Americans. "We are sovereign, and we will not take orders from the victors of past wars."

Looking Toward the Future

Back in 1903, sociologist W. E. B. Du Bois said, "The problem of the twentieth century is the problem of the color line—the relation of the darker to the lighter races." Incredibly, over a hundred years later, the color line remains one of the most volatile topics facing the nation. From time to time, the color line takes on a different complexion, as with the war on terrorism and the corresponding discrimination directed against people of Middle Eastern descent.

In another hundred years, will yet another sociologist lament that the color of people's skin still affects human relationships? Given our past, it seems that although racial-ethnic walls will diminish, even crumble at some points, the color line is not likely to disappear. Let's close this chapter by looking at two issues we are currently grappling with, immigration and affirmative action.

pan-Indianism a movement that focuses on common elements in the cultures of Native Americans in order to develop a cross-tribal self-identity and to work toward the welfare of all Native Americans

The Immigration Debate

Throughout its history, the United States has both welcomed immigration and feared its consequences. The gates opened wide (numerically, if not in attitude) for waves of immigrants in the 1800s and early 1900s. During the past 20 years, a new wave of immigration has brought close to a million new residents to the United States each year. Today, more immigrants (34 million) live in the United States than at any time in the country's history (*Statistical Abstract* 2007:Tables 5, 45).

In contrast to earlier waves, in which immigrants came almost exclusively from Western Europe, the composition of this current wave is more diverse. In fact, it is changing the U.S. racial-ethnic mix. If current trends in immigration (and birth) persist, in about 50 years the "average" American will trace his or her ancestry to Africa, Asia, South America, the Pacific Islands, the Middle East—almost anywhere but white Europe. This change is discussed in the Cultural Diversity box on the next page.

In some states, the future is arriving much sooner than this. In California, racial-ethnic minorities constitute a large majority. California has 20 million minorities and 16 million whites (*Statistical Abstract* 2007:Table 23). Californians who request new telephone service from Pacific Bell can speak to customer service representatives in Spanish, Korean, Vietnamese, Mandarin, Cantonese—or in English.

As in the past, there is concern that "too many" immigrants will change the character of the United States. "Throughout the history of U.S. immigration," write sociologists Alejandro Portés and Ruben Rumbaut (1990), "a consistent thread has been the fear that the 'alien element' would somehow undermine the institutions of the country and would lead it down the path of disintegration and decay." A hundred years ago, the widespread fear was that the immigrants from southern Europe would bring communism with them. Today, some fear that Spanish-speaking immigrants threaten the primacy of the English language. In addition, the age-old fear that immigrants will take jobs away from native-born Americans remains strong. Finally, minority groups that struggled for political representation fear that newer groups will gain political power at their expense.

Affirmative Action

The role of affirmative action in our multicultural society lies at the center of a national debate about race and ethnic relations. In this policy, initiated by President Kennedy in 1961, goals based on race (and sex) are used in hiring, promotion, and college admission. Sociologist Barbara Reskin (1998) examined the results of affirmative action. She concluded that although it is difficult to separate the results of affirmative action from economic booms and busts and the greater numbers of women in the work force, affirmative action has had a modest impact.

The results may have been modest, but the reactions to this program have been anything but modest. Affirmative action has been at the center of controversy for almost two generations. Liberals, both white and minority, say that this program is the most direct way to level the playing field of economic opportunity. If whites are passed over, this is an unfortunate cost that we must pay if we are to make up for past discrimination. In contrast, conservatives, both white and minority, agree that opportunity should be open to all, but claim that putting race (or sex) ahead of an individual's training and ability to perform a job is reverse discrimination. Because of their race (or sex), qualified people who had nothing to do with past inequity are discriminated against. They add that affirmative action stigmatizes the people who benefit

Cultural Diversity *in the* United States

Glimpsing the Future: The Shifting U.S. Racial-Ethnic Mix

DURING THE NEXT TWENTY-FIVE years, the population of the United States is expected to grow by about 22 percent. To see what the U.S. population will look like at the end of that time, can we simply multiply the current racial-ethnic mix by 22 percent? The answer is a resounding no. As you can see from Figure 9.11, some groups will grow much more than others, giving us a different-looking United States. Some of the changes in the U.S. racial-ethnic mix will be dramatic. In twenty-five years, one of every nineteen Americans is expected to have an Asian background, and one of every four or five a Latino background.

Two basic causes underlie this fundamental shift: immigration and birth rates. Immigration is by far the more important. The racial-ethnic groups have different rates of immigration and birth, and these will change their proportions of the U.S. population. From Figure 9.11, you can see how the proportion of non-Hispanic whites is expected to shrink, that of Native Americans to remain the same, and that of African Americans to increase slightly. With both vast immigration and higher-than-average birth rates, in fifty years almost one of four Americans is expected to be of Latino ancestry.

for your Consideration

This shifting racial-ethnic mix is one of the most significant events occurring in the United States. To better understand its implications, apply the three theoretical perspectives.

Use the *conflict perspective* to identify the groups that are likely to be threatened by this change. Over what resources are struggles likely to develop? What impact do you think this changing mix might have on European Americans? On Latinos? On African Americans? On Asian Americans? On Native Americans? What changes in immigration laws (or their enforcement) can you anticipate?

To apply the *symbolic interactionist perspective*, consider how groups might perceive one another differently as their proportion of the population changes. How do you think that this changed perception will affect people's behavior?

To apply the *functionalist perspective*, try to determine how each racial-ethnic group will benefit from this changing mix. How will other parts of society (such as businesses) benefit? What functions and dysfunctions can you anticipate for politics, economics, education, or religion?

Figure 9.11 Projections of the Racial-Ethnic Makeup of the U.S. Population

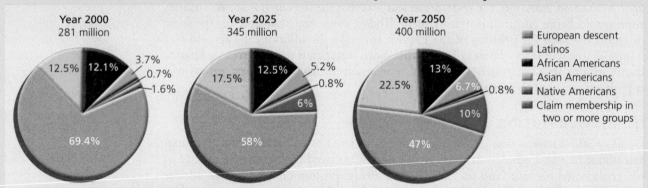

Sources: By the author. Based on Bernstein and Bergman 2003; *Statistical Abstract* 2004:Table 16; 2005:Table 16. The projections I modified are the projections based on the new census category of membership in two or more groups and trends in interethnic marriage.

from it, because it suggests that they hold their jobs because of race (or sex), rather than merit.

This national debate crystallized with a series of controversial rulings. One of the most significant was *Proposition 209*, a 1996 amendment to the California state constitution. This amendment banned preferences to minorities and women in hiring, promotion, and college admissions. Despite appeals by a coalition of civil rights groups, the U.S. Supreme Court upheld this California law.

A second significant ruling was made by the Supreme Court of Michigan in 2003. White students who had been denied admission to the University of Michigan claimed that they had been discriminated against because less qualified applicants had been admitted on the basis of their race. The Court ruled that universities can give minorities an edge in admissions, but there must be a meaningful review of individual applicants. Mechanical systems, such as giving extra points because of race, are unconstitutional. This murky message satisfied no one, as no one knew what it really meant.

To remove ambiguity, opponents of affirmative action in Michigan proposed *Proposition 2,* an amendment to the state constitution that would make it illegal for public institutions to even consider race or sex in college admissions, in hiring, or in awarding contracts. Like the proposal in California, *Proposition 2* became law (Lewin 2007).

With opponents and proponents of affirmative action gearing up for similar battles in other states, this issue of the proper role of affirmative action in a multicultural society is likely to remain center stage for quite some time.

Toward a True Multicultural Society

The United States has the potential to become a society in which racial-ethnic groups not only coexist, but also respect one another—and thrive—as they work together for mutually beneficial goals. In a true multicultural society, the minority groups that make up the United States will participate fully in the nation's social institutions while maintaining their cultural integrity. Reaching this goal will require that we understand that "the biological differences that divide one race from another add up to a drop in the genetic ocean." For a long time, we have given racial categories an importance they never merited. Now we need to figure out how to reduce them to the irrelevance they deserve. In short, we need to make real the abstraction called equality that we profess to believe (Cose 2000).

The United States is the most racially-ethnically diverse society in the world. This can be our central strength, with our many groups working together to build a harmonious society, a stellar example for the world. Or it can be our Achilles heel, with us breaking into feuding groups, a Balkanized society that marks an ill-fitting end to a grand social experiment. Our reality will probably fall somewhere between these extremes.

Summary *and* Review

Laying the Sociological Foundation

How is race both a reality and a myth?

In the sense that different groups inherit distinctive physical traits, race is a reality. There is no agreement regarding what constitutes a particular race, however, or even how many races there are. In the sense of one race being superior to another and of there being pure races, race is a myth. The *idea* of race is powerful, shaping basic relationships among people. Pp. 262–263.

How do race and ethnicity differ?

Race refers to inherited biological characteristics; **ethnicity,** to cultural ones. Members of ethnic groups identify with one another on the basis of common ancestry and cultural heritage. Pp. 262–266.

What are minority and dominant groups?

Minority groups are people who are singled out for unequal treatment by members of the **dominant group,** the group with more power, privilege, and social status. Minorities originate with migration or the expansion of political boundaries. Pp. 266–267.

What heightens ethnic identity, and what is "ethnic work"?

A group's relative size, power, physical characteristics, and amount of discrimination heighten or reduce ethnic identity. **Ethnic work** is the process of constructing an ethnic identity. For people with strong ties to their culture of origin, ethnic work involves enhancing and maintaining group distinctions. For those without a firm ethnic identity, ethnic work is an attempt to recover one's ethnic heritage. P. 267.

Prejudice and Discrimination

Why are people prejudiced?

Prejudice is an attitude, and **discrimination** is an action. Like other attitudes, prejudice is learned in association with others. Prejudice is so extensive that people can show prejudice against groups that don't even exist. Minorities also internalize the dominant norms, and some show prejudice against their own group. Pp. 268–269.

How do individual and institutional discrimination differ?

Individual discrimination is the negative treatment of one person by another, while **institutional discrimination** is negative treatment that is built into social institutions. Institutional discrimination can occur without the awareness of either the perpetrator or the object of discrimination. Discrimination in health care is one example. Pp. 269–270.

Theories of Prejudice

How do psychologists explain prejudice?

Psychological theories of prejudice stress the **authoritarian personality** and frustration displaced toward **scapegoats.** P. 271.

How do sociologists explain prejudice?

Sociological theories focus on how different social environments increase or decrease prejudice. *Functionalists* stress the benefits and costs that come from discrimination. *Conflict theorists* look at how the groups in power exploit racial and ethnic divisions in order to control workers and maintain power. *Symbolic interactionists* stress how labels create **selective perception** and self-fulfilling prophecies. Pp. 271–273.

Global Patterns of Intergroup Relations

What are the major patterns of minority and dominant group relations?

Beginning with the least humane, they are **genocide, population transfer, internal colonialism, segregation, assimilation,** and **multiculturalism (pluralism).** Pp. 273–277.

Race and Ethnic Relations in the United States

What are the major ethnic groups in the United States?

From largest to smallest, the major ethnic groups are European Americans, Latinos, African Americans, Asian Americans, and Native Americans. Pp. 277–278.

What are some issues in racial-ethnic relations and characteristics of minority groups?

Latinos are divided by social class and country of origin. African Americans are increasingly divided into middle and lower classes, with two sharply contrasting worlds of experience. On many measures, Asian Americans are better off than white Americans, but their well-being varies with their country of origin. For Native Americans, the primary issues are poverty, nationhood, and settling treaty obligations. The overarching issue for minorities is overcoming discrimination. Pp. 279–292.

Looking Toward the Future

What main issues dominate U.S. racial-ethnic relations?

The main issues are immigration, affirmative action, and how to develop a true multicultural society. The answers affect our future. Pp. 292–295.

Thinking Critically
about Chapter 9

1. How many races do your friends think there are? Do they think that one race is superior to the others? What do you think their reaction would be to the sociological position that racial categories are primarily social?

2. A hundred years ago, sociologist W. E. B. Du Bois said, "The problem of the twentieth century is the problem of the color line—the relation of the darker to the lighter races." Why do you think that the color line remains one of the most volatile topics facing the nation?

3. If you were appointed head of the U.S. Civil Service Commission, what policies would you propose to reduce racial-ethnic strife in the United States? Be ready to explain the sociological principles that might give your proposals a higher chance of success.

Additional Resources

What can you use MySocLab for?  www.mysoclab.com

- **Study and Review:** Pre-and Post-Tests, Practice Tests, Flash Cards, Individualized Study Plans.

- **Current Events:** *Sociology in the News*, the daily *New York Times*, and more.

- **Research and Writing:** *Research Navigator, Writing About Sociology*, and more.

Where Can I Read More on This Topic?

Suggested readings for this chapter are listed at the back of this book.

Marriage and Family

Michael Escoffery, *Circle of Love,* 1996

"Hold still. We're going to be late," said Sharon as she tried to put shoes on 2-year-old Michael, who kept squirming away.

Finally succeeding with the shoes, Sharon turned to 4-year-old Brittany, who was trying to pull a brush through her hair. "It's stuck, Mom," Brittany said.

"Well, no wonder. Just how did you get gum in your hair? I don't have time for this, Brittany. We've got to leave."

Getting to the van fifteen minutes behind schedule, Sharon strapped the kids in, and then herself. Just as she was about to pull away, she remembered that she had not checked the fridge for messages.

"Just a minute, kids. I'll be right back."

Running into the house, she frantically searched for a note from Tom. She vaguely remembered him mumbling something about being held over at work. She grabbed the Post-It and ran back to the van.

"He's picking on me," complained Brittany when her mother climbed back in.

"Oh, shut up, Brittany. He's only 2. He can't pick on you."

"Yes, he did," Brittany said, crossing her arms defiantly as she kicked her brother's seat.

"Yes, he did," Brittany said, crossing her arms defiantly as she stretched out her foot to kick her brother's seat.

"Oh, no! How did Mikey get that smudge on his face? Did you do that, Brit?"

Brittany crossed her arms again, pushing out her lips in her classic pouting pose.

As Sharon drove to the day care center, she tried to calm herself. "Only two more days of work this week, and then the weekend. Then I can catch up on housework and have a little relaxed time with the kids. And Tom can finally cut the grass and buy the groceries," she thought. "And maybe we'll even have time to make love. Boy, that's been a long time."

At a traffic light, Sharon found time to read Tom's note. "Oh, no. That's what he meant. He has to work Saturday. Well, there go those plans."

What Sharon didn't know was that her boss had also made plans for Sharon's Saturday. And that their emergency Saturday babysitter wouldn't be available. And that Michael was coming down with the flu. And that Brittany would follow next. And that . . .

polygyny a form of marriage in which men have more than one wife

polyandry a form of marriage in which women have more than one husband

family two or more people who consider themselves related by blood, marriage, or adoption

household people who occupy the same housing unit

nuclear family a family consisting of a husband, wife, and child(ren)

extended family a nuclear family plus other relatives, such as grandparents, uncles, and aunts

family of orientation the family in which a person grows up

family of procreation the family formed when a couple's first child is born

"There just isn't enough time to get everything done!" Most of us have this complaint, but it is especially true for working parents of young children. Unlke the past, today's young partents find themselves without the support systems that parents used to take for granted: stay-at-home moms who provided stability to the neighborhood, husbands whose sole income was enough to support a wife and several children, a safe neighborhood where even small children could play outside, and grandmas who could pitch in during emergencies.

Those days are gone, most likely forever. Today, more and more families are like Sharon and Tom's. They are harried, working more but staying in debt, and seeming to have less time for one another. In this chapter, we shall try to understand what is happening to the U.S. family, and to families worldwide.

Marriage and Family in Global Perspective

To better understand U.S. patterns of marriage and family, let's first look at how customs differ around the world. This will give us a context for interpreting our own experience in this vital social institution.

What Is a Family?

"What is a family, anyway?" asked William Sayres at the beginning of an article on this topic. In posing this question, Sayres (1992) meant that although the family is so significant to humanity that it is universal—every human group in the world organizes its members in families—the world's cultures display so much variety that the term *family* is difficult to define. For example, although the Western world regards a family as a husband, wife, and children, other groups have family forms in which men have more than one wife (**polygyny**) or women more than one husband (**polyandry**). How about the obvious? Can we define the family as the approved group into which children are born? Then we would be overlooking the Banaro of New Guinea. In this group, a young woman must give birth *before* she can marry—and she *cannot* marry the father of her child (Murdock 1949).

What if we were to define the family as the unit in which parents are responsible for disciplining children and providing for their material needs? This, too, is not universal. Among the Trobriand Islanders, it is not the parents but the wife's eldest brother who is responsible for providing the children's discipline and their food (Malinowski 1927).

Such remarkable variety means that we have to settle for a broad definition. A **family** consists of people who consider themselves related by blood, marriage, or adoption. A **household,** in contrast, consists of people who occupy the same housing unit—a house, apartment, or other living quarters.

We can classify families as **nuclear** (husband, wife, and children) and **extended** (including people such as grandparents, aunts, uncles, and cousins in addition to the nuclear unit). Sociologists also refer to the **family of orientation** (the family in which an individual grows up) and the **family of procreation** (the family that is formed when a couple have their first child).

What Is Marriage?

We have the same problem here. For just about every element you might regard as essential to marriage, some group has a different custom.

Consider the sex of the bride and groom. Until recently, this was a taken-for-granted assumption. Then in the 1980s and 1990s, several European countries legalized same-sex marriages. In 2003, so did Canada, followed by the state of Massachusetts in 2004.

Often one of the strongest family bonds is that of mother–daughter. The young artist, an eleventh grader, wrote: "This painting expresses the way I feel about my future with my child. I want my child to be happy and I want her to love me the same way I love her. In that way we will have a good relationship so that nobody will be able to take us apart. I wanted this picture to be alive; that is why I used a lot of bright colors."

These, however, were not the first groups to approve marriage between people of the same sex. When Columbus landed in the Americas, some Native American tribes were already practicing same-sex marriage. A man or woman who wanted to be a member of the opposite sex went through a ceremony (*berdache*) that officially *declared* that their sex was changed. The "new" man or woman then wore the clothing of the opposite sex, performed the tasks associated with his or her new sex, and was allowed to marry.

Even sexual relationships don't universally characterize marriage. The Nayar of Malabar never allow a bride and groom to have sex. After a three-day celebration of the marriage, they send the groom packing—and never allow him to see his bride again (La Barre 1954). (In case you're wondering, the groom comes from another tribe. Nayar women are allowed to have sex, but only with approved lovers—who can never be the husband. This system keeps family property intact—along matrilineal lines.)

At least we can be certain that a man and a woman have to be alive to get married. Or so it would seem. Even here, however, we find an exception. On the Loess Plateau in China, if a man dies without a wife, his parents look for a dead woman to be his bride. After finding one—and there are families who sell their dead unmarried daughters—the dead man and woman are married and then buried together. The parents, who feel that having a bride gives their son comfort and support in the afterlife, celebrate the marriage by inviting friends to a reception (Fremson 2006).

With such cultural variety, we can conclude that, regardless of its form, **marriage** is a group's approved mating arrangements—usually marked by a ritual of some sort (the wedding) to indicate the couple's new public status.

marriage a group's approved mating arrangements, usually marked by a ritual of some sort

endogamy the practice of marrying within one's own group

Common Cultural Themes

Despite this diversity, several common themes run through marriage and family. As Table 10.1 illustrates, all societies use marriage and family to establish patterns of mate selection, descent, inheritance, and authority. Let's look at these patterns.

Mate Selection   Each human group establishes norms to govern who marries whom. If a group has norms of **endogamy,** it specifies that its members must marry *within* their group. For example, some groups prohibit interracial marriage. In some societies, these

Table 10.1   Common Cultural Themes: Marriage in Traditional and Industrialized Societies

Characteristic	Traditional Societies	Industrial (and Postindustrial) Societies
What is the structure of marriage?	*Extended* (marriage embeds spouses in a large kinship network of explicit obligations)	*Nuclear* (marriage brings fewer obligations toward the spouse's relatives)
What are the functions of marriage?	Encompassing (see the six functions listed on pp. 464 and 466)	More limited (many functions are fulfilled by other social institutions)
Who holds authority?	*Patriarchal* (authority is held by males)	Although some patriarchal features remain, authority is divided more equally
How many spouses at one time?	Most have one spouse (*monogamy*), while some have several (*polygamy*)	One spouse
Who selects the spouse?	Parents, usually the father, select the spouse	Individuals choose their own spouse
Where does the couple live?	Couples usually reside with the groom's family (*patrilocal residence*), less commonly with the bride's family (*matrilocal residence*)	Couples establish a new home (*neolocal residence*)
How is descent figured?	Usually figured from male ancestors (*patrilineal kinship*), less commonly from female ancestors (*matrilineal kinship*)	Figured from male and female ancestors equally (*bilateral kinship*)
How is inheritance figured?	Rigid system of rules; usually patrilineal, but can be matrilineal	Highly individualistic; usually bilateral

norms are written into law, but in most cases they are informal. In the United States most whites marry whites and most African Americans marry African Americans—not because of any laws but because of informal norms. In contrast, norms of **exogamy** specify that people must marry *outside* their group. The best example of exogamy is the **incest taboo,** which prohibits sex and marriage among designated relatives.

As you can see from Table 10.1, how people find mates varies around the world, from the father selecting them, with no choice by the individuals, to the highly individualistic, personal choices of members of Western cultures. Changes in mate selection are the focus of the Sociology and the New Technology box on the next page.

Descent   How are you related to your father's father or to your mother's mother? The answer to this question is not the same all over the world. Each society has a **system of descent,** the way people trace kinship over generations. We use a **bilineal system,** for we think of ourselves as related to *both* our mother's and our father's sides of the family. "Doesn't everyone?" you might ask. Ours, however, is only one logical way to reckon descent. Some groups use a **patrilineal system,** tracing descent only on the father's side; they don't think of children as being related to their mother's relatives. Others follow a **matrilineal system,** tracing descent only on the mother's side, and not considering children to be related to their father's relatives. The Naxi of China, for example, don't even have a word for father (Hong 1999).

Inheritance   Marriage and family—in whatever form is customary in a society—are also used to compute rights of inheritance. In a bilineal system, property is passed to both males and females, in a patrilineal system only to males, and in a matrilineal system (the rarest form), only to females. No system is natural. Rather, each matches a group's ideas of justice and logic.

Authority   Historically, some form of **patriarchy,** a social system in which men dominate women, has formed a thread that runs through all societies. Contrary to what some think, there are no historical records of a true **matriarchy,** a social system in which women as a group dominate men as a group. Our marriage and family customs, then, developed within a framework of patriarchy. Although U.S. family patterns are becoming more **egalitarian,** or equal, some of today's customs still reflect their patriarchal origin. One of the most obvious examples is U.S. naming patterns. Despite some changes, the typical bride still takes the groom's last name, and children usually receive the father's last name.

Marriage and Family in Theoretical Perspective

As we have seen, human groups around the world have chosen numerous forms of mate selection, ways to trace descent, and ways they view the parent's responsibility. Although these patterns are arbitrary, each group perceives its own forms of marriage and family as natural. Now let's see what picture emerges when we view marriage and family theoretically.

The Functionalist Perspective: Functions and Dysfunctions

Functionalists stress that to survive, a society must fulfill basic functions (that is, meet its basic needs). When functionalists look at marriage and family, they examine how they are related to other parts of society, especially the ways they contribute to the well-being of society.

Why the Family Is Universal   Although the form of marriage and family varies from one group to another, the family is universal. The reason for this, say functionalists, is that the family fulfills six needs that are basic to the survival of every society. These needs, or functions, are (1) economic production, (2) socialization of children,

exogamy the practice of marrying outside one's group

incest taboo the rule that prohibits sex and marriage among designated relatives

system of descent how kinship is traced over the generations

bilineal (system of descent) a system of reckoning descent that counts both the mother's and the father's side

patrilineal (system of descent) a system of reckoning descent that counts only the father's side

matrilineal (system of descent) a system of reckoning descent that counts only the mother's side

patriarchy a society or group in which men dominate women; authority is vested in males

matriarchy a society in which women as a group dominate men as a group

egalitarian authority more or less equally divided between people or groups, in this instance between husband and wife

Finding a Mate: Not the Same as It Used to Be

THINGS HAVEN'T CHANGED ENTIRELY. Boys and girls still get interested in each other at their neighborhood schools, and men and women still meet at college. Friends still serve as matchmakers and introduce friends, hoping they might click. People still meet at churches and bars, at the mall and at work.

But technology is bringing about some fundamental changes.

Among traditional people—Jews, Arabs, and in the villages of China and India—for centuries matchmakers have brought couples together. They carefully match a prospective couple by background—or by the position of the stars, whatever their tradition dictates—arranging marriages to please the families of the bride and groom, and, hopefully, the couple, too.

In China, this process is being changed by technology. Matchmakers use computerized records—age, sex, education, personal interests, and, increasingly significant, education and earnings—to identify compatibility and predict lifelong happiness.

But parents aren't leaving the process up to technology. They want their input, too. In one park in Beijing, hundreds of mothers and fathers gather twice a week to try to find spouses for their adult children. They bring photos of their children and share them with one another, talking up their kids' virtues while evaluating the sales pitch they get from the other parents. Some of the parents even sit on the grass, next to handwritten ads they've written about their children (Ang 2006).

Closer to home, Americans are turning more and more to the Internet. Numerous sites advertise that they offer thousands of potential companions, lovers, or spouses. For a low monthly fee, you, too, can meet the person of your dreams.

The photos are fascinating in their variety. Some seem to be lovely people, attractive and vivacious, and one wonders why they are posting their photos and personal information online. Do they have some secret flaw that they need to do this? Others seem okay, although perhaps, a bit needy. Then there are the pitiful, and one wonders if they will ever find a mate, or even a hookup, for that matter. Some are desperate, begging for someone—anyone—to make contact with them: women who try for sexy poses, exposing too much flesh, suggesting the promise of at least a good time; and men who try their best to look like hulks, their muscular presence promising the same.

The Internet dating sites are not filled with losers, although there are plenty of them. A lot of regular, ordinary people post their profiles, too. And some do so successfully. More and more, Internet postings are losing their stigma, and couples are finding mates via electronic matchmaking.

A frustrating aspect of these sites is that the "thousands of eligible prospects" that they tout are spread over the nation. You might find that a person who piques your interest lives in another part of the country. You can do a search for your area, but there are likely to be few from it.

Not to worry. Technology to the rescue.

The latest is dating on demand. You sit at home, turn on your TV, and search for your partner. Your local cable company has already done all the hard work. They have hosted singles events at bars and malls and helped singles make three-to-five minute tapes talking about themselves and what they are looking for in a mate (Grant 2005).

You can view the videos free—which is often more interesting than watching reruns of old TV shows. But if you get interested, for a small fee—again—you have the opportunity to contact the individuals who have caught your interest.

Now all you need is to get a private detective service—also available by online contact, for another fee—to see if this engaging person is already married, has a dozen kids, has been sued for paternity or child support, or is a child molester or a rapist.

Hmm, maybe the old village matchmaker wasn't such a bad idea, after all.

for your Consideration

What is your opinion of electronic dating sites? Would you consider using an electronic dating site (if you were single and unattached)?

(3) care of the sick and aged, (4) recreation, (5) sexual control, and (6) reproduction. To make certain that these functions are performed, every human group has adopted some form of the family.

Functions of the Incest Taboo   Functionalists note that the incest taboo helps families to avoid *role confusion*. This, in turn, facilitates the socialization of children. For example, if father-daughter incest were allowed, how should a wife treat her daughter—as a daughter, as a subservient second wife, or even as a rival? Should the daughter consider her mother as a mother, as the first wife, or as a rival? Would her father be a father or a lover? And would the wife be the husband's main wife, a secondary wife—or even the "mother of the other wife" (whatever role that might be)? And if the daughter had a child by her father, what relationships would everyone have? Maternal incest would also lead to complications every bit as confusing as these.

The incest taboo also forces people to look outside the family for marriage partners. Anthropologists theorize that *exogamy* was especially functional in tribal societies, for it forged alliances between tribes that otherwise might have killed each other off. Today, exogamy still extends both the bride's and the groom's social networks by adding and building relationships with their spouse's family and friends.

Isolation and Emotional Overload   As you know, functionalists also analyze dysfunctions. One of those dysfunctions comes from the relative isolation of today's nuclear family. Because extended families are enmeshed in large kinship networks, their members can count on many people for material and emotional support. In nuclear families, in contrast, the stresses that come with crises such as the loss of a job—or even the routine pressures of a harried life, as depicted in our opening vignette—are spread among fewer people. This places greater strain on each family member, creating *emotional overload*. In addition, the relative isolation of the nuclear family makes it vulnerable to a "dark side"—incest and various other forms of abuse, matters that we examine later in this chapter.

The Conflict Perspective: Struggles Between Husbands and Wives

Anyone who has been married or who has seen a marriage from the inside knows that—regardless of a couple's best intentions—conflict is a part of marriage. It is inevitable that conflict will arise between two people who live intimately and who share most everything in life—from their goals and checkbooks to their bedroom and children. At some point, their desires and approaches to life clash, sometimes mildly and sometimes quite harshly. Conflict among married people is so common that it is the grist of soap operas, movies, songs, and novels.

Throughout the generations, power has been a major source of conflict between wives and husbands: Husbands have had more power, and wives have resented it. Power differences show up throughout marriage, from disagreements over responsibilities for doing housework and taking care of children to quarrels about spending money and the lack of attention, respect, and sex.

As you know well, divorce is one way that couples try to end marital conflict. Divorce can mark the end of hostilities, or it can merely indicate a changed legal relationship within which the hostilities persist as the couple continues to quarrel about finances and children. We will return to the topic of divorce later in this chapter.

The Symbolic Interactionist Perspective: Gender, Housework, and Child Care

Throughout the generations, housework has been regarded as "women's work," and men have resisted getting involved. Child care, too, has traditionally been considered women's work. As more women began to work for wages, however, men came to feel pressure to do housework and to be more involved in the care of their children. But no man wanted to be labeled a sissy or be accused of being under the control of a woman. That would conflict with his culturally rooted feelings of manhood and the reputation he wanted to maintain in the community, especially around his friends.

As women put in more hours at paid work, men gradually began to do more house-work and to take on more responsibility for the daily care of their children. When men first began to change diapers—at least openly—it was big news. Comedians even told jokes about Mr. Mommy, giving expression to common concerns of what the future would be like if men continued to be feminized.

Ever so slowly, cultural ideas changed. Eventually, doing housework and helping care for children came to be regarded in terms of fairness. No longer was it a sissy thing, but it became the right thing to do for husbands whose wives were in the paid labor force. Husband/fathers who refused to participate in these activities were labeled Neander-thals, and their wives pitied.

Now this is quite a change. This fundamental reorientation does not apply across the board, of course. Not all segments of the population have undergone the same change to the same degree, and we have not reached equality in housework and child care, but this is the general direction of our changing orientations.

One of the best indicators of this change is the research sociologists have done on how husbands and wives divide up housework and child care. If you look at Table 10.2, you can see how husbands have increased the amount of housework they do, and how wives have decreased the amount they do. Look at the changes in child care. Husbands are spending more time taking care of the children, and so are wives. This is fascinating: *Both* husbands and wives are spending more time in child care.

Contrary to popular assumptions, then, children are getting *more* attention from their parents than they used to. This flies in the face of common ideas of the *Leave It to Beaver* and *Ozzie and Harriet* families, part of our mythical past that colors our percep-tion of the present. But if wives are working so many more hours in paid jobs *and* spending more time with their children, just where is the time coming from?

Today's parents have squeezed out more hours for their children by visiting other couples less and by reduc-ing their participation in organizations. But this ac-counts for only a little bit. Look again at Table 10.2, but this time focus on women's hours at housework. You can see how women have cut down the amount of time they spend doing housework. Although husbands are doing more housework than they used to, the combined hours that husbands and wives spend doing housework have dropped from 38.9 to 29.1 hours a week. One explana-tion is that today's parents aren't as fussy as their parents were, leaving today's houses dirtier and messier. Another explanation is that the microwaves, more efficent wash-ing machines and clothes dryers, and wrinkle-free cloth-ing have saved hours of drudgery, leaving home hygiene about the same as before (Bianchi et al. 2006).

With the many changes in how married couples divide up family responsibilities, today's husbands and wives put in about the same number of hours per week at supporting the family. Wives spend more of their time in housework and child care but less in paid work. Hus-bands, in contrast, spend less of their time in housework and child care but more in paid work. Husbands and wives are following what sociologists call a *gendered divi-sion of labor;* that is, husbands remain primarily responsi-ble for earning the income and wives primarily responsi-ble for the house and children. If you follow the changes over time, shown in Figure 10.1 on the next page, you can see something more significant than a growing equality in the time that husbands and wives spend in supporting the family: The trend is for wives to take on

Table 10.2 Husbands and Wives: Who Does What?

	HOURS PER WEEK				
	1965	1975	1985	1995	2000
Housework					
Husbands	4.4	5.6	10.7	10.9	9.7
Wives	34.5	25.2	22.5	21.6	19.4
Child Care					
Husbands	2.6	2.7	3.0	5.0	6.5
Wives	10.6	8.8	9.3	11.0	12.9
Paid Work					
Husbands	47.8	47.2	42.5	39.8	42.5
Wives	6.0	15.2	19.7	24.9	23.8
Other Services to the Family					
Husbands	5.3	3.7	5.2	5.1	5.3
Wives	7.7	5.8	7.9	7.9	8.8
Total Hours					
Husbands	60.1	59.2	61.4	60.8	64.0
Wives	58.8	55.0	59.4	65.4	64.9

Note: Housework includes cooking, cleaning, and laundry, as well as plant and pet care. Husbands/wives refers to married couples who have children and are living together. Other services includes shopping, paying bills, and running errands.

Source: By the author. Based on Bianchi et al. 2006. Housework hours are from Table 5.1, child care from Table 4.1, and total hours from Table 3.4. Other services is derived by subtracting the hours for housework, child care, and paid work from total hours.

romantic love feelings of erotic attraction accompanied by an idealization of the other

Figure 10.1 In Two Paycheck Marriages, How Do Husbands and Wives Divide Up the Responsibilities?

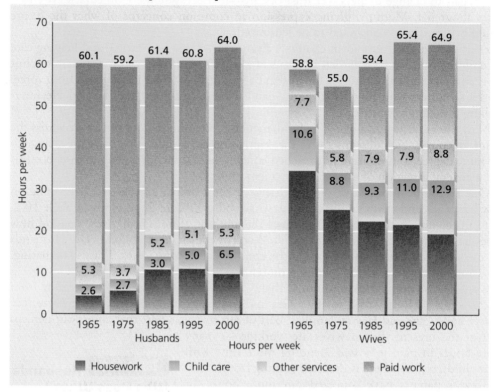

Source: By the author. Based on Bianchi et al. 2006. Housework hours are from Table 5.1, child care from Table 4.1, and work hours and total hours from Table 3.4. Other services is derived by subtracting the hours for housework, child care, and paid work from the total hours.

more of the responsibility for earning the income and for husbands to take on more of the responsibilty for household and child care. This trend is firmly in place, and we can anticipate more changes like this in the future.

The Family Life Cycle

We have seen how the forms of marriage and family vary widely, and we have examined marriage and family theoretically. Now let's discuss love, courtship, and the family life cycle.

Love and Courtship in Global Perspective

Until recently, social scientists thought that romantic love originated in western Europe during the medieval period (Mount 1992). When anthropologists William Jankowiak and Edward Fischer (1992) surveyed the data available on 166 societies around the world, however, they found that this was not so. **Romantic love**—people being sexually attracted to one another and idealizing each other—showed up in 88 percent (147) of these groups. The role of love, however, differs from one society to another. As the Cultural Diversity box on the next page details, for example, Indians don't expect love to occur until *after* marriage.

In Hindu marriages, the roles of husband and wife are firmly established. Neither this woman, whom I photographed in Chittoor, India, nor her husband question whether she should carry the family wash to the village pump. Women here have done this task for millennia. As India industrializes, as happened in the West, who does the wash will be questioned—and may eventually become a source of strain in marriage.

East Is East and West Is West: Love and Arranged Marriage in India

AFTER ARUN BHARAT RAM returned to India with a degree from the University of Michigan, his mother announced that she wanted to find him a wife. Arun would be a good catch anywhere: 27 years old, educated, well mannered, intelligent, handsome—and, not incidentally, heir to a huge fortune.

Arun's mother already had someone in mind. Manju came from a middle-class family and was a college graduate. Arun and Manju met in a coffee shop at a luxury hotel—along with both sets of parents. He found her pretty and quiet. He liked that. She was impressed that he didn't boast about his background.

After four more meetings, including one at which the two young people met by themselves, the parents asked their children whether they were willing to marry. Neither had any major objections.

The Prime Minister of India and fifteen hundred other guests came to the wedding.

"I didn't love him," Manju says. "But when we talked, we had a lot in common." She then adds, "But now I couldn't live without him. I've never thought of another man since I met him."

Although India has undergone extensive social change, Indian sociologists estimate that parents still arrange 90 to 95 percent of marriages. Today, however, as with Arun and Manju, couples have veto power over their parents' selection. Another innovation is that the prospective bride and groom are allowed to talk to each other before the wedding—unheard of just a generation ago.

Why do Indians have arranged marriages? And why does this practice persist today, even among the educated and upper classes? We can also ask why the United States has such an individualistic approach to marriage.

The answers to these questions take us to two sociological principles. First, *a group's marriage practices match its values.* Individual mate selection matches U.S. values of individuality and independence, while arranged marriages match the Indian value of children deferring to parental authority.

To Indians, allowing unrestricted dating would mean entrusting important matters to inexperienced young people.

Second, *a group's marriage practices match its patterns of social stratification.* Arranged marriages in India affirm caste lines by channeling marriage within the same caste. Unchaperoned dating would encourage premarital sex, which, in turn, would break down family lines. Virginity at marriage, in contrast, assures the upper castes that they know the fatherhood of the children. Consequently, Indians socialize their children to think that parents have superior wisdom in these matters. In the United States, where family lines are less important and caste is an alien concept, the practice of young people choosing their own dating partners mirrors the relative openness of our social class system.

These different backgrounds have produced contrasting ideas of love. Americans idealize love as being mysterious, a passion that suddenly seizes an individual. Indians view love as a peaceful feeling that develops when a man and a woman are united in intimacy and share common interests and goals in life. For Americans, love just "happens," while Indians think of love as something that can be created between two people by arranging the right conditions. Marriage is one of those right conditions.

The end result is this startling difference: *For Americans, love produces marriage—while for Indians, marriage produces love.*

This billboard in Chennai, India, caught my attention. As the text indicates, even though India is industrializing, most of its people still follow traditional customs. This billboard is a sign of changing times.

for your Consideration

What advantages do you see to the Indian approach to love and marriage? Do you think that the Indian system could work in the United States? Why or why not? Do you think that love can be created? Or does love suddenly "seize" people? What do you think love is?

Sources: Based on Gupta 1979; Bumiller 1992; Sprecher and Chandak 1992; Dugger 1998; Gautham 2002; Derne 2003; Easley 2003, Berger 2004.

Because love plays such a significant role in Western life—and often is regarded as the *only* proper basis for marriage—social scientists have probed this concept with the tools of the trade: experiments, questionnaires, interviews, and observations. In a fascinating experiment, psychologists Donald Dutton and Arthur Aron discovered that fear can produce romantic love (Rubin 1985). Here's what they did.

> About 230 feet above the Capilano River in North Vancouver, British Columbia, a rickety footbridge sways in the wind. It makes you feel like you might fall into the rocky gorge below. A more solid footbridge crosses only ten feet above the shallow stream.
>
> The experimenters had an attractive woman approach men who were crossing these bridges. She told them she was studying "the effects of exposure to scenic attractions on creative expression." She showed them a picture, and they wrote down their associations. The sexual imagery in their stories showed that the men on the unsteady, frightening bridge were more sexually aroused than were the men on the solid bridge. More of these men also called the young woman afterward—supposedly to get information about the study.

You may have noticed that this research was really about sexual attraction, not love. The point, however, is that romantic love usually begins with sexual attraction. Finding ourselves sexually attracted to someone, we spend time with that person. If we discover mutual interests, we may label our feelings "love." Apparently, then, *romantic love has two components*. The first is emotional, a feeling of sexual attraction. The second is cognitive, a label that we attach to our feelings. If we attach this label, we describe ourselves as being "in love."

Marriage

In the typical case, marriage in the United States is preceded by "love," but, contrary to folklore, whatever love is, it certainly is not blind. That is, love does not hit us willynilly, as if Cupid had shot darts blindly into a crowd. If it did, marital patterns would be unpredictable. An examination of who marries whom, however, reveals that love is socially channeled.

The Social Channels of Love and Marriage   The most highly predictable social channels are age, education, social class, and race-ethnicity. For example, a Latina with a college degree whose parents are both physicians is likely to fall in love with and marry a Latino slightly older than herself who has graduated from college. Similarly, a girl who drops out of high school and whose parents are on welfare is likely to fall in love with and marry a man who comes from a background similar to hers.

Sociologists use the term **homogamy** to refer to the tendency of people who have similar characteristics to marry one another. Homogamy occurs largely as a result of *propinquity,* or spatial nearness. That is, we tend to "fall in love" with and marry people who live near us or whom we meet at school, church, or work. The people with whom we associate are far from a random sample of the population, for social filters produce neighborhoods, schools, and places of worship that follow racial-ethnic and social class lines.

As with all social patterns, there are exceptions. Although 93 percent of Americans who marry choose someone of their same racial-ethnic background, 7 percent do not. Because there are 60 million married couples in the United States, those 7 percent add up, totaling over 4 million couples (*Statistical Abstract* 2007:Table 58).

One of the more dramatic changes in U.S. marriage patterns is a sharp increase in marriages between African Americans and whites. Today it is difficult to realize how norm shattering such marriages are, but in some states they used to be illegal and carry a jail sentence. In Mississippi, the penalty for interracial marriage was life in prison (Crossen 2004b). The last law of this type (called *antimiscegenation* laws) was not repealed until 2000. It had been a part of the Alabama constitution (Lee and Edmonston 2005).

There always have been a few couples who crossed the "color line," but the social upheaval of the 1960s broke this barrier permanently.

Figure 10.2 illustrates this increase. Look at the racial-ethnicity of the husbands and wives in these marriages. You can see that here, too, Cupid's arrows strike far from random. If you look closely, you can see an emerging change. Since 2000, marriages between African American women and white men are increasing faster than those between African American men and white women.

Childbirth

Marital Satisfaction   Sociologists have found that after the birth of a child marital satisfaction usually decreases (Rogers and Amato 2000; Twenge et al. 2003). To understand why, recall from Chapter 5 that a dyad (two persons) provides greater intimacy than a triad (after adding a third person, interaction must be shared). In addition, the birth of a child unbalances the roles that the couple have worked out (Knauth 2000). To move from the abstract to the concrete, think about the implications for marriage of coping with a fragile newborn's 24-hour-a-day needs of being fed, soothed, and diapered—while having less sleep and heavier expenses.

Yet husbands and wives continue to have children, not because they don't know how to avoid conceiving them, but because having their own child brings them so much satisfaction. New parents bubble over with joy, saying things like, "There's no feeling to compare with holding your own child in your arms. Those little hands, those tiny feet, those big eyes, that little nose, that sweet face . . ." and they gush on and on.

This is why there really is no equivalent to parents. It is *their* child, and no one else takes such delight in a baby's first steps, its first word, and so on. Let's turn, then, to child rearing.

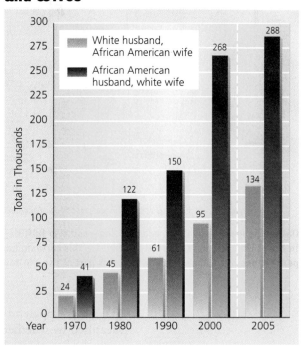

Source: By the author. Based on *Statistical Abstract* 1990:Table 53; 2007:Table 58.

Figure 10.2 | **Marriages Between Whites and African Americans: The Race-Ethnicity of the Husbands and Wives**

No adequate substitute has been found for the family. Although its form and functions vary around the world, the family remains the primary socializer of children.

"Your attitude is sucking all the fulfillment out of motherhood."

One of the most demanding, exasperating—and also fulfilling—roles in life is that of parent. To really appreciate this cartoon, however, perhaps one has to have experienced this part of the life course.

Child Rearing

As you saw in Figure 10.1 and Table 10.2, today's parents—both mothers and fathers—are spending more time with their children than parents did in the 1970s and 1980s. Despite this trend, with mothers and fathers spending so many hours away from home at work, we must ask: Who's minding the kids while the parents are at work?

Married Couples and Single Mothers Figure 10.3 on the next page compares the child care arrangements of married couples and single mothers. As you can see, their overall arrangements are similar. A main difference is the role of the child's father while the mother is at work. For married couples, about one of five children is cared for by the father, while for single mothers, care by the father drops to one of ten. As you can see, grandparents help fill the gap left by the absent father. Single mothers also rely more on organized day care.

Day Care Figure 10.3 also shows that about one of four or five children is in day care. The broad conclusions of research on day care were reported in Chapter 3 (page 84). Apparently only a minority of U.S. day care centers offer high-quality care as measured by whether they provide stimulating learning activities, safety, and emotional warmth (Bergmann 1995; Blau 2000). A primary reason for this dismal situation is the low salaries paid to day care workers, who average only about $15,000 a year (*Statistical Abstract* 2007:Table 561, adjusted for inflation).

It is difficult for parents to judge the quality of day care, since they don't know what takes place when they are not there. If you ever look for day care, however, two factors best predict that children will receive quality care: staff who have taken courses in early childhood development and a low ratio of children per staff member (Blau 2000; Belsky et al. 2007). If you have nagging fears that your children might be neglected or even abused, choose a center that streams live Web cam images on the Internet. While at work, you can "visit" each room of the day care center via cyberspace, and monitor your toddler's activities and care.

Nannies For upper-middle-class parents, nannies have become a popular alternative to day care centers. Parents love the one-on-one care. They also like the convenience of in-home care, which eliminates the need to transport the child to an unfamiliar environment, reduces the chances of their child catching illnesses, and eliminates the hardship of parents having to take time off from work when their child becomes ill. A recurring problem, however, is tensions between the parents and the nanny: jealousy that the nanny might see the first step, hear the first word, or—worse yet—be called "mommy." There are also tensions over different discipline styles; disdain on the part of the nanny that the mother isn't staying home with her child; and feelings of guilt or envy as the child cries when the nanny leaves but not when the mother goes to work.

Social Class Social class makes a huge difference in child rearing. If you thought about it, you probably would guess that people's views on how children develop affect their child-rearing practices. Sociologists have found this to be true—and that the working and middle classes hold different views of how children develop (Lareau 2002). Working-class parents think of children as wild flowers that develop naturally, while middle-class parents think of children as garden flowers that need a lot of nurturing if they are to bloom. Consequently, working-class parents are more likely to set limits on their children and then let them choose their own activities. Middle-class parents, in contrast, are more likely to try to involve their children in leisure activities that they think will develop the children's thinking and social skills.

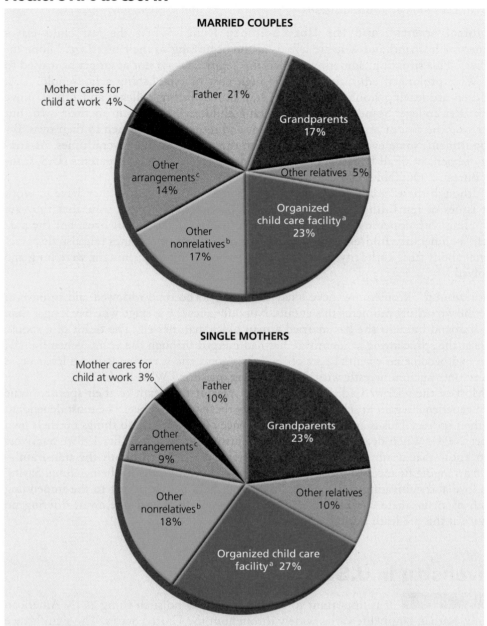

MARRIED COUPLES

Mother cares for child at work 4%

Father 21%

Grandparents 17%

Other relatives 5%

Other arrangements[c] 14%

Organized child care facility[a] 23%

Other nonrelatives[b] 17%

SINGLE MOTHERS

Mother cares for child at work 3%

Father 10%

Grandparents 23%

Other arrangements[c] 9%

Other relatives 10%

Other nonrelatives[b] 18%

Organized child care facility[a] 27%

[a] Includes in-home babysitters and other non-relatives providing care in either the child's or the provider's home.

[b] Includes self-care and no regular arrangements.

[c] Includes daycare center, nursery schools, preschools, and Head Start programs.

*Source: America's Children 2005:*Table POP8.B.

Sociologist Melvin Kohn (1963, 1977; Kohn and Schooler 1969) also found that the type of work that parents do has an impact on how they rear their children. Because members of the working class are closely supervised on their jobs, where they are expected to follow explicit rules, their concern is less with their children's motivation and more with their outward conformity. These parents are more apt to use physical punishment—which brings about outward conformity without regard for internal attitude. Middle-class workers, in contrast, are expected to take more initiative on the job. Consequently, middle-class parents have more concern that their children develop curiosity and self-expression. They are also more likely to withdraw privileges or affection than to use physical punishment.

Family Transitions

The later stages of family life bring their own pleasures to be savored and problems to be solved. Let's look at two transitions.

"Adultolescents" and the Not-So-Empty Nest When the last child leaves home, the husband and wife are left, as at the beginning of their marriage, "alone together." This situation, sometimes called the *empty nest*—is not as empty as it used to be. With prolonged education and the high cost of establishing a household, U.S. children are leaving home later. Many stay home during college, and others move back after college. Some (called "boomerang children") strike out on their own, but then find the cost or responsibility too great and return home. Much to their own disappointment, some even leave and return to the parent's home several times. As a result, 42 percent of all U.S. 25- to 29-year-olds are living with their parents (U.S. Census Bureau 2006:Table A2).

Although these "adultolescents" enjoy the protection of home, they have to work out issues of remaining dependent on their parents at the same time that they are grappling with concerns and fears about establishing independent lives. For the parents, "boomerang children" mean not only a disruption of routines but also disagreements about turf, authority, and responsibilities—items they thought were long ago resolved.

Widowhood Women are more likely than men to become widowed and to have to face the wrenching problems this entails. Not only does the average wife live longer than her husband but also she has married a man older than herself. The death of a spouse tears at the self, clawing at identities that had merged through the years. When the one who had become an essential part of the self is gone, the survivor, as in adolescence, is forced once again to wrestle with the perplexing question "Who am I?"

Most of the widowed adjust well within a year of the death of their spouse. Some even experience a gain in self-esteem, especially those who had been the most dependent on their spouse. This is apparently a consequence of learning to do things on their own (Carr 2004). When death is expected, the adjustment is easier (Hiltz 1989). Survivors who know that death is impending make preparations that smooth the transition—from arranging finances to preparing themselves psychologically for being alone. Saying goodbye and cultivating treasured last memories help people adjust to the impending death of an intimate companion. Sudden death rips the loved one away, offering no chance at this predeath healing process.

Diversity in U.S. Families

It is important to note that there is no such thing as *the* American family. Rather, family life varies widely throughout the United States. The significance of social class, noted earlier, will continue to be evident as we examine diversity in U.S. families.

African American Families

Note that the heading reads African American *families,* not *the* African American family. There is no such thing as *the* African American family any more than there is *the* white family or *the* Latino family. The primary distinction is not between African Americans and other groups, but between social classes (Willie and Reddick 2003). Because African Americans who are members of the upper class follow the class interests reviewed in Chapter 7—preservation of privilege and family fortune—they are especially concerned about the family background of those whom their children marry (Gatewood 1990). To them, marriage is viewed as a merger of family lines. Children of this class marry later than children of other classes.

Middle-class African American families focus on achievement and respectability. Both husband and wife are likely to work outside the home. A central concern is that

There is no such thing as *the* African American family, any more than there is *the* Native American, Asian American, Latino, or Irish American family. Rather, each racial-ethnic group has different types of families, with the primary determinant being social class.

their children go to college, get good jobs, and marry well—that is, marry people like themselves, respectable and hardworking, who want to get ahead in school and pursue a successful career.

African American families in poverty face all the problems that cluster around poverty (Wilson 1987, 1996; Anderson 1990/2006; Venkatesh 2006). Because the men are likely to have few skills and to be unemployed, it is difficult for them to fulfill the cultural roles of husband and father. Consequently, these families are likely to be headed by a woman and to have a high rate of births to single women. Divorce and desertion are also more common than among other classes. Sharing scarce resources and "stretching kinship" are primary survival mechanisms. People who have helped out in hard times are considered brothers, sisters, or cousins to whom one owes obligations as though they were blood relatives; and men who are not the biological fathers of their children are given fatherhood status (Stack 1974; Fischer et al. 2005). Sociologists use the term *fictive kin* to refer to this stretching of kinship.

From Figure 10.4 you can see that, compared with other groups, African American families are the least likely to be headed by married couples and the most likely to be headed by women. Because African American women tend to go farther in school than African American men, they are more

Figure 10.4 **Family Structure: The Percentage of U.S. Families Headed by Men, Women, and Married Couples**

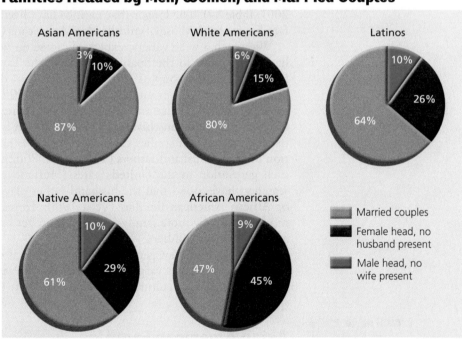

Asian Americans: Married couples 87%, 10%, 3%

White Americans: Married couples 80%, 15%, 6%

Latinos: Married couples 64%, 26%, 10%

Native Americans: Married couples 61%, 29%, 10%

African Americans: Married couples 47%, 45%, 9%

Legend:
- Married couples
- Female head, no husband present
- Male head, no wife present

Sources: By the author. For Native Americans, "American Community . . ." 2004. For other groups, *Statistical Abstract* 2007:Tables 41, 44, 62. Data for Asian Americans are for families with children under 18, while the other groups don't have this limitation. Totals may not equal 100 percent due to rounding.

As with other groups, there is no such thing as *the* Latino family. Some Latino families have assimilated into U.S. culture to such an extent that they no longer speak Spanish. Others maintain Mexican customs, such as this family, which is celebrating *quincianera*, the "coming of age" of girls at age 15 (traditionally, an announcement to the community that a girl is eligible for courtship).

likely than women in other racial-ethnic groups to marry men who are less educated than themselves (South 1991; Eshleman 2000).

Latino Families

As Figure 10.4 on page 313 shows, the proportion of Latino families headed by married couples and women falls in between that of whites and African Americans. The effects of social class on families, which I just sketched, also apply to Latinos. In addition, families differ by country of origin. Families from Mexico, for example, are more likely to be headed by a married couple than are families from Puerto Rico (*Statistical Abstract* 2007:Table 44). The longer that Latinos have lived in the United States, the more their families resemble those of middle-class Americans (Saenz 2004).

With such a wide variety, experts disagree on what is distinctive about Latino families. Some point to the Spanish language, the Roman Catholic religion, and a strong family orientation coupled with a disapproval of divorce. Others add that Latinos emphasize loyalty to the extended family, with an obligation to support the extended family in times of need (Cauce and Domenech-Rodriguez 2002). Descriptions of Latino families used to include **machismo**—an emphasis on male strength, sexual vigor, and dominance—but current studies show that *machismo* now characterizes only a small proportion of Latino husband-fathers (Torres et al. 2002). *Machismo* apparently decreases with each generation in the United States (Hurtado et al. 1992; Wood 2001). Some researchers have found that the husband-father plays a stronger role than in either white or African American families (Vega 1990; Torres et al. 2002). Apparently, the wife-mother is usually more family-centered than her husband, displaying more warmth and affection for her children.

It is difficult to draw generalizations because, as with other racial–ethnic groups, individual Latino families vary considerably (Contreras et al. 2002). Some Latino families, for example, have acculturated so such an extent that they are Protestants who do not speak Spanish.

machismo an emphasis on male strength and dominance

Asian American Families

As you can see from Figure 10.4 on the previous page, Asian American children are more likely than children in any other racial-ethnic group to grow up with both parents.

As with the other groups, family life also reflects social class. In addition, because Asian Americans emigrated from many different countries, their family life reflects those many cultures (Xie and Goyette 2004). As with Latino families, the more recent their immigration, the more closely their family life reflects the patterns in their country of origin (Kibria 1993; Glenn 1994).

Despite such differences, sociologist Bob Suzuki (1985), who studied Chinese American and Japanese American families, identified several distinctive characteristics of Asian American families. Although Asian Americans have adopted the nuclear family structure, they have retained Confucian values that provide a framework for family life: humanism, collectivity, self-discipline, hierarchy, respect for the elderly, moderation, and obligation. Obligation means that each member of a family owes respect to other family members and is responsible never to bring shame on the family. Conversely, a child's success brings honor to the family (Zamiska 2004). To control their children, Asian American parents are more likely to use shame and guilt rather than physical punishment.

The ideal does not always translate into the real, however, and so it is here. The children born to Asian immigrants confront a bewildering world of incompatible expectations—those of the new culture and those of their parents. As a result, they experience more family conflict and mental problems than do children of Asian Americans who are not immigrants (Meyers 2006).

Native American Families

Perhaps the single most significant issue that Native American families face is whether to follow traditional values or to assimilate into the dominant culture (Garrett 1999). This primary distinction creates vast differences among families. The traditionals speak native languages and emphasize distinctive Native American values and beliefs. Those who have assimilated into the broader culture do not.

Figure 10.4 on page 313 depicts the structure of Native American families. You can see how close it is to that of Latinos. In general, Native American parents are permissive with their children and avoid physical punishment. Elders play a much more active role in their children's families than they do in most U.S. families: Elders, especially grandparents, not only provide child care but also teach and discipline children. Like others, Native American families differ by social class.

To search for *the* Native American family would be fruitless. There are rural, urban, single-parent, extended, nuclear, rich, poor, traditional, and assimilated Native American families, to name just a few. Shown here is a Shoshone family in Fort Hall, Idaho.

IN SUM From this brief review, you can see that race-ethnicity signifies little for understanding family life. Rather, social class and culture hold the keys. The more resources a family has, the more it assumes the characteristics of a middle-class nuclear family. Compared with the poor, middle-class families have fewer children and fewer unmarried mothers. They also place greater emphasis on educational achievement and deferred gratification.

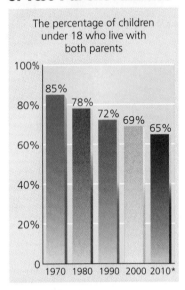

Figure 10.5 The Decline of Two-Parent Families

The percentage of children under 18 who live with both parents

*Author's estimate

Source: By the author. Based on *Statistical Abstract* 1995:Table 79; 2007:Table 62.

One-Parent Families

Another indication of how extensively U.S. families are changing is the increase in one-parent families. From Figure 10.5, you can see that the percentage of U.S. children who live with two parents (not necessarily their biological parents) has dropped sharply. The concerns that are often expressed about one-parent families may have more to do with their poverty than with children being reared by one parent. Because women head most one-parent families, these families tend to be poor. Most divorced women earn less than their former husbands, yet about 85 percent of children of divorce live with their mothers ("Child Support" 1995; Aulette 2002).

To understand the typical one-parent family, then, we need to view it through the lens of poverty, for that is its primary source of strain. The results are serious, not just for these parents and their children but also for society as a whole. Children from one-parent families are more likely to drop out of school, to get arrested, to have emotional problems, and to get divorced (McLanahan and Sandefur 1994; Menaghan et al. 1997; McLanahan and Schwartz 2002; Amato and Cheadle 2005). If female, they are more likely to become sexually active at a younger age and to bear children while still unmarried teenagers.

Families Without Children

While most married women give birth, about one of five (19 percent) do not (DeOilos and Kapinus 2003). The number of childless couples has *doubled* from what it was 20 years ago. As you can see from Figure 10.6, this percentage varies by racial-ethnic group, with whites and Latinas representing the extremes. Some couples are infertile, but most childless couples have made a *choice* to not have children. Why do they make this choice? Some women believe they would be stuck at home—bored, lonely, with dwindling career opportunities. Some couples perceive their marriage as too fragile to withstand the strains that a child would bring (Gerson 1985). A common reason is to attain a sense of freedom—to pursue a career, to be able to change jobs, to travel, and to have less stress (Lunneborg 1999; Letherby 2002).

With trends firmly in place—more education and careers for women, advances in contraception, legal abortion, the high cost of rearing children, and an emphasis on possessing more material things—the proportion of women who never bear children is likely to increase. Consider this statement in a newsletter:

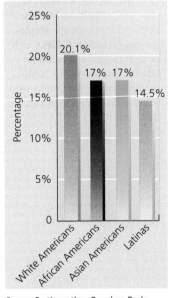

Figure 10.6 What Percentage of U.S. Married Women Never Give Birth?

Percentage

White Americans, African Americans, Asian Americans, Latinas

Source: By the author. Based on Bachu and O'Connell 2000:Table A.

> We are DINKS (Dual Incomes, No Kids). We are happily married. I am 43; my wife is 42. We have been married for almost twenty years. . . . Our investment strategy has a lot to do with our personal philosophy: "You can have kids—or you can have everything else!"

Many childless couples, in contrast, are not childless by choice. Desperately wanting to have children, they keep trying to do so. Coming to the soul-searching conclusion that they can never bear children, the most common solution is adoption. As featured in the Sociology and the New Technology box on the next page, some turn to solutions not available to previous generations.

The Brave New World of High-Tech Reproduction: Where Technology Outpaces Law and Sometimes Common Sense

JAYCEE HAS FIVE PARENTS—or none, depending on how you look at it. The story goes like this. Luanne and John Buzzanca were infertile. Although they spent more than $100,000 on treatments, nothing worked. Then a fertility clinic mixed a man's sperm with a woman's egg. Both the man and the woman remained anonymous. Pamela Snell agreed to be a surrogate mother, and a surgeon implanted the fertilized egg in Pamela, who gave birth to Jaycee (Davis 1998a; Foote 1998).

At Jaycee's birth, Pamela handed Jaycee over to Luanne, who was waiting at her bedside. Luanne's husband, John, decided not to be there. He had filed for divorce just a month before.

Luanne asked John for child support. John refused, and Luanne sued. The judge ruled that John didn't have to pay. He said that because Jaycee had been conceived in a petri dish with an egg and sperm from anonymous donors, John wasn't the baby's father. The judge added that Luanne wasn't the baby's mother either.

Five parents—or none? Welcome to the brave—and very real—new world of high-tech reproduction. Reproductive technologies have laid a trap for the unsuspecting, calling into question even what a mother is. Although Pamela Snell gave birth to Jaycee, she is not a mother. How about the donor of the egg? Biologically, yes, but legally, no. Is Luanne a mother? Fortunately, for Jaycee's sake, a higher court ruled that she is.

What is a father? Consider this case. Elizabeth Higgins of Jacksonville, Indiana, had difficulty conceiving. She gave eggs to Memorial Hospital. Her husband gave sperm. A hospital technician mistakenly mixed someone else's sperm with Mrs. Higgins' eggs. The fertilized eggs were implanted in

Mrs. Higgins, who gave birth to twin girls. Mrs. Higgins is white, her husband black. Mr. Higgins was bothered because the girls had only Caucasian features, and he couldn't bond with them. Mr. and Mrs. Higgins separated. They sued the hospital for child support, arguing that the hospital, not Mr. Higgins, is the father (Davis 1998b).

If a hospital can be a father in this brave new world, then what's a grandparent? A man in New Orleans donated sperm to a fertility clinic. He died, and his girlfriend decided to be artificially inseminated with his sperm. The grieved parents of the man were upset that their son, although dead, could still father children. They also feared that those children, who would be their grandchildren, would have a legal claim to their estate (Davis 1998b).

How would you apply common sense to these situations?

for your Consideration

With artificial insemination becoming more common, many children are aware of their conception and want to meet the other children from the same sperm donor. To help locate their (half) brothers and sisters, they can consult a Web site, the Donor Sibling Registry. If your biological father were a sperm donor, would you want to meet him? How about your biological siblings? Why or why not?

The Goslin family of Pennsylvania: Cara, Madelyn (twins 7), Alexis, Hannah, Aaden, Collin, Leah, and Joel (sextuplets).

Blended Families

blended family a family whose members were once part of other families

The **blended family,** one whose members were once part of other families, is an increasingly significant type of family in the United States. Two divorced people who marry and each bring their children into a new family unit become a blended family. With divorce common, millions of children spend some of their childhood in blended families. One result is more complicated family relationships. Consider this description written by one of my students:

> I live with my dad. I should say that I live with my dad, my brother (whose mother and father are also my mother and father), my half sister (whose father is my dad, but whose mother is my father's last wife), and two stepbrothers and stepsisters (children of my father's current wife). My father's wife (my current stepmother, not to be confused with his second wife who, I guess, is no longer my stepmother) is pregnant, and soon we all will have a new brother or sister. Or will it be a half brother or half sister?
>
> If you can't figure this out, I don't blame you. I have trouble myself. It gets very complicated around Christmas. Should we all stay together? Split up and go to several other homes? Who do we buy gifts for, anyway?

Gay and Lesbian Families

In 1989, Denmark became the first country to legalize marriage between people of the same sex. Since then, several European countries have passed such laws. In 2004, Massachusetts became the first of the U.S. states to legalize same-sex marriages. Walking a fine conceptual tightrope, other states have passed laws that give legal rights to "registered domestic partnerships." This is an attempt to give legal status to same-sex unions and yet sidestep controversy by not calling them marriages.

At this point, most gay and lesbian couples lack both legal marriage and the legal protection of registered "partnerships." Although these couples live throughout the United States, about half are concentrated in just twenty cities. The greatest concentrations are in San Francisco, Los Angeles, Atlanta, New York City, and Washington, D.C. About one-fifth of gay and lesbian couples were previously married to heterosexuals. Twenty-two percent of female couples and 5 percent of male couples have children from their earlier heterosexual marriages (Bianchi and Casper 2000).

What are same-sex relationships like? Like everything else in life, these couples cannot be painted with a single brush stroke. As with opposite-sex couples, social class is significant, and orientations to life differ according to education, occupation, and income. Sociologists Philip Blumstein and Pepper Schwartz (1985) interviewed same-sex couples and found their main struggles to be housework, money, careers, problems with relatives, and sexual adjustment—the same problems that face heterosexual couples. Some also confront discrimination at work, which can add stress to their relationship (Todosijevic et al. 2005). Same-sex couples are more likely to break up, and one argument for legalizing gay marriages is that the marriage contract will make these relationships more stable. If they were surrounded by laws, same-sex marriages would be like opposite-sex marriages—to break them would require negotiating around legal obstacles.

A major issue that has caught the public's attention is whether same-sex couples should have the right of legal marriage. This issue will be decided not by public protest but by legislation and the courts.

Trends in U.S. Families

As is apparent from this discussion, marriage and family life in the United States is undergoing a fundamental shift. Let's examine other indicators of this change.

Postponing Marriage and Childbirth

Figure 10.7 below illustrates one of the most significant changes in U.S. marriages. As you can see, the average age of first-time brides and grooms declined from 1890 to about 1950. In 1890, the typical first-time bride was 22, but by 1950, she had just left her teens. For about twenty years, there was little change. Then in 1970, the average age started to increase sharply. *Today's average first-time bride and groom are older than at any other time in U.S. history.*

Since postponing marriage is today's norm, it may come as a surprise to many readers to learn that *most* U.S. women used to be married by the time they reached age 24. To see this remarkable change, look at Figure 10.8 on the next page. Postponing marriage has become so extensive that the percentage of women of this age who are unmarried is now more than *double* what it was in 1970. Another consequence of postponing marriage is that the average age at which U.S. women have their first child is also the highest in U.S. history (Mathews and Hamilton 2002).

Why have these changes occurred? The primary reason is cohabitation (Michael et al. 2004). Although Americans have postponed the age at which they first marry, they have *not* postponed the age at which they first set up housekeeping with someone of the opposite sex. Let's look at this trend.

Cohabitation

Figure 10.9 on the next page shows the increase in **cohabitation,** adults living together in a sexual relationship without being married. This figure is one of the most remarkable

Figure 10.7 **The Median Age at Which Americans Marry for the First Time**

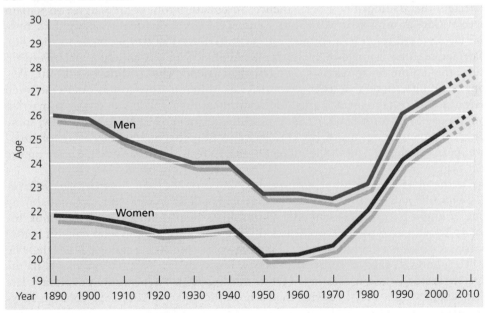

Note: The broken lines indicate the author's estimate.

Source: By the author. Based on *Statistical Abstract* 1999:Table 158 (table dropped in later editions); U.S. Bureau of the Census 2003; Fields 2004.

Figure 10.8 Americans Ages 20–24 Who Have Never Married

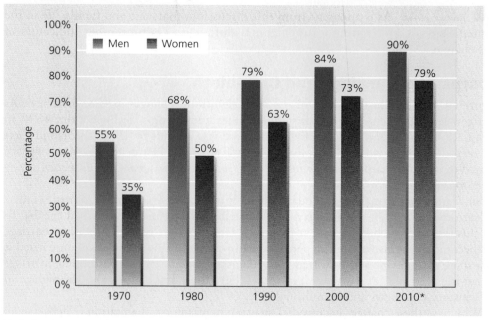

*Author's estimate.

Source: By the author. Based on *Statistical Abstract* 1993:Table 60; 2002:Table 48; 2007:Table 55.

Figure 10.9

Cohabitation in the United States

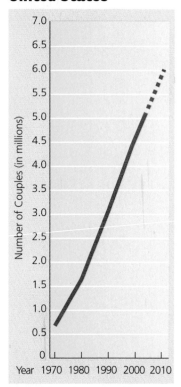

Note: Broken line indicates author's estimate.

Source: By the author. Based on *Statistical Abstract* 1995:Table 60; 2007:Table 61.

in sociology. Hardly ever do we have totals that rise this steeply and consistently. Cohabitation is *almost ten times* more common today than it was 30 years ago. Today, 60 percent of the couples who marry for the first time have lived together before marriage. A generation ago, it was just 8 percent (Bianchi and Casper 2000; Batalova and Cohen 2002). Cohabitation has become so common that about 40 percent of U.S. children will spend some time in a cohabiting family (Scommegna 2002).

Commitment is the essential difference between cohabitation and marriage. In marriage, the assumption is permanence; in cohabitation, couples agree to remain together for "as long as it works out." For marriage, individuals make public vows that legally bind them as a couple; for cohabitation, they simply move in together. Marriage requires a judge to authorize its termination; if a cohabiting relationship sours, the couple separates and they tell their friends that it didn't work out. Perhaps the single statement that pinpoints the difference in commitment between marriage and cohabitation is this: Cohabiting couples are less likely than married couples to have a joint bank account (Brines and Joyner 1999). As you know, some cohabiting couples do marry. But do you know how this is related to what cohabitation means to them? This is the subject of our Down-to-Earth Sociology box on the next page.

Are the marriages of couples who cohabited stronger than the marriages of couples who did not live together before they married? It would seem that cohabiting couples might have worked out a lot of problems prior to marriage. To find out, sociologists compared their divorce rates. It turns out that couples who cohabit before marriage are *more* likely to divorce. This presented another sociological puzzle. The key to solving it, suggest some sociologists, is the greater ease of ending a cohabiting relationship than a marriage (Dush et al. 2003). As a result, people are less picky about whom they live with than whom they marry. After they cohabit, however, they experience a push toward marriage—from having common possessions, pets, and children to pressures from friends and family. Many end up marrying a partner that they would not otherwise have chosen.

"You Want Us to Live Together? What Do You Mean By That?"

WHAT HAS LED TO the surge of cohabitation in the United States? Let's consider two fundamental changes in U.S. culture.

The first is changed ideas of sexual morality. It is difficult for today's college students to grasp the sexual morality that prevailed before the 1960s sexual revolution. Almost everyone used to consider sex before marriage to be immoral. Premarital sex existed, to be sure, but it took place furtively and often with guilt. To live together before marriage was called "shacking up," and the couple was said to be "living in sin." A double standard prevailed. It was the woman's responsibility to say no to sex before marriage. Consequently, she was considered to be the especially sinful one in cohabitation.

The second cultural change is the high U.S. divorce rate. Although the rate has declined since 1980, today's young adults have seen more divorce than any prior generation. This makes marriage seem fragile, as if it is something that is not likely to last regardless of how much you devote yourself to it. This is scary. Cohabitation reduces the threat by offering a relationship of intimacy in which divorce is impossible. You can break up, but you can't get divorced.

From the outside, all cohabitation may look the same, but not to the people who are living together. As you can see from Table 10.3, for about 10 percent of couples, cohabitation is a substitute for marriage. These couples consider themselves married but for some reason don't want a marriage certificate. Some object to marriage on philosophical grounds ("What difference does a piece of paper make?"); others do not yet have a legal divorce from a spouse. Almost half of cohabitants (46 percent) view cohabitation as a step on the path to marriage. For them, cohabitation is more than "going steady" but less than engagement. Another 15 percent of couples are simply "giving it a try." They want to see what marriage to one another might be like. For the least committed, about 29 percent, cohabitation is a form of dating. It provides a dependable source of sex and emotional support.

Do these distinctions make a difference in whether couples marry? Let's look at these couples a half dozen years after they began to live together. As you can see from Table 10.3, couples who view cohabitation as a substitute for marriage are the least likely to marry and the most likely to continue to cohabit. For couples who see cohabitation as a step toward marriage, the outcome is just the opposite: They are the most likely to marry and the least likely to still be cohabiting. Couples who are the most likely to break up are those who "tried" cohabitation and those for whom cohabitation was a form of dating.

for your Consideration

Can you explain why the meaning of cohabitation makes a difference in whether couples marry? Can you classify cohabiting couples you know into these four types? Do you think there are other types? If so, what would they be?

Table 10.3	Commitment in Cohabitation: Does It Make a Difference?				
				After 5 to 7 years	
				Of those still together	
Level of Commitment	Percent of Couples	Split Up	Still Together	Married	Cohabitating
Substitute for Marriage	10%	35%	65%	37%	63%
Step toward Marriage	46%	31%	69%	73%	27%
Trial Marriage	15%	51%	49%	66%	34%
Coresidential Dating	29%	46%	54%	61%	39%

Source: Recomputed from Bianchi and Casper 2000.

Unmarried Mothers

Births to single women in the United States have increased steadily during the past decades, going from 10 percent in 1970 to 36 percent today (*Statistical Abstract* 1995:Table 94; 2007:Table 84). Let's place these births in global perspective. As Figure 10.10 shows, the

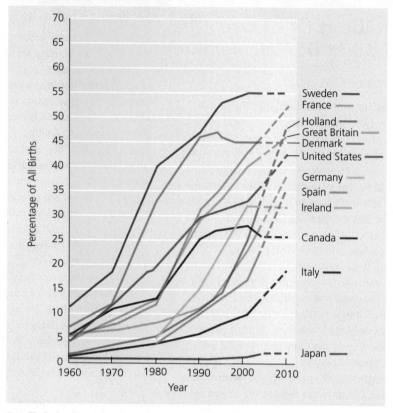

Figure 10.10 **Births to Unmarried Women in Ten Industrialized Nations**

Sweden
France
Holland
Great Britain
Denmark
United States
Germany
Spain
Ireland
Canada
Italy
Japan

Percentage of All Births

Year

Note: The broken lines indicate the author's estimates.

Source: By the author. Based on *Statistical Abstract* 1993:Table 1380; 2001:Table 1331; 2007:Table 1311.

United States is not alone in its increase. Of the twelve nations for which we have data, all except Japan have experienced sharp increases in births to unmarried mothers. As you can see, the U.S. rate falls higher than average but not at the extreme.

From this figure, it would seem fair to conclude that industrialization sets in motion social forces that encourage out-of-wedlock births. There are several problems with this conclusion, however. Why was the rate so much lower in 1960? Industrialization had been in process for many decades before that time. Why are the rates of Japan and Italy so much lower than the other nations? Why does Japan's rate remain low? Why is Sweden's rate so high? Why have the rates of some nations leveled off—and all at about the same time? Industrialization is too simple an answer. A fuller explanation must focus on customs and values embedded within these cultures. For those answers, we will have to await further research.

Grandparents as Parents

It is becoming more common for grandparents to rear their grandchildren. About 4 percent of white children, 7 percent of Latino children, and 14 percent of African American children are being reared by their grandparents (Waldrop and Weber 2001). The main reason for these *skipped-generation families* is that the parents are incapable of caring for their children (Goldberg-Glen et al. 1998). Some of the parents have died, but the most common reasons are that the parents are ill, homeless, addicted to drugs, or in prison. In other instances, the grandparents stepped in when the parents neglected or abused their children.

Caring for grandchildren can bring great satisfaction. The grandparents know that their grandchildren are in loving hands, they build strong emotional bonds with them, and they are able to transmit their family values. But taking over as parents also brings stress: the unexpected responsibilities of parenthood, the squeezed finances, the need to continue working when they were anticipating retirement, and conflict with the parents of the children (Waldrop and Weber 2001). This added wear and tear takes its toll, and these grandmothers are 55 percent more likely to have heart disease (Lee et al. 2003). (We don't have these data for the grandfathers.)

The "Sandwich Generation" and Elder Care

The *"sandwich generation"* refers to people who find themselves sandwiched between two generations, responsible for both their children and their own aging parents. Typically between the ages of 40 and 55, these people find themselves pulled in two compelling directions. Overwhelmed by two sets of competing responsibilities, they are plagued with guilt and anger because they can be only in one place at a time and have little time to pursue personal interests.

Concerns about elder care have gained the attention of the corporate world, and half of the 1,000 largest U.S. companies offer elder care assistance to their employees (Hewitt Associates 2004). This assistance includes seminars, referral services, and flexible work schedules to help employees meet their responsibilities without missing so much work. Why are companies responding more positively to the issue of elder care than to child care? Most CEOs are older men whose wives stayed home to take care of their children, so they don't understand the stresses of balancing work and child care. In contrast, nearly all have aging parents, and many have faced the turmoil of trying to cope with both their parents' needs and those of work and their own family.

With people living longer, this issue is likely to become increasingly urgent.

Divorce and Remarriage

The topic of family life would not be complete without considering divorce. Let's first try to determine how much divorce there really is.

Problems in Measuring Divorce

You probably have heard that the U.S. divorce rate is 50 percent, a figure that is popular with reporters. The statistic is true in the sense that each year about half as many divorces are granted as there are marriages performed. The totals are 2.2 million marriages and about 1.1 million divorces (*Statistical Abstract* 2007:Tables 17, 76, 119).

What is wrong, then, with saying that the divorce rate is about 50 percent? Think about it for a moment. Why should we compare the number of divorces and marriages that take place during the same year? The couples who divorced do not—with rare exceptions—come from the group that married that year. The one number has *nothing* to do with the other, so these statistics in no way establish the divorce rate.

What figures should we compare, then? Couples who divorce are drawn from the entire group of married people in the country. Since the United States has 60,000,000 married couples, and only about 1 million of them obtain divorces in a year, the divorce rate for any given year is less than 2 percent. A couple's chances of still being married at the end of a year are over 98 percent—not bad odds—and certainly much better odds than the mass media would have us believe. As the Social Map on the next page shows, the "odds"—if we want to call them that—depend on where you live.

Over time, of course, each year's small percentage adds up. A third way of measuring divorce, then, is to ask, "Of all U.S. adults, what percentage are divorced?" Figure 10.12 on the next page answers this question. You can see how divorce has increased

Figure 10.11 The "Where" of U.S. Divorce

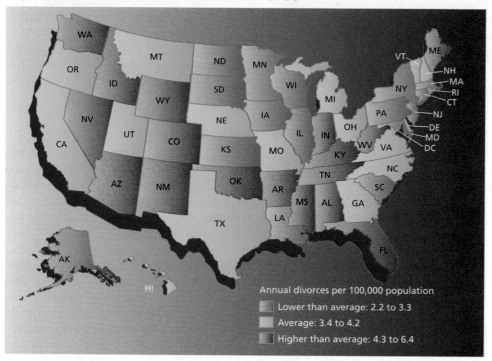

Annual divorces per 100,000 population

Lower than average: 2.2 to 3.3
Average: 3.4 to 4.2
Higher than average: 4.3 to 6.4

Note: Data for California, Georgia, Hawaii, Indiana, and Louisiana, based on the earlier editions in the source, have been decreased by the average decrease in U.S. divorce.

Source: By the author. Based on *Statistical Abstract* 1995:Table 149; 2002:Table 111; 2007:Table 119.

over the years and how race-ethnicity makes a difference for the likelihood that couples will divorce. If you look closely, you can also see that the rate of divorce has slowed down.

Figure 10.12 shows us the percentage of Americans who are currently divorced, but we get yet another answer if we ask the question, "What percentage of Americans have *ever* been divorced?" This percentage increases with each age group, peaking when people reach their 50s. Forty percent of women in their 50s have been divorced at some point in their lives; for men, the total is 43 percent ("Marital History . . ." 2004).

Figure 10.12 What Percentage of Americans Are Divorced?

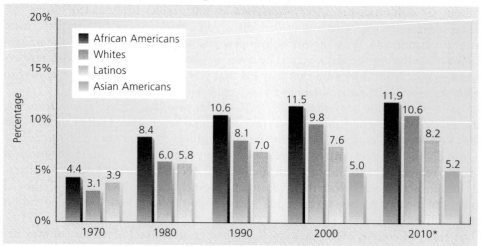

Note: This figure shows the percentage who are divorced and have not remarried, not the percentage who have *ever* divorced. Only these racial-ethnic groups are listed in the source. The source only recently added data on Asian Americans. *Author's estimate

Source: By the author. Based on *Statistical Abstract* 1995:Table 58; 2007:Table 54.

What most of us want to know is what *our* chances of divorce are. It is one thing to know that a certain percentage of Americans are divorced, but have sociologists found out anything that will tell me about *my* chances of divorce? This is the topic of the Down-to-Earth Sociology box below.

Children of Divorce

Each year, more than 1 million U.S. children learn that their parents are divorcing. Numbers like this are cold. They don't tell us what divorce feels like, what the children experience. In the Down-to-Earth Sociology box on the next page, we try to catch a glimpse of this.

Down-to-Earth Sociology

"What Are Your Chances of Getting Divorced?"

IT IS PROBABLY TRUE that over a lifetime about half of all marriages fail (Whitehead and Popenoe 2004). If you have that 50 percent figure dancing in your head, you might as well make sure that you have an escape door open even while you're saying "I do."

Not every group carries the same risk of divorce. Some have a much higher risk, and some much lower. Let's look at some factors that reduce people's risk. As Table 10.4 shows, sociologists have worked out percentages that you might find useful (Whitehead and Popenoe 2004).

As you can see, people who go to college, participate in a religion, wait to get married before having children and earn more, have a much better chance that their marriage will last. You can also see that having parents who did not divorce is significant. If you reverse these factors, you will see how the likelihood of divorce increases for people who have a baby before they marry, who marry in their teens, and so on. It is important to note, however, that these factors reduce the risk of divorce for groups of people, not for any certain individual.

Here are two other factors that increase the risk for divorce (Aberg 2003). For these, sociologists have not computed percentages. Having co-workers who are of the opposite sex (I'm sure you can figure out why) and working with people who are recently divorced increase the risk of divorce. Apparently, divorce is "contagious," following a pattern like measles. Perhaps being around divorced people makes divorce more acceptable. This would increase the likelihood that married people will act on their inevitable dissatisfactions and attractions. Or it could be that divorced people are more likely to "hit" on their fellow workers—and human nature being what it is . . .

for your Consideration

Why do you think that people who go to college have a lower risk of divorce? How would you explain the other factors shown in Table 10.4? What other factors discussed in this chapter indicate a greater or lesser risk of divorce?

Why can't you figure your own chances of divorce by starting with some percentage (say 30 percent likelihood of divorce for the first 10 years of marriage) and then reducing it according to this table (subtracting 13 percent of the 30 percent for going to college, and so on)? To better understand this, you might want to read the section on the misuse of statistics on page 332.

Table 10.4 What Reduces the Risk of Divorce?	
Factors that Reduce People's Chances of Divorce	**How Much Does This Decrease the Risk of Divorce?**
Some college (vs. high-school dropout)	−13%
Affiliated with a religion (vs. none)	−14%
Parents not divorced	−14%
Age 25 or over at marriage (vs. under 18)	−24%
Having a baby 7 months or longer after marriage (vs. before marriage)	−24%
Annual income over $50,000 (vs. under $25,000)	−30%

Note: These percentages apply to the first ten years of marriage.

Caught Between Two Worlds: The Children of Divorce

THE STATISTICS CAN TELL you how many couples divorce, how many children these couples have, and other interesting information. But the numbers can't tell what divorce is like—how children feel that their world is falling apart when they learn their parents are going to get a divorce. Or how torn apart they feel when they shuffle from one house to another.

Elizabeth Marquardt, a child of divorce herself, did a national study of children of divorce. In her book, *Between Two Worlds* (2005), she skillfully weaves her own experiences with those of the people she interviewed, taking us into the thought world of children who are being pulled apart by their parents.

It's the many little things that the statistics don't touch. The children feel like they are growing up in two families, not one. This creates painful complications that make the children feel like insiders *and* outsiders in their parents' worlds. They are outsiders when they look or act like one of the parents. This used to be a mark of an insider, a part of the family to which the child and the two parents belonged. But now it reminds one parent of their former spouse, the one they want to forget. And those children who end up with different last names than one of their parents—what a dramatic symbol of *outsider* that is. And when children learn something about one parent that they can't tell the other parent—which happens often—how uncomfortable they feel at being unable to share this information. Outsider-insider again.

What information do you share, anyway—or what do you *not* dare to share—as you travel from one world to the other? What do you say when dad asks if mom has a boyfriend? Is this supposed to be a secret? Will dad get mad if you tell him? Will he feel hurt? You don't want him to get angry or to feel hurt. Yet you don't want to keep secrets. And will mom get mad if you tell dad? It's all so complicated for a kid.

Marquardt says that as a child of divorce she tried to keep her two worlds apart, but they sometimes collided forcefully. At her mom's house, she could say that things were "screwed up." But if she used "screwed up" at her dad's house, he would correct her, saying, "*Messed up.*" He meant the best for her, teaching her better language, but this left her feeling silly and ashamed. Things like this, little to most people, are significant to kids who feel pinched between their parents' differing values, beliefs, and ways of living.

To shuttle between two homes is to enter and leave different worlds—feeling things in common with each, but also sensing differences from each. And then come the strangely evolving relationships—their parent's girlfriends or boyfriends. Eventually, come the new blended families, which may not blend so easily, those that bring the new stepmom or stepdad, and perhaps their children. And then there are the new break-ups, with a recurring cycle of supposedly permanent relationships. What a complicated world for a child to traverse.

Marquardt pinpoints the dilemma for the child of divorce when she says: Being with one parent always means *not* being with the other.

for your Consideration

If you are a child of divorce, did you have two worlds of experience? Were your experiences like those mentioned here? If you lived with both parents, how do you think your life has been different because your parents didn't divorce?

Children whose parents divorce are more likely than children reared by both parents to experience emotional problems, both during childhood and after they grow up (Amato and Sobolewski 2001; Weitoft et al. 2003). They are also more likely to become juvenile delinquents (Wallerstein et al. 2001), and less likely to complete high school, to attend college, and to graduate from college (McLanahan and Schwartz 2002). Finally, the children of divorce are themselves more likely to divorce (Wolfinger 2003), perpetuating a marriage-divorce cycle.

Is the greater maladjustment of the children of divorce a serious problem? This question initiated a lively debate between two researchers, both psychologists. Judith Wallerstein claims that divorce scars children, making them depressed and leaving them with insecurities that follow them into adulthood (Wallerstein et al. 2001). Mavis Hetherington

It is difficult to capture the anguish of the children of divorce, but when I read
these lines by the fourth-grader who drew these two pictures, my heart was touched:

Me alone in the park . . .
All alone in the park.
My Dad and Mom are divorced
that's why I'm all alone.

This is me in the picture with my son.
We are taking a walk in the park.
I will never be like my father.
I will never divorce my wife and kid.

replies that 75 to 80 percent of children of divorce function as well as children who are reared by both of their parents (Hetherington and Kelly 2003).

Without meaning to weigh in on either side of this debate, it doesn't seem to be a simple case of the glass being half empty or half full. If 75 to 80 percent of children of divorce don't suffer long-term harm, this leaves one-fourth to one-fifth who do. Any way you look at it, one-fourth or one-fifth of a million children each year is a lot of kids who are having a lot of problems.

What helps children adjust to divorce? Children of divorce who feel close to both parents make the best adjustment, and those who don't feel close to either parent make the worst adjustment (Richardson and McCabe 2001). Other studies show that children adjust well if they experience little conflict, feel loved, live with a parent who is making a good adjustment, and have consistent routines. It also helps if their family has adequate money to meet its needs. Children also adjust better if a second adult can be counted on for support (Hayashi and Strickland 1998). Urie Bronfenbrenner (1992) says this person is like the third leg of a stool, giving stability to the smaller family unit. Any adult can be the third leg, he says—a relative, friend, or even a former mother-in-law—but the most powerful stabilizing third leg is the father, the ex-husband.

As mentioned, when the children of divorce grow up and marry, they are more likely to divorce than are adults who grew up in intact families. Have researchers found any factors that increase the chances that the children of divorce will have successful marriages? Actually, they have. They are more likely to have a lasting marriage if they marry someone whose parents did not divorce. In these marriages, the level of trust is higher and the amount of conflict is less. If both husband and wife come from broken families, however, it is not good news. Those marriages are likely to be marked by high distrust and conflict, leading to a higher chance of divorce (Wolfinger 2003).

Grandchildren of Divorce

Paul Amato and Jacob Cheadle (2005), the first sociologists to study the grandchildren of divorced parents, found that the effects of divorce continue across generations. Using a national sample, they compared children whose grandparents divorced with those whose grandparents did not divorce. Their findings are astounding. The grandchildren of divorce have weaker ties to their parents, they don't go as far in school, and they don't get along as well with their spouses. As these researchers put it, when parents divorce, the consequences ripple through the lives of children who are not yet born.

The Absent Father and Serial Fatherhood

serial fatherhood a pattern of parenting in which a father, after divorce, reduces contact with his own children, acts as a father to the children of the woman he marries or lives with, then ignores these children, too, after moving in with or marrying another woman

With divorce common and mothers usually granted custody of the children, a new fathering pattern has emerged. In this pattern, known as **serial fatherhood,** a divorced father maintains high contact with his children during the first year or two after the divorce. As the man develops a relationship with another woman, he begins to play a fathering role with the woman's children and reduces contact with his own children. With another breakup, this pattern may repeat. Only about one-sixth of children who live apart from their fathers see their dad as often as every week. Actually, *most* divorced fathers stop seeing their children altogether (Ahlburg and De Vita 1992; Furstenberg and Harris 1992; Seltzer 1994). Apparently, for many men, fatherhood has become a short-term commitment.

The Ex-Spouses

Anger, depression, and anxiety are common feelings at divorce. But so is relief. Women are more likely than men to feel that divorce is giving them a "new chance" in life. A few couples manage to remain friends through it all—but they are the exception. The spouse who initiates the divorce usually gets over it sooner (Kelly 1992; Wang and Amato 2000). This spouse also usually remarries sooner (Sweeney 2002).

Divorce does not necessarily mean the end of a couple's relationship. Many divorced couples maintain contact because of their children (Fischer et al. 2005). For others, the "continuities," as sociologists call them, represent lingering attachments (Vaughan 1985; Masheter 1991; author's file 2005). The former husband may help his former wife hang a picture, paint a room, or move furniture; she may invite him over for a meal or to watch television. They might even go to dinner or to see a movie together. Some couples even continue to make love after their divorce.

" I NOW PRONOUNCE YOU SECOND
HUSBAND AND FOURTH WIFE."

This fanciful depiction of marital trends may not be too far off the mark.

Reprinted with special permission of King Features Syndicate

After divorce, the ex-spouses' cost of living increases—two homes, two utility bills, and so forth. But the financial impact hits women the hardest. For them, divorce often spells economic hardship. This is especially true for mothers of small children, whose standard of living drops about a third (Seltzer 1994). Finally, as you would expect, women with more education cope better financially.

Remarriage

Despite the number of people who emerge from divorce court swearing "Never again!" many do remarry. The rate at which they remarry, however, has slowed, and today only half of women who divorce remarry (Bramlett and Mosher 2002). Figure 10.13 shows how significant race-ethnicity is in determining whether women remarry. Comparable data are not available for men.

As Figure 10.14 shows, most divorced people marry other divorced people. You may be surprised that the women who are most likely to remarry are young mothers and those with less education (Glick and Lin 1986; Schmiege et al. 2001). Apparently women who are more educated and more independent (no children) can afford to be more selective. Men are more likely than women to remarry, perhaps because they have a larger pool of potential mates.

How do remarriages work out? The divorce rate of remarried people *without* children is the same as that of first marriages. Those who bring children into a new marriage, however, are more likely to divorce again (MacDonald and DeMaris 1995). Certainly these relationships are more complicated and stressful. A lack of clear norms to follow may also play a role (Coleman et al. 2000). As sociologist Andrew Cherlin (1989) noted, we lack satisfactory names for stepmothers, stepfathers, stepbrothers, stepsisters, stepaunts, step-uncles, stepcousins, and stepgrandparents. At the very least, these are awkward terms to use, but they also represent ill-defined relationships.

Two Sides of Family Life

Let's first look at situations in which marriage and family have gone seriously wrong and then try to answer the question of what makes marriage work.

The Dark Side of Family Life: Battering, Child Abuse, Marital Rape, and Incest

The dark side of family life involves events that people would rather keep in the dark. We shall look at spouse battering, child abuse, rape, and incest.

Spouse Battering To study spouse abuse, some sociologists have studied just a few victims in depth (Goetting 2001), while others have interviewed nationally representative samples of U.S. couples (Straus and Gelles 1988; Straus 1992). Although not all sociologists agree (Dobash et al. 1992, 1993; Pagelow 1992), Murray Straus concludes that husbands and wives are about equally likely to attack one another. If gender equality exists here, however, it certainly vanishes when it comes to the effects of violence—85 percent of the injured are women (Rennison 2003). A good part of the reason, of course, is that most husbands are bigger and stronger than their wives, putting women at a physical disadvantage in this literal battle of the sexes. The Down-to-Earth Sociology box on the next page discusses why some women remain with their abusive husbands.

Violence against women is related to the sexist structure of society, which we reviewed in Chapter 8, and to the socialization that we analyzed in Chapter 3. Because they grew up with norms that encourage aggression and the use of violence, some men feel that it is their right to control women. When frustrated in a relationship—or even by events outside it—some men become violent. The basic sociological question is how to socialize males to handle frustration and disagreements without resorting to violence (Rieker et al. 1997). We do not yet have this answer.

Child Abuse

> I answered an ad about a lakeside house in a middle-class neighborhood that was for sale by owner. As the woman showed me through her immaculate house, I was surprised to see a plywood box in the youngest child's bedroom. About 3 feet high, 3 feet wide, and 6 feet long, the box was perforated with holes and had a little door with a padlock. Curious, I asked what it was. The woman replied matter-of-factly that her son had a behavior problem, and this was where they locked him for "time out." She added that other times they would tie him to a float, attach a line to the dock, and put him in the lake.
>
> I left as soon as I could. With thoughts of a terrorized child filling my head, I called the state child abuse hotline.

As you can tell, what I saw upset me. Most of us are bothered by child abuse—helpless children being victimized by their parents and other adults who are supposed to love, protect, and nurture them. The most gruesome of these cases make the evening news:

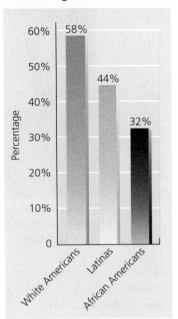

Figure 10.13 The Probability that Divorced Women Will Remarry in Five Years

Note: Only these groups are listed in the source.

Source: By the author. Based on Bramlett and Mosher 2002.

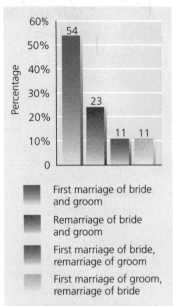

Figure 10.14 The Marital History of U.S. Brides and Grooms

- First marriage of bride and groom
- Remarriage of bride and groom
- First marriage of bride, remarriage of groom
- First marriage of groom, remarriage of bride

Source: By the author. Based on *Statistical Abstract* 2000:Table 145. Table dropped in later editions.

"Why Doesn't She Just Leave?" The Dilemma of Abused Women

"WHY WOULD SHE EVER put up with violence?" is a question on everyone's mind. From the outside, it looks so easy. Just pack up and leave. "I know I wouldn't put up with anything like that."

Yet this is not what typically happens. Women tend to stay with their men after they are abused. Some stay only a short while, to be sure, but others remain in abusive situations for years. Why?

Sociologist Ann Goetting (2001) asked this question, too. To learn the answer, she interviewed women who had made the break. She wanted to find out what it was that set them apart. How were they able to leave, when so many women couldn't seem to? She found that

1. They had a positive self-concept.
   Simply put, they believed that they deserved better.
2. They broke with traditional values.
   They did not believe that a wife had to stay with her husband no matter what.
3. They found adequate finances.
   For some, this was easy. But to move out, others had to save for years, putting away just a dollar or two a week.
4. They had supportive family and friends.
   A support network served as a source of encouragement to help them rescue themselves.

If you take the opposite of these four characteristics, you can understand why some women put up with abuse: They don't think they deserve anything better, they believe it is their duty to stay, they don't think they can make it financially, and they lack a supportive network. These four factors are not of equal importance to all women, of course. For some, the

Why do women stay with husbands who abuse them? This question has been a topic of sociological research.

lack of finances is the most important, while for others, it is their low self-concept. The lack of a supportive network is also significant.

There are two additional factors: The woman must define that what her husband is doing is abuse that warrants her leaving, and she must decide that he is not going to change. If she defines her husband's acts as normal, or perhaps as deserved in some way, she does not have a motive to leave. If she defines his acts as temporary, thinking that her husband will change, she is likely to stick around to try to change her husband.

Sociologist Kathleen Ferraro (2006) reports that when she was a graduate student, her husband "monitored my movements, eating, clothing, friends, money, make-up, and language. If I challenged his commands, he slapped or kicked me or pushed me down." Ferraro was able to leave only after she defined her husband's acts as intolerable abuse—not simply that she was caught up in an unappealing situation that she had to put up with—and after she decided that her husband was not going to change. Fellow students formed the supportive network that Ferraro needed to act on her new definition. Her graduate mentor even hid her from her husband after she left him.

for your Consideration

On the basis of these findings, what would you say to a woman whose husband is abusing her? How do you think battered women's shelters fit into this explanation? What other parts of this puzzle can you think of—such as the role of love?

The 4-year-old girl who was beaten and raped by her mother's boyfriend, who passed into a coma and then three days later passed out of this life; the 6- to 10-year-old children whose stepfather videotaped them engaging in sex acts. Unlike these cases, which made headlines in my area, most child abuse is never brought to our attention: the children who live in filth, who are neglected—left alone for hours or even days at a time—or who are beaten with extension cords—cases like the little boy I learned about when I went house hunting.

Child abuse is extensive. Each year, about 3 million U.S. children are reported to the authorities as victims of abuse or neglect. About 900,000 of these cases are substantiated (*Statistical Abstract* 2007:Table 333). The excuses that parents make are incredible. Of those I have read, one I can only describe as fantastic is this statement, made by a mother to a Manhattan judge, "I slipped in a moment of anger, and my hands accidentally wrapped around my daughter's windpipe" (LeDuff 2003).

Marital or Intimacy Rape   Sociologists have found that marital rape is more common than is usually supposed. For example, between one-third and one-half of women who seek help at shelters for battered women are victims of marital rape (Bergen 1996). Women at shelters, however, are not representative of U.S. women. To get a better answer of how common marital rape is, sociologist Diana Russell (1990) used a sampling technique that allows generalization. She found that 14 percent of married women report that their husbands have raped them. Similarly, 10 percent of a representative sample of Boston women interviewed by sociologists David Finkelhor and Kersti Yllo (1985, 1989) reported that their husbands had used physical force to compel them to have sex. Compared with victims of rape by strangers or acquaintances, victims of marital rape are less likely to report the rape (Mahoney 1999).

With the huge numbers of couples who are cohabiting, the term marital rape needs to include sexual assault in these relationships. Perhaps, then, we should use the term *intimacy rape*. And intimacy rape is not limited to men who sexually assault women. In pathbreaking research, sociologist Lori Girshick (2002) interviewed lesbians who had been sexually assaulted by their partners. In these cases, both the victim and the offender were women. Girshick points out that if the pronoun "he" were substituted for "she" in her interviews, a reader would believe that the events were being told by women who had been battered and raped by their husbands (Bergen 2003). Like wives who have been raped by their husbands, these victims, too, suffered from shock, depression, and self-blame.

Incest   Sexual relations between certain relatives (for example, between brothers and sisters or between parents and children) constitute **incest**. Incest is most likely to occur in families that are socially isolated (Smith 1992). Sociologist Diana Russell (n.d.) found that incest victims who experience the greatest trauma are those who were victimized the most often, whose assaults occurred over longer periods of time, and whose incest was "more intrusive," for example, sexual intercourse as opposed to sexual touching.

Who are the offenders? The most common incest is apparently between brothers and sisters, with the sex initiated by the brother (Canavan et al. 1992; Carlson et al. 2006). With no random samples, however, we do not know how common incest is, and researchers report different results. Russell found that uncles are the most common offenders, followed by first cousins, fathers (stepfathers especially), brothers, and, finally, other relatives ranging from brothers-in-law to stepgrandfathers. From the studies we have, we can conclude that incest between mothers and their children is rare, more so than between fathers and their children.

The Bright Side of Family Life: Successful Marriages

Successful Marriages   After examining divorce and family abuse, one could easily conclude that marriages seldom work out. This would be far from the truth, however, for about three of every five married Americans report that they are "very happy" with their marriages (Whitehead and Popenoe 2004). (Keep in mind that each year divorce removes the most unhappy marriages from this population.) To find out what makes marriage successful, sociologists Jeanette and Robert Lauer (1992) interviewed 351 couples who had been married fifteen years or longer. Fifty-one of these marriages were unhappy, but the couples stayed together for religious reasons, because of family tradition, or "for the sake of the children."

Of the others, the 300 happy couples, all:

1. Think of their spouse as their best friend
2. Like their spouse as a person
3. Think of marriage as a long-term commitment
4. Believe that marriage is sacred
5. Agree with their spouse on aims and goals

incest sexual relations between specified relatives, such as brothers and sisters or parents and children

6. Believe that their spouse has grown more interesting over the years

7. Strongly want the relationship to succeed

8. Laugh together

Sociologist Nicholas Stinnett (1992) used interviews and questionnaires to study 660 families from all regions of the United States and parts of South America. He found that happy families:

1. Spend a lot of time together

2. Are quick to express appreciation

3. Are committed to promoting one another's welfare

4. Do a lot of talking and listening to one another

5. Are religious

6. Deal with crises in a positive manner

Sociologists have uncovered two other factors: Marriages are happier when couples get along with their in-laws (Bryant et al. 2001) and when they do leisure activities that they both enjoy (Crawford et al. 2002).

Symbolic Interactionism and the Misuse of Statistics   Many students express concerns about their own marital future, a wariness born out of the divorce of their parents, friends, neighbors, relatives—even their pastors and rabbis. They wonder about their chances of having a successful marriage. Because sociology is not just about abstract ideas, but is really about our lives, it is important to stress that you are an individual, not a statistic. That is, if the divorce rate were 33 percent or 50 percent, this would *not* mean that if you marry, your chances of getting divorced are 33 percent or 50 percent. That is a misuse of statistics—and a common one at that. Divorce statistics represent all marriages and have absolutely *nothing* to do with any individual marriage. Our own chances depend on our own situations—especially the way we approach marriage.

To make this point clearer, let's apply symbolic interactionism. From a symbolic interactionist perspective, we create our own worlds. That is, because our experiences don't come with built-in meanings, we interpret our experiences, and act accordingly. As we do so, we can create a self-fulfilling prophecy. For example, if we think that our marriage might fail, we are more likely to run when things become difficult. If we think that our marriage is going to work out, we are more likely to stick around and to do things to make the marriage successful. The folk saying "There are no guarantees in life" is certainly true, but it does help to have a vision that a good marriage is possible and that it is worth the effort to achieve.

The Future of Marriage and Family

What can we expect of marriage and family in the future? Despite its many problems, marriage is in no danger of becoming a relic of the past. Marriage is so functional that it exists in every society. Consequently, the vast majority of Americans will continue to find marriage vital to their welfare.

Certain trends are firmly in place. Cohabitation, births to single women, age at first marriage, and parenting by grandparents will increase. As more married women join the work force, wives will continue to gain marital power. The number of elderly will increase, and more couples will find themselves sandwiched between caring for their parents and rearing their own children.

Our culture will continue to be haunted by distorted images of marriage and family: the bleak ones portrayed in the mass media and the rosy ones perpetuated by cultural myths. Sociological research can help to correct these distortions and allow us to see how our own family experiences fit into the patterns of our culture. Sociological research can also help to answer the big question: How can we help formulate social policy that will support and enhance family life?

To conclude this chapter, in the Down-to-Earth Sociology box on the next page we look at a subtle but fundamental change that may have begun to impact the family.

Down-to-Earth Sociology

When Work Becomes Home and Home Becomes Work

WORKERS CAN'T STAND THEIR bosses, and almost everyone would quit work and stay home if they had the chance, right? Don't be too sure.

As sociologist Arlie Hochschild (1997, 2006) did participant observation at a company she calls Amerco, she found that both work and family are changing. The family has become harried, with two working parents juggling their schedules around their work and personal lives as well as their children's school and after-school activities. As with Sharon and Tom in this chapter's opening vignette, parents can feel overwhelmed by responsibilities that come flying at them from several directions at once. Hochschild puts it this way:

> [A]t home . . . the emotional demands have become more baffling and complex. In addition to teething, tantrums and the normal developments of growing children, the needs of elderly parents are creating more tasks for the modern family—as are the blending, unblending, reblending of new stepparents, stepchildren, exes and former in-laws.

At the same time that pressures at home have increased, work for many has become less demanding and more rewarding. As Hochschild says,

> [N]ew management techniques so pervasive in corporate life have helped transform the workplace into a more appreciative, personal sort of social world . . . many companies now train workers to make their own work decisions, and . . . [many workers] feel recognized for job accomplishments. Amerco regularly strengthens the family-like ties of co-workers by holding "recognition ceremonies" . . . Amerco employees speak of "belonging to the Amerco family". . . . The education-and-training division offers free courses (on company time) in "Dealing with Anger," "How to Give and Accept Criticism," and "How to Cope with Difficult People."

What sort of "recognition ceremonies" do family members have? Or free courses on "How to Cope with Mom" or "How to Understand Your Two-Year-Old—or Unruly Teenager"? With pressures increasing at home and decreasing at work, Hochschild found that some workers volunteer for overtime "just to get away from the house." As Linda, one of the women Hochschild talked to, said,

> When I get home, and the minute I turn the key, my daughter is right there. Granted she needs somebody to talk to about her day. . . . The baby is still up. He should have been in bed two hours ago, and that upsets me. The dishes are piled in the sink. My daughter comes right up to the door and complains about anything her stepfather said or did, and she wants to talk about her job. My husband is in the other room hollering to my daughter, "Tracy, I don't ever get any time to talk to your mother, because you're always monopolizing her time before I even get a chance!" They all come at me at once.

Reflecting on what she observed, Hochschild says that for many people, the worlds of home and work have begun to reverse places. Home is becoming more like work, and work is becoming more like home. The key phrase, of course, is "for many people"—because many workplaces are not supportive, and workers still find them disagreeable places (Ducharme et al. 2004).

for your Consideration

It is difficult to pinpoint changes as they first occur, although some sociologists have been able to do so. As mentioned in Chapter 1, sociologist William Ogburn noted in 1933 that personality was becoming more important in mate selection, and in 1945 sociologists Ernest Burgess and Harvey Locke observed that mutual affection and compatibility were becoming more important in marriage. The change has been so complete that today it is difficult to conceive of getting married apart from affection and compatibility.

Could Hochschild have also put her finger on a historical shift just as it has begun to occur? Are the ways we view home and work in the process of reversing? In 50 years or so, will this be the taken-for-granted life for most of us? What do you think?

King Features, James Cavett; 800-708-7311 x 246; Orlando, FL

The cartoonist has aptly picked up the findings of sociologist Arlie Hochschild on the reversal of home and work.

Summary *and* Review

Marriage and Family in Global Perspective

What is a family—and what themes are universal?

Family is difficult to define. There are exceptions to every element that one might consider essential. Consequently, **family** is defined broadly—as people who consider themselves related by blood, marriage, or adoption. Universally, **marriage** and family are mechanisms for governing mate selection, reckoning descent, and establishing inheritance and authority. Pp. 300–302.

Marriage and Family in Theoretical Perspective

What is a functionalist perspective on marriage and family?

Functionalists examine the functions and dysfunctions of family life. Examples include the **incest taboo** and how weakened family functions increase divorce. Pp. 302–304.

What is a conflict perspective on marriage and family?

Conflict theorists focus on inequality in marriage, especially unequal power between husbands and wives. P. 304.

What is a symbolic interactionist perspective on marriage and family?

Symbolic interactionists examine the contrasting experiences and perspectives of men and women in marriage. They stress that only by grasping the perspectives of wives and husbands can we understand their behavior. Pp. 304–306.

The Family Life Cycle

What are the major elements of the family life cycle?

The major elements are love and courtship, marriage, childbirth, child rearing, and the family in later life. Most mate selection follows predictable patterns of age, social class, race-ethnicity, and religion. Childbirth and child-rearing patterns also vary by social class. Pp. 306–312.

Diversity in U.S. Families

How significant is race-ethnicity in family life?

The primary distinction is social class, not race-ethnicity. Families of the same social class are likely to be similar, regardless of their race-ethnicity. Pp. 312–316.

What other diversity in U.S. families is there?

Also discussed are one-parent, childless, **blended,** and gay and lesbian families. Each has its unique characteristics, but social class is significant in determining their primary characteristics. Poverty is especially significant for single-parent families, most of which are headed by women. Pp. 316–318.

Trends in U.S. Families

What major changes characterize U.S. families?

Three changes are postponement of first marriage, an increase in **cohabitation,** and more grandparents serving as parents to their grandchildren. With more people living longer, many middle-aged couples find themselves sandwiched between rearing their children and taking care of their aging parents. Pp. 319–323.

Divorce and Remarriage

What is the current divorce rate?

Depending on what numbers you choose to compare, you can produce almost any rate you wish, from 50 percent to less than 2 percent. Pp. 323–325.

How do children and their parents adjust to divorce?

Divorce is difficult for children, whose adjustment problems often continue into adulthood. Most divorced fathers do not maintain ongoing relationships with their children. Financial problems are usually greater for the former wives. Although most divorced people remarry, their rate of remarriage has slowed. Pp. 325–329.

Two Sides of Family Life

What are the two sides of family life?

The dark side is abuse—spouse battering, child abuse, marital rape, and **incest.** All these are acts that revolve around the misuse of family power. The bright side is that most people find marriage and family to be rewarding. Pp. 329–332.

The Future of Marriage and Family

What is the likely future of marriage and family?

We can expect cohabitation, births to unmarried women, age at first marriage, and parenting by grandparents to increase. The growing numbers of women in the work force are likely to continue to shift the balance of marital power. Pp. 332–333.

Thinking Critically

about Chapter 10

1. Functionalists stress that the family is universal because it provides basic functions for individuals and society. What functions does your family provide? Hint: In addition to the section "The Functionalist Perspective," also consider the section "Common Cultural Themes."

2. Explain why social class is more important than race-ethnicity in determining a family's characteristics.

3. Apply this chapter's contents to your own experience with marriage and family. What social factors affect your family life? In what ways is your family life different from that of your grandparents when they were your age?

Additional Resources

What can you use MySocLab for?  www.mysoclab.com

- **Study and Review:** Pre- and Post-Tests, Practice Tests, Flash Cards, Individualized Study Plans.

- **Current Events:** *Sociology in the News,* the daily *New York Times,* and more.

- **Research and Writing:** *Research Navigator, Writing About Sociology,* and more.

Where Can I Read More on This Topic?

Suggested readings for this chapter are listed at the back of this book.

EPILOGUE: WHY MAJOR IN SOCIOLOGY?

As you explored social life in this textbook, I hope that you found yourself thinking along with me. If so, you should have gained a greater understanding of why people think, feel, and act as they do—as well as insights into why *you* view life the way you do. Developing your sociological imagination was my intention in writing this book. I have sincerely wanted to make sociology come alive for you.

Majoring in Sociology

If you feel a passion for peering beneath the surface—for seeking out the social influences in people's lives, and for seeing these influences in your own life—this is the best reason to major in sociology. As you take more courses in sociology, you will continue this enlightening process of social discovery. As your sociological imagination grows, you will become increasingly aware of how social factors underlie human behavior.

In addition to people who have a strong desire to continue this fascinating process of social discovery, there is a second type of person whom I also urge to major in sociology. Let's suppose that you have a strong, almost unbridled sense of wanting to explore many aspects of life. Let's also assume that because you have so many interests, you can't make up your mind about what you want to do with your life. You can think of so many things you'd like to try, but for each one there are other possibilities that you find equally as compelling. Let me share what one student who read this text wrote me:

> I'd love to say what my current major is—if only I truly knew. I know that the major you choose to study in college isn't necessarily the field of work you'll be going into. I've heard enough stories of grads who get jobs in fields that are not even related to their majors to believe it to a certain extent. My only problem is that I'm not even sure what it is I want to study, or what I truly want to be in the future for that matter.
>
> The variety of choices I have left open for myself are very wide, which creates a big problem, because I know I have to narrow it down to just one, which isn't something easy at all for me. It's like I want to be the best and do the best (medical doctor), yet I also wanna do other things (such as being a paramedic, or a cop, or firefighter, or a pilot), but I also realize I've only got one life to live. So the big question is: What's it gonna be?

This note reminded me of myself. In my reply, I said:

> You sound so much like myself when I was in college. In my senior year, I was plagued with uncertainty about what would be the right course for my life. I went to a counselor and took a vocational aptitude test. I still remember the day when I went in for the test results. I expected my future to be laid out for me, and I hung on every word. But then I heard the counselor say, "Your tests show that mortician should be one of your vocational choices."
>
> Mortician! I almost fell off my chair. That choice was so far removed from anything that I wanted that I immediately gave up on such tests.
>
> I like your list of possibilities: physician, cop, firefighter, and paramedic. In addition to these, mine included cowboy, hobo, and beach bum. One day, I was at the dry cleaners (end of my sophomore year in college), and the guy standing next to me was a cop. We talked about his job, and when I left the dry cleaners, I immediately went to the police station to get an application. I found out that I had to be 21, and I was just 20. I went back to college.
>
> I'm very happy with my choice. As a sociologist, I am able to follow my interests. I was able to become a hobo (or at least a traveler and able to experience different cultural settings). As far as being a cop, I developed and taught a course in the sociology of law.
>
> One of the many things I always wanted to be was an author. I almost skipped graduate school to move to Greenwich Village and become a novelist. The problem was that I was too timid, too scared of the unknown—and I had no support at all—to give it a try. My ultimate choice of sociologist has allowed me to fulfill this early dream.

It is sociology's breadth that is so satisfying to those of us who can't seem to find the limit to our interests, who can't pin ourselves down to just one thing in life. Sociology covers *all* of social life. Anything and everything that people do is part of sociology. For those of us who feel such broad, and perhaps changing interests, sociology is a perfect major.

But what if you already have a major picked out, yet you really like thinking sociologically? You can *minor* in sociology. Take sociology courses that continue to pique your sociological imagination. Then after college, continue to stimulate your sociological interests through your reading, including novels. This ongoing development of your sociological imagination will serve you well as you go through life.

But What Can You Do With a Sociology Major?

I can just hear someone say: "That's fine for you, since you became a sociologist. I don't want to go to graduate school, though. I just want to get my bachelor's degree and get out of college and get on with life. So, how can a bachelor's in sociology help me?"

This is a fair question. Just what can you do with a bachelor's degree in sociology?

A few years ago, in my sociology department we began to develop a concentration in applied sociology. At that time, since this would be a bachelor's degree, I explored this very question. I was surprised at the answer: *Almost anything!*

It turns out that most employers don't care what you major in. (Exceptions are some highly specialized fields such as nursing, computers, and engineering.) *Most* employers just want to make certain that you have completed college, and for most of them one degree is the same as another. *College provides the base on which the employer builds.*

Because you have your bachelor's degree—no matter what it is in—employers assume that you are a responsible person. This credential implies that you have proven yourself: You were able to stick with a four-year course, you showed up for classes, listened to lectures, took notes, passed tests, and carried out whatever assignments you were given. On top of this base of presumed responsibility, employers add the specifics necessary for you to perform their particular work, whether that be in sales or service, in insurance, banking, retailing, marketing, product development, or whatever.

If you major in sociology, then, you don't have to look for a job as a sociologist. If you ever decide to go on for an advanced degree, that's fine. But such plans are not necessary. The bachelor's in sociology can be your passport to most types of work in society.

Final Note

I want to conclude by stressing the reason to major in sociology that goes far beyond how you are going to make a living. It is the sociological perspective itself, the way of thinking and understanding that sociology provides. Wherever your path in life may lead, the sociological perspective will accompany you.

You are going to live in a fast-paced, rapidly-changing society that, with all its conflicting crosscurrents, is going to be in turmoil. The sociological perspective will cast a different light on life's events, allowing you to perceive them in more insightful ways. As you watch television, attend a concert, converse with a friend, listen to a boss or co-worker—you will be more aware of the contexts that underlie such behavior. The sociological perspective that you develop as you major in sociology will equip you to view what happens to you in life differently from someone who does not have your sociological background. Even events in the news will look different to you.

The final question that I want to leave you with, then, is, "If you enjoy sociology, why not major in it?"

With my best wishes for your success in life,

Jim Henslin

Glossary

agents of socialization people or groups that affect our self-concept, attitudes, behaviors, or other orientations toward life

aggregate individuals who temporarily share the same physical space but who do not see themselves as belonging together

agricultural revolution the second social revolution, based on the invention of the plow, which led to agricultural societies

agricultural society a society based on large-scale agriculture; plows drawn by animals are the source of food production

anticipatory socialization because one anticipates a future role, one learns parts of it now

applied sociology the use of sociology to solve problems—from the micro level of family relationships to the macro level of crime and pollution

ascribed statuses positions an individual either inherits at birth or receives involuntarily later in life

assimilation the process of being absorbed into the mainstream culture

authoritarian leader an individual who leads by giving orders

authoritarian personality Theodor Adorno's term for people who are prejudiced and rank high on scales of conformity, intolerance, insecurity, respect for authority, and submissiveness to superiors

back stage where people rest from their performances, discuss their presentations, and plan future performances

background assumptions deeply embedded common understandings of how the world operates and of how people ought to act

bilineal (system of descent) a system of reckoning descent that counts both the mother's and the father's side

biotech society a society whose economy increasingly centers around the application of genetics—human genetics for medicine, and plant and animal genetics for the production of food and materials

blended family a family whose members were once part of other families

body language the ways in which people use their bodies to give messages to others

bonded labor, (indentured service) a contractual system in which someone sells his or her body (services) for a specified period of time in an arrangement very close to slavery, except that it is voluntarily entered into

bourgeoisie Marx's term for capitalists, those who own the means of production

capital punishment the death penalty

capitalist class the wealthy who own the means of production and buy the labor of the working class

caste system a form of social stratification in which one's status is determined by birth and is lifelong

category people who have similar characteristics

class conflict Marx's term for the struggle between capitalists and workers

class consciousness Marx's term for awareness of a common identity based on one's position in the means of production

class system a form of social stratification based primarily on the possession of money or material possessions

clique a cluster of people within a larger group who choose to interact with one another; an internal faction

closed-ended questions questions that are followed by a list of possible answers to be selected by the respondent

coalition the alignment of some members of a group against others

cohabitation unmarried couples living together in a sexual relationship

common sense those things that "everyone knows" are true

compartmentalize to separate acts from feelings or attitudes

conflict theory a theoretical framework in which society is viewed as composed of groups that are competing for scarce resources

control group the group of subjects who are not exposed to the independent variable

control theory the idea that two control systems—inner controls and outer controls—work against our tendencies to deviate

corporate crime crimes committed by executives in order to benefit their corporation

counterculture a group whose values, beliefs, and related behaviors place its members in opposition to the broader culture

crime the violation of norms written into law

criminal justice system the system of police, courts, and prisons set up to deal with people who are accused of having committed a crime

cultural diffusion the spread of cultural characteristics from one group to another

cultural goals the legitimate objectives held out to the members of a society

cultural lag Ogburn's term for human behavior lagging behind technological innovations

cultural leveling the process by which cultures become similar to one another; refers especially to the process by which U.S. culture is being exported and diffused into other nations

cultural relativism not judging a culture but trying to understand it on its own terms

cultural universal a value, norm, or other cultural trait that is found in every group

culture the language, beliefs, values, norms, behaviors, and even material objects that are passed from one generation to the next

culture of poverty the assumption that the values and behaviors of the poor make them fundamentally different from other people, that these factors are largely responsible for their poverty, and that parents perpetuate poverty across generations by passing these characteristics to their children

culture shock the disorientation that people experience when they come in contact with a fundamentally different culture and can no longer depend on their taken-for-granted assumptions about life

degradation ceremony a term coined by Harold Garfinkel to describe an attempt to remake the self by stripping away an individual's self-identity and stamping a new identity in its place

democratic leader an individual who leads by trying to reach a consensus

dependent variable a factor that is changed by an independent variable

deviance the violation of rules or norms

differential association Edwin Sutherland's term to indicate that associating with some groups results in learning an "excess of definitions" of deviance, and, by extension, in a greater likelihood that one will become deviant

discrimination an act of unfair treatment directed against an individual or a group

division of labor the splitting of a group's or a society's tasks into specialties

domestication revolution the first social revolution, based on the domestication of plants and animals, which led to pastoral and horticultural societies

dominant group the group with the most power, greatest privileges, and highest social status

downward social mobility movement down the social class ladder

dramaturgy an approach, pioneered by Erving Goffman, in which social life is analyzed in terms of drama or the stage; also called *dramaturgical analysis*

dyad the smallest possible group, consisting of two persons

egalitarian authority more or less equally divided between people or groups, in this instance between husband and wife

ego Freud's term for a balancing force between the id and the demands of society

electronic community individuals who regularly interact with one another on the Internet and who think of themselves as belonging together

endogamy the practice of marrying within one's own group

ethnic cleansing a policy of population elimination, including forcible expulsion and genocide

ethnic work activities designed to discover, enhance, or maintain ethnic and racial identification

ethnicity (and **ethnic**) having distinctive cultural characteristics

ethnocentrism the use of one's own culture as a yardstick for judging the ways of other individuals or societies, generally leading to a negative evaluation of their values, norms, and behaviors

ethnomethodology the study of how people use background assumptions to make sense out of life

exchange mobility about the same numbers of people moving up and down the social class ladder, such that, on balance, the social class system shows little change

exogamy the practice of marrying outside one's group

experiment the use of control and experimental groups and dependent and independent variables to test causation

experimental group the group of subjects who are exposed to the independent variable

expressive leader an individual who increases harmony and minimizes conflict in a group; also known as a *socioemotional leader*

extended family a nuclear family plus other relatives, such as grandparents, uncles, and aunts

face-saving behavior techniques used to salvage a performance that is going sour

false class consciousness Marx's term to refer to workers identifying with the interests of capitalists

family two or more people who consider themselves related by blood, marriage, or adoption

family of orientation the family in which a person grows up

family of procreation the family formed when a couple's first child is born

feminism the philosophy that men and women should be politically, economically, and socially equal; organized activities on behalf of this principle

(the) feminization of poverty most poor families being headed by women

feral children children assumed to have been raised by animals, in the wilderness, isolated from other humans

folkways norms that are not strictly enforced

front stage where performances are given

functional analysis a theoretical framework in which society is viewed as composed of various parts, each with a function that, when fulfilled, contributes to society's equilibrium; also known as *functionalism* and *structural functionalism*

functional requisites the major tasks that a society must fulfill if it is to survive

Gemeinschaft a type of society in which life is intimate; a community in which everyone knows everyone else and people share a sense of togetherness

gender the behaviors and attitudes that a society considers proper for its males and females; masculinity or femininity

gender role the behaviors and attitudes considered appropriate because one is a female or a male

gender socialization the ways in which society sets children onto different courses in life *because* they are male or female

gender stratification males' and females' unequal access to power, prestige, and property on the basis of their sex

generalized other the norms, values, attitudes, and expectations of people "in general"; the child's ability to take the role of the generalized other is a significant step in the development of a self

genetic predisposition inborn tendencies to some particular attitude or behavior

genocide the systematic annihilation or attempted annihilation of a people because of their presumed race or ethnic group

Gesellschaft a type of society that is dominated by impersonal relationships, individual accomplishments, and self-interest

gestures the ways in which people use their bodies to communicate with one another

glass ceiling the mostly invisible barrier that keeps women from advancing to the top levels at work

glass escalator the mostly invisible accelerators that push men into higher-level positions, more desirable work assignments, and higher salaries

globalization the extensive interconnections among nations due to the expansion of capitalism

globalization of capitalism capitalism (investing to make profits within a rational system) becoming the globe's dominant economic system

group people who have something in common and who believe that what they have in common is significant; also called a *social group*

group dynamics the ways in which individuals affect groups and the ways in which groups influence individuals

groupthink a narrowing of thought by a group of people, leading to the perception that there is only one correct answer, in which to even suggest alternatives becomes a sign of disloyalty

hate crime crimes to which more severe penalties are attached because they are motivated by hatred (dislike, animosity) of someone's race-ethnicity, religion, sexual orientation, disability, or national origin

homogamy the tendency of people with similar characteristics to marry one another

Horatio Alger myth the belief that due to limitless possibilities anyone can get ahead if he or she tries hard enough

horticultural society a society based on cultivating plants by the use of hand tools

hospice a place (or services brought to someone's home) for the purpose of giving comfort and dignity to a dying person

household people who occupy the same housing unit

hunting and gathering society a human group that depends on hunting and gathering for its survival

hypothesis a statement of how variables are expected to be related to one another, often according to predictions from a theory

id Freud's term for our inborn basic drives

ideal culture the ideal values and norms of a people; the goals held out for them

ideology beliefs about the way things ought to be that justify social arrangements

illegitimate opportunity structure opportunities for crimes that are woven into the texture of life

impression management people's efforts to control the impressions that others receive of them

incest sexual relations between specified relatives, such as brothers and sisters or parents and children

incest taboo the rule that prohibits sex and marriage among designated relatives

income money received, usually from a job, business, or assets

independent variable a factor that causes a change in another variable, called the dependent variable

individual discrimination the negative treatment of one person by another on the basis of that person's perceived characteristics

Industrial Revolution the third social revolution, occurring when machines powered by fuels replaced most animal and human power

industrial society a society based on the harnessing of machines powered by fuels

in-groups groups toward which one feels loyalty

inflation an increase in prices

institutional discrimination negative treatment of a minority group that is built into a society's institutions; also called *systemic discrimination*

institutionalized means approved ways of reaching cultural goals

instrumental leader an individual who tries to keep the group moving toward its goals; also known as a *task-oriented leader*

intergenerational mobility the change that family members make in social class from one generation to the next

internal colonialism the policy of economically exploiting minority groups

labeling theory the view that the labels people are given affect their own and others' perceptions of them, thus channeling their behavior either into deviance or into conformity

laissez-faire leader an individual who leads by being highly permissive

language a system of symbols that can be combined in an infinite number of ways and can represent not only objects but also abstract thought

latent functions unintended beneficial consequences of people's actions

leader someone who influences other people

leadership styles ways in which people express their leadership

life course the stages of our life as we go from birth to death

looking-glass self a term coined by Charles Horton Cooley to refer to the process by which our self develops through internalizing others' reactions to us

machismo an emphasis on male strength and dominance

macro-level analysis an examination of large-scale patterns of society

macrosociology analysis of social life that focuses on broad features of society, such as social class and the relationships of groups to one another; usually used by functionalists and conflict theorists

manifest functions the intended beneficial consequences of people's actions

marginal working class the most desperate members of the working class, who have few skills, little job security, and are often unemployed

marriage a group's approved mating arrangements, usually marked by a ritual of some sort

mass media forms of communication, such as radio, newspapers, and television that are directed to mass audiences

master status a status that cuts across the other statuses that an individual occupies

material culture the material objects that distinguish a group of people, such as their art, buildings, weapons, utensils, machines, hairstyles, clothing, and jewelry

matriarchy a society in which women as a group dominate men as a group

matrilineal (system of descent) a system of reckoning descent that counts only the mother's side

means of production the tools, factories, land, and investment capital used to produce wealth

mechanical solidarity Durkheim's term for the unity (a shared consciousness) that people feel as a result of performing the same or similar tasks

medicalization of deviance to make deviance a medical matter, a symptom of some underlying illness that needs to be treated by physicians

melting pot the view that Americans of various backgrounds would blend into a sort of ethnic stew

meritocracy a form of social stratification in which all positions are awarded on the basis of merit

micro-level analysis an examination of small-scale patterns of society

microsociology analysis of social life that focuses on social interaction; typically used by symbolic interactionists

minority group people who are singled out for unequal treatment and who regard themselves as objects of collective discrimination

mores norms that are strictly enforced because they are thought essential to core values or the well-being of the group

multiculturalism (also called *pluralism*) a philosophy or political policy that permits or encourages ethnic difference

negative sanction an expression of disapproval for breaking a norm, ranging from a mild, informal reaction such as a frown to a formal reaction such as a prison sentence or an execution

networking using one's social networks for some gain

new technology the emerging technologies of an era that have a significant impact on social life

nonmaterial culture (also called *symbolic culture*) a group's ways of thinking (including its beliefs, values, and other assumptions about the world) and doing (its common patterns of behavior, including language and other forms of interaction)

nonverbal interaction communication without words through gestures, use of space, silence, and so on

norms expectations, or rules of behavior, that reflect and enforce values

nuclear family a family consisting of a husband, wife, and child(ren)

open-ended questions questions that respondents answer in their own words

operational definition the way in which a researcher measures a variable

organic solidarity Durkheim's term for the interdependence that results from the division of labor; people depending on others to fulfill their jobs

out-groups groups toward which one feels antagonism

pan-Indianism a movement that focuses on common elements in the cultures of Native Americans in order to develop a cross-tribal self-identity and to work toward the welfare of all Native Americans

participant observation (or **fieldwork**) research in which the researcher participates in a research setting while observing what is happening in that setting

pastoral society a society based on the pasturing of animals

patriarchy a society or group in which men dominate women; authority is vested in males

patrilineal (system of descent) a system of reckoning descent that counts only the father's side

peer group a group of individuals of roughly the same age who are linked by common interests

personality disorders the view that a personality disturbance of some sort causes an individual to violate social norms

pluralistic society a society made up of many different groups

police discretion the practice of the police, in the normal course of their duties, to either arrest or ticket someone for an offense or to overlook the matter

polyandry a form of marriage in which women have more than one husband

polygyny a form of marriage in which men have more than one wife

population the target group to be studied

population transfer forcing a minority group to move

positive sanction a reward or positive reaction for following norms, ranging from a smile to a prize

positivism the application of the scientific approach to the social world

poverty line the official measure of poverty; calculated to include incomes that are less than three times a low-cost food budget

power the ability to carry out your will, even over the resistance of others

power elite C. Wright Mills' term for the top people in U.S. corporations, military, and politics who make the nation's major decisions

prejudice an attitude or prejudging, usually in a negative way

prestige respect or regard

primary group a group characterized by intimate, long-term, face-to-face association and cooperation

proletariat Marx's term for the exploited class, the mass of workers who do not own the means of production

race physical characteristics that distinguish one group from another

racism prejudice and discrimination on the basis of race

random sample a sample in which everyone in the target population has the same chance of being included in the study

real culture the norms and values that people actually follow

recidivism rate the proportion of released convicts who are rearrested

reference group a group that we use as a standard to evaluate ourselves

reliability the extent to which research produces consistent or dependable results

replication repeating a study in order to test its findings

research method (or **research design**) one of six procedures that sociologists use to collect data: surveys, participant observation, secondary analysis, documents, experiments, and unobtrusive measures

reserve labor force the unemployed; unemployed workers are thought of as being "in reserve"—capitalists take them "out of reserve" (put them back to work) during times of high production and then put them "back in reserve" (lay them off) when they are no longer needed

resocialization the process of learning new norms, values, attitudes, and behaviors

respondents people who respond to a survey, either in interviews or by self-administered questionnaires

rising expectations the sense that better conditions are soon to follow, which, if unfulfilled, increases frustration

role the behaviors, obligations, and privileges attached to a status

role conflict conflicts that someone feels *between* roles because the expectations attached to one role are incompatible with the expectations of another role

role performance the ways in which someone performs a role within the limits that the role provides; showing a particular "style" or "personality"

role strain conflicts that someone feels within a role

romantic love feelings of erotic attraction accompanied by an idealization of the other

sanctions expressions of approval or disapproval given to people for upholding or violating norms

sample the individuals intended to represent the population to be studied

Sapir-Whorf hypothesis Edward Sapir's and Benjamin Whorf's hypothesis that language creates ways of thinking and perceiving

scapegoat an individual or group unfairly blamed for someone else's troubles

science the application of systematic methods to obtain knowledge and the knowledge obtained by those methods

secondary analysis the analysis of data that have been collected by other researchers

secondary group compared with a primary group, a larger, relatively temporary, more anonymous, formal, and impersonal group based on some interest or activity. Its members are likely to interact on the basis of specific statuses

segregation the policy of keeping racial–ethnic groups apart

selective perception seeing certain features of an object or situation, but remaining blind to others

self the unique human capacity of being able to see ourselves "from the outside"; the views we internalize of how others see us

serial fatherhood a pattern of parenting in which a father, after divorce, reduces contact with his own children, acts as a father to the children of the woman he marries or lives with, then ignores these children, too, after moving in with or marrying another woman

serial murder the killing of several victims in three or more separate events

sex biological characteristics that distinguish females and males, consisting of primary and secondary sex characteristics

sexual harassment the abuse of one's position of authority to force unwanted sexual demands on someone

shaman the healing specialist of a tribe who attempts to control the spirits thought to cause a disease or injury; commonly called a witch doctor

sign-vehicles the term used by Goffman to refer to how people use social setting, appearance, and manner to communicate information about the self

significant other an individual who significantly influences someone else's life

slavery a form of social stratification in which some people own other people

small group a group small enough for everyone to interact directly with all the other members

social class according to Weber, a large group of people who rank close to one another in wealth, prestige, and power; according to Marx, one of two groups: capitalists who own the means of production or workers who sell their labor

social construction of reality the use of background assumptions and life experiences to define what is real

social control a group's formal and informal means of enforcing its norms

social environment the entire human environment, including direct contact with others

social inequality a social condition in which privileges and obligations are given to some but denied to others

social institution the organized, usual, or standard ways by which society meets its basic needs

social integration the degree to which members of a group or a society feel united by shared values and other social bonds; also known as social cohesion

social interaction what people do when they are in one another's presence

social location the group memberships that people have because of their location in history and society

social mobility movement up or down the social class ladder

social network the social ties radiating outward from the self that link people together

social order a group's usual and customary social arrangements, on which its members depend and on which they base their lives

social stratification the division of large numbers of people into layers according to their relative power, property, and prestige; applies to both nations and to people within a nation, society, or other group

social structure the framework that surrounds us, consisting of the relationships of people and groups to one another, which gives direction to and sets limits on behavior

socialization the process by which people learn the characteristics of their group—the knowledge, skills, attitudes, values, and actions thought appropriate for them

society people who share a culture and a territory

sociobiology a framework of thought that views human behavior as the result of natural selection and considers biological factors to be the fundamental cause of human behavior

sociological perspective understanding human behavior by placing it within its broader social context

sociology the scientific study of society and human behavior

split labor market workers split along racial, ethnic, gender, age, or any other lines; this split is exploited by owners to weaken the bargaining power of workers

status the position that someone occupies in society or in a social group

status consistency ranking high or low on all three dimensions of social class

status inconsistency ranking high on some dimensions of social class and low on others, also called *status discrepancy*

status set all the statuses or positions that an individual occupies

status symbols items used to identify a status

stereotype assumptions of what people are like, whether true or false

stigma "blemishes" that discredit a person's claim to a "normal" identity

strain theory Robert Merton's term for the strain engendered when a society socializes large numbers of people to desire a cultural goal (such as success), but withholds from many the approved means of reaching that goal; one adaptation to the strain is crime, the choice of an innovative means (one outside the approved system) to attain the cultural goal

street crime crimes such as mugging, rape, and burglary

structural mobility movement up or down the social class ladder that is due to changes in the structure of society, not to individual efforts

subculture the values and related behaviors of a group that distinguish its members from the larger culture; a world within a world

superego Freud's term for the conscience, the internalized norms and values of our social groups

survey the collection of data by having people answer a series of questions

symbol something to which people attach meanings and then use to communicate with others

symbolic culture another term for nonmaterial culture

symbolic interactionism a theoretical perspective in which society is viewed as composed of symbols that people use to establish meaning, develop their views of the world, and communicate with one another

system of descent how kinship is traced over the generations

taboo a norm so strong that it often brings revulsion if violated

taking the role of the other putting oneself in someone else's shoes; understanding how someone else feels and thinks and thus anticipating how that person will act

teamwork the collaboration of two or more people to manage impressions jointly

techniques of neutralization ways of thinking or rationalizing that help people deflect (or neutralize) society's norms

technology in its narrow sense, tools; its broader sense includes the skills or procedures necessary to make and use those tools

theory a general statement about how some parts of the world fit together and how they work; an explanation of how two or more facts are related to one another

Thomas theorem William I. and Dorothy S. Thomas' classic formulation of the definition of the situation: "If people define situations as real, they are real in their consequences."

total institution a place in which people are cut off from the rest of society and are almost totally controlled by the officials who run the place

transitional adulthood a term that refers to a period following high school when young adults have not yet taken on the responsibilities ordinarily associated with adulthood; also called *adultolescence*

triad a group of three people

underclass a group of people for whom poverty persists year after year and across generations

unobtrusive measures ways of observing people who do not know they are being studied

upward social mobility movement up the social class ladder

validity the extent to which an operational definition measures what it was intended to measure

value cluster values that together form a larger whole

value contradiction values that contradict one another; to follow the one means to come into conflict with the other

value free the view that a sociologist's personal values or biases should not influence social research

values the standards by which people define what is desirable or undesirable, good or bad, beautiful or ugly

variable a factor thought to be significant for human behavior, which can vary (or change) from one case to another

WASP White Anglo-Saxon Protestant; narrowly, an American of English descent; broadly, an American of western European ancestry

wealth the total value of everything someone owns, minus the debts

white ethnics white immigrants to the United States whose cultures differ from that of WASPs

white-collar crime Edwin Sutherland's term for crimes committed by people of respectable and high social status in the course of their occupations; for example, bribery of public officials, securities violations, embezzlement, false advertising, and price fixing

working class those people who sell their labor to the capitalist class

world system theory economic and political connections that tie the world's countries together

Suggested Readings

CHAPTER 1 The Sociological Perspective

Allan, Kenneth D. *Explorations in Classical Sociological Theory: Seeing the Social World.* Thousand Oaks, Calif.: Pine Forge Press, 2006. The author's emphasis is that sociological theory can be a guide for selecting research projects and for interpreting the results.

Bartos, Otomar J., and Paul Wehr. *Using Conflict Theory.* New York: Cambridge University Press, 2003. In this application of the conflict perspective, the author's primary concerns are the causes of social conflicts and how to manage or resolve conflict.

Berger, Peter L. *Invitation to Sociology: A Humanistic Perspective.* New York: Doubleday, 1972. This analysis of how sociology applies to everyday life has become a classic in the field.

Best, Joel. *More Damned Lies and Statistics: How Numbers Confuse Public Issues.* Berkeley: University of California Press, 2004. The author shows how special-interest groups manipulate and misrepresent statistics in order to promote their agendas.

Charon, Joel M. *Symbolic Interactionism: An Introduction, an Interpretation, an Integration,* 9th ed. Upper Saddle River, N.J.: Prentice Hall, 2007. The author lays out the main points of symbolic interactionism, providing an understanding of why this perspective is important in sociology.

Hedstrom, Peter. *Dissecting the Social: On the Principles of Analytical Sociology.* New York: Cambridge University Press, 2005. By examining the personal perspective of each theorist, the author shows how theoretical and historical perspectives apply to our understanding of the world.

Henslin, James M., ed. *Down to Earth Sociology: Introductory Readings,* 14th ed. New York: Free Press, 2007. This collection of readings about everyday life and social structure is designed to broaden the reader's understanding of society, and of the individual's place within it.

Mills, C. Wright. *The Sociological Imagination.* New York: Oxford University Press, 2000. First published in 1960, this classic analysis provides an overview of sociology from the framework of the conflict perspective.

Ritzer, George. *Classic Sociological Theory,* 5th ed. New York: McGraw-Hill, 2008. To help understand the personal and historical context of how theory develops, the author includes biographical sketches of the theorists.

How Sociologists Do Research

Bryman, Alan. *Social Research Methods,* 2nd ed. Oxford: Oxford University Press, 2005. An overview of the research methods used by sociologists, with an emphasis on the logic that underlies these methods.

Creswell, John W., and Vicki L. Plano Clark. *Designing and Conducting Mixed Methods Research.* Thousand Oaks, Calif.: Sage Publications., 2006.The authors explain how to do research that combines research methods.

Drew, Paul, Geoffrey Raymond, and Darin Weinberg. *Talk and Interaction in Social Research Methods.* Thousand Oaks, Calif.: Sage Publications, 2006. The authors stress the importance of talk in a variety of social research methods.

Gosselin, Denise Kindschi. *Heavy Hands: An Introduction to the Crimes of Family Violence,* 3rd ed. Upper Saddle River, N.J.: Prentice Hall, 2005. Explores causes, consequences, and prevalence of domestic violence; also has an emphasis on law enforcement.

Lee, Raymond M. *Unobtrusive Methods in Social Research.* Philadelphia: Open University Press, 2000. This overview of unobtrusive ways of doing social research summarizes many interesting studies.

Lomand, Turner C. *Social Science Research: A Cross Section of Journal Articles for Discussion and Evaluation,* 4th ed. Los Angeles: Pyrczak Publishing, 2005. This overview of the methods of research used by sociologists includes articles on current topics.

Neuman, W. Lawrence. *Social Research Methods: Qualitative and Quantitative Approaches,* 6th ed. Boston: Allyn and Bacon, 2006. This "how-to" book of sociological research describes how sociologists gather data and the logic that underlies each method.

Scully, Diana. *Understanding Sexual Violence: A Study of Convicted Rapists.* New York: Routledge, 1994. This analysis of how rapists rationalize their acts helps us to understand why some men rape.

Whyte, William Foote. *Creative Problem Solving in the Field: Reflections on a Career.* Lanham, Md.: AltaMira Press, 1997. Focusing on his extensive field experiences, the author provides insight into the researcher's role in participant observation.

Wysocki Diane Kholos, ed. *Readings in Social Research Methods,* 3rd ed. Belmont, Calif.: Wadsworth, 2008. The authors of these articles provide an overview of research methods.

Journals

Applied Behavioral Science Review, Clinical Sociology Review, International Clinical Sociology, Journal of Applied Sociology, The Practicing Sociologist, Sociological Practice: A Journal of Clinical and Applied Sociology, and *Sociological Practice Review* report the experiences of sociologists who work in applied settings, from peer group counseling and suicide prevention to recommending changes to school boards.

Contexts, published by the American Sociological Association, uses a magazine format to present sociological research in a down-to-earth fashion.

Humanity & Society, the official journal of the Association for Humanist Sociology, publishes articles intended "to advance the quality of life of the world's people."

Electronic Journals

Electronic Journal of Sociology (http://www.sociology.org) and *Sociological Research Online* (http://www.socresonline.org.uk) publish articles on various sociological topics. Access is free.

Writing Papers for Sociology

Cuba, Lee J. *A Short Guide to Writing about Social Science,* 4th ed. Boston: Pearson Longman, 2002. The author summarizes the types of social science literature, presents guidelines on how to organize and write a research paper, and explains how to prepare an oral presentation.

Richlin-Klonsky, Judith, and Ellen Strenski, eds. The Sociology Writing Group. *A Guide to Writing Sociology Papers,* 5th ed. New York: St. Martin's Press, 2001. The guide walks students through the steps in writing a sociology paper, from choosing the initial assignment to doing the research and turning in a finished paper. Also explains how to manage time and correctly cite sources.

About Majoring in Sociology

You like sociology and perhaps are thinking about majoring in it, but what can you do with a sociology major? Be sure to check the epilogue of this book (pages 336–337). Also check out the resources that are available from the American Sociological Association. Go to www.asanet.org. This will bring you to the ASA's home page. Here, you can click around and get familiar with what this professional association offers students.

On the menu at the top of ASA's home page, click Students. This will bring you to a page that has links to resources for students. You may be interested in *The Student Sociologist,* a newsletter for students. The link, *Careers,* will take you to several free online publications, including those that feature information on careers in both basic and applied sociology. You will also see such links as the student forum, student involvement, and funding.

If you want to contact the ASA by snail mail or by telephone or fax, here is that information: American Sociological Association, 1307 New York Avenue NW, Suite 700, Washington, D.C. 20005-4701. Tel. (202) 383-9005. Fax (202) 638-0882. E-mail: Executive.Office@asanet.org

You might also be interested in this book. If your library doesn't have it, I'm sure they'll order it if you request it.

Stephens, W. Richard, Jr. *Careers in Sociology,* 4th ed. Boston: Pearson Education, 2004. How can you make a living with a major in sociology? The author explores careers in sociology, from business and government to health care and the law.

CHAPTER 2 Culture

Berger, Peter L., and Samuel P. Huntington, eds. *Many Globalizations: Cultural Diversity in the Contemporary World.* New York: Oxford University Press, 2002. One of the recurring themes of this book is how globalization is changing cultures.

Borofsky, Robert, and Bruce Albert. *Yanomani: The Fierce Controversy and What We Can Learn from It.* Berkeley: University of California Press, 2006. The authors criticize the research on the Yanomani, including that by Chagnon in the next book, with an emphasis on anthropologists' inconsideration of human rights.

Chagnon, Napoleon A. *Yanomamö: The Fierce People,* 5th ed. New York: Harcourt, Brace, Jovanovich, 1997. This account of a tribal people whose customs are extraordinarily different from ours will help you to see how arbitrary the choices are that underlie human culture.

Edgerton, Robert B. *Sick Societies: Challenging the Myth of Primitive Harmony.* New York: Free Press, 1993. The author's thesis is that cultural relativism is misinformed, that we have the obligation to judge cultures that harm their members as inferior to those that do not.

Hull, John R., Mary Jo Neitz, and Marshall Battani. *Sociology on Culture.* New York: Routledge, 2003. The authors present an overview of sociological approaches to culture.

Inglis, David. *Culture and Everyday Life.* Oxford, UK: Routledge, 2006. An overview of how culture shapes, influences, and structures our everyday lives.

Jacobs, Mark D., and Nancy Weiss Hanrahan, eds. *The Blackwell Companion to the Sociology of Culture.* Malden, Mass.: Blackwell Publishing, 2005. The authors of these articles explore cultural systems, everyday life, identity, collective memory, and citizenship in a global economy.

Phillips, Anne. *Multiculturalism without Culture.* Princeton, N.J.: Princeton University Press, 2007. Examines the issue of individual choice within cultural constraints and the arguments of multiculturalism versus cultural differences.

Sullivan, Nikki. *Tattooed Bodies: Subjectivity, Textuality, Ethics, and Pleasure.* Westport, Conn.: Praeger, 2001. A sociological analysis of this very old and very new custom.

Wolf, Mark J. P., and Bernard Perron, eds. *The Video Game: Theory Reader.* New York: Routledge, 2003. The authors of these articles on gamers and games examine sociological and economic issues that surround gaming.

Zellner, William W. *Countercultures: A Sociological Analysis.* New York: St. Martin's Press, 1995. The author's analysis of skinheads, the Ku Klux Klan, survivalists, satanists, the Church of Scientology, and the Unification Church (Moonies) helps us understand why people join countercultures.

Journal

Cultural Sociology and *Space for Difference* focus on sociological analyses of culture, with crossovers into art history, gender studies, human geography, racism, literary studies, and social activism.

CHAPTER 3 Socialization

Ariès, Philippe. *Centuries of Childhood: A Social History of Family Life.* New York: Vintage Books, 1972. The author analyzes how childhood in Europe during the Middle Ages differs from childhood today.

Blumer, Herbert. *George Herbert Mead and Human Conduct.* Lanham, Md.: AltaMira Press, 2004. An overview of symbolic interactionism by a sociologist who studied and taught Mead's thought all of his life.

Corsaro, William, A. *The Sociology of Childhood,* 2nd ed. Thousand Oaks, Calif.: Pine Forge Press, 2004. This sociological analysis of childhood includes social indicators of children in the United States and the world.

Handel, Gerald, Spencer Cahill, and Frederick Elkin. *Children and Society: The Sociology of Children and Childhood Socialization.* New York: Oxford University Press, 2007. A symbolic interactionist perspective of childhood from birth to adolescence with an emphasis on the development of the self.

Hunt, Stephen J. *The Life Course: A Sociological Introduction.* New York: Palgrave McMillan, 2006. Gives an overview of the life course while considering what is distinct about a sociological approach to this topic.

Lareau, Annette. *Unequal Childhoods: Class, Race, and Family Life.* Berkeley: University of California Press, 2003. The author documents differences in child rearing in poor, working-class, and middle-class U.S. families.

Rymer, Russ. *Genie: A Scientific Tragedy.* New York: Harper Perennial Library, 1994. This account of Genie includes the battles to oversee Genie among linguists, psychologists, and social workers, all of whom claimed to have Genie's best interests at heart.

Settersten, Richard A., Jr., and Timothy J. Owens, eds. *New Frontiers in Socialization.* Greenwich, Conn.: JAI Press, 2003. The authors of these articles focus on the adult years in the life course, examining the influence of families, neighborhoods, communities, friendship, education, work, volunteer associations, medical institutions, and the media.

Sociological Studies of Child Development: A Research Annual. Greenwich, Conn.: JAI Press, published annually. Along with theoretical articles, this publication reports on sociological research on the socialization of children.

Walters, Glenn D. *Criminal Belief Systems: An Integrated-Interactive Theory of Lifestyles.* Westport, Conn.: Greenwood Publishing Group, 2003. The author analyzes how five belief systems (self-view, world-view, past-view, present-view, future-view) explain crime initiation and maintenance.

CHAPTER 4 Social Structure and Social Interaction

Goffman, Erving. *The Presentation of Self in Everyday Life.* New York: Peter Smith, Publisher, 1999. First published in 1959. This classic statement of dramaturgical analysis provides a different way of looking at everyday life. As a student, this was one of the best books I read.

Johnson, Kim K. P., and Sharron J. Lennon, eds. *Appearance and Power.* Oxford, England: Berg Publishers, 2000. The authors of these articles analyze how significant appearance, especially clothing, is for what happens to us in social life.

LeBesco, Kathleen. *Revolting Bodies: The Struggle to Redefine Fat Identity.* Amherst: University of Massachusetts Press, 2004. This analysis of the political struggle over the cultural meaning of fatness examines oppression and negative stereotypes.

Schauer, Frederick. *Profiles, Probabilities, and Stereotypes.* Cambridge, Mass.: Belknap Press, 2004. The focus of this book is the question of whether we can generalize about members of a group on the basis of statistical tendencies of that group.

Schmidt, Kimberly D., Diane Zimmerman Umble, and Steven D. Reschly, eds. *Strangers at Home: Amish and Mennonite Women in History.* Baltimore: Johns Hopkins University Press, 2002. These accounts of the experiences of Amish and Mennonite women provide a window onto history, as well as insight into how social structure influences social interaction.

Seidman, Steven. *The Social Construction of Sexuality.* New York: W.W. Norton, 2004. The author explores how society influences our sexual choices, our beliefs about sexuality, and our sexual standards.

Tönnies, Ferdinand. *Community and Society (Gemeinschaft und Gesellschaft).* New York: Dover Publications, 2003. Originally published in 1887, this classic work, focusing on social change, provides insight into how society influences personality. Rather challenging reading.

Waskul, Dennis, and Phillip Vannini, eds. *Body/embodiment: Symbolic Interaction and the Sociology of the Body.* London: Ashgate, 2006. Using a symbolic interactionist perspective, the authors explore the interrelationship of the body, the self, and social interaction.

Whyte, William Foote. *Street Corner Society: The Social Structure of an Italian Slum,* 4th ed. Chicago: University of Chicago Press, 1993. Originally published in 1943. The author's analysis of interaction in a U.S. Italian slum demonstrates how social structure affects personal relationships.

Journals

Qualitative Sociology, Symbolic Interaction, and *Urban Life* feature articles on symbolic interactionism and analyses of everyday life.

CHAPTER 5 Societies to Social Networks

Cross, Robert, and Andrew Parker. *The Hidden Power of Social Networks: Understanding How Work Really Gets Done in Organizations.* Cambridge, Mass: Harvard Business School Press, 2004. Based on their research and experience in organizations, the authors explain how understanding networks can improve communication and productivity.

Homans, George C. *The Human Group.* New Brunswick, N.J.: Transaction Publishers, 2001. First published in 1950. In this classic work, the author develops the idea that all human groups share common activities, interactions, and sentiments.

Hughes, Richard L., Robert C. Ginnett, and Gordon J. Curphy. *Leadership: Enhancing the Lessons of Experience,* 5th ed. New York: McGraw-Hill, 2006.

Supplementing empirical studies with illustrative anecdotes, the authors focus on what makes effective leaders.

Janis, Irving L. *Groupthink: Psychological Studies of Policy Decisions and Fiascoes,* 2nd ed. New York: Houghton Mifflin, 1982. Janis analyzes how groups can become cut off from alternatives, interpret evidence in light of their preconceptions, and embark on courses of action that they should have seen as obviously incorrect.

CHAPTER 6 Deviance and Social Control

Conklin, John E. *Why Crime Rates Fell.* Boston: Allyn and Bacon, 2003. The author analyzes the reasons that experts have suggested for why crime rates have fallen: changes in policing, imprisonment, drugs and gun usage, age, and social institutions.

Fox, James Alan, and Jack Levin. *Extreme Killing: Understanding Serial and Mass Murder.* Thousand Oaks, Calif.: Sage, 2005. As the authors analyze the various types of serial and mass murders, they examine the characteristics of both killers and their victims.

Goffman, Erving. *Stigma: Notes on the Management of Spoiled Identity.* New York: Simon & Schuster, 1986. First published in 1968. The author outlines the social and personal reactions to "spoiled identity," appearances that—due to disability, weight, ethnicity, birth marks, and so on—do not match dominant expectations.

Heiner, Robert, ed. *Deviance Across Cultures.* Oxford: Oxford University Press, 2007. Cross-cultural norms and behavior are the focus of this collection of classic and contemporary articles on deviance.

Lintner, Bert. *Blood Brothers: The Criminal Underworld of Asia.* New York: Palgrave MacMillan, 2004. Maps out the topography of organized crime in East Asia.

Lombroso, Cesare, Guglielmo Ferrero, Nicole Hahn Rafter, and Mary Gibson. *Criminal Woman, the Prostitute, and the Normal Woman.* Durham, N.C.: Duke University Press, 2005. This translation of a classic work from the 1800s on women and crime is put in current social context by two researchers on female criminals.

Paul, Pamela. *Pornified: How Pornography Is Transforming Our Lives, Our Relationships, and Our Families.* New York: Henry Holt, 2005. Based on interviews, the author's thesis is that for many people pornography is replacing intimacy and creating emotional isolation.

Rathbone, Cristina. *A World Apart: Women, Prison, and Life Behind Bars.* New York: Random House, 2006. A journalist's account of the four years she spent investigating MCI Framingham, the oldest women's prison in the United States.

Reiman, Jeffrey. *The Rich Get Richer and the Poor Get Prison: Ideology, Class, and Criminal Justice,* 8th ed. Boston: Allyn and Bacon, 2007. An analysis of how social class works to produce different types of criminals and different types of justice.

Rodriguez, Luis J. *The Republic of East L. A.: Stories.* Los Angeles: Rayo, 2003. These hard-hitting vignettes let the reader know what life is like in this poverty-plagued section of Los Angeles.

Silberman, Matthew, ed. *Violence and Society: A Reader.* Upper Saddle River, N.J.: Prentice Hall, 2003. As the authors of these articles analyze the social factors that underlie violence, they focus on social inequality, culture, and family, sexual, and criminal violence.

Journals

Criminal Justice Review: Issues in Criminal, Social, and Restorative Justice and *Journal of Law and Society* examine the social forces that shape law and justice.

CHAPTER 7 Social Stratification

Beeghley, Leonard. *The Structure of Social Stratification in the United States,* 5th ed. Boston: Pearson, 2008. The author presents a concise overview of the U.S. social classes.

Bowles, Samuel, Herbert Gintis, and Melissa Osborne Groves, eds. *Unequal Chances: Family Background and Economic Success.* Princeton, N.J.: Princeton University Press., 2005. The authors of these articles focus on how our economic origins affect our social destination as adults.

Deliege, Robert. *The Untouchables of India.* Oxford, U.K.: Berg, 2001. An overview of India's caste system, with an emphasis on the *Dalits,* or untouchables.

Florida, Richard. *The Rise of the Creative Class: And How It's Transforming Work, Leisure, Community and Everyday Life.* New York: Basic Books, 2004.

The author's thesis is that a new social class has evolved, consisting of scientists, engineers, architects, educators, writers, artists, and entertainers, and that this class needs to become cohesive and work for the common good.

Gatewood, Willard B. *Aristocrats of Color: The Black Elite, 1880–1920.* Fayetteville: University of Arkansas Press, 2000. Analyzing the rise and decline of the African American upper class that developed after the Civil War, the author focuses on marriage, occupations, education, religion, clubs, and relationships with whites and with African Americans of lower classes.

Hartmann, Heidi I., ed. *Women, Work, and Poverty: Women Centered Research for Policy Change.* Binghamton, N.Y.: Haworth Press, 2006. The authors present research on women living at or below the poverty line. Major themes are work, marriage, motherhood, and welfare reform.

Huggins, Martha K., Mika Haritos-Fatouros, and Philip G. Zimbardo. *Violence Workers: Police Torturers and Murderers Reconstruct Brazilian Atrocities.* Berkeley: University of California Press, 2002. If you want an insider's perspective in order to understand how ordinary people can rape, torture, and kill, this book will provide it.

Iceland, John. *Poverty in America, A Handbook,* 2nd ed. Berkeley, Calif.: University of California Press, 2006. This picture of poverty in the United States shows how both poverty and its related public policies have changed over time.

Neckerman, Kathryn. *Social Inequality.* New York: Russell Sage, 2004. The author examines implications of the increasing economic inequality analyzed in this chapter for the quality of family and neighborhood life, access to education and health care, job satisfaction, and political participation.

Perucci, Robert, and Earl Wyson. *The New Class Society,* 3rd ed. Lanham, Md.: Rowman and Littlefield, 2007. An overview of the U.S. social class structure, with the suggestion that no longer is there a middle class.

Ritzer, George. *The Globalization of Nothing.* Thousand Oaks, Calif.: Pine Forge Press, 2004. The author expresses concerns about the short- and long-term effects of globalization.

Sachs, Jeffrey D. *The End of Poverty: Economic Possibilities for Our Time.* East Rutherford, N.J.: Penguin Press, 2005. After visiting 100 countries, representing 90 percent of the world's population, the author suggests ways that we can end global poverty.

Sernau, Scott. *Worlds Apart: Social Inequalities in a Global Economy,* 2nd ed. Thousand Oaks, Calif.: Pine Forge Press, 2005. The author's thesis is that the market-driven global economy contributes to rather than reduces social inequality.

Sherman, Rachel. *Class Acts: Service and Inequality in Luxury Hotels.* Berkeley, Calif.: University of California Press, 2007. Based on participant observation, the author explores the relationship between workers and guests at a luxury hotel.

Wilson, William Julius, and Richard P. Taub. *There Goes the Neighborhood: Racial, Ethnic, and Class Tensions in Four Chicago Neighborhoods and Their Meaning for America.* New York: Alfred A. Knopf, 2007. This study of four working- and lower-middle class neighborhoods in Chicago is enlivened with personal narratives that provide insight into how race, class, and ethnicity influence our lives.

Journals

Journal of Children and Poverty and *Journal of Poverty* analyze issues that affect the quality of life of people who live in poverty.

Race, Gender, and Class publishes interdisciplinary articles on the topics listed in its title.

CHAPTER 8 Sex and Gender

Andersen, Margaret L. *Thinking about Women: Sociological Perspectives on Sex and Gender,* 7th ed. New York: Allyn and Bacon, 2006. An overview of the main issues of sex and gender in contemporary society, ranging from sexism and socialization to work and health.

Brettell, Caroline B., and Carolyn F. Sargent, eds. *Gender in Cross-Cultural Perspective,* 4th ed. Upper Saddle River, N.J.: Prentice Hall, 2005. The net is spread wide as the authors examine gender and biology, in prehistory, at home, and the division of labor, property, kinship, religion, politics, and the global economy.

Colapinto, John. *As Nature Made Him: The Boy Who Was Raised as a Girl, P.S.* New York: Harper Perennial, 2006. A detailed account of the event summarized in this chapter of the boy whose penis was accidentally burned off.

Edwards, Tim. *Cultures of Masculinities.* London: Routledge, 2006. An analysis of the variations of masculinity as it is shaped by culture.

Gilbert, Paula Ruth, and Kimberly K. Eby, eds. *Violence and Gender: An Interdisciplinary Reader.* Upper Saddle River, N.J.: Prentice Hall, 2004. The authors of these articles examine violence and youth, the human body, war, intimacy, sports, the media, and how to prevent violence.

Gilman, Charlotte Perkins. *The Man-Made World or, Our Androcentric Culture.* New York: Charlton, 1911. Reprinted in 1971 by Johnson Reprint. This early book on women's liberation provides an excellent view of female-male relations at the beginning of the last century.

Goldberg, Steven. *Why Men Rule: A Theory of Male Dominance.* Chicago: Open Court, 1994. A detailed explanation of the author's theory of male dominance featured in this chapter.

Johnson, Allan G. *Privilege, Power, and Difference,* 2nd ed. New York: McGraw-Hill, 2006. The author helps us see the nature and consequences of privilege and our connection to it.

Kimmel, Michael S., ed. *The Gendered Society Reader,* 2nd ed. New York: Oxford University Press, 2004. The authors of these articles examine the relationship of gender and violence in the contexts of culture, family, classroom, workplace, and intimacy.

Kimmel, Michael S., and Michael A. Messner, eds. *Men's Lives,* 7th ed. Boston: Allyn and Bacon, 2007. The authors of these articles examine issues of sex and gender as they affect men. Often provides different views from those presented in the Anderson book.

Lorber, Judith, and Lisa Jean Moore. *Gender and the Social Construction of Illness,* 2nd ed. Lanham, Md.: Rowman and Littlefield, 2003. Taking the position that both gender and medicine are social institutions, the author examines their interrelationships.

Renzetti, Claire, and Daniel J. Curran. *Women, Men, and Society,* 5th ed. Boston: Allyn and Bacon, 2003. A basic text that summarizes major issues in the sociology of gender.

Wharton, Amy S. *The Sociology of Gender: An Introduction to Theory and Research.* Medford, Mass.: Blackwell Publishers, 2005. Research on gender is viewed through three frameworks: the individual, the interactional, and the institutional.

Wolf, Naomi. *The Beauty Myth: How Images of Beauty Are Used Against Women.* New York: Harper Perennial, 2003. The author analyzes the unrealistic images of female beauty portrayed in the media.

Journals

These journals focus on the role of gender in social life: *Feminist Studies; Gender and Behavior; Gender and Society; Forum in Women's and Gender Studies; Gender and History; Gender, Place and Culture: A Journal of Feminist Geography; Journal of Gender, Culture, and Health; Journal of Interdisciplinary Gender Studies; Journal of Men's Health and Gender; Sex Roles;* and *Signs: Journal of Women in Culture and Society.*

CHAPTER 9 Race and Ethnicity

Acosta, Teresa Palomo, and Ruthe Winegarten. *Los Tejanas: 300 Years of History.* Austin: University of Texas Press, 2003. An account of how Tejanas in the colonial period and from the Republic of Texas up to 1900 overcame obstacles to their success.

Blee, Kathleen M. *Inside Organized Racism: Women in the Hate Movement.* Berkeley: University of California Press, 2002. Why and how do people join hate groups? The author's research provides answers to this troubling question.

Deutscher, Irwin, and Linda Lindsey. *Preventing Ethnic Conflict: Successful Cross-National Strategies.* Lanham, Md.: Lexington Books, 2005. Instead of focusing on what doesn't work, the authors examine positive ethnic relationships around the world.

Dray, Phillip. *At the Hands of Persons Unknown: The Lynching of Black America.* New York: The Modern Library, 2004. Examines the history of the lynching of African Americans and the social background behind these acts.

Du Bois, W. E. B. *Black Reconstruction in America: An Essay Toward a History of the Part Which Black Folk Played in the Attempt to Reconstruct Democracy in America, 1860–1880.* New York: Harcourt, Brace 1935; New York: The Free Press, 2000. This analysis of the role of African Americans in the Civil War and during the years immediately following provides a glimpse into a neglected part of U.S. history.

Hallett, Michael A. *Private Prisons in America: A Critical Race Perspective.* Champaign, Ill.: University of Illinois Press, 2006. The author's thesis is that the growth of private prisons in the United States is due more to racial discrimination than to increasing crime rates.

Hilberg, Raul. *The Destruction of the European Jews,* 3rd ed. New Haven: Yale University Press, 2003. The focus of this book is the machinery of death that the Nazis put together to annihilate the Jewish community of Europe.

Mander, Jerry. *In the Absence of the Sacred: The Failure of Technology and the Survival of the Indian Nations.* New York: Pete Smith, Publisher, 1999. With a focus on the impact of technology, the author analyzes past and present relations of Native Americans and the U.S. government.

Mueller, Timothy, and Sarah Sue Goldsmith. *Nations Within: The Four Sovereign Tribes of Louisiana.* Baton Rouge: Louisiana State University Press, 2004. Analyzes the relationship of four sovereign nations to the dominant, colonizing governmental power.

Parrillo, Vincent N. *Strangers to These Shores: Race and Ethnic Relations in the United States,* 8th ed. Boston: Allyn and Bacon, 2006. This text reviews the experiences of more than 50 racial-ethnic groups.

Ryan, Nick. *Into a World of Hate.* New York: Routledge, 2005. The author spent six years exploring the underworld of hatred in Europe and the United States.

Sowell, Thomas. *Black Rednecks and White Liberals.* San Francisco: Encounter Books, 2005. In this provocative and controversial analysis, the author places ghetto culture, slavery, the education of African Americans, and the exportation of democracy in sociohistorical context.

Walker, Samuel, Cassia Spohn, and Miriam Delone. *The Color of Justice: Race, Ethnicity, and Crime in America,* 4th ed. Belmont, Calif.: Wadsworth, 2007. The authors analyze racial, ethnic, and gender discrimination in the criminal justice system.

Wilson, William Julius. *The Bridge over the Racial Divide: Rising Inequality and Coalition Politics.* Berkeley: University of California Press, 2000. The author analyzes how monetary, trade, and tax policies increase social inequality; includes recommendations to increase multiracial political cooperation.

CHAPTER 10 Marriage and Family

Agger, Ben, and Beth Anne Shelton. *Fast Families, Virtual Children: A Critical Sociology of Families and Schooling.* Boulder, Colo.: Paradigm Publishers, 2007. The authors analyze how technology has changed the way families conduct their lives, raise their children, and try to maintain a boundary between work and home.

Bianchi, Suzanne M., John P. Robinson, and Melissa A. Milkie. *Changing Rhythms of American Family Life.* New York: Russell Sage, 2006. Based on time-diaries, the authors conclude that despite their greater participation in the paid labor force U.S. mothers spend just as much time with their children as the previous generation of women did.

Contreras, Josefina M., Kathryn A. Kerns, and Angela M. Neal-Barnett. *Latino Children and Families in the United States: Current Research and Future Directions.* New York: Praeger, 2003. The authors consider how parenting beliefs and practices of Latinos differ by socioeconomic and cultural backgrounds and try to identify family values that can be considered "Latino."

Coontz, Stephanie. *Marriage, a History: From Obedience to Intimacy or How Love Conquered Marriage.* New York: Viking, 2005. This analysis of how the fundamental orientations to marriage have changed contains enlightening excerpts from the past.

Edin, Kathryn, and Maria Kefalas. *Promises I Can Keep: Why Poor Women Put Motherhood Before Marriage.* Berkeley: University of California Press, 2005. The author's interviews provide insight into how low-income single mothers think about marriage and family.

Epstein, Cynthia Fuchs, and Arne L. Kalleberg, eds. *Fighting for Time: Shifting Boundaries of Work and Social Life.* New York: Russell Sage, 2005. Explores changes in the time people spend at work and the consequences of those changes for individuals and families.

Johnson, Leonor Boulin, and Robert Staples. *Black Families at the Crossroads: Challenges and Prospects.* New York: Jossey-Bass, 2005. After placing today's black families in historical context, the authors analyze the impact of economic policies and social change.

Marquardt, Elizabeth. *Between Two Worlds: The Inner Lives of Children of Divorce.* New York: Crown, 2005. The author deftly weaves her own experiences as a child of divorce into her summary of interviews with children who have had this experience.

Romano, Renee Christine. *Race Mixing: Black-White Marriage in Postwar America*. Cambridge, Mass.: Harvard University Press, 2003. Provides the legislative background on these marriages, plus social trends, accompanied by first-person accounts.

Wallace, Harvey. *Family Violence,* 4th ed. Boston: Allyn and Bacon, 2005. This overview examines family violence through three perspectives: legal, medical, and social.

Journals

Family Relations, The History of the Family, International Journal of Sociology of the Family, Journal of Comparative Family Studies, Journal of Divorce, Journal of Divorce and Remarriage, Journal of Family and Economic Issues, Journal of Family Issues, Journal of Family Violence, Journal of Marriage and the Family, and *Marriage and Family Review* publish articles on almost every aspect of marriage and family life.

References

All new references are printed in blue.

AAUP (American Association of University Professors). "2006–07 Report on the Economic Status of the Profession," April 2007.

Aberg, Yvonne. *Social Interactions: Studies of Contextual Effects and Endogenous Processes.* Doctoral Dissertation, Department of Sociology, Stockholm University, 2003.

Aberle, David F., A. K. Cohen, A. K. David, M. J. Leng, Jr., and F. N. Sutton. "The Functional Prerequisites of a Society." *Ethics, 60,* January 1950:100–111.

Addams, Jane. *Twenty Years at Hull-House.* New York: Signet, 1981. First published in 1910.

Adler, Patricia A., and Peter Adler. *Peer Power: Preadolescent Culture and Identity.* New Brunswick, N.J.: Rutgers University Press, 1998.

Adorno, Theodor W., Else Frenkel-Brunswick, D. J. Levinson, and R. N. Sanford. *The Authoritarian Personality.* New York: Harper & Row, 1950.

Aeppel, Timothy. "More Amish Women Are Tending to Business." *Wall Street Journal,* February 8, 1996:B1, B2.

Ahlburg, Dennis A., and Carol J. De Vita. "New Realities of the American Family." *Population Bulletin, 47,* 2, August 1992:1–44.

Akol, Jacob. "Slavery in Sudan." *New African,* September 1998.

Alba, Richard, and Victor Nee. *Remaking the American Mainstream: Assimilation and Contemporary Immigration.* Cambridge, Mass.: Harvard University Press, 2003.

Albanese, Jennifer. Personal research for the author. March 2007.

Albert, Ethel M. "Women of Burundi: A Study of Social Values." In *Women of Tropical Africa,* Denise Paulme, ed. Berkeley: University of California Press, 1963:179–215.

Aldrich, Nelson W., Jr. *Old Money: The Mythology of America's Upper Class.* New York: Vintage Books, 1989.

Alexander, Gerianne M., and Melissa Hines. "Sex Differences in Response to Children's Toys in Nonhuman Primates." *Evolution and Human Behavior, 23,* 2002:467–479.

Allport, Floyd. *Social Psychology.* Boston: Houghton Mifflin, 1954.

Amato, Paul R., and Jacob Cheadle. "The Long Reach of Divorce: Divorce and Child Well-Being Across Three Generations." *Journal of Marriage and Family, 67,* February 2005:191–206.

Amato, Paul R., and Juliana M. Sobolewski. "The Effects of Divorce and Marital Discord on Adult Children's Psychological Well-Being." *American Sociological Review, 66,* 6, December 2001:900–921.

America's Children: Key National Indicators of Well-Being 2005. Washington, D.C.: Federal Interagency Forum on Child and Family Statistics, 2005.

"American Community Survey 2003." Washington, D.C.: U.S. Census Bureau, 2004.

American Sociological Association. "An Invitation to Public Sociology." 2004.

Andersen, Margaret L. *Thinking About Women: Sociological Perspectives on Sex and Gender.* New York: Macmillan, 1988.

Anderson, Chris. "NORC Study Describes Homeless." *Chronicle,* 1986:5, 9.

Anderson, Elijah. "Streetwise." In *Exploring Social Life: Readings to Accompany Essentials of Sociology, Sixth Edition,* 2nd ed., James M. Henslin, ed. Boston: Allyn and Bacon, 2006:147–156.

Anderson, Elijah. *Streetwise: Race, Class, and Change in an Urban Community.* Chicago: University of Chicago Press, 1990.

Anderson, Elijah. *A Place on the Corner.* Chicago: University of Chicago Press, 1978.

Anderson, Nels. *Desert Saints: The Mormon Frontier in Utah.* Chicago: University of Chicago Press, 1966. First published in 1942.

Andersson, Hilary. "Born to Be a Slave in Niger." BBC News, World Edition, February 11, 2005.

Ang, Audra. "In China, High-Tech Mixes With Tradition to Make Matches." *Houston Chronicle,* February 13, 2006.

Angler, Natalie. "Do Races Differ? Not Really, DNA Shows." *New York Times,* August 22, 2000.

Annin, Peter. "Big Money, Big Trouble." *Newsweek,* April 19, 1999:59.

Annin, Peter, and Kendall Hamilton. "Marriage or Rape?" *Newsweek,* December 16, 1996:78.

Aptheker, Herbert. "W. E. B. Du Bois: Struggle Not Despair." *Clinical Sociology Review, 8,* 1990:58–68.

Ariès, Philippe. *Centuries of Childhood.* R. Baldick, trans. New York: Vintage Books, 1965.

Arlacchi, P. *Peasants and Great Estates: Society in Traditional Calabria.* Cambridge, England: Cambridge University Press, 1980.

Armstrong, David. "Hard Case: When Academics Double as Expert Witnesses." *Wall Street Journal,* June 22, 2007.

"ASA Council Statement on the Causes of Gender Differences in Science and Math Career Achievement." *Footnotes,* March 2005:10.

Asch, Solomon. "Effects of Group Pressure Upon the Modification and Distortion of Judgments." In *Readings in Social Psychology,* Guy Swanson, Theodore M. Newcomb, and Eugene L. Hartley, eds. New York: Holt, Rinehart and Winston, 1952.

Associated Press. "Military Sex Assault Reports Rose by 24 Percent." March 21, 2007.

Aulette, Judy Root. *Changing American Families.* Boston: Allyn and Bacon, 2002.

Avery, Robert B., Glenn B. Canner, and Robert E. Cook. "New Information Reported Under FMDA and Its Application in Fair Lending Enforcement." *Federal Reserve Bulletin,* Summer 2005:344–394.

Ayittey, George B. N. "Black Africans Are Enraged at Arabs." *Wall Street Journal,* interactive edition, September 4, 1998.

Bachu, Amara, and Martin O'Connell. "Fertility of American Women: Population Characteristics." *Current Population Reports.* Washington, D.C.: U.S. Bureau of the Census, September 2000.

Bales, Robert F. "The Equilibrium Problem in Small Groups." In *Working Papers in the Theory of Action,* Talcott Parsons et al., eds. New York: Free Press, 1953:111–115.

Bales, Robert F. *Interaction Process Analysis.* Reading, Mass.: Addison-Wesley, 1950.

Baltzell, E. Digby. *Puritan Boston and Quaker Philadelphia.* New York: Free Press, 1979.

Baltzell, E. Digby, and Howard G. Schneiderman. "Social Class in the Oval Office." *Society, 25,* Sept/Oct, 1988:42–49.

Banerjee, Neela. "Rape (and Silence About It) Haunts Baghdad." *New York Times,* July 16, 2003.

Barnes, Fred. "How to Rig a Poll." *Wall Street Journal,* June 14, 1995:A14.

Barnes, Helen. "A Comment on Stroud and Pritchard: Child Homicide, Psychiatric Disorder and Dangerousness." *British Journal of Social Work, 31,* 3, June 2001.

Barnes, Julian E. "A Bicycling Mystery: Head Injuries Piling Up." *New York Times,* July 29, 2001.

Barstow, David, and Lowell Bergman. "Death on the Job, Slaps on the Wrist." *Wall Street Journal,* January 10, 2003.

Bartlett, Donald L., and James B. Steele. "Wheel of Misfortune." *Time,* December 16, 2002:44–58.

Bartos, Otomar J., and Paul Wehr. *Using Conflict Theory.* New York: Cambridge University Press, 2002.

Batalova, Jeanne A., and Philip N. Cohen. "Premarital Cohabitation and Housework: Couples in Cross-National Perspectives." *Journal of Marriage and the Family, 64,* 3, August 2002: 743–755.

Bates, Marston. *Gluttons and Libertines: Human Problems of Being Natural.* New York: Vintage Books, 1967. Quoted in Crapo, Richley H. *Cultural Anthropology: Understanding Ourselves and Others,* 5th ed. Boston: McGraw Hill, 2002.

Beals, Ralph L., and Harry Hoijer. *An Introduction to Anthropology,* 3rd ed. New York: Macmillan, 1965.

Bean, Frank D., Jennifer Lee, Jeanne Batalova, and Mark Leach. "Immigration and Fading Color Lines in America." Washington, D.C.: Population Reference Bureau, 2004.

Bearman, Peter S., and Hannah Bruckner. "Opposite-Sex Twins and Adolescent Same-Sex Attraction." *American Journal of Sociology, 107,* March 2002:1179–1205.

Becker, Howard S. *Outsiders: Studies in the Sociology of Deviance.* New York: Free Press, 1966.

Beeghley, Leonard. *The Structure of Social Stratification in the United States,* 5th ed. Boston: Allyn and Bacon, 2008.

Begley, Sharon. "Twins: Nazi and Jew." *Newsweek, 94,* December 3, 1979:139.

Bell, David A. "An American Success Story: The Triumph of Asian-Americans." In *Sociological Footprints: Introductory Readings in Sociology,* 5th ed., Leonard Cargan and Jeanne H. Ballantine, eds. Belmont, Calif.: Wadsworth, 1991:308–316.

Belsky, Jay. "Early Child Care and Early Child Development: Major Findings of the NICHD Study of Early Child Care." *European Journal of Developmental Psychology, 3*, 1, 2006:95–110.

Belsky, Jay, Deborah Lowe Vandell, Margaret Burchinall, K. Alison Clarke-Stewart, Kathleen McCartney, and Margaret Tresch Owen. "Are There Long-Term Effects of Early Child Care?" *Child Development, 78*, 2, March/April 2007:681–701.

Bergen, Raquel Kennedy. Review of Lori B. Girshick, *Woman-to-Woman Sexual Violence: Does She Call It Rape?* In *Contemporary Sociology, 32*, 2, March 2003:173–174.

Bergen, Raquel Kennedy. *Wife Rape: Understanding the Response of Survivors and Service Providers.* Newbury Park, Calif.: Sage, 1996.

Berger, Arthur Asa. *Video Games: A Popular Culture Phenomenon.* New Brunswick, N.J.: Transaction Publishers, 2002.

Berger, Joseph. "Family Ties and the Entanglements of Caste." *New York Times,* October 24, 2004.

Berger, Peter. "Invitation to Sociology." In *Down to Earth Sociology: Introductory Readings,* 14th ed., James M. Henslin, ed. New York: The Free Press, 2007. First published in 1963.

Bergmann, Barbara R. "The Future of Child Care." Paper presented at the 1995 meetings of the American Sociological Association.

Bernard, Jessie. "The Good-Provider Role." In *Marriage and Family in a Changing Society,* 4th ed., James M. Henslin, ed. New York: Free Press, 1992:275–285.

Bernard, Viola W., Perry Ottenberg, and Fritz Redl. "Dehumanization: A Composite Psychological Defense in Relation to Modern War." In *The Triple Revolution Emerging: Social Problems in Depth,* Robert Perucci and Marc Pilisuk, eds. Boston: Little, Brown, 1971:17–34.

Bernstein, Robert, and Mike Bergman. "Hispanic Population Reaches All-Time High of 38.8 Million, New Census Bureau Estimates Show." *U.S. Department of Commerce News,* June 18, 2003.

Bertrand, Marianne, and Sendhil Mullainathan. "Are Emily and Brendan More Employable than Lakish and Jamal? A Field Experiment on Labor Market Discrimination." Unpublished paper, November 18, 2002.

Bianchi, Suzanne M., and Lynne M. Casper. "American Families." *Population Bulletin, 55*, 4, December 2000:1–42.

Bianchi, Suzanne M., John P. Robinson, and Melissa A. Milkie. *Changing Rhythms of American Family Life.* New York: Russell Sage Foundation, 2006.

Bird, Chloe E., and Patricia P. Rieker. "Gender Matters: An Integrated Model for Understanding Men's and Women's Health." *Social Science and Medicine, 48*, 6, March 1999:745–755.

Bishop, Jerry E. "Study Finds Doctors Tend to Postpone Heart Surgery for Women, Raising Risk." *Wall Street Journal,* April 16, 1990:B4.

Bjerklie, David, Andrea Dorfman, Wendy Cole, Jeanne DeQuine, Helen Gibson, David S. Jackson, Leora Moldofsky, Timothy Roche, Chris Taylor, Cathy Booth Thomas, and Dick Thompson. "Baby, It's You: And You, and You . . . " *Time,* February 19, 2001:47–57.

Blau, David M. "The Production of Quality in Child-Care Centers: Another Look." *Applied Developmental Science, 4*, 3, 2000:136–148.

Blau, Peter M., and Otis Dudley Duncan. *The American Occupational Structure.* New York: John Wiley, 1967.

Blee, Kathleen M. "Inside Organized Racism." In *Life in Society: Readings to Accompany Sociology A Down-to-Earth Approach, Seventh Edition,* James M. Henslin, ed. Boston: Allyn and Bacon, 2005:46–57.

Blumer, Herbert George. *Industrialization as an Agent of Social Change: A Critical Analysis,* David R. Maines and Thomas J. Morrione, eds. Hawthorne, N. Y.: Aldine de Gruyter, 1990.

Blumstein, Alfred, and Joel Wallman. "The Crime Drop and Beyond." *Annual Review of Law and Social Science, 2,* December 2006:125–146.

Blumstein, Philip, and Pepper Schwartz. *American Couples: Money, Work, Sex.* New York: Pocket Books, 1985.

Bond, Rod. "Group Size and Conformity." *Group Processes and Intergroup Relations, 8*, 4, 2005:331–354.

Booth, Alan, and James M. Dabbs, Jr. "Testosterone and Men's Marriages." *Social Forces, 72*, 2, December 1993:463–477.

Booth, Alan, David R. Johnson, and Douglas A. Granger. "Testosterone, Marital Quality, and Role Overload." Paper presented at the 2004 meetings of the American Sociological Association.

Bosman, Ciska M., et al. "Business Success and Businesses' Beauty Capital." National Bureau of Economic Research Working Paper: 6083, July 1997.

"The Boss's Pay." *Wall Street Journal,* April 7, 2007.

Boulding, Elise. *The Underside of History.* Boulder, Colo.: Westview Press, 1976.

Boxer, Sarah. "When Emotion Worms Its Way Into Law." *New York Times,* April 7, 2001.

Boyle, Elizabeth Heger, Fortunata Songora, and Gail Foss. "International Discourse and Local Politics: Anti-Female-Genital-Cutting Laws in Egypt, Tanzania, and the United States," *Social Problems, 48*, 4, November 2001:524–544.

Bradford, Phillips Verner, and Harvey Blume. *Ota Benga: The Pygmy in the Zoo.* New York: Delta, 1992.

Brajuha, Mario, and Lyle Hallowell. "Legal Intrusion and the Politics of Fieldwork: The Impact of the Brajuha Case." *Urban Life, 14*, 4, January 1986:454–478.

Bramlett, M. D., and W. D. Mosher. "Cohabitation, Marriage, Divorce, and Remarriage in the United States." Hyattsville, Md.: National Center for Health Statistics, Vital Health Statistics, Series 23, Number 22, July 2002.

Brannon, Linda. *Gender: Psychological Perspectives,* 2nd ed. Boston: Allyn and Bacon, 1999.

Bray, Rosemary L. "Rosa Parks: A Legendary Moment, a Lifetime of Activism. *Ms., 6*, 3, November-December 1995:45–47.

"Brazil Arrests U.S. Pilot Over Obscene Gesture." Associated Press, January 15, 2004.

Bretos, Miguel A. "Hispanics Face Institutional Exclusion." *Miami Herald,* May 22, 1994.

Brines, Julie, and Kara Joyner. "The Ties That Bind. Principles of Cohesion in Cohabitation and Marriage." *American Sociological Review, 64,* June 1999:333–355.

Brinkley, Joel. "U.S. Faults 4 Allies Over Forced Labor." *New York Times,* June 4, 2005.

Broder, Michael S., David E. Kanouse, Brian S. Mittman, and Steven J. Bernstein. "The Appropriateness of Recommendations for Hysterectomy." *Obstetrics and Gynecology, 95*, 2, February 2000: 199–205.

Bronfenbrenner, Urie. "Principles for the Healthy Growth and Development of Children." In *Marriage and Family in a Changing Society,* 4th ed., James M. Henslin, ed. New York: Free Press, 1992:243–249.

Brooks-Gunn, Jeanne, Greg. J. Duncan, and Lawrence Aber, eds. *Neighborhood Poverty, Volume 1: Context and Consequences for Children.* New York: Russell Sage Foundation, 1997.

Browne, Beverly A. "Gender Stereotypes in Advertising on Children's Television in the 1990s: A Cross-National Analysis." *Journal of Advertising, 27*, 1, Spring 1998:83–96.

Browning, Christopher R. *Ordinary Men: Reserve Police Battalion 101 and the Final Solution in Poland.* New York: HarperPerennial, 1993.

Brunello, Giorgio, and Beatrice D'Hombres. "Does Body Weight Affect Wages? Evidence From Europe." *Economics and Human Biology, 5*, 2007:1–19.

Bryant, Chalandra M., Rand D. Conger, and Jennifer M. Meehan. "The Influence of In-Laws on Changes in Marital Success." *Journal of Marriage and the Family, 63*, 3, August 2001:614–626.

Budrys, Grace. *Unequal Health: How Inequality Contributes to Health or Illness.* Lanham, Md.: Rowman and Littlefield, 2003.

Bumiller, Elisabeth. "First Comes Marriage—Then, Maybe, Love." In *Marriage and Family in a Changing Society,* 4th ed., James M. Henslin, ed. New York: Free Press, 1992:120–125.

Buraway, Michael. "The Field of Sociology: Its Power and Its Promise." In *Public Sociology: Fifteen Eminent Sociologists Debate Politics and the Profession in the Twenty-first Century.* Berkeley: University of California Press, 2007:241–258.

Buraway, Michael. "Public Sociologies: Reply to Hausknecht." *Footnotes,* January 2003:8.

Burris, Val. "Interlocking Directorates and Political Cohesion Among Corporate Elites." *American Journal of Sociology, 111*, 1, 2005:249–283.

Burris, Val. "The Myth of Old Money Liberalism: The Politics of the *Forbes* 400 Richest Americans." *Social Problems, 47*, 3, August 2000:360–378.

Bush, Diane Mitsch, and Robert G. Simmons. "Socialization Processes Over the Life Course." In *Social Psychology: Sociological Perspectives,* eds. Morris Rosenberger and Ralph H. Turner. New Brunswick, N.J.:Transaction, 1990:133–164.

Butterfield, Fox. "Prison Rates Among Blacks Reach a Peak, Report Finds." *New York Times,* April 7, 2003.

Canavan, Margaret M., Walter J. Meyer, III, and Deborah C. Higgs. "The Female Experience of Sibling Incest." *Journal of Marital and Family Therapy, 18*, 2, 1992:129–142.

Carlson, Bonnie E., Katherine Maciol, and Joanne Schneider. "Sibling Incest: Reports from Forty-One Survivors." *Journal of Child Sexual Abuse, 15*, 4, 2006:19–34.

Carlson, Lewis H., and George A. Colburn. *In Their Place: White America Defines Her Minorities, 1850–1950.* New York: Wiley, 1972.

Carnevale, Anthony P., and Stephen J. Rose. "Socioeconomic Status, Race/Ethnicity, and Selective College Admissions." New York: The Century Foundation, March 2003.

Carpenito, Lynda Juall. "The Myths of Acquaintance Rape." *Nursing Forum, 34,* 4, October-December 1999:3.

Carr, Deborah. "Gender, Preloss Marital Dependence, and Older Adults' Adjustment to Widowhood." *Journal of Marriage and Family, 66,* February 2004:220–235.

Carr, Deborah, Carol D. Ryff, Burton Singer, and William J. Magee. "Bringing the 'Life' Back into Life Course Research: A 'Person-Centered' Approach to Studying the Life Course." Paper presented at the 1995 meetings of the American Sociological Association.

Cartwright, Dorwin, and Alvin Zander, eds. *Group Dynamics,* 3rd ed. Evanston, Ill.: Peterson, 1968.

Case, Anne, and Christina Paxson. "Stature and Status: Height, Ability, and Labor Market Outcomes." Working Paper, August 2006.

Cassel, Russell N. "Examining the Basic Principles for Effective Leadership." *College Student Journal, 33,* 2, June 1999:288–301.

Cauce, Ana Mari, and Melanie Domenech-Rodriguez. "Latino Families: Myths and Realities." In *Latino Children and Families in the United States: Current Research and Future Directions,* Josefina M. Contreras, Kathryn A. Kerns, and Angela M. Neal-Barnett, eds. Westport, Conn.: Praeger, 2002:3–25.

Center for American Women and Politics. "Women in Elective Office 2007." April 2007.

Centers for Disease Control and Prevention. "Native American Suicides per 100,000, Ages 0–19, IHS Areas, 1989–1998." June 13, 2007b.

Chafetz, Janet Saltzman. *Gender Equity: An Integrated Theory of Stability and Change.* Newbury Park, Calif.: Sage, 1990.

Chafetz, Janet Saltzman. *Masculine/Feminine or Human? An Overview of the Sociology of Sex Roles.* Itasca, Ill: F. E. Peacock, 1974.

Chafetz, Janet Saltzman, and Anthony Gary Dworkin. *Female Revolt: Women's Movements in World and Historical Perspective.* Totowa, N.J.: Rowman & Allanheld, 1986.

Chagnon, Napoleon A. *Yanomamo: The Fierce People,* 2nd ed. New York: Holt, Rinehart and Winston, 1977.

Chaker, Anne Marie, and Hilary Stout. "After Years off, Women Struggle to Revive Careers." *Wall Street Journal,* May 6, 2004.

Chalkley, Kate. "Female Genital Mutilation: New Laws, Programs Try to End Practice." *Population Today, 25,* 10, October 1997:4–5.

Chambliss, Daniel F. "The World of the Hospital." In *Down to Earth Sociology: Introductory Readings,* 12th ed., James M. Henslin, ed. New York: The Free Press, 2003:434–446.

Chambliss, William J. "The Saints and the Roughnecks." In *Down to Earth Sociology: Introductory Readings,* 14th ed., James M. Henslin, ed. New York: The Free Press, 2007. First published in 1973.

Chambliss, William J. *Power, Politics, and Crime.* Boulder: Westview Press, 2000.

Chandra, Vibha P. "Fragmented Identities: The Social Construction of Ethnicity, 1885–1947." Unpublished paper, 1993a.

Chandra, Vibha P. "The Present Moment of the Past: The Metamorphosis." Unpublished paper, 1993b.

Chen, Edwin. "Twins Reared Apart: A Living Lab." *New York Times Magazine.* December 9, 1979:112.

Chen, Kathy. "China's Women Face Obstacles in Workplace." *Wall Street Journal,* August 28, 1995:B1, B5.

Cherlin, J. Andrew. "Remarriage as an Incomplete Institution." In *Marriage and Family in a Changing Society,* 3rd ed., James M. Henslin, ed. New York: Free Press, 1989:492–501.

"Child Support for Custodial Mothers and Fathers." *Current Population Reports,* Series P60–187. Washington, D.C.: U.S. Bureau of the Census, 1995.

Chin, Nancy P., Alicia Monroe, and Kevin Fiscella. "Social Determinants of (Un)Healthy Behaviors." *Education for Health: Change in Learning and Practice, 13,* 3, November 2000:317–328.

Chivers, C. J. "Officer Resigns Before Hearing in D. W. I. Case." *New York Times,* August 29, 2001.

Chodorow, Nancy J. "What Is the Relation Between Psychoanalytic Feminism and the Psychoanalytic Psychology of Women?" In *Theoretical Perspectives on Sexual Difference,* Deborah L. Rhode, ed. New Haven, Conn.: Yale University Press, 1990:114–130.

Chung, He Len, and Laurence Steinberg. "Relations Between Neighborhood Factors, Parenting Behaviors, Peer Deviance, and Delinquency Among Serious Juvenile Offenders." *Developmental Psychology, 42,* 2, 2006:319–331.

Churchill, Ward. *A Little Matter of Genocide: Holocaust and Denial in the Americas, 1492 to the Present.* San Francisco: City Lights Books, 1997.

Clark, Candace. *Misery and Company: Sympathy in Everyday Life.* Chicago: University of Chicago Press, 1997.

Cloud, John. "For Better or Worse." *Time,* October 26, 1998:43–44.

Cloward, Richard A., and Lloyd E. Ohlin. *Delinquency and Opportunity: A Theory of Delinquent Gangs.* New York: Free Press, 1960.

Cohen, Patricia. "Forget Lonely. Life Is Healthy at the Top." *New York Times,* May 15, 2004.

Colapinto, John. *As Nature Made Him: The Boy Who Was Raised as a Girl.* New York: HarperCollins, 2001.

Cole, Elizabeth R., and Safiya R. Omari. "Race, Class and the Dilemmas of Upward Mobility for African Americans." *Journal of Social Issues, 59,* 4, 2003:785–802.

Coleman, Marilyn, Lawrence Ganong, and Mark Fine. "Reinvestigating Remarriage: Another Decade of Progress." *Journal of Marriage and the Family, 62,* 4, November 2000:1288–1307.

Collins, Randall. "Socially Unrecognized Cumulation." *American Sociologist, 30,* 2, Summer 1999:41–61.

Collins, Randall. *Theoretical Sociology.* San Diego, Calif.: Harcourt, Brace Jovanovich, 1988.

Collins, Randall, Janet Saltzman Chafetz, Rae Lesser Blumberg, Scott Coltrane, and Jonathan H. Turner. "Toward an Integrated Theory of Gender Stratification." *Sociological Perspectives, 36,* 3, 1993:185–216.

Collymore, Yvette. "Conveying Concerns: Women Report on Gender-Based Violence." Washington, D.C.: Population Reference Bureau, 2000.

Conklin, John E. *Why Crime Rates Fell.* Boston: Allyn and Bacon, 2003.

Connors, L. "Gender of Infant Differences in Attachment: Associations with Temperament and Caregiving Experiences." Paper presented at the Annual Conference of the British Psychological Society, Oxford, England, 1996.

Conrad, Peter. "Public Eyes and Private Genes: Historical Frames, New Constructions, and Social Problems." *Social Problems, 44,* 2, May 1997:139–154.

Contreras, Josefina M., Kathryn A. Kerns, and Angela M. Neal-Barnett, eds. *Latino Children and Families in the United States: Current Research and Future Directions.* Westport, Conn.: Praeger, 2002.

Cookson, Peter W., Jr., and Caroline Hodges Persell. "Preparing for Power: Cultural Capital and Elite Boarding Schools." In *Life in Society: Readings to Accompany Sociology A Down-to-Earth Approach, Seventh Edition,* James M. Henslin, ed. Boston: Allyn and Bacon, 2005:175–185.

Cooley, Charles Horton. *Social Organization.* New York: Schocken Books, 1962. First published by Scribner's, 1909.

Cooley, Charles Horton. *Human Nature and the Social Order.* New York: Scribner's, 1902.

Copeland, Libby. "Click Clique: Facebook's Online College Community." *Washington Post,* December 28, 2004.

Corcoran, Mary. "Mobility, Persistence, and Consequences of Poverty for Children: Child and Adult Outcomes." In *Understanding Poverty,* Sheldon H. Danziger and Robert H. Haveman, eds. New York: Russell Sage, 2001:127–161.

Cortese, Anthony. *Provocateur: Images of Women and Minorities in Advertising,* 2nd ed. Boulder, Colo: Rowman and Little Publishers, 2003.

Cose, Ellis. "Black Versus Brown." *Newsweek,* July 3, 2006:44–45.

Cose, Ellis. "What's White Anyway?" *Newsweek,* September 18, 2000:64–65.

Coser, Lewis A. *Masters of Sociological Thought: Ideas in Historical and Social Context,* 2nd ed. New York: Harcourt Brace Jovanovich, 1977.

Coughlan, Sean. "If Your Face Fits." *BBC News Magazine,* June 2006.

Cowell, Alan. "4 Suspects in '94 Massacres of Rwanda Tutsi Are Held in London to Face Extradition." *New York Times,* November 30, 2006.

Cowen, Emory L., Judah Landes, and Donald E. Schaet. "The Effects of Mild Frustration on the Expression of Prejudiced Attitudes." *Journal of Abnormal and Social Psychology.* January 1959:33–38.

Cowley, Geoffrey. "Attention: Aging Men." *Newsweek,* November 16, 1996:66–75.

Cowley, Joyce. *Pioneers of Women's Liberation.* New York: Merit, 1969.

Crawford, Duane W., Renate M. Houts, Ted L. Huston, and Laura J. George. "Compatibility, Leisure, and Satisfaction in Marital Relationships." *Journal of Marriage and Family, 64,* May 2002:433–449.

Crossen, Cynthia. "How Pygmy Ota Benga Ended Up in Bronx Zoo as Darwinism Dawned." *Wall Street Journal,* February 6, 2006.

Crossen, Cynthia. "Déjà Vu." *New York Times,* February 25, 2004b.

Crossen, Cynthia. "Deja Vu." *Wall Street Journal,* March 5, 2003.

Crossen, Cynthia. "Margin of Error: Studies Galore Support Products and Positions, But Are They Reliable?" *Wall Street Journal,* Nov 14, 1991:A1.

Crossette, Barbara. "Caste May Be India's Moral Achilles' Heel." *New York Times,* October 20, 1996.

Dabbs, James M., Jr., and Robin Morris. "Testosterone, Social Class, and Antisocial Behavior in a Sample of 4,462 Men." *Psychological Science, 1,* 3, May 1990:209–211.

Dabbs, James M., Jr., Marian F. Hargrove, and Colleen Heusel. "Testosterone Differences Among College Fraternities: Well-Behaved vs. Rambunctious." *Personality and Individual Differences, 20,* 1996: 157–161.

Dabbs, James M., Jr., Timothy S. Carr, Robert L. Frady, and Jasmin K. Riad. "Testosterone, Crime, and Misbehavior Among 692 Male Prison Inmates." *Personality and Individual Differences, 18,* 1995:627–633.

Dao, James. "Instant Millions Can't Halt Winners' Grim Side." *New York Times,* December 5, 2005.

Darley, John M., and Bibb Latané. "Bystander Intervention in Emergencies: Diffusion of Responsibility." *Journal of Personality and Social Psychology, 8,* 4, 1968:377–383.

Darweesh, Suzanne. "Use Your Buying Power to Promote Ethics." *Los Angeles Times,* November 5, 2000.

Darwin, Charles. *The Origin of Species.* Chicago: Conley, 1859.

Dasgupta, Nilanjana, Debbie E. McGhee, Anthony G. Greenwald, and Mahzarin R. Banaji. "Automatic Preference for White Americans: Eliminating the Familiarity Explanation." *Journal of Experimental Social Psychology, 36,* 3, May 2000:316–328.

Davies, W. Martin. "Cognitive Contours: Recent Work on Cross-Cultural Psychology and Its Relevance for Education." *Studies in the Philosophy of Education, 26,* 2007:13–42.

Davis, Ann. "Artificial Reproduction Arrangers Are Ruled Child's Legal Parents." *Wall Street Journal,* March 11, 1998a:B2.

Davis, Ann. "High-Tech Births Spawn Legal Riddles." *Wall Street Journal,* January 26, 1998b:B1.

Davis, Ann, Joseph Pereira, and William M. Bulkeley. "Security Concerns Bring Focus on Translating Body Language." *Wall Street Journal,* August 15, 2002.

Davis, Kingsley. "Extreme Isolation." In *Down to Earth Sociology: Introductory Readings,* fourteenth ed., James M. Henslin, ed. New York: The Free Press, 2007.

Davis, Kingsley. "Extreme Social Isolation of a Child." *American Journal of Sociology, 45,* 4 Jan. 1940:554–565.

Davis, Kingsley, and Wilbert E. Moore. "Reply to Tumin." *American Sociological Review, 18,* 1953:394–396.

Davis, Kingsley, and Wilbert E. Moore. "Some Principles of Stratification." *American Sociological Review, 10,* 1945:242–249.

Davis, Nancy J., and Robert V. Robinson. "Class Identification of Men and Women in the 1970s and 1980s." *American Sociological Review, 53,* February 1988:103–112.

Davis, Stan. *Lessons From the Future: Making Sense of a Blurred World.* New York: Capstone Publishers, 2001.

Dawley, Richard Lee. *Amish in Wisconsin.* New Berlin, Wis.: Amish Insight, 2003.

Deck, Leland P. "Buying Brains by the Inch." *Journal of the College and University Personnel Association, 19,* 1968:33–37.

DeCrow, Karen. Foreword to *Why Men Earn More* by Warren Farrell. New York: AMACOM, 2005:xi–xii.

Deegan, Mary Jo. "W. E. B. Du Bois and the Women of Hull-House, 1895–1899." *American Sociologist,* Winter 1988:301–311.

Deflem, Mathieu, ed. *Sociological Theory and Criminological Research: Views from Europe and the United States.* San Diego: JAI Press, 2006.

Deliege, Robert. *The Untouchables of India.* New York: Berg Publishers, 2001.

DeMartini, Joseph R. "Basic and Applied Sociological Work: Divergence, Convergence, or Peaceful Co-existence?" *The Journal of Applied Behavioral Science, 18,* 2, 1982:203–215.

DeMause, Lloyd. "Our Forebears Made Childhood a Nightmare." *Psychology Today 8,* 11, April 1975:85–88.

Denney, Nancy W., and David Quadagno. *Human Sexuality,* 2nd ed. St. Louis: Mosby, 1992.

DeOilos, Ione Y., and Carolyn A. Kapinus. "Aging Childless Individuals and Couples: Suggestions for New Directions in Research." *Sociological Inquiry, 72,* 1, Winter 2003:72–80.

Derne, Steve. "Arnold Schwarzenegger, Ally McBeal and Arranged Marriages: Globalization on the Ground in India." *Contexts,* Summer 2003:12–18.

Deutscher, Irwin. *Accommodating Diversity: National Policies that Prevent Ethnic Conflict.* Lanham, Md.: Lexington Books, 2002.

Diamond, Milton, and Keith Sigmundson. "Sex Reassignment at Birth: Long-term Review and Clinical Implications." *Archives of Pediatric and Adolescent Medicine, 151,* March 1997:298–304.

Dickey, Christopher, and John Barry. "Iran: A Rummy Guide." *Newsweek,* May 8, 2006.

Dietz, Tracy L. "An Examination of Violence and Gender Role Portrayals in Video Games." *Women and Language, 23,* 2, Fall 2000:64–77.

DiSilvestro, Roger L. *In the Shadow of Wounded Knee: The Untold Final Chapter of the Indian Wars.* New York: Walker & Co., 2006.

Doane, Ashley W., Jr. "Dominant Group Ethnic Identity in the United States: The Role of 'Hidden' Ethnicity in Intergroup Relations." *The Sociological Quarterly, 38,* 3, Summer 1997: 375–397.

Dobash, Russell P., R. Emerson Dobash, Margo Wilson, and Martin Daly. "The Myth of Sexual Symmetry in Marital Violence." *Social Problems, 39,* 1, February 1992:71–91.

Dobash, Russell P., R. Emerson Dobash, Margo Wilson, and Martin Daly. "Marital Violence Is Not Symmetrical: A Response to Campbell." *SSSP Newsletter, 24,* 3, Fall 1993:26–30.

Dobriner, William M. "The Football Team as Social Structure and Social System." In *Social Structures and Systems: A Sociological Overview.* Pacific Palisades, Calif.: Goodyear, 1969a:116–120.

Dobriner, William M. *Social Structures and Systems.* Pacific Palisades, California: Goodyear, 1969b.

Dobyns, Henry F. *Their Numbers Became Thinned: Native American Population Dynamics in Eastern North America.* Knoxville: University of Tennessee Press, 1983.

Dodds, Peter Sheridan, Roby Muhamad, and Duncan J. Watts. "An Experimental Study of Search in Global Social Networks." *Science, 301,* August 8, 2003:827–830.

Dollard, John, et al. *Frustration and Aggression.* New Haven, Conn.: Yale University Press, 1939.

Domhoff, G. William. *Who Rules America? Power, Politics, and Social Change,* 5th ed. New York: McGraw-Hill, 2006.

Domhoff, G. William. "The Bohemian Grove and Other Retreats." In *Down to Earth Sociology: Introductory Readings,* 10th ed., James M. Henslin, ed. New York: Free Press, 1999a:391–403.

Domhoff, G. William. "State and Ruling Class in Corporate America (1974): Reflections, Corrections, and New Directions." *Critical Sociology, 25,* 2–3, July 1999b:260–265.

Domhoff, G. William. *The Power Elite and the State: How Policy Is Made in America.* Hawthorne, N. Y.: Aldine de Gruyter, 1990.

Donaldson, Stephen. "A Million Jockers, Punks, and Queens: Sex Among American Male Prisoners and Its Implications for Concepts of Sexual Orientation." February 4, 1993. Online.

Douglas, Carol Anne, et al. "Kenya: FGM Increasingly Occurring in Hospitals." *Off Our Backs, 35,* January-February 2005:5.

Dowd, Maureen. "The Knife Under the Tree." *New York Times,* December 5, 2002.

Drivonikou, G. V., P. Kay, T. Regler, R. B. Ivry, A. L. Gilbert, A. Franklin, and I. R. L. Davies. "Further Evidence That Whorfian Effects Are Stronger in the Right Visual Field Than in the Left." *PNAS, 104,* 3, January 16, 2007:1097–1102.

Du Bois, W. E. B. *Black Reconstruction in America: An Essay Toward a History of the Part Which Black Folk Played in the Attempt to Reconstruct Democracy in America, 1860–1880.* New York: Atheneum, 1992. First published in 1935.

Du Bois, W. E. B. *The Autobiography of W. E. B. Du Bois: A Soliloquy on Viewing My Life from the Last Decade of Its First Century.* New York: International, 1968.

Du Bois, W. E. B. *The Souls of Black Folk: Essays and Sketches.* Chicago: McClurg, 1903.

Ducharme, Lori J., Hannah K. Knudsen, J. Aaron Johnson, and Paul M. Roman. "Work as Haven? Modeling the Work-Related Attitudes of Dual-Earner Parents." Paper presented at the 2004 meetings of the American Sociological Association.

Duff, Christina. "Superrich's Share of After-Tax Income Stopped Rising in Early '90s, Data Show." *Wall Street Journal,* November 22, 1995:A2.

Dugger, Celia W. "Wedding Vows Bind Old World and New." *New York Times,* July 20, 1998.

Duneier, Mitchell. *Sidewalk.* New York: Farrar, Straus and Giroux, 1999.

Durkheim, Emile. *Suicide: A Study in Sociology.* John A. Spaulding and George Simpson, trans. New York: Free Press, 1966. First published in 1897.

Durkheim, Emile. *The Rules of Sociological Method.* Sarah A. Solovay and John H. Mueller, trans. New York: Free Press, 1938, 1958, 1964. First published in 1895.

Durkheim, Emile. *The Division of Labor in Society.* George Simpson, trans. New York: Free Press, 1933. First published in 1893.

Dush, Claire M. Kamp, Catherine L. Cohan, and Paul R. Amato. "The Relationship Between Cohabitation and Marital Quality and Stability:

Change Across Cohorts?" *Journal of Marriage and Family, 65*, 3, August 2003:539–549.

Dye, Jane Lawler. "Fertility of American Women, June 2004." U.S. Bureau of the Census. *Current Population Reports,* December 2005.

Dyer, Gwynne. "Anybody's Son Will Do." In *Down to Earth Sociology: Introductory Readings,* 14th ed., James M. Henslin, ed. New York: The Free Press, 2007.

Easley, Hema. "Indian Families Continue to Have Arranged Marriages." *The Journal News,* June 9, 2003.

Ebaugh, Helen Rose Fuchs. *Becoming an EX: The Process of Role Exit.* Chicago: The University of Chicago Press, 1988.

Ebner, Johanna. "Fighting International Terrorism with Social Science Knowledge." *Footnotes,* February 2005.

Eder, Donna. "On Becoming Female: Lessons Learned in School." In *Down to Earth Sociology: Introductory Readings,* 14th ed., James M. Henslin, ed. New York: The Free Press, 2007.

Eder, Donna. *School Talk: Gender and Adolescent Culture.* New Brunswick, N.J.: Rutgers University Press, 1995.

Edgerton, Robert B. *Sick Societies: Challenging the Myth of Primitive Harmony.* New York: Free Press, 1992.

Edgerton, Robert B. *Deviance: A Cross-Cultural Perspective.* Menlo Park, Calif.: Benjamin/Cummings, 1976.

Ehrenreich, Barbara, and Deidre English. *Witches, Midwives, and Nurses: A History of Women Healers.* Old Westbury, N. Y.: Feminist Press, 1973.

Eibl-Eibesfeldt, Irrenäus. *Ethology: The Biology of Behavior.* New York: Holt, Rinehart, and Winston, 1970.

Eisenhart, R. Wayne. "You Can't Hack It, Little Girl: A Discussion of the Covert Psychological Agenda of Modern Combat Training." *Journal of Social Issues, 31,* Fall 1975:13–23.

Ekman, Paul. *Faces of Man: Universal Expression in a New Guinea Village.* New York: Garland Press, 1980.

Ekman, Paul, Wallace V. Friesen, and John Bear. "The International Language of Gestures." *Psychology Today,* May 1984:64.

Elder, Glen H., Jr. *Children of the Great Depression: Social Change in Life Experience.* Boulder: Westview Press, 1999.

Elder, Glen H., Jr. "Age Differentiation and Life Course." *Annual Review of Sociology, 1,* 1975:165–190.

Elias, Paul. " 'Molecular Pharmers' Hope to Raise Human Proteins in Crop Plants." *St. Louis Post-Dispatch,* October 28, 2001:F7.

Elkins, Stanley M. *Slavery: A Problem in American Institutional and Intellectual Life,* 2nd ed. Chicago: University of Chicago Press, 1968.

Elson, Jean. *Am I Still a Woman? Hysterectomy and Gender Identity.* Philadelphia: Temple University Press, 2004.

England, Paula. "The Impact of Feminist Thought on Sociology." *Contemporary Sociology: A Journal of Reviews,* 2000:263–267.

Epstein, Cynthia Fuchs. "Great Divides: The Cultural, Cognitive, and Social Bases of the Global Subordination of Women." *American Sociological Review, 72,* February 2007:1–22.

Epstein, Cynthia. "Similarity and Difference: The Sociology of Gender Distinction." In *Handbook of the Sociology of Gender,* Janet Saltzman Chafetz, ed.. New York: Kluwer Academic/Plenum Publishers, 1999.

Epstein, Cynthia Fuchs. *Deceptive Distinctions: Sex, Gender, and the Social Order.* New Haven, Conn.: Yale University Press, 1988.

Eshleman, J. Ross. *The Family,* 9th ed. Boston: Allyn and Bacon, 2000.

"Ethiopia: Fighting Female Circumcision at Local Level." African News Service, February 16, 2005.

Ezekiel, Raphael S. *The Racist Mind: Portraits of American Neo-Nazis and Klansmen.* New York: Viking, 1995.

Ezekiel, Raphael S. *The Racist Mind: Portraits of American Neo-Nazis and Klansmen.* New York: Viking, 2002.

Fabrikant, Geraldine. "Old Nantucket Warily Meets the New." *New York Times,* June 5, 2005.

Fadiman, Anne. *The Spirit Catches You and You Fall Down.* Farrar, Straus and Giroux, 1997.

Fagot, Beverly I., Richard Hagan, Mary Driver Leinbach, and Sandra Kronsberg. "Differential Reactions to Assertive and Communicative Acts of Toddler Boys and Girls." *Child Development, 56,* 1985: 1499–1505.

Faris, Robert E. L., and Warren Dunham. *Mental Disorders in Urban Areas.* Chicago: University of Chicago Press, 1939.

Farley, John E., and Gregory D. Squires. "Fences and Neighbors: Segregation in twenty first Century America." *Contexts,* Winter 2005:33–39.

Fattah, Hassan M. "After First Steps, Saudi Reformers See Efforts Stall." *New York Times,* April 26, 2007.

Feagin, Joe R. "The Continuing Significance of Race: Antiblack Discrimination in Public Places." In *Majority and Minority: The Dynamics of Race and Ethnicity in American Life,* 6th ed., Norman R. Yetman, ed. Boston: Allyn and Bacon, 1999:384–399.

Feagin, Joe R., and Karyn D. McKinney. *The Many Costs of White Racism.* Lanham, Md.: Rowman and Littlefield, 2003.

Featherman, David L. "Opportunities Are Expanding." *Society, 13,* 1979:4–11.

Featherman, David L., and Robert M. Hauser. *Opportunity and Change.* New York: Academic Press, 1978.

Feder, Barnaby. "Billboards That Know You by Name." *New York Times,* January 29, 2007.

Feldman, Saul D. "The Presentation of Shortness in Everyday Life—Height and Heightism in American Society: Toward a Sociology of Stature." Paper presented at the 1972 meetings of the American Sociological Association.

Felsenthal, Edward. "Justices' Ruling Further Defines Sex Harassment." *Wall Street Journal,* March 5, 1998:B1, B2.

Felton, Lee Ann, Andrea Gumm, and David J. Pittenger. "The Recipients of Unwanted Sexual Encounters Among College Students." *College Student Journal, 35,* 1, March 2001:135–143.

Ferraro, Kathleen J. "Intimate Partner Violence." In *Social Problems,* 7th ed., by James M. Henslin. Upper Saddle River, N. J.: Prentice Hall, 2006:373.

Fields, Jason. "America's Families and Living Arrangements: 2003." *Current Population Reports,* November 2004.

Finer, Jonathan. "Faculty Group Rebukes Harvard President With Vote." *Washington Post,* March 16, 2005.

Finkelhor, David, and Kersti Yllo. "Marital Rape: The Myth Versus the Reality." In *Marriage and Family in a Changing Society,* 3rd ed., James M. Henslin, ed. New York: Free Press, 1989:382–391.

Finkelhor, David, and Kersti Yllo. *License to Rape: Sexual Abuse of Wives.* New York: Henry Holt, 1985.

Fischer, Tamar F. C., Paul M. De Graaf, and Matthijs Kalmijn. "Friendly and Antagonistic Contact Between Former Spouses After Divorce." *Journal of Family Issues, 26,* 8, November 2005:1131–1163.

Fish, Jefferson M. "Mixed Blood." *Psychology Today, 28,* 6, November–December 1995:55–58, 60, 61, 76, 80.

Fisher, Marla Jo. "California College Grapples with Title IX Compliance." *Community College Week, 14,* 20, May 13, 2002:18.

Fisher, Sue. *In the Patient's Best Interest: Women and the Politics of Medical Decisions.* New Brunswick, N.J.: Rutgers University Press, 1986.

Flavel, John H., et al. *The Development of Role-Taking and Communication Skills in Children.* New York: Wiley, 1968.

Flavel, John, Patricia H. Miller, and Scott A. Miller. *Cognitive Development,* 4th ed. Upper Saddle River, N.J.: Prentice Hall, 2002.

Flexner, E. *Century of Struggle.* Cambridge, Mass.: Belknap, 1971. In Claire M. Renzetti and Daniel J. Curran, *Women, Men, and Society,* 4th ed. Boston: Allyn and Bacon, 1999.

Flink, James J., *The Automobile Age.* Cambridge, Mass.: MIT Press, 1990.

Flippen, Annette R. "Understanding Groupthink From a Self-Regulatory Perspective." *Small Group Research, 30,* 2, April 1999:139–165.

Foley, Douglas E. "The Great American Football Ritual." In *Society: Readings to Accompany Sociology: A Down-to-Earth Approach, Core Concepts,* James M. Henslin, ed. Boston: Allyn and Bacon, 2006: 64–76. First published in 1990.

Foote, Donna. "And Baby Makes One." *Newsweek,* February 2, 1998: 68–69.

Fraser, Graham. "Fox Denies Free Trade Exploiting the Poor in Mexico." *Toronto Star,* April 20, 2001.

Freedman, Jane. *Feminism.* Philadelphia: Open University Press, 2001.

Fremson, Ruth. "Dead Bachelors in Remote China Still Find Wives." *New York Times,* October 5, 2006.

Friedl, Ernestine. "Society and Sex Roles." In *Conformity and Conflict: Readings in Cultural Anthropology,* James P. Spradley and David W. McCurdy, eds. Glenview, Ill.: Scott, Foresman, 1990: 229–238.

Fuhrmans, Vanessa, and Carol Hymowitz. "WellPoint's CEO Takes the Reins, Facing Challenges." *Wall Street Journal,* June 6, 2007.

Fuller, Rex, and Richard Schoenberger. "The Gender Salary Gap: Do Academic Achievement, Internship Experience, and College Major Make a Difference?" *Social Science Quarterly, 72,* 4, December 1991:715–726.

Furstenberg, Frank F., Jr., and Kathleen Mullan Harris. "The Disappearing American Father? Divorce and the Waning Significance of Biological Fatherhood." In *The Changing American Family: Sociological and Demographic Perspectives,* Scott J. South and Stewart E. Tolnay, eds. Boulder, Colo.: Westview Press, 1992: 197–223.

Furstenberg, Frank F., Jr., Sheela Kennedy, Vonnie C. McLoyd, Ruben G. Rumbaut, and Richard A. Settersten, Jr. "Growing Up Is Harder to Do." *Contexts, 3,* 3, Summer 2004:33–41.

Galbraith, John Kenneth. *The Nature of Mass Poverty.* Cambridge Mass.: Harvard University Press, 1979.

Galliher, John F., Wayne Brekus, and David P. Keys. *Laud Humphreys: Prophet of Homosexuality and Sociology.* Madison, Wisconsin: University of Wisconsin Press, 2004.

Gallmeier, Charles P. "Methodological Issues in Qualitative Sport Research: Participant Observation among Hockey Players." *Sociological Spectrum, 8,* 1988:213–235.

Gallup Poll. "Americans More Likely to Believe in God Than the Devil, Heaven More Than Hell." June 13, 2007.

Gans, Herbert. J., "Public Sociologies: Reply to Hausknecht." *Footnotes,* January 2003:8.

Garfinkel, Harold. *Studies in Ethnomethodology.* Englewood Cliffs, N.J.: Prentice Hall, 1967.

Garfinkel, Harold. "Conditions of Successful Degradation Ceremonies." *American Journal of Sociology, 61,* 2, March 1956: 420–424.

Garrett, Michael Tlanusta. "Understanding the 'Medicine' of Native American Traditional Values: An Integrative Review." *Counseling and Values, 43,* 2, January 1999:84–98.

Gatewood, Willard B. *Aristocrats of Color: The Black Elite, 1880–1920.* Bloomington, Ind.: Indiana University Press, 1990.

Gautham S. "Coming Next: The Monsoon Divorce." *New Statesman, 131,* 4574, February 18, 2002:32–33.

Gerhard, Jane. "Revisiting 'The Myth of the Vaginal Orgasm': The Female Orgasm in American Sexual Thought and Second Wave Feminism." *Feminist Studies, 26,* 2, Fall 2000:449–477.

Gerson, Kathleen. *Hard Choices: How Women Decide about Work, Career, and Motherhood.* Berkeley: University of California Press, 1985.

Gerth, H. H., and C. Wright Mills. *From Max Weber: Essays in Sociology.* New York: Galaxy, 1958.

Gerth, Jeff. "Two Companies Pay Penalties for Improving China Rockets." *New York Times,* March 3, 2003.

Giele, Janet Zollinger. *Women and the Future: Changing Sex Roles in Modern America.* New York: Free Press, 1978.

Gilbert, Dennis L. *The American Class Structure in an Age of Growing Inequality,* 6th ed. Belmont, Calif.: Wadsworth Publishing, 2003.

Gilbert, Dennis, and Joseph A. Kahl. *The American Class Structure: A New Synthesis.* 4th ed. Belmont, Calif.: Wadsworth Publishing, 1998.

Gilligan, Carol. *The Birth of Pleasure.* New York: Knopf, 2002.

Gilligan, Carol. *Making Connections: The Relational World of Adolescent Girls at Emma Willard School.* Cambridge, Mass.: Harvard University Press, 1990.

Gilligan, Carol. *In a Different Voice: Psychological Theory and Women's Development.* Cambridge, Mass.: Harvard University Press, 1982.

Gilman, Charlotte Perkins. *The Man-Made World or, Our Androcentric Culture.* New York: 1971. First published 1911.

Girshick, Lori B. *Woman-To-Woman Sexual Violence: Does She Call It Rape?* Boston: Northeastern University Press, 2002.

Gitlin, Todd. *The Twilight of Common Dreams: Why America Is Wracked by Culture Wars.* New York: Metropolitan Books, 1997.

Glascock, Jack. "Gender Roles on Prime-Time Network Television: Demographics and Behaviors." *Journal of Broadcasting and Electronic Media, 45,* Fall 2001:656–669.

Gleason, Carmen L. "Officials Emphasize Zero Tolerance of Sexual Assault." Army News Service, April 5, 2007.

Glenn, Evelyn Nakano. "Chinese American Families." In *Minority Families in the United States: A Multicultural Perspective,* Ronald L. Taylor, ed. Englewood Cliffs, N.J.: Prentice Hall, 1994:115–145.

Glick, Paul C., and S. Lin. "More Young Adults Are Living with Their Parents: Who Are They?" *Journal of Marriage and Family, 48,* 1986: 107–112.

Goetting, Ann. *Getting Out: Life Stories of Women Who Left Abusive Men.* New York: Columbia University Press, 2001.

Gofen, Anat. "Family Capital: How First-Generation Higher-Education Students Break the Intergenerational Cycle." Institute for Research on Poverty, Discussion Paper 1322–07, 2007.

Goffman, Erving. *Stigma: Notes on the Management of Spoiled Identity.* Englewood Cliffs, N.J.: Prentice Hall, 1963.

Goffman, Erving. *Asylums: Essays on the Social Situation of Mental Patients and Other Inmates.* Chicago: Aldine, 1961.

Gold, Ray. "Janitors Versus Tenants: A Status-Income Dilemma." *American Journal of Sociology, 58,* 1952:486–493.

Goldberg, Steven. *Fads and Fallacies in the Social Sciences.* Amherst, N. Y.: Humanity/Prometheus, 2003.

Goldberg, Steven. *Why Men Rule: A Theory of Male Dominance.* Chicago: Open Court, 1993.

Goldberg, Steven. "Reaffirming the Obvious." *Society,* September–October 1986:4–7.

Goldberg, Steven. *The Inevitability of Patriarchy,* rev. ed. New York: Morrow, 1974.

Goldberg, Susan, and Michael Lewis. "Play Behavior in the Year-Old Infant: Early Sex Differences." *Child Development, 40,* March 1969: 21–31.

Goldberg-Glen, Robin, Roberta G. Sands, Ralph D. Cole, and Carolyn Cristofalo. "Multigenerational Patterns and Internal Structures in Families in Which Grandparents Raise Grandchildren." *Families in Society: The Journal of Contemporary Human Services, 79,* 5, September 1998:477–489.

Goleman, Daniel. "Pollsters Enlist Psychologists in Quest for Unbiased Results." *New York Times,* September 7, 1993:C1, C11.

Gonzales, Alberto R. "Memorandum for Albert R. Gonzales, Counsel to the President: Re: Standards of Conduct for Interrogation Under *18 U.S.C. 2340–2340A.*" August 2, 2002.

Goode, Erica. "Study Says 20% of Girls Reported Abuse by a Date." *New York Times,* August 1, 2001.

Goozen, Stephanie H. M. van, Graeme Fairchild, Heddeke Snoek, and Gordon T. Harold. "The Evidence for a Neurobiological Model of Childhood Antisocial Behavior." *Psychological Bulletin, 133,* 1, 2007: 149–182.

Gottfredson, Michael R., and Travis Hirschi. *A General Theory of Crime.* Stanford, Calif.: Stanford University Press, 1990.

Grant, Peter. "Looking for Love (Or a Date) on Cable TV." *Wall Street Journal,* December 15, 2005.

Greenhouse, Linda. "Justices Uphold Long Prison Terms in Repeat Crimes." *New York Times,* March 6, 2003.

Greenwald, Anthony G., and Linda Hamilton Krieger. "Implicit Bias: Scientific Foundations." *California Law Review,* July 2006.

Gross, Jan T. *Neighbors.* New Haven: Yale University Press, 2001.

Gross, Jane. "In the Quest for the Perfect Look, More Girls Choose the Scalpel." *New York Times,* November 29, 1998.

Guensburg, Carol. "Bully Factories." *American Journalism Review, 23,* 6, 2001:51–59.

Gupta, Giri Raj. "Love, Arranged Marriage, and the Indian Social Structure." In *Cross-Cultural Perspectives of Mate Selection and Marriage,* George Kurian, ed. Westport, Conn.: Greenwood Press, 1979.

Haas, Jack. "Binging: Educational Control Among High-Steel Iron Workers." *American Behavioral Scientist, 16,* 1972:27–34.

Hacker, Helen Mayer. "Women as a Minority Group." *Social Forces, 30,* October 1951:60–69.

Hall, Edward T. *The Hidden Dimension.* Garden City, N. Y.: Anchor Books, 1969.

Hall, Edward T. *The Silent Language.* New York: Doubleday, 1959.

Hall, Edward T., and Mildred R. Hall. "The Sounds of Silence." In *Down to Earth Sociology: Introductory Readings,* 14th ed., James M. Henslin, ed. New York: The Free Press, 2007.

Hall, G. Stanley. *Adolescence: Its Psychology and Its Relations to Physiology, Anthropology, Sociology, Sex, Crime, Religion, and Education.* New York: Appleton, 1904.

Hall, Ronald E. "The Tiger Woods Phenomenon: A Note on Biracial Identity." *The Social Science Journal, 38,* 2, April 2001: 333–337.

Hamermesh, Daniel S., and Jeff E. Biddle. "Beauty and the Labor Market." *American Economic Review, 84,* 5, December 1994:1174–1195.

Hamid, Shadi. "Between Orientalism and Postmodernism: The Changing Nature of Western Feminist Thought Towards the Middle East." *HAWWA, 4,* 1, 2006·76–92.

Harlow, Harry F., and Margaret K. Harlow. "The Affectional Systems." In *Behavior of Nonhuman Primates: Modern Research Trends,* Vol. 2, Allan M. Schrier, Harry F. Harlow, and Fred Stollnitz, eds. New York: Academic Press, 1965:287–334.

Harlow, Harry F., and Margaret K. Harlow. "Social Deprivation in Monkeys." *Scientific American, 207,* 1962:137–147.

Harris, Kim, Dwight R. Sanders, Shaun Gress, and Nick Kuhns. "Starting Salaries for Agribusiness Graduates From an AASCARR Institution: The Case of Southern Illinois University." *Agribusiness, 21,* 1, 2005: 65–80.

Harris, Marvin. "Why Men Dominate Women." *New York Times Magazine,* November 13, 1977:46, 115, 117–123.

Harrison, Paul. *Inside the Third World: The Anatomy of Poverty,* 3rd ed. London: Penguin Books, 1993.

Hart, Paul. "Groupthink, Risk-Taking and Recklessness: Quality of Process and Outcome in Policy Decision Making." *Politics and the Individual, 1,* 1, 1991:67–90.

Hartley, Eugene. *Problems in Prejudice.* New York: King's Crown Press, 1946.

Hayashi, Gina M., and Bonnie R. Strickland. "Long-Term Effects of Parental Divorce on Love Relationships: Divorce as Attachment Disruption." *Journal of Social and Personal Relationships, 15,* 1, February 1998, 23–38.

Heames, Joyce Thompson, Michael G. Harvey, and Darren Treadway. "Status Inconsistency: An Antecedent to Bullying Behavior in Groups." *International Journal of Human Resource Management, 17, 2,* February 2006:348–361.

Heilman, Madeline E. "Description and Prescription: How Gender Stereotypes Prevent Women's Ascent Up the Organizational Ladder." *Journal of Social Issues, 57,* 4, Winter 2001:657–674.

Hellinger, Daniel, and Dennis R. Judd. *The Democratic Facade.* Pacific Grove, Calif.: Brooks/Cole, 1991.

Hemmings, Annette. "The 'Hidden' Corridor Curriculum." *High School Journal, 83,* December 1999:1–12.

Hendrix, Lewellyn. "What Is Sexual Inequality? On the Definition and Range of Variation." *Gender and Society, 28,* 3, August 1994:287–307.

Henslin, James M., and Mae A. Biggs. "Behavior in Pubic Places: The Sociology of the Vaginal Examination." In *Down to Earth Sociology: Introductory Readings,* 14th ed., James M. Henslin, ed. New York: The Free Press, 2007.

Henslin, James M. "On Becoming Male: Reflections of a Sociologist on Childhood and Early Socialization." In *Down to Earth Sociology: Introductory Readings,* 14th ed., James M. Henslin, ed. New York: The Free Press, 2007.

Henslin, James M. "Author's File on a Divorce." 2005.

Henley, Nancy, Mykol Hamilton, and Barrie Thorne. "Womanspeak and Manspeak." In *Beyond Sex Roles.* Alice G. Sargent, ed. St. Paul, Minn.: West, 1985.

Herring, Cedric. "Is Job Discrimination Dead?" *Contexts.* Summer 2002:13–18.

Hetherington, Mavis, and John Kelly. *For Better or For Worse: Divorce Reconsidered.* New York: W. W. Norton, 2003.

Hewitt Associates. *Worklife Benefits Provided by Major U.S. Employers, 2003–2004.* Lincolnshire, Ill.: Hewitt Associates, 2004.

Higginbotham, Elizabeth, and Lynn Weber. "Moving with Kin and Community: Upward Social Mobility for Black and White Women." *Gender and Society, 6,* 3, September 1992:416–440.

Hill, Andrew J. "Motivation for Eating Behaviour in Adolescent Girls: The Body Beautiful." *Proceedings of the Nutrition Society, 65,* 2006: 376–384.

Hill, Mark E. "Skin Color and the Perception of Attractiveness Among African Americans: Does Gender Make a Difference?" *Social Psychology Quarterly, 65,* 1, 2002:77–91.

Hiltz, Starr Roxanne. "Widowhood." In *Marriage and Family in a Changing Society,* 3rd ed., James M. Henslin, ed. New York: Free Press, 1989:521–531.

Hirschi, Travis. *Causes of Delinquency.* Berkeley: University of California Press, 1969.

Hochschild, Arlie. "When Work Becomes Home and Home Becomes Work." In *Society: Readings to Accompany Sociology: A Down-to-Earth Approach, Core Concepts,* James M. Henslin ed. Boston: Allyn and Bacon, 2006:182–191.

Hochschild, Arlie Russell. *The Time Bind: When Work Becomes Home and Home Becomes Work.* New York: Henry Holt, 1997.

Hochschild, Arlie Russell. *The Managed Heart: Commercialization of Human Feeling.* Chicago: University of Chicago Press, 1983.

Hochschild, Arlie Russell. "The Sociology of Feeling and Emotion: Selected Possibilities." In *Another Voice: Feminist Perspectives on Social Life and Social Science,* Marcia Millman and Rosabeth Moss Kanter, eds. Garden City, N. Y.: Anchor Books, 1975.

Honeycutt, Karen. "Disgusting, Pathetic, Bizarrely Beautiful: Representations of Weight in Popular Culture." Paper presented at the 1995 meetings of the American Sociological Association.

Hong, Lawrence. "Marriage in China." In *Til Death Do Us Part: A Multicultural Anthology on Marriage,* Sandra Lee Browning and R. Robin Miller, eds. Stamford, Conn.: JAI Press, 1999.

hooks, bell. *Where We Stand: Class Matters.* New York: Routledge, 2000.

Horn, James P. *Land As God Made It: Jamestown and the Birth of America.* New York: Basic Books, 2006.

Horowitz, Ruth. "Studying Violence Among the 'Lions.' " In James M. Henslin, *Social Problems.* Upper Saddle River, New Jersey: Prentice Hall, 2005:135.

Horowitz, Ruth. *Honor and the American Dream: Culture and Identity in a Chicano Community.* New Brunswick, N.J.: Rutgers University Press, 1983.

Hossfeld, Karen J. " 'Their Logic Against Them': Contradictions in Sex, Race, and Class in Silicon Valley." In *Gender Through the Prism of Difference,* 2nd ed., Maxine Baca Zinn, Pierrette Hondagneu-Sotelo, and Michael A. Messner, eds. Boston: Allyn and Bacon, 2000:388–400.

Hostetler, John A. *Amish Society,* 3rd ed. Baltimore: Johns Hopkins University Press, 1980.

"House Divided." *People Weekly,* May 24, 1999:126.

Houtman, Dick. "What Exactly Is a 'Social Class'?: On the Economic Liberalism and Cultural Conservatism of the 'Working Class'." Paper presented at the 1995 meetings of the American Sociological Association.

Howe, Henry, John Lyne, Alan Gross, Harro VanLente, Aire Rip, Richard Lewontin, Daniel McShea, Greg Myers, Ullica Segerstrale, Herbert W. Simons, and V. B. Smocovitis. "Gene Talk in Sociobiology." *Social Epistemology, 6,* 2, April-June 1992:109–163.

Howells, Lloyd T., and Selwyn W. Becker. "Seating Arrangement and Leadership Emergence." *Journal of Abnormal and Social Psychology, 64,* February 1962:148–150.

Hsu, Francis L. K. *The Challenge of the American Dream: The Chinese in the United States.* Belmont, Calif.: Wadsworth, 1971.

Huber, Joan. "Micro-Macro Links in Gender Stratification." *American Sociological Review, 55,* February 1990:1–10.

Huggins, Martha K., and Sandra Rodrigues. "Kids Working on Paulista Avenue." *Childhood, 11,* 2004:495–514.

Huggins, Martha K., Mika Haritos-Fatouros, and Philip G. Zimbardo. *Violence Workers: Police Torturers and Murderers Reconstruct Brazilian Atrocities.* Berkeley: University of California Press, 2002.

Hughes, Everett C. "Good People and Dirty Work." In *Life in Society: Readings to Accompany Sociology: A Down-to-Earth Approach, Seventh Edition,* James M. Henslin, ed. Boston: Allyn and Bacon, 2005: 125–134. Article originally published in 1962.

Hughes, Kathleen A. "Even Tiki Torches Don't Guarantee a Perfect Wedding." *Wall Street Journal,* February 20, 1990:A1, A16.

Humphreys, Laud. "Impersonal Sex and Perceived Satisfaction." In *Studies in the Sociology of Sex,* James M. Henslin, ed. New York: Appleton-Century-Crofts, 1971:351–374.

Humphreys, Laud. *Tearoom Trade: Impersonal Sex in Public Places,* enlarged ed. Chicago: Aldine, 1970, 1975.

Hundley, Greg. "Why Women Earn Less Than Men in Self-Employment." *Journal of Labor Research, 22,* 4, Fall 2001:817–827.

Hurtado, Aída, David E. Hayes-Bautista, R. Burciaga Valdez, and Anthony C. R. Hernández. *Redefining California: Latino Social Engagement in a Multicultural Society.* Los Angeles: UCLA Chicano Studies Research Center, 1992.

Huttenbach, Henry R. "The Roman *Porajmos:* The Nazi Genocide of Europe's Gypsies." *Nationalities Papers, 19,* 3, Winter 1991: 373–394.

Hymowitz, Carol. "Raising Women to Be Leaders." *Wall Street Journal,* February 12, 2007.

Hymowitz, Carol. "Through the Glass Ceiling." *Wall Street Journal,* November 8, 2004.

Itard, Jean Marc Gospard. *The Wild Boy of Aveyron.* Translated by George and Muriel Humphrey. New York: Appleton-Century-Crofts, 1962.

Jacobs, Charles. "Money Talks." *The Boston Globe,* February 19, 1999.

Jacobs, Jerry A. "Detours on the Road to Equality: Women, Work and Higher Education." *Contexts,* Winter 2003:32–41.

Jacobs, Margaret A. " 'New Girl' Network Is Boon for Women Lawyers." *Wall Street Journal,* March 4, 1997:B1, B7.

Jaffee, Sara, and Janet Shibley Hyde. "Gender Differences in Moral Orientation: A Meta-Analysis." *Psychological Bulletin, 126,* 5, 2000: 703–726.

Jaffrelot, Christophe. "The Impact of Affirmative Action in India: More Political than Socioeconomic." *India Review, 5,* 2, April 2006:173–189.

Jaggar, Alison M. "Sexual Difference and Sexual Equality." In *Theoretical Perspectives on Sexual Difference,* Deborah L. Rhode, ed. New Haven, Conn.: Yale University Press, 1990:239–254.

Janis, Irving. L. *Groupthink: Psychological Studies of Policy Decisions and Fiascoes.* Boston: Houghton Mifflin, 1982.

Janis, Irving L. *Victims of Groupthink.* Boston, Mass.: Houghton Mifflin, 1972.

Jankowiak, William R., and Edward F. Fischer. "A Cross-Cultural Perspective on Romantic Love." *Journal of Ethnology, 31,* 2, April 1992:149–155.

Jankowski, Martín Sánchez. *Islands in the Street: Gangs and American Urban Society.* Berkeley: University of California Press, 1991.

Johansson, Perry. "Consuming the Other: The Fetish of the Western Woman in Chinese Advertising and Popular Culture." *Postcolonial Studies, 2,* 3, November 1999.

Johnson-Weiner, Karen. *Train Up a Child: Old Order Amish and Mennonite Schools.* Baltimore: Johns Hopkins University Press, 2007.

Johnston, David Cay. "Is Live Sex On-Demand Coming to Hotel TVs?" *New York Times,* January 17, 2007.

Jones, James H. *Bad Blood: The Tuskegee Syphilis Experiment,* 2nd ed. New York: Free Press, 1993.

Jones, Steve. "Let the Games Begin: Gaming Technology and Entertainment Among College Students." Washington, D.C.: PEW Internet and American Life Project, 2003.

"Judge Rules Against Ford in Discrimination Lawsuit." *New York Times,* March 17, 2005.

Judge, Timothy A., and Daniel M. Cable. "The Effect of Physical Height on Workplace Success and Income: Preliminary Test of a Theoretical Model." *Journal of Applied Psychology, 89,* 3, 2004:428–441.

Kaebnick, Gregory E. "On the Sanctity of Nature." *Hastings Center Report, 30,* 5, September-October 2000:16–23.

Kagan, Jerome. "The Idea of Emotions in Human Development." In *Emotions, Cognition, and Behavior,* Carroll E. Izard, Jerome Kagan, and Robert B. Zajonc, eds. New York: Cambridge University Press, 1984:38–72.

Kalof, Linda. "Vulnerability to Sexual Coercion Among College Women: A Longitudinal Study." *Gender Issues, 18,* 4, Fall 2000:47–58.

Kanazawa, Satoshi, and Jody L. Kovar. "Why Beautiful People Are More Intelligent." *Intelligence, 32,* 2004:227–243.

Katz, Sidney. "The Importance of Being Beautiful." In *Down to Earth Sociology: Introductory Readings,* 14th ed., James M. Henslin, ed. New York: The Free Press, 2007.

Kaufman, Joanne. "Married Maidens and Dilatory Domiciles." *Wall Street Journal,* May 7, 1996:A16.

Kefalas, Maria. "Looking for the Lower Middle Class." *City and Community, 6,* 1, March 2007:63–68.

Kelly, Joan B. "How Adults React to Divorce." In *Marriage and Family in a Changing Society,* 4th ed., James M. Henslin, ed. New York: Free Press, 1992:410–423.

Keniston, Kenneth. *Youth and Dissent: The Rise of a New Opposition.* New York: Harcourt, Brace, Jovanovich, 1971.

Kent, Mary, and Robert Lalasz. "In the News: Speaking English in the United States." Population Reference Bureau, January 18, 2007.

Kephart, William M., and William W. Zellner. *Extraordinary Groups: An Examination of Unconventional Life-Styles,* 7th ed. New York: Worth Publishing, 2001.

Khattak, Mizuko Ito. "Anime's 'Transnational Geekdom.'" UCLA's Asia Institute, January 23, 2007.

Kibria, Nazli. *Family Tightrope: The Changing Lives of Vietnamese Americans.* Princeton, N.J.: Princeton University Press, 1993.

Kifner, John. "Building Modernity on Desert Mirages." *New York Times,* February 7, 1999.

Kilbourne, Jean. "Beauty and the Beast of Advertising." In *Down to Earth Sociology: Introductory Readings,* 12th ed., James M. Henslin, ed. New York: The Free Press, 2003:421–424.

Kingston, Maxine Hong. *The Woman Warrior.* New York: Vintage Books, 1975:108. Quoted in Frank J. Zulke and Jacqueline P. Kirley. *Through the Eyes of Social Science,* 6th ed. Prospect Heights, Ill.: Waveland Press, 2002.

Kleinfeld, Judith S. "Gender and Myth: Data about Student Performance." In *Through the Eyes of Social Science,* 6th ed., Frank J. Zulke and Jacqueline P. Kirley, eds. Prospect Heights, Ill.: Waveland Press, 2002a:380–393.

Kleinfeld, Judith S. "The Small World Problem." *Society,* January–February, 2002b:61–66.

Kluegel, James R., and Eliot R. Smith. *Beliefs About Inequality: America's Views of What Is and What Ought to Be.* Hawthorne, N. Y.: Aldine de Gruyter, 1986.

Knapp, Daniel. "What Happened When I Took My Sociological Imagination to the Dump." *Footnotes,* May–June, 2005:4.

Knauth, Donna G. "Predictors of Parental Sense of Competence for the Couple During the Transition to Parenthood." *Research in Nursing and Health, 23,* 2000:496–509.

Kohlberg, Lawrence. "A Current Statement on Some Theoretical Issues." In *Lawrence Kohlberg: Consensus and Controversy,* Sohan Modgil and Celia Modgil, eds. Philadelphia: Falmer Press, 1986:485–546.

Kohlberg, Lawrence. *The Psychology of Moral Development: Moral Stages and the Life Cycle.* San Francisco: Harper and Row, 1984.

Kohlberg, Lawrence. "Moral Education for a Society in Moral Transition." *Educational Leadership, 33,* 1975:46–54.

Kohlberg, Lawrence, and Carol Gilligan. "The Adolescent as a Philosopher: The Discovery of the Self in a Postconventional World." *Daedalus, 100,* 1971:1051–1086.

Kohn, Melvin L. *Class and Conformity: A Study in Values,* 2nd ed. Homewood, Ill.: Dorsey Press, 1977.

Kohn, Melvin L. "Occupational Structure and Alienation." *American Journal of Sociology, 82,* 1976:111–130.

Kohn, Melvin L. "Social Class and Parent-Child Relationships: An Interpretation." *American Journal of Sociology, 68,* 1963:471–480.

Kohn, Melvin L. "Social Class and Parental Values." *American Journal of Sociology, 64,* 1959:337–351.

Kohn, Melvin L., and Carmi Schooler. "Class, Occupation, and Orientation." *American Sociological Review, 34,* 1969:659–678.

Kohn, Melvin L., Kazimierz M. Slomczynski, and Carrie Schoenbach. "Social Stratification and the Transmission of Values in the Family: A Cross-National Assessment." *Sociological Forum, 1,* 1, 1986:73–102.

Korda, Michael. *Male Chauvinism: How It Works.* New York: Random House, 1973.

Krane, Vikki, Julie A. Stiles-Shipley, Jennifer Waldron, and Jennifer Michalenok. "Relationships Among Body Satisfaction, Social Physique Anxiety, and Eating Behaviors in Female Athletes and Exercisers." *Journal of Sport Behavior, 24,* 3, September 2001: 247–264.

Kraybill, Donald B. *The Riddle of Amish Culture.* Revised edition. Baltimore, Md.: Johns Hopkins University Press, 2002.

Kristoff, Nicholas D. "Interview With a Humanoid." *New York Times,* July 23, 2002.

Kroeger, Brooke. "When a Dissertation Makes a Difference." *New York Times,* March 20, 2004.

Krugman, Paul. "White Man's Burden." *New York Times,* September 24, 2002.

Kubrin, Charis E., and Ronald Weitzer. "Retaliatory Homicide: Concentrated Disadvantage and Neighborhood Culture." *Social Problems, 50,* 2, May 2003:157–180.

Kurian, George Thomas. *Encyclopedia of the Third World,* Vols. 1, 2, 3. New York: Facts on File, 1992.

Kurian, George Thomas. *Encyclopedia of the Second World.* New York: Facts on File, 1991.

Kurian, George Thomas. *Encyclopedia of the First World,* Vols. 1, 2. New York: Facts on File, 1990.

La Barre, Weston. *The Human Animal.* Chicago: University of Chicago Press, 1954.

Lacayo, Richard. "The 'Cultural' Defense." *Time,* Fall 1993b:61.

Lacey, Marc. "Tijuana Journal: Cities Mesh Across Blurry Border, Despite Physical Barrier. *New York Times,* March 5, 2007.

LaFraniere, Sharon. "Africa's World of Forced Labor, in a 6-Year-Old's Eyes." *New York Times,* October 29, 2006.

Landtman, Gunnar. *The Origin of the Inequality of the Social Classes.* New York: Greenwood Press, 1968. First published in 1938.

Lareau, Annette. "Invisible Inequality: Social Class and Childrearing in Black Families and White Families." *American Sociological Review, 67,* October 2002:747–776.

Larson, Jeffry H. "The Marriage Quiz: College Students' Beliefs in Selected Myths About Marriage." *Family Relations,* January 1988:3–11.

Larson, Mary Strom. "Interactions, Activities and Gender in Children's Television Commercials: A Content Analysis." *Journal of Broadcasting and Electronic Media, 45,* Winter 2001:41–51.

Lauer, Jeanette, and Robert Lauer. "Marriages Made to Last." In *Marriage and Family in a Changing Society,* 4th ed., James M. Henslin, ed. New York: Free Press, 1992:481–486.

Leacock, Eleanor. *Myths of Male Dominance.* New York: Monthly Review Press, 1981.

LeDuff, Charlie. "Handling the Meltdowns of the Nuclear Family." *New York Times,* May 28, 2003.

Lee, Nick. *Childhood and Society: Growing Up in an Age of Uncertainty.* Buckingham: Open University Press, 2001.

Lee, Raymond M. *Unobtrusive Methods in Social Research.* Philadelphia: Open University Press, 2000.

Lee, Sharon M. "Asian Americans: Diverse and Growing." *Population Bulletin, 53,* 2, June 1998:1–39.

Lee, Sharon M., and Barry Edmonston. "New Marriages, New Families: U.S. Racial and Hispanic Intermarriage." *Population Bulletin, 60,* 2, June 2005:1–36.

Lee, Sunmin, Graham Colditz, Lisa Berkman, and Ichiro Kawachi. "Caregiving to Children and Grandchildren and Risk of Coronary Heart Disease in Women." *American Journal of Public Health, 93,* November 2003:1939–1944.

Leland, John, and Gregory Beals. "In Living Colors." *Newsweek,* May 5, 1997:58–60.

Lenski, Gerhard. *Power and Privilege: A Theory of Social Stratification.* New York: McGraw-Hill, 1966.

Lenski, Gerhard. "Status Crystallization: A Nonvertical Dimension of Social Status." *American Sociological Review, 19,* 1954:405–413.

Lenski, Gerhard, and Jean Lenski. *Human Societies: An Introduction to Macrosociology,* 5th ed. New York: McGraw-Hill, 1987.

Lerner, Gerda. *The Creation of Patriarchy.* New York: Oxford, 1986.

Lerner, Gerda. *Black Women in White America: A Documentary History.* New York: Pantheon Books, 1972.

Lester, David. "Adolescent Suicide from an International Perspective." *American Behavioral Scientist, 46,* 9, May 2003:1157–1170.

Letherby, Gayle. "Childless and Bereft? Stereotypes and Realities in Relation to 'Voluntary' and 'Involuntary' Childlessness and Womanhood." *Sociological Inquiry, 72,* 1, Winter 2002:7–20.

Levinson, D. J. *The Seasons of a Man's Life.* New York: Knopf, 1978.

Levinson, Wendy, and Nicole Lurie. "When Most Doctors Are Women: What Lies Ahead." *Annals of Internal Medicine, 141,* 2004:471–474.

Lewin, Tamar. "Colleges Regroup After Voters Ban Race Preferences." *New York Times,* January 26, 2007.

Lewin, Tamar. "Little Sympathy or Remedy for Inmates Who Are Raped." *New York Times,* April 15, 2001b.

Lewis, Neil A. "Justice Dept. Toughens Rules on Torture." *New York Times,* January 1, 2005.

Lewis, Oscar. "The Culture of Poverty." *Scientific American, 115,* October 1966a:19–25.

Lewis, Oscar. *La Vida.* New York: Random House, 1966b.

Lichter, Daniel T., and Martha L. Crowley. "Poverty in America: Beyond Welfare Reform." *Population Bulletin, 57,* 2, June 2002:1–36.

Liebow, Elliott. *Tally's Corner: A Study of Negro Streetcorner Men.* Boston: Little, Brown, 1999. Originally published in 1967.

Lightfoot-Klein, A. "Rites of Purification and Their Effects: Some Psychological Aspects of Female Genital Circumcision and Infibulation (Pharaonic Circumcision) in an Afro-Arab Society (Sudan)." *Journal of Psychological Human Sexuality, 2,* 1989:61–78.

Lind, Michael. *The Next American Nation: The New Nationalism and the Fourth American Revolution.* New York: Free Press, 1995.

Linton, Ralph. *The Study of Man.* New York: Appleton-Century-Crofts, 1936.

Linz, Daniel, Paul Bryant, et al. "An Examination of the Assumption that Adult Businesses Are Associated with Crime in Surrounding Areas: A Secondary Effects Study in Charlotte, North Carolina." *Law & Society, 38,* 1, March 2004:69–104.

Lippitt, Ronald, and Ralph K. White. "An Experimental Study of Leadership and Group Life." In *Readings in Social Psychology,* 3rd ed., Eleanor E. Maccoby, Theodore M. Newcomb, and Eugene L. Hartley, eds. New York: Holt, Rinehart and Winston, 1958: 340–365. (As summarized in Olmsted and Hare 1978:28–31.)

Lipset, Seymour Martin. "Democracy and Working-Class Authoritarianism." *American Sociological Review, 24,* 1959:482–502.

Liu, Haiyong. "Growing Up Poor and Childhood Weight Problems." Institute for Research on Poverty, Discussion Paper. DP 1324-07, April 2007.

Lombroso, Cesare. *Crime: Its Causes and Remedies,* H. P. Horton, trans. Boston: Little, Brown, 1911.

Lorber, Judith. *Paradoxes of Gender.* New Haven, Conn.: Yale University Press, 1994.

Lublin, Joann S. "Living Well." *Wall Street Journal,* April 8, 1999.

Lublin, Joann S. "Women at Top Still Are Distant from CEO Jobs." *Wall Street Journal,* February 28, 1996:B1.

Luhnow, David. "As Jobs Move East, Plants in Mexico Retool to Compete." *Wall Street Journal,* March 5, 2004.

Lunneborg, Patricia. *Chosen Lives of Childfree Men.* Westport, Conn.: Bergin and Garvey, 1999.

Lurie, Nicole, Jonathan Slater, Paul McGovern, Jacqueline Ekstrum, Lois Quam, and Karen Margolis. "Preventive Care for Women: Does the Sex of the Physician Matter?" *New England Journal of Medicine, 329,* August 12, 1993:478–482.

Mabry, Marcus. "The Price Tag on Freedom." *Newsweek,* May 3, 1999: 50–51.

MacDonald, William L., and Alfred DeMaris. "Remarriage, Stepchildren, and Marital Conflict: Challenges to the Incomplete Institutionalization Hypothesis." *Journal of Marriage and the Family, 57,* May 1995: 387–398.

Mack, Raymond W., and Calvin P. Bradford. *Transforming America: Patterns of Social Change,* 2nd ed. New York: Random House, 1979.

Madigan, Nick. "Judge Questions Long Sentence in Drug Case." *New York Times,* November 17, 2004.

Maher, Sarah. *Salvadorans in Suburbia: Symbiosis and Conflict,* Boston: Allyn and Bacon, 1996.

Mahoney, John S., Jr., and Paul G. Kooistra. "Policing the Races: Structural Factors Enforcing Racial Purity in Virginia (1630–1930)." Paper presented at the 1995 meetings of the American Sociological Association.

Mahoney, Patricia. "High Rape Chronicity and Low Rates of Help-Seeking Among Wife Rape Survivors in a Nonclinical Sample: Implications for Research and Practice." *Violence Against Women, 5,* 9, September 1999:993–1016.

Main, Jackson Turner. *The Social Structure of Revolutionary America.* Princeton, N.J.: Princeton University Press, 1965.

Malinowski, Bronislaw. *Sex and Repression in Savage Society.* Cleveland, Ohio: World, 1927.

Mander, Jerry. *In the Absence of the Sacred: The Failure of Technology and the Survival of the Indian Nations.* San Francisco, Calif.: Sierra Club Books, 1992.

"Marital History for People 15 Years Old and Over by Age, Sex, Race and Ethnicity: 2001." Annual Demographic Survey, Bureau of Labor Statistics and the Bureau of the Census. 2004.

Marquardt, Elizabeth. *Between Two Worlds: The Inner Lives of Children of Divorce.* New York: Crown Publishers, 2005.

Marshall, Samantha. "Vietnamese Women Are Kidnapped and Later Sold in China as Brides." *Wall Street Journal,* August 3, 1999.

Marshall, Samantha. "It's So Simple: Just Lather Up, Watch the Fat Go Down the Drain." *Wall Street Journal,* November 2, 1995:B1.

Martin, William G., and Mark Beittel. "Toward a Global Sociology: Evaluating Current Conceptions, Methods, and Practices." *Sociological Quarterly, 39,* 1, 1998:139–161.

Marx, Karl, and Friedrich Engels. *Communist Manifesto.* New York: Pantheon, 1967. First published in 1848.

Marx, Karl. "Contribution to the Critique of Hegel's Philosophy of Right." In *Karl Marx: Early Writings,* T. B. Bottomore, ed. New York: McGraw-Hill, 1964:45. First published in 1844.

Masheter, Carol. "Postdivorce Relationships Between Ex-spouses: The Role of Attachment and Interpersonal Conflict." *Journal of Marriage and the Family, 53,* February 1991:103–110.

Massey, Douglas S., and Garvey Lundy. "Use of Black English and Racial Discrimination in Urban Housing Markets: New Methods and Findings." *Urban Affairs Review, 36,* 2001:451–468.

Mathews, T. J., and Brady E. Hamilton. "Mean Age of Mother, 1970–2000." *National Vital Statistics Report, 51,* 1, December 11, 2002.

Mayer, John D. *Personality: A Systems Approach.* Boston: Allyn and Bacon, 2007.

McCall, Michael. "Who and Where Are the Artists?" In *Fieldwork Experience: Qualitative Approaches to Social Research,* William B. Shaffir, Robert A. Stebbins, and Allan Turowetz, eds. New York: St. Martin's, 1980:145–158.

McCormick, John. "The Sorry Side of Sears." *Newsweek,* February 22, 1999a:36–39.

McGee, Glenn. "Cloning, Sex, and New Kinds of Families." *Journal of Sex Research, 37,* 3, August 2000:266–272.

McIntosh, Peggy. "White Privilege and Male Privilege: A Personal Account of Coming to See Correspondences through Work in Women's Studies." Working Paper #189. Wellesley College Center for Research on Women, 1988.

McIntyre, Jamie. "Army Rape Case Renews Debate on Coed Training." April 30, 1997: CNN Internet article.

McLanahan, Sara, and Gary Sandefur. *Growing Up with a Single Parent: What Hurts, What Helps.* Cambridge, Mass.: Harvard University Press, 1994.

McLanahan, Sara, and Dona Schwartz. "Life Without Father: What Happens to the Children?" *Contexts, 1,* 1, Spring 2002: 35–44.

McLemore, S. Dale. *Racial and Ethnic Relations in America.* Boston: Allyn and Bacon, 1994.

McShane, Marilyn, and Frank P. Williams, III., eds. *Criminological Theory.* Upper Saddle River, N.J.: Prentice Hall, 2007.

Mead, George Herbert. *Mind, Self and Society.* Chicago: University of Chicago Press, 1934.

Mead, Margaret. *Sex and Temperament in Three Primitive Societies.* New York: New American Library, 1950. First published in 1935.

Meese, Ruth Lyn. "A Few New Children: Postinstitutionalized Children of Intercountry Adoption." *Journal of Special Education, 39,* 3, 2005:157–167.

Meltzer, Scott A. "Gender, Work, and Intimate Violence: Men's Occupational Spillover and Compensatory Violence." *Journal of Marriage and the Family, 64,* 2, November 2002:820–832.

Menaghan, Elizabeth G., Lori Kowaleski-Jones, and Frank L. Mott. "The Intergenerational Costs of Parental Social Stressors: Academic and Social Difficulties in Early Adolescence for Children of Young Mothers." *Journal of Health and Social Behavior, 38,* March 1997:72–86.

Mende, Nazer, and Damien Lewis. *Slave: My True Story.* New York: Public Affairs, 2005.

Merton, Robert K. *Social Theory and Social Structure.* Glencoe, Ill.: Free Press, 1949, Enlarged ed., 1968.

Merton, Robert K. "The Social-Cultural Environment and *Anomie*." In *New Perspectives for Research on Juvenile Delinquency,* Helen L. Witmer and Ruth Kotinsky, eds. Washington, D.C.: U.S. Department of Health, Education, and Welfare, 1956:24–50.

Merwine, Maynard H. "How Africa Understands Female Circumcision." *New York Times,* November 24, 1993.

Messner, Michael. "Boyhood, Organized Sports, and the Construction of Masculinities." *Journal of Contemporary Ethnography, 18,* 4, January 1990:416–444.

Messner, Michael A., Margaret Carlisle Duncan, and Cheryl Cooky. "Silence, Sports Bras, and Wrestling Porn." *Journal of Sport and Social Issues, 27,* 1, February 2003:38–51.

Meyers, Laurie. "Asian-American Mental Health." *APA Online,* February 2006.

Mezentseva, E. *Russian Social Science Review, 42,* 4, July-August 2001:4–21.

Michael, Robert T., John H. Gagnon, Edward O. Laumann, and Gina Kolata. "How Many Sexual Partners Do Americans Have?" In *Exploring Social Life: Readings to Accompany Essentials of Sociology: A Down-to-Earth Approach* 5th ed., James M. Henslin, ed. Boston: Allyn and Bacon, 2004:166–174.

Milgram, Stanley. "The Small World Problem." *Psychology Today, 1,* 1967:61–67.

Milgram, Stanley. "Some Conditions of Obedience and Disobedience to Authority." *Human Relations, 18,* February 1965: 57–76.

Milgram, Stanley. "Behavioral Study of Obedience." *Journal of Abnormal and Social Psychology, 67,* 4, 1963:371–378.

Milkie, Melissa A. "Social World Approach to Cultural Studies." *Journal of Contemporary Ethnography, 23,* 3, October 1994: 354–380.

Miller, Laura L. "Women in the Military." In *Down to Earth Sociology: Introductory Readings,* 14th ed., James M. Henslin, ed. New York: The Free Press, 2007. First published in 1997.

Miller, Walter B. "Lower Class Culture as a Generating Milieu of Gang Delinquency." *Journal of Social Issues, 14,* 3, 1958:5–19.

Mills, C. Wright. *The Sociological Imagination.* New York: Oxford University Press, 1959.

Mills, C. Wright. *The Power Elite.* New York: Oxford University Press, 1956.

Mills, Karen M., and Thomas J. Palumbo. *A Statistical Portrait of Women in the United States: 1978.* U.S. Bureau of the Census, *Current Population Reports,* Series P-23, no. 100, 1980.

Mohawk, John C. "Indian Economic Development: An Evolving Concept of Sovereignty." *Buffalo Law Review, 39,* 2, Spring 1991: 495–503.

Money, John, and Anke A. Ehrhardt. *Man and Woman, Boy and Girl.* Baltimore: Johns Hopkins University Press, 1972.

Montagu, M. F. Ashley, ed. *Race and IQ: Expanded Edition.* New York: Oxford University Press, 1999.

Montagu, M. F. Ashley. *The Concept of Race.* New York: Free Press, 1964.

Montagu, M. F. Ashley. *Introduction to Physical Anthropology,* 3rd ed. Springfield, Ill.: Thomas, 1960.

Moore, Elizabeth S. *Advergaming and the Online Marketing of Food to Children.* Kaiser Family Foundation Report, July 2006.

Morris, Joan M., and Michael D. Grimes. "Moving Up from the Working Class." In *Down to Earth Sociology: Introductory Readings,* 13th ed., James M. Henslin, ed. New York: The Free Press, 2005:365–376.

Mosher, William D., Anjani Chandra, and Jo Jones. "Sexual Behavior and Selected Health Measures." *Advance Data from Vital and Health Statistics, 362,* September 15, 2005:1–56.

Mount, Ferdinand. *The Subversive Family: An Alternative History of Love and Marriage.* New York: Free Press, 1992.

Moynihan, Daniel Patrick. "Social Justice in the *Next* Century." *America,* September 14, 1991:132–137.

Murdock, George Peter. *Social Structure.* New York: Macmillan, 1949.

Murdock, George Peter. "The Common Denominator of Cultures." In *The Science of Man and the World Crisis,* Ralph Linton, ed. New York: Columbia University Press, 1945.

Murdock, George Peter. "Comparative Data on the Division of Labor by Sex." *Social Forces, 15,* 4, May 1937:551–553.

Murray, Christopher J. L., Sandeep C. Kulkarni, Catherine Michard, Niels Tomijima, Maria T. Bulzaccheili, Terrell J. Landiorio, and Majid Ezzati. "Eight Americas: Investigating Mortality Disparities across Races, Counties, and Race-Counties in the United States." *PLoS Medicine, 3,* 9, September 2006:1513–1524.

Naik, Gautam. "Doing Hard Time in Greenland Isn't Really That Hard." *Wall Street Journal,* January 13, 2004.

Nakamura, Akemi. "Abe to Play Hardball with Soft Education System." *The Japan Times,* October 27, 2006.

Nakao, Keiko, and Judith Treas. "Occupational Prestige in the United States Revisited: Twenty-Five Years of Stability and Change." Paper presented at the annual meetings of the American Sociological Association, 1990. (As referenced in Kerbo, Harold R. Social Stratification and Inequality: *Class Conflict in Historical and Comparative Perspective,* 2nd ed. New York: McGraw-Hill, 1991:181.)

Nash, Gary B. *Red, White, and Black.* Englewood Cliffs, N.J.: Prentice Hall, 1974.

National Institute of Child Health and Human Development. "Child Care and Mother-Child Interaction in the First 3 Years of Life." *Developmental Psychology, 35,* 6, November 1999: 1399–1413.

National School Safety Center. "School Associated Violent Deaths." Westlake Village, California, 2007.

National Women's Political Caucus. "Factsheet on Women's Political Progress." Washington, D.C., June 1998.

Navarro, Mireya. "For New York's Black Latinos, a Growing Racial Awareness." *New York Times,* April 28, 2003.

Navarro, Vicente, ed. *The Political Economy of Social Inequalities: Consequences for Health and Quality of Life.* Amityville, N. Y.: Baywood Publishing, 2002.

Needham, Sarah E. "Grooming Women for the Top: Tips from Executive Coaches." *Wall Street Journal,* October 31, 2006.

Nestar, Russell, and Robert Gregory. "Making the Undoable Doable: Milgram, the Holocaust, and Modern Government." *The American Review of Public Administration, 35,* December 1, 2005:327–349.

Neugarten, Bernice L. "Personality and Aging." In *Handbook of the Psychology of Aging,* James E. Birren and K. Warren Schaie, eds. New York: Van Nostrand Reinhold, 1977:626–649.

Neugarten, Bernice L. "Middle Age and Aging." In *Growing Old in America,* Beth B. Hess, ed. New Brunswick, N.J.: Transaction, 1976: 180–197.

Neuman, W. Lawrence. *Social Research Methods: Qualitative and Quantitative Approaches,* 6th ed. Boston: Allyn and Bacon, 2006.

Nisbett, Richard E. *The Geography of Thought: How Asians and Westerners Think Differently . . . and Why.* New York: The Free Press, 2003.

Nussenbaum, Evelyn. "Video Game Makers Go Hollywood. Uh-Oh." *New York Times,* August 22, 2004.

O'Brien, John E. "Violence in Divorce-Prone Families." In *Violence in the Family,* Suzanne K. Steinmetz and Murray A. Straus, eds. New York: Dodd, Mead, 1975:65–75.

O'Brien, Timothy L. "Fed Assesses Citigroup Unit $70 Million in Loan Abuse." *New York Times,* May 28, 2004.

O'Hare, William P. "A New Look at Poverty in America." *Population Bulletin, 51,* 2, September 1996a:1–47.

O'Hare, William P. "U.S. Poverty Myths Explored: Many Poor Work Year-Round, Few Still Poor After Five Years." *Population Today: News, Numbers, and Analysis, 24,* 10, October 1996b:1–2.

Offen, Karen. "Feminism and Sexual Difference in Historical Perspective." In *Theoretical Perspectives on Sexual Difference,* Deborah L. Rhode, ed. New Haven, Conn.: Yale University Press, 1990:13–20.

Ogburn, William F. *Social Change with Respect to Culture and Human Nature.* New York: W. B. Huebsch, 1922. (Other editions by Viking in 1927, 1938, and 1950.)

Okamoto, Dina G., and Lynn Smith-Lovin. "Changing the Subject: Gender, Status, and the Dynamics of Topic Change." *American Sociological Review, 66,* 6, December 2001:852–873.

Olmsted, Michael S., and A. Paul Hare. *The Small Group,* 2nd ed. New York: Random House, 1978.

"On History and Heritage: John K. Castle." *Penn Law Journal,* Fall 1999.

Orme, Nicholas. *Medieval Children.* New Haven: Yale University Press, 2002.

Osborne, Lawrence. "Got Silk." *New York Times Magazine,* June 15, 2002.

Pagelow, Mildred Daley. "Adult Victims of Domestic Violence: Battered Women." *Journal of Interpersonal Violence, 7,* 1, March 1992:87–120.

Pager, Devah. "Blacks and Ex-Cons Need Not Apply." *Context, 2,* 3, Fall 2003:58–59.

Partington, Donald H. "The Incidence of the Death Penalty for Rape in Virginia." *Washington and Lee Law Review, 22,* 1965: 43–75.

Pascoe, C. J. "Multiple Masculinities: Teenage Boys Talk About Jocks and Gender." *American Behavioral Scientist, 46,* 10, June 2003:1423–1438.

Patterson, Orlando. "The Root of the Problem." *Time,* April 26, 2007.

Pearlin, L. I., and Melvin L. Kohn. "Social Class, Occupation, and Parental Values: A Cross-National Study." *American Sociological Review, 31,* 1966:466–479.

Peña, Maria. "Patrullaje de voluntarios destaca urgencia de aprobar reforma." EFE. April 3, 2005.

Perry, Barbara. "Nobody Trusts Them! Under- and Over-Policing Native American Communities." *Critical Criminology, 14,* 2006:411–444.

Peters, Jeremy W., and Danny Hakim. "Ford's Lending Practices Challenged in a Lawsuit." *New York Times,* March 1, 2005.

Peterson, Iver. "1993 Deal for Indian Casino Is Called a Model to Avoid." *New York Times,* June 30, 2003.

Pfann, Gerard A., et al. "Business Success and Businesses' Beauty Capital." *Economics Letters, 67,* 2, May 2000:201–207.

Piaget, Jean. *The Construction of Reality in the Child.* New York: Basic Books, 1954.

Piaget, Jean. *The Psychology of Intelligence.* London: Routledge & Kegan Paul, 1950.

Pines, Maya. "The Civilizing of Genie." *Psychology Today, 15,* September 1981:28–34.

Portés, Alejandro, and Ruben G. Rumbaut. *Immigrant America.* Berkeley: University of California Press, 1990.

Pratt, Laura A., Achintya N. Dey, and Alan J. Cohen. "Characteristics of Adults with Serious Psychological Distress as Measured by the K6 Scale: United States, 2001–04." *Vital and Health Statistics, 382,* March 30 2007:1–18.

Prystay, Cris, and Geoffrey A. Fowler. "They Shun Hard-Body Look, Preferring Pills, Teas and Gels." *Wall Street Journal,* October 9, 2003.

Quadagno, Jill. *Aging and the Life Course: An Introduction to Gerontology,* 4th ed. New York: McGraw-Hill, 2007.

Rainwater, Lee, and Timothy M. Smeeding. *Poor Kids in a Rich Country: America's Children in Comparative Perspective.* New York: Russell Sage, 2003.

Raisfeld, Robin, and Rob Patronite. "Shirako Season." *New York Magazine,* December 25, 2006.

Ramos, Jorge. "Project Minuteman Is Meaningless." *Oakland Tribune.* April 10, 2005.

Ray, J. J. "Authoritarianism Is a Dodo: Comment on Scheepers, Felling and Peters." *European Sociological Review, 7,* 1, May 1991:73–75.

Reckless, Walter C. *The Crime Problem,* 5th ed. New York: Appleton, 1973.

Regalado, Antonio. "Seoul Team Creates Custom Stem Cells from Cloned Embryos." *Wall Street Journal,* May 20, 2005.

Reiman, Jeffrey. *The Rich Get Richer and the Poor Get Prison: Ideology, Class, and Criminal Justice,* 7th ed. Boston: Allyn and Bacon, 2004.

Reiser, Christa. *Reflections on Anger: Women and Men in a Changing Society.* Westport, Conn.: Praeger Publishers, 1999.

Rennison, Callie Marie. "Intimate Partner Violence, 1993–2001." Washington, D.C.: Bureau of Justice Statistics, February 2003.

Reskin, Barbara F. *The Realities of Affirmative Action in Employment.* Washington, D.C.: American Sociological Association, 1998.

Resnik, David B. "Financial Interests and Research Bias." *Perspectives on Science, 8,* 3, Fall 2000:255–283.

Reuters. "Fake Tiger Woods Gets 200-Years-To-Life in Prison." April 28, 2001.

Richardson, Stacey, and Marita P. McCabe. "Parental Divorce During Adolescence and Adjustment in Early Adulthood." *Adolescence, 36,* Fall 2001:467–489.

Richman, Joe. "From the Belgian Congo to the Bronx Zoo." National Public Radio, September 8, 2006.

Ricks, Thomas E. "'New' Marines Illustrate Growing Gap Between Military and Society." *Wall Street Journal,* July 27, 1995:A1, A4.

Rideout, Victoria J., and Elizabeth A. Vandewater. "Zero to Six: Electronic Media in the Lives of Infants, Toddlers and Preschoolers." Kaiser Family Foundation, Fall 2003.

Rieker, Patricia P., Chloe E. Bird, Susan Bell, Jenny Ruducha, Rima E. Rudd, and S. M. Miller, "Violence and Women's Health: Toward a Society and Health Perspective." Unpublished paper, 1997.

Robertson, Ian. *Sociology,* 3rd ed. New York: Worth, 1987.

Rodriguez, Richard. "Searching for Roots in a Changing Society." In *Down to Earth Sociology: Introductory Readings,* 8th ed., James M. Henslin, ed. New York: Free Press, 1995:486–491.

Rodriguez, Richard. "Mixed Blood." *Harper's Magazine, 283,* November 1991:47–56.

Rodriguez, Richard. "The Late Victorians: San Francisco, AIDS, and the Homosexual Stereotype." *Harper's Magazine,* October 1990:57–66.

Rodriguez, Richard. *Hunger of Memory: The Education of Richard Rodriguez.* Boston: Godine, 1982.

Rodriguez, Richard. "The Education of Richard Rodriguez." *Saturday Review,* February 8, 1975:147–149.

Roediger, David R. *Colored White: Transcending the Racial Past.* Berkeley: University of California Press, 2002.

Rogers, Joseph W. *Why Are You Not a Criminal?* Englewood Cliffs, N.J.: Prentice Hall, 1977.

Rogers, Stacy J., and Paul R. Amato. "Have Changes in Gender Relations Affected Marital Quality?" *Social Forces, 79,* December 2000:731–748.

Rohwedder, Cecilie. "London Parents Scramble for Edge in Preschool Wars." *Wall Street Journal,* February 12, 2007.

Rosaldo, Michelle Zimbalist. "Women, Culture and Society: A Theoretical Overview." In *Women, Culture, and Society,* Michelle Zimbalist Rosaldo, and Louise Lamphere, eds. Stanford: Stanford University Press, 1974.

Rosenfeld, Richard. "Crime Decline in Context." *Contexts, 1,* 1, Spring 2002:25–34.

Rosenthal, Elisabeth. "Cat Lovers Lining Up for No-Sneeze Kitties." *New York Times,* October 6, 2006.

Rosenthal, Elisabeth. "Harsh Chinese Reality Feeds a Black Market in Women." *New York Times,* June 25, 2001b.

Rosenthal, Elisabeth. "China's Chic Waistline: Convex to Concave." *New York Times,* December 9, 1999.

Ross, Casey. "Jackpot Grandma Busy Eluding Moochers." *Boston Herald,* July 14, 2004:2.

Rossi, Alice S. "Gender and Parenthood." *American Sociological Review, 49,* 1984:1–18.

Rossi, Alice S. "A Biosocial Perspective on Parenting." *Daedalus, 106,* 1977:1–31.

Roth, Louise Marie. "Selling Women Short: A Research Note on Gender Differences in Compensation on Wall Street." *Social Forces, 82,* 2, December 2003:783–802.

Rotstein, Arthur H. "Minuteman Volunteers May Have Played Prank." Associated Press, April 7, 2005.

Rubin, Zick. "The Love Research." In *Marriage and Family in a Changing Society,* 2nd ed., James M. Henslin, ed. New York: Free Press, 1985.

Ruggles, Patricia. "Short and Long Term Poverty in the United States: Measuring the American 'Underclass.'" Washington, D.C.: Urban Institute, June 1989.

Russell, Diana E. H. "Preliminary Report on Some Findings Relating to the Trauma and Long-Term Effects of Intrafamily Childhood Sexual Abuse." Unpublished paper.

Russell, Diana E. H. *Rape in Marriage.* Bloomington: Indiana University Press, 1990.

Sadler, Anne G., Brenda M. Booth, Brian L. Cook, and Bradley N. Doebbeling. "Factors Associated With Women's Risk of Rape in the Military Environment." *American Journal of Industrial Medicine, 43,* 2003:252–273.

Saenz, Rogelio. "Latinos and the Changing Face of America." Washington, D.C.: Population Reference Bureau, 2004:1–28.

Sahlins, Marshall D. *Stone Age Economics.* Chicago: Aldine, 1972.

Sales, Leila. "Facebook Is the Greatest Thing Since Marx." *Chicago Maroon,* May 4, 2004.

Salopek, Paul. "Shattered Sudan: Drilling for Oil, Hoping for Peace." *National Geographic, 203,* 2, February 2003:30–66.

Samor, Geraldo, Cecilie Rohwedder, and Ann Zimmerman. "Innocents Abroad?" *Wall Street Journal,* May 5, 2006.

Sampson, Robert J., Jeffrey D. Morenoff, and Felton Earls. "Beyond Social Capital: Spatial Dynamics of Collective Efficacy for Children." *American Sociological Review, 64,* October 1999: 633–660.

Sampson, Robert J., Gregory D. Squires, and Min Zhou. *How Neighborhoods Matter: The Value of Investing at the Local Level.* Washington, D.C.: American Sociological Association, 2001.

Samuelson, Paul Anthony, and William D. Nordhaus. *Economics,* 18th ed. New York: McGraw Hill, 2005.

Sanchez-Jankowski, Martin. "Gangs and Social Change." *Theoretical Criminology, 7,* 2, 2003:191–216.

Sapir, Edward. *Selected Writings of Edward Sapir in Language, Culture, and Personality.* David G. Mandelbaum, ed. Berkeley, Calif.: University of California Press, 1949.

Saranow, Jennifer. "The Snoop Next Door." *Wall Street Journal,* January 12, 2007.

Sayres, William. "What Is a Family Anyway?" In *Marriage and Family in a Changing Society,* 4th ed., James M. Henslin, ed. New York: Free Press, 1992:23–30.

Schackner, Bill. "How to Win New 'Friends' With a Click." *Pittsburgh Post-Gazette.* November 28, 2004.

Schaefer, Richard T. *Racial and Ethnic Groups,* 9th ed. Upper Saddle River, N.J.: Prentice Hall, 2004.

Schaefer, Richard T. *Sociology,* 3rd ed. New York: McGraw-Hill, 1989.

Schellenberg, James A. *Conflict Resolution: Theory, Research, and Practice.* Albany: New York University Press, 1996.

Schemo, Diana Jean. "Rate of Rape at Academy Is Put at 12% in Survey." *New York Times,* August 29, 2003b.

Schemo, Diana Jean. "Women at West Point Face Tough Choices on Assaults." *New York Times,* May 22, 2003a.

Schmiege, Cynthia J., Leslie N. Richards, and Anisa M. Zvonkovic. "Remarriage: For Love or Money?" *Journal of Divorce and Remarriage,* May-June 2001:123–141.

Schmitt, Eric. "Rapes Reported by Servicewomen in the Persian Gulf and Elsewhere." *New York Times,* February 26, 2004.

Schulz, William F. "The Torturer's Apprentice: Civil Liberties in a Turbulent Age." *The Nation,* May 13, 2002.

Scommegna, Paola. "Increased Cohabitation Changing Children's Family Settings." *Population Today, 30,* 7, October 2002:3, 6.

Scott, Monster Cody. *Monster: The Autobiography of an L. A. Gang Member.* New York: Penguin Books, 1994.

Scully, Diana. "Negotiating to Do Surgery." In *Dominant Issues in Medical Sociology,* 3rd ed., Howard D. Schwartz, ed. New York: McGraw-Hill, 1994:146–152.

Scully, Diana, and Joseph Marolla. "'Riding the Bull at Gilley's': Convicted Rapists Describe the Rewards of Rape." In *Down to Earth Sociology: Introductory Readings,* 14th ed., James M. Henslin, ed. New York: The Free Press, 2007.

Scully, Diana, and Joseph Marolla. "Convicted Rapists' Vocabulary of Motive: Excuses and Justifications." *Social Problems, 31,* 5, June 1984: 530–544.

Segal, Nancy L., and Scott L. Hershberger. "Virtual Twins and Intelligence." *Personality and Individual Differences, 39,* 6, 2005:1061–1073.

Seltzer, Judith A. "Consequences of Marital Dissolution for Children." *Annual Review of Sociology, 20,* 1994:235–266.

Sharp, Deborah. "Miami's Language Gap Widens." *USA Today,* April 3, 1992:A1, A3.

Shenon, Philip. "Arguments Conclude in Army Sex Hearing." *New York Times,* August 26, 1997.

Sherif, Muzafer, and Carolyn Sherif. *Groups in Harmony and Tension.* New York: Harper & Row, 1953.

Sherman, Spencer. "The Hmong in America." *National Geographic,* October 1988:586–610.

Shields, Stephanie A. *Speaking from the Heart: Gender and the Social Meaning of Emotion.* New York: Cambridge University Press, 2002.

Shively, JoEllen. "Cowboys and Indians: Perceptions of Western Films Among American Indians and Anglos." *American Sociological Review, 57,* December 1992:725–734.

Shively, JoEllen. "Cultural Compensation: The Popularity of Westerns Among American Indians," Paper presented at the annual meetings of the American Sociological Association, 1991.

"Sierra Leone: Female Circumcision Is a Vote Winner." African News Service, March 21, 2005.

Silverman, Eric K. "Anthropology and Circumcision." *Annual Review of Anthropology, 33,* 2004:419–445.

Simmel, Georg. *The Sociology of Georg Simmel,* Kurt H. Wolff, ed. and trans. Glencoe, Ill.: Free Press, 1950. First published between 1902 and 1917.

Simpson, George Eaton, and J. Milton Yinger. *Racial and Cultural Minorities: An Analysis of Prejudice and Discrimination,* 4th ed. New York: Harper & Row, 1972.

Skeels, H. M. *Adult Status of Children with Contrasting Early Life Experiences: A Follow-up Study.* Monograph of the Society for Research in Child Development, *31,* 3, 1966.

Skeels, H. M., and H. B. Dye. "A Study of the Effects of Differential Stimulation on Mentally Retarded Children." *Proceedings and Addresses of the American Association on Mental Deficiency, 44,* 1939:114–136.

Skinner, Jonathan, James N. Weinstein, Scott M. Sporer, and John E. Wennberg. "Racial, Ethnic, and Geographic Disparities in Rates of Knee Arthroplasty Among Medicare Patients." *New England Journal of Medicine, 349,* 14, October 2, 2003:1350–1359.

Sklair, Leslie. *Globalization: Capitalism and Its Alternatives,* 3rd ed. New York: Oxford: University Press, 2001.

Smedley, Brian D., Adrienne Y. Stith, and Alan R. Nelson eds. *Unequal Treatment: Confronting Racial and Ethnic Disparities in Health Care.* Washington, D.C.: The National Academies Press, 2003.

Smith, Beverly A. "An Incest Case in an Early 20th-Century Rural Community." *Deviant Behavior, 13,* 1992:127–153.

Smith, Craig S. "Abduction, Often Violent, a Kyrgyz Wedding Rite." *New York Times,* April 30, 2005.

Smith-Lovin, Lynn, and Charles Brody. "Interruptions in Group Discussions: The Effects of Gender and Group Composition." *American Sociological Review, 54,* 1989:424–435.

Snyder, Mark. "Self-Fulfilling Stereotypes." In *Down to Earth Sociology: Introductory Readings,* 7th ed., James M. Henslin, ed. New York: Free Press, 1993:153–160.

Solomon, Charlene Marmer. "Cracks in the Glass Ceiling." *Workforce, 79,* 9, September 2000:87–91.

Soss, Joe. "Lessons of Welfare: Policy Design, Political Learning, and Political Action." *American Political Science Review, 93,* 1999:363–380.

Sourcebook of Criminal Justice Statistics. Washington, D.C.: U.S. Government Printing Office, published annually.

South, Scott J. "Sociodemographic Differentials in Mate Selection Preferences." *Journal of Marriage and the Family, 53,* November 1991:928–940.

Spector, Tim. "Ageing Linked to Social Status." *BBC News,* March 29, 2007.

Spickard, P. R. S. *Mixed Blood: Intermarriage and Ethnic Identity in Twentieth Century America.* Madison: University of Wisconsin Press, 1989.

Spitzer, Steven. "Toward a Marxian Theory of Deviance." *Social Problems, 22,* June 1975:608–619.

Spivak, Gayatri Chakravorty. "Feminism 2000: One Step Beyond." *Feminist Review, 64,* Spring 2000:113.

Sprecher, Susan, and Rachita Chandak. "Attitudes About Arranged Marriages and Dating Among Men and Women from India." *Free Inquiry in Creative Sociology, 20,* 1, May 1992:59–69.

Srole, Leo, et al. *Mental Health in the Metropolis: The Midtown Manhattan Study.* Albany, N. Y.: New York University Press, 1978.

Stack, Carol B. *All Our Kin: Strategies for Survival in a Black Community.* New York: Harper, 1974.

Stampp, Kenneth M. *The Peculiar Institution: Slavery in the Ante-Bellum South.* New York: Vintage Books, 1956.

Statistical Abstract of the United States. Washington D.C.: Bureau of the Census, published annually.

Stenner, Karen. *The Authoritarian Dynamic.* New York: Cambridge University Press, 2005.

Stephens, Bret. "The Foreign Brides." *Wall Street Journal,* May 2, 2006.

"Sticky Ticket: A New Jersey Mother Sues Her Son Over a Lottery Jackpot She Claims Belongs to Them Both." *People Weekly,* February 9, 1998:68.

Stiles, Daniel. "The Hunters Are the Hunted." *Geographical, 75,* June 2003:28–32.

Stinnett, Nicholas. "Strong Families." In *Marriage and Family in a Changing Society,* 4th ed., James M. Henslin, ed. New York: Free Press, 1992:496–507.

Stockard, Jean, and Miriam M. Johnson. *Sex Roles: Sex Inequality and Sex Role Development.* Englewood Cliffs, N.J.: Prentice Hall, 1980.

Stodgill, Ralph M. *Handbook of Leadership: A Survey of Theory and Research.* New York: Free Press, 1974.

Stolberg, Sheryl Gay. "Blacks Found on Short End of Heart Attack Procedure." *New York Times,* May 10, 2001.

Stouffer, Samuel A., Arthur A. Lumsdaine, Marion Harper Lumsdaine, Robin M. Williams, Jr., M. Brewster Smith, Irving L. Janis, Shirley A. Star, and Leonard S. Cottrell, Jr. *The American Soldier: Combat and Its Aftermath,* Vol. 2. New York: Wiley, 1949.

Stout, David. "Pentagon Toughens Policy on Sexual Assault." *New York Times,* January 5, 2005.

Straus, Murray A. "Explaining Family Violence." In *Marriage and Family in a Changing Society,* 4th ed., James M. Henslin, ed. New York: Free Press, 1992:344–356.

Straus, Murray A., and Richard J. Gelles. "Violence in American Families: How Much Is There and Why Does It Occur?" In *Troubled Relationships,* Elam W. Nunnally, Catherine S. Chilman, and Fred M. Cox, eds. Newbury Park, Calif.: Sage, 1988:141–162.

Stryker, Sheldon. "Symbolic Interactionism: Themes and Variations." In *Social Psychology: Sociological Perspectives,* Morris Rosenberg and Ralph H. Turner, eds. New Brunswick, N.J.: Transaction, 1990.

Suizzo, Marie-Anne. "The Social-Emotional and Cultural Contexts of Cognitive Development: Neo-Piagetian Perspectives." *Child Development, 71,* 4, August 2000:846–849.

Sullivan, Andrew. "What's So Bad about Hate?" *New York Times Magazine,* September 26, 1999.

Sumner, William Graham. *Folkways: A Study in the Sociological Importance of Usages, Manners, Customs, Mores, and Morals.* New York: Ginn, 1906.

Sutherland, Edwin H. *White Collar Crime.* New York: Dryden Press, 1949.

Sutherland, Edwin H. *Principles of Criminology,* 4th ed. Philadelphia: Lippincott, 1947.

Sutherland, Edwin H. *Criminology.* Philadelphia: Lippincott, 1924.

Sutherland, Edwin H., Donald R. Cressey, and David F. Luckenbill. *Principles of Criminology,* 11th ed. Dix Hills, N. Y.: General Hall, 1992.

Suzuki, Bob H. "Asian-American Families." In *Marriage and Family in a Changing Society,* 2nd ed., James M. Henslin, ed. New York: Free Press, 1985:104–119.

Sweeney, Megan M. "Remarriage and the Nature of Divorce: Does It Matter Which Spouse Chose to Leave?" *Journal of Family Issues, 23,* 3, April 2002:410–440.

Sykes, Gresham M., and David Matza. "Techniques of Neutralization." In *Down to Earth Sociology: Introductory Readings*, 5th ed., James M. Henslin, ed. New York: Free Press, 1988: 225–231. First published in 1957.

Szasz, Thomas S. *Cruel Compassion: Psychiatric Control of Society's Unwanted.* Syracuse: Syracuse University Press, 1998.

Szasz, Thomas S. "Mental Illness Is Still a Myth." In *Deviant Behavior 96/97,* Lawrence M. Salinger, ed. Guilford, Conn.: Dushkin, 1996:200–205.

Szasz, Thomas S. *The Myth of Mental Illness,* rev. ed. New York: Harper & Row, 1986.

Tafoya, Sonya M., Hans Johnson, and Laura E. Hill. "Who Chooses to Choose Two?" Washington, D.C.: Population Reference Bureau, 2005.

Taneja, V., S. Sriram, R. S. Beri, V. Sreenivas, R. Aggarwal, R. Kaur, and J. M. Puliyel. " 'Not by Bread Alone': Impact of a Structured 90-Minute Play Session on Development of Children in an Orphanage." *Child Care, Health & Development, 28,* 1, 2002: 95–100.

Tannen, Deborah. " 'But What Do You Mean?' Women and Men in Conversation." In *Down to Earth Sociology: Introductory Readings,* 14th ed., James M. Henslin, ed. New York: The Free Press, 2007.

Tannen, Deborah. *You Just Don't Understand: Women and Men in Conversation.* New York: Morrow, 1990.

Tappan, Mark B. "Moral Function as Mediated Action." *Journal of Moral Education, 35,* 1, March 2006:1–18.

Taylor, Chris. "The Man Behind Lara Croft." *Time,* December 6, 1999:78.

Taylor, Howard F. "The Structure of a National Black Leadership Network: Preliminary Findings." Unpublished manuscript, 1992. As cited in Margaret L. Andersen and Howard F. Taylor, *Sociology: Understanding a Diverse Society.* Belmont, Calif.: Wadsworth, 2000.

Thayer, Stephen. "Encounters." *Psychology Today,* March 1988: 31–36.

Thomas, Paulette. "Boston Fed Finds Racial Discrimination in Mortgage Lending Is Still Widespread." *Wall Street Journal,* October 9, 1992:A3.

Thomas, Paulette. "U.S. Examiners Will Scrutinize Banks with Poor Minority-Lending Histories." *Wall Street Journal,* October 22, 1991:A2.

Thomas, W. I., and Dorothy Swaine Thomas. *The Child in America: Behavior Problems and Programs.* New York: Alfred A. Knopf, 1928.

Thompson, Ginger. "Chasing Mexico's Dream into Squalor." *New York Times,* February 11, 2001.

Thompson, William. "Handling the Stigma of Handling the Dead." In *Down to Earth Sociology: Introductory Readings,* 14th ed., James M. Henslin, ed. New York: The Free Press, 2007.

Thornton, Russell. *American Indian Holocaust and Survival: A Population History Since 1492.* Norman: University of Oklahoma Press, 1987.

Todosijevic, Jelica, Esther D. Rothblum, and Sondra E. Solomon. "Relationship Satisfaction, Affectivity, and Specific Stressors in Same-Sex Couples Joined in Civil Unions." *Psychology of Women Quarterly, 29,* 2005:158–166.

Tönnies, Ferdinand. *Community and Society (Gemeinschaft und Gesellschaft),* with a new introduction by John Samples. New Brunswick, N.J.: Transaction, 1988. First published in 1887.

Torres, Jose B., V. Scott H. Solberg, and Aaron H. Carlstrom. "The Myth of Sameness Among Latino Men and Their Machismo." *American Journal of Orthopsychiatry, 72,* 2, 2002:163–181.

Treiman, Donald J. *Occupational Prestige in Comparative Perspective.* New York: Academic Press, 1977.

Tresniowski, Alex. "Payday Or Mayday?" *People Weekly,* May 17, 1999: 128–131.

Trice, Harrison M., and Janice M. Beyer. "Cultural Leadership in Organization." *Organization Science, 2,* 2, May 1991:149–169.

Tuhus-Dubrow, Rebecca. "Rites and Wrongs." *Boston Globe,* February 11, 2007.

Tumin, Melvin M. "Some Principles of Social Stratification: A Critical Analysis." *American Sociological Review 18,* August 1953:394.

Turner, Jonathan H. *The Structure of Sociological Theory.* Homewood, Ill.: Dorsey, 1978.

Twenge, Jean M., W. Keith Campbell, and Craig A. Foster. "Parenthood and Marital Satisfaction: A Meta-Analytical Review." *Journal of Marriage and Family, 65,* August 2003:574–583.

U.S. Bureau of the Census. *Statistical Abstract of the United States: The National Data Book.* Washington, D.C.: U.S. Government Printing Office. Published annually.

U.S. Bureau of the Census. "Annual Social and Economic Supplement to Current Population Survey." Washington, D.C.: U.S. Government Printing Office, 2006.

Uchitelle, Louis. "How to Define Poverty? Let Us Count the Ways." *New York Times,* May 28, 2001.

Udry, J. Richard. "Biological Limits of Gender Construction." *American Sociological Review, 65,* June 2000:443–457.

UNESCO. *Education for All Global Monitoring Report,* 2006.

Usdansky, Margaret L. "English a Problem for Half of Miami." *USA Today,* April 3, 1992:A1, A3, A30.

Useem, Michael. *The Inner Circle: Large Corporations and the Rise of Business Political Activity in the U.S. and U. K.* New York: Oxford University Press, 1984.

Vartabedian, Ralph, and Scott Gold. "New Questions on Shuttle Tile Safety Raised." *Los Angeles Times,* February 27, 2003.

Vaughan, Diane. "Uncoupling: The Social Construction of Divorce." In *Marriage and Family in a Changing Society,* 2nd ed., James M. Henslin, ed. New York: Free Press, 1985:429–439.

Vega, William A. "Hispanic Families in the 1980s: A Decade of Research." *Journal of Marriage and the Family, 52,* November 1990:1015–1024.

Venkatesh, Sudhir Alladi. *Off the Books: The Underground Economy of the Urban Poor.* Cambridge: Harvard University Press, 2006.

Volti, Rudi. *Society and Technological Change,* 3rd ed. New York: St. Martin's Press, 1995.

Von Hoffman, Nicholas. "Sociological Snoopers." *Transaction 7,* May 1970:4, 6.

Wade, Nicholas. "In Dusty Archives, a Theory of Affluence." *New York Times,* August 7, 2007.

Wagley, Charles, and Marvin Harris. *Minorities in the New World.* New York: Columbia University Press, 1958.

Wald, Matthew L., and John Schwartz. "Alerts Were Lacking, NASA Shuttle Manager Says." *New York Times,* July 23, 2003.

Waldrop, Deborah P., and Joseph A. Weber. "From Grandparent to Caregiver: The Stress and Satisfaction of Raising Grandchildren." *Families in Society: The Journal of Contemporary Human Services,* 2001:461–472.

Walker, Alice, and Pratibha Parmar. *Warrior Marks: Female Genital Mutilation and the Sexual Blinding of Women.* New York: Harcourt Brace, 1993.

Wallerstein, Immanuel. "Culture as the Ideological Battleground of the Modern World-System." In *Global Culture: Nationalism, Globalization, and Modernity,* Mike Featherstone, ed. London: Sage, 1990:31–55.

Wallerstein, Immanuel. *The Capitalist World-Economy.* New York: Cambridge University Press, 1979.

Wallerstein, Immanuel. *The Modern World System: Capitalist Agriculture and the Origins of the European World-Economy in the Sixteenth Century.* New York: Academic Press, 1974.

Wallerstein, Judith S., Sandra Blakeslee, and Julia M. Lewis. *The Unexpected Legacy of Divorce: A 25-Year Landmark Study.* Concord, N. H.: Hyperion Press, 2001.

Walsh, Catherine. "The Life and Legacy of Lawrence Kohlberg." *Society, 37,* 2, January-February 2000:38–44.

Wang, Hongyu, and Paul R. Amato. "Predictors of Divorce Adjustment: Stressors, Resources, and Definitions." *Journal of Marriage and the Family, 62,* 3, August 2000:655–668.

Wang, Yong, and Carl W. Roberts. "*Schadenfreude:* A Case Study of Emotion as Situated Discursive Display." *Comparative Sociology, 5,* 1, 2006:45–63.

Wark, Gillian R., and Dennis L. Krebs. "Gender and Dilemma Differences in Real-Life Moral Judgment." *Developmental Psychology, 32,* 1996:220–230.

Watson, J. Mark. "Outlaw Motorcyclists." In *Society: Readings to Accompany Sociology: A Down-to-Earth Approach, Core Concepts,* James M. Henslin ed. Boston: Allyn and Bacon, 2006:105–114. First published in 1980 in *Deviant Behavior, 2,* 1.

Wayne, Julie Holliday, Christine M. Riordan, and Kecia M. Thomas. "Is All Sexual Harassment Viewed the Same? Mock Juror Decisions in Same- and Cross-Gender Cases." *Journal of Applied Psychology, 86,* 2, April 2001:179–187.

Weber, Max. *Economy and Society,* G. Roth and C. Wittich, eds. Berkeley: University of California Press, 1978. First published in 1922.

Weber, Max. *The Protestant Ethic and the Spirit of Capitalism.* New York: Scribner's, 1958. First published in 1904–1905.

Weiss, Rick. "Mature Human Embryos Cloned." *Washington Post,* February 12, 2004:A1.

Weitoft, Gunilla Ringback, Anders Hjern, Bengt Haglund, and Mans Rosen. "Mortality, Severe Morbidity, and Injury in Children Living with Single Parents in Sweden: A Population-Based Study." *Lancet, 361,* January 25, 2003:289–295.

Werbner, Pnina. "Veiled Interventions in Pure Space: Honour, Shame and Embodied Struggles among Muslims in Britain and France." *Theory, Culture, Society, 24,* 2007:161–186.

Werner, Erica. "Indian Casinos Gross $25 Billion in 2006." Associated Press, June 5, 2007.

West, Candace, and Angela Garcia. "Conversational Shift Work: A Study of Topical Transitions Between Women and Men." *Social Problems, 35,* 1988:551–575.

Wheaton, Blair, and Philippa Clarke. "Space Meets Time: Integrating Temporal and Contextual Influences on Mental Health in Early Adulthood." *American Sociological Review, 68,* 2003:680–706.

White, Joseph B., Stephen Power, and Timothy Aeppel. "Death Count Linked to Failures of Firestone Tires Rises to 203." *Wall Street Journal,* June 19, 2001:A4.

White, Richard D., Jr. "Are Women More Ethical? Recent Findings on the Effects of Gender Upon Moral Development." *Journal of Public Administration Research and Theory, 9,* 3, July 1999: 459–471.

Whitehead, Barbara Dafoe, and David Popenoe. "The Marrying Kind: Which Men Marry and Why." Rutgers University: The State of Our Unions: The Social Health of Marriage in America, 2004.

Whorf, Benjamin. *Language, Thought, and Reality,* J. B. Carroll, ed. Cambridge, MA: MIT Press, 1956.

Williams, Christine L. *Still a Man's World: Men Who Do Women's Work.* Berkeley: University of California Press, 1995.

Williams, Robin M., Jr. *American Society: A Sociological Interpretation,* 2nd ed. New York: Knopf, 1965.

Willie, Charles Vert. "Caste, Class, and Family Life Experiences." *Research in Race and Ethnic Relations, 6,* 1991:65–84.

Willie, Charles Vert, and Richard J. Reddick. *A New Look at Black Families,* 5th ed. Walnut Creek, Calif.: AltaMira Press, 2003.

Wilson, Edward O. *Sociobiology: The New Synthesis.* Cambridge, Mass.: Harvard University Press, 1975.

Wilson, James Q., and Richard J. Herrnstein. *Crime and Human Nature.* New York: Simon & Schuster, 1985.

Wilson, William Julius. *The Bridge over the Racial Divide: Rising Inequality and Coalition Politics.* Berkeley: University of California Press, 2000.

Wilson, William Julius. *When Work Disappears: The World of the New Urban Poor.* Chicago: University of Chicago Press, 1996.

Wilson, William Julius. *The Truly Disadvantaged: The Inner City, the Underclass, and Public Policy.* Chicago: University of Chicago Press, 1987.

Wilson, William Julius. *The Declining Significance of Race: Blacks and Changing American Institutions.* Chicago: University of Chicago Press, 1978.

Wirth, Louis. "The Problem of Minority Groups." In *The Science of Man in the World Crisis,* Ralph Linton, ed. New York: Columbia University Press, 1945.

Wise, Raul Delgado, and James M. Cypher. "The Strategic Role of Mexican Labor Under NAFTA: Critical Perspectives on Current Economic Integration." *Annals of the American Academy of Political and Social Science, 610,* March 2007:120–142.

Wolfinger, Nicholas H. "Family Structure Homogamy: The Effects of Parental Divorce on Partner Selection and Marital Stability." *Social Science Research, 32,* 2003:80–97.

"Women in Politics: 60 Years in Retrospect." Geneva, Switzerland: Inter-Parliamentary Union, 2006.

"Women of Our World." Washington, D.C.: Population Reference Bureau, 2002.

Wood, Daniel B., "Latinos Redefine What It Means to Be Manly." *Christian Science Monitor, 93,* 161, July 16, 2001.

Wright, Lawrence. "Double Mystery." *New Yorker,* August 7, 1995:45–62.

Wright, Lawrence. "One Drop of Blood." *New Yorker,* July 25, 1994: 46–50, 52–55.

Xie, Yu, and Kimberly A. Goyette. "A Demographic Portrait of Asian Americans." Washington, D.C.: Population Reference Bureau, 2004:1–32.

Yat-ming Sin, Leo, and Hon-ming Yau, Oliver. "Female Role Orientation and Consumption Values: Some Evidence from Mainland China." *Journal of International Consumer Marketing, 13,* 2, 2001:49–75.

Yinger, J. Milton. *Toward a Field Theory of Behavior: Personality and Social Structure.* New York: McGraw-Hill, 1965.

Yonas, Michael A., Patricia O'Campo, Jessica G. Burke, and Andrea C. Gielen. "Neighborhood-Level Factors and Youth Violence: Giving Voice to the Perception of Prominent Neighborhood Individuals." *Health, Education, and Behavior OnlineFirst,* July 21, 2006.

Zamiska, Nicholas. "Pressed to Do Well on Admissions Tests, Students Take Drugs." *Wall Street Journal,* November 8, 2004.

Zellner, William W. *Countercultures: A Sociological Analysis.* New York: St. Martin's, 1995.

Zernike, Kate. "The Harvard Guide to Happiness." *New York Times,* April 8, 2001.

Zerubavel, Eviatar. *The Fine Line: Making Distinctions in Everyday Life.* New York: Free Press, 1991.

Zielbauer, Paul. "Study Finds Pequot Businesses Lift Economy." *New York Times,* November 29, 2000.

Subject Index

Photo Credits